SECRET DREAMS

SECRET DREAMS

The Biography of Michael Redgrave

ALAN STRACHAN

Weidenfeld & Nicolson

LONDON

First published in Great Britain in 2004
by Weidenfeld & Nicolson

A CIP catalogue record for this book
is available from the British Library.

ISBN 0 297 60764 2

Typeset by Selwood Systems, Midsomer Norton

Printed and bound by Butler & Tanner Ltd,
Frome and London

Weidenfeld & Nicolson

The Orion Publishing Group Ltd
Orion House
5 Upper Saint Martin's Lane
London WC2H 9EA

This book is in memory of
MICHAEL

*L'acteur n'est pas seulement
interprète, il est un inspirateur...
et le grand acteur: un grand
inspirateur*

Jean Giraudoux, *Giraudoux par lui-même*

and for
JENNIFER

The actor was busy wiping face and neck with a towel already stiff with rouge and grease-paint. . . . This then – such was the tenor of my thoughts – this grease-smeared individual is the charmer at whom the twilight crowd was just now gazing so soulfully! This repulsive worm is the reality of the glorious butterfly in whom those deluded spectators believe they were beholding the realisation of their own secret dreams of beauty, grace and perfection!

Thomas Mann, *Confessions of Felix Krull, Confidence Man*

CONTENTS

ILLUSTRATIONS

John Fowler at his Hampshire hunting-lodge with Michael
Michael in the film of Graham Greene's *The Man Within*, 1947
Making-up as Shylock at Stratford, 1953, with Glen Byam Shaw
Michael as Antony at Stratford, 1953
The Redgraves at a 1960s film premiere
Michael as the elder Leo in *The Go-Between*, 1971
Dick Green
Noël Coward
With Fred Sadoff
Michael, Rachel, Fred and Iris Tree in Ischia, 1957
Shakespeare's People – Michael with Elizabeth Counsell, David Dodimead,
    Philip Bowen and Rod Wilmott
As Jasper in *Close of Play*, National Theatre, 1979 (photograph by Nobby
    Clark)
Uncle Vanya – Michael with Sybil Thorndike, Fay Compton and Joan
    Plowright, at Chichester, 1963
Michael, Vanessa and Corin outside Liverpool Playhouse, 1982
With Rachel, Corin, Kika Markham, Jemma Redgrave and Luke
    Redgrave, at the Foyle's Literary Luncheon for *In My Mind's Eye*, 1983

The author and the publishers offer their thanks to the Theatre Museum
(the National Museum of the Performing Arts) for their kind permission
to reproduce images in their possession.

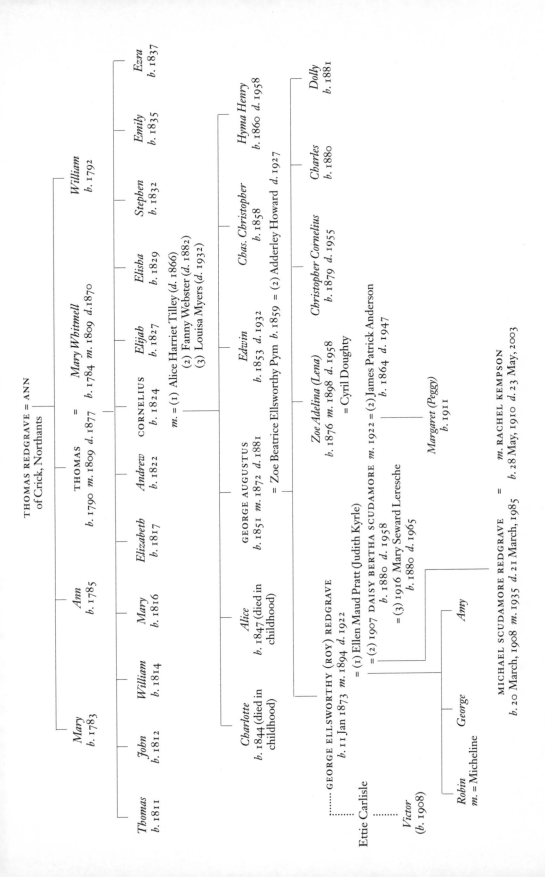

THOMAS REDGRAVE = ANN
of Crick, Northants

THOMAS = Mary Whitmell
b. 1790 m. 1809 d. 1877   b. 1784 m. 1809 d. 1870

Mary   Ann   William
b. 1783   b. 1785   b. 1792

Thomas   John   William   Mary   Elizabeth   Andrew   CORNELIUS   Elijah   Elisha   Stephen   Emily   Ezra
b. 1811   b. 1812   b. 1814   b. 1816   b. 1817   b. 1822   b. 1824   b. 1827   b. 1829   b. 1832   b. 1835 b. 1837

m. = (1) Alice Harriet Tilley (d. 1866)
     (2) Fanny Webster (d. 1882)
     (3) Louisa Myers (d. 1932)

Charlotte   Alice   GEORGE AUGUSTUS   Edwin   Chas. Christopher   Hyma Henry
b. 1844 (died in b. 1847 (died in b. 1851 m. 1872 d. 1881   b. 1853 d. 1932   b. 1858   b. 1860 d. 1958
childhood)   childhood)   = Zoe Beatrice Ellsworthy Pym b. 1859 = (2) Adderley Howard d. 1927

                                                                            Christopher Cornelius   Charles   Dolly
                                                                            b. 1879 d. 1955   b. 1880   b. 1881

                  GEORGE ELLSWORTHY (ROY) REDGRAVE   Zoe Adelina (Lena)
                  b. 11 Jan 1873 m. 1894 d. 1922   b. 1876 m. 1898 d. 1958
                  = (1) Ellen Maud Pratt (Judith Kyrle)   = Cyril Doughty
....   b. 1880 d. 1958
                  = (2) 1907 DAISY BERTHA SCUDAMORE m. 1922 = (2) James Patrick Anderson
Ettie Carlisle   b. 1880 d. 1965   b. 1864 d. 1947
                  = (3) 1916 Mary Seward Leresche
....   Margaret (Peggy)
Victor   b. 1911
(b. 1908)

                                    MICHAEL SCUDAMORE REDGRAVE   =   m. RACHEL KEMPSON
Robin   George   Amy   b. 20 March, 1908 m. 1935 d. 21 March, 1985   b. 28 May, 1910 d. 23 May, 2003
m. = Micheline

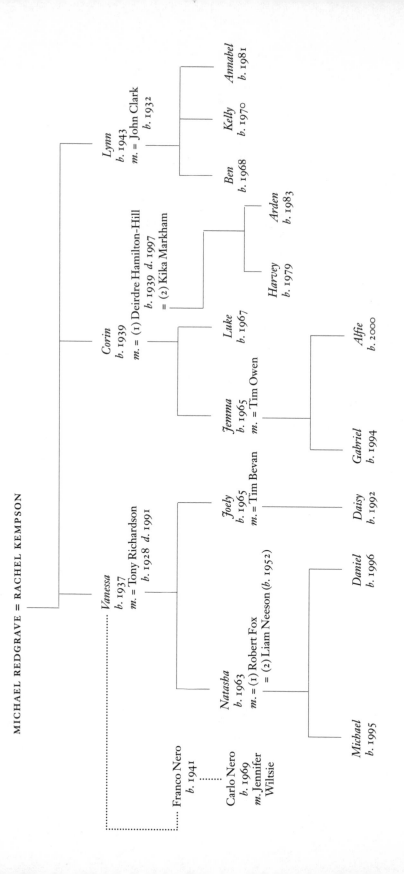

MICHAEL REDGRAVE = RACHEL KEMPSON

Vanessa
b. 1937
m. = Tony Richardson
b. 1928 d. 1991

Corin
b. 1939
m. = (1) Deirdre Hamilton–Hill
b. 1939 d. 1997
= (2) Kika Markham

Lynn
b. 1943
m. = John Clark
b. 1932

Franco Nero
b. 1941

Carlo Nero
b. 1969
m. Jennifer
Wiltsie

Natasha
b. 1963
m. = (1) Robert Fox
= (2) Liam Neeson (b. 1952)

Joely
b. 1965
m. = Tim Bevan

Jemma
b. 1965
m. = Tim Owen

Luke
b. 1967

Harvey
b. 1979

Arden
b. 1983

Ben
b. 1968

Kelly
b. 1970

Annabel
b. 1981

Michael
b. 1995

Daniel
b. 1996

Daisy
b. 1992

Gabriel
b. 1994

Alfie
b. 2000

PROLOGUE

Actors, said William Hazlitt, the essayist and chronicler of the early nineteenth-century stage, 'can show us all that we are, all that we wish to be and all that we dread to be', adding, 'Actors are the only honest hypocrites. Their life is a voluntary dream.' While Ralph Richardson, unrivalled modern interpreter of the mysteries behind the quotidian, always insisted, 'The actor must *dream* – dream constantly.'

Dreams infuse the imaginative landscape of many artists; for actors, who need to charge their unconscious with as much awareness of the characters they play as possible before allowing the acting fuel to flow, significantly so. The theatre superstition of sleeping with the script under the pillow during rehearsals, as if bedtime study of the lines will fix them in the memory by some mysterious osmosis of dreams, still lingers (less fanciful than it may seem – the theory that dreams may consolidate memory goes back two centuries). And most actors have had experience of some form of the 'Actor's Nightmare' – recurrent dreams of exposure and nakedness, humiliation and dread.

Michael Redgrave's version of the Actor's Nightmare was a plunge into authentic terror, as clammy as anything in his film *Dead of Night*. He rarely discussed it, but gave it vivid fictional form in his 1958 novel, *The Mountebank's Tale*, a story shot through with dreams, the most compelling of which describes an actor seated at his dressing table during that sacred time before the rise of the curtain and his call:

It was hot, unbearably hot, in my dressing room. My hands trembled as I applied make-up and the grease paint would not stay in place, but would slide around my face into my ears and hair like drops of oil on a pond. I had the dresser turn on electric fans and sat shivering while I applied chalk-dry sticks of grease. ... At last the make-up was done. I rose from the table and reached for my shirt. As I did the electric fans stopped and instantly I started to sweat again. I looked in dismay at the mirror and then I could see the make-up slowly start to drain down my face, over my chin down my neck and onto my chest! When the greasepaint reached this point it recomposed itself and there, amid the hair on my chest, was the grease-paint portrait of my face. I stared at it in horror.

This fictional re-creation – a loss of face, an identity crisis as disturbing as any horror film – crystallised his recurrent dream, ironically most potent during his especially successful years of the 1950s.

Throughout his life, Michael Redgrave was fascinated by dreams. In the 1930s like many contemporaries – Graham Greene included – he kept a Dream Diary noting the detail and texture of his dreams. He knew his Freud; one of his early literary efforts, *The Battle of the Book*, written as a Cambridge undergraduate, an operetta based on a time-travelling Samuel Pepys in a dream, has the couplet, satiric in its time:

> A dream, you know, may be enjoyed
> Without the help of Doktor Freud.

However, his scrutinising attitude to his dreams arguably stemmed less from Freud than from the analytical thrust of so much Cambridge teaching during his undergraduate years. Often on waking he would follow the advice of J. W. Dunne, the writer on time theory and the language of dreams, fixing the most immediately recalled detail before exploring the dream backwards.

He also had reason to be grateful for the power of dream when working on his adaptation of Henry James's *The Aspern Papers*, in which for dramatic purposes he slightly heightened the background of the American poet who so obsesses the narrator-scholar. When revising the play in 1959, in a dream there came to him not only the idea of a military song translated by Aspern but also the complete lyrics for its four verses, his 'Coleridgian Experience' as he described it.

Dreams, too, pervade the diaries which he kept sporadically throughout his life (the first was at school aged sixteen). In them he often notes the nature of his dreams – and frequent nightmares – alongside attempts to anatomise his complex, often troubled nature. One of his old school-teaching colleagues from the 1930s voiced the feelings of many of his friends when he wrote to Michael thirty years later: 'I was puzzled when you told one of those smooth interviewers that you were puzzled about your own personality. For a man whose "success story" owes everything to talent, dedication and sheer hard work, I should have thought you have every right to sit back and purr.' But that sense of puzzlement ran through his life, to some extent surely the reason he found it so difficult to write his own story. Twice he came to sign contracts with publishers but neither book was delivered, although his claims that he had begun work seem genuine. His son, Corin, who acted as patient amanuensis to his father in

collaborating on what in 1983 became his published autobiography at a
time when illness prevented any further work on stage or screen, said –
rightly to my mind – that the early chapters of the book, vivid writing
evoking the Edwardian respectability of his stepfather's Belgravia house,
were written much earlier, probably in the early 1950s.

Even then, as his diaries corroborate, he was considering work on his
memoirs, jotting down occasional working titles. Apart from a couple
(*Out of Character* and, intriguingly, *The Trouble with Me*) all his suggestions
were from *Hamlet* quotations with *The Motive and the Cue* just finally
losing out to *In My Mind's Eye*:

HAMLET: My father! Methinks I see my father.
HORATIO: Where, my lord?
HAMLET: In my mind's eye, Horatio.

Both the play and his chosen title had resonance for Michael. Roy
Redgrave, his actor-father, was best known for his performances in
romantic melodrama but his one major Shakespearean performance in
London was as Hamlet. His mother, Daisy Scudamore, as a beginner
had 'walked on' in *Hamlet* during a London season by Sarah Bernhardt
in black tights giving her Dane. Michael himself played Hamlet when
teaching at Cranleigh in 1933; he played Horatio in his first rep season
with Liverpool Playhouse and Laertes to Laurence Olivier's Hamlet at
the Old Vic in 1937 during which Vanessa Redgrave was born. He
played the title role twice – at the Old Vic (1950) and Stratford (1958) –
before later taking on Polonius for television and Claudius in the
inaugural production of the National Theatre. Only illness in later
years prevented him from appearing as the Player King (imagine that
incomparable voice, 'in a dream of passion', in the 'Hecuba' speech)
for Peter Hall. In addition Michael's wife, Rachel Kempson, had played
Ophelia early in her career and only pregnancy prevented her from
repeating it opposite Olivier in 1937. The Redgraves' younger daughter
Lynn was a Court Lady for the inaugural National Theatre Company,
while Michael's last visit to the theatre, only a few weeks before his
death in 1985, was to see his granddaughter Natasha Richardson as
Ophelia in a Young Vic *Hamlet*.

But for all the appositeness of the title, *In My Mind's Eye*, published
to coincide with Michael's seventy-fifth birthday, was a somewhat
incomplete book. This was no fault on the part of Corin, without whom
it is unlikely that it would have been completed, but by the early 1980s
Michael was restricted by the effects of Parkinson's disease. It affected
his movement, memory, voice, handwriting – an elegant, distinctive
hand reduced to the trail of an anarchic spider – and, crucially, his

energy. Corin coaxed some engrossing material but there were inevitable lacunae, sometimes frustrating (with some key performances barely mentioned), sometimes puzzling. Only very obliquely, for instance, did he refer to the tensions in his life caused by his divided nature. He had said to Corin before they embarked on the book that he intended in it to address the question of his sexuality, but only in the most indirect way was it finally mentioned. He belonged, of course, to a generation conditioned to certain codes of reticence and he had, moreover, been educated in the English public-school system, that ideal training ground for the masking of secrets. He was not – *au fond* – ashamed of his bisexuality, but he was often shamed and dismayed by the problems it could create for those he most loved. Also, for the greater part of his adult life an area of his sexual conduct was, in the eyes of the law, a crime. It is understandable, then, that he finally backed away from a confrontation with that aspect of his life in any public confessional even in old age. However, he did not, as far as can be ascertained, destroy any of his diaries, as surely he would have done – he did destroy some later letters from his mother, written in her final distressing years – had he wished to block the tracks for any future biographer.

Back in 1956 the critic Richard Findlater wrote the excellent *Michael Redgrave, Actor*, an interim progress report on a career rather than a biography. Corin in 1995 produced a brief and touching memoir, *Michael Redgrave, My Father*, while Rachel Kempson's *A Family and its Fortunes*, Vanessa Redgrave's *Autobiography* and Lynn Redgrave's theatrical voyages round her parents in *The Mandrake Root* and *Shakespeare for My Father* also, in various ways, refract the family's central figure. But this, surprisingly to me, is the first full published biography.

Michael himself always wryly predicted – mostly rightly as it transpired – that his obituaries would describe him as an 'intellectual' actor, which had become a wearisomely familiar label attached to him (the very word 'intellectual' seems still to carry a pejorative ring in the English theatre). It was also his bad luck that the two most influential dramatic critics of his time – James Agate and Kenneth Tynan – both subscribed to that theory. They were, of course, conscious not only of his Cambridge degree and teaching career but also of his early *engagé* political stance, his published articles – including a memorable debate with London's dramatic critics launched by his provocative stance (which offended Agate deeply) in 1942 in the *New Statesman* – not to mention his enthusiasm for the work of Konstantin Stanislavsky. This, more than any other single factor, lay behind the 'intellectual' label.

Michael indeed discussed Stanislavsky and the craft of acting in general, in two books and in many articles and interviews. Always he was anxious to stress that for him Stanislavsky's writing on acting was a key – not *the* key – to unlocking specific acting problems. It was, fundamentally, 'an inspiration towards an ideal', to the kind of almost Utopian life in the theatre sought by any dedicated actor. What he was always equally anxious to stress was that he would never claim that Stanislavsky's work could be reduced to a comprehensive single system or 'Method'. Much as Michael admired individual talents from the Actors' Studio, he was never a devout 'Method-ist'. He regarded himself as an actor who used his emotions (behind the reserve he was in life a man of extremely strong emotions and passions) just as much as his mind. For him the best actor's maxim – he often quoted it – was from the nineteenth-century American star, Joseph Jefferson: 'I act best when my heart is warm but my head is cool.' Yet the labels, epitomised by *Variety*'s 'Egghead Actor', remained branded on to his name in the cuttings libraries until his death.

Even if one rejects – as I do – the 'cerebral' descriptions attached to Redgrave the actor, an air of controversy, however civilised, still attracts itself to his work. He remained always difficult to categorise, having from the outset of his career (and he was a late beginner) consciously decided to aim for as richly varied a theatrical life as possible, to be – in the Louis Jouvet sense – an *acteur* as opposed to the *comédien* of the personality star actor. Critics of his day tended palpably to throb in the presence of outsize star performances – the *monstres sacrés* of the French stage or Henry Irving for Agate (Harold Hobson, his *Sunday Times* successor, was, if anything, even more Francophile), Olivier pre-eminently for Tynan (even after his Brechtian 'conversion') – while Michael's whole *raison d'être* as an actor was different. It was rooted in his early cradling, artistic and political, in the 1920s and 1930s, including periods in Heidelberg and Cambridge, in the company work at his first professional home in Liverpool, at the Old Vic, in the West End company of John Gielgud of which he was a key member and the short-lived company at the Phoenix Theatre which Michael formed with the director Michel Saint-Denis just before the war. It was an ethic of theatre fundamentally antipathetic to the glamorous hierarchy and the glorious assertions of self of the commercial theatre. Even though for a good part of his career he was a bankable West End and Broadway star with his name in lights, his inclinations were essentially towards the ensemble ideal. When he joined the first company of the National Theatre – returning to his beloved Old Vic – he readily agreed to play 'as cast', exactly as he had been contracted to do thirty years before at Liverpool.

As an established star he liked to seek out directors who might shake up a moribund English system. In the 1950s, a time when the London commercial sector seemed, in Arthur Miller's phrase, 'hermetically sealed off from life', he worked with American directors such as Sam Wanamaker and Harold Clurman from New York's Group Theater. He was also responsible for giving the work of Joan Littlewood and Theatre Workshop a first London showing in the early 1950s, while in a hidebound British cinema he was prepared to take risks with unfamiliar talent such as Joseph Losey.

Illness denied him the kind of Indian summer enjoyed by contemporaries such as John Gielgud and Ralph Richardson in new writing. And when Gielgud – last of his generation of stage greats – died, virtually all his obituaries reduced a quartet to a trinity of great actors (Gielgud, Olivier, Richardson) with Michael almost airbrushed out of theatrical history. To a large extent, this book attempts the reclamation of a great actor.

He had most of the ideal natural attributes – a commanding physical presence, an expressive voice, wide in range with a rich timbre, overlaid by an occasional husky catch, and piercingly blue, wide-set eyes. Although he had an undervalued comic gift he seemed, as he owned, to have a special affinity with men 'in, as it were, invisible chains'. He excelled at characters haunted by spectres, revenants or their own demons – Hamlet, Macbeth, Strindberg's *The Father*, the modern Orestes – figures of T. S. Eliot's *The Family Reunion* or, on film, Eugene O'Neill's *Mourning Becomes Electra*, other haunted screen personae including the schizophrenic ventriloquist of *Dead of Night* or the elder Leo, eyes unforgettably pursued by the past, in *The Go-Between*.

Duplicity is another hallmark of his best work, not just the split personality of some of his most memorable stage and screen characters, but also in his subtly realised version of James's *The Aspern Papers*, its literary sleuth resorting to duplicity to reach his obsession, or in the hypnotic doppelgänger motif central to *The Mountebank's Tale*.

There were, of course, dualities and bifurcations in his own personality, those private demons which informed the public work with so much of its uniquely troubling intensity. At the front of a diary for 1945, in very bold handwriting he transcribed a piece from Benjamin Constant: 'This duplicity was far from my natural character, but man becomes depraved as soon as he has in his heart a single thought which he is constantly obliged to dissimulate.' Michael comprehended his bisexuality early, although of the guilts and tensions it could cause he never would be entirely free. His marriage to Rachel Kempson – it endured for just under half a century – was, despite inevitable strains and much speculation and gossip, a continuing love story, however unorthodox to the outside world.

He once wrote in his diary of his misery and distress at what he described as his 'cruelty' to Rachel at one period, even though she had from the outset known of his divided nature, and how, in talking to her of his father in an attempt to explain his conduct, he realised that he had often had the 'obscure' feeling that he, like Harry in *The Family Reunion*, was 'the consciousness' of his family:

'Its bird sent flying through the purgatorial flame...'

One
ANCESTRAL VOICES

On Sunday, 24 April 1960, Michael Redgrave must have felt at the pinnacle of both personal and professional success. He was given that evening the particular accolade – aged fifty-two – of a Garrick Club dinner in his honour. It was a packed house – the event had been fully subscribed well ahead – with the guests including fellow actor members such as Robert Morley, Donald Sinden and Michael Hordern alongside leading critics, impresarios and writers.

He was the newest theatrical knight, invested the previous year. Only the night before he had given his final performance in his own Comedy of Letters, an adaptation of Henry James's *The Aspern Papers*, at the Queen's Theatre which he had also directed and co-presented; his remarkably subtle, insinuating performance as James's duplicitous literary sleuth in late nineteenth-century Venice had given him one of the most satisfying successes of his career.

After the Château Magdelaine St Emilion (acknowledging his Cambridge college) with the Suprême de Volaille à la Kiev (either a nod to his leadership of the Stratford Memorial Theatre Company's recent visit to the USSR or a Garrick Club wag's sly reference to his politics), the guests settled to their brandies and cigars as Michael rose to reply to the toast from Sir Julian Hall. Always surprisingly nervous on such occasions, his speech – initially hesitant but progressively graceful and wryly funny – surprised many of those present as the tall, elegant figure, immaculate in perfectly cut evening dress and speaking in that unmistakable voice with its trademark tones of the Auden generation, gave in describing his early years a picture worlds removed from the patina of success in the candlelit room hung with gilt-framed portraits of the theatrical greats.

Michael told his audience that he had been initially averse to the stage, far from intoxicated by his parents' unsettled profession: 'Between the ages of three and six I lived in Islington or Kennington and was farmed out at points north and south to places such as Sheffield and Portsmouth. I spoke with a pronounced London accent and though not exactly a street-urchin I played in the streets.' He also touched on his 'devoted, dutiful and determined' mother's pursuit of his 'less devoted, less dutiful but equally determined' father around Australia in his early childhood. This was mostly new information to the Garrick guests, who possibly knew of his public-school education and would be aware of his Cambridge degree (he slyly acknowledged that some of those present probably considered that he would have been a better actor without either). But while Michael's own theatrical reputation was formed primarily in the classics, his parents made theirs in the far less rarefied world of fit-up tours, stock companies, melodrama and the music halls. And it secretly always rather pleased him that the story of Roy Redgrave and Daisy Scudamore rivalled anything in the most coincidence-packed melodramas, full of buried secrets and late revelations, in which they had appeared.

Roy would have objected to appearing first, preferring a long, anticipatory build-up to a showy first entrance, sometimes on horseback as in one of his special favourites, an adaptation of Rolf Bolderwood's *Robbery Under Arms* in the leading role of Captain Starlight. His story is more complex than Daisy's, however, and must take precedence.

Like Daisy's, Roy's family history involves some strange gaps and unexplained mysteries. Michael became aware of much of his parents' lineage only after their deaths and a good deal of the rest is in frustratingly incomplete (and usually undated) letters. Also, several incidents in his ancestry, because of Edwardian convention, were only euphemistically related by surviving members of what he gradually came to realise was a more extended family – some of whom he got to know only in later life – than he had imagined.

Michael's paternal family can be traced back with certainty as far as the eighteenth century and to his great-great-great-grandfather Thomas Redgrave of Crick in Northamptonshire. A successful farmer, he and his wife Ann had five children, the second of whom, also named Thomas (born in 1790), remained in Crick as a prosperous cordwainer and shoemaker. This Thomas had a long and happy marriage to Mary Whitmell, also from Crick (she died in 1870 and Thomas, aged eighty-seven, in 1877). They had twelve children – nine boys and three girls – of whom the seventh child and fifth boy, Cornelius (born in 1824), developed into one of the more colourful Redgrave ancestors.

Cornelius – Michael's great-grandfather – was a formidable character, married three times altogether. His first wife, London-born Alice Tilley, bore him six children before her death in 1866 aged forty-two. Cornelius's early career is uncertain, although most likely he worked for his father, but by 1850 he and Alice were in London, initially in the Tottenham Court Road, and by 1861 they were living at Brydges Street, Covent Garden, not then the most salubrious of London addresses. His profession

in the Census of that year is given as 'Theatrical Agent', a misleading term
in that he did not represent actors but was more akin to a modern ticket
broker. From his tobacco shop in Drury Lane Cornelius sold tickets for
the nearby giant 'monopoly' theatres – Covent Garden and Drury Lane's
Theatre Royal – the only two houses then licensed to stage 'legitimate'
drama, although there was a thriving market and below-the-counter trade
especially centred around the Covent Garden area and the teeming streets
of Holborn in 'illegitimate' theatre, presenting everything from pantomime to boxing matches. Cornelius would shrewdly buy up blocks of
tickets for the likely popular attractions, selling them on at a tidy profit.
When the Licensing Authorities tried to clamp down on this practice,
Cornelius quickly organised a gathering of his associates and cronies – an
intimidating posse – in the Drury Lane stalls, all of them primed with
detailed instructions at a given signal to raise their newspapers simultaneously to obscure the stage. Faced with the near riot this caused –
almost a replay of the 'Old Price' riots at Covent Garden in 1809 – the
Licensors prudently withdrew their objections.

For a while Cornelius continued to flourish in business, running the
Metropole in the Edgware Road too for a time, although he seems to have
been less than prudent with money, whether other people's or his own.
Both daughters born to Cornelius and Alice died in childhood. The
surviving boys were George, Edward, Charles and the exotically named
Hyma Henry, who met Michael for the first time in the 1930s during
Michael's first Old Vic season and was able to tell him more about his
scattered family. George, the third of Cornelius's and Alice's children, was,
as the eldest boy, a 'big brother to the whole family' according to Hyma,
who described him as 'a typical Redgrave – volatile, agile, sensitive,
impetuous and supremely kindly'. According to Hyma, there were often
'financial exigencies' in Cornelius's household, involving 'frequent migra-
tions' and more than one moonlight flit. As a result George's education
in particular was neglected, although Hyma added of his brother: 'He
made up by his natural genius for any disadvantages accruing from that
misfortune. He had a poetic and artistic temperament and was passionately
fond of music.'

When Alice died, Cornelius did not remain a widower long, marrying
Fanny Webster, a farmer's daughter, and the family moved to the Waterloo
Road near the Old Vic in the days when the road was considered a
relatively 'posh' residential highway. Before long, however, they all moved
to near their stepmother's home in Cambridgeshire where for a time the
children were happy enough in the country. George made something of
a name for himself as an ace swimmer and diver; his brothers would vividly
recall his famous exploit at a village fête in front of a huge crowd, when

he dived under a paddle steamer churning its way upstream, to emerge triumphantly on the other side.

Soon, however, there were tensions between Fanny and her eldest stepson, and it was at this time, when he was in his mid-teens, that George decided to leave England and sail for Canada. He travelled a good deal – family legend had it that he became a crony of William 'Buffalo Bill' Cody – throughout Canada, often sleeping rough, which led to a serious attack of rheumatic fever, forcing his return to England.

Cornelius found George a job managing a small hotel in Greenwich and, at twenty-one, Michael's grandfather fell in love, almost at first sight, with a local girl, ambitious for a stage career, named Zoe Beatrice Ellsworthy Pym, daughter of Edward Pym, a Devon-born baker, and his wife Anne, a butcher's daughter. A family boast on their side was that Zoe was a descendant of the actress Zoe Ellsworthy of the Lyceum Theatre in the mid-nineteenth century who had once played Gertrude to the Hamlet of the great Charles Fechter. That Zoe was enchantingly beautiful is clear but Hyma seems to have been wary of his brother's sweetheart ('Ambition burnt in her heart like the fires of a restless volcano,' he said), pointing out that she was glad ('I know her *mother* was') to have found so eligible a suitor. With eloquently delicate circumlocution, Hyma stated that marriage between Zoe and George ('much too soon for him') was, as he understood, 'owing to circumstances deemed necessary without further delay'. Hyma remembered being fetched out of school by his stepmother to run to St John's Church in the Waterloo Road for the wedding. On the marriage certificate of 8 February 1872 George is described as 'Licensed Victualler' and Zoe as 'of full age' although, as she was born in 1857, she could have been only just sixteen, which explains Hyma's 'circumstances': Zoe may not have been pregnant (her first child was not born until 1873) but possibly pressure was brought to bear on George who could have been prosecuted for 'unlawful carnal knowledge' of a minor. The wedding certificate was witnessed by Cornelius whose profession now is given – he seems to have been quite a jack-of-all-trades – as 'Billiard-Board Maker'.

George and Zoe began married life in Stamford Street, just off the Waterloo Road, later moving to Kennington. They had five children, the eldest – George Ellsworthy Redgrave, born in 1873 – always, from babyhood, being called Roy. There were two other boys, Charles and Christopher Cornelius, and two girls, Zoe Adelina (known as Lena) and Dolly, the baby. It was a trying early married life for such a young bride – five pregnancies in eight years, a husband in increasingly poor health and the shock of her father abandoning her mother Anne to become a ship's chef, never to see his family again ('Conjugal affection was not a conspicuous virtue in him,' sniffed Hyma). Zoe's deserted mother was reduced to working as a seamstress in an East End sweatshop.

The young family's circumstances were aggravated by George's increasing ill health and the need for Zoe often to care for her mother. Hyma was regularly deputed to act as surrogate nursemaid to Roy and to entertain his nephew he had a cabinet-maker friend make a portable stage. He would set Roy up in his baby chair and 'compel him to witness my novel, original and *thrilling* creations'. Enraptured, the baby 'would stare with wide-opened and fearful eyes' as the plots developed.

Roy caught the theatre virus in his high chair. Lena later remembered how her big brother (she was three years his junior) would subsequently dragoon her and her brothers into his theatricals:

> Acting was his life. Under a big round table covered with a long cloth Roy would have his dressing room – mirror, candles, make-up. His brothers were his scene shifters. He made the plays, programmes, tickets and admission – stalls 1d, sofa seats 2d, home-made lemonade (much diluted) $\frac{1}{2}$d a glass.

Lena was the leading lady in Roy's plays – always 'Tragedies' – although she also had to look sharp and nip behind the scenes as soon as she had made an exit to stage-manage Roy's carefully orchestrated Special Effects. She used old tin trays to shake for thunder, dried peas rattled in a box for rain and magnesium paper (which often burnt her fingers) for the lightning with which Roy liked to underscore his solo speeches.

George's early death – he was just thirty – completely altered the family's structure. Although he had never been in robust health since his return from Canada, it still came as a devastating shock. He died early on a November morning, sitting fully dressed in the wheelchair he had finally had to use; only the night before, according to Lena, he had told Roy to keep to his acting 'and some day you will be as great as Henry Irving or Beerbohm Tree'. Hyma, then at divinity college, never could forget the bleak grey day when his brother's coffin was taken from Kennington Road to his funeral.

The home broke up almost immediately. Zoe, taking Lena with her, joined a touring company, the boys were sent to a boarding school while Dolly, still only a toddler, was taken in by her cousin, a dancer at the Empire in the West End (Dolly later worked in vaudeville before retiring to run a Southampton hotel). Things were to deteriorate further, however. According to Lena, family funds – such as they were – were gambled away by grandfather Cornelius who had been made George's executor and joint guardian (with Zoe) of the children. Christopher and Charles were sent to Dr Barnardo's, although their maternal grandmother, Anne, soon removed them and took them to live with her in her one room in Poplar, while Roy was apprenticed to a barber with a shop off the Walworth Road.

Roy was to 'live in' with his own bedroom (actually a large landing cupboard) on 1s 6d a week, his first task being to lather customers' chins for shaving, although he was still too small to cope without standing on a box. Every Thursday he was allowed time off between 4 and 10 p.m., when he would walk all the way to Poplar to see his brothers. It was at this point, when Roy had been at the barber's shop for a few years, that Hyma, who had lost touch with the scattered family and was now a young married curate at the Abbey Church of Waltham Abbey, encountered his nephew again: 'Passing the cheapest barber's shop in town, the fat, bibulous boss of the shop – a vulgar tonsor – told me "a relative of mine" was working for him as an apprentice.'

At which point Roy, now 'a bright, rosy-faced and smiling chappie', appeared. Hyma arranged to meet him privately later, when he tried to persuade him to leave the barber's and come to lodge with him and his wife. But Zoe had recently remarried ('some actor – not a *noted* one,' remarked Hyma), giving the children a stepfather, the actor-dramatist Adderley Howard. Convinced that he had spotted possibilities in some of his adopted family, Howard polished the elocution of Lena and Roy in particular, giving them rudimentary acting classes and training them in his own sketches. Lena's description of their stepfather as 'harsh and cruel' seems justified; all the children were soon planning to leave and Zoe, after only a few years of marriage, eventually divorced him. Christopher joined the Navy (he was killed at sea in his twenties) while Charles took Holy Orders and later left for America. Roy and Lena were forced to take off separately; Lena joined the respected Maggie Norton's fit-up company at £1 a week, while Roy managed 5s more in his professional theatrical debut, playing small parts on tour in the melodrama *The Divers*. Lena idolised her brother and tried to fix up acting engagements for them jointly whenever possible, admiring both his talent and his sense of dedication: 'Steadily, he climbed the ladder. Poverty did not trouble him, he was on the stage. To me he was all and everything. What a lovely personality he had; everyone loved him, especially the women.'

From the evidence of the handful of surviving recollections and photographs it is clear that Lena was not blindly biased. Of moderate height but with a sturdy physique and a full head of auburn-brown hair, Roy was strikingly handsome, blessed with the open good looks ideal for so many of the strapping heroes for which he was so often cast. Men liked his stage personality as much as women; he was athletic and virile, particularly noted for his prowess at sword fights and stage combat, and recklessly heedless of injury, although he did one finger permanent damage during a stage duel. Lena remembered his reply – it could have been a line from one of his plays – to a doctor advising its amputation: 'Oh, no! Never! I brought it into this world with me and I shall take it out with me into the next.'

Gradually Roy's career began to take off. Although he never acted in London in the West End, which he loftily professed to disdain as a closed shop patronising provincial actors (it is, of course, possible that he preferred to be a big fish in a smaller pool), he became a major attraction at several of the many flourishing suburban theatres of late-Victorian London.

Eventually he was billed often as 'The Dramatic Cock of the North', not because of fame in Scotland or the North of England but because for several seasons in the 1890s he was the popular leading man at the Britannia Theatre in Hoxton, north London. Affectionately known as 'The Brit', the theatre had been run for more years than anyone could remember by its much-loved manageress Sara Lane, a legendary Principal Boy in the Brit's annual pantomimes (running from Boxing Day until Easter) until she was in her seventies.

Roy's most popular roles at the Brit included his speciality of Captain Starlight in the rousing Australia-set *Robbery Under Arms*, Rudolf Rassendyll in *The Prisoner of Zenda* – he loved Anthony Hope's novel and all its Ruritanian trappings – and one of the many sailor heroes he tackled, William in his own version of Douglas Jerrold's nautical melodrama *Black Ey'd Susan*, using Dibdin's music for the songs. Among his possessions Michael always kept one of the few things of Roy's he owned – a tattered script of *Black Ey'd Susan*, heavily revised and cut by Roy to highlight the bravery of its mettlesome hero. Press-ganged by the dastardly guardian of his sweetheart Susan, William has such ringing curtain-lines as: 'I will come back. I shall! Neither God nor man nor devil shall stand 'twixt me and my revenge!'

Michael heard in the 1950s from the son of an actress who had been friends with his aunt Lena:

> As a boy I was enormously impressed by your Father in the role of a Jack Tar 'hero' with a tattoo over the five and nine Leichner greasepaint on his muscular arms. He really looked the part and would have commanded a colossal 'fan club' had he lived in these days.

Also at the Brit, in what was almost certainly his only London appearance in Shakespeare, he played Hamlet in one of the theatre's comparatively rare classical excursions. According to Michael's mother later, Roy seemed to take an unusually relaxed attitude to it: 'He was going to play in *Hamlet* at Mrs Lane's theatre, and had not troubled to read it till he heard one of the costers in the market reciting some of it and then he thought he had better get on with the words.'

Although Daisy granted Roy the looks of a leading man, she felt that he was essentially a character actor and doubted whether he could have got near what she called 'the *soul* of Hamlet'. Hyma, who saw Roy's performance, tactfully blamed an indifferent production for Roy's less than triumphant version of 'the pale Dane'.

It was during his time at the Brit that Roy met his first wife. 'A delightful woman caught him,' was Hyma's version, while even Daisy later conceded that she was very pretty, although adding the tart rider, '*Not* a very good actress.' This was Ellen Maud Pratt – wisely, perhaps on Roy's advice, she changed her name to Judith Kyrle – who on occasion had played opposite Roy at the Brit. Utterly captivated, Roy married Judith at the same age – twenty-one – that his father had been on his marriage; the wedding was in the bride's old home town of Littleham near Exmouth in Devon.

From the outset this seemed destined to be a passionate but stormy relationship, with Judith's jealousy of Roy's greater popularity causing many of the problems ('Fame is a jealous jade,' said Lena, who seems to have shared Hyma's gift for the telling phrase). They had three children – two boys and a girl. When it came to what Hyma described as 'certain troubles in Roy's conjugal relations', Judith asked Hyma to intervene. Perhaps wisely he chose to abstain, although the decision alienated him from the family.

The problems of which Hyma spoke may well have been exacerbated by Roy's roving eye or by his drinking; even the ever loyal Lena admitted that as well as women 'being often in his way' it had to be acknowledged that 'Roy sometimes drank too much'. The marriage, for whatever reason or combination of reasons, seemed to be disintegrating after only a few years.

In early 1901 Roy began a season at Sadler's Wells Theatre in Islington, playing a demanding series of major roles, taking him through until February 1902, billed as 'The title-role ruler of "The Britannia" that rules Hoxton'. The opening play, billed as a new 'thrilling French drama of deep and dark dungeon horrors', was *The Executioner's Son*, with other attractions including *The Great Detective* (Roy as Sherlock Holmes) and *I Am Innocent* (Roy as Captain Dreyfus), many productions trumpeting Roy's stage partnership with 'the luscious Leading Lady of the "Wells", Miss Louisa Peach'. Only in one production during that season, his final Wells appearance in *Under the Flag of France*, was Judith Kyrle featured and it seems likely that this was the last time they acted together before the collapse of their marriage.

Certainly Judith did not accompany Roy to South Africa where he worked until the summer of 1903, touring the country with a local company in an ambitious repertoire. Some of his roles – Rudolf Rassendyll included – were old favourites but he also had to take on a whole string of new parts including Rawdon Crawley in a *Vanity Fair* adaptation, more ambitious than his work at the Brit or the Wells. Judging by the few surviving accounts, he was extremely popular.

More than forty years later Michael was touched to receive a letter from an old soldier from Boer War days, a Yorkshireman named Archie Cormack, who stayed on in South Africa working as a 'super' at the Pietermaritzburg Theatre:

> I had no speaking part, but I watched with envy one grand actor, commanding, who could hold the audience (and me) spellbound. I can see him now, Roy Redgrave, strutting across the stage with tight black trousers and a loose blouse-effect shirt, pure white.

This 'presence' or star quality – an ineluctable gift on stage – was Roy's most valuable attribute as an actor, helped by his almost childlike identification with the simplified morality and large-scale emotions of his roles in the kind of play he liked best. He simply believed so totally in the situations, however exaggerated, of those stirring old plots that his audiences believed them too, with Roy transmitting a communicable relish from stage to auditorium.

At the end of the South African tour in Durban Roy sailed on the *Walmer Castle* 'to be back in good time in good old London town' as he wrote to his new employers, the respected Melville Brothers management. It is not known whether he met Judith and his children – it would seem unlikely – and he stayed for only a short time in London, appearing in the autumn of 1903 in Walter Melville's new play *A Girl's Cross Roads* at the Standard in Bishopsgate, one review of which mentioned his warm reception from 'a large amount of Hoxtonian admirers'. A rip-roaring melodrama on the evils of alcohol, it had a female version of Emile Zola's Copeau at its centre – a beautiful woman unloved by her wealthy husband (Roy) whose alcoholism climaxes in scenes of delirium tremens and hallucinations of giant spiders before her terrible death. Roy perhaps for once was content to be second fiddle as the stuffed-shirt spouse with no part to play in the final episodes, which could not have been easy for the actress playing Barbara, the bibulous heroine. According to one review: 'The unsuppressed joy with which the gallery hailed her discovery of an unsuspected store of whisky did not greatly assist the effect of tragedy doubtless intended.' The supporting part in this piece may well have represented some difficulty for Roy in finding a continuous supply of leading roles. His love life too was, as ever, somewhat complicated. He certainly seemed itchy to be off again, accepting immediately when offered a ten-week engagement with the leading Australian management of J. C. Williamson Ltd. He ended up staying in Australia for over three years.

His first work for the Williamson organisation was as leading man opposite the company's latest imported star, the wonderfully named Minnie Tittell Brune, billed as 'The Bernhardt of America', her plays largely consisting of versions of the Divine Sarah's vehicles including Sardou's *Theodora*, Rostand's *L'Aiglon* and Dumas's *La Dame aux camélias*. La Brune's publicity photographs, all in extremely soft focus, show a Mary Pickford-ish face of considerable winsomeness, framed by clouds of hair and cascades of lace at her throat. Roy thought little of her first vehicle, a cloying piece called *Sunday* with Miss Brune as the eponymous child of nature christened for the day of her birth, an orphan cared for by brawny Californian miners out of Bret Harte until her arrival – by coincidence's unusually long arm – at Brinthorpe Abbey in the Home Counties where this 'wild flower of the Californian goldfields' finds true love in the shape of Roy as the stalwart, pious brother of a scoundrel who has tried to seduce her. He enjoyed much more the chance to steal the show in Coquelin's old role of Flambeau opposite Miss Brune *en travesti* as Napoleon's son in *L'Aiglon*.

The greatest personal success of Roy's first period in Australia was his Mercutio in *Romeo and Juliet*, although the reviews – dazzling for Roy with glowing praise for his athletic swordplay – were at best only respectful for Miss Brune's somewhat mature-looking Juliet. A fellow actor and one-time crony of Roy's wrote of this performance to Michael over fifty years later: 'His Mercutio is still regarded as the most brilliant Australia has ever seen. Despite his faults – God knows he had many – your father was a great actor. He had the rare gift of losing himself in the character he was playing.'

With his star in the ascendant in Australia – between Williamson engagements he found work on the music hall stage, sometimes in his own sketches – it seems initially surprising that Roy should have returned to England. No records exist of his passage home and the family reports are silent on the subject too, but it must have been at some point towards the end of 1906 or early 1907. He had obviously not managed before leaving to fix any engagement for his return and there was no available place for him in the companies of his old homes at the Brit or the Wells, for his next traceable recorded appearance – marking something of a downturn in prestige for him – was during the memorably glorious summer of 1907 when he signed a contract for a six-week season of repertory in Brighton.

Roy's marriage to Judith Kyrle was well behind him, although he had been by no means solitary during the years since he had left her and their young children. And one of his intervening attachments was shortly to create a very uncomfortable dilemma for him. But in the sea air of Brighton as Roy began the short rehearsal period for his rep season he met for the first time his new leading lady, seven years younger, slim, tall and fair-haired, with a delightful smile.

Like Roy, Daisy Scudamore had gone on the stage in her teens. Born in 1880 she grew up as the youngest daughter of William George Scudamore (originally from the Isle of Wight), a boatbuilder, and his wife Clara (they married in 1864) in Portsea in Portsmouth. A pretty girl with wide blue eyes, she was affectionately known as 'the flower of mother's flock' and much indulged as a late child. From a very young age she adored stories – those of Hans Christian Andersen in particular – and music, including brass band concerts on Clarence Pier.

Educated first at the Circus school attached to the Circus Church, she was soon reciting at school concerts, her pièce de résistance a sentimental poem called 'Father's Letter'. Subsequently she attended St Luke's School where her love of Shakespeare was kindled. Daisy's imagination was fired quickly; she loved the excitement of being taken to the circus by a lodger in the household and of sitting on a wooden stool early in the morning in front of the fire while her mother told her stories of the exploits of Franklin, the explorer: 'I think I had enough imagination to feel the snowy and icy territory that he explored, and she had enough drama in her voice to make the tale exciting.'

However, as it emerged it was not so much Clara from whom Daisy had inherited her taste for drama as a key figure in her life whom she was shortly to meet. When she was about fifteen, as Daisy remembered, 'I had been staying in the Isle of Wight with some distant relatives who had friends staying with them. They liked my singing and one of the guests, a friend of Sylvia Leslie's, then a dancer at the Gaiety, said "You should go on the stage".' With £3 given to her by this guest, who also passed on the names of a few London actors' agents, Daisy ran away from home to try her luck in London. Lodging with a cousin in Camden Town, sleeping on the sitting-room couch, she found her way to the Covent Garden area where in those days most theatrical agents were based. One of the grandest was Blackmore's, where actors were not encouraged to hang about; most of those trying their luck there would gather in a Bedford Street pub where cheese came free with the beer. Daisy had no success at Blackmore's and she then called on St John Denton whose offices were next door to Rules Restaurant in Maiden Lane. With remarkable resourcefulness for her age Daisy got to the head of the line ('Actors all the way up the stairs') waiting for casting news, bluffing her way through by pretending to be delivering an urgent message, past Denton's secretary and into his inner sanctum.

Like an Edwardian version of *Gypsy*'s Baby June – and without a Mama Rose to push her – Daisy promptly launched into her 'act', rapidly seguing, when it was clear that her rendition of 'Jerusalem' was finding no favour, into a chirpy version of 'Merry Goes the Heart'. The agent loved her second song, declared she was ideal for the chorus in *Babes in the Wood* in Aberdeen, scheduled to begin rehearsals in London shortly, and fixed it with the pantomime's producer in the adjacent office. Returning to note down Daisy's details, when he heard her name St John Denton looked at her more closely, then laughed delightedly, saying with a twinkle, 'So, you must be Scudie's little girl.' Daisy, of course, assumed she was the daughter of William Scudamore of Portsmouth but thinking there might be some family connection she took 'Scudie's' address from St John Denton and crossed London to Castlenau in Barnes to visit him.

Unsurprisingly, Daisy never forgot the ensuing encounter and she recorded the essentials of it years later when she was lonely and unhappy, encouraged by Michael to put down some of her recollections in a couple of flimsy school notebooks. 'Scudie' – Fortunatus Augustus Scudamore (shortened, usually, to F. A.) – was a moderately prosperous author and manager, having graduated from a touring character actor's career to presenting his own melodramas on the road. When he opened the door to Daisy's knock, before she even had a chance to speak, F. A. flung out his arms to enfold her in an emotional embrace, with the startling line (recalling more than a few from his own dramas): 'If you are not my daughter, then I do not know whose daughter you may be!'

Unfortunately Daisy never wrote down the conversation that followed. But piecing together all the evidence – the strong physical resemblance, F. A.'s subsequent letters to her addressed to 'My child Daisy' or 'My own pet girl', her acknowledgement of him from that time as 'dear Dadda' and as her father in her later entry in *Who's Who in the Theatre*, together with a 1907 letter from F. A.'s kind (and, one would guess, long-suffering) wife Ellen ('You are nearly as dear to me as my own children – I took you to my heart years ago') – it seems certain that Daisy was F. A.'s illegitimate daughter. But the identity of her mother is far from clear (no birth certificate for Daisy has been traced) and the connection between F. A. Scudamore and the Scudamores of Victory Villas in Portsmouth is impossible to establish accurately. *882,035/920 | RFD*

Daisy was the 'child aged four months' listed on the 1881 Census for the Portsmouth address of William George and Clara Scudamore. It is possible that Clara had an affair with another man with the surname Scudamore and just possibly that man was F. A., who conceivably may have lodged with the family when touring locally in the early part of 1880, although no documentary proof exists of any appearance in the area by F. A. at that time. Of Clara very little can be established with certainty; she would have been over forty (she was born in 1839) in 1880, old for further childbearing for the period but not impossibly so. Clara (née Linington) was, like her husband, originally from the Isle of Wight and she was an illegitimate child. Beyond that and the facts that she spent a brief time in London as a young woman, most likely in domestic service, that she married William George Scudamore in Marylebone in 1864 and that she bore him four legitimate children in Portsmouth, little else can be definitely established about her. The whole issue of Daisy's parentage clouds even further with the discovery that her father F. A. was not in fact christened Scudamore.

His real name was Frank Davis, born in 1846 in Stroud, Gloucestershire, son of James Davis, a Dissenting Minister, and his wife Hepzibah. When Frank married Ellen Sheridan Gillet in 1874 in Bristol, where both were living, his name on the wedding certificate is still Davis and he is described as an 'Elocutionist'. The certificate was witnessed by his brother James, a tailor. Then, in 1877, on the birth certificate of their son Lionel (there was later a daughter, Mabel), F. A. is now described as 'Theatrical Proprietor' and his name is written as Fortunatus Augustine Davis Scudamore.

A possible scenario is that, given that young Frank was destined to follow his father into the Church but succumbed to a yearning to act (he claimed to have made his first stage appearance aged seventeen) and the likelihood that a Dissenter would have strongly disapproved of a son becoming an actor (his brother's signature on Frank's wedding certificate suggests that his parents did not attend the ceremony) he decided to change his name. Daisy must have been conceived during early 1880 when F. A. was still a touring actor (Daisy – not uniquely in her profession - could be extremely vague about her age, but the most likely date of her birth is November 1880). Possibly William Scudamore of Portsmouth was a cousin or relation, and he and Clara accepted Daisy as a fourth daughter and fifth child of their own to add to May, Annie, Bea and Willie. They were far from well-off, taking in lodgers at times, and F. A. perhaps contributed financially to his daughter's upbringing.

There is also no absolutely certain way of knowing what passed between Daisy and her 'parents' when she returned briefly to Portsmouth after her momentous first visit to London. All she ever said of this was that Clara was distraught ('I would bring down her grey hairs with sorrow to the grave'), although whether Clara was referring to Daisy's announcement of a stage career or to the revelation that she had met her real father is unclear. Clara did, however, give Daisy a thick cape to take to Aberdeen, and her 'sister' May came to see her off on her return to London.

The excitement that any actor feels and never forgets about a first job informs Daisy's recollections of that winter, of the two weeks of London rehearsals for *Babes in the Wood* (she lodged again in Camden Town) and of 'chumming up' with another newcomer in the chorus, Kitty Gibbs, both of them going off to Thomas's in Long Acre to buy their first sticks of greasepaint. Daisy and Kitty found rooms in Aberdeen for 16s a week each (meals included) and they used the hot water in their dressing room (a luxury then) to wash. This 1895 pantomime paid Daisy £1 a week.

She was now incurably stage-struck. Back in London she found another job almost immediately, again in the chorus, in a musical comedy aptly titled *The Runaway Girl*. This time she was also given a tiny part as one of a quartet backing the star, Charlie Brown, in a brisk little number 'The Sort of Girl I Care About' which boosted her pay to 30s. At the end of the tour she was happy – for £1 a week, but with a room in Pimlico for 8s – to 'walk on' in *Hamlet* and *Camille* at the Adelphi during a Sarah Bernhardt season. It is a pity that Daisy did not write down more of her memories of actors – she paints some vivid pictures of stars such as Bernhardt (crawling over the stage just before Hamlet's death to stroke the dead Gertrude's long fair hair) or the elder Coquelin, in whose *Cyrano de Bergerac* she also appeared as an extra, and whose voice in Cyrano's great proxy wooing scene she described as 'seeming to sound of gentle bells'. Daisy was an avid learner, too, visiting all the major London theatres, seeing Beerbohm Tree's sumptuous *Henry VIII* at Her Majesty's ('all golden glitter and excitement') and Henry Irving in *Faust* at the Lyceum. Like Roy, Daisy never appeared in significant West End roles then, and also like him came to believe in a snobbish 'closed shop' attitude to touring actors. But she was still young enough to enjoy the variety of touring life, even the train calls and Sunday changes at Crewe when most of the girls put on their best outfits to travel in, hoping they might be noticed by an important manager: 'Actresses did not make up in those days in the daytime. I was quite shocked when I saw a young woman who travelled with Bernhardt, in the daytime with *lips* heavily made up.'

Daisy began to tour in her father's productions with Lionel (who acted also as business manager), Ellen and Mabel also often in the casts. F. A. – tubby, with impeccably waxed moustache and impish, bright-blue eyes – was an exacting director, orchestrating the 'big moments' in his plays with great care. He had grown up in the theatre in stock companies before touring – in such parts as Touchstone and Dogberry – with the Irish actor-manager, Barry Sullivan (Bernard Shaw's favourite), from whom he learnt all about the arts of holding a pause and making an exit tell. His own plays, exuberantly theatrical, had splendid titles – *The Beautiful Avenger*,

The Inside Track (popular overseas, this became billed as 'The *East Lynne* of America') and *Because I Love You* – the last, as one critic noticed, causing 'a considerable sensation', as well it might with a principal character 'endowed by a freak of nature with the talons of a vulture'.

In London Daisy mostly lodged with the Scudamores in Barnes, sharing a room with her half-sister Mabel. She had a long period as leading lady at a theatre every bit as remarkable as Roy's the Brit, the Pavilion in the Mile End Road, known locally as 'The Drury Lane of the East'. For years the Pavilion was run by Isaac Cohen, a patriarch figure with white hair, long beard and electric dark eyes, who stamped out the rhythm of the lines with his cane at rehearsals. It was a friendly theatre; Cohen paid above average wages and there were perks including the call-boy's arrival on Friday evenings with a cardboard box of fish fried Jewish style, a present from his mother. The repertoire was fairly standard – *East Lynne*, several of F. A.'s plays, nautical melodramas and an occasional new play – but although it took Daisy over an hour on the Underground train to reach Mile End, she was pleased with her £5 a week salary and thrilled to see her name billed on the big poster at Mile End station.

It was during Daisy's 1904 Pavilion season that a traumatic event took place *chez* Scudamore. She and F. A. quarrelled violently – both were strong-willed and stubborn – and Daisy stormed out of Castlenau Mansions vowing not to perform in his play that night. She was, of course, too professional not to go on but, smarting still from the row, stayed away from Barnes for two nights before returning on a Sunday afternoon. According to press reports of subsequent proceedings at Mortlake Coroner's Court, Daisy (described as F. A.'s 'niece') arrived at the flat to find the blinds down and could get no reply to her knock (the rest of the family were on tour). On calling a neighbour and forcing an entry, they found F. A. 'stretched on his back on the floor, quite dead' aged fifty-eight. What the reports did not go on to describe was the telling scene in F. A.'s memorabilia-stuffed study, where he had turned the many photographs of Daisy and all the posters on which her name appeared to the wall – except for one high up in a corner which was probably what he was reaching for when he had his fatal heart attack and fell. Daisy always felt acute guilt – 'my heart ached with loss and shock' – although there were no reproaches from the Scudamore clan.

Her touring life continued after her period at the Pavilion. She never mentioned any romantic attachments during this time; when in London she loved to walk along the Strand, savouring the smells and sounds from institutions such as Romano's Restaurant and the Tivoli music hall: 'Men sometimes made eyes at me, and even sometimes spoke to me; if they did that I ran as fast as I could.'

It was in the Strand in the summer of 1907 that she celebrated landing two jobs in one day – a brief rep season at Brighton (a 'fill-in' as Daisy saw it), followed by the plum role of the wayward Glory Quayle in Hall Caine's popular drama, *The Christian*, on a long tour:

> There was a shellfish shop next door to the Adelphi ... I loved shellfish and although I was very hard up I decided to have a really good lunch and into the shop I went and ordered a dressed crab. This seemed like food of the gods to me. It was a lovely summer day and one of the happiest in my life.

Soon afterwards she was in Brighton, rehearsing the season's opening production, *Their Wedding Day*: 'It was at Brighton that I met Roy, a lovely year, full of sunshine, one of those warm English summers which now seem a thing of the past.'

No letters or notes survive from this first period when Daisy and Roy were working together, but then they would have been in each other's company rehearsing or playing most of the time. Nor, sadly, do the first few letters of what became a voluminous correspondence over the succeeding months. They both had jobs lined up to follow the Brighton engagement – Daisy on tour with *The Christian* and Roy also touring as one of six in a company called George Seymour's Comedians in a bill of 'Novelties and Sketches'. Both tours were booked to start in Scotland, but Roy definitely did not keep the letter he received there from Daisy in which she sent him the news that she was pregnant.

Two

FAMILY SECRETS

Most of the letters which flew between Daisy and Roy over the next few months, written in digs, dressing rooms and on trains, are undated and often almost indecipherable, so urgently scribbled are they at times. Daisy's handwriting is always dashingly extravagant, flowing and boldly looped, her punctuation full of dashes, while Roy's varies from confident flourishes to shaky, pencilled scrawls on paper ranging from embossed sheets to ripped-out scraps of scripts. The early weeks of both their tours saw them in Scotland and it is fairly certain that the first of Roy's letters to reach an anxious Daisy was from Coatbridge. It contained what was for Daisy a very unexpected and unwelcome shock.

In a highly emotional letter Roy apologises for hurting her, however much 'this other trouble of yours hurts me' (his single reference to her pregnancy) but abjectly tries to explain that despite her condition and 'although I know it seems brutal to you for me to write like this' he cannot marry her. Not only does Roy have a 'commitment' to another woman, 'Miss C.', she has also recently borne his child – 'the boy' – and her awaited divorce is about to come through. It is hardly surprising that Roy refers to himself as 'your old worried Roy', but he ends on a high moral tone with the assertion that 'My first duty is to her and the boy'.

This mysterious 'other woman' is always referred to as 'Miss C.' or 'the lady' in this correspondence, although just once Roy drops his guard and calls her 'Carlisle' and gives his new son's name as Victor. Roy at one point tells Daisy that he and 'Miss C.' had had 'six years together' and so he had definitely met her before he went on tour in South Africa. 'Miss C.' was in fact an actress called Ettie Carlisle (born Esther Mary Cooke into a circus family) with whom Roy began an affair while he was still married to Judith Kyrle. Ettie was appalled at the prospect of being named as 'the other woman' in a divorce case (Judith was threatening to divorce Roy) and she accepted a job in South Africa where she married an actor in the company, Henry Parrett. Not long afterwards Roy simply walked out of Judith's life, leaving her and their three children to follow Ettie, whose resistance to Roy's charms melted under his persuasion almost instantly. She left Parrett to run off with Roy and she accompanied him back to

England for his brief first period with the Melville Brothers and then to Australia when he accepted his offer from Williamson in late 1903.

Finding herself pregnant there, Ettie decided to come home – her father paid her passage – and Roy, with what degree of alacrity it is hard to estimate, accompanied her. Their return from Australia must have been in late 1906 or early 1907, by which point the process of Henry Parrett's divorce from Ettie had begun. Now, in August 1907, with three children by Judith and Victor by Ettie, Roy was facing the prospect of further fatherhood rather more imminently than he might have imagined.

Daisy's reply to Roy's bombshell is also unfortunately missing, but as their son later said, 'I am certain that few men would have wanted to be in Roy's shoes when he received it.' Roy must have felt, like Captain Macheath, a role subsequently played by Michael:

> How happy could I be with either
> Were t'other dear charmer away.

Whatever Daisy's letter contained – threats or imprecations – it produced, written in Roy's finest hand, a complete capitulation in which he now offers the suggestion that they should be married 'the next time we meet, in Glasgow'. At considerable length and with a sober reasoning poles apart from his first self-dramatising letter, after acknowledging that he is 'not a saint but with the right hand at the helm I can and will steer straight', he touches on 'the sacrifice' he will be making in giving up his rights to 'the boy' by marrying Daisy rather than Ettie, and closes with a magnificent curtain-line flourish:

> I *can't* have the boy. We *must* have our own!
> My love, dear wife,
> Your
> Roy

Daisy's reply – by return, clearly – is a rapturous outpouring of unconditional love, declaring that after receiving Roy's letter she had gone on stage and acted on air: 'I'm the happiest woman in the world. Oh, I feel I want to shout it tonight from the rooftops – I love you and you love me.'

By now Roy seems to be moving with urgency to get them married as soon as possible. With Daisy in Dundee with *The Christian* and he in Govan with the other five Comedians, he proposes marrying the following Monday morning in Glasgow before he has to leave for his next date, Bradford, using a Scottish marriage ceremony which he claims 'is allowed by a special revision of the marriage laws' recently 'designed for mariners, travellers, etc.', a ceremony 'to hold legal and binding the world over'. Michael's later suspicions about his father's stress on 'the *great* advantage' of this plan being that he need not produce any papers in evidence of his divorce from Judith Kyrle ('which will take trouble and time to get') were probably well founded; certainly no record of that divorce has been traced and it is extremely likely that Roy's wedding in such hole-in-the-corner circumstances (well away from Ettie in London, too) usefully cloaked a bigamous marriage.

Roy carefully stressed to Daisy that it must be her responsibility to find two friendly and discreet witnesses from *The Christian* company ('We don't want any more "outside members" than we can help to know the exact date of our marriage on account of the future event'). When Daisy sent her immediate agreement to every point in his plan he wrote an ecstatic reply from his Govan digs – 'the last letter I shall write you before you are really my wife' – jokily playing word games by underlining their respective landladies' names, his Mrs Mc*Bride* and Daisy's Mrs *Fortune*, adding that they should take this as a good omen. Presumably in their joy neither took note of Mrs McBride's Govan address, ominous for actors, always superstitious about *Macbeth* – 38 Birnam Terrace.

Roy told his touring manager and friend Percy Hammond the news, although he got him and his wife to promise secrecy ('and then they mustn't know when we were married,' he told Daisy). There was time only for the tiny group of the bridal couple and Daisy's two girlfriends from *The Christian* to enjoy a snatched wedding breakfast at the station buffet before Roy had to catch his train for Bradford. From there he wrote a total of five letters in a week; never again would he be so prolific.

Daisy in Glasgow was rhapsodic – 'a very proud and happy girl' – clinging to the memory of her wedding and of her Sunday pre-nuptial night in Glasgow with Roy, tanned still from their Brighton summer: 'I found your old gloves on the table in the bedroom – I hugged them in my arms and felt I had a little bit of my dear brown boy.'

The sexual charge between Roy and an awakened Daisy was powerful; every time there was a possibility of their dates offering a chance of a snatched Sunday together, they would spend it in bed, and Daisy's early letters convey palpable longing as she counts the days and nights until she can be again in his 'big arms'. Writing from Perth she promises: 'You can come to me straight from the train and into bed and into your wife's arms.'

Roy's letters rarely match Daisy's in ardour. She could not have failed to notice a distinct tendency to hypochondria (a trait inherited by Michael); Roy is often out of sorts – neuralgia, liver attacks and colds – to which a solicitous Daisy would anxiously react with recommendations of Bovril or sugar and lemon (neither a likely beverage of Roy's choice) and advice on properly airing his beds.

At times Roy could be tactless, reporting in his letters his visits whenever his tour brought him within striking distance of London to 'the boy' in Clapham and, on one occasion when Daisy was staying in old digs of his in Liverpool, recalling his time there with Robin, his first child by Judith Kyrle: 'You would have laughed to have seen me bathing him, but he was so good he seemed to understand that daddy was daddy and mummy in one then.'

Daisy was far from amused, referring to Ettie always only as 'the lady' and making it clear that whenever Roy visited Victor, 'I do hope *she* won't be anywhere near at the time'. The advance of her pregnancy and the discipline of playing a demanding part eight times a week on a long tour could not have made for an easy time for Daisy. She slept poorly, suffering from nightmares, reporting an especially troubling one which took place in their old meeting ground of Brighton but in which another man's head was superimposed on Roy's body. Cheering herself up from 'this horrid dream' she told Roy: 'Well, sweetheart, they say dreams go by contraries, so it must mean that we are going to be very happy.'

Of course, although passionate lovers physically, in reality they scarcely knew each other. They exchanged photographs with their letters in a kind of post-matrimonial courtship and began to probe each other's interests. Daisy, then a dabbler in a vaguely Fabian brand of socialism, sent Roy a copy of *The Open Road*, a book mainly on eugenics by the radical Ibsenite actress Elisabeth Robins, but Roy was clearly perturbed by such an 'advanced' book from a woman, much preferring his current reading of Anthony Hope's *Tristram of Blent*.

Politically, too, they seem some distance apart, as Roy outlined in a letter from Hull which also contained some ancestral claims of dubious authenticity:

> I must tell you that if I am anything at all I am very Conservative. Why? Only my father's blood can answer because on my mother's side I am descended from a celebrated Irish rebel and before that Rob Roy the Scottish outsider and earlier still John Pym, one of the Notorious Four who defied King Charles in the House of Commons. ... I *should* be a red hot Socialist, shouldn't I? And yet, somehow I have a supreme Conservative contempt for the Masses as a Mass.

After a paean of praise for the British aristocracy, Roy encloses a poem written for Daisy, anticipating her reaching out to their newborn child:

> The outstretched hand, the feeble clutch
> Around my fingers tight,
> Till soothed by Mother's gentle touch,
> Our loved one sleeps. Good-night!

By January 1908, with her baby due in late March, Daisy was preparing to take up the digs she had reserved in Bristol (a favourite date of both Roy and Daisy) for the time when she could no longer work. Roy's tour ended at the time Daisy had to leave *The Christian*, and he was back in London preparing to rehearse a brand-new Melville Brothers production of *Robbery Under Arms* at Daisy's old stamping ground of the Pavilion in Mile End.

Daisy was at once suspicious when a letter arrived from Roy without an address in London, forcing him on to the defensive: 'As to not giving you my address – No, darling, it was *not* because I am staying in the same house as Miss C. I am *not* with her.' He was telling the truth here; he was in familiar digs in Clapham at a favourite indulgent landlady's, Mrs Loader ('such a good soul') in Sandmore Road, assuring Daisy that he was 'safe and sound in the big smoke' and only lodging so far from Mile End to be near Victor ('my little bit of joyful trouble'). But he had obviously had a difficult scene over Victor with Ettie Carlisle and was, not unusually, feeling very sorry for himself: 'It rather upset me and I confess to you, my girl, that like the silly duffer I was, I went to the Club and proceeded to drink myself as tight as I could.'

How much comfort this was to Daisy, heavily pregnant in her room above a newspaper shop in Horfield Road in the St Michael's Mount district of Bristol, is debatable. She was having to work at times in the shop; Roy sent only the occasional £1 postal order and seemed much more interested in his new venture. This *Robbery Under Arms* was, Roy told Daisy excitedly, to be entirely under his supervision and he was thrilled to discover that in this version 'more is made of Starlight – he is the pivot and dominates everything'; and that there would be new sets and costumes with a high spectacle quotient, involving a bush fire, a mail coach ambush and a racetrack scene before a climactic fight in a swamp.

With Roy unable to be with her for the birth ('Not that I should be of much use ... the woman has to get through it by herself'), Daisy had comfort from her friend Mabel Russell, then appearing in pantomime in Bristol. Daisy saw the show the night before Michael was born: 'I came back to the room at the paper-shop and made myself a Welsh rarebit. I don't think I expected you so soon, but you came and a big, bouncing fellow you were.'

It was another of Daisy's friends, Hulow Hodgson – then appearing in music hall at Bristol – who suggested the baby's name, after St Michael's Church across the road ('she said it would be lucky for you'), although Roy was less keen, worried that his son might end up called Mickie or Mike. He seemed pleased enough at the news of the birth on 20 March, writing to Daisy (on the 22nd): 'Fancy young Master Redgrave having a

lot of hair and dark at that. Poor girlie, I expect he is a big fellow. I thought
it must be that or "two of a kind!" by the way things were going.'

Roy let Mabel and the rest of Daisy's families know the news. Their
marriage had been handled with considerable cloaked discretion. Daisy,
who had written to Ellen, F. A.'s widow, received a letter from that
remarkable woman, on tour in Newcastle: 'I have by this time got so
used to receiving *shocks* from all the family of the Scudamores that your
astonishing news did not surprise me as it might have done. I could never
judge you. I love you.'

While Daisy recuperated in Bristol, Roy was in poor health yet again,
being mothered by Mrs Loader who was clearly charmed by him, bringing
him milk puddings, hot lemon drinks and lighting coal fires for him.
During rehearsals he was apologising to Daisy for sending only the occasional postal order: 'Oh dear, oh dear – your poor old man is earning his
little bit of corn with a vengeance.'

When Michael was just over two weeks old Daisy travelled with him to
London ('Roy could not send any more money') to join Roy at Mrs
Loader's ('the landlady practically kept us'). As was beginning to happen
with increasing frequency with managements, Roy had quarrelled with
the Melville Brothers and his only work at this time was the occasional
'special week' with a stock company ('and they were *not* paying salaries,'
Daisy remembered grimly). Money was so tight that despite Mrs Loader's
kindness Michael was becoming progressively thinner, so worrying Daisy
that she took him to her 'sister' May, now married and living in Sheffield,
where he was nursed back to health on Nestlé's milk.

Realising by now that Roy was feckless about fixing work and that she
would have to take charge, Daisy persuaded Wentworth Croake, the
manager preparing *The Christian* for another tour, again with Daisy as
Glory, to cast Roy as the hero John Storm (a case of art reversing life – in
Hall Caine's torrid piece, Glory is the impulsively capricious one, John
the doggedly faithful clergyman who remains constant). Starting in August
1908 and booked until the following June, it began happily; the dates were
excellent, business healthy and Roy, as Daisy restrainedly phrased it, was
'fairly well behaved'.

Then about halfway through the tour Roy abruptly announced that he
was going back to Australia; he had, without telling Daisy, been in touch
with a new Australian management, the Anderson company, who had
cabled him with an offer conditional on his immediate acceptance. Daisy
was devastated: 'I was simply distraught, but as he had seen so little of
you, I sent for you and you reached me in Cardiff. I know I wondered at
the time if I should ever see him again.' Despite all Daisy's entreaties and
the emotional pressure of Michael's presence, Roy was adamant and

departed for Australia on the first available ship. Daisy and Michael, left behind for Daisy to complete *The Christian* tour, received a cable as he sailed from Plymouth: 'Goodbye, my darlings. Roy.'

On board the RSM *Ophir* of the Orient Royal Mail Line Roy wrote occasionally asking after both 'my old girlie' and 'sonnie boy', but mostly complaining at length about his health, suffering ever since 'the effects of eating fruit at Naples', and insisting that the ship's doctor said 'this voyage has saved my life'. Arriving in Melbourne and living in some style at the Union Club Hotel, he seemed to pick up remarkably rapidly; he had been flattered by being met by the Anderson company's representatives before various equally flattering press interviews. His spirits climbed further at the sight of his first script, even although it involved learning a big leading role with a short rehearsal period. He knew that in the role of Dave Gouldburn in a new Australian drama *The Man from the Outback* he had a chance as showy as anything Captain Starlight had to offer: 'I roll down precipices, extending from the flies to the footlights – I'm locked in a burning hut, set free by dogs, released by my faithful horse. Fights, shots, struggles galore.' By his own account he scored a triumph ('I had to bow and bow until I thought they'd never stop') but after only a few performances his health took a turn for the worse, as he wrote in a shakily pencilled note, adding faintly, 'Give Nutty a big kiss from Daddy.'

Throughout the summer of 1909 Roy's letters veer from euphoria as the applause lifts him up to despair as he lies prostrate, ill and hurt by what he sees as managerial indifference to his condition, undoubtedly coloured by suspicions of his drinking ('ungrateful beggars'). Excuses to Daisy come thick and fast – for not being able to send for her and Michael as planned, for sending so little money ('But Brand's essence is 2/6d out here!') or for the lack of vacancies for actresses in the Australian companies. Different tactics were in evidence by August: 'I am coming back to you by the first ship I can get on. This illness has cost me a "mint of money". One *week* alone – when I had two doctors – cost £29!'

Daisy's letters to Roy from this period have not survived, but she was having a hard time at home. There was no immediate prospect of work after *The Christian* tour and Mrs Scudamore, Mabel and Lionel (together with Lionel's actress wife Nettie) were also all out of work. They shared digs together in West Square in Lambeth and finally Daisy landed a job touring in a poor melodrama, poorly paid (£3 10s) on the suburban theatre circuit: 'The salary kept us all in food but I think we had to keep on selling odds and ends to pay the rent. Getting to the theatres took a long time and I remember coming home one night and sitting on the steps and crying my eyes out from sheer exhaustion.'

Roy by now was sending no money. Mabel, one of the few women indifferent to Roy's magnetism, flatly refused to believe his excuses and would tell Daisy bluntly that he was spending his money on a good time and that the suggestions of his possible return were a ruse to put her off following him to Australia. Daisy, of course, was too besotted to believe her half-sister: 'You see, Roy was tremendously erratic and could not be relied on. I always knew this in my heart but thrust it away. Men loved him and women went mad for him.'

The infant Michael had had no chance to get to know either parent, having spent most of his first year and more with his 'aunt' May, but Daisy was now planning decisive action. Roy had told her en passant in a letter that William Anderson, his Australian manager, was due in London to cast some additional company members. Daisy found out the address of the London agency where he could be contacted and invited him to see her in her melodrama, and although Anderson had already signed one leading actress, she was persuasive enough for him to take her on too, and to give her a £20 advance until they sailed: 'That £20 had to cover everything – I had plenty of stage clothes but not many day dresses and none for hot climates. But I managed.' Michael, now fifteen months old, was still in Sheffield with May and cried bitterly when Daisy collected him ('You were leaving May and I was a stranger') to take him with her on board a new vessel, the *Orson*. Once at sea, however, he settled down, happily playing for hours with corks in the scuppers and being fussed over when they stopped briefly at Gibraltar where May's sister-in-law lived. Intrepid as she surely was, it must have been a lonely voyage for Daisy – she always remembered the stars in the Indian Ocean and the blood-red sunsets she saw alone on deck in the evenings – something of a trip into the unknown with little idea of her new life in Australia.

Roy – showing few signs of all his ailments – was waiting to meet the *Orson* at Fremantle and then the little family travelled across Australia by train to Melbourne where Roy now had digs with another gem of a landlady, Mrs Becket ('large and large-hearted,' said Daisy) who adored the infant Michael, often babysitting when Roy and Daisy were working.

Perhaps naturally enough in the light of events, Daisy was always comparatively reticent about her time in Australia. At first, everything seemed bathed in a rosy glow – 'the old joy seemed to come back' – but once the Anderson company started rehearsals she began to feel less secure. Although the top managements – Williamson and the Taits – had imported English and American actors for years, this was the first time the Andersons had done so and Daisy always felt that the Australian actors resented her ('they felt neglected and outclassed'), although Roy was always popular in a company or at the bar with his hail-fellow-well-met breeziness.

Roy even enjoyed the endless touring and the often epic train journeys between dates, which tired and bored Daisy, anxious about Michael's welfare in temperatures which could reach 100 degrees in the shade. Nor was the Anderson repertoire much to Daisy's taste. Most of her parts were in 'Bush Dramas', plays such as *The Bushwoman* ('A Tale of the Outback') with Daisy in the title role and Roy as a strapping farmer, or the major success of *The Squatter's Daughter* in which Daisy's feisty heroine had to fight off villains pursuing a map indicating buried treasure. These plays were enormously popular and were lavishly mounted with real waterfalls and even real sheep, with many elaborate set changes; *The Bushwoman*, for instance, had no less than eleven different settings, from 'Dead Tree Swamp' to an opulent drawing room.

'Roy, of course, loved it all,' said Daisy – the primitive dramas with their bare-knuckle fights, the camaraderie of touring life, the late nights drinking after the show in outback hotels. In between tours Roy often appeared in his own sketches or one-act plays in music hall in Adelaide (one Australian city which Daisy really liked) or Melbourne, and it was in the latter city that Michael, then aged two and a half, made his first stage appearance, at the music hall where Roy was performing one of his popular rhyming monologues, planned to end with a big sentimental finish as Michael ran on to shout 'Daddy!'. Michael always kept his father's copy of this piece, addressed to 'Little X', an actor's son, which ended:

> This drama called 'Life' you have got to appear in
> Has plenty of howlin' and lots more of cheerin'
> And although but a 'callboy' to start with you'll need
> To remember that some day you're sure to be 'lead'.
> Then, when pa and ma's played out and you see 'em pause
> And you walk to the centre and hear the applause,
> Don't forget, lad – in front – maybe up in 'the gods'
> The old folk will be watching – you jest bet the odds,
> And amid the applause that your ear then devours,
> You will hear them both whisper, 'He's splendid! He's ours!'

Daisy was waiting with Michael in the wings for his debut: 'It was a full house and his monologue went well, but trying to get you on to the stage was an ordeal, poor lamb, you were so terribly frightened. However, I pushed you on as far as I could – you rushed over to Roy and burst into tears. You did not say "Daddy!" but the tears were just as effective. It brought the house down.'

When his parents were touring long-distance Michael was often left with Mrs Becket. Daisy trusted few other landladies, often less congenial; one, in Sydney, kept snakes and pet magpies, the birds terrifying Daisy by darting at the toddler's eyes. His own memories of Australia were inevitably both few and dim – recollections of being hosed down by Mrs Becket in her backyard and left, fully clothed, to dry off in the broiling Melbourne sun, and of a rousing fight with a boy named Cyril at a children's party when Cyril's flaxen curls stole the limelight. He also could remember being taken, dressed up in a white frock and brimmed hat, by Daisy to a matinée of an American musical and insisting at the end, shouting with delight, on walking down the vestibule stairs on his own as the crowd parted to make way, one woman's remark quoting a popular song of the day – 'His Majesty the Baby!'.

Of his father Michael had only two faint recollections – one of Roy bending over him to examine a new pair of shoes, and a similarly fragmentary memory of looking through the bars of his cot in a room with a fire in a grate, before which a man and a woman argued with raised voices. Just possibly Roy and Daisy were going through the lines of a play, but it is much more likely that it was a marital row. It would hardly be surprising. Roy, always restless, was now accepting solo bookings for his sketches in outback theatres prior to another Anderson season, allowing him to leave wife and son behind. There is something infinitely touching in the way Daisy kept always the few communications from Roy during this time – mainly bills from hotels and bar tabs. Roy's extravagances got him into such trouble that Daisy had to come to an arrangement with a firm of Adelaide solicitors for his debts to be paid off in monthly instalments.

Left behind with Michael in Melbourne, she once again had to make a major decision:

> When our contract ended Roy said he would not come back to England. But I felt if I renewed my contract I should never get home again. The management, of course, had to pay our fares at the end of the first contract but not if we stayed on, on our own as it were. I knew I could never save enough to get the fares back, so I decided after careful thinking to come home.

A good deal of emotion – desolating sadness, no doubt injured pride too – is behind this sober explanation, written many years later. Daisy still loved – always would love – Roy ('he affected my whole life') but she was clear-eyed enough to see that he was essentially 'flotsam and jetsam', and that her life and Michael's would be unsettled always if they remained in Australia. Furthermore, although she had thrilled to 'the old joy' when she was first reunited with Roy, she could see, as she explained to Michael in words that must have stung and hurt, even although written after Roy's death: 'But then the old joy failed, principally I think because he did not care for you.'

Daisy did not record if Roy came to see her and Michael sail off back to England, when their son was almost three years old. In any event, neither of them was to see Roy again. Travelling second class on an Orient Line ship, Daisy and Michael shared a double-bunk cabin for the voyage home. Daisy's sadness was relieved by the discovery that a congenial company of English actors, headed by a well-known comedy specialist, Kenyon Musgrave, returning first class from an Australian tour, was also on board. The ship's captain allowed Daisy and Michael to join the company in first, except at mealtimes.

Another key passenger, joining the ship at Colombo, was J. P. Anderson (friends called him Andy), returning to England after a long period working in tea and rubber for the Ceylon and Eastern Agency. Scottish by birth, he was sixteen years older than Daisy, comfortably off, tall, balding and moustached, with ramrod posture and impeccable manners. Before long, greatly taken by Daisy, he was spending much of his time with her, confiding in her one night over a brandy on deck in the moonlight after she had told him something of her life with Roy ('but I never reviled him') that he had cohabited with a Sinhalese woman who had borne him two daughters, adding that of course they had been left 'provided for'. At the ship's Fancy Dress Ball, which Daisy helped organise – she went costumed as George du Maurier's Trilby, Michael as a little pierrot – she had supper with Andy and won the first prize, a handkerchief of Maltese lace which he had donated. Before the ship docked Andy had told her that he very much wanted to meet her again and he gave her the address of his London club – the Badminton – where he could be contacted before he established himself with a London house.

The years between Daisy's return to England – in 1910 – and the outbreak of war in 1914 are barely touched on in her memories of her early life. She once told Michael: 'I wish I could tell you more of yourself as a young child but alas you were not with me nearly as much as I wished, but you were a very docile child and I'm afraid I frightened you a good deal.' As he discovered subsequently, there were reasons other than Daisy's professional engagements or absences on tour which were to keep him from his mother for much of this period. Initially they were together most of the time. For the first months after returning from Australia, the only job she could find – work for any actor always being harder to obtain after an absence – was in a sketch by Roy's stepfather, Adderley Howard, on the halls. Living in a cheap room in Pimlico with no contact from Roy – he wrote, according to Daisy, only once after she returned to England and she said that she destroyed the letter – she was 'sore distressed' at having to leave Michael in her digs, putting him to bed before going off to the theatre. This was a particularly bleak time for Daisy.

Luckily she was able to find better digs in Faunce Street, Kennington, with a landlady well known in theatrical circles, Mrs Gold ('gold by name, gold by nature ... many of "our calling" she helped to keep going'), a motherly woman who ran a cheerful establishment where Daisy and Michael had a big, light, first-floor room. A good-natured blonde cockney maid-of all-work, Florrie, helped run the household, bringing up hot water and trays; Daisy felt secure there, knowing that she could safely leave Michael with Florrie to keep an eye on him (he developed a distinct cockney accent for a while) as he played on the pavement or when Daisy was at the theatre. It was Mrs Gold who lent Daisy 3s 6d for a taxi one evening when she went, dressed in her best stage evening dress, to the Café Royal in Regent Street for a first dinner in London with Andy. Watching the meter anxiously all the way – it came to precisely that sum – she was touched that 'Andy, good man' paid the fare. And Mrs Gold also gave Daisy a coat – for an older boy and much too large, but warm – for Michael when, that first chilly winter back in England, Daisy went on tour, taking her son with her, in a sentimental drama, *Two Little Vagabonds*.

The production opened up north. After a delayed and freezing train journey they arrived late at night in Sunderland, their first date, where it poured with rain and where digs were hard to find: 'You walked around with me with not a word of complaint – finally we were taken in at a public house and given a bedroom with a four-poster bed and a feather mattress. You loved that feather bed. The landlady brought us some supper – a Working Man's Club were celebrating, so we got some of their fish and cockle sauce – It was sheer delight.'

There were rough patches on this tour, weeks when the business manager had no petty cash to advance (an occasional occupational hazard of touring still) when suppers would be herrings or simply bread. But Michael seemed happy enough according to Daisy: 'You were sweet at night when I got home from the play and we sang together, and cuddled up like "two birds in the nest".' Often she would recite Shakespeare or Tennyson to him – partly responsible for his early response to poetry – or he would demand his favourite song of the time, 'The Little Newsboy', a little boy singing to his sister:

> If I were a poor little newsboy
> Like those whom we see in the street,
> With old worn-out clothes and so ragged
> And old tattered shoes on my feet,
> Amid all the struggles and hardship
> The comforts of life might be few

But still I'd have one ray of sunshine
In such a dear sister as you.

For Daisy, this life meant poverty – 'poverty in so much as every single penny had to be watched' – but there were many happy periods, such as a balmy summer week with *Two Little Vagabonds* in Chester where they stayed at the Ring of Bells pub and strolled along the city walls after supper.

On returning to London Daisy moved into new lodgings in Shepherd Market, still one of London's oases then, with another treasure of a landlady who would babysit Michael as well as run up long flights of stairs with tin baths and trays, and whose son made Michael a long-treasured model theatre. With no straight part on offer, Daisy at this time occasionally appeared on the music hall stage, working with Augustus York and Robert Leonard (the original Potash and Perlmutter) when the American comics had a London success at the Coliseum. Then – at last – she finally secured a West End engagement. Her shipboard friend Kenyon Musgrave had kept a promise to introduce her to the actor-manager Arthur Bourchier who employed her at the Garrick Theatre. Mainly she was playing only small roles and understudying Bourchier's wife, the popular star Violet Vanbrugh, but as she was often 'off' with colds, Daisy had many opportunities to go on for her as well as taking home a regular, if hardly lavish, salary.

And yet it was at just this time that Michael was finding himself less and less with Daisy, spending increasing amounts of time with his various 'aunts'. Sometimes he was back with his kind, bustling Auntie May in her sooty house in Sheffield, sometimes with Auntie Bea at Wem in Shropshire where her husband, Uncle Norman, was a dairy farmer. Most of all he enjoyed visiting the Scudamores, when he was sent off on the train with a label – 'M. S. Redgrave, Portsmouth' – prominently pinned to his lapel, sent by what Daisy considered the safer system of parcel post (surely, when he played Jack Worthing in *The Importance of Being Earnest*, giving an extra subtext to his scene with Lady Bracknell and her outraged refusal to allow her daughter 'to form an alliance with a parcel'). Michael loved no. 8 Victoria Villas, a small back-to-back with an outside lavatory and a tin bath in the scullery. The Scudamores, with the exception of his deaf 'Grandpa' William, now retired from the boatyards and spending his days reading the *Strand Magazine* in the kitchen, were loving and demonstrative, fussing over him as a prodigy when he played his party piece of Grieg's 'The Watchman's Song' on the upright piano in the front parlour. His Auntie Annie allowed him to dress up in clothes from her second-hand shop on the corner of the street and Uncle Willie, who worked in the boatyards and was mad about the theatre, took Michael to pierrot shows on Clarence Pier and on Saturday nights to the music hall, sitting way up high in the gallery for George Robey or Little Tich. He always bought a programme for Michael, who would roll it up and bring it to his eye like a telescope: 'So that all I could see when the curtain rose was one face in the chorus. A sort of concentrated excitement gradually unfolded and flooded over me as I unfurled my programme wide enough to see the whole stage.'

Daisy, since soon after returning to England, had been worried about the possibilities of a European war. Now, with Zeppelins hovering, she moved from her digs in central London to near the park in Battersea, to a flat rather than digs, bringing Michael home for a time to be with her in her surprisingly improved circumstances. But before long he was packed off again: 'Poor lamb, life was not all beer and skittles for you and I think I was a somewhat temperamental mother.' He was sent briefly to a boys' boarding school at Leigh-on-Sea, home of one of Daisy's heroes, the socialist writer and editor of *Clarion* magazine, Robert Blatchford ('a *true* socialist, he had no class feelings' as Daisy described him), but as soon as German shells began to hit the east coast, Daisy swooped down to rescue Michael, this time depositing him with two spinster sisters – they became known as Auntie Lou and Auntie Gwen – who had a big Victorian house in Cricklewood in north London which was home to about a dozen children of various ages, the lodgers including a little girl some three years younger than Michael, Peggy, who was so shy that she hardly ever spoke and was rarely included in the children's games. Lou was especially fond of children, but tended to be somewhat scatty, once peroxiding Michael's and Peggy's hair for no discernible reason.

Michael was first sent to nearby St Ursula's School, convent-run, from which he was sent home after less than the first morning in deep disgrace for continually addressing the Mother Superior as 'Mummy'. Another nearby establishment, Mr Dove's school, proved more congenial; Michael quickly learnt to read and was soon devouring G. A. Henty and James Fenimore Cooper. If he missed his mother or wondered why they could not be together in London he did not show it in the few little notes to her which she lovingly preserved. One, a smudged few lines illustrated by a drawing of a teacher at a blackboard, is dated New Year's Eve of 1915:

I got best marks at school. Auntie Lou is going to take me to the pantomime. I am in a little play at school on Thursday. With love from your loving
    Michael
    With Kisses
PS The cat walked on my paper.

He began to write stories, winning 2s 6d from *Puck*, a children's paper, for an essay on 'My Christmas Holidays'. Daisy transcribed and proudly preserved in an exercise book a short story 'The Hidden Treasure' ('by Michael Scudamore, aged eight and a half years'), a Christmas-set tale borrowing imaginatively from F. Anstey's *Vice Versa* and from Lewis Carroll, moving from fogbound London to a wonderland of realms of ice where a waif-child is reunited with her long-lost father. Daisy was now appearing at the Savoy Theatre in the company run by H. B. Irving (son of Sir Henry) whose repertoire included his father's greatest vehicle, *The Bells* (Michael loved watching this from the flies and helping with the snow effects), and J. M. Barrie's *The Professor's Love Story*. She sent Michael's story to Barrie, who wrote a diplomatic reply:

> i expect some day u will be the author of printed books if there is nothing better for u to do.
>   Your fellow scribe,
>   J. M. Barrie

In 1917, not long before Christmas, one day 'Uncle Andy' – J. P. Anderson (or 'Captain' in his Middlesex Regiment uniform, although he was too old for active service) – pulled up outside the house in Cricklewood in a shiny black open-top car, taking off Michael along with – much to Michael's bemusement – quiet little Peggy, now all prettied up in her best frock with ribbons in her hair. Michael's bewilderment increased; he had assumed they were going to his mother's flat, instead of which she was standing, somewhat anxious-looking, in the doorway of a grander house in Chapel Street, Belgravia, not far from Hyde Park. Gradually he understood, as an Irish maidservant, Mary, took in the two puzzled children and showed him 'his room' and then 'Miss Peggy's room', that they were to stay. Finally, when he was left alone with Daisy, she folded him unusually close in her arms (she was less demonstrative after his toddling days) to tell him that Peggy was his sister, or rather half-sister, and that 'Uncle' Andy – from now on to be called 'Daddy' – and she were married.

Here Daisy was being economical with the truth; Roy was still alive and Andy and she did not marry until after his death. Daisy had made another of her decisions; even if she did not love Andy he was, as she had described him at that Café Royal evening, a 'good man' and he could provide security for her and Michael as well as their own Peggy. Michael dutifully obeyed Daisy, going off to Andy's pipe-bedecked study to kiss him on his tobacco-scented moustache and call him 'Daddy'. It would, of course, be some time before the picture became clearer for him. But how much can a boy of less than ten take on board of adult secrets and duplicity? Not enough, surely – even if Michael now had to share Daisy – to effect an instant transformation into a juvenile Prince Hamlet figure (and Andy, with his mild reticence, made an unlikely 'bloat-King' usurper). Since their homeward voyage from Australia, Michael had met his new 'Daddy' only three times while Daisy had kept her secrets well. There had been a Café Royal dinner from Andy for him and Daisy and, more significantly – certainly in retrospect and enough to cause a frisson even at the time for an observant child – there had been a brief encounter, no more than a snapshot moment, when Michael had caught a fleeting glimpse of Andy stealing out from the Battersea flat early one morning. More recently Andy had taken Daisy and Michael round the Middlesex Regiment barracks, when a fellow officer had said of Michael to Andy: 'So, this is the son and heir?' It would also be some time before another memory of a few summers before – when he and Daisy were staying at a friend's house in Pinner and he challenged her to a race on the lawn and was surprised to win so easily, looking back and noticing 'how heavy she had become and out of breath' – would become fully focused.

There were other changes around this time. Professionally Daisy now became Margaret Scudamore, a name more dignified in keeping with the more respectable 'legitimate' West End actress she had always wanted to be, although Andy – whose idea of good evening's entertainment was to sit at home with one of his beloved P. G. Wodehouse novels – did not greatly care for the theatre. Michael was also sent to a new school, Gladstone's and Vipan's in nearby Eaton Gate off Sloane Square, a respectable small prep school at which he most enjoyed Mr Gladstone himself, a gentle soul who preferred, late in the afternoon, to abandon formal teaching and simply tell stories or read colourful passages from history or literature. When the Germans began to bomb London once more, although Chapel Street had a basement area where the household could shelter together with Mary the parlourmaid enlivening the atmosphere with tales of County 'Wickerlow', Andy decided it would be prudent to rent a furnished villa in Windsor for Daisy and the two children, where they stayed until close to the end of the war. Michael would go each day into London on the train by himself – Mr Gladstone agreeing that it would help him to 'rely on himself' – and he learnt to swim in the Thames with lessons from a Windsor boatman. There were walks after school with his mother and occasional boating trips, Michael learning to row while Daisy fed the swans with their sandwich crusts. Once more he had Daisy almost to himself, Andy joining them only at weekends.

The night before peace was officially declared Daisy took Michael, already a keen film fan, to see *Intolerance* at the old Stoll Theatre: 'The theatre was packed and I nearly lost you as we were coming out but the usherette found you. ... We got a bus and got off at Hyde Park Corner and as we went along Chapel Street we saw an aeroplane with a light upon it and I knew that the War was over.'

To Michael, the searchlights raking the London sky somehow seemed less real than D. W. Griffith's film. There was a big party at Chapel Street for the victory celebrations with the house full of people, mostly Daisy's theatrical chums – Andy seemed to have comparatively few friends of his own – and a buffet of cold salmon and chicken, followed by the Victory Procession. This was watched in Belgrave Square and was an impressive parade (Michael loved the martial music) headed by Field Marshal Haig, although Daisy thought Marshal Foch by far the more commanding figure.

Michael continued happily enough at Gladstone's, although even more he enjoyed his piano lessons from the imperious Miss Smith who also taught John Casson, son of Sybil Thorndike and Lewis Casson. Daisy doted on Michael's musical talent, of course, but she was not so idolatrous as to overlook that while John's playing and technique were obviously superior to Michael's, at Miss Smith's concerts Michael somehow seemed to receive double John's applause. Miss Smith enlightened her: 'Ah, yes. Well, you see, when Michael starts to play he starts to *act* and that covers a multitude of sins.' Daisy emphatically did not want Michael to act – 'No life for a man,' she always said, more frequently now in her newly exalted social position – and she had been frightened deeply when for a period as a child Michael would point with his middle finger (startlingly similar to a gesture of Roy's, resulting from the old damage to his finger), terrified that history might repeat itself. Michael knew very little about his real father and heard nothing about him at home except on the occasions when Aunt Mabel ('Miggles' as Daisy called her half-sister – she was 'Diggles' to Mabel) stayed at Chapel Street, chain-smoking and gossiping at the breakfast table (Daisy was served breakfast in bed when working while Andy, with several directorships to occupy him, left each morning for the City at exactly 9.30 a.m.). Mabel doted on Michael and gave him his favourite toy – a raggedy doll made out of hairpins with a red bobble cap on its head, called 'Impy' – and sometimes naughtily fed him titbits of family gossip, giggling subversively one morning: 'I think Roy maybe only touched Diggles once and you, my dearest little Mickey-Doodlums, were the result!'

Much later Michael remembered: 'Aunt Mabel's information, though somewhat stunning, elated me. My father now seemed a sort of Jove, descending lustfully on his unsuspecting love. I became a Perseus or a Minos, chance offspring of one improbable but gaudy night.' This fresh perspective on the mysterious but magic figure of Roy slowly helped confirm Michael's growing sense of oppression in the Chapel Street house with its predictability ruled by Andy's – as Michael then saw it – humdrum and bourgeois lack of imagination. All his life he was able to recall, in remarkably minute detail, every aspect of the atmosphere of the dark, heavy dining room, scene of so many identical breakfasts, so vivid in the memory that he could almost taste the Ceylon 'Breakfast' tea and evoke the embossed wallpaper, heavy dark-red damask curtains, oppressive glass-fronted dark furniture, square-cut glassware and dull silver ('a terrible room'), although the drawing room, gold-wallpapered, L-shaped and always whenever possible filled with Daisy's favourite chrysanthemums, was a brighter, lighter space.

Andy, who did not actively dislike children but simply did not really understand them, was no doubt keen to see Michael packed off to public school, although he had been overseas for so long that he had no idea as to which school would be suitable. Nor did Daisy, none of whose family had ever been to public school, but she was extremely eager that Michael should go to one (Daisy was most zealous always to see the standing of actors improve). It was a combination of a passing recommendation from Daisy's friend, the writer Clemence Dane, and the fact that another of Daisy's friends, Ruthie Harker, had a son who seemed fairly content at Clifton College in Bristol which decided Michael's academic fate. He was duly put down for Clifton's Dakyns House, which was Geoffrey Harker's house.

Before that Michael had a last near-perfect summer – the cloudless months of mid-1921 – at Stratford-upon-Avon, with his mother all to himself once again. Daisy, in the Festival Theatre's company that summer, was thrilled to be playing in classical work at last – Mistress Page in *The Merry Wives of Windsor* was her best part that season – although she was well aware that the organisation of the ramshackle little old Victorian-Gothic theatre on the river was fairly chaotic and that artistic standards, with little rehearsal time and routine designs, left a lot to be desired. She liked her fellow actors, however, taking especially to the imposing Dorothy Green, the powerfully voiced Shakespearean who became a great friend, and she remembered the summer as one of her happiest. She rented a charming small villa about a mile from the town ('to me Shakespeare was still there') and she enjoyed taking Michael to sights such as Anne Hathaway's cottage and on long walks in the Warwickshire countryside.

Michael was allowed to 'walk on' that season for some performances of *Henry IV, Part 2*, which he enjoyed most in the final scene when he had to dash on, fists full of rose petals to hurl at the newly crowned Henry V. For him it was a summer always to be preserved in a kind of Proustian amber:

It was that long, dry blazing sunflower of a season, the shimmer of 1921. Of all the seasons I have spent at Stratford since then, that one remains to me the most memorable, the most exciting. To this day, a wasp buzzing around a bottle of lime-juice on a sunny window evokes a midsummer night's dream.

Andy and Peggy came for several weekends – Andy in his 'country' summer garb of white sharply pressed flannels – but largely Daisy and Michael were together. Possibly she engineered the arrangement, knowing that she would see Michael only in the school holidays after he began at Clifton. She, too, never forgot that summer, fixing especially in the memory their final Stratford Sunday when they punted a good distance upstream and met a couple, Percy Rhodes and his wife, from the theatre punting back: 'We tied the punts together and you and Mrs Percy Rhodes poled us home. Oh, how tired you were. You just fell into bed and went fast asleep – though you said once you remembered the stars so vividly as you poled us home.'

Back in Belgravia Michael found his necessary clothes and sports equipment, all the garments with Cash's name-tapes painstakingly sewn in by Mary, packed up – not into the regulation conventional school trunk but into a stout wicker costume skip from Daisy's days on the road (a sense of economy never entirely leaves a touring actor), his name boldly stencilled on the lid. Michael was ready to be sent off again, this time returning to Bristol for the first time since his infancy.

Three
BRISTOL-FASHIONED

His birthplace – along with his first professional home of Liverpool and Edinburgh, always a favourite touring date – retained a special place among British cities for Michael. He belonged to a generation many of whom seemed more than usually marked by their public-school days, producing a vast literature, mostly of violently negative reactions, on the subject. That was not Michael's attitude, nor was he one, like Cyril Connolly, always looking back at his Eton days as a prelapsarian idyll, for whom nothing in later life could ever match past glories. He never completely lost touch with Clifton – he returned several times in adult life and opened a new school theatre in the 1960s – where he was mostly happy, although it was the memory of particular masters and what he owed to them that was important to him, nostalgia playing only a minor part.

He could certainly have been sent to worse places; the 1920s was an undistinguished decade in English public-school history, with Wellington and Marlborough in particular housing regimes of gulag-like misery, marked by primitive sanitation, disgusting food and sadistic bullying. Clifton may not then have been considered one of the élite public schools but its balance between hearty athleticism and scholastic excellence was remarkable for the period. Its site was a great plus, high above the city in the leafy Clifton district of wide streets and charming squares of elegant villas. The school buildings were fairly typical Victorian-Gothic but inside it was light, comparatively warm (almost unique in that regard), surrounded by generous acres of playing fields and trees.

Clifton's founding headmaster had been the strong-willed John Percival, later headmaster of Rugby and then Bishop of Hereford, very much the Arnoldian autocrat presiding over a regime of conventional muscular Christianity with a strong bias towards sport. By the time Michael arrived for his first term in 1922, the reign of Percival's successor Norman Whately (1918–39) was well established. Respected by both masters and pupils, Whately was humane and simpatico with the rare gift of being able genuinely to motivate his staff, considering himself more the captain of a team of masters rather than an austerely remote figure. Games were still taken with ferocious seriousness, but Whately encouraged music (still today a Clifton trademark) and drama, supporting the foundation of a Dramatic Society the year prior to Michael's arrival. Subsequently others, including Trevor Howard, John Cleese and Simon Russell Beale, followed Michael from Clifton on to the stage.

Michael had no Latin and so was placed on the Modern Side, which had been at something of a post-war ebb but was gradually being transformed, not least by the housemaster of Dakyns, the master who had by far the most impact on Michael, the remarkable R. P. Keigwin – 'Keggers' to the boys – who later, more affectionately known as Dick, would remain one of Michael's lifelong friends. Keigwin was an old Cliftonian, leaving in 1902 with an Exhibition to Cambridge where he edited *Granta* and became a quadruple Blue – cricket, rackets, hockey and Association Football – while establishing himself as a brilliant linguist. After a naval wartime career and a spell teaching at Osborne, he had returned to Clifton to teach Modern Languages. His regime at Dakyns House was remarkably tolerant for the time, with only rare beatings allowed and with boys encouraged to pursue their own interests. Other masters could be somewhat wary of him; his own head of department, Bernard Yaudell, was never entirely convinced that Keigwin's teaching of grammar was quite rigorous enough and often had to reprimand him for being late for his own classes (Keigwin always professed contrition, blaming his unpunctuality on his 'rather strong Celtic strain'). Michael and he took to each other from the start; Michael never forgot his housemaster's dictum, quoting it in a *Times* obituary of Keigwin: 'You can't teach boys anything much. But you can encourage them to learn. Encouragement is what matters.'

Michael needed no special protection at Clifton. There was surprisingly little bullying there, although Daisy's costume skip came in for some initial ribbing, and he soon settled in, sharing his first study with four others, his only real alarms being the initially unexpected nocturnal shrieks of the peacocks from Bristol's nearby zoo. His first letter to Daisy was brave enough: 'I am by far the youngest in my form and am finding things rather difficult. It all seems like a dream and it seems very funny to wake up in the night and wonder where I am. We have a very nice little study and everything is comfy – barring the beds!'

It was as well that Michael was adapting without too much trouble to life at Clifton, because before long Daisy had another surprise for him, forced to reveal the truth about Roy. On 1 June 1922 she had received a cable from Australia, baldly and shockingly announcing 'Redgrave dead', followed by a brief letter from the Melbourne office of the Tait management confirming the news.

Roy had worked fairly steadily after Daisy returned with Michael to

England, appearing most frequently for the Williamson management. In the infancy of the Australian cinema industry he had worked for the Lincoln-Cass Film Group making various shorts as early as 1913 and even a silent version, much abridged, of his old standby *Robbery Under Arms* in 1920, although by far his most popular screen appearances were in some of a series of folksy family films known as *The Hayseeds*. By the 1920s, however, mainly because of his uncertain health, on which years of drinking and heavy smoking had taken considerable toll, he was working less regularly on stage and then only in supporting or minor roles, often in routine musical productions. In 1921 he toured for the Williamsons as Alif Bey, Keeper of the Harem, in the Otto Harbach–Rudolf Friml musical *Katinka* and later he had been employed by the Taits to play a small role in the old warhorse *The Maid of the Mountains*. The actor Carl Falb, who starred as Baldasarre in the production, remembered:

> At rehearsal an elderly actor whom I had to catch by the neck to throw down, apparently very violently, when he brings in some bad news, asked me, as he wasn't very well, would I not be too rough with him in this scene? On the last night, he came to me and said, 'Thank you for never hurting me. Your fingers were like feathers round my neck.' A few days later he was dead. He was Roy Redgrave.

The 'elderly' actor Falb recalled was in fact not quite fifty. Daisy received further details from Sister Cyril of the Sisters of Charity at the Sacred Heart Hospice for the Dying in Darlinghurst, Sydney, telling her that Roy had been in the Sisters' care for just three days, the cause of death being given as 'Pulmonary Tuberculosis complicated by Carcinoma of the Scalp and Throat': 'He had kept to his profession until two weeks before he died. His death was very peaceful and the suffering he endured with most heroic patience. There were several of his professional friends with him at the end.' Sister Cyril went on to inform Daisy that after his death on 25 May, his remains had been interred at the Roman Catholic cemetery of South Head in Sydney ('There were many floral tributes'). She also enclosed what was in effect Roy's 'obituary', a posthumously published final gallant flourish of the old Roy style, the last of his poetic efforts, written shortly before his death and printed after it in the *Sydney Morning Herald*. He gave it the title of 'One of the Best':

> One of the best! Held his own 'in a crowd',
> Lived like the best (when finances allowed),
> Slapped on the back as a jolly fine sport,
> Drank any tack from bad whisky to port.
> Fool to himself – that's the worst you can say;

Cruel to himself, for the health has to pay.
Months back he died and we've only just heard,
No friends by his side just to say the kind word.
No relatives near and no assets at all,
Quite lonely, I fear, when he answered the call.
One of the best. Held his own while he could.
Died like the rest, just when life seemed so good.

Daisy's reaction to the news and to reading Roy's last poem can only be guessed at. Michael was at Chapel Street when he was told the bare facts; that evening Andy took Daisy in evening finery to the Ritz to celebrate the news, which for him meant that they finally could marry (which they did, quietly, on 26 June). Michael's reaction to their behaviour can also only be guessed at. His mother's second marriage was hardly effected with the 'most wicked speed' of Gertrude's to Claudius in *Hamlet* (Daisy had seen and heard nothing of Roy for over a decade) but his attitude to his stepfather, ambivalent at best then, was from that point onwards in his private thoughts and soon, in his occasional diaries, ironically hostile.

Reactions all round might have been somewhat different had any of them known that Roy's lachrymose predictions of his own end were not entirely accurate. Not only were there 'friends by his side' (several fellow actors) but there was also – although neither Daisy nor Michael ever knew this – 'one relative near' at the deathbed. In the Registrar General's offices in Chancery Square in Sydney is the dusty evidence that the irrepressible Roy, without bothering about any divorce from Daisy, married yet again. Giving his name on the certificate for what was very likely his second bigamous marriage as 'Royal' Redgrave of 11 Woolcott Street in Darlinghurst, Sydney, he married on 30 May 1916 one Mary Seward Leresche, known as 'Minnie' and described as 'of independent means'. She had been born in Limerick, the daughter of a surveyor and although a Catholic (which explains Roy's dying address and resting place) she described herself as 'Divorced', as Roy did blithely too. At the time of her marriage she was living just along Woolcott Street from Roy, at no. 2B. Seven years his junior, Minnie survived Roy by thirty-six years, never contacting any of his family and dying in Sydney aged eighty-five; she, too, was buried at South Head. As Roy exited from Daisy's life – although she on more than one occasion tried to bring him back in seances when she dabbled in the spirit world – he might well have allowed himself some spectral glee at the thought of Daisy remaining resolutely unremarried until after his death, without ever knowing of Minnie's existence.

On his return to Clifton Michael found his musical education being taken well in hand. He was musically precocious for his age; Keigwin encouraged his further special tuition under the school's distinguished head of music, Dr R. O. Beachcroft, another of Clifton's 'enthusers'. Soon Michael was playing – Debussy, Bach and Chopin featuring most regularly – in house concerts and, word inevitably having leaked out of his mother's profession, he was also wooed into joining in the 1922 school play, Sheridan's *The Critic*. At this stage Michael definitely had no burning ambition to act; to any suggestion that he might consider a stage career the reply invariably was 'Good Lord, no!', followed by 'My stepfather would never permit it!' Still, it was flattering to be pursued, although his Clifton stage debut was in the unrewarding part of Second Niece, with only a few lines.

He enjoyed rehearsals under another of Clifton's encouragers, the indefatigable A. C. K. Toms, who took overall responsibility for each school play. Remarkably – it was one of the secrets of his success – he treated everyone the same, whether actors, carpenters or stagehands. Everyone involved was made to feel equally important and Toms had the talent for communicating and infecting a whole group with his own sense of total commitment. As in most public schools then, there was no proper theatre in the buildings; school plays were presented in 'Big School', a vast, high-ceilinged hall with appalling acoustics and dreadful sight lines. It was also unventilated and the heatwave that particular summer was such that Toms had to arrange in the wings bathtubs filled with ice blocks with electric fans blowing over them. This cooled the actors but only made the echoing acoustics even worse with the sound of the fans.

Toms recognised at once a real gift in Michael and he gave him a major promotion in the next school play by casting him in the leading female role of Lady Mary in J. M. Barrie's social comedy *The Admirable Crichton*, his story of role-reversal on a desert island when Lord Loam's family is shipwrecked, with the butler Crichton rising to the top as leader and Loam and family demoted, resulting in Lady Mary falling in love with Crichton, to the extent that she begs him ('Let the ship go, Guv! Let the ship go!') not to hail a passing ship to rescue them. In playing Lady Mary, Michael discovered in that scene that the emotion of the situation made him cry real tears ('Blubbing again!' disapproved a nearby rugger hearty, playing a marine, on the second night) and the reality of 'her' confused distress at that moment was especially picked out by the enthusiastic reviews of Michael's Lady Mary ('remarkable – he can divest of himself and put on a character' noted *The Cliftonian*).

The 1924 play – Goldsmith's *She Stoops to Conquer* with Michael as a delightfully befuddled Mrs Hardcastle – catapulted him into a position of real regard within the school. He never properly distinguished himself at games, although – urged on by Keigwin – he tried hard at cricket. Keigwin had some unorthodox coaching methods; perhaps only a supreme athlete could have persuaded public-school boys to take fielding practice seriously when the ball was delivered from a wickerwork pelota racket (less energetic for the batsman, of course, and considerably more accurate). But cricket never really became Michael's game and he only tolerated rugby when he grew so tall (by seventeen he had reached his adult height) that he could shine effortlessly in the line-outs, but his long legs gave him a useful advantage in his best sport, cross-country running. Secretly he yearned to be awarded his 'sixties' – Cliftonese for sports 'colours', little woollen tags tucked into socks – and was ecstatic to receive them to indicate that he was among the sixty best rugby footballers in the school.

At the piano, on stage and in print he was now established as a Clifton personality. He had begun writing for *The Cliftonian*, initially contributing some wryly Aesopian fables and the occasional poem, sometimes adopting the nom de plume of 'Moonshine', sometimes signing his contributions 'M. S. R.'. At Keigwin's suggestion he was even competing with one of the masters, J. A. Muirhead ('The Chop'), who had previously written the Dakyns House plays, delivering a successful if shamelessly derivative one-act farce, *Pigs in Straw*, set in a country inn (he had recently seen Ben Travers's Aldwych farce *A Cuckoo in the Nest*), cleverly writing characters tailored to his cast's personalities, playing a 'silly-ass' part himself as well as directing.

Until that summer all his holidays had been spent at Chapel Street – there was no repetition of his golden Stratford summer with his mother to himself – with occasional summer seaside breaks, one at Bexhill. Michael was increasingly finding Andy's unshakeable Conservatism acutely grating and his relationship with his half-sister Peggy was still uncomfortable, settling at this stage into a routine of mutually sarcastic banter. But the summer of 1924 was a departure – it also marked a sea change in Michael's development – with Andy's decision to take the family to Normandy for a three-week-long holiday. He chose, unsurprisingly, Veules-les-Roses, a resort not far from Dieppe and a hotel, L'Hôtel des Bains et de la Plage (not quite the setting for *The Boy Friend* that it may sound), much favoured by English visitors. Shingle beaches backed by steep chalk cliffs and the drearily mediocre food at L'Hôtel perhaps recalled familiar English south coast resorts. But for Michael the 'Casino' with its dance floor, even if not much more than a shack, the scratchy orchestra playing in the evening, the banks of poppies on the clifftops, all marked it as 'Abroad' and the time at Veules-les-Roses developed, for him, into a memorable summer.

To begin with he fell in love – or, as he said later, 'I imagined myself to be in love' – with a gravely beautiful, tall, dark American girl a year or two his senior, with the beguilingly Shakespearean name of Mary Arden

Stead. They went on long walks through the poppy fields together and in the evenings they would go along to the dance floor at the Casino where they danced energetically to the countless reprises of that summer's hot favourite, 'Yes, we have no bananas'. But he spent less time with Mary after meeting one of the strongest influences of his most impressionable adolescent years when new visitors, three young men, arrived at L'Hôtel des Bains.

The eldest of the trio, Oliver Baldwin, had visited Veules-les-Roses before when his parents brought the family there in the summers of 1905 and 1906. This time he was accompanied by his close friend from Eton days, Johnny Boyle, together with another young man who made a bizarre sight in sleepy 1924 Normandy. A kind of Quentin Crisp figure *avant le jour*, Sidney had bright-orange stubble where his hair had evidently been recently close-cropped, wore long, filmy scarves trailing behind him ('Mr Silk Scarf' a boggling Andy dubbed him) and glided along with a willowy, languid carelessness. Nobody knew quite how to react to this outré figure and he did not last very long. Sidney taunted Michael for being unable to play the piano by ear and after loudly, with considerable rubato, demonstrating his own showy keyboard skills, spun him unlikely tearful tales of how his mother had paid for the trio's holiday and of his disgraceful treatment as a skivvy by his travelling companions. After his abrupt departure back to England, Oliver Baldwin gently enlightened Michael; in fact Sidney's worried mother, a family friend of the Baldwins, had begged Oliver to take her adored but problem only child with them, to which Oliver and Johnny had reluctantly agreed, on condition that he cut his luxurious peroxided hair and abandoned his usual elaborate *maquillage*. At home, it transpired, he had been known as 'The Painted Lady of Sidmouth'.

Initially Andy approved of Oliver Baldwin even less, considering him 'beyond the pale'. Slim, tall, with smoothly parted auburn-gold hair, he had the kind of good looks Michael described as 'Pre-Raphaelite' and had packed an awesome amount of experience into twenty-five years. His ancestry was distinguished; a great-aunt was his beloved Georgiana Burne-Jones, widow of the artist, and John Kipling (Rudyard Kipling's son) was a cousin, but he had rebelled early against his background of privilege. At Eton he was wretched ('I have never been more pleased to leave anywhere, except prison, than I was to leave Eton,' he wrote in his later autobiography) and he despised the whole class-ridden public-school system which he believed to be ruled by totally false values. Further disillusioned and deeply affected by his experiences in the trenches of 1914–18 (including John Kipling's death at Loos) and the muddy slaughter of his time with the Irish Guards, he chose in the immediately post-war years to travel widely through Greece, Georgia and Turkey, was imprisoned by the Bolsheviks when captured in Turkey, rearrested after escaping to Armenia and then imprisoned by the Turks when fleeing to Constantinople. He spent time in six consecutive jails, more than once under threat of death, experiences which provided the material for his book *Six Prisons and Two Revolutions*. Michael was captivated by him and by his passionate involvement in Armenian affairs; Oliver had been appalled when acting as an adviser to the British Delegation (including Lord Curzon and Harold Nicolson) to the 1922 Lausanne Conference to witness what he saw as a cynical betrayal of Armenia to pacify the Turks.

Oliver's father, Stanley Baldwin, became Prime Minister for the first time in 1923 but Oliver, who had studied Karl Marx in depth (although his personal hero was William Morris), regarded Conservatism as hopelessly stagnant and joined the Labour Party. Not long before his arrival in Normandy he had incurred a storm of abuse at home for daring to stand (unsuccessfully) as a Labour candidate in Dudley, Worcestershire, an industrial constituency of rigid Tory tradition. Andy – and many like him in England – saw Oliver as 'the Bolshie', a traitor to his father, a 1920s Angry Young Man who blamed his father's generation for betraying his own in the war. But Michael said, 'I cannot recall ever seeing Oliver angry,' and realised that Oliver in fact admired many things about his father, not least his 'clear conscience' in such matters as giving every penny (some £125,000, a huge sum then) of profits from shares during the war to the nation.

Michael was dazzled by the spell of this charismatic figure – 'Oliver was my first hero' – and began to spend as much time as possible in his company. After an evening of charades at L'Hôtel, which Michael organised with Peggy, Oliver and Johnny treated all the youngsters to orangeade and then led them into a beach hut in the dark where they sat on the floor, listening spellbound to Oliver telling ghost stories in his mesmerising voice, cleverly underplaying the narratives and never condescending to his young audience. He also related Mark Twain's story 'The Jumping Frog of Colevas County' before they walked back, Michael staying close to him all the way while Oliver identified the constellations and gave them the names of the stars. Saying goodnight, Michael told him that he ought to be an actor, to which Oliver only laughed in reply, saying that perhaps Michael should.

Oliver was bisexual – he married in 1933 – and he and the ruddy, genial Johnny (who called Oliver 'Noll') had been lovers for some years. When Oliver felt that his socialist beliefs meant he could no longer stay with his parents, he went to live with Johnny in his house at Shirburn, Oxfordshire, close to his sister's place of Shirburn Castle, and it was there that he wrote the journalism which kept him financially afloat while Johnny bred Alsatians. They invited Michael to visit them later that summer and it was Johnny, more socialite than socialist, anticipating Andy's opposition, who handled the situation with aplomb ('John Boyle, when he set out to charm, seldom had a failure,' Michael had noticed). Johnny used blatant aristocratic name-dropping with Andy, let slip a little casual information about Oliver's wartime record, enquired – apparently fascinated – about Andy's fishing plans for the summer and, playing his trump card, tantalisingly dangled the possibility of a trip to Chequers for Michael should he stay at Shirburn.

Andy at once gave his permission and Michael spent a happy weekend with Oliver and Johnny (although Chequers had to wait until a later visit) before returning to Clifton for the 1924–5 year. Stopping overnight in Chapel Street before travelling to Bristol, he was surprised when Daisy, who had been very subdued on the family holiday, came to his room while he was reading in bed, anxiously warning him not to be easily persuaded politically by Oliver. She had had her own socialist principles when young, but she knew that Andy simply could never understand such youthful convictions. If there was a subtext to this unusual bedtime discussion, Daisy did not air it. However, noticing that Michael had propped a snapshot of Oliver in front of a framed photograph of her, she picked it up – without comment – and laid it flat on the mantelpiece before leaving the room.

Michael then was at that awkward teenage stage of being no longer a boy but not quite yet a man, touchingly evident from a scribbled list – 'Books I Have Read' – in a 1924 notebook. Aged sixteen, he was still reading Stanley Weyman, Zane Grey, R. L. Stevenson and Roy's favourite, Anthony Hope (also, along with many another English adolescent he was thumbing through Elinor Glyn's scandalous *Three Weeks*). But in addition, that year he devoured most of Shakespeare and Shaw, Yeats's poetry (to remain a lifelong passion), Ibsen, Galsworthy, Rupert Brooke and most of Pepys. He developed, too, an enthusiasm for H. G. Wells, reading virtually all – fiction and non-fiction alike – that he had published. His hero-worship of Oliver survived his return to school and for many more years. Taking up art and carpentry, he only ever finished one piece of the latter, a pair of bookends carved to resemble hollowed-out books, on the spines of which could be seen the titles of two of Oliver's books.

Michael's penultimate Clifton year was marked by friendships of a new intensity and one romantic attachment. At the OTC camp in the summer before going to Normandy he had found the routine not entirely his cup of tea ('Only till one has been on an OTC parade can one realise how boring boredom can be'), the high spots for him being the late-night campfire sing-songs. But at the camp he had become close to another Clifton boy, a year older, Geoffrey Hayward. Michael felt that he had never been 'unselfishly friendly' in the past but that now 'I love from a purely unselfish point of view'. Hayward went so far as to show Michael the diaries he had kept for two years – 'full of dreadful confessions, so that I might know all about him and, if I could, still love him' – and when Michael told Hayward that he wanted to continue the friendship, Hayward bought two identical leather-bound notebooks for them to use as 1925–6 diaries ('I dedicate this volume to my friend G. M. H., by whose inspiration it is written,' inscribed Michael on the front page of his, which he began dutifully, tailing off gradually over the terms). He and Hayward were together as much as possible, Hayward being now privileged as the first to read Michael's literary efforts, including his stoutly Kiplingesque poem 'En Avant!' for *The Cliftonian*:

> Don't ask to linger in your happy state,
> Don't dread the world before you! do not fear
> The mournful eyes, the quaver, nor the tear,
> Go forth with speed and learn your unknown fate.

Hayward also joined Michael to play Caithness in A. C. K. Toms's pro-duction of *Macbeth*, in which Michael had his greatest Clifton stage success in another female role, as Lady Macbeth, wearing a sea-green dress from his mother's stage wardrobe. The logistics of such a large-scale enterprise made this the most demanding of Toms's ventures to date and the general reaction to a production which had the full-blooded commitment of all involved was highly enthusiastic. Even decades later boys who saw or took part in *Macbeth* could remember in old age details of Michael's performance; Abel Phelps, a younger boy in Dakyns House, recalled Lady Macbeth's sleepwalking scene and her handwashing: 'He put into the action a sort of natural disgust, so real that it stuck in my young mind.' Daisy saw Michael act for the first time in *Macbeth* – attracting gratifying local press attention in the front row – and she too picked out that scene: 'You not only seemed to be asleep, you bowed your head just before the end of the scene and your head seemed to droop as though you were tired to death – a lovely bit of business.' However, when Toms suggested to her that Michael had the makings of a fine actor – as did Keigwin, genuinely struck by this particular performance – Daisy was aghast at the thought of Andy's disapproval. She felt in any event that Michael was too tall for the stage, also reaffirming her belief that the theatre was 'no place for a man', which Michael knew stemmed from her feelings for Roy ('The shadow of my father haunted her until she was an old woman') and her deep-rooted dread that Michael might grow to be like him.

Michael's diary became fuller when in August 1925 he, Andy and Peggy went abroad again, this time to Pornic, a delightful, sleepily isolated little town at the south end of the Loire. Daisy was working – 'How I miss her warm soft breast, athrob with sympathy,' wrote Michael, whose language in his early diaries can be more than slightly self-conscious. As at Veules-les-Roses, the Pornic beaches were shingle, but their hotel was directly opposite a charming little bathing *plage* and near by was a café which had dancing and classical-music concerts on alternate nights. They crossed to France by ferry but this time en route Michael had his first glimpse of Paris, where he felt that 'Peggy and her father seemed strangely out of place' and where, briefly alone to walk round the centre of the city, he experienced one of those exhilarating surges of the boundless expectation of adolescence: 'I felt truly happy, happier than I had been for a long, long time, I think happier than I had ever been before.'

Awaiting their arrival in Pornic was a friend of Daisy's, Margaret Chute (briefly mentioned as Margot Dempster in Michael's autobiography), a smart, sophisticated woman in her early thirties who had recently been to tea at Chapel Street. Margaret knew Pornic from the previous summer when she had rented a house with her sister, but this year she was in the same hotel as Andy's party, and alone. Before very long the atmosphere in the lazy summer heat subtly developed into something out of a Colette novel, as Michael began to spend most of his time with Margaret – they hired bicycles for long rides along the headlands, bathed and played tennis – with Margaret joining the family for dinner, usually the last to come down, to the punctilious Andy's indignation ('Late again, Margaret?'). Soon Michael's diary was recording a sharp, brittle atmosphere, fused with unvoiced thoughts, at their meals: 'Waves of thought from each of the party of four exuded from each other with steely clearness and, melting, crashed into fragments over the dismal board.'

Margaret became a magnet for Michael, an alluring alternative to Andy's regimented routine. Intriguingly, in the occasional later entries for this time, Michael's diary slips into the third person, as if he were observing his own behaviour: 'Watch the boy get up and slip along to talk to Margaret about 8.00. Margaret is sitting up in bed reading or, more likely, writing letters. The boy squeezes a lemon and orange juice into a glass. That is her breakfast and it amuses him to watch her drink it.' Their days were spent – not entirely to the approval of Andy, who was ill at ease with Margaret's emancipated chic and glamour – swimming out to a raft, racing each other through the waves and after dinner they would walk slowly to the end of the jetty, sitting watching the stars, with the low sounds of the waves on the shore and the faint, insistent music from the beach café in the background. Michael listened to Margaret talk of her loneliness and of her life in London where she lived with her mother, while he opened up to her about his literary ambitions and his frustrations at the narrowness of his life at home, which bound his actions, his thoughts:

> He feels he is understood at last – Then they talk in Margaret's bedroom by the dim light of the shaded bed-lamp. Margaret becomes more amorous. He kisses her and then goes back to bed. What is it she wants of him? He thinks he knows, somehow. But he likes her – she seems to understand.

At Michael's age when he was sexually inexperienced and fairly ignorant (sex education, of course, did not then feature on any public-school curriculum) – he probably knew no more than what he had gleaned from dirty jokes and dormitory sniggers and fumbles – Margaret, older and to him worldly, was irresistible. For her part, a tall, handsome and charming seventeen-year-old (Michael was lucky to escape the spotty physical blots of adolescence) was more than an idle holiday flirtation and she promised that she would get in touch when both were back in London, where she returned a week before the family.

Michael had been thrilled when Andy had planned a two-night stop in Paris on the way home, staying at the Hôtel Terminus, reassuringly close to the Gare St Lazare, even if Andy's idea of a night out in Paris was an outing to the cinema (Mary Pickford in *Annie Rooney*). They were allowed to visit the Grand Exposition on their second afternoon, followed by dinner (*le rosbif*) in the British Pavilion, walking back via the Pont d'Alexandre to watch the illuminations before Andy bustled them back to the hotel by 10 p.m. But, probably without even knowing quite what he was looking for, Michael later slipped out into the dark and near deserted streets, 'feeling rotten in mind and thoughts'. He noticed a man 'cruising' him and then he went with the man, an Italian, to his room in a dark street behind the rue de Clichy. But suddenly he took flight, suffocated by panic in the tiny room heavy with the smell of garlic: 'After five minutes I seized my hat, shoved a few francs in his face and, rushing out of the room, tumbled down the Stygian staircase, across the courtyard, into the street, with panting chest and burning, shameful cheeks.' The episode ends with Michael recording his relief to be back in London with his mother – 'A balm for hurt pride, a fortifier to diseased morals'.

As if to muddle his emotions and his sexual confusion further, waiting for him at Chapel Street Michael found several long letters from Geoffrey Hayward (who had left Clifton that summer), which made him wonder 'if there was anybody who was going to be a *Grande Affaire* friend?' for him at Clifton in his final year. But he was also spending time with Margaret Chute although their meetings were clandestine; anything sexual seemed of necessity covert then: 'She was very sweet and kind but the knowledge that even Mother would have disapproved of such intimacy (let alone Father, who nearly had a fit when I told him I was going to see *The Rat* film with M) made me keep our relation secret.'

Back at Clifton he spent the Christmas term sharing a study with Douglas Wilkie, a bright boy who had already achieved his School Certificate, which it was fast becoming clear – and which a concerned Keigwin kept stressing – would be unlikely in Michael's case if he did not buckle down to some serious academic work. He vowed to do so in 5B under the deaf but kindly Major Burbey ('always fond of boys who were good-looking' and much too indulgent to Michael), but there were many distractions, including a craze for keeping white mice with Wilkie: 'I imagine that about that age everybody feels the urge to take an active interest in someone or something living. There are many boys whose sensitiveness to public feeling makes it impossible for them to pursue the obvious outlet for this, smaller boys.'

In the spring term Michael developed his first major 'crush' on another boy, Cyril White, who was in neighbouring Watson's House. Cyril was Michael's age but smaller, with a sturdy build, large dark eyes and soft, floppy fair hair (Michael besottedly noted, 'I used to describe his nose as "wouffly"') and for most of that term it was a thrillingly secret 'affair'. Michael would daringly break the rules by slipping into Watson's House, braving the vigilance of 'The Mug' (H. B. Mayor, Watson's housemaster) to stay with Cyril for the whole 'Prep' period before being let out through the furnace door ('It became a regular thing – we spent every spare minute together'). Michael was deliriously happy when Cyril invited him to spend part of the Easter holidays at his home in Somerset.

Practically the only other person Michael in his enraptured state seemed even to notice at that time was the new, unusually young school chaplain, David Loveday, who had arrived at Clifton the previous term. Michael had been initially apathetic, to say the least, at the prospect of being confirmed on his eighteenth birthday, but in his discussions on the subject with Loveday, the chaplain had impressed him with his keen intelligence and unexpectedly acerbic humour. But even his last school play seemed to rouse him less than usual. Toms had selected another Sheridan, *The Rivals*, with Michael uncharacteristically dithering between Bob Acres and Jack Absolute as his first school play male role before choosing the latter, although he was unusually uneasy during rehearsals: 'I felt that everyone thought I was effeminate. They didn't really, but I was very sensitive to a critical atmosphere.' Again, despite the technical challenges and Michael's collywobbles, the scene changes were as applauded as the magical change from Belgravia to desert island in *Crichton* and the whole production a roaring success, but his mood continued uncertain, not helped by an unsatisfactory reunion with Hayward in London where they visited Kew Gardens together: 'He was cynical, bitter and depressing. I was joyful because of my coming visit to Somerset – he was out of keeping with the sunlit future.' After another awkward meeting they quarrelled – poor Hayward must have felt ill-used, but adolescent loves are often ruthless – and afterwards Michael visited a Turkish bath for the first time: 'I was the only boy there at first, amidst a lot of horrible men, some old, some middle-aged, some quite young. But they all stared at me and each tried to get me into conversation. The openness of their intentions was what was so beastly.' But he went on, recording: 'I went home to tea with a good-looking Austrian boy who was there too. I was a fool but I could hardly help myself.'

His impatiently anticipated week with Cyril in Timbercombe, about six miles from Taunton, he wrote of as 'almost the most enjoyable I have ever spent'. With Cyril's mother and brother away on a cycling tour, they were alone except for an aunt of Cyril's, free to enjoy trips to Minehead (with Cyril's dog Rover) Lyme Regis and Exmoor, riding ponies, playing tennis, picnics in the Quantocks and a visit to the operetta *Merrie England*: 'Each morning I would wake up, hear the birds singing and count the number of days I still had left in Paradise, as it seemed.'

London without Cyril seemed wan, although there was great excitement in Chapel Street surrounding a bold venture of Daisy's. Genuinely passionate about Elizabethan and Jacobean drama, and now with both money and time, she had set up a company, the Fellowship of Players, to present plays of those periods both familiar and neglected. She had been encouraged and helped by her old employer at the Garrick, Arthur Bourchier, who also made one of a most impressive list of Patrons and Supporters, including Lilian Baylis of the Old Vic, Dame Ellen Terry, Sybil Thorndike, Dorothy Green ('Greenie'), the actor-manager Robert Atkins and the distinguished scholar-director William Poel. Michael dutifully went to the anonymous *Fratricide Punished*, a first Fellowship production – a version of *Hamlet* reputed to have been acted by English actors touring the Continent in Shakespeare's day – directed by Poel with Esmé Percy as Hamlet and Daisy as the Queen ('she was very good,' Michael loyally noted). He was privately more interested in meeting up secretly with Margaret Chute to see Sybil Thorndike in *Saint Joan*.

At the Fellowship's first dinner-dance at the Hyde Park Hotel he had to do without Margaret's company but, back at Chapel Street where his mother invited some friends for a nightcap afterwards, one of the group, a vivacious actress called Tonie Bruce, got rather merry: 'Tonie came up to my bedroom to show me some photos of Rye. She became very loving and I kissed her several times ... What is it that these no-longer-young beautiful women like about us boys?' Michael by now must have gleaned at least an idea of the answer to that question. But he was still ill prepared for the emotional torments which marked his final term at Clifton.

As the summer went by, the careless rapture of his relationship with Cyril was under threat: 'Each got the stupid desire to show the other that he had lots of friends and both of us got a bit jealous.' Deep down Michael knew, abjectly, that he would make things worse by continual entreaties, but he was unable to help himself: 'I said that if he was going to start again and come to stay with me he was to play a song from *Merrie England* on his gramophone at such and such a time. He failed to do so.' Michael was devastated. He had a friend in Dakyns House, Peter Bartrum, who was now the head of house (Peter had had to help deliver the one Clifton beating Michael had when he and a few others were thrashed – a caning on the bare buttocks – for keeping forbidden Primus stoves in their rooms) and he was very sympathetic to Michael in this crisis: 'I found him in tears – Cyril had turned him down or something and he was trying to write a letter to Cyril but was crying too much.' Peter Bartrum agreed to act as a go-between or mediator between the boys, although privately he thought little of Cyril ('he had a younger brother who was much nicer', for which Michael was grateful). As he was for the distraction of David Loveday's company; sensing Michael's low spirits, David took him in his car on trips to Glastonbury and Gloucester: 'He is very interesting. His sermons are very good. Especially one on Friendship which he preached at my request.'

Michael's final days at Clifton were filled with goodbyes. He was especially sorry to say farewell to Mr and Mrs Montague who lived in Beaufort Road with their daughter Thyre, all of whom had been so kind to him at Clifton. Passionate about music and impressed by Michael's musical talent, Mrs Montague had taken him to many Bristol concerts, often featuring great artists such as Paderewski, Myra Hess, Chaliapin or Thomas Beecham with the LSO, and had also frequently invited him and other boys to Sunday lunches at their book- and music-filled house. Keigwin had tried his best to make Michael 'cram' for his School Certificate, but the exams passed in a kind of dazed blur ('I don't know at all whether I have got one'), although he could remember every detail of the Dakyns House music competition in July. At this, in a packed hall, Michael's solo was Brahms's Rhapsody in B Minor; the points awarded helped make Dakyns 'Cock House' in music, to wild applause. Crowning that achievement, Michael's playing won him the handsome Kadoorie Cup, which he was slightly disconcerted later to find at Chapel Street being used as a vase for more of Daisy's chrysanthemums.

He also won the T. E. Browne Prize for an original English poem, a strenuously iambic threnody on 'The Death of Abel' reminiscent of Matthew Arnold at his most sonorous ('I am not very proud of it as a poem,' he confessed). He had won some of the glittering prizes but what he did not have on leaving school was any sense of his future. Unlike many of the people he would soon meet, Michael while at school had not fully grown into – or invented – a persona for himself. Keigwin felt bitterly disappointed – and partly blamed himself – at the possibility that Michael would not gain his School Certificate and worried what his future might be. At his leaving interview with Mr Whately, Michael admitted a vague notion about going into publishing, firmly rebutting the headmaster's tentative probing about a stage career. Whately, who had been at school with Nicholas Hannen, an actor's son who had also initially repudiated the idea of the theatre, smiled, saying, 'Still, I shouldn't be surprised to see you there some day soon.'

While supposedly debating his future and waiting for his School Certificate results, Michael enjoyed the first weeks of the summer at Chapel Street with Cyril staying for a while; they were on friendly terms again, although romance had cooled, and they had a crowded time of theatre-going, including a sneak visit to the torrid Tallulah Bankhead in *They Knew What They Wanted* ('pleasantly unpleasant'), Peter Bartrum occasionally joining them. Cyril and Michael were together at their last OTC camp, at Tonbridge in a sunburning heatwave, with a memorable final communal sing-song round the bonfire until 1 a.m.

Instead of a foreign holiday that summer, Andy's plans included only a stultifyingly dull month – to Michael's mind – in a drizzly Scotland in Cupar, Fife, where Andy rented 'Dalgairn', a dourly stolid villa from which Michael could barely wait to return to join Cyril in Somerset for 'one of the jolliest weeks I have ever spent'. He then went on to Shipston-on-Stour, met by David Loveday to be driven to Arlescote where David lived. A tall, spare man with piercing eyes and an urbane, ironic manner, David Loveday had been a brilliant schoolboy at Shrewsbury with an equally dazzling Cambridge career at Magdalene before taking Holy Orders. He was very discreetly homosexual and it is clear that Michael was the love of his life, although the relationship was most likely platonic. He belonged to a dauntingly bright family, living with two sisters and a bibliophile brother at the Manor House in Arlescote, in the shadow of Edgehill. The four Lovedays treated Michael as an adult throughout his stay, and there were organised outings to Stratford and Blenheim. On the last evening of his visit David took Michael alone for dinner to the Lygon Arms in Broadway.

On the next stage of this mini-Grand Tour, David drove him to Oxford, giving him a present of *The Oxford Book of English Verse and Prose* and as they said goodbye Michael wrote, 'I realised how he would miss me.' He was met by Johnny Boyle who drove him for another visit to Shirburn ('that dear little farm cottage with a nice garden and lots of hens'); Oliver was away for a few days, during which Michael was with Johnny, of whom he wrote somewhat earnestly, using an oddly dated word – even for the time – for homosexual: 'He is an Uranian. His anxiety of the most trivial household matters is absurd. He fills the role of housekeeper almost to perfection.'

When Oliver arrived Michael was at first suddenly somewhat nervous, almost afraid of him – 'as I am with all people who seem to know my limitations' – but soon relaxed under the older man's genuinely friendly interest. It seems most unlikely that Oliver ever made any sexual overtures to Michael. Possibly recognising in him another person, at a confusing age, of a similar divided nature, he gently tried to make him think more deeply, more originally. Sitting together in a little home-made wooden gazebo in the garden where he did his writing, a peacock strolling on the lawn, Oliver first questioned Michael about politics and his beliefs, refusing to allow him to get away with woolly answers and claims of thinking himself a socialist. For Oliver, thinking was not enough; belief was what mattered. He promised Michael that he need not talk or argue with him – he could *show* him, take him to Dudley and prove to him that England still, in the phrase from Disraeli's novel *Sybil*, was 'Two Nations' – the Rich and the Poor. The conviction which informed Oliver's autobiography, written after he later left the Labour Party to become an Independent, with its simple assertions – 'I still seek the socialist state; I still seek the International Brotherhood of Man. I shall always fight hypocrisy and humbug' – burnt strongly behind his conversations with Michael. Gradually Michael understood how rooted was Oliver's belief that the object of life was to develop the individual soul and make it as good as one can. Oliver also had a conversational habit, deliberately disconcerting, of asking an occasional question out of left field, as he did once with Michael when he asked him if he had ever been to bed with a woman. Michael shook his head slowly in silent reply, to which Oliver quietly said, 'I think, if I were you, I would.'

On this visit he was taken over to Chequers, sitting with Oliver and Johnny after dinner in the handsome oak-panelled smoking room with its high mullioned windows framed by rich red curtains; later Michael played the piano and they all sang before his solo party piece of 'Sucking Zyder Through a Straw'. Michael subsequently wrote of this Shirburn visit: 'When I returned home I was already a different fellow to what I was before I visited Shirburn ... from that day I could not politically call myself anything but a socialist.'

Back at Chapel Street, however, awaited the cold shower of the news that he had failed his School Certificate. Somewhat unexpectedly, although Michael's Clifton education had cost him no small amount, Andy made no reproaches; he never entirely trusted 'brainy' people and the lack of a School Certificate, he would point out, had done him no harm. Michael himself cheerfully carried on with his social round – lots of cinema and theatre visits, including going to the Everyman, Hampstead to see Robert Loraine (an actor with a superb voice and effortless command, one of his favourites) in a revival of Shaw's *Arms and the Man* with Daisy as Mrs Petkoff. He noted privately that he thought Daisy had rather overacted and indeed this was becoming something of a problem; her inability, or reluctance, to throw off the 'grand manner' in an era of increasing naturalism on stage was potentially a liability. Also, Michael was playing a good deal of tennis with Peter Bartrum and Cyril White, with whom he now seemed disillusioned ('Really, that boy is a fatuous ass. Peter is fed up with him').

Peter Bartrum joined Michael for his first paid (£1 per performance) appearances on the stage, for two matinées at the Apollo, Shaftesbury Avenue in a Fellowship of Players production of *The Taming of the Shrew* with Loraine as Petruchio and Dorothy Green as Kate in September 1926. Michael and Peter had non-speaking parts as the Cook and Nathaniel, a servant, respectively. They had one brief rehearsal for their scene, directed by the veteran traditionalist Ben Greet, who was especially fond of a piece of inherited comedy business involving the Cook twirling along a line of servants, passed from one to another until he lands in Petruchio's arms. Perhaps unwisely up against such an old pro as Loraine, Michael in performance embellished the idea by eluding Petruchio's grasp and falling winded at his feet, winning and holding a gratifying big laugh. Loraine said nothing although he must have realised that this was no amateur's stumble, and at the second performance, with Michael all set to repeat and even improve on his big moment, Loraine bested him by moving away and beginning his next line, taking the audience's focus with him. Still, the two boys enjoyed the whole experience; Michael helped Peter with his make-up in a dressing room shared with an actor who excitingly talked 'a continuous stream of filthy language' and they were both treated by Peter's parents afterwards to a slap-up tea at the Piccadilly Lyons Corner House.

As for Michael's future, acting was never mentioned. Andy at one stage posited – perhaps hopefully – that his old agency might come up with some post in Ceylon, although he did add the qualification that it would involve a ride of twenty miles should Michael fancy a game of bridge. In the meantime, nonchalantly unconcerned – he always retained this

Micawberish streak – Michael was happily earning some pin money from occasional light secretarial work for Margaret Chute who had reappeared in his life after a spell working in public relations in Hollywood and was now beginning to do similar work in British studios. She seemed even more cosmopolitan and smart after America, giving chic cocktail parties in her West End flat, serving daring transatlantic concoctions such as Manhattans or Clover Clubs, worlds away from Chapel Street and Andy's watery Martinis. It was after one of Margaret's parties, with the room empty of guests at last but filled with sticky glasses and cigarette stubs, that a slightly tipsy Michael, in thrall once again to Margaret, alluring in then unusual black nylon stockings ('I've a friend who likes me in them,' she teased) lost his virginity, in a version of countless adolescent boys' fantasies, on the hearthrug before the fire. He was to find himself on the rug – enthusiastically varying positions – a good few times over the next weeks.

Daisy, innocent as to Michael's sentimental education, was nudging him in the direction of a Fleet Street career and he dutifully trotted off to various interviews arranged for him – he seemed at this stage to initiate little himself – armed with various letters of introduction which she had solicited. Without the magic School Certificate the best opening that seemed remotely forthcoming was a suggestion from the publishing magnate Sir Ernest Benn that a place might be found for him on the *Western Farmer's Journal*. Providentially, another publisher, Ivor Nicholson of *Nash's* magazine, suggested that he might profitably improve his employment prospects by polishing his languages during a period abroad and even volunteered to put the notion to Andy. Much to Michael's surprise, Andy made no objection; only much later did it occur to him that Andy, for a relatively modest outlay, would be getting an often irritating teenager out of the way. Andy's friends George and Vera Orbach, a jolly couple who lived in nearby Chesham Street, came round for an animated debate on the best place for Michael to polish his German, with the respective merits of Berlin, Munich and Leipzig discussed at length before George, who returned to Germany on occasion, insisted that Michael would be better served in a more intimate, artistic milieu, forcefully pushing Heidelberg as the perfect place. The perpetually beaming George also advised on and helped arrange tutors, travel plans and living arrangements, fixing remarkably quickly every detail so that Michael could leave for Heidelberg in early November.

Although his arrival there – before dawn after a delayed and long journey – was inauspicious, Michael was so enchanted by the town from the outset that he could have adopted for himself the slogan seen on mugs, postcards and chocolate boxes in the countless souvenir shops: '*Mein Herz ist in Heidelberg verloren'*. It had its kitsch *Student Prince* side but more seductive to him were the river, the rose-pink stone castle, the monument to Bismarck halfway up the hill and the staggeringly beautiful panoramic views from the top to the distant mountains of Alsace-Lorraine.

Throughout his stay he lodged with the stout, motherly Fraulein Rau of the Pension Sylvana where the long, bare corridors and large, spartan rooms reminded him of a house in an English public school. Michael hired a piano for his rooms, often playing with a German lodger who had the Beethoven septets arranged as duets. He was soon writing enthusiastically to Peter Bartrum about Heidelberg, his German lessons with Professor Wildhage ('A dear old thing, but so dirty – his odour is devastating') and about the town's Stadttheater ('small, but the most beautiful and perfectly run theatre I have ever seen'). Much of his spare time was spent in the town's many cinemas, seeing everything from *Ben-Hur* and Harold Lloyd in *Mädchenscheu* (*Girl Shy*) to his astonished discoveries of a new world, the masterpieces of contemporary German cinema then emerging in an extraordinary stream during the golden age of Berlin's Ufa Studios. He was completely bowled over by the daring of so many of those films, with the stylised gestures of the Expressionist stage carried into the cinema, particularly in the films of F. W. Murnau and Fritz Lang, whose *Doktor Mabuse*, *Der Müde Tod*, with its amazing final conflagration, and both parts of *Die Nibelungen* came to fascinate him. He saw many of these films several times in the Heidelberg cinemas, smoke-filled and filtering unforgettable images of immolation, fire, desire and death; they also, crucially, introduced him to a generation of German actors – Lil Dagover, Elisabeth Bergner, Emil Jannings, Conrad Veidt – by whose work, so completely different in amperage from anything in British or even Hollywood cinema, he was similarly captivated.

The theatre in and around Heidelberg had a good deal to offer him also. Opera was well catered for and within easy reach was Mannheim where he saw Richard Strauss's *Elektra* for the first time. But as he wrote to Margaret Chute, he was most impressed by some of the Stadttheater's dramatic productions, especially those featuring Maria Andor ('grave of face and sweet of tongue'), an unusually restrained and truthful actress whose style many compared with that of Eleanora Duse, by whom Michael was enchanted, although he never plucked up the courage to speak to her at the stage door. He wrote with passionate enthusiasm to Margaret about the Stadttheater's *Much Ado About Nothing*, which for him was superior to the heavy overdressed Shakespeare he was used to at home, staged simply against three large, graceful Italian arches ('without any fussy ornamentation') backed by a deep blue backcloth, with costumes in primary colours, Benedick in crimson, Beatrice in pink, Hero in blue-grey: 'The ensemble was like a beautiful Titian, lit with that lovely, brilliant yellow sunlight that one imagines to be an inherent quality of Italy.'

He remained in Heidelberg over Christmas; Daisy's present of a Christmas pudding was suspiciously inspected at Customs but appreciated at the Pension Sylvana. Also he attended a Weihnacht, a boisterous knees-up with Heidelberg's student fraternity after a stiffly formal start with a line of students all offering him a handshake and a bow to almost forty-five degrees. Exuberant polkas, Michael dancing with a girl he described as 'round and splodgy with an aggressive sniff and a laugh like the death-rattle of a winkle' and copious wine cup kept the party going until after dawn.

Early in the new year David Loveday arrived to visit Michael for a few days. They went all over the sights together in the snow, their trip to the deserted Schloss making Michael genuinely regret that he would have left Heidelberg before the annual summer open-air production by Berlin actors of *Sommernachtstraum*. They visited Mannheim's galleries and churches, and also there saw Wagner's *Lohengrin*, which David enjoyed more than Michael. By now in his occasional diaries – although his time in Heidelberg has few entries – Michael was beginning to frame his own opinions more freely, as Oliver Baldwin had encouraged, admitting that after *Lohengrin* and *Tannhäuser*: 'I have had enough of these aesthetic, silver-and-white Grail-serving, pancake-faced Wagner heroes and heroines with their swans and their doves and paunched choruses.' Even superior productions never totally won him over to Wagner; he remained a devout Mozartian and a Richard Strauss and Beethoven man. The difference of opinions caused no rift in his friendship with David, however. They walked up the snowy Königstuhl and along the lamplit banks of the Neckar in the town at night before talking for hours over long meals in the Weinrestaurants. Whether or not David said on this visit anything directly of his love for Michael is uncertain, but they discussed, among many other topics, homosexuality and bisexuality, parting on intimately tender terms: 'We kissed each other solemnly before he left and David squeezed my hand and asked me to pray for him.'

The comparatively few entries in his diary at this period express distinctly more original opinions, shaped and expressed with discernibly increased confidence. He seemed to be sensing for himself that his return to England would mark some kind of transition in his life and that he was ready for it. The last – and longest – entry in Heidelberg reflected, after a period of dreams more vivid than usual, on his future:

Dreams are strange things. For dreams are illogical and life seldom is. Dreams are not such worthless things, and dreamers do not miss so much as the world likes to think. Shall I be a doer or a dreamer? Logicality says do, do and do again! The task is to combine them both.

This resolve may have been stimulated by David Loveday's visit, which had spurred David himself to lead a 'Save Michael' campaign, determined that a failure in the School Certificate must not stand in Michael's way. Not only his own feelings for Michael underpinned his plans; he sensed ability in him, despite the School Certificate failure, and he knew that most Clifton masters agreed with him. David now plotted a strategy to get Michael into Cambridge and into his own old college, Magdalene. In those days candidates lacking a School Certificate had to pass the University Examination familiarly known as 'Little Go' as well as a College Examination, a tough prospect for a boy hopeless at maths, one of the requirements, but David for all his diffidence was not a timid man and he persuaded Andy of the scheme; he volunteered to coach Michael in Latin (another potential hurdle) himself and to find another tutor to 'cram' him in maths, followed by a period in France to polish his French.

Few Cambridge candidates can have had such back-up as Michael once David swung into action. After Andy had made the formal application for Michael to study for the Modern Languages tripos at Magdalene, the College received a remarkably united front of support with letters, all written on the same day, from Norman Whately ('he may do something remarkable in later life'), Dick Keigwin, with unusual candour blaming Clifton rather than Michael for academic failure ('a criticism less of himself than of our system') and David himself in a long, passionately argued letter, strategically dropping a few Magdalene names, stressing Michael's poor prep school grounding and underlining what he insisted were 'special circumstances'.

Although Magdalene's list of candidates had closed two weeks previously and despite the College tutor pointing out to Andy that over sixty candidates would be competing for at most fifteen places and that 'frankly, I think his chances would be small', he did cave in to David's pressure and agreed, as a concession to him, that Michael could sit the College Examination and Little Go together in June. Michael understood the efforts David had put in on his behalf and was determined not to let him or himself down. Back in Bristol, in digs in Clifton's St John's Road, he buckled down to the grinding maths tuition designed to allow him at least to scrape through in his worst subject. He sat the examinations in Cambridge, staying in Magdalene, emerging convinced that he had, despite his efforts, failed maths. Then, by now a seasoned traveller for one so young, he set out for France for the rest of the summer.

The surroundings of his French 'finishing school' were idyllic, at the unpretentiously attractive Château de Lestiou near Avary in the Loire-et-Cher district, its gardens sloping down gently to the river. It was run by Monsieur Sémézies, described as '*Ancien professeur de L'École Berlitz*', leading Michael to expect a greybeard pedant; he was rather surprised to be met by a friendly young man and his attractive wife. There were only a handful of other pupils, including two German boys (with whom Michael had to make a conscious effort not to speak German), and the chateau's regime was relatively relaxed, with morning French classes and the afternoons spent relaxing, punting on the Loire or walking through the surrounding fields. Most evenings involved music, either gramophone records or Michael and one of the German students on piano and cello.

There was one memorable break, when M. Sémézies organised a weekend trip to Touraine to see the great French actor Louis Jouvet in Jules Romains' *Doctor Knock*. Jouvet's impact on Michael was similar to the innovatory shock of the stars of German cinema, so different from the genteel restraint of so much Anglo-Saxon acting. Immensely impressed by Jouvet as 'a true artist, a real *homme du théâtre*', Michael was fascinated to find him not at all the pedagogic elocutionist some of his critics alleged, but a constantly involving actor, with a relaxed ease inside a formidable and totally assimilated technique, seemingly inhabiting each moment as if for the first time. He only saw Jouvet again on film but he was to remain for Michael another 'hero' figure – the ideal actor, 'a true artist' impervious to compromise, always an *acteur* rather than a *comédien* – throughout his own career.

While Michael was at the chateau, David Loveday was working away on his behalf at home. He wrote to Michael in early July that he had been talking to his Magdalene chums, including the College tutor, and that the news on the Little Go front was 'good so far' with only the dreaded maths, as yet unmarked, to worry about, encouraging him with: 'You have good friends at Magdalene now, not one alone.' No wonder, then, that Michael was beginning to see David, as he had regarded others – Oliver, Clifton masters, even barely older boys – as a kind of father figure and substitute for Andy.

A week later, when he was playing croquet in the garden one glorious afternoon, a telegram arrived for him announcing '*Accepté par la Madeleine*'. For a moment or two he was puzzled – what did either the great white church in Paris or Proust's little sponge cake have to do with him? – before the penny dropped with the realisation that at least his immediate future was firmly fixed.

Four
TREADING THE WIND

Halfway through his time at Cambridge – originally intending the normal undergraduate three years, he stayed for four – Michael was 'profiled' in various university magazines. In the lightest of these – *Granta* – his inclusion in the series 'Those in Authority', illustrated by a photograph of Michael in his rooms, posed soulfully reading a book, brought him some playful teasing, with the suggestion that his birthplace above a Bristol paper shop was surely a forecast of his Cambridge literary stardom, adding: 'He spent five years at Clifton. Work and games whispered their siren syllables in his ear. Sternly he rejected their advances and confined himself to piano, poetry and plays.'

During his first academic year, however, it seemed as if the Clifton pattern was to be totally reversed. His first lodgings at Cambridge were close to Magdalene's gates, just across the river in Bridge Street, in rooms below those of a fellow Cliftonian, Robin Fedden. In different houses, they had scarcely known each other at school, although Michael did confess that once he had cribbed so glaringly from Robin while sitting next to him during a maths exam that he only escaped a beating by flagrant perjury. Robin's father was a distinguished writer and painter – his watercolours were particularly prized – Romilly Fedden, whose pictures decorated Robin's rooms. Michael's decor was rather more austere, enlivened only by a few Bakst reproductions of ballet prints, framed in passe-partout, the ubiquitous hired piano and some bunches of flowers. Robin was reserved, even shy, but he and Michael – each knowing very few others at Cambridge, they were initially much together – became real friends, very much through a shared love of poetry, especially that of Keats.

Also soon after arrival Michael became friends with another Magdalenian, Humphrey Browne, a gregarious Reptonian who, like Michael, had a good light baritone voice useful for the College's Choral Society, and whose passion for music exceeded even Michael's. His other close Magdalene friend was an Anglophile, impeccably mannered French student Louis le Breton, who had studied briefly at the Sorbonne prior to applying to Cambridge to read Geography. Like Michael – and many of his friends (and lovers) then and later – Louis was fatherless; his father had died when he was a young boy and he was extremely close to his mother Hélène, who divided her time between a Paris apartment and the family chateau.

Michael was determined initially to concentrate predominantly on his academic work and to resist the temptations of more frivolous pursuits. Word of his Clifton theatrical successes had reached the ears of the university's Amateur Dramatic Club (the ADC) and David Loveday had not failed, in singing Michael's praises to his Cambridge friends, to mention his acting ability. He was politely non-committal when the ADC's representative called on him in his rooms to sound out his interest, but as he told Thyre Montague back in Bristol: 'I refused a speaking part in *King Arthur*, Purcell's opera which is being done at the theatre next week. I refused Volumnia in the Marlowe Society's *Coriolanus* which comes off at the end of this term. This was a great renunciation and I am justly proud of it.'

His few outside activities during most of that first year were either musical – he was soon on the committee of the Magdalene College Music Club and played occasionally at College concerts – or, more unexpectedly, athletic. Rejecting the blandishments of the rowing team, for a brief period in the spring term he enthusiastically took up athletics, turning out for Magdalene against Trinity and then Sidney Sussex, coming third in the mile on both occasions.

This plunge into athletics might well have continued had he not, during his second term, fallen in love – no Clifton 'crush' or tentative fumblings this time, but his first real passionate adult love affair – and it absorbed him to the exclusion of everything else but his work. This was with Michael Garrett who had arrived at Magdalene at the same time as Michael. His father also had died when he was a child and his mother had moved from their first home in Suffolk to live in Eastbourne, which he loathed. Garrett had been a bright pupil at Rugby, effortlessly sailing through his Oxford and Cambridge Joint Board exams, and he had also been a strong all-round sportsman. He was reading History, having switched from his original choice of Classics, in which he had shone at Rugby. His physique was impressive – an unusually squarish head on a powerful body with a dazzling smile – although some found his offhand, laconic brand of humour somewhat disconcerting. But Michael was totally intoxicated by him, physically and mentally, at least in the early stages of their affair and Garrett, with his quicksilver intelligence and throwaway wit, for two years continued to cast a spell on Michael that was not easily broken. Their letters have mostly disappeared but it is clear that at Cambridge they were then in each other's company as much as possible.

They studied together – Garrett, too, was determined to do well aca-demically – which helped Michael concentrate enough on his own work to achieve a 2/1 in French and, somewhat disappointingly, a 2/2 in German in the first part of the Modern Languages tripos in the summer of 1928. He was already debating the possibility of switching to English, partly because of his disillusion with the uninspired teaching in Modern Languages, more significantly because of his instinct that he would respond more positively to and learn more from those beginning to make an impact in the Cambridge English faculty.

Shortly before the end of his first summer term Michael had an informal but crucial interview with I. A. Richards, the Magdalene don who was unquestionably more instrumental than any other then at Cambridge in transforming the university's approach to the teaching of English, moving it away from the belle-lettrisme of its past under the great 'Q', Sir Arthur Quiller-Couch, towards a radical, almost scientifically based discipline rooted in precision, the primacy of the word and, as a seminal Richards book put it, *The Meaning of Meaning*.

Cambridge then was informed widely by this attitude of neo-scientific analytical scrutiny, perhaps to some degree stemming from the university's reputation for the spirit of enquiry in the work of such scientist-dons as Ernest Rutherford or J. B. S. Haldane. Richards was still developing the work which would result in *Practical Criticism* (published in 1929), but already he had more than a few devoted disciples, none more fervent than the astonishingly precocious Magdalene undergraduate William Empson, already a published poet and hard at work on the book that would become *Seven Types of Ambiguity*. Michael had read Empson's work and admired him – this was another case of near hero-worship – as the most talented writer of his own generation he had encountered. They had discussed poetry together, with Empson occasionally reading his verse out loud, rolling his enormous saucer eyes like the mythical dog in Hans Christian Andersen's 'The Tinder-box', but Michael then remained too shy to show Empson his own work. His talks with Empson and his meeting to discuss his future with Richards made Michael – with Richards's encouragement – decide to change to English even although he would not be taught by Richards who was leaving for a period to teach in Japan.

With exams and that major decision out of the way, suddenly Michael seemed to emerge from the cocoon which had encased him to date, waking up to Cambridge's alternative possibilities, and he thoroughly enjoyed the last weeks of that summer term. He began to write for *Granta*, the most light-hearted student publication – film criticism to begin with, often acutely funny – and he made his first appearance on the Cambridge stage. In the relaxed atmosphere of May Week the ADC produced Goldoni's comedy *The Servant of Two Masters* directed – very much towards farce – by Frank Birch, who had directed at the Cambridge Festival Theatre and who handled large student casts (all male in those days) extremely efficiently. This Venice-set romp, using Scarlatti and Galuppi as scene-setting music, had Robert Eddison, a craggily tall Trinity undergraduate, the club's secretary and already established as a leading student actor, as the heroine Beatrice (usefully disguised as her own brother for much of the action) and Michael as her pursuing lover Florindo. It was an ideal summer choice and a big success, Michael's assured and charming performance being noted with interest by the leading figures in undergraduate theatre.

Also during the final weeks of term while walking – appropriately enough – to Rupert Brooke's Grantchester with Robin Fedden one afternoon, they had jointly the idea to start a Cambridge literary magazine, designed as an outlet for the original talent (not only poetic) surely abundant enough to make a viable addition to both *Granta* and the quasi-official (and extremely sober) magazine, the *Cambridge Review*. By the end of term Michael had fixed up with R. L. Severs, the Cambridge printers, to produce *The Venture*, as they decided to call it, while Robin suggested a third co-editor, Anthony Blunt, a second-year Trinity student whose air of somewhat aloof, mandarin hauteur made him distinctly intimidating, but who could be helpful in selecting material on art and in advising on the design aspect of the publication. Blunt accepted the proposal immediately and the three co-editors met during the last days of term, each agreeing to solicit poems, articles, drawings and – not the least important – subscriptions. It was planned to produce the first issue of *The Venture* in October.

Michael visited Chapel Street briefly at the start of the long vacation, bringing Michael Garrett to stay. The atmosphere in the household was uneasy; already the early signs of Daisy's battle with alcohol were occasionally evident. She still had her drinking mostly under control but the combination of professional disappointments – she did not work as much as she felt she ought to and a recent performance as Lady Bracknell in a modern-dress production of *The Importance of Being Earnest* had been less than a triumph – and boredom, especially when out of work, could make her querulously difficult to handle after a few gins. Michael and Peggy had grown much closer; the alliance in a common cause over Daisy's drinking no doubt helped, and Peggy was grateful for Michael's understanding over her frustrations when an adolescent love affair with a young German was firmly squashed by a disapproving Andy. But Michael was too restlessly impatient to remain in London for long; he and Michael Garrett were off on holiday to France, initially to the area around Mont St-Michel.

This shared holiday was blissfully happy, full of pagan days in the sun, bathing and passionate love. Michael wrote to his Magdalene tutor, F. D. Scott: 'Michael Garrett and I are in Brittany for a fortnight and enjoying this lovely place immensely. The exterior of Mont St-Michel disappointed us, but inside the Abbey is wonderful. The village is enchanting, full of curio shops, strawberries and lobsters.' The two Michaels often found deserted coves where they could swim naked and read the long days away, with only the rare upset – Mont St-Michel showed its appreciation of its namesake by providing a bad lobster at one dinner – to cloud the horizon.

When Garrett returned to England Michael moved on to join Louis le Breton at the family chateau – the Château de Beaucé near Sable – where Louis's mother Hélène was also staying. The balance of Michael's intense friendship with Louis was always uneven, although never uneasy. Michael was extremely fond of Louis with his gentle, old-world courtesy and found his knowledge and appreciation of English poetry, and his painting, remarkable whereas for Louis Michael had the status of an ideal, a kind of English Apollo, and he loved him unconditionally, without ever asking for or expecting his feelings to be returned. Beaucé was an idyllic, peaceful haven with abundant flower-filled gardens – Louis was also a gifted horti-culturist – and Michael always felt restored and happy staying there. After that first brief Beaucé visit Louis wrote resignedly to Michael of the pangs of separation: 'Le sentiment, fortifié ces jours ci, que ma vie serait vide et complètement démicé de sens et d'intérêt si je ne t'amais pas. Je pense tout le temps à la vie que tu dois mener avec Michael G.'

Michael's summer travels continued with a brief visit to Sicily, then on to a distinctly rum interlude at the Villa Romana on the shores of Lake Garda, where it had been arranged by his Cambridge friend Francis Cook that he should spend a week or so as the guest of an elderly aesthete, a kind of expatriate 'beauty lover' in the John Addington Symonds mould, called Fothergill Robinson. The villa was comfortable, decked with photo-graphs of musical celebrities – Melba, Caruso, John McCormack – and little was demanded of villa guests, always personable Oxbridge under-graduates, except to keep Robinson company as he talked and reminisced, at length, after dinner. Food was Lucullan, served by Robinson's 'servant', introduced as 'Marco', although it transpired that he was actually Sam from Leamington Spa where he had been a chorister before being taken up by Robinson. On hearing Michael sing, Robinson became convinced that he had spotted a musical prodigy, a second Steuart Wilson, offering to pay for Michael to study in Berlin; he turned decidedly chilly when Michael confessed that his ambition was to be a poet and brought the visit to an abrupt close.

The last leg of this extended European holiday took him back to France, to Chantemesle, about twenty miles from Paris, where the Fedden family had a delightful house which had previously been the home of another artist, Charles Conder 'the English Impressionist'. Once again the French weather was cloudless; Michael spent most days reading Proust in French for the first time and discussing possible material for *The Venture* with Robin who had already drummed up a good few subscriptions.

The Michael who returned to Cambridge to share new digs – further out from the centre in Victoria Road – with Louis le Breton and Michael Garrett was different, more assured than the teenager who had gone up the previous year. The period of his Cambridge stardom was beginning, with a whirlwind of activity and a whole new group of friends, the most significantly enduring of whom was Dick Green, a new Magdalene arrival, introduced to Michael by Dick's fellow Reptonian Humphrey Browne. Tall, distinctly stork-like, already a chain smoker and an elusive mixture of gentle shyness and breathtakingly flagrant misrule, Dick was initially suspicious of Michael and his popularity, but during one long winter walk they came to respond to each other and relax in each other's company. Dick, too, had literary ambitions but was shy in the extreme of showing his work to others (he wrote virtually nothing for undergraduate publications). He was homosexual – in his first Cambridge term he went through agonies, he confessed to Michael, over a German dancer, Ernst – but he and Michael were never lovers, one reason perhaps why their friendship, often a puzzle to outsiders, was so unusually close and so steadfast. Although Michael was slightly the elder – it was he who introduced Dick to alcohol, something he had later cause to regret – Dick was oddly the more mature in some ways. Somewhat like Oliver Baldwin he detested woolly or sentimental thinking; he had absolutely no sense of conventional religion ('Good old humanism' did for him) but over the years his Stoic sensibility – Marcus Aurelius and Zeno were, even at Cambridge, his most admired writers – came to influence Michael deeply. Dick's other great Cambridge friend also became close to Michael – Gervase Smith, an eccentric Byronic figure even then, eschewing electric light for candelabra in his rooms, which were decorated in a unique mixture of the rococo and Victoriana. Both Dick and Gervase became part of a group known satirically as 'Michael and his Angels' (after Henry Arthur Jones's play *Michael and his Lost Angel*) which met in his digs for play readings, music or simply animated talk.

Michael now was fully inhabiting his role as aesthete. In *Granta* during that term he contributed to a group parody of Virginia Woolf's recently published novel *Orlando*, creating a cross-gender heroine named Verandah in what emerged as a rather mild pastiche of Bloomsbury mannerisms, illustrated by several striking photographs of Anthony Blunt in pensive drag as the squib's eponymous heroine. That term's issue of the *Magdalene*

College Magazine included his poem 'From a Sequence', full of Empsonian characteristics, notably a penchant for compound words ('ice-rain', 'sinew-frozen') but it seems a wan piece compared with the real thing of Empson's 'Fighting for Duck' in the same issue. The Jubilee number of the *Cambridge Review*, appearing at the same time, carried a poem of Michael's, a yearning ode titled 'To Beauty Dead'; it also announced the imminent publication of the first issue of *The Venture* at 1s 6d. There was another announcement, too, which the co-editors of *The Venture* had not anticipated, trumpeting a rival new publication to appear almost simultaneously, called *Experiment*, to be edited by Empson and Jacob Bronowski, one of the very few non-public-school boys (and one of the even fewer also Jewish) at Cambridge then, although Alfred Cooke from Blackpool (soon to change his name to Alistair) was making a mark as a critic on *Granta*.

The so-called 'battle' between *Experiment* and *The Venture* was more a rivalry in the minds of their respective editors and contributors, although broadly speaking *The Venture* tended to be more traditionalist while *Experiment* took its cue from its name, much helped by the *réclame* from Empson's name and the hard work from 'the dynamic gnome' as his friend Julian Trevelyan called Bronowski, who was brilliant at sweet-talking people into taking subscriptions. But in reality there were quite a few cross-overs among contributors (even Empson published in *The Venture*) although Michael encouraged the assumed rivalry in publicity. Later he was hard on *The Venture* ('a farrago of juvenile trifles') – too hard in the light of some later issues – but certainly the first issue was a disappointment.

Only Blunt of the co-editors had any experience of running a magazine; at Marlborough with John Betjeman he had co-edited a short-lived school publication, *The Heretick*, which had the bonus of advice from Blunt's great friend at school, Louis MacNeice, whose poems were now beginning to establish his reputation. But for *The Venture* original submissions over the vacation had been thin on the ground, so much so that Michael in desperation to pad out the first number had solicited from Oliver Baldwin a John Drinkwater sonnet and a poem by old Magdalenian J. R. Ackerley (both dismal efforts). Of the poems, only the two contributions provided by Blunt from Louis MacNeice – an Oxford undergraduate – had any merit, rather undermining the magazine's claim to be a showcase for new Cambridge literary talent. By far the best pieces were a tightly argued essay on Blake, icily dismissive of Lytton Strachey's view of the poet, by Alister Watson, a friend of Blunt's and one of the few openly Marxist students at Cambridge then, and from Blunt himself a lapidary, maturely cool piece on 'Self-Consciousness in Modern Art', very much influenced by the scientific approach to art criticism of the Bloomsbury writer Clive Bell. However, far too much of the first *Venture* carried a pungent aroma of

shopworn Bloomsbury, evidenced most strongly in two dreadful poems –
'Nostalgiques Demons d'Automne', mistily evoking 'diaphanous shrouds
of autumn dusk' – by George Rylands.

George – always known as Dadie (from his early inability to pronounce
'baby') – Rylands, after Eton and a dazzling undergraduate career at
King's College, Cambridge, had worked on his thesis in the very heart of
Bloomsbury at the Hogarth Press under Leonard and Virginia Woolf. He
had recently become the youngest don at King's, in part because of
the influence of King's bursar and leading Bloomsberry, the economist
Maynard Keynes. King's, the academic cradle of so many of Bloomsbury's
key figures and home of Keynes, Rylands and E. M. Forster, was the
epicentre of Bloomsbury's Cambridge branch and Dadie, passionate about
the theatre, would also over the next half-century open doors for many
talented theatrically leaning undergraduates.

A magnetic personality with his good looks crowned by corn-coloured
golden hair, he had a tongue both eloquent and feline (as undergraduates
he and the historian Steven Runciman led a coterie dubbed 'Tea Party
Cats'). He was, inevitably, an 'Apostle' – G. E. Moore, Ludwig Witt-
genstein, Bertrand Russell, Strachey and Keynes had been or were too –
a member of that surprisingly well-known 'secret' society of the Apostles,
centred round King's, to which Blunt would shortly be elected. Dadie
shared all the conventionally unconventional Apostolic attitudes, especially those of a period when Cambridge was markedly behind Oxford in
its recognition of the equal status of women. A paramount credo was that
homosexual love ('The Higher Sodomy' in Apostle-ese) could be both
morally and aesthetically superior to heterosexual love. Bloomsbury
stressed the supreme importance of personal relationships and that found
loud echoes among Apostolic Cambridge dons such as Keynes, Rylands,
the kindly but troubled Trinity economics don Dennis Robertson and
King's Goldsworthy Lowes Dickinson, all of whom became captivated by
Michael's good looks and charm.

Dadie was no poet – although he would keep trying – but he was an
excellent, even inspiring, teacher. Despite the gauzy tosh of his verse his
book *Words and Poetry* was, in its own way, as rigorous as I. A. Richards's
work in its emphasis on the value to each line of poetry of the weight of
the individual word. Michael enjoyed and learnt considerably from his
tutorials – they certainly disciplined his own thinking and analytical
ability – and of course he could not help but be flattered when Dadie
began to woo him to appear in his Marlowe Society production of *King
Lear*, scheduled for the spring term. Dadie was extremely ambitious for
this production and desperately needed a strong actor for one of *Lear*'s
most difficult roles, Edgar (Peter Hannen, son of actors Nicholas Hannen

and Athene Seyler, had already been cast in the title role). Dadie wrote an extremely clever, flattering letter to Michael:

> Without you, my task as a producer will be doubly, terribly hard. *King Lear* is to my mind (and Lytton has often agreed with me) the most terrific work that the English literary genius has produced ... you will get to know Shakespeare by taking the part of Edgar in exactly the same way you would get to know Mozart by playing first violin in a symphony.

Michael initially resisted Dadie's blandishments to concentrate on work, although he did agree to take part in an enterprise less time-consuming, over which both Dadie and Maynard Keynes hovered benevolently. The hitherto robustly homosexual Keynes had married – to Bloomsbury's surprise and no little initial disapproval – the entrancing Russian ballerina Lydia Lopokova who had bewitched London in Diaghilev's company, especially dancing the cancan with Massine in *La Boutique Fantasque*. She was no intellectual – to Strachey she was a 'half-witted canary' while for Virginia Woolf she had 'a very limited head-piece' – often scandalising supposedly unshockable Bloomsbury with her unorthodox behaviour (she liked to sit inside the refrigerator during a heatwave) but to undergraduates Mrs Keynes, whenever she came to Cambridge, was a seductive presence. Her dancing days were coming to a close and Keynes was now ambitious for the acting abilities of Caesar's wife to be recognised.

For the ADC Dennis Arundell, well known in Cambridge artistic circles, supervised an evening consisting of Stravinsky's *A Soldier's Tale* and a first staging of Shakespeare's poem *A Lover's Complaint*, followed by three short dances arranged for Lopokova. Michael was cast as the Soldier opposite Lydia as Stravinsky's non-speaking Princess and as the Lover to her Afflicted Fancy in the Shakespeare. It was altogether a high-class evening, with Bloomsbury helping out its own – Duncan Grant elegantly designed *A Lover's Complaint* and Vanessa Bell the closing dances; *The Soldier's Tale* was the work of a multi-talented undergraduate, Humphrey Jennings (later a brilliant documentary film maker and co-founder of Mass Observation) who came up with a simple monochrome set with touches of red in the rooftops echoing the colour of the Soldier's uniform. Michael was captivated by Lydia's childlike enthusiasm, gurgling laugh and unexpectedly complete lack of ego. He tried to help her overcome the metronomical scansion which her pre-rehearsal coaching from Keynes had produced, and all three performances were extremely successful.

Dadie turned up the heat in pursuit of Michael for *Lear* after this production and when Michael was staying with David Loveday during part of the Christmas vacation wrote yet again in persuasion. David Loveday was an old friend of Dadie's from Cambridge and he, too, was urged by Dadie to help coax Michael into the production. Finally, up against such pressure, Michael caved in and agreed to play Edgar.

Perhaps because of his increasing involvement in so many extra-curricular activities, the inevitable cracks in his relationship with Michael Garrett began to appear. New friends were crowding in on Michael and the 1929 spring term was by far his most frenetic to date. He was appointed for a term as editor of the *Cambridge Review* (John Lehmann, an aspiring poet who had contributed to *The Venture*, was appointed as assistant editor), its routine mandatory pages (deaths of alumni, the university sermon) and advertising (mostly for teaching agencies, including the graduates' graveyard of Messrs Gabbitas and Thring) under Michael being much enlivened by some innovative articles. A new friend, passionate about film (another talented film maker subsequently), Basil Wright, contributed a first-rate piece on modern Soviet cinema and Michael published more than the customary number of poems, including several by Julian Bell whose work he admired almost as much as that of Empson. Son of Clive and Vanessa Bell, he was an untidy, tousle-haired charmer (although otherwise heterosexual he got Anthony Blunt at least once into bed, then – in best Bloomsbury manner – told his mother all about it, warning her only not to tell her sister Virginia Woolf, which would be tantamount to proclaiming it in a *Times* advertisement). Passionate about eighteenth-century poetry – Michael caught some of this then unfash-ionable enthusiasm, particularly for Pope's verse – Bell showed signs of becoming a major talent; he was killed in the Spanish Civil War.

Simultaneously, Michael had to work on *The Venture*'s second issue, keen to atone for the first. This issue saw poems and essays of real vigour, with work from Bell and a muscular long poem, 'Autumn', by John Davenport. A bibulous polymath, Davenport had become friends with Michael in the spring term and they often now drank together in Cam-bridge's pubs. A man of enormous promise – never quite fulfilled – the rampantly heterosexual Davenport was not at all to Michael Garrett's taste and Garrett resented the time Michael was spending with him. Also in this *Venture* Michael contributed his poem 'Waking to Sleep', a haunting dreamscape, while Blunt produced another forensic piece, anatomising William Beckford's Fonthill in 'The Gothic Revival'. Altogether in this issue, *The Venture* gave *Experiment* a good run for its money, although with Empson's departure from Cambridge (he was sent down when condoms were discovered in his rooms) the rival publication suffered a major setback.

Michael also had to fit in *Lear* rehearsals and Dadie held long and arduous sessions. Never an innovative director, although he valued the ideas of Harley Granville-Barker and William Poel in encouraging simple settings and swift, continuous action in Shakespeare, Dadie was a stickler for the verse, often going over sections countless times. In Michael he knew that he had a natural at handling the iambic line and left him fairly much alone. With the Cambridge tradition of all-male productions (although Alistair Cooke and a new group, the Mummers, were set to challenge that) Dadie also played Regan. Sadly, Arthur Marshall, still decades away from the rotund star of *Call My Bluff* on television and then almost sylphlike, fast becoming famous for his performances in female roles (Dadie had reviewed one of his performances by suggesting that his legs should be insured at Lloyds while he was an ADC member), was forbidden by Christ's College to act any more that term. Marshall, like several other members, seemed practically to live in the cosy club room beneath the intimate ADC theatre in Park Street, but he had to drop out of playing Cordelia (mutinously, he insisted on acting as prompter).

Peter Hannen's Lear was considered an excellent performance by a young actor but Michael's Edgar completely dominated the evening, surprising everyone (even Dadie) in performance by his authority and mature handling of the verse. This was a startlingly 'lived' performance, at its most powerful as a virtually naked 'poor Tom' in the heath scenes amid the storm and heart-rending in the episodes with his blinded father, informed by both pity and love. David Loveday came over from Clifton to see the production and confessed himself 'mute' after the performance; he had not been prepared for such maturity from Michael in such a demanding part. National newspapers then reviewed Oxbridge productions; this *Lear* was judged superior to a recent OUDS version directed by the iconoclastic Russian Theodore Komisarjevsky.

During the Easter holiday Michael for the first time went on a Magdalene reading party organised by the don Francis Turner; they stayed at the Castle Rock Hotel in Mortehoe, north Devon, which became one of his favourite places in England, as it did for Dick Green, also in the party. It looks out to the island of Lundy, with long and then deserted beaches close by. They returned there often separately or together after Cambridge; for both it became a place of reflection and renewal, always treasured.

Such absences, together with the amount of time devoted to rehearsals and editorial meetings, brought the tensions between Michael and Michael Garrett to the boil. They had simmered throughout most of the previous term, when Michael first worked with John Lehmann on the *Cambridge Review*. Another charismatic Cambridge figure – tall, magnetically blue-eyed and fair-haired – Lehmann in many ways was physically similar to Michael in Nordic good looks, although his terse, reserved manner (some said chilly, others arrogant) was at a polar extreme from

Michael's exuberant enthusiasm at that time. Lehmann carried also a nimbus of reflected glamour; his elder sister Rosamond, who had been at Girton (she was Dadie's closest female friend) had recently published her first novel, *Dusty Answer*, to much publicity and the Eton-educated John (he had co-edited *College Days* there) was fiercely ambitious for his own literary career. He was then inexperienced emotionally and sexually gauche but he fell heavily for Michael. The subsequent brouhaha caused them both a good deal of anguish.

For all Bloomsbury's lofty pronouncements, it is extraordinary how messy so many of their own love lives – and those of the people they advised – could be. Dadie himself was repressed to the extent that his sex life was conducted almost exclusively when he was either abroad or drunk; for him, like so many of his circle, it seemed that love and sex were incompatible. Lehmann's personality and inexperience and Michael's guilt over his feelings of betrayal towards Michael Garrett made a recipe for emotional mayhem, but when Lehmann confided in Dadie, confessing that he was in love with Michael, Dadie – who did not like Michael Garrett – was ready to play agony uncle, urging Lehmann to write at once to Michael: 'You should think more about Michael than about yourself; he is a dear creature and by that means you will turn his great liking for you into love.' Lehmann obviously acted on Dadie's advice, but his letter to Michael has not survived.

Michael wrote a very frank reply, acting on the Bloomsbury principle of complete candour in personal relationships:

> I will try to be honest with you. I love you and respect you vastly; I want to be with you and talk to you and see you. But there is this, which I should tell you: I am not at all what you think me; I am shallow, selfish (horribly), jealous to a torturing degree, greedy, proud and self-centred; I have grasped at people's love and done vain and stupid things to get it; I am at times hideously immoral.

The following day Dadie, like some Pandarus of King's, was pushing his argument further to Lehmann: 'I am very fond of you and very fond of Michael and I am sure this is a wonderful opportunity for him as well as for you and I don't want to see it missed and muffed. Michael has all your tastes and interests but of course he is not an easy person – what young man worth loving is easy?'

Encouraged so by Dadie, Lehmann embarked on what turned out to be a brief – and by Lehmann's own admission – physically clumsy love affair, blighted by his inhibitions and inexperience. But Michael was at least initially caught up in the intoxication of a new love, writing to Lehmann from Mortehoe of his problems with Michael Garrett (who in his hurt had gone off with a new boyfriend) and of how he missed Lehmann: 'I feel it so much at night when I blow out the candle and let in the starlight and the smoke of the wick mingles with my breath and sickens me; I could cry for you. Each day makes me find something more in this love, so long forgotten.'

Perhaps the spectre of Michael Garrett was also palpable for Lehmann; he seemed to retreat emotionally from Michael almost as soon as he had committed to him. By April Lehmann's apparent distance made Michael write once more: 'Our love is beautiful to me, and I pray for the sunshine of you to make it grow.' And Michael opened up further to Lehmann, admitting that although now Michael Garrett had a new lover (a woman this time) he still loved him, although he desperately wanted also to keep Lehmann's friendship, almost pleading with Lehmann to understand his dilemma:

> Don't think I have been deceiving you. Only occasionally did I suspect that my love for M.G. was not quite dead ... suddenly the stars change, the whole world collapses and time slips back, and I am sick at the inevitability of this awful love, that will not let me be ... Oh John, I have been hurt and I have hurt you.

The always prickly Lehmann – his lovers often mentioned how he separated emotional and physical feelings – took this simply as a rejection of his own feelings and although Michael could assure him soon afterwards that his sexual relationship with Garrett was conclusively over, their affair was not resumed and the intimacy between them was never the same again, although they were, cautiously, friends in later life.

As if to escape all this angst, Michael spent the latter part of his second Cambridge year in a madly social whirl. He was now often seen in the town's gathering places – the Copper Kettle, the Dorothy Café ('The Dot') – and at ADC 'Smokers', well-wined, dinner-jacketed affairs (all male, of course), with revue-style cabaret, often featuring the Christ's College double act of Geoffrey Toone, a tall, impressive actor, and Arthur Marshall –

> 'Are you feeling hysterical?'
> 'No – he's feeling mine.'

– or Arthur in solo drag, already perfecting his Angela Brazil schoolgirl impersonations, oozing doubles entendres, or playing his dragon-schoolmistress ('I shall be running through your parts in a minute!').

The hothouse camp of the Smokers evaporated when many of the participants met up at the various salons which existed in Cambridge then, run by figures such as the Clare don Mansfield Forbes (in his day as influential as I. A. Richards) whose house (Finella) on the Backs, mundanely Victorian outside, was filled with art deco, all chrome and smoked glass, and by dons' wives or widows, the most exclusive of whom, Charlotte ('Chattie') Haldane, wife of the biochemist J. B. S. Haldane, liked to entertain young Cambridge's *crème de la crème*. John Davenport first took Michael there and he immediately became one of Chattie's 'regulars', others including Arthur Marshall, the ebullient Hugh Sykes Davies (who wrote for both *The Venture* and *Experiment*), a delicate beauty, Kathleen Raine, then the Zuleika Dobson-poetess of Cambridge (she married Hugh Sykes Davies shortly afterwards) and the future dramatist Wynyard Browne.

It was at Chattie's that Michael became friends with the moodily brilliant Malcolm Lowry of St Catherine's, even then much travelled and a published poet and, along with Davenport, also already inhabiting the Manichaean world of the committed drinker. He and Michael seemed unlikely friends – Lowry was burly, pugnacious and resolutely macho – but in addition to his passions for poetry and American literature Lowry was mad about German cinema, particularly the films of Murnau and Lang. Expressionist cinema was a major influence on his prose – he was experimenting even then in the writing of what became *Ultramarine* – and he and Michael argued over the Ufa films of the 1920s, frame by frame, with equal fervour. Invited to join him on Cambridge pub crawls round what Lowry called 'taverns measureless to man', Michael warmed to the funny, tender Lowry underneath the tough-guy exterior.

Another intimate to join this circle became the painter Julian Trevelyan, then much under the sway of Bloomsbury's Roger Fry, whom he saw as a kind of Diaghilev of Post-Impressionism. Like most of the group – despite the later revelations of the activities of Blunt and his associates and Julian Bell's commitment – even in an era of growing Fascist menace following a cataclysmic General Strike he took less interest in politics than in the arts (the succeeding Cambridge generation reversed this). Trevelyan bicycled around Cambridge wearing a black 'artist's' hat; similarly, Michael lived up to his aesthetic image by taking care always in public to have a book under his arm. They would all meet in Michael's digs or in Davenport's rooms in Corpus, filled with books, all the latest literary periodicals and copious drink, with Lowry weaving in after the Mayflower pub closed, sometimes strumming on his banjo. Another favourite meeting place, where Dick Green would often join them, was Humphrey Jennings's flat. Married and living in rooms above an art gallery, Jennings – extremely fond then, like most of the set, of the word *Weltanschauung* – would hold forth in torrents of polymathic monologue on everything from Petrarch to Picasso, although he was as fond of gossip as the rest.

Occasionally they would all go in a group to productions of a bold new venture at the Festival Theatre, run by the bearded, saturnine Terence Gray. The theatre was decidedly avant-garde, not remotely like a provincial 'rep', with an apron stage and sets made up of 'units' of wooden cubes and rostra in various configurations. The auditorium was painted ink-black and emerald-green, and there was also a strange, somewhat more bilious green beer available at the bar. The repertoire was quite remarkable for its uncompromising range at the time – often featuring British premières of plays by Pirandello or O'Neill – and some of the young talents there during Michael's time included Flora Robson, Robert Donat and Tyrone Guthrie, the latter already embarked on a directing career as well as acting.

With all this activity the production of another *Venture* was inevitably something of a scramble but somehow it emerged as easily the best of its six issues. Blunt had written to Michael from Paris during the vacation, loftily rebuking him for his enthusiasm ('My <u>dear</u>, you mustn't underline <u>every</u> word you write') as he discussed his article on 'the Barock', a cogent piece on the architect Johann Michael Fischer's fusion of Italian baroque and French rococo. The issue was especially strong on poetry, with work from Bell, Davenport and Lehmann. Michael's contribution, 'Love's Tightrope, or the Triumph of Blondin' subtitled 'A Dream of Crystal Palaces', is one of his best poems, comparing himself ('In dreams thus do I tread the wind') with the high-wire artiste, 'forgetful of gravity'. A pugnacious brief 'Manifesto' at the back of this issue promised a continuation of the magazine (with a veiled taunt at *Experiment*) – 'as a protest against the more licentious forms of Free Verse, Surréalisme and Art Without Tears'.

Throughout the summer of 1929 Michael was on his travels – Andy's allowance could never be described as mean – taking four separate trips that summer, all unsettling in different ways and to different degrees. His restlessness seemed more than physical; although Michael kept no diaries for his undergraduate years he made a few jottings in a small notebook covering this summer, and it is clear that he was in the middle of a period of doubt and indecision.

First he went briefly to the oasis of Beaucé where the doggedly adoring Louis was writing many poems, often addressed to Michael, '*le plus tendre ami*', praising his eyes ('*le soleil de tes yeux*') and lamenting his own spiritual and emotional isolation ('*mes nuits solitaires*'). Louis rather relished his melancholy – the Rodgers and Hart song 'Glad to be Unhappy' might have been written for him – a good deal of which infused his poetry and the study of the Ganymede myth on which he was engaged. Michael slept a great deal, began – urged on by Louis – to read André Gide and talked over his emotional problems with Louis who was, as ever, a wonderful listener, tactful not to probe too deeply about Michael Garrett or John Lehmann.

Michael travelled on from Beaucé, leaving Louis to continue what he called his 'vegetable life', to join the Fedden family once more at Chantemesle. The original plan for that summer had been Romilly Fedden's scheme for a production of the opera *The Immortal Hour* with Michael to sing the role of Midir and when plans were shelved Michael nearly cancelled his visit, only to change his mind when Robin intrigued him by his teasing information that two American girls – the Coss sisters – one of whom was 'in love' with Michael, Robin added, were also staying and that their visit would overlap with Michael's arrival. Michael had met Mary and Margaret Coss before, when they had visited Robin in his Cambridge rooms; Margaret was then finishing a year's course at Cambridge and Mary was visiting her elder sister before they returned to the States together. He remembered Mary especially for her grave, quiet beauty enhanced on that occasion by a simple brown dress.

The events of the next few days at Chantemesle are compressed in Michael's notebook of the time into a kind of feverish, impressionistic pen picture mixed with the draft version of a letter to Mary, his writing markedly more impatient and scribbled than usual. He recalls Mrs Fedden saying to him what 'a lovely child' she thought Mary and how she could draw every line of her face, Michael adding: 'O, Mary, so could I. Never shall I forget your face, your hair, your hands and your sweet, sweet body.' In a crowded room after dinner, having lost an opportunity to be alone with her earlier in the evening, he suddenly blurts out that he wants to go for a walk and asks Mary to join him. They walk slowly together in the moonlight:

> Talk of M.G. – she says his attitude is wrong – spontaneously, which rather gratifies me. I explain why I like him – I tell her what I thought when I first saw her … she explains that she came precisely to see me. I did not know she had seen me before we met at Robin's. We are sitting on a low stone wall, banked with vines. She continues, 'I remember when I first saw you, in Magdalene Gardens. Suddenly you came across with a book in your hand. I said "Who's that?". Margaret said: "That is Michael Redgrave." "O", I said, "isn't he beautiful?" I decided that I must meet you. So it was arranged that I come to call for Margaret at Robin's.'

Soon Michael impulsively takes her hand and 'after a very long pause':

> She moves towards me. I kissed her. Suddenly a consciousness – Indescribable feeling of panic. A sweetness, a *tenderness* that I have never felt

before – we embrace with passion. Another wave of panic … we move along the road, entwined, but each minute we stop and cannot help embracing – There is a little lightning, cooling like a dash of soda. I kiss her again and again, on the shoulders, almost on the breast.

After swearing their mutual love, they creep back to their rooms at 3.30 a.m., although Michael cannot sleep ('The scent of her is in my hands, my face').

Next morning Michael and Mary go for a walk and sit by a stream out of the scorching sun. As they embrace once more:

> Tells her doesn't want to break up his family but inevitable if he wants to write – explain, as far as possible, my family, the disaccord, the envy, hatred, malice and all uncharitableness. She is silent but seems to understand. A pause. Then – 'And have *you* no faults?' she asked, without the slightest irony in her voice, as if it really seemed to her that I was perfect. I replied: 'I am selfish, above all selfish. Proud. Weak in needing encouragement. Living in the present. Sensual.' 'And vain,' I add. She smiles. I tell her about Cyril White and hint about Michael G. She says she is going to work, work, work then one day she will come back to England and we will go to a tea-party together and she will astound me with her knowledge.

The Coss sisters had to leave to begin the journey back to America the following day. It was a miserable parting for Michael and Mary, she mostly silent in a blue sailor-style dress, sitting close to him on the drive to the station at Nantes and gazing at him, still silent, throughout the leave-takings and as the train pulled away: 'Her eyes only leave me for a second. The train draws out and her eyes, as if fastened inside me, draw away something.'

On the drive back, Robin was sympathetic and understanding when Michael was 'quite unable to control the flood of tears' and listened as Michael voiced his thoughts:

> I feel convinced that the two years I have been loving Michael G. have not been wasted. They strengthened me for this most perfect love – I tell Robin, explaining why, I think, my life has been so unbalanced sexually. This is now righted, I am certain. This purely physical sex, which I have so often enjoyed in my life, mostly with men, once with a woman, seems no trouble now, and, moreover I trace to it all my failings.

A few further rambling jottings in his notebook confirm this sense of almost willing himself to erase the past, protesting (perhaps too much) that the Michael Garrett affair was essentially physical, the kind of involvement he must turn his back on: 'So I must just try and forget about all that except as a necessary state of purgatory.'

As well as Robin, Michael could confide, too, in David Loveday in their regular correspondence. Earlier that year, on Michael's twenty-first birthday, David had celebrated also what he always remembered as their 'other anniversary', the date of Michael's confirmation at Clifton, with the gift of a beautiful specially bound edition of Thomas à Kempis's *Imitation of Christ* and an accompanying note: 'The days between have brought me through you more happiness than I ever could have believed possible. God bless you, darling, and give you more "happy days".'

David, intuiting Michael's state of mind and longing to see more of him *à deux*, had invited him on a trip to Italy (David contributed to Michael's expenses) and this was now scheduled for August 1929. Arriving in Rome to meet David, staying in a modest little hotel on the Via de Principi Amedia, drinking alfresco and 'talking of my future with a gloomy vigour', followed by a long stroll around the moonlit Colosseum, Michael's spirits began to revive. He always loved Italy – almost as much as he came to love America – and could swiftly relax into its more sensuous rhythm, although for the first few days of that visit he became a gawping tourist as David took him all over St Peter's, the Sistine Chapel and the Protestant cemetery. Standing by Shelley's grave, suddenly his thoughts turned to Michael Garrett: 'Turning behind a tree I cried, almost *howled*, for three minutes.' Their relaxed mealtimes – Michael was developing a taste for Italian sparkling red wines – revolved around intense, Apostolic-style conversations on personal relationships, God and atheism: 'For David the most wonderful experience, mental and emotional, is the belief in God, the poetry of the Church service and the interpretation of Christ's Gospel – whereas the Church service means nothing to me, as I am too self-centred to believe in God.'

In Capri, well-known Mecca for gay men then, after crossing with 'Nuns, nancy-boys and flashy women', Michael was enchanted by the island's relaxed, sensual atmosphere, sitting watching couples dance closely in the square after dinner, and by the clear blue water in which he and David swam naked. They then travelled down to Sicily where Michael again fell in love with Palermo – 'a city of gold against bronze mountains' – and took David on a favourite walk, to Monte Pellegrino, described by Goethe as the most beautiful promontory in the world and where, at the Temple of Concord: 'We had a feeling of standing on a planet looking into the void – we felt like some rulers of the skies.'

David was as understanding as Louis and Robin had been, patiently listening whenever Michael talked about Michael Garrett, as he did often to David. During their Italian days there was a good deal of nude bathing and wrestling ('Changing in our room, we fought and got very hot – good exercise. D. routed'); this may well have spilt over into some sexual activity, but even if it did what is clear is that in this friendship David genuinely loved Michael and certainly later could sublimate his longings into a platonic love for a younger man. Michael's old Clifton 'crush', Geoffrey Hayward, now at Oxford, had kept in touch with him (they occasionally exchanged poems) and had written to him of David: 'What a terrible thing it is to have the life of a schoolmaster, these interests, and have to go on facing them.' For David, however, the Italian journey had been a glimpse of paradise and he treasured its memory for the rest of his life. He wrote to thank Michael after their return for some snapshots of their summer idyll: 'a time of such perfect and glorious happiness as I did not know could be – If it is not blasphemous, I may call it my moment of Transfiguration.'

Michael returned via Paris to London before embarking on his final jaunt of the summer, a somewhat uneasy cruise, the atmosphere crackling with unspoken tremors, along the Norwegian fjords with Andy, Daisy and Peggy, joined by the recently engaged Margaret Chute, still working in film public relations but more subdued than usual. Again, only a few scattered notebook jottings cover this time but Michael seems distinctly unsettled: 'All Bergen appears to be homosexual. Curious people. Worried about bi-sexuality. Know that I love Mary and want to marry her. Why have been so long homosexual? This I cannot understand.' At shipboard receptions he danced with Margaret, telling her about Mary Coss while she spoke of her imminent marriage. But the familiar relaxed ease between Margaret and him had evaporated; he was made uneasy sitting beside her at meals and neither visited the other's cabin. Michael enjoyed being with Peggy more – she taught him how to waltz – but they both noticed with unease how much Daisy tended to drink.

With only a short time to kill in London before returning to Cambridge, he made just one notebook entry in that time, on attending a Beethoven concert:

> Afterwards I allow myself to speak to a male prostitute, and am glad he is so disgusting.
>
> I have only to remember Mary now and there is no difficulty. How could I love her and yet think of such things as these?

That paradox, central to his existence, seemed nevertheless to trouble him less when back in Cambridge. Mary wrote regularly, in her extraordinarily angled sloping handwriting, from Bryn Mawr where she was now studying, telling him that when driving through the Pennsylvania countryside she would mark out 'all the places and the most beautiful approaches to them which I should show you, just in case you were suddenly to appear. My every thought is prompted by you, Michael.'

Living in new digs in the Chesterton Road, Michael was trying hard to focus on his studies, faithfully attending lectures and tutorials, avoiding last-minute essay writing. Outside activities were confined to his collaboration on the fourth *Venture*, strong on verse but still suffering from a dearth of advertising revenue. He also was writing book reviews and film criticism for *Granta*, whose many pages of lucratively sybaritic advertisements (Piper-Heidseck champagne, Hawks of Savile Row) must have made *The Venture*'s co-editors envious. One evening off work was spent as the star guest at a boisterous *Granta* dinner, the menu of which with defiant frivolity offered 'Fillet of Editor's Soul', held the same night as the Union was debating the motion, proposed by Gilbert Harding, 'That England Requires a Mussolini'.

There was no theatre for him that term but he was again tempted by Dadie, for a Christmas vacation project consisting of scenes from Milton's masque *Comus* as another showcase for Lydia Lopokova for a private performance in the very heart of Bloomsbury, at the Keyneses' house, 46 Gordon Square. Lydia played the Lady, with Dadie as Comus and Robert Eddison and Michael as the Brothers, in a simple classical design by Vanessa Bell and Duncan Grant. Both Michael and Eddison were thrilled by the chance to observe Bloomsbury at close range and the audience – Bernard Shaw, Walter Sickert, Virginia Woolf, the *New Statesman* critic Raymond Mortimer, Lytton Strachey – did not disappoint. In the circumstances Dadie's private November report to Magdalene on Michael's academic progress – 'Considering his great sensibility, his essays are curiously disappointing. I suspect that he has too many irons in the fire' – was rather naughty, given that it was Dadie's pursuit which had persuaded Michael into so many theatrical ventures, not to mention his role in the Lehmann affair.

Milton and *Comus* had reactivated Michael's drive, however, and the spring of 1930 was the most hectic time of his Cambridge years. With John Davenport and Hugh Sykes Davies he co-edited for the Hogarth Press 'Living Poets' series a volume of *Cambridge Poetry*, which included work by Lehmann, Davenport, Julian Bell's witty 'Imitation of Pope' and, strikingly, Malcolm Lowry's poem on one of his heroes, 'For Nordahl Grieg, Ship's Fireman'. Michael's contribution was 'Proteus and the Fountain', contrasting the freshness of dawn with the bifurcated unrest of 'Proteus, poor youth, the mask and mind'. The collection was reviewed by the *Times Literary Supplement*; the critic rightly mentioned the heavy influences of Empson and T. S. Eliot but praised the work as more fresh than a companion recent Oxford volume.

In the same term *The Venture*'s fifth issue, with a strong emphasis on Julian Bell's verse, appeared while Michael also returned to Dadie and the Marlowe Society for *Henry IV, Part 2*, doubling Prince Hal and Rumour, the Chorus. In later years he would disparage this as one of his worst efforts but although Dadie's production clearly did not make for a Marlowe Society thriller, Michael's performance was unanimously praised, the notices all mentioning Hal's impressive transition from hot youth into remote regality.

Somehow he found the time and energy, too, to write script and lyrics for an operetta which he also directed, playing in it as Samuel Pepys, with music by Francis Turner. A programme note mock-belittled *The Battle of the Book* as 'merely a Pepys show' but he took great pains over the production, which involved many of his circle – designs were by Louis le Breton and Gervase Smith, and the cast included John Davenport, Humphrey Browne and Robert Eddison (as 'an American beauty'). A farrago set in Magdalene's Pepys Library and travelling between the future (1940) and 1653, it involved gangsters, tourists and Pepys in a fast-moving plot centred round the attempted theft of the Library's rare editions. Michael had learnt a lot from A. C. K. Toms at Clifton of the logistics of large-scale projects and he marshalled his huge cast and orchestra extremely capably; his piece of escapist drollery was packed at all performances.

It was just at this time that Michael wrote to propose marriage to Mary Coss. Besides her own letters, he had had regular news of her from Francis Cook, his Magdalene friend now on a Commonwealth Fellowship at Harvard who had met Mary. Cook stressed to Michael how he had sung his praises to Mary's parents and how much Mary reminded him of his – and Cyril Connolly's – great friend Noel Blakiston ('the best compliment I know') by which he meant that Mary could be gay or serious and 'in either mood she is completely enchanting', adding, 'I never saw such adoration as she reserves for you, Michael.' Mary's reply to Michael's proposal gently temporised: 'Michael, dearest, do you *really* want to marry me? I'm stunned. Nothing so important has ever happened to me or will happen to me again.'

There had been some talk of Michael also trying for a Commonwealth Fellowship so that he could join Mary in America, although money would have been tight (Mary had a tiny personal income but her father's finances suffered lasting damage in the 1929 crash). In the meantime they would wait to see the results in the second part of the tripos and for Mary's planned visit to England the following year. Perhaps Mary was – or both were – feeling a transatlantic change in the intensity of their feelings after what had been such a brief interlude in such very different surroundings in the French moonlight. Michael undoubtedly thought then that he loved Mary and that he wanted to marry her; she was at this stage the more aware that perhaps both had been more in love with being in love at Chantemesle. But the stasis in the relationship made Michael uneasy and agitated; he worked during the summer term but with no real conviction, refusing all ADC overtures and even contributing little to any of the student magazines. That term Michael Garrett was editor of the *Magdalene College Magazine*, and for one of Garrett's issues Michael contributed his most striking Cambridge poem, a mordantly Empsonian version of a Donald McGill postcard, called 'Seaside':

> Bang! On a tub the thumper boosts up God,
> Five pierrots scream, the steamer's siren blows,
> The mind a blank, Mother bathes her quad-
> rilateral feet, Papa his rhomboid toes.

He was conspicuous by his absence at the usual gatherings of his set or in the town's watering holes. By the end of that summer term his mood of disenchantment and unease had manifested itself, dramatically, in physical terms with severe abdominal pains, finally after considerable worry diagnosed as stomach ulcers. Michael spent most of that long vacation in a Kensington convalescent-cum-nursing home, comforted by visits from friends and letters from Mary and Francis Cook in America. Once out of acute pain, he was able to strike a nonchalant note, writing to Dennis Robertson, the Trinity don who had developed a definite crush on him:

> I am not despondent, only resigned. Turgenev says that the man who is angry with his disease gets well quicker. I am not. The enforced hermitage has done me a great deal of good and people are incredibly kind. I have read all European literature and am beginning on the Koran.

Allowing for exaggeration he still had read Turgenev (to remain a cherished favourite), more of Gide, Henry James (another in his pantheon) and many modern novels, most impressed by Henry Green's *Loving*. He was touched by Dennis Robertson's anxiety – he found Dennis less devious than Dadie – and genuinely regretted that his illness prevented him from accepting Dennis's invitation to join him at the Salzburg Festival.

David Loveday was a regular correspondent and also visited Michael several times from Bristol, although he remained concerned that Michael seemed still unsettled when he returned to Cambridge for a fourth year to read for part two of the English tripos:

> I got the impression when I saw you last that you were utterly miserable and in a *new* way – you seemed *resentful* against your circumstances and I

thought I saw a hardness in your expression which I had never seen before.
My dear, you were made for love – to love and be loved – and you may
have to undergo a good deal of the suffering that love involves – but I don't
think you can bludgeon against life and love. You are not like that.

Certainly Michael seemed still troubled. Mary had returned to England
and they spent a good deal of time together, often in London at the
theatre, both of them much taken by the Japanese Players' visit and by an
Othello with Paul Robeson in which he was impressed most by an actress
unknown to him ('Desdemona was lovely, I thought'), a young Peggy
Ashcroft. But it was soon transparently evident to Mary and himself
that on both sides, totally without rancour, the love of the Chantemesle
summer had cooled. They remained friends – Mary soon afterwards, not
entirely to Michael's surprise, married Francis Cook (although they later
divorced, after which Mary joined the American Communist Party).

Michael also heard at this time from Michael Garrett, who had left
Cambridge without the First expected of him. There was no bitterness in
their relationship now either; shortly before leaving to work in the Pacific
Islands, Garrett wrote to Michael: 'Cambridge retrospectively seems a
pretty good waste of time; anything there I have got or saved from these
three years is due to you – I would still infinitely rather see you and be
with you than with anybody else.' He later married and settled happily in
Australia.

His first Clifton 'romance', Geoffrey Hayward, also still wrote to him,
soon to leave Oxford, uncertain of his future ('I have so *many* dreams'),
compounding Michael's sense of melancholy, a feeling of experiencing
endings but with no new beginning in view. *The Venture* was drawn to a
close after a good innings of six issues, the valedictory number appropriately full of autumnal poems and an overall world-weary tone. Michael
wrote next to nothing then, spending most of his free time with Dick
Green, ideal companion for moods of melancholy.

However, he had to stir himself in the Christmas holidays, rehearsing
hard again to honour a promise to Dadie. In partnership with the bal-
letomane Arnold Haskell, Maynard Keynes briefly turned impresario to
present, at the intimate Arts Theatre in London, another programme to
showcase Lydia Lopokova, this time for a metropolitan public. *A Lover's
Complaint* was revived (Dadie this time bagged the role of the Poet,
wearing rather too much bronze make-up) together with an extended
Comus (Eddison and Michael repeating the Brothers) plus various dances
for Lydia. Few such enterprises can have boasted a more impressive group
of young talent; it included Frederick Ashton, just launching himself on a
great choreographic career, costume designers William Chappell and

Beatrice ('Bumble') Dawson, musical director Constant Lambert, and Cecil Beaton, who took the production photographs, not to mention Michael, Eddison and Wynyard Browne, all of whom went on to theatrical success.

It was hardly surprising that the *Nation* should describe this rarefied evening as 'blue-blooded'. Special praise was given to the spell of *A Lover's Complaint* as 'almost the last word in aristocratic fantasy', its staging (with significant contributions from Ashton) mixing mime and recitation to bring out the orchidaceous bloom of a neglected Renaissance masterpiece, while the verse speaking of *Comus* took critics and public by surprise in making Milton so accessible. The week-long Arts run was packed with fashionable figures and covered by all major newspapers, the spotlight naturally on Lydia but also all praising the undergraduate talent; the *Evening Standard* singled out Michael for his superb voice, pleasing him greatly by referring to him as 'a manly young actor'. The Cambridge players all received a crisp £5 note, personally slipped into the hand by Keynes.

Now fully restored to health and understandably buoyed up by his Arts success, Michael during his penultimate term kept up a phenomenal pace. Recently more than a few of his friends, including the Magdalene don Francis Turner, had urged him to consider the prospect of an academic career, but this was an option he seemed never to take seriously, even if he had no other career prospects in sight. His outside activities therefore continued unabated, including his final ADC bow in Dadie's summer 1931 production of Shaw's *Captain Brassbound's Conversion*, although Shaw was never a favourite playwright and he knew that his title role was inferior to that of the briskly commonsensical Lady Cicely Waynefleet, written for Ellen Terry and for Dadie played by Arthur Marshall, also in an ADC farewell.

Dadie set this 1890s play in modern dress, the better no doubt to give Arthur, to whom he had taken an instant shine, a last chance to dazzle Cambridge with his legs. They, and Arthur, predictably stole the show, although Michael was widely admired and certainly looked suitably exotic. As did the sets, also much admired, the work of an old Etonian undergraduate at Trinity, Guy Burgess. He looked then like an only slightly debauched Botticelli angel and had immense, electrifying energy; unabashedly and promiscuously homosexual, he delighted the ADC with his outrageous jokes but he took his work on *Brassbound* extremely seriously and all involved were impressed by his attention to detail. The production was such a success that extra shows had to be added, with cars and trains bringing social London to see it, giving Michael's goodbye to undergraduate theatre an aura of unusual glamour.

Even with final examinations looming he seemed blithely unconcerned and even busier, often making lightning descents on London; a BBC producer, Hilda Matheson, had been so impressed by Michael's voice when she was taken to *Comus* in London by her then lover, Vita Sackville-West, that she offered him a Savoy Hill studios audition. Throughout that final term Michael became almost an old hand at the microphone, doing several poetry and prose readings, working usually for a laconically informal producer, Lionel Fielden, his assignments including Lord Chesterfield's *Letters*, Kipling's verse and, most dauntingly, T. S. Eliot's *The Waste Land*. It was almost as if he had begun to shake off Cambridge – although its influence would never wholly leave him – before officially going down, and in the circumstances his 2/1 in the second part of the English tripos was respectable enough.

Resplendent in fur-trimmed coat, Daisy came to watch Michael take his BA in the Senate House, accompanied by Andy, no doubt keen to see some solid evidence of (and now, hopefully, some return on) his not inconsiderable investment. A group photograph taken outside Michael's digs shows Daisy beaming and Andy, cigarette in hand, smilingly benevolently but probably wondering what Michael might profitably (and, hopefully, at no further cost to him) do with his degree. Michael looks only mildly cheerful; he was possibly wondering exactly the same thing.

Five

EARLY STAGES

In 'Love's Tightrope' Michael may have felt himself invincible, a Blondin able to 'tread the wind' with no safety net, but that was in a poem, about a dream. The reality of post-Cambridge life was more bleakly prosaic, compounded by the inevitable sense of anticlimactic isolation with his tight-knit university group's dispersal. Michael Garrett had gone to the Pacific, Malcolm Lowry had signed on as a fireman on a tramp streamer bound for Russia, Dick Green – who would be peripatetic for years – was at his parents' Derbyshire home while Robin Fedden, Julian Trevelyan and Louis le Breton were all in France, the last doing his long-delayed military service ('I sleep my military duties away'). With John Davenport, who was writing – or procrastinating about writing – near Andover, Michael kept up a jocular correspondence in the personae of two affluent 'literary Johnnies' with horticultural leanings – Michael as Trench, Davenport as George Nathaniel Booth – allowing Davenport to indulge his love of bawdy innuendo: 'I took your advice about the Priapus; it drooped badly. But the primula syphillida and the penus distendae are doing very well.'

For a few weeks after taking his degree in the summer there was no immediate cause for worry. Dennis Robertson took him on holiday, with a brief return to Heidelberg before Salzburg, where they saw a performance of what instantly became and remained Michael's favourite opera, Strauss's *Der Rosenkavalier*. Dennis, too, was happy to be with Michael with no favours expected in return; he had always told Michael to come to him for help should he ever need it (Michael promptly borrowed £15, although he repaid it as soon as possible) and Michael came to sympathise with Dennis's own troubles – he was subject to periods of depression, what he called 'fits of darkness and terror' – and to value his counsel as much as David Loveday's: 'I know of no-one I would sooner unburden myself than to you, my dear Dennis.'

Life at Chapel Street was often edgy. Andy had settled Michael's outstanding Cambridge debts (the largest being the bill owed to Severs, *The Venture*'s printers) but of course now waited for him to find a job. Daisy waited too, although she had no advice to offer except occasional vague messages from the spirit world, counselling him to preserve all his writing and to prepare for great things. She and Michael were still very close, although he was irked by the increasing amount of time she spent in the company of her friend Bess Tait, a staunch believer in the Life Beyond, attending seances or sessions round the ouija board in pursuit of news of Roy (as elusive in death as he had been in life) or of Michael's likely future.

In 1931, after the collapse of Ramsay MacDonald's Labour government and the election of a National government, there were nearly 3 million unemployed in the country. Jobs for poets were not advertised at any Labour Exchange (the National government had almost at once cut the dole) and Michael was clear-eyed enough to know that he could not expect to make a proper living out of his writing in anything like the immediate future. His only asset was his BA, armed with which he followed the familiar path of countless idealistic graduates adapting to the real world to the offices of the Gabbitas and Thring teaching agency, which had advertised so lavishly in the *Cambridge Review* when he was editor.

They found him a job as tutor to a smart Brazilian boy, Miguel, but he was back on the job market almost immediately when the boy's guardian objected to Miguel improving his English at the cinema (the suggestion had come from Miguel, whose English was virtually perfect already). Messrs Gabbitas and Thring were not unused to frequent appearances by clients; they next came up with a Modern Languages teaching post in Highgate although 'references would be required'. Michael contacted Dennis Robertson and David Loveday, who had that year left Clifton to take up the headmastership of Cranleigh School near Guildford in Surrey. Instead of a reference David was able to offer a job teaching Modern Languages and some English at £225 per annum (board and lodging in term-time) initially for two terms. Michael wrote to Daisy, away on tour, in the wildly theatrical terms (addressing her as 'my darling', signing off 'your adoring Mike') they both used in letters then:

> You say you do not know if you want me to be a schoolmaster, and I agree: I do not want to be one much, myself. But it would really be better to have that than nothing; it would be good experience; I should be saving money, if only a little; and besides, were not Verlaine and Rimbaud and a dozen other great people schoolmasters?

Whether or not Daisy knew much of the relationship between Rimbaud and Verlaine, the matter was all arranged at lightning speed and at the beginning of the next term Michael was settled in the folds of the Surrey Downs. Two terms became nearly three years.

The Cranleigh governors had been unusually enlightened in appointing

David Loveday to the headmastership at only thirty-four and it proved an inspired choice. Cranleigh had opened its doors in 1865, part of the boom in Victorian public-school expansion, capitalising on the rise of the mercantile classes and the growth of a Home Counties commuter belt coinciding with the spread of the railways, but it had been going through difficult times. The previous headmaster, the Revd Herbert A. Rhodes (nicknamed 'Searchlights' after his protuberant eyes), had begun a process of reform, overseeing the building of new science labs and a prep school, but the emphasis under him at Cranleigh was still very much along traditionalist lines, with games a top priority (Rhodes had been a Football Blue at Oxford, and a school song, by a previous headmaster, included the line: 'Footer's but a game of life, the same for you and me'). David Loveday, like Rhodes, was a churchman, a bachelor and a Salopian but he arrived at Cranleigh with a mission, determined to update academic standards (very few boys went on to university then) and effectively to modernise a school still preserved to a degree in the world of *Goodbye, Mr Chips*, with its arcane rituals, fagging and initiation rites, all the regulations of a well-oiled hierarchy. When Rhodes had been stolid and phlegmatic, David was razor-sharp and caustic, sailing into Morning Assembly to the shout of 'School!', the signal for all to rise, while he strode in with a senior prefect behind him carrying a rug to keep his legs warm.

Cranleigh was run on a kind of 'hostel' system, a House being a dormitory and a House-room rather than a self-contained geographical unit. The original main building was pleasingly Victorian neo-Tudor structured round a quadrangle, and Michael's rooms as house tutor in 2 & 3 South in that building gave him a commanding view over Cranleigh village and to the Downs. He tended to disparage his teaching abilities in later years, but every surviving boy from his time there seemed to remember him with affection, perhaps because – consciously or unconsciously – he followed Dick Keigwin's Clifton notion of trying to enthuse his classes rather than just routinely teach them. Norman Paul in 1983 said after half a century, 'I remember the breath of fresh air you brought into your classes. You were a very good and very kind schoolmaster,' while Vivian Cox, who was later to become a film producer and a lifelong friend of Michael's, vividly recalled the impact of his arrival at the school: 'It always reminded me of the lines in Keats's *Hyperion* – "The morning-bright Apollo! Young Apollo!" – for he was indeed a striking figure, six-feet three, athletically built, fair haired. The whole school was completely *bouleversé.*'

Within weeks of his arrival, rather as at Cambridge a kind of informal 'court' had gathered around him, everyone competing for his attention, including Cox: 'The greatest thing of all was to be invited for one of his discussion evenings held in his rooms. Usually about a play, or literature, sometimes politics.'

For the boys there was the added frisson of the illicitly adult; against all the rules Michael would serve his disciples alcohol – actually an extremely low-proof and dirt-cheap South African hock called Paarl Amber – along with omelettes cooked on a tiny stove, and this was enough to send his glamour rating soaring.

The only real drawback for Michael was the acute cold of the rooms in the winter; any prospective guest was strongly advised to bring a hot-water bottle. But on the whole he found he was enjoying himself, writing to Dennis Robertson: 'The teaching of boys is amusing and instructive. The common room has its moments, and I have my walks, with the extreme beauty of the hills and the fields on frosty mornings.'

He even began to take up sport again, playing hockey with great enthusiasm on realising that his height and long reach with the hockey stick allowed him on the wing to cut like a scythe through the opposition. And there were occasional trips to London to continue his radio work for the BBC, still mainly for Lionel Fielden, including a series of readings from his favourite Keats, when he would catch the train from Guildford to Waterloo and then walk across Waterloo Bridge – always the London bridge he liked best – to the old BBC Savoy Hill Studios, followed perhaps by a meal at Gow's in the Strand, possibly meeting an old Cambridge friend like Dick Green if he was in London for 'crazing' as he called his occasional descents into a metropolitan *vie de Bohème*. Mary Smith, Gervase's adoring sister, had a little flat in Denbigh Street (known to regulars as 'Denbigh Hall') and around this Trilby figure would gather friends such as Dick and young aspiring writers including the critic Philip Hope-Wallace. Their other haunt, where Michael and John Davenport often joined them, was in Fitzrovia at the Fitzroy Tavern where they rubbed shoulders with literary Bohemia and such exotics as the painter Nina Hamnett, rumoured to be Picasso's discarded mistress, or Mayfair's notorious drug addict, the one-time Bright Young Person, socialite Brenda Dean Paul. All this added to what Michael described as 'a feeling of dizzy festivity' around this period of his life.

With David's encouragement, Michael now began to plan theatrical productions for Cranleigh, ambitious from the start to establish the school as a centre for Elizabethan English drama just as Bradfield had built a reputation for the staging of classical Greek plays.

As at Clifton, there was no really suitable building and, indeed, the acoustics of the Speech Hall, which had an awkward, wide stage, were so bad that at one point Michael – distinctly ahead of his time – envisaged his first Cranleigh venture of *As You Like It* as an outdoor promenade-style production to be staged all over the grounds before deciding to attempt the taming of the Speech Hall. He retained some of his ambitious non-naturalistic initial concept, with a division of the playing area into two stages and by using the auditorium aisles and doorways as exits and entrances. Soon he was writing to Dennis Robertson that 'files of pretty choristers come to simper their way through Rosalind', with the most talented one regrettably losing two front teeth on the rugby pitch. In his first production, apart from directing and designing, Michael limited himself to the small part of Hymen, while everything he had absorbed from A. C. K. Toms's Clifton productions came into play as he charmed everyone he wanted to take part.

As You Like It was his first collaboration with Tom Bowyer, the classics master, as composer, a tubby, G. K. Chesterton-like figure with a fringe of ginger hair (he also supervised the set building) and with the school's brilliant head of music, Maurice Allen, as musical director, and he also managed to persuade several masters including J. S. ('Tum') Purvis, North's housemaster who had supervised Cranleigh's past occasional excursions into plays, to take part with no resentment whatsoever. In addition, he cast several rugger hearties, including a school idol, the good-looking South African-born Paul Jacklin as Silvius, a clever ploy *pour encourager les autres*. The whole school seemed swept up in the communal enthusiasm surrounding the project, the success of which was crowned by Michael's own appearance in the closing scene, staging Hymen's entrance very much as the arrival of a deus ex machina to a burst of glorious Bowyer music for the school orchestra. He made his entrance from the back of the auditorium, down the central aisle, dressed from head to foot in gold with a golden make-up including glittering golden sequins on his eyelids and followed by a retinue of near-naked golden putti. No wonder, as Vivian Cox remembered, 'the audience simply gasped'.

Few school productions could match this but Cranleigh then, although it had always had a vigorous musical tradition, was leading the way in school drama, with only Clifton, Bradfield and, recently, the Whitgift School in Croydon under an equally enthusiastic John Garrett, providing serious competition. There was no stopping Michael now. Hardly had *As You Like It*'s set been taken down before he was planning and casting Gilbert and Sullivan's *HMS Pinafore*, for which virtually the whole of Cranleigh village was marshalled too, for the female roles and for back-stage activity. Nobody was busier than Mrs Louch in the High Street, a jolly currant bun of a woman who made every costume for *Pinafore* and for all Michael's subsequent Cranleigh productions, so devoted to him that she made new curtains and loose covers for his rooms, and patched his jackets (regularly holed then until he mastered the art of pipe-smoking less dangerously).

With Michael taking the lead role of Ralph Rackstraw he left the design to Tom Bowyer while Maurice Allen supervised a twenty-six-strong orchestra. Michael drilled the chorus so well – in rehearsal shrewdly devising individual characters for everyone so that nobody felt just 'one of the chorus' – that the whole show had a communicable effervescent zest, brimming with fresh comic invention worlds away from the ossified D'Oyly Carte routines, so that normally restrained Home Counties audiences were howling their delight. Nothing Michael touched at this period of his life seemed to go wrong, and he refreshed himself with happy Easter returns to Mortehoe, where Francis Turner organised reunions for regulars including Michael, Dick, John Davenport and Gervase Smith. One Easter Michael spent a whole afternoon after a long reading session devoted to the Metaphysical Poets making, with Robin Fedden, a monument to John Donne, a stone cairn decorated with ivy and daffodils, the poet's initials spelt out in gorse ('unhappily everyone thought it was for John Davenport').

The exhilaration of these breaks, combined with his Cranleigh success and the brief, intoxicating visits to London, seemed to inject him again with his old feelings of infinite expectations. Every moment of every day was filled – nights too, as his admiring classes noted on many mornings when he only just made the first lesson, often uncombed and barely shaven, clearly just back from London in the nick of time. At this period Michael was in the throes of a fairly long and passionate affair with an attractive young actress, Ruth Lodge, who had a flat in Pimlico. In addition, according to Vivian Cox, his love life nearer home was fairly hectic too, including a fling with Paul Jacklin ('his great Cranleigh love,' Cox said), now rugger captain (Jacklin was as busy as Michael – he was rumoured also to be having an affair with a woman who ran a Cranleigh tea shop) and also an affair with Maurice Allen who told Cox later that Michael had 'initiated' him 'into the joys of love as if it was the most natural thing in the world' in this time of uninhibited if necessarily clandestine pagan delight in his sexuality.

Crowded and seemingly fulfilled as his life seemed to be, the entries in Michael's Dream Diary, a notebook from this time, intriguingly detail many dreams of flight – literally, recalling the desire to 'tread the wind' of his Blondin poem in *The Venture* – and of escape. And theatre buildings, or in some cases buildings transforming themselves into theatres, also figure often in his vivid, frequently surreal, dreams, in which he can resemble an Ariel-figure out of a feverish *Tempest*, yearning to fly alone and to be free, as he records in a dream during his second Cranleigh year:

Am performing Hamlet in a large white hall with balconies and pillars, immensely high. Also Ariel, and for this I fly, to the amazement of all, diving off the level of the top gallery.

When he realised that John Milton's great epic poetic drama, *Samson Agonistes*, a School Certificate text, even using Robert Bridges' *Milton's Prosody* as an aid, was boring his class, Michael had the idea of staging it, which must have seemed to most involved initially a dubious project. Even Michael himself had doubts, telling Dennis Robertson that he had started it to try to bring Milton alive 'rather forlornly, as a rather exclusive sort of charade', but that soon 'It seems to have won over all sorts of odd people to our side. Gaza has fallen, it appears.' What helped him in his production of a work supposedly never intended for the stage (Michael always insisted that Milton may have meant only that it was not suited to the stage of his Cromwellian age) was undoubtedly the impact on him shortly before his *Samson* rehearsals of a trip with a few of his most dedicated French-class pupils to see a visiting theatre company's London season. This was the Compagnie des Quinze, a spin-off from the heritage of the great actor-director Jacques Copeau, whose own work Michael had seen just once, in 1928, when he visited Cambridge with his company Les Copiaus with *L'Illusion*, a revelation in committed ensemble work. When Copeau disbanded Les Copiaus, his nephew Michel Saint-Denis, also then an actor-director, regrouped with a core number of actors into Les Quinze, still along the lines of Copeau's non-star ensemble ideal, integrating all the skills of the actor – voice, mime, music, acrobatics – and travelling a collapsible and adaptable rostrum stage in a kind of forerunner of Peter Brook's international 'empty-space' language of theatre. The impresario Bronson Albery had admired their work in France and brought Les Quinze to London for two seasons, during which they presented work by their regular dramatist André Obey (*Noah*, *Lucrèce*) and Molière's *Don Juan* with Pierre Fresnay as the Don and Saint-Denis as Leporello. Many English actors and directors – Peggy Ashcroft, John Gielgud, Tyrone Guthrie, George Devine – were delighted by Les Quinze's relaxed versatility, while for Michael the performances he saw with his pupils at the Ambassador's and then at Wyndham's Theatre marked a crucial signpost on his personal Damascus road: 'In their bright light, all obstacles – my stepfather's disapproval, the warnings that I was too tall, the insecurity which I would be exchanging for a "safe" job – melted away.' He finally knew what he wanted – or what he was destined – to do.

In the meantime, the inspiration of Les Quinze's work, so striking in its unshowy physicality, helped him crack the problems of making *Samson Agonistes* accessible. He worked more than usually closely with Tom

Bowyer, devising a musical score, heavy on the inventive use of percussion, which would underscore many speeches, and spent hours of gruelling rehearsal working with the all-important chorus on their movement as well as their speech, conceiving them as a section of a 'tribe' and choreographing the mass of their combined bodies into a single body which could threaten or cower (as in terror at the meeting of Samson and Harapha) alternately. He also devised a pattern of sinuous movement for his golden-robed and masked Dalila, using circles and curves to elicit a serpentine character. His own Samson was an awesome presence, using every note of his voice to mine caverns of defiance or despair, holding the audience even through some lengthy speeches (Samson's opening speech is over five minutes long). Vivian Cox played Samson's father, Manoa, and remembered at the first performance after Bowyer's last long timpani rolls reverberated to silence, synchronised with a slow lighting fade to blackness: 'There was dead silence for a full minute. The Speech Hall had been packed. Were the audience all asleep? Was there still an audience? Then the applause began.'

By now word was spreading about the extraordinary innovations at Cranleigh. Michael had contacted leading Shakespearean scholars – G. Wilson Knight, J. Dover Wilson and Daisy's friend William Poel were those he respected on questions of staging Shakespeare – and they all supported his ideas, promising to try to come to future productions. Now Michael aimed for the big ones – in succession Hamlet, Prospero and King Lear.

The photographs of his Cranleigh Hamlet bear out his own feeling that it resembled – too much – that of John Gielgud, the great 1930s Hamlet (he had already played it twice); he certainly bears a strong physical resemblance, very pale and abstractedly pensive, although from the notices – his productions were now beginning to attract more than local critical coverage – it would seem that even this first charting of the arc of the role was rooted in the overpowering, near paralysing grief of a son for a dead father. He risked a remarkably full text (three and a half hours), staging it against his own very simple stepped and columned set with a minimum of furniture which allowed seamless fluidity of action (his Cranleigh script time and again urges 'Speed here!'). Bowyer again composed and also contributed a funny, practical countryman of a gravedigger (the Yorick scene was another highlight noted by critics, as was the remarkably athletic final duel with Paul Jacklin as Laertes), other masters involved including H. R. Jacob, Cranleigh's most famous England rugby international, as Fortinbras.

Hamlet was an especially happy production, cast and rehearsed in a glorious summer, often outdoors underneath the willows in South Fields, adjourning after rehearsals to the garden of the Tuck Shop in Horse-shoe Lane. Most of Michael's friends – Dennis, Gervase Smith, Dick (Dick's mother Isabel also appeared, driving a noisy box of a car Michael christened 'The Bride's Bath'), Wynyard Browne and John Davenport – along with smart London friends of David Loveday's, including Cyril Connolly, Noel Blakiston and Christopher Isherwood, came down for the production.

Daisy arrived for his penultimate Cranleigh starring vehicle, *The Tempest*, over which he took even more pains with the music – using eerie, ethereal off-stage voices often; although Tom Bowyer, an ideal collaborator, loved the whole process of revising and experimenting; he wrote to Michael on the first night: 'This is the most marvellous moment. It's partly owing to you that I have been set free, like those at the end of the play. My brain at the moment is a white hot fiery ball of love for everything and everybody.' Michael was unhappy with his Prospero, although again the notices were superb, partly because he felt hampered by a cumbersome magic staff, partly because he had put so much effort into the production that he knew he had somewhat neglected his own performance. Daisy's notes to him, written back at Chapel Street after a performance, seem very much those of a fellow professional, advising on problems practical and interpretative: 'A long, long, twig of a tree would be the best magic wand – like a water diviner's rod. Don't be afraid to *let go*, and remember the plot of the play is in your opening speech to Miranda. Every word *must* strike home.'

Daisy was perhaps beginning to realise that Michael would make an actor, although until the spring term of 1934 he said nothing to her or to David Loveday about his growing conviction that he should leave Cranleigh to try his luck on the professional stage. By then he had widened his outside activities to include several appearances with the semi-professional Guildford Repertory Company, deliberately testing himself in a variety of parts which included Jack in *The Importance of Being Earnest*, Robert Browning in Rudolph Besier's *The Barretts of Wimpole Street* and, most adventurously, Menelaus in Euripides' *The Trojan Women*. It made for a hectic life – either Bowyer in his little open-top sports car or, in a race against time, on 'Boanerges', his thunderous motorbike with a tiny sidecar into which Michael jacknifed his long legs, or Maurice Allen, who had a sharp red roadster, would drive him at speed through the Surrey lanes to Guildford and then back to Cranleigh in the moonlight. The Guildford company performed – for a silver collection towards costs – in St Nicholas Hall, off the High Street, in a draughty, cheerless auditorium with crim-inally hard seating (the programme for *The Importance* announced that 'cushions can be hired for 2d', while for the audience's bravery for attending Greek tragedy it was 'cushions can be hired for 1d'). Michael's usual Guildford director was the affable Alan Kitching, who was most encouraging, telling him that he definitely would have a good chance of success as a professional actor.

A letter Michael received from Dennis Robertson ('I hope there has been no contretemps with David of the kind you feared') suggested that he was dragging his feet in informing David Loveday of his decision to leave Cranleigh, perhaps dreading any accusation of ingratitude. In the event David, who must have been anticipating some such news in time, was completely understanding. From that point, and after he had let Daisy know, another campaign on Michael's behalf was launched. His mother set about asking for advice on his future while he prepared his swansong showcase at Cranleigh.

His notebook-prompt script for *King Lear*, a thick, canvas-covered volume, makes evident how carefully he planned the production, down to a rehearsal schedule with the availabilities of all his cast charted out (including days when the first Fifteen and first Eleven were playing away), many grouping and staging diagrams, and a large number of music notes for the unusual score which he and Bowyer worked out, using an effective mixture stressing horns, drums and cors anglais. Significantly, his script is prefaced by a boldly inscribed quotation from Jacques Copeau: 'Shake-speare on the stage needs – "*des grands acteurs, ou des acteurs supérieurement stylés, ou tout naïfs*".' Michael, of course, had the task of trying to make *naïfs* more *stylés*, and of all his Cranleigh ventures none was so scrupulously prepared or rehearsed as *Lear*. He felt always that it was an essentially pagan play – at one with Granville-Barker here – with Edgar emerging as a Christian gentleman. His costume and make-up reinforced this – he looked truly old, an Ancient of Days out of William Blake – and this time he had not neglected his own performance, shattering the house with his vocal power and stamina in the storm scenes, memorably touching as Lear subsequently moves towards a world of purification and redemption after suffering and pain. It was acclaimed in the press unanimously while Dadie Rylands, who came from Cambridge with Dennis Robertson, insisted he had only one note (he felt the Dover scene was slightly 'underpowered') for what he later described to Michael as 'a performance of exceptional beauty and understanding'. G. Wilson Knight and William Poel were also full of praise, while David Loveday wrote him a touching note after the first night:

Dearest Michael,
    King Lear has been a noble end to a noble series.
    Probably no school has had equal good fortune in having such

geniuses to co-operate as yourself and Bowyer. You have made Cranleigh widely known in a new way.

Daisy had swung into action by now. Her friend Alice Fredman
('Freddie'), the manager of London's Rudolf Steiner Hall, had admired
Michael's Hamlet, telling Daisy that she believed he could match or
outstrip actors such as Gielgud and Leslie Howard. She had returned to
Cranleigh for *Lear* and reported to Daisy: 'A truly wonderful performance – stupendous, bearing in mind that he bore the weight of the
production on his shoulders.'

Daisy had already contacted her friends Lilian Baylis at the Old Vic
and William Armstrong, artistic director of the Liverpool Playhouse, on
Michael's behalf but neither was able to see *King Lear*. She had even gone
up to Liverpool – she had acted at the Playhouse in its old days as the
Star, a melodrama house – armed with a portfolio of Michael's production
photographs, which certainly impressed Armstrong although, as a Scot in
the middle of a recession his advice was: 'Oh, Margaret! Don't let him go
on the stage. He can have a good job as a schoolmaster and that's so safe,
you know.' Similarly, Tyrone Guthrie – Michael and he had met several
times when Guthrie worked at the Festival Theatre in Cambridge – had
advised Michael, 'I do think you'd be rather a mug to leave Cranleigh.'
Freddie's advice to Daisy was that Michael should aim for the Old Vic and
with Daisy's permission she wrote to Lilian Baylis who would soon be
auditioning for a new season with the Vic's director, Henry Cass, strongly
recommending Michael: 'He takes the stage in the manner of an experienced actor and in my opinion is the most promising player of Shakespeare
that I have seen for a very long while. Please see him.'

An audition was duly arranged, although Michael's heart sank when he
was given the precise time of 10.40 a.m. (obviously meaning they were
seeing a mass of people that day). He had decided as an audition speech
on Rumour's prologue ('Painted full of tongues') from *Henry IV, Part 2*,
which he had played for the Marlowe Society, repeating his very physical
performance, a busily choreographed pattern of body and hand movement. After only a few lines he was stopped – always disconcerting at an
audition – and the dumpy, bespectacled Lilian Baylis waddled down the
aisle complaining that she could not follow the words because of his busy
hands, and suggested he try another piece. Gamely going into *Samson
Agonistes*' opening speech, he had only uttered a few words before realising
that as the blind Samson, again he was using his hands to grope his way.
Baylis stopped him in mid-flow once more and told him that he should
have to work on his hand movements. And that she could offer no salary
(Henry Cass whispered to Michael that this was an old ploy by the

notoriously penny-pinching Baylis to get him into the company for
nothing and not to accept). But Michael, still beglamoured by the idea of
making his professional debut in London on the Old Vic stage, said that
he would accept if she could give him a few small parts because he was
too old to carry a spear. The Old Vic audition seemed to end encouragingly
when the stage director, Murray Macdonald, who knew Daisy well, mur-
mured to Michael as he left, 'I expect you'll be with us.'

And yet, during his last weeks at Cranleigh, he heard nothing from the
Waterloo Road and by Whitsun had decided to go to Liverpool on the
Saturday to see William Armstrong. He called at Chapel Street en route
for Euston to find among his mail a letter from the Old Vic offering him
a play-as-cast contract at £3 a week. He had booked a seat for the Liverpool
matinée so decided still to keep the appointment with Armstrong who
was characteristically warm and friendly but still non-committal, telling
Michael that his company for the following season was virtually settled
but that he would bear him in mind. As he rose to leave, some boldness
made Michael play an unplanned trump card, asking only that Armstrong
let him know one way or another very shortly because he already had an
offer from the Old Vic. Armstrong, canny Scot that he was, paused only
fractionally before asking how much the Old Vic were offering. 'Three
pounds,' admitted Michael, to which Armstrong, without even the frac-
tional pause this time, replied, 'I'll give you four.'

Many people thought Michael was making a wrong choice in putting
Liverpool before the Old Vic but – as at other crucial points in his life (he
once said later that often 'you make your own luck') – he intuitively felt
happy with the decision, writing to Dennis Robertson:

> The work is so good there from what I saw and from what I've heard and
> it seems to me that I am most in need of all kinds of work, rather than just
> Shakespeare, so I am going at the end of August. Liverpool is pretty
> alarming and of course one would love to go to 'The Vic' – but I am sure I
> am doing right.

His 'alarm' at Liverpool may have stemmed from the fastidious David
Loveday's recollection of it as having 'a gin palace on every corner', but
after watching the Playhouse matinée following his talk with Armstrong
he had walked down to the seafront and the Liver Building, experiencing
once more that swell of boundless expectation for his future. He had also
sensed an omen in meeting at the Playhouse stage door the tall, handsome
actor Lyn Harding who, unprompted, reassured him that he was not too
tall for the stage. Michael, he said, at six foot three was the same height
as the great Lucien Guitry ('and you never noticed his height when he
was on the stage').

It was left to Daisy to handle the slightly awkward matter of telling the Old Vic that Michael had opted for Liverpool (Lilian Baylis seemed unconcerned) and, with rather more trepidation, the problem of presenting Andy with what would look like a fait accompli. To her – and to Michael – his reaction came as a surprise: 'Andy had been salmon fishing in Scotland all of May and had had much luck, and perhaps due to that he did not seem to mind very much that you had decided to become an actor.'

Daisy had swallowed all her previous objections – like others she had been surprised and deeply affected by Michael's Cranleigh work – although she still gave him what she considered her most important piece of advice: 'Most people go into the theatre for what they can get out of it. Not enough think about what they can put into it.' And before he left Cranleigh after what was inevitably an emotional farewell to so many colleagues and to David Loveday, she also reminded him – and he did not forget this either – 'It takes twenty years to make an actor.'

William Armstrong – 'Willie' to everyone who worked with him – would have agreed with Daisy. Scottish-born, his voice still retaining traces of its original genteel Morningside, tall, rather stooped and sandy-haired, Willie had originally been an actor, with both Beerbohm Tree and Sir Frank Benson and then with the redoubtable Mrs Patrick Campbell – Shaw's 'Stella' and first Eliza Doolittle, Pinero's original shocking Mrs Tanqueray – in her touring company when she was ageing, faded and fat but, for him, still trailing some remnants of authentic glory ('She was great when she could be bothered,' Willie said, which by the time he worked with her was rarely). She took a shine to Willie, nicknaming him 'Fanny' (he was often alleged to be one of the two young men in her company said to be unusually close, leading Mrs Patrick Campbell to remark that she didn't care what people did 'provided they don't do it in the streets and frighten the horses'). Willie had acted at the Liverpool Playhouse in its early days but in 1922 had nervously to tell Mrs Patrick Campbell that he would be leaving her employment to take up the job of its director. She said nothing at the time and then, a few nights later, sweeping upstage of him in *Hedda Gabler* she startled him (and the audience) by hissing loudly: 'I could have made an actor of you! Now you throw me on to the *trottoir* like an old *cocotte!*'

Willie had had a hard act to follow at Liverpool. The Playhouse had as its first director the tyrannical innovator Basil Dean who had gone on to great power and success as a West End and film producer and director. Famed – and feared – for his whiplash tongue, Dean had acted and directed for Miss Horniman at the very start of the British repertory movement. The powers behind the Liverpool repertory theatre, part of an explosion of civic pride in the city in the early years of the century, seeing a new university, a great cathedral, art galleries and libraries, supported by all the major shipping and commercial families of the city with considerable financial help from the soap magnate Lord Leverhulme, having raised the cash to convert the old Star in Williamson Square, gave the young Dean the job as director when the Playhouse opened its doors in 1911. He had built it up into indubitably the outstanding British regional repertory theatre, the little building in the square tucked away opposite Lime Street station and the great bulk of the Adelphi Hotel becoming a genuine powerhouse. Dean was fascinated by European theatre and its technical advances (he was something of a genius in the area of lighting) and the Playhouse became famed for its scenic and technical standards too.

Under Willie the theatre's reputation continued to soar. He would never be an innovator like Dean – his temperament too, benign and gentle, was poles apart from Dean's sarcastic irascibility – but he was a superb talent spotter (Rex Harrison, Robert Donat, Diana Wynyard were just some of his discoveries) with an unrivalled knack of picking harmonious companies and, with his own fairly cosily conservative tastes, he was the ideal director of a repertoire which by the 1930s consisted mainly of solid, middlebrow fare, recent West End successes often, with the occasional new or American play and an annual Shakespeare production. Willie always did his homework – vital with the turnover of rep – and his rehearsals were famously relaxed, with many tea breaks when he enchanted his actors with stories of the Acting Greats, while in rehearsal he was constantly encouraging (not such a bad way of getting good work out of a company) and, above all, indefinably communicating a priceless sense of common enterprise.

His colleague, and the ideal counterbalance to his sometimes volatile Celtic temperament – he cried at the drop of a hat – was the pragmatic (dour at first meeting) Maud Carpenter, the shingle-haired business manager who had been with the Playhouse since the beginning, first as box office assistant, then as Dean's secretary. Maud was resolutely unimpressed by the classics or 'highbrow' plays – she once sat phlegmatically all through Ibsen's *A Doll's House* until Nora loudly slammed her door towards the end before realising that she had seen it before – much preferring a 'nice play' with a beginning, middle and end which would keep the box office busy and Liverpool's theatregoers happy. She became a familiar sight during the intervals in the Playhouse's shell-shaped foyer, meeting and greeting, noting comments, 'working the room'. Between them Willie and Maud kept the theatre a vital part of Liverpool life.

When Michael arrived for the 1934–5 season, the auditorium had just been given a facelift – Maud insisted the fabric of the building be maintained in pristine condition – repainted dark green with the white plasterwork round the two circles of the inviting horseshoe-shaped auditorium picked out in gold, and a new walnut wood frontage to the orchestra pit. Immediately before arriving, Michael had had a long, healthy walking tour with Dick Green, centred round Grange-in-Borrowdale, and then had caught some of that season's Stratford productions, impressed especially by Fabia Drake as Beatrice and Rachel Kempson as an androgynous, seaweed-clad Ariel in *The Tempest*.

His digs throughout his time in Liverpool were in Falkner Street, up the hill quite near the cathedral, where the landlady was the welcoming and theatre-struck Mrs Rankin. At once, taking a long walk on his first evening, he realised that his own first impression of Liverpool had been right and he came truly to love the city. It was a noisy place then – the centre a cacophony of clanging trams, seagulls, stallholders' competitive cries in the Square's market, ferry boats hooting as they nipped between the huge ocean-going liners – and very much dirtier, all the beautiful Georgian houses on his walk down into the town centre veiled in a patina of factory soot. But the sheer vigour and vibrancy of Liverpool and its constantly changing skies seduced him; it was packed then with picture houses (the Tatler Cinema became his favourite) and cafés and restaurants ranging from the Blue Bird, the Brasserie and, best lunchtime value, the Bon Marché near the theatre to Quinns for oysters or the Adelphi Hotel grill room for special occasions. It was just about possible to get through the week on his £4 salary.

All his early parts were relatively undemanding *jeune premier* roles, which required little other than a handsome presence and good diction. By far the most challenging was his very first Liverpool role in the large-cast American play *Counsellor-at-Law* by Elmer Rice. Michael knew about the play; he had become a subscriber to *Theater Arts Monthly*, the American magazine, and it had reported on the piece's success in New York, produced by the dynamic Group Theater with Paul Muni in the title role of a powerful New York lawyer threatened by a past scandal. Moving between the law firm's inner and outer offices, the play was packed with juicy parts – lovelorn secretary, revolutionary immigrant, heartless socialite wife, wisecracking switchboard girl – and, for Michael, a smooth Ivy League seducer, Roy Darwin, with two good scenes with the Park Avenue wife. Willie staged it – fast, often funny – with just the right touch and Michael found himself unexpectedly relaxed and focused inside the WASP accent and dapper suits of this suave chancer.

It was a strong company, including Geoffrey Edwards (brother of an already successful actor, Alan Webb), Robert Flemyng and an outstanding character actor, Lloyd Pearson; the women included a stylish leading actress of casual aplomb, Ena Burrill ('Auntie Ena' to younger actors), tall, with a camp wit, often trailing her leopard-skin coat, and a clever character actress, Deirdre Doyle (she reminded Michael of the great Abbey Theatre actress Sara Allgood), who helped Michael with make-up tips including how to use Leichner No. 20 on his hair to add some years for *Counsellor-at-Law*. She also tried to kill one of his laughs one night by upstaging him but Daisy, wise to all the old tricks, simply advised him that on the next occasion he should just walk upstage with her until they both reached the back of the set and she would never do it again. He did and she didn't. All this was part of an apprenticeship which he soon realised he would never have got at the Old Vic in minor roles. His only worries were when he was cast in the conventional juvenile-lead roles of which he had quite a few – he opened a lot of scripts to find his character described like Charles Hubbard, 'a well-dressed suave young man of thirty', in John van Druten's *The Distaff Side*; having to rely only on his own personality he often felt maladroit and uninventive, although Willie seemed happy enough. Daisy – a regular visitor to Liverpool where she felt something of the excitement of her own early days – kept urging him to 'smile more' in such roles, but at that time and indeed until movies and money could provide a top-flight dentist, Michael remained self conscious about the gap in his front teeth.

He soon realised, too, how physically demanding the schedule of rep could be. On afternoons when he was not called for rehearsal he often took ferry trips, usually to Seacombe, gulping in huge lungfuls of Mersey ozone, or went to the gym, Ned Tarleton's in Bold Street (Tarleton was then the popular British Featherweight Champion), his workouts sometimes under the supervision of 'the Great Tarleton' himself. At weekends he varied his routine. Some Sundays he would catch the early train to London to spend the day with Ruth Lodge in her Warwick Square flat, returning to Liverpool on the last train; the diary, which he resumed for a time on 1 January 1935, records a few Sundays when he spent the morning with Ruth, went over to Belgravia alone for a Chapel Street lunch and then returned to Ruth's flat for the evening before his train. A fairly exhausting routine, so much so that he was beginning to suggest her name to Willie as a possible future company member. Otherwise he would visit Buxton in Derbyshire where Dick Green's parents now lived, in a beautiful house in the Square and where Dick – barely solvent, agonising over his writing and his love life a hopeless mess, all fairly usual for him – was staying then. Dick had a local friend, a writer called Patrick Railton (he wrote detective novels as Patrick Carleton), a frequently heavy boozer like Dick and often wildly funny (Dick's parents thought him something of a reprobate). Dick and Paddy often came to see the Playhouse productions, while both Maurice Allen and Tom Bowyer from Cranleigh were loyal regular visitors too.

When Michael resumed his diary – no time for introspection, mostly notes of plays and engagements – he was in the middle of rehearsals for a supporting but challenging role, Melchior Feydak in the American comedy by S. N. Behrman, *Biography*, a recent Broadway hit with Ina Claire as Marian, the central Bohemian artist figure (Ena Burrill at Liverpool). Feydak was her confidant, an urbane, mature operetta composer, full of avuncular wisdom, left alone on stage at one point to play the piano. That was no problem for Michael but he found the tone of the part – Feydak was written for an actor of fifty – extremely elusive and was convinced that he was falling back on Mittel-European cliché. But then in the second week of rehearsals, perhaps helped by seeing *Jew Süss* (starring Conrad Veidt) at the Tatler, the part began to swim into focus for him. He noted after a further rehearsal: 'Act 1 – good in parts. Want to repeat and repeat things. There appears to be no time for this.' But despite the frustrations of rep's schedules, later he wrote: 'Opening of *Biography*. Lunch with mother. Walk. Bath. Theatre. Performance better than hoped. Very much from within! Mother v. pleased.' The reference to a performance from 'within' may have something to do with the fact that as well as watching Veidt, his old Heidelberg favourite, and subscribing to *Theatre Arts*, Michael had been reading Komisarjevsky (who had known Stanislavsky in Moscow) and Stanislavsky himself (the first mention of reading Stanislavsky is in January 1935, when he was rehearsing a French frivol, Sacha Guitry's *Villa for Sale*). At this stage, with the kind of workload he faced, Michael had no time for intensive study or practice of Stanislavsky's precepts, but the keen interest alone is an earnest of his resolve to use his time at Liverpool to make himself as grounded an actor as possible. He loved his work, writing of *Theater Arts Monthly*'s latest issue, 'It continues to induce pleasant dreams of being in a delightful profession.' He was pleased, too, by Willie's words to him after the dress rehearsal of *Villa for Sale*: 'W.A. pleased. Talks about "advancing leaps and bounds" . . . Cheered by this.' He was also cheered by Willie raising his salary to £6 per week.

While rehearsing the courtroom play *Libel* and aware that Willie would soon be planning the forthcoming production of John van Druten's *Flowers of the Forest*, which had a meaty female role still uncast, Michael invited Ruth Lodge to Liverpool for a few days. They stayed at the Hoylake Hotel in West Kirby and Michael, offhandedly casual, engineered introducing her to Willie, suggesting equally casually that she would be good as Naomi in *Flowers of the Forest*, only for Willie to tell them he had already cast Rachel Kempson. Michael was put out, not just because of Ruth's disappointment but also because he remembered Rachel Kempson as a tiny Ariel from Stratford ('I should have to go down on my knees to kiss her,' he protested).

'Ruth back to London' is the last we hear of Ruth Lodge in Michael's diary. The next entry is for Tuesday, 12 March: 'Rehearse *Flowers of the Forest*. Rachel Kempson Naomi. Taller than I had feared. To lunch with her at Bon Marché.'

At that first lunch after the read-through of *Flowers of the Forest* Rachel had to take some medicine – she had been suffering from gastric trouble – which, with his own history of ulcers and his hypochondria, was immediately fascinating for Michael and they shared over lunch the most intimate digestive confidences, so delighted with each other's company that they left for afternoon rehearsal blithely singing songs from *The Beggar's Opera*.

From that point the 1935 entries become more sporadic, tapering off for fairly lengthy periods. The 'R' in his entries is now Rachel rather than Ruth; there are a few 'Lunch R. Bon Marché' entries and a longer one after the first night of the play: 'Accident with lights. To comfort R. afterwards. Extraordinary meeting. To Adelphi with Geoff, Valerie and R. then home with R.' There are a couple of 'to tea with R' entries – her digs in Gambia Terrace were close to his – and then silence between 4 and 17 April except for two pencilled entries – 'Eric Kempson' on 4 April and on 17 April, 'Become engaged to R.' A whirlwind romance, it raised a few company eyebrows, although Deirdre Doyle burst into tears – Willie joined her – when the engagement was announced.

Rachel Kempson was two years younger than Michael. She was the only daughter and eldest child (she had two brothers, Nicholas and Robin) of Eric Kempson who, after a teaching career of mixed fortunes, including a spell at Rugby, had become headmaster of the Royal Naval College at Dartmouth. His marriage to Beatrice (known familiarly as 'Beanie') Ashwell was often uneasy, shaken badly by Eric's absence in the war and by Beatrice's unconsummated wartime infatuation with a Herefordshire farmer. Rachel later diagnosed the problem with her parents' troubled marriage – although they grew closer in their final years – as sexual incompatibility. The tensions at home, plus her own deep insecurity, her lifelong feeling of never quite belonging anywhere, due surely in some measure to an unsettled, peripatetic childhood with no fixed home for years and many schools including a particularly joyless convent school, had resulted in a history of digestive and gastric ailments. She had been a nervous child and teenager, subject to a recurring dream of insecurity: 'I would find myself at the end of a breakwater, far out in the sea, surrounded by a thick white mist. I could not see to go back and knew that if I went forward I would step off into the sea and be drowned. So I stood on the end of the breakwater enveloped in the silent mist unable to move until I woke tearful and shaken.'

Witness of many parental rows – she was always closer to her father than to her mother – Rachel became convinced when quite young of a theory distinctly unorthodox for her era:

> If only married partners would generously allow each other a little latitude, how much more easily marriages could stay together. A person *may* only love one man or woman in the world; that is fortunate. But it is an extraordinary rule that once married no man or woman should ever have some of the love that men or women have in them to give. For a man never to experience any other woman or for a woman never to experience love with another man can be a kind of imprisonment.

In acting Rachel found an escape from her own dreads. She was helped and encouraged by the retired actor-manager Cyril Maude who lived near Dartmouth; he helped arrange a partial scholarship for her to attend RADA (although, with money tight, her diet was ludicrously inadequate, only exacerbating her ailments and hyper-acidity). Also of immense help was the director of the Memorial Theatre, Stratford, W. Bridges Adams, who gave her a first break there in the 1933 season when she played small parts in *Macbeth* and *Richard II*, directed by Theodore Komisarjevsky and Tyrone Guthrie respectively, early in their careers as 1930s theatrical *enfants terribles*. She also rose to the occasion when cast as Juliet for Adams, who invited her back the next season to repeat her Juliet and to play Ariel and Titania. Her porcelain, delicate beauty could seem so fragile that it might shatter, and her health was still a worry, leading her father to note in his unpublished journal: 'Bridges spoke of his doubt as to whether Rachel should go on with the stage. No doubt as to her artistic power, but a feeling that she herself was not of the theatre world, a world which called for something hard-boiled in its citizens.'

Rachel admitted herself that she never had 'a tough ego', but what Adams missed was a tensile cord right through her, an inner strength which would help her through later troubled times and which even then led her to refuse the security of an offer from W. Bridges Adams's successor, Ben Iden Payne, of the next Stratford season, when she felt the parts on offer were not good enough compared with what she had already played. It also drove her on to write to directors, including Willie, to find the kind of work which she wanted to develop her craft.

For Rachel, Michael was, almost at first sight, 'my young god'. They spent most of the *Flowers of the Forest* rehearsal time together, their growing attraction magnified by the intensity of their scenes. *Flowers of the Forest* had had a modest London success the previous year when a startling young actor, Stephen Haggard, had stolen most of the notices as a tubercular pacifist in the first and third acts. It is a stilted play for the most part, although intriguingly its structure is an anticipatory variation on the time scheme of J. B. Priestley's *Time and the Conways* (1938) with Acts I and III set in the present (1934), the middle act flashing back to the war years.

Rachel had the taxing part of Naomi, married and cocooned in affluent hardness; twenty years earlier we see her ardent and tender, in love with a much-admired young poet about to leave for the trenches, Richard Newton-Clare (Michael), and then her shock at his cynical disillusion when he returns, driving her to abort the child he never knows he fathered. In the play's best scene, in the second act, Richard turns off a lamp so that the room is lit only by the flickering firelight and moonlight through the window, then admits to Naomi his secret fears about what he would be dying for should he be killed, going on into a tender love scene. The 'accident with lights' noted in Michael's diary was an opening-night blunder by the electrician, who forgot the cue to switch off the lamp, and then as Michael wisely decided to carry on with the touching dialogue, suddenly remembered and switched the light off, leaving Michael with Rachel in his arms amid laughter from the audience. Then what he noted as an 'extraordinary meeting' when he went to comfort Rachel in her dressing room was Rachel suddenly saying, as he consoled her, 'Oh Mike, I love you so!' They joined Geoffrey Edwards and Valerie Tudor from the company at the Adelphi for supper, Rachel wearing a white camellia from Michael as a corsage, although it barely survived the evening: 'I didn't care, since it was Michael's embrace that had killed it.'

That evening brought the relationship to a different plane. Rachel ached with longing to sleep with Michael but, still virgin, she was anxious to avoid pregnancy although besottedly in love. Michael had fallen deeply in love with Rachel, too, but on one occasion when they were in a passionate embrace in Falkner Street he talked, very openly, to her about his bisexuality – 'difficulties in his nature' – which perhaps might be a reason not to marry. Rachel – who had fallen in love two years before with her Stratford Romeo, John Wyse, who was also bisexual – insisted to Michael that this made no difference. She admitted herself: 'The fact that I loved Michael so much meant that I was sure I could overcome his difficulties. I would have done anything for him. And, indeed, it was probably this sensitivity in his nature that made me love him so.'

On Michael's part, he wanted to be – as he had been in his Cambridge and Cranleigh affairs – as honest as possible. If he married it would not be as a smokescreen for the conventional world. He did want a real marriage, he wanted children, but he never deceived himself or Rachel that marriage would overnight make him completely heterosexual. He knew that his bisexuality was part of who and what he was.

Rachel's reassurance convinced Michael that they should marry (Rachel had spotted that the photograph of Ruth Lodge on his mantelpiece had vanished) and she was 'delirious with joy'. Eric Kempson journeyed to Liverpool to meet this sudden prospect of a son-in-law over lunch at the Stork Hotel; within days *The Times* announced the engagement and the wedding was scheduled for the break between the Playhouse's seasons, taking place at Dartmouth.

Michael had to swallow his ambitions – and keep quiet about his Cranleigh version – while Geoffrey Edwards played Hamlet in April, although he admitted to his diary after the opening 'Great ovation for Geoffrey' and that 'I determine to improve Horatio'. He used the off-stage dressing-room waits during *Hamlet* to finish a one-act play, which Willie promised to consider as a curtain-raiser (still popular in those days). *The Seventh Man* was a taut adaptation of a short story by 'Q' – Sir Arthur Quiller-Couch – with a haunting evocation of an atmosphere not unlike that of 'The Ancient Mariner' or the predicament of Captain Scott when he and his team became aware of some presence in the Arctic. It involves six sailors, one dying, stranded in a hut built out of their ship, wrecked by pack ice, all of them exhausted in a kind of grim living death. The tensions between the men steadily mount towards a climax when they become aware of 'a seventh man', and as they fling back the massive trapdoor to seek him, they find instead the long dark Arctic night over and the sun returned. Willie thought it first-rate and put it on before a tactlessly titled comedy, *Too Young to Marry*. Subsequently it had many performances by amateur companies – it was ideal for all-male groups – at drama festivals.

At the end of the season – Playhouse end-of-season last nights then were always great affairs, with speeches, flowers and big crowds at the stage door – Michael went briefly to Chapel Street, catching up with London theatre; the first thing he rushed to see was the London pro-duction of *Noah* for John Gielgud's company directed once again by Michel Saint-Denis. Rachel had previously met Andy, whose Edwardian gallantry and puns relaxed her, and Daisy, whose sometimes peremptory attitude and proprietary treatment of Michael did not. Inevitably, when they separated after such a short, intense courtship, doubts set in, par-ticularly for Rachel, who developed a bad case of pre-wedding jitters not long before the ceremony. Not at all unusually, they suddenly felt like strangers to each other after such intense intimacy; Rachel described later how she unpacked Michael's wedding clothes, holding the trousers to herself thinking that garments which had been close to his body would rekindle her feelings.

An air of slightly strained gaiety arrived with Daisy's, Andy's and Peggy's descent on Dartmouth, heightened when Beatrice was shocked by one of the wedding presents (from Dick Green on the groom's side), a painting of a nude which she insisted be turned to the wall, and by a minor huff from Peggy, who could still be awkwardly truculent and who took against her bridesmaid's outfit until firmly squashed by Michael. Dick Green was Michael's best man, repeating his recent role for Humphrey Browne ('Nothing – with its eight bridesmaids – was so out of my line') and his laconic good humour helped defuse the tension around an affair which finally went off perfectly satisfactorily, crowned by a witty, affectionate speech from Cyril Maude at the reception.

A chauffeured car took the couple as far as Exeter where they transferred to Eric Kempson's car; even though Michael never properly learnt to drive he managed – L-plates clanking – to get them to Lyme Regis. Rachel had begun to relax ('was it the final loosening of mother's long domination?') and although both were naturally nervous their wedding night, by their separate accounts, was a success, followed by ten days of a happiness at Hamble neither would forget, swimming, walking and playing records on the gramophone given them as a wedding present by W. Bridges Adams. And, as Rachel put it: 'We became happy in the big double-bed in the pretty bow-fronted bedroom' of the house they had been lent.

They had arranged to rent extra rooms at Mrs Rankin's back in Falkner Street so that they could have room for the inevitable hired piano as well as the vast double bed which had been Daisy's present. Their combined salaries of £15 per week allowed them to enjoy a fairly comfortable life-style. The company gave the couple a belated wedding party and a present of Victorian porcelain doorknobs presented by a moist-eyed Willie.

That season's productions again balanced the box office certainties with some more stretching work, although Michael still found himself lumbered with some unrewarding parts. He and Rachel had looked forward to a new work, *Miss Linley of Bath*, Mary Sheridan's play about her dramatist ancestor, but it emerged an undernourished piece and Willie, Michael and Rachel (playing Sheridan and his runaway bride Elizabeth) had a frustrating time trying to animate it. Willie had asked Michael to write another play for the company, suggesting something for the Christmas period that would entertain a family audience, and he came up with *Circus Boy* ('An Adventure in Three Acts'), a fast-moving play with a colourful cast of circus characters – Bobo the clown and Sophie, an enterprising chimpanzee – along with gypsies, village bobbies and intrepid children. The latter included Janet, a tomboy who wants to be a gypsy, her Lord Snooty-ish wimp of a half-brother ('I have very sensitive ganglia') and the title character, Ludo, whose dead father once owned the circus now run by the villain of the piece, Gaspar, who, it transpires, tricked Ludo's father to deprive the boy of his inheritance. The children's exploits include kidnapping, escaping from a prison cell aided by the resourceful chimp (shades of Roy's melodramas) and a thrilling climax at a moonlit Deadwater Mill when Gaspar's crimes are exposed by the king of the gypsies. Ludo is finally restored to ownership of the circus, his dream realised at the end as the stage dims and then, underneath circus music and Bobo's 'walk-up' routine, the electric sign flashes through the darkness – 'LUDO'S CIRCUS'. It was artfully tailored to suit the company – with a young Patricia Hayes giving a magical portrait of Ludo – and audiences loved it and the box office boomed (Maud, who had been sceptical, was delighted with the box office returns).

Some of Michael's finest Liverpool performances were to follow, often in unusual character parts, none more unexpected than a virtuoso comic turn as a complacently vain minister in an Ulster village full of gossiping spinsters (Deirdre Doyle in her element as a tattling Miss McClurg); cheaply eloquent and smarmy as *Boyd's Shop*'s Revd Dunwoody, slyly making a play for a shopkeeper's daughter, Michael delighted the audience and the author, St John Ervine. And in Merton Hodge's *The Wind and the Rain*, playing a fairly stereotypical 'silly-ass' role, he invested it with such self-satisfied glee, hair glistening like patent leather, chin seemingly vanishing, he took part and play into a P. G. Wodehousian comic dimension. Best of all, remembered for years by those who saw it, was *Cornelius*, in the title role, one of the slightly baffled Everyman figures which J. B. Priestley wrote so well. It is a clumsy play often – dealing with a small aluminium business whose boss slowly comes to comprehend the cumulatively dehumanising effects of the business routine – with dangerous passages of near bathos, not least a tricky scene for Cornelius and a trusting young secretary who has set him thinking: 'It's as if it's been dark here … and you carried a little light with you. There was a light around your head … How small and clear you are – like the flame of a candle.' By the utter conviction and simple, direct truth of his playing, Michael negotiated those awkward passages, even pulling off a final scene when, talked out of suicide in his despair by the conveniently to hand office charlady, Cornelius leaves the office to begin his romantic quest, his dream of finding the lost city of the Incas. What could have seemed almost risibly sentimental passed in pin-drop silence, so deeply involving was Michael's communication of the emotions of an ordinary man, troubled by the strength of his inner feelings.

Sometimes he could make light of the work, writing to Dennis Robertson, for instance, when the Playhouse was presenting the family chronicle of G. B. Stern's *The Matriarch*: 'Everyone rushes to the dressing-room between each scene to change and add 5 or 20 years. I came back in the last act – after 10 years in South America – looking what I think is the dead spit of Frank Harris.' More and more, however, he was making the kind of discovery so exciting to a young actor – just as John Gielgud had found when playing Trofimov in *The Cherry Orchard* in his first rep job – that acting is so much more than display, that it is possible to inhabit a character completely different from one's own.

Michael mentioned to Dennis Robertson that he intended to stay on – as did Rachel – for a third season, but the final plays during the spring of 1936 altered all their plans. During the run of another family drama, *A Hundred Years Old*, Jane Baxter, who had joined the company, introduced Michael to her agent, Bill Linnit, smoothly sophisticated and a powerful name in London theatre then; he had begun as a call-boy before joining Edgar Wallace and his company and now worked with the O'Brien and Dunfee management as well as running his agency. Michael had been cast in the title role of the forthcoming *Richard of Bordeaux*, Gordon Daviot's chronicle play tracing Richard II's life from boy-king of volatile hysteria to soldier-statesman of thirty, which had catapulted Gielgud to major West End stardom the previous year. It was a wonderful opportunity for Michael to display his range and Linnit, who had admired Michael's performance (heavily 'aged-up') in *A Hundred Years Old*, promised to catch his performance as Richard and that he would bring with him a new young West End impresario, H. M. Tennent's Hugh Beaumont (the name meant nothing to Michael). Willie who also co-designed, gave the play royal treatment, and both Michael and Rachel (as Anne of Bohemia who becomes Richard's Queen) scored huge successes – Liverpool audiences liked seeing them play lovers – but on the evening of Linnit's visit, two sombre-looking men entered Michael's dressing room after the show. He was convinced that they had disliked his performance but they were in fact desolate – their car had broken down – that they had only caught the final ten minutes (since Anne dies, plague-stricken, well before the end, they missed Rachel altogether). Everyone cheered up over an informal smoked salmon and white Burgundy supper back at Falkner Street, Michael and Rachel both taking to the voluble, worldly Beaumont (always known as 'Binkie'), just then at the start of his climb to a near monopoly in the West End in the post-war decades. Before leaving, Binkie had offered Michael what he described as 'a leading role' in his next presentation, a version of Kate O'Brien's novel *The Ante-Room* starring Diana Wynyard (ex-Playhouse, now a West End star), directed by the leading American director, husband of Broadway's Katharine Cornell, Guthrie McClintic: 'The next morning, Rachel and I were up and out, searching every bookshop in Liverpool for Kate O'Brien's novel.'

Binkie was shrewd in his perception of sometimes unexplored aspects of an actor's range, but he had been unusually canny to spot after only ten minutes of Michael's Richard how much potential he might have for playing a divided character. O'Brien's novel was centred round a middle-class Tipperary family, the underlying frictions caused by a repressed woman's passion for her sister's doctor husband. Binkie already had Wynyard and Jessica Tandy cast as the sisters, but he knew very well how much depended on the casting of the austere but magnetic doctor, his surface charm cloaking a troubled, complex personality. And on reading the novel Michael could see what a rich part it could be – and how crucial – in an adaptation.

The next Liverpool play also had good parts for both Michael and Rachel. James Bridie's *Storm in a Teacup*, set in a small Scottish seaside town, was loosely based on Bruno Frank's *Storm im Wasserglass*, whisked into a feather-light comedy, a simple affair of the threat to a pillar of respectability, the Lord Provost, by a poor Irish hawker (Deirdre Doyle having a field day in a part created by Sara Allgood). Michael played Frank Burdon, an idealistic cub reporter covering the story, while Rachel was the Provost's young disillusioned wife who falls for him. This was the kind of material at which Willie excelled – keeping it light and sparkling without losing the emotional sincerity underlying the scenes between Michael and Rachel. Following one performance, next morning they found a letter addressed to them both at the stage door from Tyrone Guthrie who had seen the previous night's show. Obviously he no longer considered Michael a mug for throwing up his Cranleigh job; now he was offering them both places in the company for the next season at the Old Vic where he was returning as director. Willie was reconciled to them leaving – although he wept, just as he always cried copiously during rehearsals of love scenes ('Oh, it's so beautiful – Oh, you're so clever!') – and over a Bon Marché lunch they filled in, positively, Guthrie's shrewdly enclosed stamped and addressed postcard:

> We are/are not interested in the idea of an Old Vic season. We are/are not available. If your salesman calls (in plain van) around May 25th, we can/cannot discuss fully.

Guthrie had Edith Evans and Laurence Olivier in place, although the plays had not been finalised. One possibility, which interested Michael especially, was Ibsen's *Ghosts* with Edith Evans as Mrs Alving and Michael as Oswald, the artist son who has inherited the venereal sins of his dead father, returning to his mother's house from Paris; he had always wanted to play Oswald and was giddy at the prospect of tackling it, especially the extraordinary closing scene with Oswald begging his mother to finish him off as he subsides into idiocy, opposite an actress such as Edith Evans. In the event, the play was dropped (Michael never played Oswald). The other news that Michael found particularly tempting was that one play in the season – probably Dekker's *The Witch of Edmonton* – would be directed by Michel Saint-Denis. After a good deal of chopping and changing on Guthrie's part, and a little horse-trading on Michael's (he surprised Guthrie by asking for Laertes in *Hamlet* to Olivier's Prince rather than the offered Horatio, which he did not want to repeat), he had also agreed to play the King of Navarre in Guthrie's production of *Love's Labour's Lost* (Rachel as the French Princess – she had also been cast as Ophelia) and the rakish seducer, Mr Horner, in Wycherley's Restoration comedy *The Country Wife*. With the possible exception of the latter, none of these offered an obvious chance to dazzle the town or to lead the company, but he knew that this was a superb introduction to London theatre. Better, certainly, than he would have had in *The Ante-Room* as it transpired. Binkie had been right about the vital casting of the doctor; Marius Goring, who opened it out of town, was sacked on the road, Laurence Olivier refused to take over and it was finally played by Clifford Evans. It ran for less than two weeks (another case of 'you make your own luck'?).

Michael also appreciated what a good first showing in London the Old Vic casting was for Rachel. Or would have been. But although she would still be able to play the Princess – *Love's Labour's* opened the season – Rachel would not, after all, be able to take on Ophelia. As they were finishing their final Liverpool production – *Twelfth Night* with Michael a Malvolio of acerbic pedantry, Rachel a glowing, romantic Viola–Cesario – Rachel discovered that she was pregnant.

Six

TAKING THE TOWN

For most actors the big rehearsal room at the top of the Old Vic is the favourite in London, even though, with its glass roof, it remains arctic in winter and a hothouse in summer. But its walls breathe history, with photographs of twentieth-century greats looking down on those aiming to succeed them; they include quite a few from a legendary 1936–7 season when Michael and Rachel arrived together on a beautiful August day to begin rehearsals for *Love's Labour's Lost*.

Their first married home in London was a small, rather dark but usefully central flat in Greycoat Mansions, Westminster, tucked away behind the Army and Navy Stores. At this time Daisy was at her best, helping Rachel fit out a bare kitchen while organising the move of their stored Liverpool furniture. She had been thrilled by the news of Rachel's pregnancy, which by the time they were settled into Greycoat Mansions was past the early stage of tiredness and nausea. They travelled by District Line on the Underground to Embankment, walking across Hungerford Bridge to Waterloo Station and the Old Vic stage door (in the Waterloo Road in those days).

Expectations were running high for Guthrie's season. London theatre in the mid-1930s was enjoying an economic boom but it was a desert of mediocrity, with Noël Coward and J. B. Priestley the leading dramatists, and the West End generally given over to the cosy, well-made play along-side escapist revues and musicals, with leading stars – Gertrude Lawrence, Lewis Waller, Robert Loraine – of understated charm. There was little to challenge this theatre of reassurance except the odd enterprising little theatre, the then equivalent of the Fringe or off-West End; there were also a few directors like Tyrone Guthrie (he was usually called Tony) or émigrés including Theodore Komisarjevsky, who had pioneered Chekhov in England at a little theatre over the bridge in Barnes, who could create some fireworks. Also just beginning to work in London was Michel Saint-Denis who, after Les Quinze had run into trouble in 1934, had come to direct *Noah* for what had emerged as the most fascinating enterprise to hit the London theatre for years.

John Gielgud, after his 1920s Old Vic seasons and the massive commercial success of *Richard of Bordeaux*, had allied himself with Bronson Albery to present a season at Albery's New Theatre in the West End with a remarkable company ranging from senior actors, some of whom went back to Sir Frank Benson's Stratford days, alongside established stars such as Edith Evans, to a pack of young talent to whom Gielgud gave generous first or early breaks; Alec Guinness, Frith Banbury, Glen Byam Shaw, Jessica Tandy and George Devine were just some of those new faces. Gielgud was fired by both the Granville-Barker English tradition and the example of Les Quinze to build up a company of like-minded ensemble actors, and in effect he created the nearest thing to a permanent company to be seen in London between the Irving–Tree era and the emergence of the main subsidised companies in the 1960s.

That 1934–35 Gielgud season – which also included his own *Hamlet* production and a *Romeo and Juliet* with himself and Laurence Olivier alternating Romeo and Mercutio to Peggy Ashcroft's Juliet – was a revelation in the possibility of an English ensemble and in stage design. All of the three-woman design-team known as Motley – two sisters, Margaret ('Percy') and Sophie Harris and their friend from art school Elizabeth Montgomery – were as committed as Saint-Denis to a philosophy of design as subservient to the text and the bold use of colour, using unconventional (and cheap) materials – unbleached calico, dishcloth material, even pipe-cleaners – in what amounted to a revolution in English theatre design, breaking away from the decorative pictorial tradition. In 1936 Gielgud was on Broadway but he was rumoured to be planning a new London season.

In the meantime Tony Guthrie was set on upgrading standards at the Old Vic. He and Lilian Baylis had a wary mutual respect. She knew that she needed his flair and ability to woo strong casts while Guthrie, a mixture of showman and puritan, genuinely admired (as Michael came to do also) this extraordinary, cottage-loaf-shaped, stubborn woman whose mission in life was to give 'our people' – the Old Vic audiences – their Shakespeare. Guthrie had managed – at last – to separate the two-way traffic between the Old Vic and Sadler's Wells so that now the Wells housed opera and the Vic only plays, but he knew that he still had battles ahead with 'The Baylis', as he called her with a kind of exasperated affection.

Guthrie had promised Michael that the old, tatty production style at the Vic would go; before him, set budgets were rarely more than £25 for a production while costumes were recycled until rabbit-fur moulted and velvet rotted. There was, however, little evidence of any dramatic change from the past, at least regarding the set, on *Love's Labour's Lost*. Guthrie was aiming for a buoyant, youthful and stylised production; he had to make do with a tented pavilion on each side of the stage, a stone well stage centre and a few steps upstage backed by a hideously painted and wrinkled skycloth (a gauze hung in front of it finally disguised all but the worst folds).

But Guthrie was nothing if not an invigorating presence in rehearsal. Lean and tall – well over six feet – his hair always short-back-and-sided, with a bristling toothbrush moustache, he was an unusual combination of a barking Montgomery of Alamein and a giggling scoutmaster with a voice – unexpected from his appearance – both high-pitched and slightly camp. His casts had quickly to get used to his finger-snapping energy and speed of working – 'On! On!', 'Pace, Rhythm, Pace!' were favourite exhortations – while most problems were greeted with a groan of 'Oh, fucky-poo!'. The big guns – Edith Evans and Laurence Olivier – were not yet involved, the *Love's Labour's Lost* company including some of London's brightest pro-spects – Margaretta Scott as Rosaline and the handsome, blue-eyed Alec Clunes as Berowne. Michael, secretly, coveted that part, by far the best younger male role; for him Navarre meant a return to the kind of part requiring little but a pleasant personality that he had been given so often at Liverpool. The company also included some senior actors such as the capricious, wildly mannered Ernest Milton, a Bensonian with the char-acteristic rich vowels of that tradition, ideally cast as the broken-down Don Quixote figure, Don Armado. Guthrie had to cope with his attempts to embellish in rehearsal, much to the younger actors' delight:

MILTON: Tawn-nay! I thought here I could sort of careen around the well here centre while I do this speech.

Slight pause.

GUTHRIE: Don't know what you mean by 'careen'. Show us, Ernest.

MILTON *performs a long and complex speech while executing a dazzlingly extravagant parade around the well, with many a baroque flourish.*

Pause.

GUTHRIE: Yes. I see. Cut the careen. On!

Michael admired Guthrie's invention in rehearsal, and he and Rachel soon got to know him and his wife (also cousin) Judith, as tall as he and fiercely protective. The Redgraves, like many others, marvelled at the mixture of civilisation and squalor in the Guthries' flat high up in Lincoln's Inn, books, music and cats all over the place, laundry dripping from ceiling racks and meals from tins (the actress Coral Browne always swore it was cat food) sloshed up in one frying pan. Other theatrical couples and groups were beginning to be part of the Redgraves' circle too – Roger Livesey and Ursula Jeans, Glen Byam Shaw and Angela Baddeley, George Devine and the Motley girls (George would soon marry Sophie Harris) and, especially, Stephen Haggard and his wife Morna, also beginning a family. Stephen Haggard was from a diplomatic family, passionately political – at this time Michael and he endlessly discussed the Spanish Civil War – and he had a rare intensity on stage. The Haggards had an airy mews flat in Notting Hill Gate and Michael and Rachel spent increasing amounts of time with them.

Love's Labour's Lost opened the Old Vic season to a great ovation – ten minutes of cheers as flowers rained down on the stage (the Vic then had a passionately loyal audience) – and reviews which mostly praised the youthful zest of both production and company (although, surprisingly when one reads through them, not one mentions the slyly aloof Boyet created by Alec Guinness). Michael collected more than a few reviews which predicted that Guthrie's description of him in the Vic-Wells magazine as 'a potential star' would be justified.

He became, however, convinced that such opinions would be revised as he toiled through rehearsals for Wycherley's *The Country Wife*. This was a set-up very different from the make-do of *Love's Labour's*; it had backing from a glitzy New York producer, Gilbert Miller, an imported Broadway star, Ruth Gordon, as Margery Pinchwife and designs by the prince of Shaftesbury Avenue sumptuousness, Oliver Messel. In effect it was a cheap way of getting a starry, stylish production tried out for Broadway, a package which, however much it may have offended their ensemble principles, neither Baylis nor Guthrie could afford to turn down (she would have a hit while the Broadway royalties would subsidise Guthrie's Old Vic £700 per annum salary). Alongside Edith Evans as the randy Lady Fidget, Guthrie also had experienced actors of great style such as Ernest Thesiger, as well as the newcomers Michael and Alec Guinness.

Michael was initially acutely nervous; Horner, the Restoration libertine at the centre of this extremely bawdy play, who feigns clap-induced impotence to cuckold London's husbands, is a difficult role and he was aware of the feisty Ruth Gordon's beady eyes on him at the read-through (she had played her role previously in summer stock in America and now was determined to show Broadway she could play more than smart broads). The ruthless ways of Broadway became more apparent on the second day when Ruth Gordon stepped out of rehearsal on stage with Alec Guinness as Mr Sparkish to tell Guthrie, 'Tony, I can't act with this man,' and insist on his replacement. Edith Evans was especially shocked by what she saw as Guthrie's lack of gumption (he shrank always from such confrontations) and by his refusal to protest against Baylis's penny-pinching over Guinness's pay-off. She went out of her way to reassure him that his talent was not in question (in truth Guinness was much too young for the role) and to make sure that the incident did not sour the production; indeed, after that initial demonstration of star power, Ruth Gordon became extremely popular at the Old Vic, much liked by her fellow actors and respected for her hard work and no-nonsense approach.

She took greatly to Michael and his increasing insecurity in *The Country Wife* had nothing to do with her. He had imagined he was on the right lines, aiming to create a lubricious, mockingly saturnine Don Juan of Mr Horner, but felt that Guthrie was constantly steering him away from such dark areas towards a squeaky-clean charmer which to Michael compromised the character and, indeed, contradicted the text. What he did not know was that Guthrie had promised Baylis, anxious about the effects of the play's bawdy strain on the ultra-traditionalist Board of Governors, that he would sanitise the play by skating over its seamier side and giving it a thorough wash and scrub-up. Baylis was far from the Victorian innocent old maid often assumed – after all it was she, following the dress rehearsal of a *Measure for Measure* with an Isabella so resolutely, purely chaste that there was not the slightest suggestion of any response to Angelo, who brusquely instructed the actress: 'Well, dear – all we can do now is get on our knees and pray for lust' – but she did not want a controversy on her hands.

By the first dress rehearsal, not cheered by his heavy wig of Restoration sausage curls, Michael was losing what little confidence he had left. Daisy watched that afternoon, afterwards criticising his lack of 'attack' and insisting that he should 'smile much more', not exactly helpful notes under the circumstances.

Guthrie had further demoralised Michael by adding a new bit of business to cover a set change, not with the originally planned drop-cloth and music but using Michael to cross the forestage, laughing all the way as the scene changed behind him, a nightmare for an actor at the best of times, let alone to be presented with at dress rehearsal stage.

Michael had also sprained his ankle badly during the previous night's *Love's Labour's* penultimate performance; by the time Rachel found him in the wings after the dress rehearsal he was in pain, his wig awry, with tears streaming down his face. She got him back to Greycoat Mansions and the understudy played for the last performance.

And then, the next day – did she time it by accident or design? – Edith Evans took his breath away as the company assembled for Guthrie's notes prior to a final dress rehearsal and opening:

She gave me a radiant smile. In her most honeyed tones, almost a whisper, as if she and I were old friends of long standing, she said 'You don't want to go to New York to play Horner on Broadway' – she made it sound as if only a great booby could possibly want such a thing – 'you want to stay here and play Orlando with me!'

It was enough to lift his spirits, although Edith was perhaps not being totally altruistic. Orlando in *As You Like It*, the next Old Vic production (Edith was never part of the Broadway deal for *The Country Wife*), was still uncast and she knew that Michael could be the ideal romantically virile Orlando to partner her Rosalind. About which there was some scepticism, even green-room sniggers. Edith was then forty-eight and she knew that not only had Guthrie not wanted to include *As You Like It* in the season (Baylis had already agreed it with Edith, however), he had flatly refused to direct it. He had told Baylis, 'Edith's too old,' but it is possible that another reason was the high emotional wattage of the play and its many variant love scenes. Guthrie understood the importance of emotion on the stage but could be frightened of and by it, not unusually leaving actors to work out love scenes by themselves; he never directed the play.

The Orlando question had to wait until *The Country Wife* had opened. Guthrie had given it the works, staging it with the speed and glitter of a musical, right through until the concluding dance of cuckolds. Messel's sets, easily the most lavish ever on that dusty old stage, included a ravishing drop-curtain in various shades of blue, like something out of Hogarth or James Thornhill, with strings of candelabra over the inner proscenium, while his costumes, shimmering with golds, crimsons and blues for Edith, pure white with blue flowers for Ursula Jeans' virtuous Alethea, created seductive stage pictures, all pristine-bright and squeaky-clean just as Guthrie had promised Baylis. To Michael's relief – he had disappointed himself – his notices all praised an 'impudent' Horner and he was mentioned as much as Ruth Gordon's sexpot Margery or Edith's exhilarating high-comedy brilliance. The exception was James Agate, then at the height of his *Sunday Times* power, the only one who spotted what Guthrie had been up to, adding of Michael: 'He was neither old enough, nor experienced enough, nor sardonic enough, and he was altogether much too nice a youth to hit upon this play's ugly and middle-aged invention.'

Gilbert Miller, a social snob, vastly corpulent and never Michael's favourite producer, was now keen to include him in the New York production for which, after sharp upwards bargaining from Miller's risible initial offer, he would have been handsomely paid. And the thought of New York – dreamt of from the movies for years – was strongly tempting. Michael instead chose to stay, for £20 per week, at the Old Vic to play Orlando.

Edith Evans, like Michael, was a late starter, twenty-five before her first stage appearance. She had absorbed a great deal from her first mentor, Daisy's old friend William Poel, but after a West End Shakespeare – an overproduced Basil Dean *A Midsummer Night's Dream* – she had determined to improve her classical work, studying with the Central School's great voice teacher Elsie Fogerty and going to the Old Vic where she played most of the leading female Shakespeare roles in the 1920s. Her West End work and Lyric, Hammersmith performances in Restoration comedy – notably a legendary Millamant in *The Way of the World* – had established her as a box-office star and the great stylist of her era. But there seemed little interest at the Old Vic for her second Rosalind (first played at the same address a decade before) and the advance barely climbed even while *The Country Wife* sold out each evening.

She had always said she could 'assume beauty', but Edith was far from convention's idea of allure, with one slightly drooping eye and a comparatively heavy figure, although she went on a rigorous diet before rehearsals. Guthrie had put Esmé Church, uninspired but safe (Michael said later that he could never remember her giving him one note), in charge of a venture he regarded as a dubious prospect, but it was evident from the early stages of rehearsal that something rare was being created. Edith always called Millamant and Rosalind 'my lovelies', her special roles, and although she was reluctant normally to talk much about her craft or a particular role, she did say later of this 1936 Rosalind: 'The part gave me a sense of ecstasy that I have never quite realised in any of the others. . . . I remember after some of the rehearsals I used to be so excited that I would run a great deal of the way home.'

Also much later, Michael used to say that the best advice he could give any prospective Orlando was to fall in love with his Rosalind. That was what happened in the top-floor rehearsal room in October 1936. It started about halfway through rehearsals. Working on the Act III wooing-lesson scene, with Orlando sitting close to Rosalind (disguised as the youth, Ganymede, but then only in rehearsal clothes) on the floor, when Rosalind–Ganymede instructs Orlando not to call him/her 'good youth' but Rosalind, Michael impulsively took Edith into his arms and kissed him/her. Nothing was said in rehearsal and Edith made no comment until she had supper with Michael at the Café Royal a few days later when, nervously, he admitted when she asked him why he had kissed her, 'Because I wanted to.' Soon he suggested another Café Royal supper; she instead invited him back to her Belgravia flat and their affair began.

After it was over Edith would refer to the episode almost self-deprecatingly as 'my five-minute love' or when she became a familiar face on television chat shows in old age she would say that Michael was in love with her 'for about five minutes'. But as her biographer Bryan Forbes has said, she kept all his notes and letters, and still talked lovingly of him until shortly before her death. It was an episode very special to her.

Edith had been married to her boyfriend from adolescent days when she was apprenticed to a hat maker ('he fell in love with a milliner and he married an actress'). Guy Booth worked for an oil company in its Venezuelan offices; they had become lovers before they married and then saw each other only during Guy's annual leaves. Guy died suddenly from an undiagnosed brain tumour in 1935 when Edith was playing on Broadway and she returned to England at once. She may have chosen to return to the Old Vic in 1936 rather than star in *The Millionairess*, which Bernard Shaw was begging her to do, so as to feel cocooned by a company in familiar surroundings, but now that the shock of unexpected widowhood had diminished the emotional life unbottled during *As You Like It* rehearsals surprised, confused and finally delighted her. Michael, with Rachel nearly seven months pregnant, simply could not control the overwhelming sense of falling in love with Edith who had helped him so much, not just by making Orlando possible but by what she had taught him of his craft during *The Country Wife* run and also by treating him implicitly as a good actor. More than anything, he was struck by her moral quality – the sense of duty to her profession, learnt from Ellen Terry with whom she had worked as a beginner – which, for him, invested Edith with a quality unique as an actress and as a woman.

It was a highly passionate physical affair. Although their notes and letters are sometimes incomplete and virtually always – maddeningly – undated, it is clear that their love affair continued for longer than supposed, for well over a year and that, for both, it was far from a fling or a brief rehearsal period romance. Almost as soon as it had begun, Edith was writing adoringly to Michael,

> If I had any doubts about being your darling, they are completely solved now. ... I do hope that you have no notion whatever of living your life without me. You simply can't do it. We have such Heavenly things in common. Rice pudding on the hearthrug and coats over the backs of chairs. Darling, please don't alter. I love you shamelessly.

In a later letter she exclaims: 'Isn't love extraordinary, the way it releases energy? I have told you that I can't live without loving, and it's true.'

The intoxication of a sexually charged affair informed *As You Like It* with a headiness that took critics and public by surprise. The production was little more than routine, in a vaguely Watteau-inspired design of misty, silvery perspectives and statuary with an air of Marie Antoinette's Petit Trianon – although the colours were more autumnal than vernal – with Edith in silk jacket and breeches, like Gainsborough's Blue Boy, as

Ganymede rather than the usual doublet and hose. And yet the energy which Edith mentioned, the sheer voltage of the performance, was extraordinarily potent. Orlando's wrestling scene with Charles (Stephen Schnabel, son of the pianist) was a thrilling, sweatily athletic affair (Michael and Schnabel worked hard on it together), while Edith's Rosalind–Ganymede was a breathtaking display of the alchemy of acting as she lifted the evening into a realm of sublimely civilised enchantment. Perhaps, too, it had something to do with her feeling: 'You have to have been desperately unhappy before you can really play comedy, so that nothing can frighten you any more.'

The students of the Old Vic School were at that time sometimes allowed to walk on. One of them, Diana Graves, watched Edith from the wings:

> I used to watch her waiting for her cue, night after night, dressed in her shirt and knee-breeches, transforming herself in a matter of seconds into a sparkling, adorable young creature. Her chin would go up, her eyes begin to shine, her body became spring-like and resilient, and full of confidence in her beauty and gaiety, she would sweep on to the stage to meet her dear love with such lightness that I used sometimes to wonder if her feet actually touched the stage at all.

Michael, fired by his Rosalind, also seemed to take wing with Orlando – often a seemingly dull part – taking him into an Arcadian maze of sexual and gender confusion, funny, touching and human. Edith had helped him find his feet on stage again after the wobble of *The Country Wife*: 'Acting with Edith Evans was heaven. It was like being in your mother's arms, like knowing how to swim, like riding a bicycle. For the first time in my life I felt completely unselfconscious.' Above all she taught him a lesson – applicable to a career and to the discipline of a particular play: 'Try not to repeat yourself,' touching on the very essence of acting, that ability to mint emotion and thought afresh at each performance.

The hats-in-the-air notices for *As You Like It*, which confirmed Michael's growing reputation, soon had the box office under siege and negotiations began for a possible remounting the following year. During the run the Redgraves moved from Westminster – their first flat was too small for a baby as well – to Bayswater, to a bright, top-floor flat in Pembridge Mansions on the Moscow Road (with rent less than £200 a year, even with Michael as sole earner on £20 a week they could still provide for a nanny and a cook-general). Daisy, indomitable as usual, had persuaded Rachel that a vegetarian regime and nursing home (run by obstetricians pleasingly named Drs Pink and White – in Blackheath) would take care of her best, but she was given next to no information or advice on childbirth or how to prepare for it, and the diet was making her feel tired and often weak.

They still saw a good deal of the Haggards and they also went on the town *à quatre* on occasion with Glen Byam Shaw and Angela Baddeley, including an after-theatre visit to Soho's Gargoyle Club where Glen, who adored pregnant women, asked Rachel to dance so he could rest her baby against him.

During the run of *As You Like It* Michael was back in the rehearsal room, again with Edith who was playing the title role of Mother Sawyer in *The Witch of Edmonton*, transforming Rosalind's androgynous beauty into gnarled, misshapen querulousness. Making a first Old Vic appearance was John Lehmann's sister Beatrix who became a close friend of both Redgraves. She was highly intelligent, witty, hopeless at disguising her opinions of poor directors (consequently somewhat feared and often out of work), and her emotional life was usually in some sort of crisis. Bisexual, she had recently had an affair with the émigré director Berthold Viertel when he was in London en route from Nazi Germany to America and she had been devastated when he left. Michael admired her work and especially her incisive handling of an awkward role in *The Witch of Edmonton*. Michel Saint-Denis, stocky, bespectacled, pipe-smoking, communicating ruminatively in English that was not so much broken as 'fractured' (Alec Guinness's word), was the antithesis of Guthrie's volcanic lightning conductor. Painstakingly he spent rehearsal time evoking a sense of community and Dekker's strange atmosphere of compassion behind the violence of a plot which involves a man's murder of his wife and a witch who sells her soul to the devil. It was an innovatory, non-naturalistic production, with Motley providing spare, bleached sets on a revolve which turned in view of the audience. For Saint-Denis, the play was another exploration of the essence of the kind of popular theatre that was his ideal; the first night was cheered and the notices mostly approving, although all along the lines of *The Times*'s 'an experiment well worth making', which meant the kiss of death at the box office.

Michael was downcast during rehearsals; having looked forward so keenly to working with Saint-Denis, he felt that the great man had hardly noticed him in his small role of Warbeck, the more unpleasant of two suitors for a rich yeoman's daughter, and that he thought little of Michael's talent. In performance he sat out his waits in Edith's dressing room – in her grotesque make-up and bald wig she would beg him not to look at her – and she did her best to reassure him, but he felt that he had somehow let Saint-Denis down.

With Edith he was more entwined than ever. He would often go back after the show with her to her West Halkin Street flat before going home to Bayswater. Rachel always said that although she had got used to what she called Michael's 'roving eye', she had at this stage no inkling of his involvement with Edith. There were, inevitably, some backstage whispers, while Edith's friends noticed how she seemed to have bloomed and, unusually, how her dress sense had dramatically improved, the beginning of her love affair with haute couture. On several weekends, when Rachel's mother was at Pembridge Mansions, and with Alec Guinness as what today would be called a 'beard', Edith took Michael to the farmhouse she and Guy had bought, Washenden Manor near Biddenden in Kent. Michael and Alec became friends gradually; both were fundamentally shy men, both had increasingly difficult maternal relationships and neither had known a father (Guinness never even knew for certain his father's identity). They also shared a dedication to an ensemble-based theatrical ideal and came greatly to admire each other's work; of all his contemporaries Guinness, who had what Michael called the great gift (especially in comedy) of 'seeming to possess an impenetrable secret' on stage, was the one he came to respect the most. Perhaps, too, each had recognised some kindred sexual ambivalence in the other, although in Guinness's case that would remain more buried or repressed. Alec, who worshipped Edith, was happy to be 'gooseberry' on these weekends, when the talk would often turn to the kind of ideal theatre each envisaged, Alec and Michael both sharing the Saint-Denis aspiration towards a kind of collective of equals. Both men felt privileged to be talking – as equals, implicitly – of their dreams to Edith, who had already been on the stage for over twenty years.

Michael wrote after one of those Washenden weekends, which always included long walks on the Romney Marshes: 'I slept heavily in the car going back for an hour and felt v. fresh, but my mind was still in the open air, under those giant skies.' While Edith's renewed vitality continued to pulse with energy, as she replied after the same weekend in one of her characteristically scribbled notes in pencil in her extravagant handwriting, 'I washed my hair, picked two rows of spinach (Spinach Pickers should be *very* highly paid), planted 12 lettuces and had my breakfast, a sort of *brunch*, on the *porch*, for Heaven's sake!' And after another Kent weekend she was opening her heart again: 'I want to say in words how heavenly happy I was on Sunday. I think, too, Michael, that we can never, never misunderstand one another again and if ever tempted to do so we must think back to Sunday and all will be well. I've ceased to analyse, I just give thanks.'

Michael and Alec were now rehearsing *Hamlet* (Alec brilliantly doubling Reynaldo and Osric) for Guthrie with Olivier's Prince.

Olivier in 1936 was already a star, although his classical performances – principally his 1934 Romeo–Mercutio with Gielgud – were controversial, his critics attacking his lack of poetry while his champions, in thrall to his scimitar cheekbones and pantherine sex appeal, insisted that his virile athleticism was, in a new age of realism, what classical acting needed. Guthrie had warned Olivier that his so-called lack of lyricism would come in for criticism on *Hamlet*, but Guthrie the iconoclast was keen to smash traditions too. Olivier was at one with Guthrie also over his deeply Freudian reading of the play. Both had read Dr Ernest Jones, Freud's exegetist, and adopted his reading of *Hamlet* as, like *Oedipus*, a drama of royal succession with the son's attachment to a beloved mother the fulcrum of the action. In this light, Hamlet's indecision basically stems from his unconscious longing to take the place of the usurper Claudius.

Michael agreed with very little of this, but wisely kept quiet. He was glad he had badgered Guthrie into giving him Laertes; all Robert Newton had to do as Horatio was moon around after Hamlet and weep a lot in the final scene. Michael saw Laertes as a more positive character than usual – a young soldier, very forceful and physically bigger than Hamlet, 'bursting with health and proper pride' and so untouched by tragedy in his life that his reactions to Ophelia's madness become, as well they might, selfish and conventional. Guthrie had opted for an uncut version (the 'Eternity Version', actors call it) and, with a relatively short rehearsal time, left Michael more or less alone to develop his character, while Michael and Olivier worked out by themselves a final duel full of Errol Flynnery.

Olivier's Hamlet was indeed accused of lacking poetry but, more crucially, it was generally also accused of putting little in its place other than a spring-heeled virility which completely overlooked the reflective, philosophical Hamlet. The overall consensus was that although this Prince might have made a useful wing three-quarter for Wittenberg University, he would have been lucky to scrape a Third in his Philosophy finals. Agate's was the bluntest review, bitchily describing it as 'the best performance of Hotspur that the present generation has seen'. Hardly anyone mentioned the Freudian subtext.

Laertes, often overlooked, came in for unusual praise, most critics taken aback by the emotional power with which Michael brought a seemingly colourless part to life. His early scene with Polonius (George Howe) conveyed not the routine politely bored son listening to Dad's dreary advice, but a living relationship. At its close, with Polonius's crowning 'This above all, to thine own self be true', Michael suddenly touched his father's hand with an unexpected gesture of affection, a moving moment in a performance packed with illuminating detail.

Michael liked Olivier, as aware of his 'Star Quality' as anyone, but he did not admire this performance: 'The truth is I thought he was a bad Hamlet – too assertive and too resolute. He lacked the self-doubting subtleties the part demands.' Olivier's ability to live his life on the grand scale intrigued him; he attended the christening of Olivier's son Tarquin by his first wife, Jill Esmond, fascinated by the splendour of a Chelsea studio with vast windows and a baronial fireplace, the kind of setting which might have dwarfed lesser men but in which Olivier seemed entirely at home. Their tastes and temperaments were essentially different, but the friendship was real and close.

Edith had kept away from *Hamlet* rehearsals, leaving a heavily pregnant Rachel to sit in Baylis's stage box. Baylis adored babies, believing they were a gift from God. And if God smiled on Rachel, Baylis would too. Rachel's pregnancy had been relatively smooth but, taken to the Blackheath nursing home on a stormy 29 January when she felt her contractions begin, she went through a long and arduous labour. Michael stayed with her until after dawn and then, with two Saturday *Hamlets* ahead, left for a shave and brief rest before the theatre. That matinée seemed genuinely an eternity; often during Laertes' long break between his departure for and return from France Michael, with a coat over his costume, would slip out for a walk (years later he admitted that on more than one occasion he had crossed Waterloo Bridge to the Gaiety Theatre and up the gallery stairs to watch Leslie Henson in some of *Seeing Stars*), but that afternoon he stayed close to the backstage telephone. It was just before the end of the matinée, with Michael still on stage for the last act, that the call came from Blackheath that Vanessa had been born, strong and healthy (a vegetarian diet had helped the baby if not her mother). Pandemonium broke out backstage; Michael and Rachel were very popular within the company. The Old Vic students ran out into the Waterloo Road, just in time to buy up all the flowers remaining before the market closed, and rushed them back to Michael's dressing room with a note: 'Love's Labour's Not Lost!' The evening show played as speedily as a farce (twenty minutes off the running time) and Olivier, making the customary Saturday-night Old Vic curtain speech, spoke with what then must have seemed emotional hyperbole but which now seems extraordinary prescience – 'A great actress has been born. Laertes has a daughter!' – to cheers, stomps and whistles from the house. Backstage the company crowded the corridors while Michael, awash with tears, clutching his flowers so that he looked like a moving bank of blossom, kissed everyone in sight. Later, still with his flowers, Olivier and his old Liverpool colleague Robert Flemyng took him off to celebrate at the Moulin d'Or in Soho, entering to cries of 'He's got a daughter!' and showering surprised diners with flowers.

After visiting Rachel next morning, weeping with delight to see his first child, Michael telephoned Chapel Street and Dartmouth and many friends. He also called Edith who wrote from Kent, 'Nothing could have made me happier than that you should have rung me to tell me that Vanessa had arrived. The room was full of people and I couldn't say what

I wanted to say and I couldn't have done so anyway, with joy and pain and everything. Michael, Michael, God bless Rachel and Vanessa always.'

As soon as Rachel and Vanessa were home in Bayswater, inevitably Michael and Edith again were with each other often. Bronson Albery had arranged a limited-season revival of *As You Like It* at his New Theatre, which involved some restaging and rehearsal. With some money spent on the physical production and with much-improved lighting, the production bewitched the West End too, playing to 'House Full' boards and ecstatic receptions, the reviews if possible even better than before. Again the excitement of off-stage life spilt into the effervescence on stage, as the lovers picked up the pattern of Michael visiting West Halkin Street and occasional Kent weekends, still accompanied by the loyal Alec (repeating his William in *As You Like It*). Whether or not Albery had any idea of the affair, he offered Michael the chance of working again with Edith as Kate in *The Taming of the Shrew*, which he was soon to present. With Leslie Banks cast as Petruchio, all that Michael could be offered was the bland Biondello which, with Edith's full agreement, he turned down.

Michael could not afford to be out of work for long after the close of *As You Like It* – an emotional final night for Edith, who knew she would never again play Rosalind on stage – with bills to pay and mouths to feed. He had to accept whatever was on offer, starting with a misbegotten resuscitation of the old comedy thriller *The Bat* at the Embassy, Swiss Cottage, with its original (and now somewhat too elderly) star, Eva Moore, as the spinster detective in an Old Dark House mystery full of weird noises and secret panels. Michael played an American detective and could barely believe it when several notices, while panning the play, still marked him out as 'a rising star'. The good thing about the show for him was the beginning of a long friendship with the farouche Irish-born character actor Max Adrian, who made him laugh off stage and tried very hard to make him laugh on it too. During its run, Vanessa was christened; Michael and Rachel asked Willie Armstrong to be godfather (he cried all through the ceremony) while Jane Baxter was godmother.

Guthrie invited Michael to return to the Old Vic briefly – as a favour – to replace Marius Goring as Chorus in *Henry V*, which he was happy to do (he always maintained that Olivier's Henry was one of the finest pieces of heroic Shakespearean acting he had ever seen). There were some discussions with Guthrie about a possible future at the Old Vic but before anything had been settled Michael had the offer – through Bill Linnit, who now represented him – to join the company being set up by Gielgud at the Queen's Theatre later in the year, the plays to include *Richard II* in Gielgud's own production (Gielgud as Richard, Michael as Bolingbroke),

Guthrie's production of *The School for Scandal* (Gielgud and Michael as the Surface brothers), *Three Sisters* to be directed by Saint-Denis who had not yet decided on definite casting, and *The Merchant of Venice* (Gielgud as Shylock in his own production, Michael as Bassanio). The company was also to include Peggy Ashcroft, Angela Baddeley, Glen Byam Shaw and Alec Guinness. It was immensely flattering – Michael had been in London less than a year – the only drawback being that, Bolingbroke excepted, his parts were, yet again, in the *jeune premier* division in which he had already had some success. What really made him accept was the carrot of Saint-Denis. *Three Sisters* was a favourite play – he assumed he would be asked to play Andrey, the sisters' brother who moves from happy idealism to premature middle age – and perhaps this would be a happier experience with Saint-Denis.

Until rehearsals began, he still had to work, although the dismal flop of a West End 'domestic comedy', *A Ship Comes Home* at the St Martin's, ran so briefly he received few pay packets. Set in a boarding house with the usual assorted 'characters', it starred Mary Clare as an actress with ambitions as a novelist, with Michael as a well-meaning doctor dithering between an older woman and her mercurial daughter. The only noteworthy aspect of this piece was that Michael, who had been reading Stanislavsky in more detail, in the middle of one performance of a scene set in his consulting room, suddenly changed all the action as directed (very little), tidying away his carelessly abandoned stethoscope and notes. He was so in character – and had that day been reading Stanislavsky on the actor's relationship with props – that it hit him (rather disconcertingly for Mary Clare) that of course his methodical character would have a tidy desk.

Edith and he had continued their affair but now she was abroad on a brief break in Cannes, from where she sent (discreetly, to the St Martin's) a postcard – '*Ne m'oubliez pas. Eternellement. E.*' – before moving on to Florence where alone she visited the Palazzo Vecchio, sending a card of the Loggia (also to the theatre) – 'I stood upon this balcony, and told you all about this Palazzo.'

Still with time to kill before the Queen's season, Michael returned to the Embassy in another unsuccessful play, *Three Set Out*, its central characters a tap-dancing duo and an architect (Michael) moving through three acts from poverty in Bohemia to success in opulence, its story if not its style echoing Coward's *Design for Living*. But he enjoyed the short run, especially the company of his co-star, the bright and beautiful American Constance Cummings, now resident in London. She and her writer husband Benn Levy were politically to the left – Levy later became a Labour MP – and Michael was impressed by Levy's succinct diagnoses of current events. For the first time he was reading Marx and the Labour-supportive *News Chronicle* became his regular newspaper; the old Oliver Baldwin-inspired political awareness gradually resurfaced as fears of a likely war increased.

There were further meetings with Edith over a brief, intense mid-summer period when she returned from holiday. Towards the end of his St Martin's run she wrote: 'I can come into the pit on Tuesday and then we can go back for supper together. I loved our last evening together as much as you did and I hope you'll play to me again often.'

Then, before the long Queen's season began, it was Michael's turn to take a break. As had become almost an annual ritual, he was off to Mortehoe to join the bachelors – Gervase Smith and a painter friend, Eric O'Dea, with Dick Green, now beginning to publish on occasion and achieving some success with his atmospheric, Derbyshire-set short stories, due slightly later. On the train he wrote to his 'Edieva', a lover's name he had coined for her:

> It certainly doesn't seem possible
> That now at last I'm free,
> Just an unemployed actor
> Who's lost his Max Factor
> And is off to the West Countree.

It was, as always at Mortehoe, a time for renewal, this year with an abundance of strawberries and wild flowers, Gervase working at times on his articles on landscape gardening, O'Dea painting for hours, Dick smoking and lazing, and Michael swimming, reading Trollope and his plays for the Queen's.

Edith was also inspired to take to verse. The energy unleashed in the last months still bubbled in her and, having astonished friends by taking driving lessons, she now went to Ross-on-Wye in Herefordshire to learn horse riding, making good progress apart from criticism from her instructor, Dick Pritchard, of her posture in the saddle ('You cut a sorry figure, Madam'). In mock rage, she wrote 'My Lament' for Michael:

> I don't mind scoldings loud or quiet
> I don't mind training, work or diet,
> I don't mind lectures – in fact, I've had 'em,
> But I'm damned if Dick shall call me Madam.

Perhaps because of this separation, Edith's scruples now began occasionally to quarrel with her happiness. She went on, writing from Ross-on-Wye:

Michael, darling, some honourable way must be found whereby we can love each other and not hurt anyone else or each other, I mean by which we can help each other to grow. You can't know how you help me. This all seems priggish and dull but darling everything sounds like that when I say it or write it. But I don't fear that you will misunderstand.

In early August, just before Michael began with Gielgud and Edith went into rehearsal for a new play by St John Ervine (in which Daisy had also been cast), they were meeting up again in London, Edith scribbling before the first encounter, 'It's impossible to believe that I am really going to see you. This absence has seemed far longer than my holiday abroad.'

When rehearsals began for *Richard II*, Michael was nervous, stumbling more than a few times in the read-through of a text he had studied hard. He had met Gielgud only on a few brief occasions previously and his initial overawed feeling took some time to evaporate. Gielgud – whose directorial boredom threshold was notoriously low – on this production changed his staging ideas comparatively rarely. He knew he had a strong cast – Peggy Ashcroft as his Queen, Leon Quartermaine in redoubtable form as John of Gaunt and an impressive gallery of young talent (Harry Andrews, Anthony Quayle and Dennis Price had also joined the company) – and he began to be impressed by the development of Michael's performance. Gielgud created a tensely atmospheric production, Richard's court full of mistrust and turbulence, simmering ambitions and jealousies. In the midst of this and against the petulant popinjay of Gielgud's Richard in the early scenes, Michael was allowed time to establish the ruthless grandeur of his Bolingbroke, tall and leonine with a neatly trimmed beard, and to build up his watchfulness. This was an active, not a passive quality; it communicated a powerful sense of the man's inner life, even during long passages when Bolingbroke is silent, his brooding, patient waiting game fascinating the house without taking the focus off Richard. Without overlooking Bolingbroke's conflicting conscience, the tension between muscular physical presence and serpentine mind fused the performance, most impressively in the deposition scene after Richard has asked for a looking-glass. Bolingbroke sat impassive, betraying not an eyelash flicker of impatience, listening to Richard's cadenzas of self-pitying grief before giving the order – with almost as much pity as contempt – 'Go, one of you, and fetch a looking-glass.'

The season, in advance, had seemed to some the return of the old actor-manager tradition in new clothes, and so it was particularly gratifying to Gielgud's company to read so many reviews which clearly went out of their way to stress the ensemble aspect of the production. Peter Fleming in the *Spectator* went so far as to claim, 'It might almost be a Russian

Company, so compact is the texture of a large cast.' Michael was thrilled to be part of this, delighting in the atmosphere within the company on stage and off. The New (now Albery) Theatre in St Martin's Lane was practically opposite the Motley Studios in Garrick Yard, reputed once to have been Thomas Chippendale's workshop; more recently the space had housed a somewhat louche nightclub with mock-medieval decor run by the outrageous drag artist ('Doris, the Goddess of Wind') Douglas Byng. The big studio, reached across the cobbled yard by an iron staircase, became a kind of informal club for the New company and for London's liveliest young theatrical talent. The Motley girls provided tea and buns, working away on their upcoming productions while arguments went on around them – about Shakespeare, Stanislavsky, the respective merits of Saint-Denis and Komisarjevsky (the Slavic Lothario's nickname of 'Come-and-seduce-me' had to be dropped during his brief marriage to Peggy Ashcroft) – as well as green-room gossip (Michael having to watch his tongue whenever Edith was mentioned).

The excitement and success of *Richard* helped carry the company through the let-down of Guthrie's work on *The School for Scandal*, on which even the loyal Gielgud had to admit his disappointment with the production. Guthrie was overextended at the time – still in charge at the Old Vic (where the Saint-Denis production of *Macbeth* with Olivier was having rehearsal problems) and also moonlighting as an actor for extra money on a terrible Charles Laughton film, *Vessel of Wrath* – but he had obviously done next to no homework, relying on his inventive instincts which, on this occasion and with this company, were not enough. Michael again felt that he was being directed against the text, with Guthrie insisting on a dishevelled, poorly dressed Charles (his servant, Trip, would have failed to raise a shilling by pawning this homespun wardrobe) while Gielgud as the seemingly sober brother Oliver was in silk and satin. Perverse touches infected the production, including a scampering curtain call which Guthrie seemed to rehearse more than some scenes and which the company loathed. Rachel, who had joined the company to play the small part of Maria, could never find her way into the character while even Peggy Ashcroft, usually so amenable, was miserable, and not just because, always hating much make-up, she had to plaster herself with it as Lady Teazle.

The production opened unhappily. Guthrie was distracted by problems at the Old Vic where Saint-Denis's *Macbeth* dress rehearsals overran, forcing for the first time an Old Vic opening's postponement. Then, on the New first night, came the news of Lilian Baylis's death; Gielgud, who had earned his classical spurs at the Old Vic and who had loved 'The Baylis' for all her exasperating habits, was thrown completely off balance.

Surprisingly, although there were a handful of dismissals, the production emerged relatively unscathed, amazing Michael again that his performance – to him under par – should be praised at all.

Edith was on a pre-West End tour with *Robert's Wife* in which she played the Spanish-born Sanchia. Still mutually besotted, she and Michael were now separately professionally preoccupied as well, and sharing their concerns, Edith anxiously fretting from Edinburgh that 'It hasn't become *subconscious* yet', that Sanchia was not yet inside what she called her 'soulcase', while Michael was pondering the unexpected casting of *Three Sisters*: 'Michel came into my dressing-room last night. I am to play Tusenbach. Which I am most happy about. He was interesting about his meetings and talks with the Russian actors in Paris.' Saint-Denis had cast Gielgud in Stanislavsky's old role (he ended up with exactly the same beard and monocle) of the Army Captain, Vershinin – Saint-Denis had seen Chekhov's widow, Olga Knipper, play Masha in Paris and had discussed the play with Stanislavsky – but he surprised some company members with other choices. The handsome, gentle Glen Byam Shaw was cast as the near psychotic Solyony, George Devine as Andrey, while Michael was given the difficult part of the ineffectual Baron Tusenbach hopelessly in love with Irina, the youngest sister.

Michael had not seen Gielgud as the Baron in Komisarjevsky's Barnes production but he knew that he was conceived as a romantic character (Komisarjevsky heavily upped the romantic stakes in his Chekhov productions, accommodating what he felt were English tastes). Michael had prepared extra hard for rehearsals and hoped on this production to please Saint-Denis but initially it seemed a repetition of *The Witch of Edmonton* experience: 'I could see that he thought very little of my work. When he gave me a note or asked a question I would answer with a show of brightness but with a miserable lack of confidence within myself.' The breakthrough came in the middle of a long day while Michael was working on Tusenbach's second-act speech about cranes and migratory birds, attempting to invest it with something of the amateur expert's enthusiasm, only to be stopped by Saint-Denis, criticising his attempt to make it 'intelligible'. When Michael ('somewhat tartly') asked, 'Isn't that what an actor is supposed to do?' he was surprised by Michel's reply: 'In this case, no.' Michael, somewhat stung, tried again, this time throwing the speech away, much more routinely, at which point – just as he began to feel the speech come alive, its rhythms seem natural – Saint-Denis beamed and said, 'You see. You 'ave eet!'

From that crucial rehearsal, although normally the hardest thing to act is a bore, the performance began to fall into place physically and in his 'soulcase'. This was no conventional juvenile lead but a rather unhealthy young man, face pallid and pitted with the traces of adolescent acne, with prominent ears, lank hair and already a slight pot belly (clever padding). The company had an unheard-of eight weeks to rehearse – a major concession to free Saint-Denis from the constraints of the English commercial system. West End diehards scoffed; the play would go stale after the usual three or four weeks, more than enough even for a Russian writer. The actors had the rare luxury of not having to make instant, perhaps wrong, choices, of individually growing into their roles and collectively into the Pozorov household, with the time to take part in exercises – focusing on the heat, or on a particular time of day – which would be commonplace rehearsal practice now but were then refreshingly releasing to Saint-Denis's cast. He had prepared, as always, meticulously – nobody could have guessed that he had just directed a flop with *Macbeth* – working exhaustively to suggest a life of the household and of the town behind the scenes, in the bustling life of doorbells, sleighs or carnival sounds in a fretful undercurrent coinciding with the shifts and eddies of the play, with one of the Motley team's most haunting designs, beautifully lit by George Devine, solving all the technical demands of a four-set play while creating a magical sense of movement from the crowded, colourful household of Act I to the arid, Vuillard-like final-act garden with its fences and recedingly perspectived trees. Peggy Ashcroft always said that she had never worked on a production which so subtly suggested the sense of the changing seasons.

For many of that cast *Three Sisters* marked a career sea change – sadly, the only off-key performance was Gielgud's own over-refined Vershinin (Rachel said it did not quite work because 'he could never quite believe himself in the part'). Alec Guinness claimed that the experience of *Three Sisters* changed his whole attitude to his profession, while Glen Byam Shaw, in one of his last performances before turning director, surprised himself almost as much as the audience with a performance of suppressed, scented violence as Solyony. George Devine was the most ardent Saint-Denis disciple of all; together they formed the London Theatre Studio as an actors' school, based initially in Diaghilev's old Beak Street premises and then in a Marcel Breuer-designed conversion in Islington.

For Michael the production was unequivocally a turning point in his development as an actor. This Tusenbach was gawky, ridiculous, boring, coltish and intensely real, consequently all the more moving as the play progressed. For many, the emotional high point of the play was the moment when Tusenbach, a straw boater, not quite fitting, on his head (Saint-Denis had also instructed the Motleys to have his uniform just slightly the wrong cut), gazed forlornly at Peggy Ashcroft's Irina before going off to his duel with Solyony, not asking for a love she cannot give, simply pleading, 'Say something to me.'

The performance was the one which most dazzled the critics, largely because it so surprised them, several of them remarking on that transforming power of great acting which not only changes the actor's personality but his very shape and bones, the physical habits (in many actors fixed, permanent) adapting themselves to the mental habits he took on with the character. Saint-Denis had succeeded with Michael in this instance in informing the performance with the right tension between emotion and technique. His favourite simile was that acting was like a hand holding a bird – 'If you clench your fist, you will kill it. If you loosen your hand too much it will fly free.'

Michael's buoyant mood, even at a grim time nationally, with the Foreign Secretary Lord Halifax talking appeasement to an ever threatening Hitler, communicated itself in a letter to Daisy, still on tour with Edith in *Robert's Wife*:

The part has a way of making me full of affection for the whole world ... oddly enough, I have been trying to grow more part of the world around me, to be more selfless, to lose myself. I can see clearly that to achieve anything really *good* in art one must lose oneself in it and that is why I know Tusenbach is the best thing I have done. I can completely lose myself in him. ... I have had a peep of the real thing, the living creation which breathes its own breath and lives now, and in the past and in the future. This is an immense encouragement to me, because I think you know how immensely self-critical I am as regards my work.

Daisy, it seems certain, was unaware of the affair between Michael and Edith (for whom she did not much care, thinking she had been lucky in 'hoodwinking' the critics). During the *Robert's Wife* provincial tour Edith was still finding the part of Sanchia difficult, not yet able to lose herself in it as Michael had submerged himself in Tusenbach. She wrote to him from Blackpool about her insomnia – her 'white nights' – at the same time letting him know the arrival time of her train to spend Sunday in London, praying that he would be able to find time to see her. But in another letter soon afterwards, Edith was clearly once again divided between her love and her moral sense:

The situation here is so odd and would be intolerable over a length of time. We all sit – your mother included – at supper, and there am I sitting in the midst, my heart singing for joy because of my share in your life and nobody knows.

Mike, why am I always the secret person? I want to come out into the open and say everything to everyone. Oh dear, I can't get it straight. Blessings always on you and your home, my heart's love to you always, always, always.

The following week Edith opened in *Robert's Wife* at the Globe, adjacent to the Queen's in Shaftesbury Avenue. Because of their respective schedules, Michael was able to see the play, sending Edith a note that he would be there with her as Sanchia and writing afterwards: 'They say you send husbands and wives away more in love with each other, do they? You sent me away more in love with the whole world and if I had never known before that I'd love you all my life, I knew it then. How I knew it! However much they love you as Sanchia, they can't love you as "Edith–Sanchia".' He added how desperately he wanted to see her: 'Any night this week you care to name. And if you'd care to name one by return so that I get it before I leave tonight so much the better. Else post a note before 12 tonight here – and hurry home.' Shortly afterwards, early in 1938, he scribbled a hasty note, another one flying from the Queen's to the Globe: 'It's a week since we saw each other. Almost last year! I think of you and think of you ... Will you let me know what night *early* next week, we can meet. My darling Edith – how I love you!'

On his birthday in March – his thirtieth – Edith sent him two mugs ('Steins' or 'Ugly Mugs' she called them), a reminder of drinking soup from them 'on our way down to the farm ... Happy Birthday, Happy everything, your loving E.' When he wrote to thank her for his present he added that Rachel was still out of London, adding a scrawled PS: 'When shall we meet. When – O, when?'

But the end of the affair was in sight. Rachel was again pregnant and it may well have been the news of this that decided Edith to end it (Bryan Forbes stressed that Edith had 'a strong sense of sin'). There was no rancour – indeed, the whole affair, with the image of a sand-glass always behind it, has an air of Michael's favourite *Der Rosenkavalier*, with him as Oktavian to Edith's Marschallin – but finally Edith could no longer enjoy an Arcadia which might involve another's unhappiness. Her letter ending it may well have been as threnodic as the Marschallin's Act III farewell in Strauss's opera, but it has not survived. His reply, however, is most lovingly tender and perhaps responded to her tone:

Dearest Edieva,

Adieu to you, farewell, au revoir. All the sad words I can think of cannot tell you how sad it felt to get your note and to know that you were going to Cornwall and that, for once, I was the last to know.

As far as can be ascertained, Michael was Edith's last love. Her friend and biographer Bryan Forbes believed that she was torn between her feminine need to feel desired and that opposite side of her nature which in the past often had deflected affection because of duty, but that Michael made her feel for the first time since she lost Guy that the self-denial attached to duty might involve waste. Michael – he always said so – had been profoundly enriched by Edith but in return he had enriched her by the gift of a love the more precious because unlooked-for and initially so unexpected.

Inevitably they saw less of each other, even professionally, although the bonds between them remained strong. Rachel had known something was afoot, but not with whom. On one occasion, when Michael had stormed out of the flat and not returned overnight after a row during his re-rehearsals for the West End *As You Like It*, Rachel rang Edith's flat to see if he had gone there. Alarmed, Edith had come round to Pembridge Mansions, Michael on his return shortly afterwards being unexpectedly confronted by the two women then in his life. It was only later that Michael told Rachel of his affair with Edith.

Forty years later, when she and Michael were helping Forbes with his biography of Edith, Rachel wrote to Forbes after he had sent her the typescript. She felt she had to object to just one thing in his book, the stress on Edith's description of the affair as 'a five-minute love' which she felt diminished it and which, as another woman, she felt was Edith's way of self-deprecating something deep and important in a humorous way. Rachel told him, 'At the time I was young, with my first child, and strangely enough I didn't know.' She described to Forbes the evening of the missing Michael and Edith's worried arrival:

> It must have been agonising for her because, if you see what I mean, I had intruded, but I hadn't really realised and was panic-stricken. ... But the chief thing for me is that it was and is true and as I said to Mike last night very wonderful to have been in love with and loved by the greatest actress of our time ... she *needed* romantic love so much, and for a time she had it.

Rachel's attitude is the more remarkable in the light of Michael's secrecy about his affair with Edith. Normally so candid emotionally with her – certainly he freely admitted all his subsequent major loves – in this instance he remained silent until the preparations for the biography of Edith (*Ned's Girl* – her father's name was Ned) forty years later. Realising that Forbes, as a conscientious biographer, would inevitably have to touch on the episode which, although not widely known, was no secret to a small circle of friends and theatre-insiders, Michael had consented to the use of extracts from his letters to Edith and he also permitted some quotation from her letters (most of them preserved) to him. When finally she did learn of the affair with Michael's admission in the late 1970s Rachel said that initially she felt foolish, understandably given that it was clearly so much more than a run-of-the-play fling or an infatuation. Also, as she came gradually to realise, the relationship was something which had been known to some of her close friends and contemporaries, while she remained in ignorance.

For all his usual honesty with Rachel, on this occasion Michael must have understood that while his affair with a man would have caused her pain and distress, it would have been – allowing for the self-confessed 'difficulties in his nature' – probably just about bearable, this intense love affair with another woman, and at a time when Rachel was pregnant (then continuing into the infancy of their first child), would have come as the most devastating news. But his betrayal was surely compounded by his subsequent failure to tell her. Having funked it at the time, he then never had the courage until the imminent biography made it necessary all these years later; had he told her earlier he might have spared her, at a most testing time in her life (and his), the pain of feeling foolish.

Rachel's attitude to Forbes' book and in her letter to him might be seen by some as that of a woman putting on her bravest face and bandaging an emotional wound. She was rarely a dissembler, however; rather, the view she took in time remains one of the most extraordinary instances of her compassionate insight and of her perspective on conventional morality. Doubtless some aftershocks from Michael's admission continued to reverberate but by the time – over a year later – she came to read the account of the episode in the text of Forbes' book she was able to see through to the essence of that unexpected but transforming love affair. Rachel had admired Edith as an actress above all those of her era (only Peggy Ashcroft came close for her) and also as a woman. They had been lifelong friends, most close during the children's earlier years; eventually Rachel could comprehend something of the intimate bond that went beyond sex in the relationship of that fevered pre-war time, allowing her to understand that, certainly on Edith's part, as her biographer phrased it in words which Rachel particularly praised: 'Her brief days in Arden were never forgotten.'

Seven
COMING OF AGE

Well before the days of instant celebrity on TV survival shows or in soap opera, Michael had shot to prominence remarkably swiftly. Then it was still possible to make an unheralded success in the theatre and although only London audiences had seen his Tusenbach, the high-profile coverage of Gielgud's season saw him interviewed and discussed in national and weekly publications.

Even before *Three Sisters* had opened he was being courted by the cinema, although his own feelings about a screen career were ambivalent. He loved the cinema – he had been a film fan even before his Heidelberg exposure to the Weimar Republic masterpieces, while his Cambridge reviewing for *Granta* and his discussions of world cinema with friends like Basil Wright and Humphrey Jennings, not to mention those escapist hours with Clara Bow or Joan Crawford in Liverpool, had all confirmed his passion for the medium. But so far as British films were concerned he admitted, 'To be honest, I suppose I was something of an intellectual snob at the time, and film acting here in England was not regarded very highly.'

The lack of native directors to rank with the great names of Ufa, Paris or Hollywood was another drawback; the fact that one of the most powerful men in British cinema and a supposedly leading director was Basil Dean (whose films were stiff to the point of rigor mortis) said it all for those who, like Michael, looked on the cinema as primarily a director's medium. Moreover, he genuinely felt that, lacking the iconic sheen of contemporary male leading men, his looks were perhaps not best suited to the camera.

His diffidence seemed to make his pursuers even more keen. One of the first film chiefs to pick him out had been Edward ('Ted') Black, executive producer of Gainsborough Studios and the savviest of the three Black brothers, so prominent in British entertainment along with the other fraternal trio of the Ostrer brothers. Ted Black had first seen Michael's work at the Old Vic in *The Country Wife* and had been even more impressed during the Queen's season. Finally – urged on by Bill Linnit, an agent with a shrewd sense of all his clients' marketability – Michael agreed to a film test for Gainsborough which was shot with

Rachel playing opposite him in a scene from Coward's *Private Lives*. The offer of a five-year contract, which Linnit pressed him to accept, came very quickly and as something of a surprise; it also involved asking Gielgud for a release from his contractual obligation to the season's final play, *The Merchant of Venice*.

In truth, the part of another handsome charmer in the shape of Bassanio was not one which would stretch Michael or that he was burning to play, but he was deeply grateful to Gielgud for the chances of the Queen's season and would have had no quarrel had Gielgud wanted him to remain as part of a hand-picked company. Gielgud himself at this stage in his career could see little attraction in films – he had made a handful including Alfred Hitchcock's *The Secret Agent*, but never truly took to the screen until years later in *Julius Caesar* after a long absence – but easily replaced Michael with Richard Ainley (son of a favourite actor of Michael's, the great Henry Ainley) and made no great objection. Peggy Ashcroft, who had gone only twice near the film studios (once for Hitchcock, in *The 39 Steps*) and had not much enjoyed it, was disappointed to lose him opposite her Portia, while Edith added, 'I'm disappointed only because you do not see that *all that* will come later.'

Michael wrote to Daisy soon afterwards:

> The film contract is being drafted. I went to see the test the other day and was rather pleased with it. I quite seriously thought there was personality and assurance and some humour too. I look my plainest, but once you make up your mind to that, it's a success. I think there was no trace of camera-consciousness – which anyway I didn't feel. They say at the studio it's one of the best tests they've seen.

Ted Black was delighted; he had had a particular part in mind all along for Michael's screen debut in a script by Frank Launder and Sidney Gilliat – Gilbert in *The Lady Vanishes*, the leading male role opposite a rising star under contract to Gainsborough, Margaret Lockwood. Michael became much more interested when he was told that the director – who had not originally been assigned the project – would be Alfred Hitchcock. Michael had seen some of Hitchcock's early British films; he especially admired *The Lodger*, which incorporated ideas and techniques that could have come out of Ufa films (indeed, as Michael discovered, Hitchcock had spent some time in Ufa's Berlin studios).

All the same, he had insisted that Bill Linnit negotiate that the Gainsborough contract should allow him enough time each year to work in the theatre, a clause which now figured large when, rather to his surprise, Michel Saint-Denis came to talk to him about the possibilities of working together again. More than that, the proposal involved establishing a company, a realisation of Michael's dream since his Cranleigh days and the visits to Les Quinze's productions. Michel had been one of the few not to suggest disapproval of Michael's 'defection' to films – he too revered the cinema, especially the work of his friends Jean Renoir and René Clair – although he warned Michael (he had to some extent assumed the role of mentor) to beware the traps of luxurious laziness waiting in the film world. Even after the success of his Tusenbach, Michael had never felt completely sure what the ruminative Frenchman really felt about his talent; the suggestion of his new closer collaboration settled his doubt. Michel admired Gielgud as *un homme du théâtre* but sensed, probably rightly, that he was of more influence on Gielgud the director than the actor and that the star wattage which Gielgud carried with him made him perhaps not best suited to Michel's ideal ensemble. Whereas something about Michael's openness as an actor, his ability to start each project from, as it were, a state of tabula rasa, both intrigued and challenged Michel. Although never one to say enormous amounts about any particular actor, Michel valued Michael, proof of which reached him years later when he had helped Michel's widow, Suria Magito (he married her after his affair with the actress Vera Lindsay finished), when she was planning a book on Michel's career. Writing to thank Michael, Madame Saint-Denis sent him the draft of an unpublished article by Michel which discussed Michael's acting:

> At work he shows himself sensitive, impressionable to the point of instability, nervous and instinctive. Rehearsals were an endlessly renewed pleasure because Michael was joyous in his work, as if possessed by his characters, concentrated and at the same time light, and so right in the abundance of his inventions.

Peggy Ashcroft was similarly enthused by the Saint-Denis project and she had greatly enjoyed acting opposite Michael at the Queen's (she especially responded to his refusal to repeat the previous evening's performance) and so, by the early part of 1938, by which time Michael was well into filming *The Lady Vanishes*, plans were consolidated. Other actors – Edith, Olivier (who had enjoyed the experience of *Macbeth* for Michel, despite its failure), Stephen Haggard and Ralph Richardson – had all expressed willingness to appear in Michel's production of *Twelfth Night*, with Olivier as Malvolio, Edith as Maria, Stephen Haggard as Feste and Richardson as Sir Toby joining Michael as Aguecheek and Peggy as Viola. Bronson Albery was attracted to the project and began negotiations for the Phoenix Theatre in the Charing Cross Road as the company's base and to raise the capital. From the outset the plan was to link the company closely to the London Theatre Studio where Michel and George Devine were teaching, using students in small parts and as understudies, and drawing on the Studio's design wing too.

Many other plays were under discussion – Edith was keen to play in Lorca's *Blood Wedding*, *Uncle Vanya* was mooted and there was a fascinating project for Michael, the tragi-comic treatment of the Trojan War by Jean Giraudoux, *La Guerre de Troie n'aura pas lieu* in which he would play Louis Jouvet's role of Hector. Giraudoux visited London briefly to meet both Michel and Michael, and although no translator had as yet been fixed, the French dramatist, keen to see his play mounted in England as the possibility of war seemed to increase, was happy to approve both Michel's production plans and Michael's casting as Hector. Michel was also passionate about a play completely unknown in England – *The White Guard* by Mikhail Bulgakov, set in the post-war, post-Revolution Russia of 1918, which had good roles for a strong company.

The project had to wait until Albery had the financing in place, which gave Michael and Rachel a breathing space to reorganise themselves. With the prospect of improved finances from his film earnings, they decided first to take on a relatively inexpensive (£750) country property for weekends and then to move in London from the Bayswater flat (top floor and exhausting without a lift with babies and prams) to a St John's Wood house, both properties giving Rachel the chance to garden, which she loved.

Rachel had been the first to spot the advertisement for a cottage (with the lure of 'windmill attached') in White Roding, a village near Great Dunmow in Essex, within comfortable commuting distance and with spectacular, wide-ranging views across the Essex fields and flatlands from the mill with its creaky sails ('*Il a un air maritime*,' said Michel). It struck neither of them at first as their ideal – 'windmill attached' meant a huge tower mill with mostly broken sails, and the water source from their well had been polluted by oil – but, as Rachel said, it grew on them ('like actors reading over a part that didn't seem very good at first sight') and the cottage itself required mostly only cosmetic work. The move in London, slightly later, was to Clifton Hill, to a large, stuccoed house with generously proportioned rooms with moulded, corniced ceilings, a handsome residence. The vogue among many of their friends at this time – the Haggards included – was towards a certain restrained austerity and lack of clutter in decor, while Rachel always needed more in the way of carpets, curtains and cushions ('my early dream of the white mist surrounding me has always affected me, so I have to upholster my background'). A good deal of money – for antique mirrors and huge sofas – went towards fitting up Clifton Hill in particular.

All this change was against a background of continuing international unease, with Hitler's annexation of Austria the most recent frightening development. Michael wrote to Daisy at this time, 'The only way we can make any headway is just to stop thinking about war. ... It still seems impossible to me and I shall go on thinking that until it is proved possible; I know that I think that way because I want to, but that one can do it is a merciful dispensation of the Almighty.' The threat was omnipresent nonetheless, and although Michael always worked to keep his closest friendships in good repair, it was surely because of an unpredictable future that at this period he was such a regular and loyal correspondent. Of course, he could see a good deal of friends such as David Loveday, taking Cranleigh to great success, Dennis Robertson and Dick Keigwin, the last still in Bristol and now with his astonishing gift for languages beginning to work on his translations of Hans Christian Andersen. They often came up to London to see his performances, as did Gervase Smith and John Davenport, who was beginning to work often for the BBC. Louis le Breton was now in Persia, working on archaeological digs, although their correspondence continued, as affectionately as before. Dick Green, Michael's closest friend – something which surprised those who could not see past his laconic exterior – continued to behave as unpredictably as ever, to nobody's surprise.

Dick always seemed to have just enough money to survive – the only proper job he seems ever to have had was as tutor (courtesy of Gabbitas and Thring) to the sons of the publisher Jonathan Cape, a post from which he was promptly fired because of his reluctance to do much more than 'sit on his arse all day and drink Cape's sherry'. At times he stayed with his patient parents in Buxton, at others moving between renting 'The Wee Hoose', really a wooden shack, just along the coast from the Magdalene set's regular bolt-hole at Mortehoe or staying with the Davenports near Andover.

Another friend on whom Dick descended at times was the writer Hector Bolitho at his sixteenth-century house on the Essex flats. Dick wrote to Michael from there as the Hitler threat was growing, after a weekend during which a German baron had also been a guest: 'And towards midnight in that shadowy room – the Baron intently smoking his cigarette, Hector going on with his Patience, I sitting – it seemed as if the whole of Hitler's Germany was coming to us over the North Sea and Essex, into that small, beamy room.' Michael's letters to Dick have not survived, although it is evident from Dick's to him that he wrote often and that Dick saw him as 'the dearest friend I know'. Dick was always a slow writer, not helped by his 'dislike of the possessive sense and the earning of money', and he used Michael as a sounding board constantly, veering between a torpid 'sluggation of the mind' when his novel of a homosexual love affair,

Peradventure, was going poorly to euphoric glee when one of his short stories, mainly Lawrentian in tone and sparely evocative of the Derbyshire landscape, sold to a magazine. John Lehmann, then working for the Hogarth Press and soon to take charge of the Penguin *New Writing* series, was always encouraging to Dick and tried to help him with agents and editors.

At this period Dick sometimes, usually unexpectedly, turned up in London when Michael would do his best to keep up with his 'crazing', wandering on Fitzrovia pub crawls, mixing with French-Canadian Marines in louche bars and staying out till all hours. Rachel liked Dick very much, realising how complex his character really was and also sensing that he and Michael, in a non-sexual sense, needed each other, but only very rarely did they have to put him up when he had Mary Smith's flat to collapse in. The problem with Dick in London was always alcohol. Away from the city his drinking was containable but in London, although he never was an aggressive drunk, he could get out of control. Paddy Railton was in touch with Michael, who had suggested to Paddy that he write a historical play for him and Edith; Paddy always worried about Dick and wrote to Michael: 'He is incapable of behaving like a grown-up person, or even like a moderately cautious child, when drunk (as always in London). Can anybody make him see sense? It's you or nobody.'

As if Dick's drinking were not problem enough, more immediately pressing a worry was Daisy, whose moods were becoming more unpredictable. She tended to watch herself when appearing in a play but otherwise nobody quite knew what to expect. She was, of course, bored – bored by Andy, for all his mildness (perhaps because of it), bored when out of work – but there was a new edge to her black moods. Daisy had never been especially welcoming to Rachel from their first meeting at Chapel Street when Daisy and her sycophantic friend Molly Terraine had patronisingly made it clear they did not consider her in Michael's league as an actor, although she had helped out when Rachel was pregnant with Vanessa. But Michael's rapid success – and Rachel, although missing some chances because of pregnancy, had also been part of those glittering Old Vic and Queen's seasons – seemed to gnaw at Daisy. As did his transparent happiness – those first years with Rachel in London were euphoric – which made her remember how close they had been when he was a child, while now she no longer seemed to be needed. Even in questions of acting or his career, mentors such as Saint-Denis had usurped her, or so it seemed to Daisy. Alcohol – gin was her usual tipple – made simmering resentments sometimes boil over, as in the spring of 1938 when she wrote to Michael in unusually shaky writing:

My Dear Son,
I telegraphed you yesterday to say I did not wish to see or hear from you again. At that moment I felt I did not, but of course it is not *so*.

She then berates him – and Rachel – for neglecting her, although she does admit, 'I am sorry that on two occasions I have spoken so roughly to Rachel.' Daisy had been under stress (her half-sister Mabel had tuberculosis) but she seemed dimly to grasp that her troubles lay deeper:

> I want help and perhaps Rachel can help me. It has been a very sad and very trying year for me so far and at times I feel there is little use in going on at all.
>   Your Mother, who loves you.

Michael was often shattered by Daisy's outbursts and such letters, and he also began to revise his perspective on Andy who never would reproach Daisy. Michael arranged, for the first of what would become many times, a 'rest-cure' for Daisy, in Brighton where she had several friends, later that summer, which at least for the time being patched up things between them. Daisy had good friends in the theatre – her old Stratford and Fellowship of Players chum Dorothy Green, the actor-manager John Clements, the impresario Firth Shepard and his mistress, the outspoken Australian-born actress Coral Browne whose whiplash wit masked great kindness, all of whom tried to help her – but one of the factors affecting Daisy's problem was that her stubborn insistence that the old-style actor-managers knew best made her difficult to cast except in revivals, which she resented without accommodating a changed era.

The Lady Vanishes was completed in a remarkably brisk five crowded weeks, and Michael even had time to ft in another film (lent out by Gainsborough – at a profit – to Paramount), *A Stolen Life*, a romantic drama opposite Elisabeth Bergner, by far the biggest 'name' Michael had worked with before 'the beginnings of Michel's great Enterprise' as he put it to Edith during a break in Pinewood filming while he was preparing to play Alexei Turbin in the Phoenix's opening production of *The White Guard*: 'I feel the excitement and zest again which you need to work well … I'm reading Trotsky on Russia to get some pictures in my mind of the Russia that Alexei had the faith to want to save.' Once again he wanted to share with Edith the actor's sense of absorbing, sponge-like, the life of a character prior to rehearsals: 'The part lies fallow in my mind and gathers all sorts of life from the oddest thought and daydreams.'

When Michael first read *The White Guard* in the version skilfully prepared by Rodney Ackland it excited him as few other modern plays had done, and both play and the little of what he could glean about its author came to fascinate him. Bulgakov, like Chekhov, was a doctor before the theatre world drew him from Kiev to Moscow. *The White Guard* began as a long, extremely ambitious novel set in the Ukraine capital of Kiev about a family of Whites, the Turbins, and in 1925 he started work on a stage adaptation. The play takes place shortly after the Armistice, following the assassination of the Romanov royal family; it is still centred round the Turbin family as warring factions hover over Kiev in the bitter winter of 1918. A German division is propping up the Hetman of the Ukraine, around whom the White Guard has rallied, while a rebel leader, Petlura, is besieging the city; as the Germans begin to withdraw and the Hetman flees, Kiev is left to the mercy of Petlura's rebels and, ultimately, of Trotsky's army.

Bulgakov's play was taken up by the Moscow Art Theatre where Stanislavsky took a keen interest in its progress. It was worked on intensively, a project which became caught up in the middle of rival MAT factions (Bulgakov's later mordant novel, *Black Snow*, is based on his experiences with the play), with many arguments over its content and its tone. Bulgakov initially incorporated a potent atmosphere of dream – a whole section dealt with Alexei Turbin falling asleep while reading Dostoevsky, confronted by a character called Nightmare who reveals to him the full import of the senseless bloodbath which Petlura's regime could involve, in an amazingly daring sequence soaring away from naturalism as the walls of the Turbin apartment disappear through the nightmare. But the MAT's suspicions of the play drove it away from such an approach, back into a quasi-naturalistic style and replacing a fascinatingly passive central character with more of an ideologue. Alexei's second-act death, the end of a hero who pays for his choice with his life, became the climax of the play which, in essence, lost a good deal of its broodingly dangerous Dostoevskian atmosphere to become more 'Chekhovian', even quoting Sonya's 'We shall rest' from the end of *Uncle Vanya*. The always irreverent Mayakovsky gibed that the MAT were plagiarising Chekhov in *The White Guard* but that oversimplification ignores the fact that the play – the dress rehearsals of which had to be attended by government representatives – remained dangerously tricky in the Russian political climate of 1926, possibly seeming to sympathise with aspects of tsarist Russia, although Stalin was one of the play's greatest admirers (it may have seemed anti-Soviet but it certainly demonstrated the mighty power of the Bolsheviks), although he had to give in to pressure from Kiev when it was banned for several years. Bulgakov managed for a time to duck and dive to survive, even when he had the sublime cheek to send to Stalin, at the very height

Fortunatus Augustus Scudamore ('F.A.') –
Michael's maternal grandfather.

Daisy Scudamore, Michael's
mother. A photograph taken
in Dundee the week before
her wedding.

Roy Redgrave, Michael's
father – 'The Dramatic Cock
of the North'.

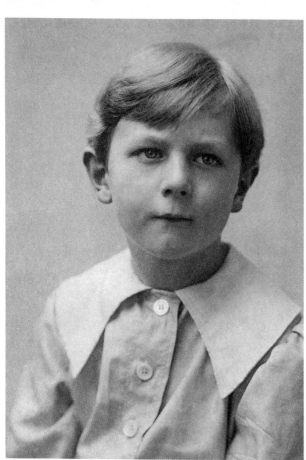

'Not exactly a street urchin' – an early photograph.

Cyril White – Michael's Clifton friend – and 'Rover'.

Top Michael as an under-graduate – the Magdalene aesthete.

Middle Oliver Baldwin, 'my first hero'; Michael Garrett (centre) at Cambridge; and the undergraduate John Lehmann.

Michael's degree day at Cambridge, 1931. His mother (centre) and Andy.

'Come, good Athenian …' – Michael in the title-role of *King Lear* at Cranleigh.

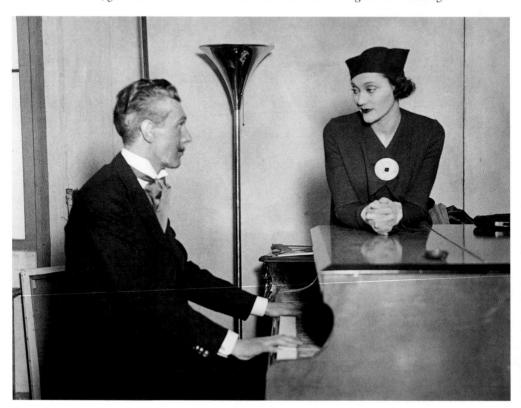

'A great deal of Leichner No 20' – Michael as Feydak in S.N.Behrman's *Biography* with Ena Burrill, Liverpool Playhouse, 1935.

Michael and Rachel Kempson in their first stage partnership – in *Flowers of the Forest*, Liverpool, 1935.

'Come, woo me, woo me …' – Michael and Edith Evans in *As You Like It*, Old Vic, 1936.

'You see, you 'ave 'eet!' –
Michael with Peggy Ashcroft
in *Three Sisters*, Queen's
Theatre, 1938.

A brace of directors –
Michel St. Denis (left) and
George Devine (right), 1939.

With Basil Radford, Dame May Whitty and Margaret Lockwood in Hitchcock's *The Lady Vanishes* – his first film.

As David Fenwick in *The Stars Look Down*, directed by Carol Reed.

With Beatrix Lehmann in *Uncle Harry*, 1944 – 'Murderers, like artists, are appreciated best when they are hung'.

Michael as the 'magnificent dinosaur' – *Jacobowsky and the Colonel*, with Diana Gould, 1945.

of the Purges, a sixtieth birthday present of his new, extremely anti-Stalin novel, *Batum*.

No wonder Michael was so enthralled, but a play by an unknown Russian writer was an audacious choice in the commercial sector of 1938. The programme sounded a brave note, prominently carrying the names of actors who had 'promised to co-operate' (including Olivier, Evans and Richardson) and adding *The Wild Duck* and Hugo von Hofmannsthal's *Christina's Journey* to the ambitious list of likely plays. Michel, Michael and Albery still planned *Twelfth Night* as the second production, although they could not announce a definite date until the likely run of *The White Guard* was clearer, which in turn made casting *Twelfth Night* awkward while actors understandably in demand tried to juggle offers and stall decisions.

The White Guard had been less a political choice for Saint-Denis, despite the play's timeliness, than another text with which to try to achieve the particular style of poetic realism towards which his work was dedicated. As with his other Russian 'family' production, *Three Sisters*, so here too Michel worked hard to achieve not only the closely textured acting he aimed for but also to suggest a seamlessly interwoven sense of a world beyond the play's set, echoing the tensions and crises of the play. Musical and sound motifs underscore the text – from the Boccherini waltz of the opening to the strains of the Internationale at the close – with folk songs, cannon, musical clocks and storms all adding to the density of this counterpoint, meticulously worked out.

The cast never felt that they were being pressed into a pre-existing mould, however; heightened by Michel's patience, his accommodating mind meeting with each actor's, all of those in *The White Guard* felt a communally thrilling sense of excitement, affected indubitably by a consciousness of racing against time, as Michael articulated: 'A feeling that our culture was going to have to come to a stop.' The actors responded to the mood in the air and to Michel's loving direction by giving uniformly magnificent performances as they again inhabited the microcosm of a family, this time (in the Marxist sense) a bourgeois one with that odd air of *vive la bagatelle* beating under the surface which Michel so cleverly teased out. Even Peggy Ashcroft's admirers were startled by the quietly devastating emotional power which she brought to her playing of a miserably married woman, shackled to a weak bully, who in desperation more than attraction gives herself to a man she knows quite well to be almost equally worthless, while the idealistic young man who admires her (Stephen Haggard) helplessly looks on. Michael, too, rose to remarkable heights: no star turn this, but a flawless piece of ensemble acting, negotiating a death scene set in the White Guard's headquarters in the

Alexandra College in the bitter cold with superb control. In that scene Alexei, leader of a forlorn hope, a man of chasm-deep feelings but comparatively few words, is shot, which could easily have turned mawkish, full of false heroics; by simply continuing fully in character, Michael made Alexei enthrallingly eloquent, never more so than when silent, using only his impressive stillness and his unblinking eyes.

After a first night to a packed and rapt house, most of the notices were hosannas – a juvenile piece from Agate excepted – full of comparisons with the best work of Les Quinze and exhortations to London to flock to a play which enriched it. Instead of which London stayed well away. There were excuses, of course – mainly the coincidental return from Germany by Neville Chamberlain – but even without Munich the play probably would still have struggled. It simply never was going to be a popular enough play at that time to cover its costs.

The commercial failure of *The White Guard* – evident very early at the box office – threw Phoenix plans into disarray, although oddly there was little of the depression which usually follows a flop. Those involved knew that they had been part of something special. *Twelfth Night* would have to go into rehearsal earlier than anticipated and Michel came down to join Michael and Rachel in Essex, accompanied by the volatile Russian-born Vera Lindsay, his partner at the time, who handled him beautifully but had, unfortunately, overambitious acting plans. Michel and Vera had rented a cottage – 'Clobbs' – also near Dunmow and they all spent a happy time planting snowdrops, daffodils and crocuses after they had grabbed the Sunday newspapers to see if a letter in support of *The White Guard* – Gielgud, Edith, Sybil Thorndike and others had grouped together as signatories – had appeared. Which it had, but not on the letters page and under the title 'A Helping Hand', so giving more the impression of what fine chaps the writers were than a leg-up for the play. Nevertheless, even knowing the production was doomed, an air of calm rather than anxiety pervaded that time:

> It was all delightful that day. Sometime back I should have been so anxious to please M that I should have been self-conscious and boring. Now, since quite recently I feel so much more certain of myself, and knowing his respect for me has helped almost as much as anything . . .
>
> The evening was very still. It was still quite light. A ribbon of birds, with an arrow head, flew across the sky and an occasional bat. The peace of sitting there with R whom I have never loved more than these last two days.

The air of feverish expectation surrounding the big adventure of the opening of the Phoenix season had inevitably abated by the time *Twelfth*

Night went into rehearsal. Even though he had not had his anticipated preparation time – he usually filled several large notebooks in advance – Michel knew the play well; under the title *La Nuit des Rois* it had been a great success for Copeau, with Louis Jouvet as Sir Andrew, before the First World War. But, perhaps still in awe of Shakespeare after the failure of his first Shakespeare production in English with *Macbeth*, he never properly took wing with this production. It did not help either that of the originally planned cast Edith had gone into an H. M. Tennent production, Richardson too was no longer available, while Olivier had taken Sam Goldwyn's offer of *Wuthering Heights* in Hollywood. Michael was never entirely clear why Stephen Haggard was no longer playing Feste and Vera Lindsay (fond as he was of her, Michael – like everyone else except Michel – had to agree 'she couldn't act for toffee') was over-parted as Olivia. The *coup de grâce* was a fussily messy and ugly set – compared variously with a municipal bathing pool and the entrance to a new block of flats in north London – the work of a London Drama Studio graduate, Vivienne Kernot. For all Michel's memories of the *commedia dell'arte* touches from Copeau and the light, colourful costumes, the production remained stubbornly earthbound and simply not funny enough. The exception – again to considerable surprise (not for those who had seen his Liverpool performances in comedy) – was Michael's Sir Andrew Ague-cheek, conceived untraditionally and inventively re-imagined as no witless chinless wonder but as a hefty maypole with long flaxen hair, in pink breeches, happy to be thought a fool, gurgling with glee at the very suggestion, but fundamentally both very, very rich and very happy. He persuasively evoked a young man who, more or less on a whim, has fantasticated his own intelligence and it delighted audiences and critics (the *Guardian*'s 'a performance for Elia's pen' pleased Michael, a Charles Lamb lover, especially). Agate continued to be whimsical about the season, to which he certainly gave no boost, firstly raving about Michael's 'glorious' fooling although he disliked the production and then, in reply to a reasoned letter from fellow critic Desmond McCarthy of the *New Statesman* accusing Agate of dismissing *Twelfth Night* as a waste of time, writing another piece insisting that the Old Vic was 'the proper place for the production of Shakespearean comedy' and adding that Michael's performance, funny as it was, amounted to 'a betrayal of the character' (Michael always agreed that in the cast which finally presented *Twelfth Night* his performance probably did overbalance the *production*, but he would fiercely defend his interpretation of Aguecheek).

The box office returns for *Twelfth Night* were much healthier than for the Bulgakov but, with the expensive seats selling more slowly, losses mounted until Albery was unable to guarantee future backing. After only two productions the Phoenix adventure was over, but there was little of the shell-shock or demoralised inertia which usually follow such failure. Writing the second of only two diary entries for 1938, Michael described the mood at White Roding with Michel and Vera after *Twelfth Night*:

> The plans, the avoiding of excuses – or, at least, the disguising of them – I remember very well that I was happy, underneath my disappointment, to be implicated with such people in misfortune ... today I was happy, having good cause and none of the usual responsibility. This is perhaps the point; that I did not feel it was my fault and besides – all the old vanity – I had not made a personal success. Michel, a much more complete and honest character, was not glum or dull, as I might have been. We only felt that he had some information about life, which he could tell us.

He goes on characteristically to put himself under a stronger lens of the microscope: 'Writing this has made me wonder whether I have not a lot of suppressed, as it were inverted conscience. A vague feeling of guilt and sin and general worthlessness impedes me a lot of the time.' Against this entry he wrote, in contrasting red ink, two verses of Yeats's '1932', concluding with the reference to things said or unsaid or done and undone from years before still weighing the poet down ('My conscience or my vanity appalled').

The mood here is eerily similar to that of T. S. Eliot's *The Family Reunion*, the next play in which Michael appeared and his last before the war. There had been hopes of presenting *Uncle Vanya* and Michael even went to Paris, taking Vera Lindsay with him as interpreter, to meet Stanislavsky's widow Idyanova and Vera's aunt who had known Stanislavsky well. He wrote to Max Adrian – they often corresponded in the guise of nineteenth-century actors, Michael adopting 'the firm, manly tone' of William Charles Macready:

> I have been obliged to give the lie, very sternly, to those malicious, *hellish* spirits who have been associating my *good* name with that of Miss L——.
> In truth, *L'affaire est assez simple*. Miss L—— has offered to introduce me to her aunt in Paris, a Russian lady of some years, who knew and revered Staninslavsky, a Russian actor and stage-manager of some standing in his own country and in America but one who never braved the frank, freer, more critical and I think I may say more *discerning* public of Albion.

As it happened, the visit to Idyanova in Stanislavsky's old apartment was not immensely helpful; first of all she told Michael his height made him more suitable for Astrov than Vanya and then, in the days he spent with her in the flat or walking in the Bois de Boulogne, all his questions about Vanya's motives were answered by an unvarying 'Because he is bored'.

The collapse of the Phoenix venture had come at another crucial stage of Michael's development. His discovery of Stanislavsky ('He went to my head like wine') combined with everything he had learnt from Michel and the Queen's company had advanced his work to change the perception of him as a hearty, extrovert Orlando figure ('all the time I was aching to play the neurotic Oswald in *Ghosts*') but he needed parts like Vanya or Hector to extend his talent as a supremely versatile leading man. When he first read *The Family Reunion* – Michel had lent him a copy one weekend at White Roding – he was *bouleversé*, reading it alone after the household had gone to bed, gripped by both the play and the central role: 'I stood reading the play, tears of fright pouring down my cheeks, so excited that I wanted to wake them up there and then.'

The play had been written during the most troubled decade of Eliot's life, but as many of his Bloomsbury friends intuited – Virginia Woolf most acutely, pinpointing a streak of underlying violence in his work and naughtily stressing his resemblance to Dr Crippen – it was precisely his cloaked, subterranean life which fuelled his excursions into 'The Sacred Wood' of poetry. The 1930s, in addition to 'The Four Quartets', also produced *Murder in the Cathedral*, *Sweeney Agonistes* and *The Family Reunion*. Eliot exegetists continue to argue the degree of autobiographical element in the play, which fuses Argos and England in recasting the Orestes myth in the context of an English country-house family drama, presenting a Furies-pursued central Orestes figure, Harry Monchensey, whose wife disappeared at sea on a transatlantic crossing, possibly murdered by Harry (her body is never found). Undoubtedly the appalling events of the committal to an asylum of the tragic Vivienne Haigh-Wood, the first Mrs Eliot, inform the play, while other commentators would add that Harry's chauffeur-manservant Downing is based on W. C. James, Eliot's ex-policeman manservant, the patient-Griselda figure of Mary on a suggested possible fiancée for the young Eliot, Emily Hale, and the austere matriarch, Amy, on Charlotte, Eliot's mother, who loathed Vivienne. The biographer Carole Seymour-Jones claims that Vivienne is 'the painted shadow' who stalked Eliot who then, in art as in life (he referred to her even before committal and divorce as 'my late wife'), tried to exorcise her, and that in *The Family Reunion* 'Eliot takes his revenge upon Vivienne and upon his mother'.

The play, set in the spring ('A season of sacrifice') throughout, stresses the need of expiation for sin, as Harry – helped by his wisest aunt, Agatha – begins to grasp that if he learns to trust rather than dread the Furies or Eumenides, they will lead him to 'the bright Angels' and purge his sense of inner decay: 'What matters is the filthiness. I can clear my skin, purify my life, void my mind, but always the filthiness, that lies a little deeper.'

Michael relished the challenge of play and part, although the dialogue, in verse which aims to negotiate the freedoms of prose, using three marked stresses in each line in an attempt to catch the cadences of conversation, is at times clotted and knotty, a fiendishly difficult discipline for the actor to make accessible, as in Harry's description of twilight: 'Where the dead stone is seen to be batrachian, the aphyllous branch ophidian.'

Aspects of the play – Harry's lack of clear knowledge of his long-dead father, the description of his role as the 'consciousness' of his 'unhappy family' having to fly through 'purgatorial flame', the family's buried secrets and the motifs from *Hamlet* – all touched something in Michael and he was very eager indeed to play Harry, cursed for his sin and fleeing the Eumenides, one of those haunted characters at which he excelled. He knew he had not been first choice for the part. Previously Eliot and the play's director, E. Martin Browne, had met John Gielgud at a sticky Reform Club lunch to discuss the play; it tended to be thought that Eliot vetoed the casting because Gielgud had no religious faith, although a more likely reason is that Gielgud's insouciant homosexual life rather alarmed the punctilious Eliot (who could not have been entirely unconscious of literary London's gossip about his own residence in the Great Ormond Street homosexual household of the novelist C. H. B. Kitchin), Michael, like Gielgud, had no deep faith but his private life at that time at least seemed conventional enough; the Edith affair had been exceedingly discreet as theatrical romances go, while his bisexuality was then known only to intimate friends. Eliot was anxious to see the play staged before the threatening clouds of war burst and Michael was cast at the head of a strong company – Catherine Lacey as Agatha, Robert Harris as Downing – to rehearse in March 1939.

Michael had been spoilt by Michel, of course, and E. Martin Browne simply was not in the same league as a director, although Eliot trusted him with most of his work. Browne, an old Etonian, had been an actor with no great success before his appointment by Bishop Bell as director of Religious Drama for Chichester and he had wooed Eliot to write *The Rock* choruses for its Sadler's Wells production, subsequently directing *Murder in the Cathedral* with Robert Speaight's memorable Becket. *The Family Reunion*, in which the drama is essentially internal, such action as there is taking place inside the characters' minds, was a very different piece, much more experimental in its verse, choric passages and fusion of Greek myth and drawing-room comedy. The comedy gave the less than jocund Browne trouble and Michael felt that the whole production was too reverent, undervaluing the vein of sly comedy in it; at times it suggests a macabre marriage of P. G. Wodehouse and Ivy Compton-Burnett, especially in the second act in the library after dinner when the absence of the dim younger brother Arthur is explained by a newspaper account of his motor accident when he demolished a roundsman's cart in Ebury Street before reversing into a shop window, explaining when challenged by the police: 'I thought it was all open country about here.'

Browne dithered, too, over the handling of the Eumenides, presenting Michael with a problem on his very first entrance, one of the most difficult in the modern theatre, when Harry returns to Wyshwood after eight years, having instantly to convey, at a glimpse of the pursuing Furies, the haunted, transfixed suffering of the character without falling into melodrama. Only once – late into rehearsals – was Michael convinced that he had captured this, only to suffer the actor's problem of trying to recapture the emotion of that rehearsal. He tried Stanislavsky concentration exercises, Komisarjevsky's advice to focus on an object to centre the senses prior to an entrance, but nothing worked. What he needed then was a good director (probably to suggest to him not to try so hard), instead of which Browne, like his author, usually sat with his head in the text, concentrating on line readings in static groupings while the drama became more frigidly inert. The Eumenides problem, admittedly very difficult (Eliot wrote once that they could look dangerously like a football team), was never cracked, although an inspired production such as Michael Elliot's for the Manchester Royal Exchange, in the round where huge, hooded figures could materialise and disappear quickly, proves that the problem of fusing ancient and modern can be solved. Browne's frozen postures and insistence on the design emphasising the classical aspect with a plethora of Ionic columns helped the actors not at all.

It was not an easy rehearsal period although all very civilised, with Michael not alone in the cast feeling that the play needed treatment a good deal less obsequious. The play came in for some ribbing in the press – 'a nice Hellenic kettle of fish' or 'Sophocles-and-soda' – while many were confused by a manifestly Christian writer's exploration of Greek myths and themes. Misleadingly compared by some with O'Neill's *Mourning Becomes Electra* – a better comparison would be his *Strange Interlude* in which on-stage characters also speak thoughts aloud – the general response echoed the lines of the play's Uncle Charles: 'It's very odd, but I'm beginning to feel that there is something I could understand, if I were told it.' Although one critic testily remarked that Michael looked 'too healthy to be hag-ridden', most were deeply impressed by his burning-glass intensity and by his febrile, haunted communication of an imprisoned soul struggling for release. For Michael, this was always to remain one that got away; he felt strongly that the production, and his performance in it, had rather short-changed the play.

Michael and Rachel celebrated the play's opening and the move to

Clifton Hill on the same night with a party, the first in their new home; a pregnant Rachel had to finish the move, prepare for the party and watch the play all on the same day. It also belatedly celebrated the opening of *The Lady Vanishes*, a big success with both critics and public, which established Michael as a star in his very first film, while *A Stolen Life* awaited imminent release. Other films were in the pipeline; Ted Black, who had ambitious plans to build up a stable of British film stars along Hollywood studio lines, was developing an idea to pair Michael again with Margaret Lock-wood – he had noticed the strong public response to the partnership – in a series of sophisticated comedy thrillers similar to the William Powell and Myrna Loy *Thin Man* combination. In the meantime, as post-Munich optimism began to ebb and with war looking now virtually certain, Michael's stage future was unresolved.

Michel Saint-Denis was already planning his return to France where he would help the Free French movement, but he had met with Michael, Vera, George Devine and others from the Queen's and Phoenix projects to see what would be done about somehow – even if at a reduced level – keeping the flame of that work alight, all of them, especially Devine, aware of 'a sense of comradeship' in what he described as 'the task' Michel had left them. Simultaneously, Michael was approached by Guthrie to return to the Old Vic for a new repertory system, alternating not only plays but parts, and throughout one of the finest summers for years they met to discuss the plans for a company potentially headed by Michael, Robert Donat, Constance Cummings and Roger Livesey. *Uncle Vanya* – again – reared its head, along with *Julius Caesar*, *Macbeth* and *Romeo and Juliet*, the last to alternate Donat and Michael as Romeo (Edith rebuked him for choosing the less difficult role but privately Michael felt he wanted to wait before tackling Macbeth, the most notoriously awkward tragic hero to crack).

Any doubts Michael had about the Old Vic scheme were less concerned with the parts than with Guthrie himself. Much as he liked him and his inventive mind, his experiences with a director such as Michel had made him a touch wary of Guthrie's gung-ho approach, as he outlined to Max Adrian:

> I think to do him justice, he's in a hell of a spot, but I don't think he has what it takes for the Vic. Perhaps that's unfair without further explanation, but let it go.
>
> I told him I was personally only prepared to go if we could get a really strong team together, and if Robert could stay, so much the better. Between Robert and Roger my casting was pretty difficult, but I was prepared to do the Orsinos and Cassiuses if we could be a *team*. Tony agreed in theory, but

I noticed that when it came to casting, his ideas are so *Tonyish*. For instance, having argued that Feste is the most difficult part to cast and that Marius is the best available, he proposes in lieu someone quite unsuitable who 'might make a shot at it'.

It saddens me because as you know I have the Old Vic bug and the Shakespeare quinsy.

He wrote to Edith (who largely concurred with him about Guthrie) too, clearly torn, 'We seem to see eye to eye in theory, but his way of putting this into practice, deliberately miscasting or misusing people, baffles me.' Undoubtedly Michael touched on Guthrie's Achilles heel here; he was prone to perverse casting wheezes and, as a born nomad, was perhaps not best suited to the grind of leading an institution. Their differences come down to fundamentally dissimilar ideas about acting; at its crudest Michael worked 'from within' while Guthrie (who tended to mock Stanislavsky and any idea that acting is much more than instinct yoked to technique) was external, the undisputed master of panache-packed display but less reliable with sheer naked emotional truth and simplicity.

During that long, suspenseful summer Michael was glad to have some time between films to reflect and also to be with Rachel when their second child was born. In the event of a boy they had planned to call him William, with either Corin (from *As You Like It*) or (after his great-grandfather) Cornelius as a middle name (Daisy did not approve – she felt that school-boy humour would mock the 'W. C.' initials, adding, 'I am rather super-stitious about the Redgraves, and old Grandpa was a bit of a devil'). Michael was at home at Clifton Hill when Corin William (as he was christened) was born, getting back just in time from Twickenham filming, and although he wrote virtually nothing in diaries throughout the 1930s he made a long entry for 16 July, noting down the preparations for the birth with 'Mackie' (the same nurse who had looked after Rachel in Blackheath when Vanessa was born) placing oilcoth around the bed, the doctor's arrival ('a tennis shirt under his mac') and Rachel's cries, while he paced round the garden, 'Thinking the silliest thoughts, including the observation that I was watching myself, which I detested.'

Michael and Rachel had wanted a boy this time, so he and Rachel ('crying with happiness and relief') hugged each other over the baby. His christening became a mixture of coincidences. Michael's great-uncle Hyma had contacted him at the Old Vic in early 1937 and the families met for the first time (Hyma had a daughter, Grace, training to be an 'acrobatic dancer') so it seemed only fitting, especially after Hyma had filled in some tantalising blanks in the family history, that Michael should ask him to officiate at the christening (on, 'in defiance of vulgar superstition', 13 August) at St John's in the Waterloo Road, close to the Old Vic. Daisy, omnipresent dead fox flung over her shoulder, attended with Andy even though she was inclined to be somewhat wary of Redgrave relations. 'Uncle Hyma spoke perhaps too many words,' she criticised afterwards to Michael, although adding: 'It was thrilling to think that William was being baptised in the church where his great-great-grand-parents were christened.' St John's was, of course, also where his great-grandfather had been married. Daisy was mightily impressed, too, by the glamorous presence of the godmother, Elisabeth Bergner (whose gift to her godson was a wildly expensive and completely impractical blue doves-kin suitcase). Michael and Rachel asked Max Adrian, even if his wicked tongue and gimlet eyes suggested more a Carabosse than a benevolent sponsor, to be godfather.

Corin was just over a month old when finally war was declared. The Clifton Hill house was closed up and the family joined Vanessa (who now was beginning to speak, with a broad Essex accent) and the nanny, Nurse Dulcie, at White Roding, which turned out to be no peaceful haven as an army of evacuees descended on the village. Michael and Rachel, as well as taking two pregnant women into an already crowded small house, spent much time driving around, on limited petrol, trying to billet many others. Most of the new arrivals chose to return to London when it became clear that there had been no sign of the anticipated German air raids, although for a time there was considerable festivity as Michael reported to Max describing a crammed nearby Bishop's Stortford: 'Of the 2 pubs there – the Whalebone resembles Babylon, the Black Horse Sodom *and* Gomorrah.'

Michael went to London by train to continue discussions with both Devine and Guthrie, but the war now threw most plans into confusion. In the event the Old Vic season was abandoned, although a revised programme headed by Donat and Constance Cummings began a tour in Buxton shortly afterwards, while little came of the plans of the Saint-Denis rump, as the group left behind by Michel might be called. With others interested – Alec Guinness and Martita Hunt included – lists of plays for possible touring were drawn up but their problem was lack of finance rather than of ideas. Looking for backing, Michael went to talk to his agent Bill Linnit, who could be of no practical help and hinted that he felt their plans were too idealistic for a wartime public. In the short term only one production, indirectly, came out of their talks – Guinness's version of *Great Expectations* with himself as Herbert Pocket at the Rudolf Steiner Hall – but in the long term, the 1930s work of the Gielgud and Phoenix seasons was astonishingly influential, that 'family' ethos carrying through after the war with Quayle and Byam Shaw at Stratford, Devine and the English Stage Company at the Royal Court and Olivier at the

National (with Michael in the first company), while Peter Hall has always acknowledged the seminal debt he owed to Peggy Ashcroft in the formation of the Royal Shakespeare Company. So, although it only existed briefly, Michael's hope for the Phoenix season, reported to the *American Theater World*, was realised after all: 'Here is something unique. It must be judged, not by the success or failure of this or that play, but by whether after a time, after trial and error, something does not emerge which will be good, and consistent, new and lasting.'

At the time, however, everything in the theatre was on hold. Finally Bill Linnit, who had been setting up a scheme with producers and touring theatres to tour plays on a new financial structure with actors, even stars, taking only basic salaries (maximum £10 per week) with the inducement of a small participation in profits, and authors of plays in copyright taking similar royalty cuts, came back to Michael to suggest that a play they had discussed – Benn Levy's comedy *Springtime for Henry*, a feather-light four-hander – would be ideal for his scheme with Michael and Rachel playing with another husband-and-wife pair, Roger Livesey and Ursula Jeans. It was hardly how Michael had envisaged his early war effort work, but knowing that he was unlikely to be called up for a time and with nothing else on offer until he began shooting his next film, he prepared to pack up for the hard slog of a ten-week provincial tour, with some long journeys on wartime trains. Before rehearsals they had several jolly sessions with Benn Levy and Constance Cummings at their unique Gropius-designed Chelsea house – Benn had the gift of inspiring laughter even in bad times – talking over *Springtime for Henry* while Vanessa and Corin were sent from London down to Dartmouth.

The Family Reunion audiences at the Westminster Theatre had combined London's literati with the more adventurous theatregoing public. But on tour with Benn's play Michael began to realise from the audiences and their reactions that the public was now coming to see him primarily because he was a Film Star.

Eight
SOUND STAGES

Michael's entry into the world of film making, for him completely new, had been somewhat stumbling and he once gratefully acknowledged: 'I have learned most of what little I know about film through my directors' – while he also always admitted that to have had Alfred Hitchcock and Carol Reed (twice) behind the camera on three out of his first four films was unusually lucky. And yet it was a generous fellow actor who gave him perhaps the wisest advice of all.

Early one morning on *The Lady Vanishes* Michael, bleary-eyed in the make-up chair, met Paul Lukas, the elegant Hungarian-born actor playing the suavely chilling Dr Herz in the film. Lukas, who had worked in the theatre for Max Reinhardt before his international film career, had been the previous evening to see *Three Sisters* and, enthusing about Michael's performance, casually implied that compared with Tusenbach, as Gilbert in the film he seemed barely to be trying. To which Michael replied that indeed he was finding filming somewhat dull since Hitchcock seemed to want him just to hit his marks, inflect his lines properly and to keep it snappy. Which is fine as far as it goes except, as the seasoned Lukas told the tyro, 'But, my dear boy, it's all going in the can! Once the director has taken the last shot of a scene it's too late to wish you could do it again.'

Michael was lucky to learn so early the vital lesson that although the eye of the camera of course photographs acting, it also photographs thought, the latter being what so often connects more potently with the multiple eyes of an audience. Some of the greatest screen stars – Garbo, Monroe, Valentino, Cooper, Tracy – had that gift, priceless on screen, of allowing an audience direct access to their minds, often without words, often without, in the strict sense, 'acting' ability. In many ways Michael, with his rooted belief in acting 'from within', for the truth, and with his proven ability to communicate a character's interior life, was potentially an ideal film actor and, indeed, he quickly became one.

To begin with, compared with the seamless playing in the theatre with which he was involved at night, the studio seemed a frustrating place, the waiting around and the fragmentary nature of filming resistant to the kind of re-creation of spontaneity which he searched for on stage. He was, too, as he confessed, initially biased by the fact that so few leading British actors took the cinema seriously (Edith, at that time, had made not one film). Ralph Richardson had told him: 'You sell to the cinema what you've learned in the theatre,' which was the general *de haut en bas* attitude of stage actors at that time. Michael came rapidly to disagree with Richardson and his theory that the actor gets nothing as an artist out of the cinema – to Richardson the film actor never really gets beyond the stage of a first rehearsal in the theatre – and he began soon to find the different disciplines of the medium totally absorbing. After trying to work on Lukas's advice, he realised: 'In the cinema, in some of the early takes, or in rehearsals, you will find something that is absolutely spontaneous or not modelled, and the camera can go right in and read your thoughts.'

The Lady Vanishes was an ideal film with which to begin a movie career. The picture did not depend on any single performance and this, together with the knowledge that the director had so thoroughly prepared and storyboarded the film, plus Hitchcock's relaxed, Buddha-like calm on set, made the actors feel at ease too. He had teased Michael – who always swore that Hitchcock did say (with a smile) 'Actors are cattle' on *The Lady Vanishes* set – by telling him on the first day that Robert Donat had wanted to play Gilbert, intending perhaps to cut him down to size but also giving him a hint that what Hitchcock was after from him was an insouciantly casual performance. His help to Michael was mostly technical – tips on how to match different shots or angles within the same scene, occasional reminders about avoiding carrying the pace of the end of one scene into the opening of another – but invaluable to a newcomer.

His actual introduction to the movie world, just before filming began, had been mildly unsettling, having to pose with Margaret Lockwood (their first meeting) for falsely intimate publicity shots at a film charity ball at the Royal Albert Hall. Despite the toothpaste smiles in the press they were slightly wary of each other initially, she of this new bright hope from the theatre, he of her screen experience, with sixteen films to her credit already. This – whether or not Hitchcock was aware of or encouraged it – actually helped the film, sparking the early scenes of sparring between heiress Iris and breezy musicologist Gilbert (luckily shot first) with a useful edge of spiky adrenalin. Similarly, as they grew to like each other as filming proceeded, their later scenes of collaboration in pursuit of the vanished lady (the redoubtable Dame May Whitty) took on a relaxed, bantering ease.

All the ingredients of the film – a cross-European train, mysterious nuns with high heels under their habits, potential Nazis in disguise – may seem fairly standard, the elements of many a routine period thriller and yet, well over half a century on, *The Lady Vanishes* still sparkles, still intrigues, still holds. Hitchcock always rather tended to disparage it later, partly because it remains one of the few films on which he had comparatively little influence before filming began, rather undermining his standing with the *auteur* film theorists (who in any case prefer his later American films with their more overt and more personal explorations of themes of Catholicism and guilt).

The foundation of the film and of its enduring appeal is the superb script by the then young and virtually unknown team of Frank Launder and Sidney Gilliat, which they adapted cunningly from Ethel Lina White's novel, *The Wheel Spins*. They developed the oneiric element in the story – Iris's feeling that she is drawn into a world of nightmare when she loses her ally Miss Froy (mischievously confused with Freud in one throwaway moment) – and, most memorably, they introduced two original characters, the cricket-mad quintessential Little Englanders Charters and Caldicot. The book's Gilbert is a stereotypical beefy hearty; the film's change to a musicologist gives him a sharper mind and tongue as well as a heightened romantic side.

The film, originally titled *Lost Lady*, had gone into production in 1936 (without Hitchcock) but was aborted when the unit shooting exteriors in Yugoslavia was deported. Ted Black rightly guessed that Hitchcock would respond to the script's marriage of comedy and suspense. Hitchcock owed Gaumont-British (Gainsborough's parent company) a film contractually and he quickly approved script (which subsequently changed only slightly) and, after seeing their respective tests, both Lockwood and Michael. Indeed, everything about the film moved quickly once it was back in production and one of its joys is its sheer kinetically charged pace. There is a sense of continuous impetus on the train and the dialogue has a rapid-fire, sometimes overlapping swiftness – the movie's speed surely reflects Hitchcock's itch to leave England and get to Hollywood for David O. Selznick as soon as possible.

Michael, nattily dressed and with a sharp, Colman-ish moustache, is in terrific form; the film gains a lot from his high-octane good humour and mental energy. He and Margaret Lockwood make a strong team – Ted Black's notion of extending the partnership before war intervened was well founded – especially fine together in one of those set-ups which Hitchcock loved directing, with an initially antagonistic couple growing closer and mutually attracted in some unusual, confined space or situation – handcuffed together in *39 Steps*, in *The Lady Vanishes* searching together in a luggage van full of clever props and an illusionist's magic cabinet: 'Don't stand there hopping about like a referee,' Gilbert scolds Iris at one point before a deftly offhand Will Hay impersonation, using the vital prop of Miss Froy's spectacles. Michael's buoyant sense of adventure also greatly boosts the narrative, especially in the closing stages on the train when the movie takes on something of a suggestion of the 'family' of England, a tight little island banding together in the climactic gunfight against the agents of Fascism (theorists who suggested in this context that the coward Todhunter's waving of his white handkerchief was a parodic gesture of appeasement to suggest Chamberlain's waving of his piece of white paper were disappointed to learn that the script and film both were finished before Munich).

Even in this action-packed sequence the script manages to fuse the comedy and the goodies v. baddies plot in an exhilarating balance (one of many things absent from the dire remake), greatly helped by Michael's casually underplayed but truthful comedic instincts. He remained dubious about his reply to the enemy soldier boasting that his command of English is due to an Oxford education, when Gilbert flattens him with a chair, adding the inconsequentially daffy explanation, 'I was at Cambridge.' Later he acknowledged that it got one of the biggest laughs in the film.

Michael grew to like Hitchcock – there was something of Willie Armstrong's avuncularly relaxed authority in him to which he responded – although he deeply disliked his more sadistically juvenile humour, which became evident only at the end-of-shoot party on set when he contrived for the teetotal Mary Clare (playing the haughty baroness) to be served a supposedly innocuous concoction which made her embarrassingly drunk. As it was his first film, there remained moments in it which always made him wince as he recalled how green he was when making it, but it was a film which grew on him to become a personal favourite.

Filming *The Lady Vanishes* was a happy time for him – he enjoyed the work once he adapted to filming's special requirements, he had financial security (£150 per week) for at least the immediate future, the freedom to continue theatre work and an unexpected bonus, linking him to his father. The old Gainsborough Studios in Islington were near Hoxton, and after viewing his *Lady Vanishes* test Michael decided to call Rachel from a nearby pub next door to the Brit, Roy's old theatrical patch and by then a cinema. The pub's landlord and his wife, it emerged, had been stagehand and dresser respectively at the Brit and remembered Roy – they clearly adored him – very well, regaling Michael with memories of his Captain Starlight and his Marcus Superbus in *The Sign of the Cross*. For Michael such encounters were to be treasured; apart from a few scripts and sepia-tinted photographs (he never knew of Roy's letters until much later) his only tangible memento of his father was a signet ring supposedly given to Roy by the Brit's manager, Sara Lane, which was stolen from Clifton Hill in a burglary during the Blitz, which also destroyed the Brit.

Word had leaked out even before *The Lady Vanishes* was completed that

Michael's screen debut was likely to mark him out as a leading man in demand, although he was surprised to be told that even before its release he would be going straight into *A Stolen Life*, loaned out to Paramount, especially when it was added that the star was to be Elisabeth Bergner. Virtually forgotten now, in her time Bergner was an authentic megastar. Viennese by birth, she was playing leading roles including Saint Joan, Rosalind and Tessa in *The Constant Nymph* in her twenties and in a legendary *Romeo and Juliet* opposite Francis Lederer for Reinhardt before leaving Germany in 1932 with her husband Paul Czinner, who had directed several of her silent films. The impresario C. B. Cochran, who had been overwhelmed by *Saint Joan*, brought her from Paris to London to star in a Tyrolean-set play written for her by the author of *The Constant Nymph*, Margaret Kennedy, *Escape Me Never*, a piece of edelweiss-and-dirndl whimsy with Bergner as the waif-like Gemma hopelessly in love with the caddish Heinrich. She became a star in England literally overnight; Cochran cleverly opened her unheralded and the play sold out for a year. Bergner was a highly strung artist; she was bisexual and could be capricious and demanding in the theatre and in life but her stage presence, a walking definition of *gemütlich*, entranced a 1930s public hungry for escapist romance. Androgyny was central to her appeal – Czinner directed a fussily decorative *As You Like It* film with Olivier as Orlando to her Rosalind and J. M. Barrie was so captivated that he wrote his final play, a rare failure, *The Boy David*, for her.

When Michael was cast in *A Stolen Life* her film popularity was still strong (*Dreaming Lips* the previous year had audiences flocking) and he remembered her spellbinding charm from the films he had seen in Heidelberg, and so he was taken aback by the banality of the script. Margaret Kennedy provided a *Peg's Paper* farrago, with Bergner cast as identical twins – 'a teasing team' as described by their beaming papa – Silvina and Martina, the only discernible difference between them being that their hair is parted on different sides, which is just as well because otherwise both girls have exactly the same huge, brimming eyes, elfin, open-mouthed smile and lispy voice ('she *talks* on tiptoe' as one critic said). Michael was saddled with the stodgy role of Alan McKenzie, a famous mountaineer who one day amid an Alpine near avalanche of cardboard studio rocks meets Silvina (surprisingly chicly dressed for such an outing) and falls for her although, of course, it is Martina who really loves him. After Alan marries Silvina and while he is on a Tibetan expedition – allowing Michael gratefully to bow out of the wilder central sequences – Silvina, who has been faithless, drowns in a boating accident on a remote lake, only for Martina to retrieve her sister's wedding ring, rapidly change her parting and switch so that she 'becomes' Silvina (by happy coincidence, at this stage of the film, papa is going blind). The film ends in Athens and after a conveniently planted line – 'Real life sometimes plays tricks that no author would ever invent' – which Michael manages to deliver straight-faced, Martina re-parts her hair, Alan realises his true love and they end in a clinch by the Acropolis overlooking a twinkling studio skyline of Athens as William Walton's music swells.

Shooting this nonsense was a very different experience from Hitchcock's economic, fast-moving style. Czinner was enslaved by Bergner and studio hours were dictated by her insistence on rest to keep her dewy-eyed freshness so that most of the cast and crew were tired from waiting around for her late arrivals on set. But Czinner was a poor director, with little sense of how to shape or pace a film, although he did his own editing. Even allowing for the period's technical shortcomings his films are clunky affairs; he once told Michael his basic approach to filming was essentially to film as many takes as possible, on the assumption that at least one would be on the right lines.

Michael realised early on in shooting that this was Bergner's film (her billing was huge) and that his best bet was to shut up and deliver his lines, full of shopworn cliché ('We can't control our hearts') with Macready's 'firm, manly tone' as convincingly as possible. Only a couple of scenes give him any real chance, principally an episode in an Athens hotel when he mistakenly believes Martina has found the man she loves in Scotland, which he plays with a forlorn, touchingly acquiescent dignity.

He had no complaints about Bergner's diva behaviour. For him, partly because of his memories of her silver image in Heidelberg ('my boyhood dream-girl' as he described her), she was a genuine star, a modern Réjane or Bernhardt, a *monstre sacrée* for whom exceptions must be made. She took greatly to him, knowing from early rushes that he made her look good on the screen; she was a bright woman, well read and an incisive judge of acting. She and Michael never lost touch and while many old colleagues dropped her when she 'bolted' to America from the set of the Canadian-British *49th Parallel* film shooting during the war in Canada when she feared a Nazi occupation of Britain, he was one of the few to keep in contact; Michael's concept of friendship had been rooted, after all, in the same Cambridge world which bred E. M. Forster's *Two Cheers for Democracy*.

Unexpectedly – at least to Michael – *A Stolen Life* did well at the box office and he was beginning to receive quantities of fan mail. Even his staunchest fan, however, must have been as dismayed as Michael by *Climbing High* into which he was rushed from Bergner's arms straight into those (literally – the first shot on the first day was their final embrace) of the reigning British musical queen, Jessie Matthews. Her hits such as

Evergreen (amazingly, scripted by Benn Levy) and *It's Love Again* had been lavish big-budget affairs but after her champion Michael Balcon left Gaumont-British to head MGM's new English company, the new regime headed by Maurice Ostrer began to cut back. Jessie was then married to the comedian Sonnie Hale who also wrote film scripts and had directed her last film, a weak effort, *Gangway*; he was scheduled to direct her next, *Asking for Trouble*, which he had also written, intended as another showy musical vehicle. Maurice Ostrer privately wanted Sonnie off the film as director – he thought little of his ability – and stalled until Sonnie's contract expired. He then swiftly ordered all the musical numbers cut and assigned the film to Carol Reed. It was a sign of Michael's immediate popularity with the public that Linnit was able to negotiate above-the-title billing with Jessie for him (she had enjoyed solo billing for seven years) although when he read the script Michael would have preferred not to have his name on the film at all.

Carol Reed was reluctant too. He had just started to make a name for himself with an unpretentious but expertly crafted film, *Bank Holiday*, with Margaret Lockwood, and the last thing he wanted to do was film a script for a musical comedy without the songs (one bizarre musical 'interlude' was retained) but contractually he was obliged to take on *Climbing High* as it had been retitled. What saved the film from total disaster – just – was the camaraderie which developed between Reed, Jessie and Michael after an uneasy start.

Filming began with Michael meeting Jessie for the first time on set saying 'How do you do? I believe I have to kiss you now, don't I?' before going into the fade-out's passionate embrace. Jessie was bright enough to know the script was witless but her husband had written it and she was irked when Michael and Reed made it clear what they thought ('Oh, God – must I say these dreadful lines?' Michael had asked at one point). Reed upset her, too, when he ordered her to change out of the elaborate Norman Hartnell gowns designed for her but she eventually had to admit that they were wrong for the more modest film it had become. Before long Jessie and Reed were having a torrid dressing-room affair and they, with Michael, agreed to try to do what they could to salvage the project.

They had a struggle. Jessie played Iris, a doe-eyed dancing instructor accidentally entangled in photographic modelling (involving a laboured running gag when she mistakes the model agency for a brothel), sharing digs with a mad revolutionary (Alastair Sim at his most relentlessly bug-eyed). Iris is accidentally knocked over by Nicholas Brooke (Michael), a wealthy sportsman, and the film spends the next ninety minutes following their tiresome misadventures as he, under an assumed name to shake off a predatory society girl, tries to woo her. It says a lot about the script that by far the best sequence in the film is silent, a long slapstick scene, when a wind machine is accidentally switched on during a photo shoot for a starch advertisement in which props, starch and underclothes on scantily dressed models go flying, inventively accelerated and paced by Reed. By far the worst is a scene of staggering political incorrectness involving an escaped lunatic (poor Francis L. Sullivan, clearly blushing even in black-and-white) with delusions that he is 'the songbird of the Alps' forcing Iris and Nick to join him in a Viennese waltz trio.

Again Michael had to do his best with near impossible material: 'You must see eye to eye with me about her eyes,' he has besottedly to insist to his chum, played by Basil Radford. In his few scenes he builds up an entertaining Drones Club double act with Michael, who throughout has an endearingly chumpish guilelessness that would have sparkled with a better script.

He did, however, come to like and greatly admire Carol Reed, a reflective, absorbed figure on the floor where he had the rare gift of creating a congenial atmosphere, also handling actors with courtesy and consideration. Michael was fascinated by him, perhaps because they were so alike in some ways – both tall, intelligent and with little conventional small talk. Reed too was illegitimate, one of five sons of the Victorian actor-manager Sir Herbert Beerbohm Tree by his mistress May Pinney, and had learnt his craft under Edgar Wallace who had brought him from the theatre into films. Michael became impressed by Reed's single-mindedness and they began a ritual of having a drink together at the end of each day's work: 'Reed is one of those dedicated beings, the artist who is completely absorbed by his dream.' Even though *Climbing High* was a poor film, he respected Reed's attempt to do the best he could and responded to the conviction below the calm demeanour: 'Underneath the gentle tone was an iron will which eleven times out of twelve would have its own way. I found that admirable. With Reed I learned for the first time how subtle the relationship between an actor and director could be.'

Michael was delighted when Gainsborough agreed to loan him out, along with Reed, to be part of a film produced by a new company, Grand National (its finance was sourced from a consortium of millionaire businessmen including the holiday camp magnate Billy Butlin), although the choice of film was a surprise from such a plutocratic set-up. *The Stars Look Down* was from a best-selling novel by A. J. Cronin, remembered now, if at all, for his *Doctor Finlay* stories, but undeservedly forgotten. He was a superior Catherine Cookson of his day, writing fat, engrossing sagas, set often in his native Scotland or the North of England. Based around a mining catastrophe – the pit owner having kept quiet about the danger of flooding – *The Stars Look Down* drew on Cronin's experiences in the early

1920s as a doctor in the Welsh pit communities and then as an inspector of mines.

The novel is long, tracing the life of its central character, David Fenwick, a miner's son who wants to educate himself to fight the miners' cause but who, snared by the social-climbing Jenny, abandons his university course to teach back home. The book is in three parts, going from early 1900s wildcat strikes and pit catastrophes through the experiences of David and Arthur, the mine owner's son, in the 1914–18 trenches on to David's election as MP in the 1929 Labour government and his fight for the nationalisation of coal. When he is defeated at the next election by his long-time rival the profiteer-spiv Joe Gowlan, David ultimately returns to the mines.

The film necessarily compresses the novel, concentrating mostly on the first third. While the book is the story of two families, the Fenwicks and the mine-owning Barrases, the script cuts much of the Barras story while whole plots (the collapse of David's marriage to Jenny and her descent into prostitution and death in a VD ward) and characters (Barras's feminist daughter Hilda and, the biggest loss, the Bible-thumping miner nick-named Jesus Wept) are excised. Yet J. B. Williams's script, vitally, is faithful to the novel's central characters and to its subversive spirit, fiercely expressed in the crucial scene of the pit disaster inquiry with David arguing: 'So long as the economic system of private ownership exists the waste of human life will continue.' By any standards it remains a remarkable film, a little-known near masterpiece, arguably Reed's finest work and containing certainly Michael's first truly major screen performance, one which in its unaffected directness has a gravitas, an understatedly implicit moral strength which can stand comparisons with anything on screen from Gary Cooper or Henry Fonda (Will Joad in John Ford's *The Grapes of Wrath* is kin to David Fenwick, but time has reinforced Pauline Kael's contention that Reed's is the finer film).

Although the 'message' of Cronin's novel is unambiguous, he wrote much more than a polemic and Reed was resolute that the film must do the same. He wanted only Michael for David while Michael, who had been impressed by both *The Citadel* (Cronin's second novel, filmed first) and *The Stars Look Down*, was ready: 'It's a remarkable opportunity. You might wait all your life for a part like this, saying "Why don't they let me play this?" without any result. And here it has fallen into my lap. No wonder I'm excited.'

Reed talked Margaret Lockwood into accepting Jenny (her formidable mother did not want her to play 'a tart'). Trusting Reed and prepared to go outside her usual range, she went on to give one of her best performances as the pitiable Jenny, a minx curdling into a discontented shrew. The supporting roles were also unerringly cast, especially Nancy Price, herself a pit boss's daughter and an actor-manager in the Baylis mould, as David's proud, defiantly unemotional mother. The only slightly off-key performance is from Emlyn Williams – the witty actor-dramatist – who is just too overtly sly and too unmistakably Welsh as Joe.

Reed insisted on a good deal of location work – he was unshakeable in his resolve to make this film as authentic and as unsentimentalised as possible – and the budget was upped to allow filming at a colliery near Workington, the nearby mining village of Great Clifton with its rows of back-to-backs standing in for the story's Sleescale, with only the climactic disaster and a few interiors shot at Twickenham Studios.

Despite a syrupy voice-over at opening and close (imposed on Reed by US distributors, sepulchrally promising at the end 'the light of the world that could and must be') Reed's aims were totally achieved and vindicated. No British film before and none again until the 1960s New Cinema had the social fervour yoked to cinematic brilliance of *The Stars Look Down*. And few other British films have used montage so well (Humphrey Jennings, especially in his film of a fire-station in the Blitz, *Fires Were Started*, could also be a master of montage); often an inert device, throughout this film Reed makes it dynamic, part of the movie's structure and movement, in such extraordinary sequences as the pit flooding or the pithead reaction to disaster, with the mine lift stopped, children racing out of school as the pit alarm sounds, shawled and aproned women silently waiting, all in images of frozen tableaux but both dramatically and cinematically active with a powerful cumulative emotional undertow.

Michael's performance retains its force and impact. For the first time – with top billing – he had to carry a film and he made it over all the hurdles without a single false or sentimental moment. Scene after scene leaps from the screen – his look of shame (or, rather, the shame of being ashamed) when his mother goes to beg from the butcher, aware that she cannot understand or share his dreams and ambitions, or another scene with Nancy Price when, in his ill-fitting 'best' clothes, he leaves his unyielding mother for Tynecastle University, gawky in gait, awkward with her. Best of all is the scene of a university debate in which his argument – that coal is not a man-made invention but a natural and national resource which should be the lifeblood of British industry – is not rhetoric but the unshowy, direct eloquence of the deep, moral conviction which brings Michael's David close to Thomas Hardy's Jude. Close-ups separate men from boys in film; Michael has many in this and all are right and true, the eyes communicating his most secret thoughts, most impressive in tiny details such as when the camera moves in on him as Jenny turns to spit out that she wishes she had married wide boy Joe instead of him and his eyes momentarily flicker with sudden, perplexed pain.

Filming was on a tight schedule, with Reed getting the final shot in the can late on 2 September, the day Hitler's troops reached Warsaw and one day before war was declared. When cinemas reopened, the film was finally premièred in February 1940 to strong reviews, with Graham Greene in the *Spectator* particularly laudatory but, perhaps unsurprisingly in that climate, only moderate business.

It was barely released in America at all; another film with a mining background, John Ford's Welsh-set *How Green Was My Valley*, had recently opened and distributors did not want to compete. Interestingly, American reaction sometimes accused the film of being *anti*-union, so unsentimental is its picture of such incidents as wildcat strikes or Nancy Price's condemnation of all strikes. But Reed's work easily surpasses a tear-jerker like Ford's film. Indeed, were it not for a certain undeniable touch of the novelette (endemic in the original) about the David–Jenny plot, the film could stand beside Pabst's *Kameradschaft*.

For Michael, David in *The Stars Look Down* was the screen equivalent of Tusenbach in *Three Sisters* on stage, the performance which signalled the breakthrough from being ranked along with all the other good-looking leading men. In the same way Carol Reed was for him the cinematic counterpart of the theatre's Michel Saint-Denis. It also marked a crucial stage in his intellectual development. He had, as war approached, again been reading radical literature, tackling Lenin's writings for the first time, and during the pre-location work and filming with Reed he had been jolted and moved by his experiences in mining villages and his times down the pits and along the cramped coalface tunnels. Oliver Baldwin's influence had never left him but that period in Workington reactivated its fervour. As did the talk on set during breaks when inevitably discussion turned to background events. Michael spent a good deal of time during filming with David Markham, playing Arthur Barras in the film (he and Michael share one excellent scene, although Arthur figures much less prominently than in the novel), already a long-time socialist, and he too helped rekindle Michael's political touchpaper (David's wife, Olive, also became friends with Michael and Rachel – she knitted a shawl for Corin during *The Stars Look Down*'s shooting).

During the filming, with his return to the theatre in *Springtime for Henry* planned, Michael gave a surprisingly candid interview:

> Whatever the result of the European crisis, it will mean the disintegration of the present economic system of the West End theatre. In the general reorganisation of working conditions which seems an inevitable aftermath,

the deadlock hold of conservatism and of profit-making will crumble and a new theatre world rise up beside the old – 'When the half-gods go, the gods arrive.'

He stresses the need to commit to touring and avoid both 'snobbery' and 'apathy', going on: 'Snobbery will die with conservatism. I'm going to use a very old-fashioned word with regard to the future of the theatre – Socialism . . . I believe it is the ultimate solution to the Theatre's economic troubles. The nationalisation of the theatre will come.' It would be easy to explain this fervour by assuming that Michael had carried David Fenwick off the set with him but in fact this was not an actor infected by the persona of his current character but an expression of his strong beliefs and hopes. He had begun to attend meetings of Equity (the actors' trade union) and had on such occasions been similarly passionate about the profession's apathy (he did not exclude himself) when it came to the need to give support to such bodies as the Legion of Audiences (Sybil Thorndike was with him there) which was campaigning to get through Parliament a Bill to get government support for the theatre.

That was definitely not going to happen overnight, however. Michael was saddened not to be joining the Old Vic (in the event he and Guthrie never worked together again) and his pangs are evident in a note just after the declaration of war to Max Adrian who had joined the Old Vic company on tour, with London theatres temporarily closed, opening in Buxton with Goldsmith's *The Good Natur'd Man*: 'I think it was the best news of this dreadful week, to think that tonight, at this very moment, something is being *acted* somewhere. . . . The dream of being near a theatre again is *so* strong.'

Nine
LOVE AND WAR

The suggestion of touring *Springtime for Henry* had been a clever notion of Bill Linnit's; it did excellent business on the road and Michael and Rachel (once her nerves – not helped by Michael as director, anxious on her behalf, pushing her over much in rehearsal – had subsided) greatly enjoyed playing light comedy with such generous experts as Roger Livesey and Ursula Jeans. They all made the best of wartime restrictions, taking picnics and hot-water bottles on long, often delayed journeys on unheated trains. Edinburgh was an especially happy date. Both of Rachel's brothers had joined up, enlisting in the Navy; Robin had been badly shell-shocked on a torpedo boat, needing convalescence at Dartmouth initially, but Nicholas, who was in destroyers, was on board his ship in Leith during the tour's Edinburgh week and was able to spend a happy time with Michael and Rachel. They both were struck at a party given at the Caledonian Hotel by Nicholas's fellow officers by the almost too hectic gaiety when even temporary freedom seemed to intoxicate the men, a reminder that in wartime the possibility of imminent death heightens such brief periods of escape.

Michael kept in touch with his friends with postcards and letters. He and Max Adrian had now invented a pair of outrageous rival opera stars, a diva – Bigolo – and a tenor – Frattocini – who figure heavily in their correspondence, the defiant frivolity another counter to the uncertainty of the time. From Scotland Michael reported on Bigolo's great success entertaining the Royal Scots in barracks with *Lucia di Lammermoor* ('She's sleeping with an interned submarine-commander. They've been given the East Wing at Glamis') and on the fun of the Edinburgh time with Nick, including two nights at 'a vulgar place called the de Guise (which is really the cloakroom of Princes Street Station disguised').

He was also keeping regularly in touch with Edith, still somewhat wistful about their affair, conveying that curious sense of suspended time in wartime, writing to her also from Edinburgh while they were both on tour:

And now, you're in Manchester at the Midland I expect, where we were such a long-short time ago, perhaps even in that same dining-room. And I suppose if we were to meet suddenly, as you came round the front of the hotel or as I came up to your table, we would find again and at once that point in time when we – you and I – were last suspended and start chattering and talking, not nearly fast enough for our thoughts. . . . Oh, Edith dearest, how I wish it could be *now*, this moment. I have never wanted to talk to you more, or be with you as I do now.

Michael still sighed after classical work, although by now he was resigned to Old Vic plans failing to work out – the nearest he ever got to *Romeo and Juliet* was one performance of the Balcony scene opposite Peggy Ashcroft the following spring at a Haymarket charity matinée – but he was more than intrigued by another offer. Glyndebourne Opera planned to move in wartime from Sussex to London, first with a new production of *The Beggar's Opera* to be directed by John Gielgud at the Haymarket. He had Peggy Ashcroft to thank for his casting; she had suggested Michael, knowing what a good light baritone voice he had, when Gielgud had mentioned to her that he wanted an actor-singer for Macheath in Gay's ballad opera, although an opera singer, Audrey Mildmay (wife of Glynde-bourne's founder, John Christie), had already been cast as Polly Peachum. While *Springtime for Henry* was in Southport Christie, together with Glyndebourne's autocratic manager, Rudolf Bing, came to hear Michael sing. They were delighted with what they heard although in order to get his voice into condition for an eight-performance week they decided to send their voice coach, Jani Strasser, out on the tour to work with Michael. This became an instant long-lasting friendship; Michael thought Jani something of a Svengali, writing to Max: 'My Hungarian singing-teacher is the wildest success imaginable and has done wonders to my voice . . . he really is a darling man and we love him.' Using sometimes bizarre – but, for his pupils, somehow appropriate – metaphors ('Now you must think that you have diarrhoea'), Jani worked essentially on his pupils' breathing and to make them connect to the sense of what they were singing (he was later of great benefit to Vanessa) and by the time the *Springtime* tour ended Michael's voice felt to him more elastic and wider-ranging than it had ever been. He was childlike in his impatience to begin rehearsals for the new project, sounding exuberantly eager in a pre-rehearsal interview: 'I'm greedy . . . I want everything. I just want to do everything there is. And I never want to stop playing Shakespeare. But if someone would only write an English *Showboat* . . .'

Gielgud was notoriously unpredictable as a director. On *Richard II*, which he had played before, he had been incisive and clear about what he wanted, but on *The Beggar's Opera*, when his mind was constantly flooding with new ideas, often hitting him before he had finished articulating first thoughts, he was both confused and confusing. Because of his ceaseless changes of mind ('Michael, come in from the left. No, no, no, I meant the other left') and the cast's mixture of actors and singers, many were muddled about the intended style.

Memories were still strong of the famous Nigel Playfair revival in the 1920s at the Lyric, Hammersmith, with its scarlet-coated Macheath in the sharply defined Lovat Fraser designs. With the Motleys designing, Gielgud chose to transplant the piece into the early nineteenth century, giving the appearance of the show a Dickensian quality, with some characters looking as if they had stepped out of a Cruikshank drawing – Filch resembling the Artful Dodger, Mrs Peachum a Mrs Gamp. Some scenes were strikingly beautiful – the gaming house, mirrored in a gilt oval frame, stopped the show regularly – but there was in Gielgud's approach a fundamental clash between the Hogarthian spirit of Gay's plot and the songs and the Victorian visual effect with, crucially, little sense of the shadow of the gibbet or the whiff of the gutter which informs the whole piece.

Michael was determined to avoid any principal-boy, strutting highwayman. He concurred with Hazlitt that Macheath was a difficult character to pitch correctly, halfway between gusto and slang, port and brandy, blackguard and gentleman. He devised an exotic, slightly Asiatic, make-up using transparent gauze connected to invisible thread under his wig at the temples to pull back the corners of his eyes (his friend the artist Feliks Topolski did a series of drawings tracing the stages of the make-up), giving him a glittering gypsy aura to match the costume of striped trousers, claret vest and black coat with a diamond earring and stove-pipe hat. The production toured, to sell-out houses, briefly before London, a tricky period while Gielgud was appearing in his own production of *The Importance of Being Earnest* with Edith and unable to be with the company but sending letters trying to direct by post. Michael got one note which suggested he should try playing a scene with Macheath's doxies 'as if chasing hens round a farmyard' while Gielgud added an attempt to convey the style he was after: 'A superimposed gusto and absurdity of style slightly larger than life, which is always present on the surface of a perfectly solemn performance continuing underneath just as we try to do in *The Importance*.'

There was widespread criticism that the production was both too long and over-sanitised with Audrey Mildmay's Polly particularly far too genteel, more Quality Street than Soho. Michael had a success with his redefined Macheath; most critics agreed that he had found an ideal tension between charmer and villain, building an increasingly dangerous effrontery right from his startling first entrance, late in the first act, bursting out of a concealed landing cupboard, jumping down into Peachum's shop, pistols cocked and sailing at once into Polly's arms for 'Pretty Polly, say'. Some purists, including Ernest Newman, fretted about the mix of operatic and dramatic voices, although the consensus was that Michael sang as well as he acted: 'The darling of the ninepennies faced his first half-guinea stall in the West End as a star – light of voice and light of foot.'

Michael felt relieved more than anything, confessing that he thought he had only just 'got away' with Macheath and that he had enjoyed himself too much on tour, staying out too late and not looking after his voice, which was true. He had been high on more than pre-London adrenalin throughout that time. In fact, he was once more in love, elated and emotionally entangled yet again. Corin, in his memoir of Michael, wrote of how, when going through his father's books after his death, he came across a copy of W. H. Auden's *Selected Poems* with an inscription (dated during the tour of *The Beggar's Opera*) on the flyleaf taken from Auden's poem 'Look, Stranger, at this Island Now', dedicated to Christopher Isherwood:

> '... the word is love.
> Surely one fearless kiss would cure the million fevers ...
> For Mike
>   From Tommie
> Liverpool
> Jan. 1940'

The handwriting looks childish and 'Tommie' sounds a childish name, but it is hardly likely that a child would know Auden's or Isherwood's work, or write such an inscription. Michael, shortly after *The Beggar's Opera* opened in London, resumed his diary in April 1940 after a gap (with very few entries) of five years. An early entry for 1940 refers to a new feeling of 'freedom' in his work now that *The Beggar's Opera* has settled down but also reflects that he had been fortunate to pull it off: 'I must face it that Macheath was not properly "prepared". I never laid the foundations of the character. John muddled me. The singing of it preoccupied me at rehearsals, but in my quiet, alone moments, those fallow moments when imagination works, I was absorbed with being in love.' A slightly later entry records the wish that he had kept his diary more regularly: 'that I had written down by day, for instances those daily hours of happiness in London. And again, some account of *The Beggar's Opera* tour and T's weekly visits.'

Corin puzzled over the relationship between Michael and 'T', examining his father's diary for clues, but it is no surprise that he could not definitely establish 'T's identity. 'Tommie' was deceptive as a lead;

Michael's new lover was known only to a very few as 'Tommie' or 'Tommy'. His name was Tony Hyndman, who had been the lover for several years in the mid-1930s of the poet and critic Stephen Spender. In Spender's autobiographical *World Within World* Tony is called 'Jimmy Younger'; he is given the same name in a later book by Spender's friend Christopher Isherwood (who also had a brief 'duet', as he called it, with Tony), *Christopher and His Kind*, while to add to the confusing multiple nomenclature, T. C. Worsley's autobiographical novel *Fellow Travellers* calls him 'Harry Watson'.

Everyone who encountered Tony Hyndman agreed that he had a genuinely beguiling charm; Vivian Cox knew him from Fitzrovia pubs and recalled him well as 'a dazzler. . . . He could charm a bird off a branch.' As he was something of a self-mythist, the actual facts of his life are hard to come by and to sort out from legend but he was Welsh, born in 1911 in Cardiff, christened Thomas and known as 'Tommy' or 'Tommie' as a boy but changing to Tony when he moved to London. His early life was unhappy, blighted by a hostile relationship with a dourly unloving and overbearing father. Tommy-Tony was the third of seven children and the only boy; his father, also Thomas, had been an Army boxing champion, who went on to run first a pub (with a boxing ring upstairs) and then the Neville Hotel in Cardiff's Bridgetown. He despised his 'sensitive' son; although robust and well built, Tommy-Tony showed no interest in boxing, leaving school to take a course at secretarial college before working briefly in Cardiff as a solicitor's clerk. Even as an adolescent, influenced certainly by the practice's work in helping defend working men charged with disturbances of the peace during the General Strike, he had become absorbed by radical politics.

Arriving in London at eighteen as Tony, he joined the Guards, although he left in 1931 after just three years, the rumour – aired in T. C. Worsley's novel – being that he had been bought out by an older, infatuated male lover. Certainly Tony – like more than a few of his fellow guardsmen – had not been averse to boosting his Guards pay with some undemanding casual prostitution with 'steamers' – educated men, often writers, including Worsley, John Lehmann, William Plomer and J. R. Ackerley – drawn to virile young working-class men.

Spender and Tony became lovers in the spring of 1933. At that time Spender – of whom there were always conflicting opinions – was still to a degree in thrall to Auden and Isherwood; he followed their path to Germany in the early 1930s, and although Hamburg was always his preferred city he spent some time with them in their Berlin haunts of the Cosy Corner 'boy bar' and the world of Sally Bowles's clubs in *Goodbye to Berlin*. Back in London trying to establish his own artistic and sexual identity Spender was soon a regular guest in Bloomsbury's salons, while his relationship with Tony was his first serious love affair at home. Virginia Woolf cattily referred to Spender (she included him in the group she liked to lump together as 'Bugger Boys') as being 'Married to a Sergeant in the guards. They have set up a new quarter in Maida Vale. I propose to call them the Lilies of the Valley.'

Tony was always described and introduced as Spender's 'secretary' – actually not the usual euphemism, given the amount of typing and organisational work he did – but the inevitable cracks in an unequal relationship were evident even early in their volatile affair. Foreign holidays seemed to exacerbate the problems; a tragi–comic stay in Portugal with Isherwood and his moody lover Heinz was especially fraught. Spender, turning increasingly to heterosexual affairs, married Inez (Marie Agnes Pearn), whom he met in Oxford while she was working for the Spanish Aid Committee and just after his own brief flirtation with the Communist Party. But even those who found Spender self-absorbed had to admit that he came through for Tony to extricate him from a dangerous situation in Spain after he had gone to join the International Brigade.

Michael very likely had met Tony before 1940. His friend Dick Green – no stranger to either Fitzrovia's bars or gay London's cruising grounds – knew Tony well in the 1930s, and his letters to Michael include many references to 'T' joining Dick and Paddy Railton in Derbyshire for weekends or to Dick meeting 'T' outside the Café Royal late one night and going on a Soho bender with him. And Michael knew Spender too – they had met at poetry readings and at the salon of Moura Budberg, once H. G. Wells's mistress. The real affair, brief but extremely intense, between Michael and Tony was in the first half of 1940, with Tony joining Michael for a time at each touring date of *The Beggar's Opera*. Spender's wife Inez had 'bolted' with the writer Charles Madge; although they were no longer sexually involved, Tony and Spender still occasionally met. At twentynine, Tony was magnetically attractive with a fit, muscular body and the most engaging smile, as Isherwood described his fictional alter ego: 'His appearance was attractive: curly, red-brown hair, sparkling yellow-brown eyes, big smiling teeth.... He was full of fun and the love of argument – left-wing political or just argument for its own sake.'

Tony's appeal, from all accounts of him, obviously lay deeper than just his good looks. He seemed to be unusually at ease in his body and quite unselfconscious about his sexuality; for him sex really was as natural and as uncomplicated as breathing, which to Michael was part of his magnetism, as was his damaged, vulnerable side, always a key element in Michael's serious affairs. With *The Beggar's Opera* playing and with Rachel and the children in Dartmouth during most of that spring, he could look forward to seeing a lot of Tony, particularly at weekends, recording in his diary at the end of April his inability to sleep 'from excitement' at the very thought of going down to Dedham on Sunday to see 'T', who was working as an artist's model at the Cedric Morris School.

This was the somewhat oddball East Anglian School of Drawing, established by the artist-botanist Cedric Morris (ninth Baronet of Claremont, as he occasionally let drop) and his lifelong partner Arthur Leff-Haines, run extremely informally and housing only a handful of students at a time. Lucian Freud, a student during Tony's time, later burnt down the school by smoking in bed (the school simply moved – Freud remained a pupil – to Morris's nearby Hadleigh House). Michael's description of his Dedham weekend with Tony is one of the longest in his diary, as if he wants to recapture and bottle some of the weekend's essence, and another of those remarkable evocations of time out in wartime; apart from one mention of a soldier called Boo, also a painter, hardly anything of the war disturbs a classically timeless English country idyll. Michael had been nervous at the thought of 'all those young people' (he was thirty-one, only three years older than Tony) but relaxed immediately with Tony, even though Spender was staying at Lavenham close by and came over on the Sunday afternoon. The edginess in Michael's relationship with Spender at that time was only partly due to the question of Tony. Michael admired some of Spender's poetry but he had never wholly taken to him personally; he felt rather at one with Cyril Connolly's second wife Barbara Skelton's suggestion about him that 'even his ill-fitting clothes struck one as having been well thought-out', although he came to like Spender more and to become a genuine friend of the writer during his second long and happy marriage.

That Sunday afternoon Michael walked with Tony through the Essex fields to Morris's house – 'a wonderful afternoon' – while on the Monday they went round the local antique shops and then for a long walk along the river:

> It was an idyllic sort of walk. I can't even now remember what we said. ... I was blissfully happy and cannot and shall not try to describe the happiness beyond noting that at one moment I said to myself: tomorrow you will be in London, but if you are wise you can still be happy to think of that walk and not *sad* and greedy. The line of Amiel's – '*Qui n'accepte pas le regret n'accepte pas la vie*' – has stuck in my head. ... The knowledge that I shall certainly see T again this week makes all the difference.

At that time Michael had been reading André Gide's *Journals* and appends a note to the description of his weekend with Tony: 'Gide says he thinks he finds the "*devoirs*" of life more interesting than the *plaisirs*. He is right. But why cannot I act on this? Lack of willpower. Lack of strength.'

The force of his feelings for Tony had taken Michael by surprise. Without any diaries for the years since his engagement to Rachel (a few scattered entries – Vanessa's and Corin's births most significantly – aside) and with the solid evidence of extramarital affairs from surviving letters being only his intense involvement with Edith, it is impossible to say whether in that time the homosexual side of his nature had surfaced at all. The most that can be even guessed at, from hints in Dick Green's letters referring to their sorties into Soho together, is that there may have been the occasional one-night stand. But that there had been no passion such as he now had for Tony seems certain. He had obviously talked of Tony to Rachel, writing the day after his return from Dedham when Rachel, just back in London, had asked him about Spender, his wife and Tony: 'I always reply to her questions as fully as I can. She understands so much, but there is so much for her to understand.' Indeed there was even more than his involvement with Tony for Rachel to understand, including his increasing financial recklessness ('I have an extravagant, incomprehensible attitude to money – après moi le deluge – which just now particularly alarms her'), the extent of which he sometimes concealed.

For the first time since he had married Rachel – and those five years had given them both boundless happiness – Michael was having seriously to confront his bisexuality, not too familiar a topic in 1940. Even today, with the advance in the studies of sex and gender, it remains a complex battleground of a subject. It also remains a surprisingly undeveloped field despite exploratory writing from a range of theorists and psychologists from Freud to Foucault, and divisively split in arguments over gender politics and modern epistemological categories of sexuality.

Some argue that there is actually no such thing as the bisexual, the reasoning based on the theory that no one person can, as it were, 'dance at two different weddings at the same time', suggesting that bisexuality is a kind of index of a person's ambiguous sexual nature rather than a thing in itself, that basically so-called bisexuals are really homosexuals with an occasional heterosexual experience. Others – extending radically from Freud – would propose that *all* human beings, not homosexuals alone, have had their polymorphous nature tamed – or, as some would put it, repressed – by rigid socio-cultural 'norms'. The very issue, suggestive as it is of a third sexual identity to add to 'gay' or 'straight', seems to alarm – perhaps in some measure because bisexuality airs and makes explicit that which the majority only dream or fantasise about – and confuse. Not least because fundamentally bisexuality is a state of mind rather than a sexual practice.

There were times when Michael wanted nothing more than to be with Rachel emotionally and sexually, and with his family, in his home. But the alternate side of his nature (the old shorthand for bisexuality – AC/DC – had a point), at this period in his life unpredictable, made him at other times desire a male body, a male's company, a desire no less real and no less intense than his heterosexual side. Sex – the sexual act – gave Michael great self-fulfilment and pleasure, but the inability (really the im-possibility) of controlling his bifurcated sexual identity increasingly was to confuse and unsettle him.

The passion for Tony at this stage was paramount and there were occa-sions that week back in London when he stayed away overnight from Clifton Hill, most likely at Tony's Battersea flat. But, by the Saturday, at home:

> Very tired and cross when we woke up, partly because R cried when we woke and we had sat till 3 or so talking things out. For 2 nights I have not been home and though I imagined that R knew where I was and accepted it, it appears that I have caused her 2 days of agony. She talked at great length. She had been to see Edith [Evans]. I felt in despair with myself and my cruelty. Told R all about Roy and his end. Tried to explain the feeling of guilt I have towards her. Always it returns to the question of split personality and I cannot feel it would be right, even if I had the will-power – which I have not – to cut off, or starve the one side of my nature. I complained, weakly, but with some sense that whereas people go to see plays like *Mourning Becomes Electra* and *Family Reunion* yet they think a person morbid who feels, as those characters feel, and as I felt last night and have obscurely felt before; that I am '... the consciousness of my unhappy family. Its bird sent flying through the purgatorial flame'.

This 'obscure' feeling of the need somehow to expiate for sin and for the sins of a father who did not want him and whom he never was allowed properly to know had increased with Daisy's drinking and her often malevolent displays, gin-fuelled, of a distressing jealousy of Michael's success and film stardom. It made indeed for an 'unhappy family', although since the spring of 1940 Andy had taken Daisy away from London and the raids to a farm near Great Missenden where she was usually more in control. Michael's half-sister Peggy – now married to a doctor and with a young son – often spent weekends there and Michael dutifully visited too. Interestingly, whereas the adolescent Michael had often mocked Andy in his diary, now he refers to him as 'an impressive character'.

His own family he could delight in, writing that same summer of the joys of watching Corin in his pram in Clifton Hill's garden: 'It is pleasant to watch him living a life of pure sensation: the noise of the birds, the leaves of the pear tree, the colour of the sky, the friendly loving sounds we make at him.' And he and Rachel were usually as bonded as ever during that uncertain time, happily taking refuge in quiet domesticity against the background of 'horrible war news' with Churchill predicting German air-raids before the summer's end. An evening in mid-May was typical: 'R. calls for me after dining at Orbach's. Home by tube. Lovely night. Cider. We talk for about two hours and I read her my Liverpool journal.' Clifton Hill for that suspended summer before the Nazi bombardments began to hit London and while waiting for news of Michael's call-up was a happy house (Vanessa, although only just over three at that time, retained vivid memories of the big, light house, the top-floor nursery and the downstairs rooms often filled with friends). Socialising was more informal with wartime restrictions, but there were many after-theatre suppers or Sunday lunches (often these days round the kitchen table) with regular friends such as the Haggards, Benn Levy and Constance Cummings or the actor Michael Gough and his wife Diana. And yet, for part of that time the dutiful son, adoring husband and doting father was also still involved in his affair with Tony. On Tony's side there was no intention of breaking up a marriage and it is also possible that Tony, who had not always been faithful to Spender, was not exclusively Michael's to love. Certainly, for a time, it was love, although – not unusually – one which Michael came to attempt to anatomise, again turning, as if a solution might lie therein, to Gide's *Journals* and the description of a man in Michael's position contrasting the abandon of his affair with wartime reality: 'To carry on being happy and comfortable one must in fact not know how many thousands are suffering in order to preserve one's happiness.' Rachel's 'agony' illustrated that for him only too graphically. The problem with loving two different people – people of different sensibilities, loved in different ways – is, as his son wrote later that 'He cannot be in two places at once'.

There are very few entries for May when the Tony affair was at its height. The main entry for that month is to record briefly a major shock, Max Adrian's imprisonment for 'cottaging' in the gents' lavatories at Victoria Station. Max had confided in Michael previously that his case would come up on the 30th and an anxious Michael waited all morning until a lunchtime telephone call: 'He had been given three months. A savage and useless, wicked sentence.' Michael understood the emotion of shame – he portrayed it better than any other actor of his time – and he knew how deeply ashamed Max would be, of letting people down and of hurting his elderly mother. He contacted Max's long-time partner, the director Laurier Lister, at once 'to see what can be done to reduce the sentence' (which was unusually harsh even for the time) although nothing was possible. Michael visited him several times in jail – Max survived the experience with courage and even wit – although he still felt unhappy that he had not been able to help more.

The case took his mind off the anxieties involved with a new play which had presented itself with unusual speed at a time when he was afraid he might have to film *Rob Roy*, a scheduled picture which he dreaded (in the event the plans were shelved). Michael normally avoided taking on a part without allowing time to let it 'lie fallow' in his mind, slowly charging his mental batteries, but on this occasion the play at once seized his imagination. *Thunder Rock* by Robert Ardrey had had a New York production by the Group Theater whose work Michael followed so keenly in *Theater Arts*. That it had failed so disastrously – it ran for one week, a rare Elia Kazan flop – Michael put down, partly correctly, to a poor production but the play also must have seemed oddly uncomfortable for Broadway audiences in then neutral America, part of its 'message' being a rallying call to fight oppression and avoid isolationism.

The play came to Michael from Norman Marshall, an enterprising director who had spent time in Moscow working with Stanislavsky and Meyerhold before going to London's left-wing Unity Theatre, directing the strike-set Clifford Odets play *Waiting for Lefty*, a big former Group Theater success. The central role of Charleson in *Thunder Rock* – a once crusading journalist, a John Reed-like figure who has retreated from the world, baffled by man's inability to learn from history – struck Michael as one of the most challenging he had been offered.

Marshall had helped form a new London theatre group, Neighbourhood Theatre, housed in the old London Academy of Music building in Harrington Road opposite South Kensington Tube station. Seating about 250, it had a glass ceiling – perilous at that time when German air raids finally began – and the theatre, it was announced, would be 'a theatre with a policy' and 'an international repertory' intent on building up a system of work with the same basic personnel, its method 'that of Stanislavsky adapted to our particular material and conditions', a bold if short-lived addition to the tiny handful of off-West End theatres such as the Torch in Knightsbridge or the Gate near Charing Cross (later blitzed) trying to keep some initiative alive in a restricted wartime theatre, with many West End theatres still closed. A paper shortage meant that newspapers did not print theatre listings then, and the Neighbourhood had no budget for leaflets; each member of the cast and crew agreed to write a hundred letters and telephone everyone they knew, while Michael did as many press interviews as possible to plug the play in advance: 'It is a good, strong play; I intend to stay in London and act until I am called up.' All the extra activity, together with a short preparation time and little opportunity to worry, contributed to the concentrated, absorbing intensity of Michael's Charleson. He and the play captured London's attention instantaneously and it became a complete sell-out at the Neighbourhood. The play had found its moment.

The title comes from the Thunder Rock lighthouse on Lake Michigan to which, as keeper, Charleson has withdrawn from the world; the action takes place in the circular limestoned living area below the light chamber, with a staircase up to it and, prominent on the wall, a memorial plaque to the memory of the *Land o' Lakes*, a ship which sank near by in 1849 with all on board drowned. The first scene is a long dialogue full of tense dialectic between Charleson and his friend Streeter, a hard-boiled airman who is making his own stand against oppression by enlisting on the Chinese side in the Sino-Japanese war, with Streeter urging Charleson to abandon his isolated retreat. Then, in a terrific *coup de théâtre*, Charleson's imagination brings to life the shipwrecked 'Forty-niners', reflections of his defeatism it seems, moving and talking with him with only their Captain, Joshua, aware that they are dead. It is Joshua who challenges Charleson to let them live as they were in actuality with their own tragedies and fears from their own time. From the courage they show, Charleson finds his faith in the knowledge of the limitations of his own finite mind. The figments of his imagination – wrongly described often as ghosts, just as, mistakenly, the play is compared with Sutton Vane's spectral *Outward Bound* – then disappear, replaced by one genuine ghost, that of Streeter, who has been killed in China, and who sees his friend reactivated and ready to re-enter the world. Baldly described, the play sounds portentously allegorical and it has to be acknowledged that a large part of its success was due to its timing at such a crucial stage of the war with America still outside the conflict, but its elements of Pirandello – the appearance of the group of Forty-niners is as eerie as that of his Six Characters – and the unfailing theatrical device, which J. B. Priestley used so effectively in *Dangerous Corner*, of replaying a scene from another perspective, give it a potent theatrical charge in its best central section.

Marshall had managed to cast the play to the hilt, with the formidable Frederick Valk immeasurably moving as the Viennese Dr Kurtz escaping with his family from prejudice and fear of his medical experiments, and giving a first major London chance to Bernard Miles (he had worked as an Embassy Theatre stage manager with Michael before) as a North Country English Jew dying of consumption. All the passengers are fleeing poverty, despair or prejudice, but the play rests on Charleson, who has only one very short section off stage throughout.

Audiences were profoundly touched by the play's grave depiction of the Forty-niners' dignity in seeking a new life in America and by Charleson's growing appreciation of human heroism and suffering. The play seemed something of a crystallisation of the national consciousness of the time, although written by an American. Critics had high praise for the palpable truth and the questing quality of his tracing of the intellectual conflict of a character at war with himself in Michael's performance of Charleson. He paced the evening cunningly, emerging slowly from a kind of despairing cynicism as he begins to comprehend that the reality of the unhappy drowned ones is as intolerable as that of the world from which he has withdrawn to the conviction, persuaded by seeing modern events through the perspective of history, that he can now once again take up the life of committed action which he renounced.

On paper it can seem a prosy, somewhat stiffly 'noble' role, but Michael, because of his basic sheer belief in the play (like Roy with Captain Starlight), took it by the throat and made Charleson the most memorable figure of wartime drama on the London stage. One critic even compared his Charleson with a Shakespearean hero: 'Charleson at the end emerges with a new vision from his dive into a hopeful past – he is like a young Lear, strong and unfettered who will do such things, what they are yet he knows not but they shall strike terror from the earth.'

Duff Cooper, recently moved to the Ministry of Information, was among those overwhelmed by the play and he was determined to help it find a wider public. Michael was summoned to the Treasury where he was grilled politely by officials deputed to work out a way of government subsidy to the production who slipped in as they agreed the figures: 'Mind you, if this comes up in the House, we should simply deny it' (the play recouped quickly and the Treasury was recompensed – with profits).

Most theatres were now reopened although *Thunder Rock* did not finally secure the Haymarket as Michael would have wished; like many actors, for him its auditorium and unique backstage atmosphere made it his London favourite. With Binkie Beaumont also involved in the transfer it instead reopened with the same cast at the epicentre of the H. M. Tennent empire, the Globe on Shaftesbury Avenue. The notices for the West End version – even if the *Evening Standard* gave more space to reviewing the audience (Somerset Maugham, and Lady Diana Cooper 'in black lace and red hat', included) than to the play – were again superb, hailing it as the best new play in London. George Orwell reviewed it for *Time and Tide*, insisting, 'This play ought not to be missed, especially in such a time of drought.' Michael had made a fervent first-night curtain speech, under-lining the play's message of encouragement and rebutting the description of its American origin as a strange irony, preferring to call it 'a blessed promise'. It was a difficult run, although houses were packed, with the Blitz now in full force. Binkie Beaumont's secretary, Kitty Black, would often come into her own on raid nights. If there had been an air raid warning but the all clear had not sounded by the curtain call, the audience would be invited to stay in the auditorium until the all clear and the cast, with any 'pros' in the audience, would stage an impromptu cabaret. Kitty

Black was an excellent pianist, often playing off-stage piano for Tennent productions, and she was kept busy: 'Michael would invite me to play to accompany him as he sang pop songs and ballads. Once Peter Ustinov was persuaded to come up and join in – he imitated all the noises from a radio if you twisted the dial across the air waves, static, and French and German and incomprehensible snatches.'

Daisy, down in Great Missenden, was as frightened of Michael performing in such conditions as she was about his possible call-up, constantly sending him cautionary notes and echoing Roy at times: 'Keep your wagon hitched to the star, Captain Starlight!'

Professionally, after his film successes, *Thunder Rock* consolidated his public profile. *Picture Post* gave him a lavish spread and their cover during the run, complete with a *Hello!* magazine-style series of 'at home' photographs – elegant drawing room with elaborately draped curtains and rococo mirrors, Michael in the garden with Vanessa – juxtaposed with a defiantly 'unstarry' quote, sounding initially something of a Roy note:

> I agree with Charles Laughton that actors' names should not be inscribed in gold on a roll of fame, but scrawled on the walls of all the public places in the world. My sympathies are with the popular as well as with the more aristocratic manifestations of art. I am glad you think I am an actor by the people's choice. That is what I want to be.

By the time *Thunder Rock* had moved to the Globe, the high point of his affair with Tony had passed. The first entry in his diary for June (on the 25th), after Tony had had lunch with him, is a long analysis of the state of play:

> Yesterday T. came to lunch. Have seen very little of him lately. The great, deep feeling of love I had is no longer there. I feel only friendly. .... He is a lonely, muddled creature, wanting always to turn back the clock. He spoke yesterday of wishing he had never left London which meant that he would now be in the Army and not have to think for himself. The real trouble also is that he cannot bring himself to work ... he talked freely about himself and said there were only 2 people he could talk to, me and S. but that S. had forbidden him to talk of themselves for some time. S. incidentally is the most astonishing mixture of genius and silliness. I admire him for his work. But dear, dear T. How can one expect him to be otherwise than he is? T's character is largely conditioned by his years with S. I have seen S. being self-indulgent with the boys he is fond of and it is sickening.

The affair had been short, but it was much more for Michael than just a fling, with a lot of tenderness as well as desire. He and Tony Hyndman continued to meet at varying degrees of frequency for years and Michael often bailed Tony out emotionally and financially. Tony seems to have been genuinely fond of Michael, certainly seeing him as much more than another useful 'steamer'. It did not bother Michael that Tony was not especially interested in the theatre; their discussions were usually political or literary (Tony's knowledge of modern poetry was impressive). But certainly by midsummer the fever of the relationship had cooled. Through all the confusions and in Michael's diary-entries of this period, the depth of his and Rachel's understanding of and love for each other shines clearly. His 'despair' at the 'agony' he sometimes caused her was real, and although the love for Tony was for its duration also true (probably the more intensely felt because transitory) his mind had never been engaged or inspired to the same degree as in his relationship with Edith. Fundamentally he still remained then yoked physically and spiritually to Rachel, as lover and as husband, as he had ever been.

Michael's immediate worries were about his family. The German raids which began that summer were the most concentrated yet and Rachel, the nanny Nurse Dulcie and the children were spending increasing amounts of time in the shored-up Clifton Hill basement listening to the sinister whines of the falling bombs before the explosions. Michael was at the theatre at night except for Sundays but he was now determined to try to get the children away from London, although Dartmouth was no longer safe. At first he thought he might succeed in finding safety for Rachel as well. He was approached by the film director Michael Powell to appear in a government-backed film about the Canadian war effort, *49th Parallel*, to be filmed partly in Canada, with Charles Boyer, Elisabeth Bergner and Leslie Howard, all the stars to be paid a flat £2000 fee. Michael was negotiating to see if it might be possible that out of his fee could be taken the cost of passage to Canada for Rachel and the children, too, so that they could stay on while he returned after filming, either in Canada or in the USA. The great Broadway acting couple Alfred Lunt and Lynn Fontanne had offered, through Ruth Gordon, to have Vanessa and Corin, although they had no children of their own, or they could have gone to Rachel's Aunt Nora, 'the rich relation', married to the millionaire art collector Paul Mellon. In the event he could not persuade Ted Black to start filming his next scheduled film, *Kipps*, slightly later ('Damn those bloody bastards. Always the same') and Eric Portman went into *49th Parallel* in his place.

Providentially, as *Thunder Rock* was reopening at the Globe, Lucy Kempson – 'Cousin Lucy' to the family – came to their aid. Lucy's mother had been Louisa Wedgwood (of the pottery family) who had married Rachel's great-uncle Alfred Kempson; he died young, leaving Louisa with four young children. The highly intelligent Lucy had gone to Oxford (she made a lifelong friend there of Dorothy L. Sayers) and became Warden of Bedford College at London University. For years her home away from London had been Birchyfield, a handsome house in Bromyard in Herefordshire which had originally belonged to Rachel's grandfather but Lucy, her brother John and widowed sister Hester had all moved to a newly built house nearby, called Whitegate. Lucy had lived on there after the deaths of John and Hester, and in her retirement.

Most people who knew it described it as, from the exterior, one of the most hideous houses imaginable, 'like a big square uncompromising box with a pitched roof'. However, halfway between Hereford and Worcester and built on a slope, Whitegate had the most spectacular views of the Malvern Hills and a splendid garden, well stocked with treats such as asparagus beds as well as herbaceous borders, lovingly tended by William Hodges who doubled as Lucy's chauffeur and gardener (she also kept a uniformed maid and two other staff). Inside, the house was faded and often chilly in winter, but it was friendly, full of Wedgwood and books and Victorian furniture, not to mention, for the time, ample food with luxuries rare in London such as eggs and cream.

Lucy, small and round with thick pebble glasses and a large mole, was much loved in Bromyard's small community. Her mind was always busy and enquiring – she was splendid company for children, genuinely interested in them – and she came to love Rachel and worship Michael, while they in return remained devoted to her. Bromyard became in effect the children's home for the next three years while Michael and Rachel increasingly looked upon it as a haven from London.

Michael saw Rachel, Vanessa, Corin and Dulcie off from Paddington, privately terrified among the crowds that there might be an air raid warning and that people could panic under the vast glass station roof. For the next two months he was on his own, sometimes staying at the Carlton Hotel in the Haymarket, which often 'rocked like a pagoda' during raids before eventually, when *Kipps* was in the studios, taking a tiny service flat in Grosvenor Square in the same building as Carol Reed. Clifton Hill for the immediate future was to be lived in and looked after by a new addition to the Redgrave household, Edith Hargreaves, who became Michael's first secretary. Incurably and practically undiscriminatingly stage-struck, she had worked in a bank before coming into an inheritance (her other passion was cricket or, more accurately, cricketers – notably Denis Compton). She had helped Edith Evans with secretarial duties and was now ecstatically happy to be working for the British male actor she admired above all others and whom she transparently and innocently adored.

On evenings when alone after *Kipps* filming, Michael often sat reading or listening to his treasured *Der Rosenkavalier* recordings while bombs fell over central London. Or he would spend the evening with Reed, talking till late about – inevitably – movies, although Michael noticed that Reed was increasingly mentioning Diana Wynyard, co-starring in *Kipps*. Michael again felt that sense of time divorced from reality of wartime; he sometimes took pills to guarantee some sleep during the raids with early calls for make-up, so that he said afterwards that his own main memory of the Blitz was 'largely of a fictitious Folkestone in Edwardian dress' such is also the actor's tunnel vision. During one of those whisky-and-soda evenings in Grosvenor Square, Reed kept returning to the subject of Diana Wynyard, maintaining that she had yet to come to terms with her beauty, that she needed 'a man to wake her up to the realisation of her glorious self' and strongly urging Michael ('Go on, Mike') that he should be the one to do so. It was the next day that Diana informed Michael during an on-set wait that she and Reed had been married a few days previously. Michael's private theory was that Reed had already fallen in love with Penelope ('Pempe') Dudley-Ward but could not think of how to extricate himself from Diana and that he wanted Diana 'looked after' while he occupied himself with Pempe (who later became the second Mrs Reed). All very odd, but although – contrary to a great deal of con-temporary whispers – Michael never did have an affair with Diana, *Kipps* marked the start of one of the strongest *amitiés amoureuses* in his life. They loved working with each other and Diana, who tended to make rotten choices of men as husbands and lovers, treasured Michael as one male friend she could rely on without sexual complications. Rachel was extremely fond of her too.

Perhaps because of tensions in her relationship with Reed, Diana is not at her best in *Kipps*; in fact, the screen never really captured her quality and she was very self-conscious too of the cast in her eye which on stage seemed to enhance her allure but could be exaggerated by the camera. Reed did everything to flatter her – soft focus, clever lighting and a whole wardrobe of Cecil Beaton's most gorgeous gowns enfolding her in foaming chiffon, crêpe de Chine and lace-edged parasols – while Beaton realised a chance to indulge that love of Edwardian opulence which he would take to its apogee in *My Fair Lady*. The famously waspish designer got on surprisingly well with Reed, probably because he was allowed his head.

But Beaton's contribution is one of the problems with the picture; so grateful for the care he lavished on Diana, Reed gave him such a free rein that shop girls look far too glamorous for a story rooted in H. G. Wells' affectionate but sharp-eyed observation of English class and snobbery.

Reed's film of Wells' 'story of a simple soul' catches the affection of the novel but his soft focus extends to missing crucially much of its sharp satirical thrust. Where the book has energy the movie has languor, while its stress on exteriors and costume slowly reduces it to a nostalgic evocation of a prelapsarian England, although the world of Wells's novel, that almost tribal solidarity of the lower middle classes, was altogether a much more awkward social minefield than Reed would suggest.

Kipps was in part US-financed, although made on location and at Shepherd's Bush Studios using many of the regular Gainsborough creative and technical team. The script was by *The Lady Vanishes* duo of Launder and Gilliat, a clever job of compression even if Wells devotees inevitably miss that wonderful early section of young Kipps's friendship with his chum Sid, an unlikely but totally successful blend of *David Copperfield* and the *Just William* books. The film inevitably concentrates on the triangle of Kipps and the two women in his life, his childhood sweetheart Ann and the aloof Folkestone woodcarving instructor Helen Walsingham, while some of Wells' most lively characters (including the memorably blowsy Mrs Chitterlow, wife of the rantipole actor-dramatist and Kipps's eventual saviour) disappear. Michael persuaded Carol Reed – against some opposition from Ted Black – to cast Max Adrian as the genteel toady Coote, while the filming's coincidence with the closure of many theatres meant that Reed had his pick of character actors including George Carney, a veteran of working the halls with Chaplin, as Kipps *père* and the ebullient farceur Arthur Riscoe as Chitterlow.

Eyebrows had been raised – including, briefly, his own – when Michael was cast as Wells' hero, the archetypal 'little man'; although there is actually nothing in the original to suggest he is small, many no doubt remembered George K. Arthur in a previous film version. Michael said to himself during filming, 'I grow to love the character. Am *not* Wells's Kipps. Do not know who could play it. John Mills?' Mills was fine on screen subsequently as Wells' Mr Polly, but Michael gives a quite beautifully measured performance as the hesitant shop assistant whose basic honesty is his final salvation. Physically, he uses his height to his advantage; his body seems loose-limbed, floppily awkward, especially ill at ease in his cage of smart upwardly mobile clothes, neck chafing at high collar like a baby giraffe, wrists at war with starched cuffs. Never playing for sympathy or easy pathos – compare and contrast with Tommy Steele in the later musical version, *Half a Sixpence* – but wearing his innocence like a magic cloak he becomes a comedic version of *Thunder Rock*'s Charleson. The chance of a replay in life – in Kipps's case a second chance of money – points him to the right path, so that even the potentially treacly final scene with Kipps and Ann bathing baby Arthur (Reed suggested using Corin but was vetoed by Michael and Rachel) is genuinely touching, not mawkish. Michael and Rachel had met Wells at the soirées given by his ex-mistress, the Russian-born translator Moura Budberg; he had totally approved of

Michael's approach to the part and was delighted with his performance in the completed film. But surprisingly, despite predominantly glowing reviews, *Kipps* did not perform strongly at the box office. The *New York Times*, marvelling at the remarkable sang-froid of the British, perhaps put its finger on the problem in its review: 'During the heaviest struggle in Britain's history, they have the mental tranquillity to make a gently satirical portrait of Victorian caste and snobbery. This is not a film for the present moment.'

Michael found Reed less relaxed on *Kipps* than previously, possibly because the director was also absorbed in his own complex emotional life. They had one major disagreement, over the set-up of a dinner table scene, and Michael, normally amenable to directors, on this occasion felt strongly enough about his point to stick to his guns. Previously Reed had never been averse to actors making suggestions or putting their point, but on this occasion he took umbrage, as Michael described to Max, writing from the studio – 'If I could believe that Carol, besides being a hell of a good director, were also infallible, or nearly so, I would not have stuck out so for my conviction' – and he was clearly hurt by the incident's repercussions – 'What mortified me and depressed me most was that in Ted's office he and Carol took the line that I was by nature temperamental and difficult and suffering from the usual pettiness of small artists who have got above themselves' – although he really cared about an important scene and was disappointed that Reed should want to 'pay me back' out of hurt pride. But they finished the film with no bad feeling, back on their normal terms of friendship; only bad luck and timing prevented their further collaborations, while Michael and Rachel saw a lot of the Reeds during their marriage.

The filming of *Kipps* continued until shortly before Christmas, when Michael at last was able to join the rest of the family at Bromyard where, according to Stephen Croft, then a young Westminster schoolboy billeted at Bromyard who became a great friend of the Redgrave children, his arrival was 'like that of a visiting potentate', laden with presents and a bottle of champagne.

It was a white Christmas that year, the countryside blanketed in deep snow with the only noise the rooks cawing in the trees. With a big tree in Whitegate's hall it was the idyllic family Christmas. Rachel's brother Robin, still recovering from his shell-shock, was also staying, his buoyancy slowly returning and entertaining the children, while Michael, getting a first chance to know Lucy properly, was enchanted by her (he loved the way she addressed everyone as 'ducky' – 'Rachel-ducky' and 'Michael-ducky') and the household custom of all meeting for a proper tea in Lucy's sitting room, with games of Beggar My Neighbour or Happy Families and the radio news at 6 p.m. For Michael, Bromyard became one of the enchanted places, like Mortehoe, as he wrote to Lucy after a reluctant return to London to begin shooting *Atlantic Ferry*: 'I really think it was the happiest Christmas *ever*. ... I feel I know a bit more about the nature of happiness than before, because of it. Your house has *grown* like its owner, as houses do, and I love both house and owner.'

Michael was still uncertain about any likely call-up date when work on *Atlantic Ferry* began; had he been summoned earlier, the forthcoming political furore which erupted around him might have been avoided.

Ten
POLITICS AND WAR

'When will this picture end?' Michael groaned in his diary in early March 1941. *Atlantic Ferry*, which had started shooting in January, was proving heavy going. Most of his friends were away – Dick Green in the Army, Gervase Smith with the Royal Marines in Sicily, Robin Fedden in Egypt, Max Adrian on tour, Paddy Railton in Wales invalided out of the Army, John Davenport an unlikely recruit to the RAF, and he saw less of friends nearer London such as David Loveday while bombing and the blackout continued. Dick and he still wrote often – Dick had looked after the Mill at White Roding for a time – comparing notes on their simultaneous reading of Flaubert ('what an old ocean of gloom – altogether after my own heart!' was Dick's response), with Dick, although moaning that physical training courses in the Army were like nightmares of returning to school as a grown-up, taking unexpectedly well to Army life. Max was a less faithful correspondent, Michael regularly scolding him as 'an old reprobate' or 'you wicked old bag' for not writing in reply to his letters which continued to embellish the behaviour of their imaginary toupeed tenor Frattocini and the soprano Bigolo, the latter behaving more than usually capriciously on discovering no reservation on a train: 'She turned the Lithuanian Ambassador out of his Pullman, the Ambassador's only retort being "D'Annunzio" under his breath, which caused Bigolo, by then overheated, to turn pale, while her Peke bit the stationmaster.'

Atlantic Ferry provided little diversion. The script had had possibilities; the original story, even if an unabashed reworking of Turgenev's *Fathers and Sons*, by the émigré Emeric Pressburger (soon, with Michael Powell, to form the innovative team, the Archers) was a strongly characterised tale of two nineteenth-century shipbuilding brothers in Liverpool, one wary, one visionary, their relationship complicated by their love for the same woman. Valerie Hobson and Griffith Jones joined Michael playing the idealistic Charles McIver, passionately committed to the development of steamships. The script subsequently had been reworked to emphasise the love triangle, the characters reduced to simpler outlines, and both Valerie Hobson and Jones were pallid in the film, Michael's best scenes being those with Hartley Power as the American Cunard whose fizzing energy gives the picture a welcome kick when he finally appears. Michael liked Walter Forde, the film's director who excelled at action scenes – a storm sequence with Michael on board an overcrowded immigrant sailing ship is extremely fine – but there was no sense of the committed quiet excitement of a Carol Reed and his role asked little of him except to wear his period costume with a dash. One scene only gives him a real opportunity – set in the Admiralty when he argues the case for steam to enhance 'the most wonderful age the world has ever known' – in which his fervour bursts through the screen.

His dissatisfaction at this time had a good deal to do with one particular worry, his involvement – innocent enough but fraught with confusions and misunderstandings – with a movement known as the People's Convention. It is remembered now only as a footnote to the earlier war years, but as Michael said, 'For some years to come I was haunted by the words "People's Convention".'

In the 1950s when the children were clearing out old records they came across a 78 rpm of Michael singing 'A New World Will be Born', credited on the label to 'Workers' Music Association', which when they were playing it brought Rachel to beg them to get rid of it and certainly never to play it within Michael's hearing ('He hates to think about it'). In his autobiography Michael gave most of a chapter to the episode, as if in a belated attempt at self-exculpation, although never quite explaining why the subject should have so 'haunted' him, even in his old age seemingly still dangerous and almost contaminating. Both Corin's memoir and Vanessa's *Autobiography* touch on it too and, obviously, it was a crucial episode, which at some psychic level marked Michael in a way he could never quite articulate.

It was early in 1941 as Michael was sitting in the garden of Clifton Hill that he first came across the People's Convention. It had been (unknown to him) first aired in the Communist Party's newspaper the *Daily Worker* some three months previously during the heaviest air raids, called 'The People's Convention for a People's Covenant'. Michael encountered it in his mail as what he took to be a manifesto of a kind against the war with two particular slogans which caught his notice – 'a people's war' and 'a people's peace'. They were key points in an appeal to arouse public consciousness of the need for 'a People's Convention'. Other points urged eminently rational details such as the need for deep bomb-proof shelters in working-class areas near docks etc. (it took a public outcry to allow London's Tube stations to serve as shelters) and 'defence of people's living standards'. It also urged 'friendship with the Soviet Union'.

Michael was not a pacifist. Like most people of his generation in his profession, he regretted the interruption to his career but he was expecting to be called up in the near future. Indeed, when his film agent, Bill Linnit's partner Jack Dunfee, tried hard to argue that he could easily be exempted and allowed to act as his war effort contribution (he had had all the necessary papers drawn up ready for signature) Michael refused to consider the option. Oliver Baldwin's talks of fifteen years before had not been forgotten and although Michael was not active in party politics, he thought of himself as a socialist (at that time on the *Atlantic Ferry* set during breaks he was reading Lenin's *Socialism and War*) and, like the Labour Party, had agreed that Hitler must be defeated. To him, the circular from the People's Convention seemed 'a good socialist document'. He signed it.

The first sign of any problem was when he heard a rumour that all signatories to the People's Convention would henceforward be banned from broadcasting by the BBC. This, in turn, had produced a piece in the *Daily Express*, the first mention of the affair in the press, insinuating that signatories (Michael, among others, was named) must be either pacifist or Communist or both. The *Express* piece had at least one person rushing to his support – another Redgrave unexpectedly appearing – with a letter from Roy's sister, Michael's Aunt Lena. She had married a wine merchant after giving up the stage and now, as Lena Doughty, in her sixties she lived in Folkestone ('there is no name more respected in Folkestone than that of Doughty') and was rather more radical politically than Roy, it would seem: 'You are a real Redgrave and I am proud of you. Your proper place is inside the Houses of Parliament. You belong to the advance guard. Men like you have spades in your hands.'

The BBC thought otherwise. Michael was summoned to Broadcasting House, not entirely to his surprise – he knew that the bandleader Lew Stone, also a Convention signatory, had been before him – for an interview every bit as civilised as the Treasury pondering how to deal with its unexpected role as theatrical 'Angels' on *Thunder Rock* but with a very different intent. Michael was politely told that the BBC governors had decided that the People's Convention was 'not in the national interest' and that they needed to know his position. Which, equally politely, he answered by pointing out that censorship was not, so far as he understood, part of the BBC's charter. His assumption that the Corporation would not wish to employ him in the future was, he was told, correct. His next question – how did that affect his contract to sing in a BBC concert broadcast from the Scala Theatre five days later? – fazed his interviewers, unaware that he had a pre-existing contract, before the reassurance: '*That* will be *quite* all right, Mr Redgrave.' He talked with the composer Berkeley Fase, also a People's Convention supporter and similarly indignant at the BBC ban, but a few days later, when lunching with his old BBC employer from Cambridge days, Lionel Fielden, Michael was disturbed by Fielden's suspicions of the People's Convention particularly because of the involvement of D. N. Pritt, an eminent lawyer who was a sponsor of the People's Convention and a known fellow traveller with the Communist Party, a man Fielden both disliked and distrusted.

Publicly, the fuss over Michael's involvement with the People's Convention blew up only after his Scala broadcast (his radio 'farewell!' as he put it) when the left-wing *News Chronicle* gave the story of Michael's BBC ban huge front-page coverage, even taking precedence over Moscow's bellicose warnings to Bulgaria. When he had a day off from filming, his telephone rang non-stop, with Bea Lehmann and Benn Levy particularly vocal in support. The Worker's Music Association, for whom he had recorded 'A New World Will Be Born', organised a protest meeting – Rachel, ever loyal, attended in his absence at the studios. The following day the story was on the front pages of most newspapers, with photographs of Rachel at the WMA meeting and coverage of the Council for Civil Liberties' plans also to hold a protest meeting.

Michael's film bosses, according to Jack Dunfee, were furious. Ted Black and Maurice Ostrer, immensely powerful in the industry and also producers of *Atlantic Ferry*, were worried too, anxious that their film's reception could be affected by any association with a political renegade. He was 'invited' to meet them to discuss the issue at Claridge's Hotel but found present only another producer, Marcel Hellman, in charge of Michael's next scheduled film, *Jeannie*, who clearly had his anxieties about that project and who kept pressing that Michael was being 'used' by the People's Convention. Quixotically perhaps, but in total earnest, Michael offered Hellman back the *Jeannie* contract, in response to which the flustered producer temporised, saying only 'he would hate to have to think about such a thing'.

Slowly the atmosphere around Michael was becoming poisoned. At the studio on *Atlantic Ferry* there was a good deal of whispering and he found, too, that someone had scrawled in chalk 'Make Peace' between his two names on the back of his canvas studio chair ('I laugh this off, but do not sit in the chair. Presently it is wiped off'). One evening he had a drink with Carol Reed, explaining his regret should the publicity harm *Kipps* (Reed was understanding), adding to Reed that he felt he seemed to be committing 'a sort of professional suicide'.

He had written to both the *News Chronicle* and the *Star* attempting to clarify the matter, explaining that he was neither pacifist nor Communist, but he was beginning to realise that mud indeed does stick. At another meeting with Marcel Hellman he also met a movie publicist, Joseph Pole, who had worked for the Labour Party in the past and who told Michael that he was sure that the People's Convention was a Communist Party affair, explaining that the Party had a way of manipulating other organisations and cynically dropping them once their purpose had been served. Others he saw during this period included the writer Geoffrey Parsons, a Communist Party member, who tried to reassure him and persuade him to keep loyal although, when Michael raised the question of the possibility of the Party simply using the People's Convention, Parsons countered, as Michael remembered, ' "So what? Aren't the Government using the Labour leaders and won't they drop them when it suits them?" These sorts of arguments and parallels exhaust me and I begin to distrust them.' He was right to do so. The Communist Party, acting on direct orders from Moscow following the Molotov–Ribbentrop pact, had reversed tactics in a complete volte-face to try to demonstrate that Germany was not so much the enemy as Britain and France combined, who had been the initial aggressors in declaring an imperialist war (even some Party members could not accommodate to this – Harry Pollitt, the British Communist Party's general secretary, resigned over the issue). What Michael had read in his circular and the Communist Party's statement of March 1941 when the affair was at its height – 'The People's Convention is not a "stop the war" movement. It is irreconcilably opposed to Fascism' – was part of a smokescreen clouding the real position. Until the USSR was invaded by German troops in June the Communist Party, controlled by Moscow, had in fact been totally opposed to siding with an anti-Fascist war.

It is hardly surprising that Michael was confused and nobody from the People's Convention or the Communist Party could allay his anxieties entirely. They certainly tried. Out of the blue he was visited by the great scientist J. B. S. Haldane (husband of Chattie, his Cambridge hostess), also a supporter of the People's Convention and a Board member of the *Daily Worker* who, like Parsons, tried to reassure him that his allegiance to the Convention was 'a right and true move'. Then, undoubtedly in a collusive move to keep Michael's valuable name on board, he was invited to lunch by the curiously sinister figure of D. N. Pritt at his house near Reading, a near surreal meeting like something out of John le Carré, with Michael met by a glossy chauffeured car, given a delicious lunch in an elegant dining room decorated with Imperial-pottery porcelain from the tsarist era, followed by a walk in the stream-bordered garden. Silver-tongued and eloquently persuasive – he was a successful KC – Pritt was a long-standing supporter of the Communist Party and had reported the 1930s Moscow trials for the *New Statesman* as one of Stalin's most devout apologists, praising the trials as portents of a new era of social justice. His charming reassurances to Michael flattered him by association with other Convention signatories such as the Dean of Canterbury, Dr Hewlett-

Johnson (later known as the 'Red Dean') – he too had had 'doubts', Michael was assured, but remained 'staunch'. The whole experience, including Pritt's jocular references to the possibilities of Michael being awarded the Order of Lenin or made an Artist of the Republic, all reinforced what seemed to Michael 'a sort of daydream', enough to make him have to remind himself that he was in England, not Russia.

That same evening, still 'not much clearer than when I started', he and Rachel attended the People's Convention dance at the Royal Hotel at which he sang and presented prizes to warm applause. The next day – 'O, a sad day!' – back at the Royal for the Convention itself, he had a long, disappointing and dismaying time while endless grievances were aired with 'snarling references' to his explanatory newspaper letters (his recording of 'A New World' often being played in the background), which added to his growing conviction that it was 'a false set-up'. And yet, when collection time came round he signed a cheque for 15 guineas.

That, of course, he found splashed over the *Daily Mail* front page the following morning and he could not begin to explain why he had made his donation when he met Marcel Hellman and *Jeannie*'s director, Harold French, for lunch. The threats to his career seemed even stronger; Hellman told him that Maurice Ostrer had tried to frighten him off using Michael on *Jeannie*. The one bright spot of that day was the Conway Hall meeting organised by the Council of Civil Liberties in protest against the BBC's ban, with eloquent speeches from E. M. Forster, stating he would break his contract for BBC broadcasts unless the ban was lifted, the Dean of Westminster, Michael's friend Beatrix Lehmann and Michael himself. He at least got a laugh with his joke about being able to find only one precedent for the politically conscious actor, Lincoln's assassin John Wilkes Booth, and he was heartened by the presence in support of Edith Evans, Roger Livesey and Ursula Jeans, Benn Levy and Constance Cummings all alongside Rachel.

The next day, with *Atlantic Ferry* at last wrapped, Michael could get away from London back to the haven of Bromyard. With Rachel booked for a film test he for once was left in sole charge of the children – rather bewildering him, with domestic matters such as potty routine to grasp – with Vanessa singing hymns at great length and Corin, who had not seen Michael for some months, quite unable to comprehend what he was doing there. That evening, after a long solo walk, he went with Cousin Lucy to the local tin-roofed cinema to see a film with his favourite Spencer Tracy, then came home, sat down and wrote several letters, one of which was to D. N. Pritt withdrawing his name from the list of People's Convention supporters.

Undoubtedly the groundswell of popular opinion, including a letter signed by forty Labour MPs organised by Harold Laski, and a Churchill speech, in addition to other protest meetings such as the Council of Civil Liberties organised, helped influence the BBC soon to drop the ban. But it seems far more likely that it was the government, understandably of the opinion that the BBC could hardly retain its reputation for independence and objectivity, especially during a war against countries using insidious propaganda weapons, with such a ban in force, which gave the final push to the BBC to lift it.

For a while the sniggers of 'Red Redgrave' were heard around the film studios and backstage, but inevitably the whole of *l'affaire* People's Convention eventually died down. Michael, had he really been convinced that its motives were, as he had – naïvely, perhaps, but in good faith – originally believed, those of 'a good socialist document', would have undoubtedly risked his career by giving Hellman back the *Jeannie* contract had he wanted it. His film career would have suffered although he would have been able to work on in the theatre. As it was, his film career suffered no lasting damage. But at some deep level Michael had damaged himself, in his own eyes at least, and the effects were enduring. The majority of people would have been embarrassed, maybe, but able to laugh off such an episode or put it behind them. For Michael that old feeling of shame was involved – shame that he might have risked the security of his wife and children, shame that he might have let people like Oliver Baldwin down and shame that he had been, or seemed to have been, weak and indecisive. Also, he remained guilty in his own eyes of his poor judgement. He must have berated himself mentally to receive a letter such as Paddy Railton wrote to him, referring to 'the atrocious behaviour of the BBC' before turning to the Convention, explaining he had not written before, not wishing to seem interfering: 'Well, Mike, you rather rouse my conscience. As soon as I saw your name associated with that racket, my first impulse was to write you imploring you to dissociate yourself from it publicly and at once.' If Paddy, miles away from the centre of things in a hospital bed, could see through to the phoney nature of the Convention, why had he been so blinkered? Michael never voted anything other than Labour in any election and he continued to involve himself in Equity affairs and theatre campaigns, and in the 1960s appeared in CND concerts. But – even when pressed in the most flattering terms – he never again took any significant part in active politics.

With no news of his call-up he had to go straight into *Jeannie*, an arch Cinderella story comedy in which he co-starred with Barbara Mullen, dark-haired and winsome long before her days as A. J. Cronin's Janet of TV's *Dr Finlay's Casebook*. The funniest thing in the film is the over-the-top first-reel turn by Wilfred Lawson; playing Jeannie's Bible-thumping

Calvinist father, he delivers broadsides against his neighbour's new English bride – 'a besom, a Jezebel, an English hussy' – at full roar in one of the worst Scottish accents to hit the screen until Mel Gibson in *Braveheart*. The rest of the picture is a tame affair, with Jeannie blowing her small inheritance on a trip to Vienna, her dream since first hearing 'The Blue Danube', meeting on the way Stanley Smith (Michael) also en route to Vienna to market his new invention, a washing machine. In the cardboard studio Vienna, Jeannie falls for an impecunious count-cum-gigolo while Stanley is briefly beguiled by Kay Hammond, voice gurgling in her plummily languorous drawl, as a mannequin always on the scrounge for a free meal ('Modelling gives me the most enormous appetite'). Long before the end the film has run out of steam, with an almost perfunctory coda when the central duo meet again at the Ideal Home Exhibition. Harold French, successful in the theatre with Terence Rattigan's early comedies, had no feel for the rhythm of film; altogether *Jeannie* was nobody's finest hour.

His call-up papers came through in the summer during *Jeannie's* final sequences. The Mill had been let – a continuing saga of flooding, bad tenants and drains – while Michael had taken a short lease on a house owned by film producer Gabriel Pascal near the *Jeannie* studios at Denham, giving him easier access to Bromyard. During one break, with the news that Paddy Railton's TB had worsened, Michael travelled to the sanatorium in Ruthin, North Wales, to visit him. Stopping overnight in Manchester at the Midland Hotel, he bumped into Noël Coward – Michael had recently joined the Committee of the Actors' Orphanage, of which Coward was president, but they had met only once – in Manchester for the pre-London try-out of his *Blithe Spirit*. Michael watched it with Coward from the author's box and, although Michael kept no diary for this period, it seems clear that it was then that his affair with Coward began.

Of all Michael's lovers, Coward seems the least likely, certainly a major contrast to Tony Hyndman. He was eight years older than Michael and easily the most successful English theatrical figure of the time. A glamorous figure, certainly, but while it is easy to understand the appeal Michael must have had for Coward – tall, virile, charming, very much the type of previous Coward lovers such as the Duke of Kent or the American Jack Wilson, now solely a business associate – the reverse attraction is harder to pinpoint, not least because of their opposite political and theatrical viewpoints.

Michael was no doubt flattered to be pursued by Coward, who oozed success and confidence – Michael always envied that – and who could be both funny (often a potent aphrodisiac) and kind. Wiseacres muttered 'father figure' and of course it is true that Michael was capable, by his own admission, of regarding even younger men than himself as father substitutes, while some of Coward's lovers, Jack Wilson ('Dabs') and, later, Graham Payn ('Little Lad'), were jokily treated as 'sons' of his close-knit theatrical 'family'. Coward had had quite a few flings since the break-up with Wilson, the actor Alan Webb included, and for a time in the summer of 1941 and briefly again later he and Michael enjoyed a dizzy, intoxicating affair. Coward's pet name for Michael for the rest of his life was 'China', after *The Country Wife*'s euphemism for Mr Horner's sexual equipment. When he heard that Michael was planning to join the Royal Navy – Coward always had a thing about sailors – he insisted that his friend Louis Mountbatten would see what he could do for him. For a while it looked as if 'Dickie' Mountbatten might manage to have Michael assigned to his new command, the aircraft carrier HMS *Illustrious*, although in the event when Michael did join her Mountbatten had been promoted to Joint Operations Commander-in-Chief and was no longer with the ship.

The affair with Coward was so consuming at that time that Michael even spent the last night before he left to report for his first day in the Navy with Coward at the Savoy. Years later, with Coward back at the Savoy from his Swiss tax exile, Rachel joined him for a late supper in his suite: 'Noël said that he hadn't wished to hurt me, and that it was no use having regrets about what you have done, but he had found Michael so irresistibly charming. I couldn't but agree with him.'

For two months at Plymouth Michael got on with his basic training, mainly at the training barracks of HMS *Raleigh* at Torpoint as an ordinary seaman, and then on the tougher HMS *Drake* at Devonport. The instincts which in the theatre always led him to ensemble-based work helped him adapt and he found the friendliness 'indescribable' (he was, probably inevitably, nicknamed 'Lofty'), guided particularly by an older hand, a Jewish ex-soldier, ex-cab driver called 'Needle' who showed him most of the ropes and alerted him to a few basic dodges. Some shipmates volunteered to help him, one offering to do his 'dhobying' for him, but in fact he enjoyed doing it, adapting to Navy life as well as Dick Green had got on in the Army. He wrote virtually every day to Rachel, missing her and finding it frustrating to know that she was sometimes very close at Dartmouth but that they could not meet until he got leave. Inevitably, he was approached by the Entertainment Officer who gratefully left him to organise a ship's concert – he got Coward to send him material, including a hot-off-the-piano 'Could You Please Oblige Us with a Bren Gun?', which he had to learn in the lavatory after lights out.

Coward combined business with pleasure by visiting Plymouth to research his planned film based on the story of Mountbatten's ship, the

Kelly, spending time with Michael whenever he could slip away. Bert Lister, Coward's valet at the time, remembered Coward's anticipation, as Friday afternoons ended, of being able to leave for Plymouth and Michael, although by September the sailors earmarked for the *Illustrious* were ready to be sent to join her.

After extensive damage in the Mediterranean, the ship was undergoing a major refit in harbour in Norfolk, Virginia. Joining the *Illustrious* there had one major lure for Michael – the possibility en route of a first, long-awaited visit to New York. They sailed from Gourock on the SS *Pasteur*, originally built as a de luxe liner sailing between France and South America, and converted into a troopship after the fall of France. Intended for a few hundred pampered passengers it now transported several thousand troops, a mixed bag including a large RAF contingent as well as the small naval draft of which Michael was a member. There were also six fabled figures from the Battle of Britain, among them Adolph 'Sailor' Malan and the formidable Robert Stanford Tuck, always remembered by Michael as one of the very few people he had ever met who both looked and talked as he had always imagined Sir Walter Raleigh might have done, all bound on a US 'goodwill' tour. Michael had to work hard on board, with constant physical training: 'I threw myself into the routine with the zest of an actor tackling a strenuous part. I felt more physically fit than at any other time in my life, before or since.'

It was a strange period, free of the weight of any professional responsibilities, although some of his shipmates – over-identifying him with Gilbert in *The Lady Vanishes* – were never to be convinced that he was not on some sort of secret mission ('Come on, Mike, you can tell us'). When the ship slowly steamed up the St Lawrence he could not help being reminded of *Thunder Rock*'s Forty-niners making the same journey. Disembarking at Montreal, they travelled by train to Toronto, before continuing immediately on another, Michael being convinced that there would be at least a couple of hours' stopover in New York: 'We approached NY and saw from the train, for just a few seconds, the celebrated skyline, lit in the sunshine of an autumn morning.' But the train vanished into a tunnel, then into another station where they transferred to yet another train before reaching Virginia.

Michael had somehow imagined that Norfolk, a port in a Southern state, would be an atmospheric, lively place, full of New Orleans wrought-iron and lazily languorous jazz, but it was very different from New Orleans, a quiet, humid, sober and uneventful little town. He grew fond of it, however, and was grateful for generous hospitality, principally from the Masergyll family who introduced him to Old-Fashioneds (although Norfolk, technically, was a 'dry' town) in their comfortable clapboard house where he spent many evenings playing the piano after meals.

The work on *Illustrious* was a mind-numbing routine, mostly spent repainting the enormous ship, frustrating for Michael, knowing that none of the time would count towards time at sea, which could reduce his chances of a later commission. Finally he organised a weekend leave and a trip to New York – the £10 which he had been allowed to take out from England just covered a plane ticket via Washington – the fabled city of his imagination. He had read Ford Madox Ford's *New York is not America* and knew that was true, but no city ever matched up to New York for him – not even Venice, which later came to rival his Manhattan passion – and on that first trip the city more than lived up to all his expectations.

Ruth Gordon – 'that tiny dynamo of warmth and friendship' – met him and put him up in her Greenwich Village town house. She was determined to show him '*theatrical* New York' and surely lived up to her promise – with tickets to Radio City Music Hall (not to see any production, just to show him the awesome interior), *Pal Joey* with Gene Kelly, the long-running *Life with Father*, a reunion with Paul Lukas, then on Broadway in Lillian Hellman's *Watch on the Rhine*, at '21' Club, which somehow involved conga-dancing, a private screening by MGM of Garbo's *Two-Faced Woman* arranged by Ruth who was in the film, with drinks, lunches, cocktails and nightclubs, meeting Ethel Barrymore, Gertrude Lawrence, Jack Warner and Ronald Colman, even having to dodge fans recognising him from *The Lady Vanishes*, and a dinner at Ruth's house, with 'Ludmilla Pitoëff – great French actress who'd fled before the Nazi occupation, not a great beauty but exuding all the beautiful mystery of a great artist. And Thornton Wilder, who became a much valued friend.' The producer Gilbert Miller, who had been so tight with money when negotiating the transfer of *The Country Wife*, now pressed dollars into his palm ('Howrya doin' for dough?') and just before his return, Ruth took him to the house of director Guthrie McClintic and his wife, Broadway star Katharine Cornell, on Beekman Place overlooking the East River, with half of Broadway arriving just as Michael, 'with a heavy heart', had to leave for La Guardia. He wrote twenty years later that although he had always loved the theatre, which was in his blood, he felt something for the first time then:

> I felt, that last day of my lost-in-wonder weekend in New York that all these theatre people had not only glamour and talent which had made them the great names they were, but that somehow I was related to them through our craft and our mutual respect for the theatre, which for such a large part of an actor's life is his home. For the first time I saw the theatre as others, not born into it, see it. I was, at last, stage-struck.

He managed to squeeze in a second New York trip, even fitting in a broadcast with Flora Robson for British War Relief, just as giddy a round as the first, before the *Illustrious* crew were called together to be told that they would be sailing off to Jamaica for the ship's gunnery trials. Michael was posted to the bridge during mock bomber attacks by American aircraft, relaying commands to the starboard guns, but there were occasional times in Jamaica when, from sly references in Dick Green's letters, it is clear that Michael had an athletically busy time of homosexual activity ('Jamaican activities' became for them a code word euphemism similar to *Private Eye*'s 'Ugandan discussions').

Once the *Illustrious* had finally finished its extensive refit and trials she sailed for home, with Michael anxious to be back; the news had reached him from England that Rachel's brother Robin, health restored and back at sea, had been on board the *Prince of Wales* in the Pacific when it went down, although news of him was contradictory. On night watch, to focus his mind and to avoid falling asleep, Michael began to concentrate on particular points in his life, training his mind to recall each incident in a sequence, the memory of which infused the early pages of his later autobiography with such sharp detail.

He was also keen to reach England so that his arm, which had been injured in Norfolk during ammunitioning and was now giving him acute pain, could be properly examined. Its stiffness could not be adequately diagnosed or treated by the ship's doctor.

The *Illustrious* docked on New Year's Eve 1941 in Liverpool ('without the Playhouse company, it was like a foreign city') and he walked the familiar streets, reorientating himself; each day after Divisions he also visited the Northern Hospital for treatment, without any sign of improvement, to his arm: 'I saw myself spending the remainder of the war in barracks in Liverpool and the rest of my career playing Richard III.' Eventually allowed a few days' leave, he was finally reunited with Rachel, and they lunched together at the Ritz at a window table overlooking Green Park to celebrate. There were drinks with Coward, about to start filming his 'story of a ship' *In Which We Serve*, a lunch with Mountbatten to talk over his future, supper with Edith, lunch with Daisy at the Ivy (where, still in uniform of course, he was somewhat startled to be hailed by James Agate with 'Hello, sailor!') and finally, with Rachel to Bromyard and the children: 'The most beautiful winter's day I ever did see. Thick frost, sun, no wind. Walking all day. V. on kiss goodnight: "Tell your master to let you come away again!"'

Bromyard for Michael always had an almost mystical power of restoration. Lucy had been thrilled to see him, laden down with American gifts, writing to him after that visit: 'There is one thing always about war –

it knocks all *sense* out of the divisions of time – 48 hours can become so heart-warming a memory that it carries us through the bare places.'

Possible film work was dangled – the new team of twin brothers Roy and John Boulting was keen to film *Thunder Rock* – but had to await a decision about his Navy future. Socialising continued, often with a new friend for both Michael and Rachel, the interior designer John Fowler who had had his own King's Road shop prior to forming a successful partnership with Sibyl Colefax and who rapidly became very central to the Redgraves' lives, sometimes to the ballet with Edith Hargreaves, on one occasion meeting Lydia Lopokova with Maynard Keynes who 'guaranteed the war would be over by the end of 1943', and a lunch with Max Adrian ('I tell him my troubles. He is a good friend to tell troubles to').

His immediate future was not the only source of his troubles, although he was torn between his wish to serve the Navy (even if he would have had to admit that he had not had a distinguished OS career) and the thought that perhaps he could be of more practical use in an entertainment division. But also the conflict between his desire for domesticity with Rachel and the physical desire for men was increasingly strong, creating more than usually divided feelings once the affair with Coward resumed, as it did at that time. Also, Daisy's drinking had become a problem again; that leave included a nightmarish Great Missenden visit with Daisy screaming abuse, telling Michael how many professional enemies he had and 'slanging Rachel which I will not stand'. Andy was mostly helpless: 'It's all right for you, damn it, but I've got to listen to it.'

Back in Liverpool his hospital treatment continued without significant improvement to his arm and he remained in a somewhat limbo-like state, sometimes passing the time with the touring company of Ivor Novello's *Dancing Years*, noting in his diary that he was becoming increasingly irritable and also transcribing a remark by V. S. Pritchett in an essay on Joseph Conrad: 'The soul may be marred by the evils it commits but it is far more commonly marred by the failure to admit that it has committed evil.' Anywhere else other than Liverpool might have been better for him then – 'half the trouble is Liverpool is full of memories' – but he determined that on his next leave he would try to get some decision on his future. Rachel was on a tour – with *Blithe Spirit* – and Clifton Hill was let while Edith Hargreaves returned to her own flat, so, repulsed by the Ritz who seemed not to want uniformed sailors in residence, he checked into the Cavendish in Jermyn Street where he was delighted to find its owner Rosa Lewis living up (and more) to her legend and to the portrait of her as Lottie Crump in Evelyn Waugh's *Decline and Fall*. He had spent a few drinking evenings there – Dick Green and Lucian Freud along with him – before the war and came now rather to relish 'the mad Cavendish atmosphere' with Veuve Clicquot, even with wartime restrictions, apparently flowing (Rosa's only overt concession to the war was to remove a portrait of the old Kaiser) and Rosa herself liable to be found burning shoes and shoelaces late at night in the grate. He ended up staying there for three months. Rosa took greatly to Michael, telling Rachel when she stayed there at weekends – 'You own the best man in the world!'

Old friends were regrouping at that time – he met up with Edith, joined by George Devine, Sophie Harris and Peggy Ashcroft ('Go into E's flat for 5 mins. How that brings back memories'), although such meetings only exacerbated his frustration in not knowing where his future lay. It was not until early March that he went through an exhaustive medical at Plymouth resulting in a provisional discharge from the Navy on medical grounds (his arm had lost a great deal of mobility), handed in his pay book and was free to resume his career (his final discharge came in October). He had not been on stage or in front of the camera for over a year.

Before anything else he joined Rachel for a week in their favourite Edinburgh where she was on tour and then went on to be with the children at Bromyard where once more he could shake off the cobwebs with long walks, joined briefly by John Fowler with whom he went on a few epic pub crawls, including one in Ludlow: 'The fascination of pubs is fatal. We drank 5 whiskies, beer, $\frac{1}{2}$ bottle of wine, 3 yellow chartreuses, 2 beers – each!' Hardly surprisingly, the only entry for the following day is 'Very sorry for ourselves'. Michael – he was not alone in wartime – was beginning to drink more at this time, although he was considerably more disciplined when *Thunder Rock*, for which he agreed to take a considerably reduced fee, started filming at Denham. Coward and David Lean were at work on an adjacent sound stage with *In Which We Serve* and Coward's affair with Michael could carry on while Michael was staying at the Bull near the studios or back in Coward's Gerald Road flat. But the dissonance in his nature now nagged more strongly. When Rachel joined him at the Cavendish one weekend he wrote: 'Wake 3.30 and feel awful. Guilt is always heaviest in the early hours. The "doom" of 3.30.' Before 1940, for all the occasional problems, Michael seemed able to accommodate his divided nature; the problem afterwards, with the shock to his moral system of the People's Convention episode, the war and the unsettling intensity of his affairs with Tony Hyndman and Coward, was the beginning of a long period in which, however well he might manage to deal with the professional side of his life, his relationship with himself became increasingly unhappy.

Thunder Rock was a difficult film to make, and not simply because of the need to adjust to new casting – James Mason, Lilli Palmer and Barbara Mullen included. The screenplay, by Bernard Miles and Jeffrey Dell, remained mainly loyal to Ardrey's play, except for some clumsy 'opening-out' sequences with flashbacks to Charleson's Spanish Civil War experience, and the sinking of the *Land o' Lakes*, but Roy Boulting was then inexperienced as a director and at times uncertain on the set ('Roy is apt to think the 3rd rehearsal is the finished offering'). Michael was patient, however, despite the often muddled atmosphere and, watching the rushes, he was often impressed by the way Mutz Greenbaum's photography eerily suggested the dual time dimension of the lighthouse. The brooding power and internal confusions of Michael's Charleson if anything gained from the close-ups of the camera, although most British critics agreed that the film had lost overall something of the intensity of the stage version (its US notices were mostly superb). Coward continued as something of a distraction then, too: 'Being driven home, N. overtakes us and indicates Drink at Bull? He dines with me there and we drink a great deal. He is in his most mischievous mood. Stays the night. Drink too much.'

Michael cheered up considerably as *Thunder Rock* proceeded more smoothly in its later stages and when Binkie Beaumont approached him about appearing in a revival of one of his favourite plays, Turgenev's *A Month in the Country*. He was even able to laugh when a BBC announcer introduced his broadcast of his old Cranleigh vehicle as *Samson Agnostes* and wryly to monitor his own recent fluctuating moods, as when reading Macready's *Journals* ('Poor old Macready with his frets and fusses – how well I sympathise').

Things were looking up all round. Although Binkie had set no definite date for the Turgenev, in the meantime Jack Dunfee had an offer for Michael to further his directing ambitions with a new play, *Lifeline*, and no sooner had that deal been done than he was asked to direct the new Patrick Hamilton play, *The Duke in Darkness*, in which there was also a striking part for him. He celebrated, after a happy reunion with Carol Reed, by taking Rachel, now back from her tour, to a slap-up dinner at the Grange ('lovely white Burgundy and day ends triumphantly!'). Family legend had it that their second daughter – born nine months later to the day – was conceived that night.

Michael now plunged into one of the busiest periods of his entire career. *Lifeline*, by Norman Armstrong (the pseudonym for a collaboration between Barbara Tay and Norman Lee), was the first play with a Merchant Navy background to be seen in London (a few nights later, Terence Rattigan's *Flare Path*, the first RAF play, opened). It was a tautly written piece set on board a tramp ship, the *Clydesdale*, crossing from Canada to Liverpool with a 10,000-ton petrol cargo. Michael had little time to prepare a complex production before rehearsals; his script is scrawled over with hasty emendations to some of the inexperienced team's stiffer dialogue and countless notes on sound and lighting effects covering mainly two major incidents, when the ship is attacked by a German sub, which it sinks, and by a bomber which forces the captain to abandon ship. The play was packed with realistic detail which Michael added to with more MN slang, helped by Vivian Cox, now a captain in the Navy – 'tin fish' for torpedo, 'grey armchair' for a U-boat's tower – although the characters, led by a dour martinet of a captain, were little more than stereotypes. At times the play comes close to overt propaganda, stressing that while the MN is always appreciated in wartime: 'Then it's good old Lifeline and God bless the Merchant Navy! – but in peace time we're just another lot of sea tramps with our arses out of our pants.' And sentimentality is never far away, the captain's dying speech after the bombing raid a shameless piece of manipulative tear-jerking: 'Get the petrol home! They need it there. We mustn't let the people down on Derby Day.'

For a director it was a challenging play. The cast included such formidable individualists as Wilfred Lawson as the Para Handy-ish skipper (drunk often – and sometimes absent – during rehearsals) and the large-scale Frank Pettingell, although Michael also shrewdly cast his old Liverpool colleague Lloyd Pearson to enliven the underwritten part of the ship's wireless operator, and it was technically challenging also with a complicated sound plot of chugging engines, swelling Atlantic, bombs dropping and submarine fire. Michael had learnt from Saint-Denis how potent sound could be in the evocation of a world beyond the play's setting; virtually all the notices remarked on its quality, Alan Dent going as far as to say that in the radio version broadcast during the run, the sound effects were inferior to those used on stage.

It had a disappointingly brief run despite wonderful reviews. Michael's Cambridge contemporary, Basil Wright, in the *Spectator* was representative in praising the play as 'one of the most exciting which London has seen since September 3rd, 1939' and in adding that Michael had 'brilliantly seized' on the challenges of the play. Michael did not have an easy time with the cast; Lawson, as was his habit, continued often belligerent and unreliable (although he gave a terrific performance), but Michael relished the experience and was more than ready to move on to *The Duke in Darkness*. He had time for a quick Bromyard visit, taking his *Der Rosenkavalier* records to listen to while he worked on Patrick Hamilton's play, even more of a challenge than *Lifeline*.

The Duke in Darkness had also come to Michael through his agents – Bill Linnit was Hamilton's agent – and the play totally absorbed him, although he knew it was another risky commercial proposition. Its author, too, fascinated him; although Michael had met Hamilton several times with their mutual friend John Davenport, a regular Hamilton drinking crony, he did not know him well then. Hamilton's reputation, after such stage successes as *Rope* and *Gaslight* and his superb wartime novel *Hangover Square*, was at its peak. He was a complex bundle of paradoxes; while his novels chronicled a seedy backstreet London or Brighton world of transients and tarts, he was as much of a bon viveur as the elegant Bill Linnit, in whose sleek Rolls he would often go off for Broadstairs golfing weekends, and although originally a committed Marxist he was moving increasingly to the right. His (unfinished) autobiography was appropriately titled *Memoirs of a Heavy Drinking Man*.

Hamilton had told Linnit that he wanted to write 'a sort of highbrow Cloak and Sword play' and the resulting *The Duke in Darkness* was quite unlike any of his previous work. All the Hamilton quintessential themes are nevertheless present – private loyalties set against a wider public cause, and the often unsettling closeness between torturer and victim – although the play intriguingly broadens into what many, including Michael, saw as an unusual political parable of the fall of France using a story of late sixteenth-century French religious and civil war to parallel the spread of Fascism.

It was another all-male play, although utterly different from *Lifeline*. It is set in a chamber high up in the fortress of the Duc de Lamorre, and the title role is that of his captured rival the Duc de Laterraine, imprisoned for over sixteen years and accompanied solely by his devoted attendant Gribaud. Forces beyond the castle walls, still looking on him as a Protestant champion, are mustering to free Laterraine who has feigned blindness to convince his jailers that he is incapable of escape. The plan is endangered by Gribaud, who has slowly been driven to madness by captivity and has to be killed to prevent him inadvertently revealing his master's plot.

Michael cast the play extremely strongly, with Leslie Banks as Laterraine and the unusually versatile Walter Fitzgerald as the vicious, homosexual Lamorre. He had not originally intended to play Gribaud; it would have been a splendid part for Stephen Haggard but he had shockingly been killed (suicide or whatever was never satisfactorily clear) in a train accident (Michael also heard that summer that Paddy Railton's tuberculosis had killed him). All his other choices for the part proved unavailable. He made an unexpected but brilliant choice of designer in Ernst Stern, a Romanian-born émigré best known for the religious spectacle *The Miracle* at Olympia in the 1920s and for lavish musicals including *White Horse Inn* or the famous Viennese set for Coward's *Bitter-Sweet*. But Michael knew, too, of his work for Reinhardt in Berlin including Alexander Moissi's *Hamlet*, and the delightfully unassuming Stern came up with a superb design, suggesting both the height of the prison chamber up in the battlements and its massively thick walls, while also solving the technical demands of hiding places and concealed entrances.

For Michael it was another complex play technically, with musical elements introducing each act, intensifying the play's growing sense of spiritual conflict and also a vital near climactic thunderstorm to orchestrate. The St James's first-night audience gave it an ovation (not so common then), clearly responding to the play's contemporary urgency, with one scene, in which Laterraine turns on his captors to denounce their cruelty and predict the inevitable success of his popular cause (a scene inspired by Lenin's *One Step Forward, Two Steps Back*), especially impressing the house. The notices were wildly contrasting. For some it was pure romantic melodrama, an enjoyable return to Stanley Weyman country, with Agate impishly setting it against Victor Hugo's *Ernani*, enjoying watching Hamilton 'make a bee-line for the Castle Rodomontade in Medieval France', while others were deeply affected by the parallels with contemporary Europe, calling it one of the most enthralling and moving plays since the war began.

Michael's production and his Gribaud both were acclaimed. The loyal servant who breaks down could have been an embarrassing role – some of the later passages of delirium and terror needed extremely finely balanced acting – but he created a pitiable character which some critics ranked as the best performance he had yet given, a tortured mass of nerves disintegrating into hysterics and final, total madness, avoiding the melodrama on the verge of which the play at times teeters. It was acting of high-wire daring fused with the electricity of truth and superbly observed physical detail.

The Duke in Darkness also had a comparatively short run – all-male plays were having little luck in London at this time – but for Michael it was another rewarding experience. On tour before London he had enjoyed the collaboration on fine-tuning and adjustments with Hamilton, and it was a happy company. And on the post-West End tour there was a Bristol reunion with Dick Keigwin from Clifton ('as great fun as ever'), with whom he attended a Clifton rugby match. The tour meant that he was away from home for New Year, beginning 1943 in Cardiff where a major surprise awaited him in the form of an invitation to stand for Parliament.

The Common Wealth Party, formed by a rich ex-Liberal MP, Sir Richard Acland, had been enjoying significant successes in wartime by-elections; it had already won three seats defeating the coalition government. Acland had moved towards socialism – which he called 'common ownership' – and his *Manifesto of the Ordinary Man* had been widely popular, selling in enormous quantities. Common Wealth was definitely annoying and worrying the Communist Party (who tried to smear it as

Fascist) and even more the Labour Party who were growing to realise as
the war progressed that they would have to break away from the coalition
in order to stop Common Wealth's emergence as the third major party
ahead of the Liberals (in the event Acland and his supporters – to Labour's
great relief – re-entered the Party fold). Jackson, the Common Wealth
Secretary, called on Michael in Cardiff with a serious proposition; they
wanted Michael to contest the seat for North Portsmouth at an imminent
by-election caused by the sitting MP's elevation to the Lords. Another
Common Wealth candidate, Wintringham, who was about to contest
Midlothian, was insisting that Michael's standing in Portsmouth would
win 25 per cent more supporters for Common Wealth over the country
as a whole: 'Jackson says I'd win any election by a 2–1 majority. Explained
why I could not undertake it.' The reasons he gave Common Wealth are
not known. He was, of course, ambitious for his career, of which he was
determined now to be more his own master, but surely, too, that haunting
shadow of the People's Convention affair influenced his decision to retreat
from any significant political involvement. Jackson had probably been
right about Michael's chances – in a recent poll of British film stars'
popularity he had been well up the list although not a single film of his
had been released in 1942 – but for Michael that window of opportunity
would now remain definitely tightly closed.

The Duke in Darkness tour finished just before *A Month in the Country*,
also destined for the St James's, went into rehearsal. Michael was to appear
in three different English productions of Turgenev's play (always in the
same role, Rakitin, once a favourite Stanislavsky part), one of which he
directed, while he also directed another production in New York. Turgenev had been a favourite author since he had first read him during his
undergraduate illness, loved for his humanity as a man and for his scru-
pulous honesty as a writer. It would be surprising if Michael had not seen
something of himself in Turgenev, *'le doux géant, l'aimable barbare'* as the
Brothers Goncourt described him; Turgenev was also tall, blue-eyed,
hypochondriacal and prone to hero-worship (Bakunin in his youth), to
put love and sex in separate compartments at times, as well as often
childlike, naïve and fascinated by his dreams. The play, too, interweaving
comedy and near tragedy in its picture of life on an 1840s Russian estate,
drawing heavily emotionally on Turgenev's *amitié amoureuse* (although
some scholars insist it was more) with the singer Pauline Viardot, has
something of the shimmering, watered-silk quality of other favourites of
Michael's such as *Twelfth Night* or *Der Rosenkavalier*.

It is a fiendishly difficult play to pitch correctly in production. Too
serious and it can become simply a story, as one of John Buchan's clubland
hero characters succinctly tells Richard Hannay, of 'a dreary hag falling

in love with a youth'. Too comedic and the romantic agony under the play's surface evaporates. Michael had wanted to direct but Emlyn Williams had insisted on directing his own version, with a mouth-watering cast including Peggy Ashcroft as the heroine Natalya Petrovna and an unusual appearance in a period play from the urbane Ronald Squire. It developed into a jinxed production; after a week of rehearsals Peggy Ashcroft broke her ankle, to be replaced quickly by Valerie Taylor who looked ravishing, like a dreamy Winterhalter portrait, but just lacked the emotional volatility of the part. Michael was thrown by the loss of Peggy – she was one of the reasons he had gone into the production – but worked hard with Valerie Taylor, discussing Stanislavsky and working on scenes with her when they were not called at her Royal Avenue home, helping her to overcome a certain brittle quality in her work.

Michael was at this point beginning to spend a good deal of time after rehearsal at what his diary refers to only as 'W.R.'. This was the White Room, a slightly louche ground-floor and basement bar and restaurant in Denman Street opposite the Piccadilly Theatre's stage door, an establishment similar to that of the club in Rodney Ackland's play *Absolute Hell* (originally called *The Pink Room*) which was based on an amalgamation of the White Room and the French Club in St James's. It was not specifically a gay bar – although homosexuals and what Coward called 'the seedier West End chorus boys' frequented it – with women also part of the clientele in a relatively sophisticated ambience (there was a white piano played by the improbably named composer-singer Marc Anthony). Michael avoided the more familiar West End pick-up places such as Piccadilly's Long Bar, the Chalice, or the First Floor of the Coventry Street Lyons Corner House (known as the Lily Pond) and found the White Room atmosphere congenial and relaxed.

Among the floating displaced-persons population of wartime, Americans seemed especially drawn there; habitués included several actors who worked for the US Army's entertainment unit. For Michael the White Room became more of a second home than the Garrick Club (to which he had been elected in 1943) for several years to come. But, with Rachel well into her pregnancy, this life made for problems: 'Again pretty late at W.R. and when I return R. is upset and tearful and I feel beastly. But after long rehearsals never feel v. like coming straight home and unless I come straight home I always stay too long and drink a little or a lot too much.'

He was unhappy with the production of *A Month in the Country* and particularly disliked – as do most actors – Emlyn Williams' habit of giving his cast inflections and line readings in the early rehearsals. Michael found the sharp-tongued Williams – another bisexual with whom he had a slightly awkward relationship – something of a conundrum. He was funny, very entertaining if slightly too much in love with West End parish-pump gossip, and undeniably clever but as a director superficial and prone to emphasise the sentimental. Michael thought that the production only skimmed the surface of the play, content to present it as a costume piece of West End confectionery, but although Binkie had pushed the boat out the sets were over-fussy and heavy. The notices were disappointing, with the production judged too slow and over-decorated ('like some Hollywood stunner with Joan Crawford in the offing,' Agate said of the drawing-room scene). Michael pleased most – but not himself – with his first sketch of Rakitin, the self-portrait into which Turgenev poured all that he had undergone on behalf of Pauline Viardot, the urbane, cultivated family friend, adoring Natalya but behaving with tortuous meanness when she falls in love with her son's handsome young tutor. What happens to Rakitin in the play is as crucial as what happens to Natalya and the production and Michael's subtle performance, captured that at least.

His Cambridge friend Wynyard Browne, his playwright's career inter-rupted by Army service, was also a great admirer of the play and made a special trip on a weekend pass from Derby to see it, writing to Michael later: 'The extraordinary thing is that all your characters have *three* levels – what they actually do and say, what they are thinking and feeling but don't show or say *and* – this is the mystery – a subconscious.' Browne is very astute here about Michael's particular genius for suggesting these under-currents in his characters. Even in that first Rakitin he was able to suggest that he is a victim not only of Natalya but of lets and hindrances in himself of which he knows nothing. Browne added that a good number of actors could work on two levels:

> But three is terrific, like prophecy or modern physics or people who play 3-dimensional chess and sometimes quite uncanny. I don't think it can be the result of 'acting' in the ordinary sense but rather of the fact that you have a much deeper insight into people than even the best actors normally have, and therefore know your characters better than they even can, however skilful they may be at showing what they do know.

With the public, *A Month in the Country* was a big success, clearly destined for a long run (Michael confessed to Max Adrian, 'It is really rather exciting to be in what Bigolo calls "a hit smash".') Michael seemed at this stage to have boundless energy, becoming very involved with the Campaign for Sunday Opening of theatres as well as taking on Peter Ustinov's new play, *Blow Your Own Trumpet*, for Bronson Albery. Then, as if that were not workload enough, including his eight performances a week at the St James's, he decided to present and direct Henri Becque's rarely revived comedy *Parisienne* for a series of matinées at the St James's.

Michael, Rachel and Bob
Michell in Hollywood, 1947.

Bob Michell

Michael, Norris Houghton,
Rachel and Vanessa in London,
1943.

Bedford House, Chiswick.

Right The family with Nanny Randall outside Bedford House.

Wilks Water, Hampshire.

John Fowler at his Hampshire hunting-lodge with Michael.

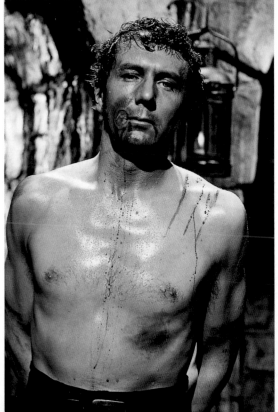

Michael in the film of Graham Greene's *The Man Within*, 1947.

'Ours is a family that rejoices in each other' – the Redgraves at a 1960s film premiere.

Right 'The past is a foreign country' – Michael as the elder Leo in *The Go-Between*, 1971.

Opposite top Making-up as Shylock at Stratford, 1953, with Glen Byam Shaw.

Opposite below 'One sees his past spread around him like a scarlet cloak' – Michael as Antony at Stratford, 1953.

Portrait of a Stoic – Dick Green.

'Dearest China' – Noël Coward.

With Fred Sadoff – to publicise FES (Plays). In the background is the Anthony Devas portrait of Rachel.

Left Michael, Rachel, Fred and Iris Tree in Ischia, 1957.

Top Shakespeare's People – Michael with Elizabeth Counsell, David Dodimead (standing), Philip Bowen (left) and Rod Wilmott.

Above 'The door is open' – as Jasper in *Close of Play*, National Theatre, 1979.

Uncle Vanya – Michael with Sybil Thorndike, Fay Compton and Joan Plowright, at Chichester, 1963.

Michael, Vanessa and Corin outside Liverpool Playhouse, 1982. His penultimate stage appearance, on the stage of his first professional home.

With Rachel, Corin, Kika Markham, Jemma Redgrave and Luke Redgrave, at the Foyle's Literary Luncheon for *In My Mind's Eye*, 1983.

He also had a new daughter, born safely at the London Clinic (which had a bomb shelter) and named after Lynn Fontanne: 'Our second daughter was born about 8.15. Sleeping when Dr Low telephoned. ... Lynn very podgy, with blue hands, blowing bubbles. R. well.' He celebrated by buying a pair of silver earrings for Rachel and finished a Pirate Ship scene for a toy theatre for the children, visiting the clinic most days during the two weeks of Rachel's stay, having pledged 'No more W.R.' in his diary just before Lynn was born. He kept up his resolution, at least for a while, but he was also spending a good deal of time with a beautiful young woman he had recently met and been entranced by.

Diana Gould was one of the two striking daughters – she and her sister Griselda were 'the beautiful Gould girls' – of a mother who was a brilliant pianist and an Irish father who worked in the Foreign Office but who died when she was a baby. She had trained as a dancer and even although tall for the ballet – nicknamed variously 'The Eiffel Tower' and, by Russians, 'Sparja' (an asparagus stalk) – she had danced for George Balanchine's company and with Anton Dolin. She had acting ambitions, but when she tried films, Alexander Korda simply chased her (literally) round the casting couch. A small success in the theatre, appearing with Peggy Ashcroft directed by Saint-Denis in *Weep for the Spring* by Stephen Haggard before the war, had led to her being cast in a revival of Barrie's *What Every Woman Knows* in which Michael first saw her act, meeting her at a party afterwards: 'Michael Redgrave came up and said charmingly: "I was in love with you when you must have been about sixteen", and proceeded to tell me that he had come to see me whenever he could.' They went together to see a matinée the next day of *Heartbreak House* with Edith and Robert Donat, marking the real beginning of what Diana described as 'a long and tender friendship'. She was fiercely intelligent and could be very funny; Michael especially enjoyed her description of a dire *Giselle* with an unfortunate Alicia Markova partnered by the ageing Serge Lifar, monstrously vain even as his figure had expanded ('His bottom looked like luggage sent by a later train').

There was a little gossip when they began to have occasional suppers together but at that stage, before anything could develop romantically, Diana was cast in *The Merry Widow*, leaving for a long European tour. Rachel at that time was at a low point, possibly suffering from some post-natal depression but also miserably unhappy about the virtual certainty that her brother Robin was dead (the full story of his heroism in death was not known until after the war). Michael, knowing too that he was the cause of at least some of Rachel's mood, was worried about her: 'She seems to have no go, no resistance, is terrified by German propaganda etc.' His own crowded schedule meant that any holiday together was impossible.

John Fowler, a rare friend who took no sides, fond equally of them both, suggested that Rachel see a psychiatrist who had helped him through a bad patch when he seemed, as usual, to be unable to find lasting love or happiness.

Charlotte Wolff had, it transpired, also seen Dick Green before the war. An extraordinary woman, she was then fifty; originally from Danzig she had left Berlin for France, settling in London in 1936. Tiny, lesbian and Jewish, she was soft-spoken and compassionate, fascinated by the study of human and animal hands, and the author of several key papers on lesbianism and bisexuality. Rachel could describe to her the recurrent feeling she had of resembling an isolated figure, like one inside a glass bubble as snow swirled round her. Over their sessions, which included talk of Michael's sexuality, Wolff helped Rachel see herself more as an individual rather than as an appendage of Michael, while Michael too – according to his diary he visited her several times ('Feel immensely better as I leave her,' he noted after one visit) – appreciated her counsel. She gradually helped them find an adjustment in a marriage both wanted to continue, still loving each other profoundly, unable to live without each other however anguished they might be separately or jointly at times.

Michael had ended up acting in as well as directing *Parisienne* for six St James's matinées in aid of British Equity War Relief. One of the greatest triumphs for the French actress Réjane, the title role of Clotilde was the plum part, played at the St James's by the witty, incisive Sonia Dresdel, with stylishly simple designs (on a shoestring budget but looking sumptuous) by John Fowler. First performed in 1885, it ironically reverses the traditional roles of lover and husband, showing – in a uniquely French way – how extremely conjugal the relationship between a married woman and her lover can be. Michael played Lafont, the lover, sublimely oblivious to any difference between himself and Clotilde's husband. Clotilde, exasperated by Lafont's jealousy, takes a younger lover but he proves such a let-down that she returns to her two 'husbands'. Adult in its view of sex and of the gulf between our view of ourselves and that taken by others, the play – like most of Becque's work – had never been popular in England, its sophisticatedly forensic irony alien to Anglo-Saxon expectations of comedy, especially when involving sex. Sonia Dresdel found something of Millamant's glorious drollery in Clotilde and Michael, looking like a Manet come to life, had a wonderfully lugubrious comical jealousy, both of them keeping the play diamond-sharp and airborne.

Some friends were puzzled by Michael's drive to direct so much at this time. The truth, as his diary indicates, was that he had a master plan for after the war, a scheme to form his own company to play in the West End in repertoire to consolidate and build upon the venture at the Phoenix cut short by the war, and he wanted to have as much experience as possible in readiness. He had talked to Binkie Beaumont of his dream and had been greeted with at least a flicker of interest from those inscrutable lizard eyes. Binkie probably calculated that another successful film or two would turn Michael into a solidly bankable and backable star and he was not going to be averse to the chance of an involvement in potentially profitable post-war ventures, although he already had Gielgud leading his stable of stars. He genuinely admired, too, the talent he had so craftily spotted ten years before at Liverpool and truthfully believed that Michael was also developing a real directorial gift.

Peter Ustinov's play, *Blow Your Own Trumpet*, unfortunately enhanced nobody's reputation. Michael had had reservations about it but was reassured that Ustinov would address any problem areas in rehearsal or on the road (he never did – once he handed Michael a supposedly rewritten scene and vanished before anyone had time to notice it was exactly the same as the old one). It was only the wunderkind Ustinov's second play and expectations were high after the promise of his Chekhovian piece of Russian émigrés in London, *House of Regrets*. He set his new play in an East End Italian Restaurant, the Santa Maria, 'during the present war' (of which there are few signs), once more involving mostly émigrés in a setting which fosters illusions. The proprietor thinks he could have been Pope had he not so strongly wished for sons; the two he has, one working in a garage, the other crazy about dirt-track racing, are often at logger-heads with him before winning the right to 'blow their own trumpets'. Michael again made some intriguing key choices, going to Feliks Topolski for an unexpectedly perspectived design cunningly tilting the play away from naturalism and casting such clever character actors as Esmé Percy as a wild conductor and Lilly Kann as the restaurant owner's mother, sadly given little to do except gibber in a corner. He spent hours painstakingly orchestrating a play which had a lot of incident but no real action. The London notices were uniformly terrible and the kind words about Michael's inventive production and a clever cast but with no box office name could not help. Business was atrocious (£14 at one matinée) and Bronson Albery withdrew the play after less than a fortnight.

No better luck was in store when he turned, again almost without a break (and still appearing in *A Month in the Country*), to direct the American play by Maxwell Anderson, *Wingless Victory*, for his agency's management, Linnit, O'Brien and Dunfee. This had been a modest success for Katharine Cornell before the war on Broadway, where she was one of the sure-fire draws, but even then the play had come in for some criticism ('tish-tosh' was George Jean Nathan's summing-up). Written in blank verse of such high-mindedness it seems on stilts, the play refashions the Medea legend

in a New England setting when the rich Nathaniel McQueston returns
to Salem with his bride from Malaya, Oparre of the Celebes, a princess at
home but now, although a Christian convert, treated with such prejudice
and bigoted hostility by her husband's family and the Salem community
that she commits suicide after killing her children. Reaching for *Medea*'s
heights, *Wingless Victory* becomes instead a bizarre mixture of *The Scarlet
Letter* and *White Cargo*, with Oparre rather more akin to the latter's
Tondelayo than to Hester Prynne. Michael cast the Czechoslovakian
actress Wanda Rotha, who had come to London with her husband Karel
Stepanek just before the war, and with her Titian hair and beauty she
certainly conveyed something of the misfit Oparre's dignified allure.
Rachel was saddled with a feeble role as Faith, the dry stick Nathaniel's
former fiancée, hurt when he fails to recognise her: 'No spark? No
glimpse? But all those fond farewells!' Not helped by a title which sounded
like that of an RAF revue, the play was doomed even before its predictably
poor notices, with Michael ruefully noting: 'Must remember never again
be persuaded by nice people to do play first instinct says *no* to.'

Michael's blood, however, was up. Not because he had had two directorial flops in succession but because the notices crystallised feelings he
had had for some time about the standard of London's dramatic criticism.
He had a point. There were, as always, some genuinely dedicated critics
around – J. C. Trewin, Ivor Brown and Philip Hope-Wallace (who still
wrote only on occasions for the *Manchester Guardian*, however) – while
mavericks like the increasingly whimsical James Agate apart, some of the
rest then were a dismal bunch and not much informed about the theatre
(one of Michael's main points). He sailed into battle first after *Blow Your
Own Trumpet* with a long article, 'An Actor to the Critics' in the *New
Statesman*.

Soberly written, cogently argued, he made his principal point that
although he knew that Ustinov's play was imperfect it deserved more
considered notice than the dismissive rejections it received. He stressed
that he was not trying to excuse failure but to persuade critics to try to
help create some much-needed theatrical renaissance and to understand
that new talent needed deliberation rather than judgement on a hit-or-
miss criterion. He challenged that good copy is not necessarily good
criticism, adding an agenda for the Critics' Circle to consider, including
advocating that all criticism should be signed (a surprising amount was
then still anonymous), that the daily press should follow the *Evening
Standard*'s practice then of holding reviews until Saturday to give critics
time to reflect and that critics should have some knowledge of past dramatic criticism such as Hazlitt's work. The essence of his broadside was
that 'professional work should be judged professionally'.

The critics' reactions to his piece varied from applause for his courage ('this St George of the theatre,' said Harold Hobson) in risking publishing it on the eve of *Wingless Victory*'s opening to accusations of sour grapes. Most thought that his points were over-idealistic or impractical and that, as Beverley Baxter put it, while suggesting he should be cheered for taking the theatre seriously he should be warned not to take himself too seriously. Agate, predictably, was outraged, writing in the *Daily Express*: 'I wrote to him and said it was an insult to all critics of standing.'

The same ground was covered – more personally – after the closure of *Wingless Victory* when Michael addressed the Critics' Circle with Sybil Thorndike's support, but he felt that he spoke poorly, sounding too censorious ('A most horrible afternoon'). The episode remained vivid in theatrical memory, however, often referred to in subsequent interviews with inevitable descriptions of Michael as 'an intellectual actor'. J. B. Priestley wrote a rousingly supportive piece in the *New Statesman* attacking what he saw as the view of the majority of critics then writing that the theatre was just a minor branch of show business. Beatrix Lehmann produced a letter of support, too – 'Shouldn't a critic know something of the cause before judging the effect?' – although privately she wrote to Michael: 'They are a bunch of old cross-bowmen defending a miasmic ditch. I believe you overestimate them by addressing them as *educated* men.'

It was Beatrix, following an Equity meeting – Michael had recently joined her on the union's council and had just chaired a meeting to discuss Equity's approach to Ernest Bevin to establish the government's priorities for wartime entertainment – who accidentally provided Michael with his next play and one of his most memorable parts. She had toured earlier in the year in the Broadway success *Uncle Harry* opposite Eric Portman in the title role but the play failed to come into London as expected. She told Michael, who was looking for a play to tour for ENSA, that it had potential but that Portman had been miscast and Willie Armstrong as director had not been able to counter that. She gave Michael a copy of the script, which reduced him to 'tears of fright', so enthusing him that he arranged to meet Binkie (who had produced the earlier tour) and persuaded him to revive (most unusually) a Tennent's flop, scheduling rehearsals for the end of the year before a joint ENSA–Tennent tour and the West End early in 1944.

Thrilled about *Uncle Harry*, Michael was even more excited when, after lunching with Anton Walbrook and dining with Peggy Ashcroft on the same day, his plans for his own company bubbled over with ideas, meeting Binkie the very next day to talk further ('Mainly satisfactorily'), possible future plays now including *Uncle Vanya* (with Walbrook as Astrov), Peggy in Ibsen's *Lady from the Sea* and Goldoni's *Lacondiera*.

Binkie, who liked to crack the whip even with stars should they step out of what he judged the line, was in no mood to smile on Michael's plans the following week, however. On a short post-West End tour of *A Month in the Country* during a Liverpool matinée he and Valerie Taylor could barely be heard over the chatter and clinking of teacups after an intermission, whereupon Michael rebuked the audience ('When you have finished your tea, we will go on with the play'), a heinous crime in the eyes of Binkie, who felt that the sacred fourth wall of illusion should never be broken. Deviously, he did not speak to Michael directly but called Rachel to say how angry he was, that he might not produce *Uncle Harry* and that he might not be able to support the idea of Michael's company, knowing that she would tell Michael, making him all the more uncertain. They patched things up over lunch at Scott's, one of Binkie's favourite power-broking venues, and so Binkie had cleverly gained the reins of control before the tour moved to Oxford; this was never Michael's favourite city (he swore Oxford audiences coughed more than any other), although he was able to have a delighted reunion with Oliver Baldwin ('charming as ever') and Johnny Boyle, joining them twice for lunch.

Before rehearsals began for *Uncle Harry*, in which Rachel too had been cast, Michael seemed, after a year of extremely hard work and see-sawing professional fortunes, much happier and more settled. The Coward affair had petered out – for Coward such affairs, even when brief, were often more to do with affection than with sex, and he and Michael remained always fond of each other – while Charlotte Wolff had helped Rachel and him alike. The household, too, now moved to a new flat (with Clifton Hill and the Mill both sold), a large apartment in Rivermead Court, Putney, overlooking the river, was much more organised. The Redgraves would always have trouble with staff – drink, drugs, theft, the lot – but now a new nanny had arrived for Lynn, Norfolk-born Kathleen Randall, who would be a mainstay for the entire family for over twenty years. Lynn that Christmas was sleeping in her parents' bedroom while Nanny Randall recovered from flu. Michael had written his last letter of the year to Rachel from Oxford, where he had bought books for the children's Christmas to which he was, as always, looking forward, signing his letter 'Mickie Muckle' (other names they used were Mikey, Misha and Mick), telling her to tell the children how much he missed them: 'Now that I am getting to know them they are often in my thoughts. They are so lovely and enchanting now that I could wish them never to grow up. Get thee behind me, Peter Pan!'

At the end of the year *Uncle Harry* began rehearsals, Michael noting after the first day: 'Rachel excellent. Home by tube together. It's like a new life together these last two weeks.'

Eleven
HURLY-BURLY

Nobody, Michael included, quite anticipated the success of *Uncle Harry*, which established him as a top West End star. With Joseph Schildkraut in the title role the play had had a good Broadway run in 1942, seen as an enjoyable period psychological thriller. The emphasis in the production steered by Michael, reunited with Willie Armstrong as co-director, was much more on the psychology and less on the thriller, rightly realising that the play's suspense is to do less with the 'how?' than with the 'why?'. They interfered very little with its basic tight structure – 'Algebra in wigs,' as the American critic John Mason Brown described it.

Thomas Job, the Welsh-born author – by 1944 working for MGM – had set his play originally in Wales while in New York it was set in a small Canadian town. Michael and Willie moved it to a close-knit small north country town, reworking the prologue in which Harry Quincey first appears like a creepy Ancient Mariner to buttonhole a commercial traveller in the local pub with the story of how his murder, cunningly ingenious in the planning (following his near namesake Thomas de Quincey's description of murder as 'a Fine Art'), backfired to haunt him.

Harry, a seemingly meek, unobtrusive man, spoilt by the two strong-willed spinster sisters with whom he has lived for years, was nicknamed 'Uncle' by the boys to whom he once taught art, a fond but also humiliating tribute to his sexlessness and his submission to his sisters' octopus tentacles. He has never forgiven his sisters for preventing his marriage to Lucy, now engaged to another man. Manipulating the need to have the family dog put down, Harry contrives the murder of the overbearing Hettie by poison, apparently administered by her sister Lettie who is tried and sentenced to death, Harry seemingly broken by the family tragedy. The powerful last scene in prison, when Lettie and Harry are left briefly together before her execution, turns on Lettie's decision to die, realising that Lucy, who has rejected Harry's renewed advances, was the cause of Harry's revenge and that now, faced with the knowledge that it was all for nothing, he wants the truth to be known: 'Just like that little trick you had of giving your toys away when you'd broken them. . . . Now you've broken your life and you want to give that away. But it won't do, Harry. Not this time.' Knowing that everyone will think that Harry's assumption of guilt is only an attempt to clear his sister, Lettie prepares to go the gallows, abandoning him to his horror for the rest of his life, leaving an hysterical Harry still with no say in his own life behind her.

Both Schildkraut and Eric Portman had emphasised the artist-manqué side of the character ('Murderers, like artists, are appreciated best when they are hung'). Michael took another route into the pathetic mind of this outwardly mild killer to whom, with his gold-rimmed spectacles and damp moustache, he gave a suggestion of Crippen. He seized on and expanded the economic dependence of Harry on his sisters – their parents' will left a handsome legacy on the condition that the siblings lived together – another factor feeding his resentment. Again, Michael's body appeared to alter with the character; he seemed almost boneless, with a weak, loose mouth and a somewhat apologetic, pigeon-toed walk, apparently happy to be his sisters' idol and slave alike but, when alone, suddenly terrifyingly malignant. The play alternates between the Quincey parlour – overstuffed and filled with ornaments, the chief of which is Harry – and the Blue Bell tavern where Harry, pillar of the community, plays piano for the local Glee Club, the songs gradually coming to seem like a macabre chorus to the play.

The other casting helped take *Uncle Harry* out of the 'Home Sweet Homicide' bracket and into unusually charged psychological depths. Bea Lehmann's rigid, flint-dry Lettie never once played for sympathy, while Ena Burrill, normally cast in sophisticated roles, was a revelation as the dragon Hettie, using padding and a brilliant make-up which made her virtually unrecognisable, and Rachel, true and touching, was Lucy. Rehearsals were intense and continued so on the pre-London tour as Michael and Willie reshaped and refined the play technically.

The pressure of work kept Michael's diary blank until the tour reached Edinburgh, usually a favourite date, but troubled now. For the first time a new initial makes an appearance in his entries. This was 'N' – not for Noël, with that affair over, but for a fresh figure in Michael's life, the first of three men, all American, who would take up much of his extramarital life over the next twenty-five years.

'N' stood for Norris – Norris Houghton – whom, it transpired, he had met at the White Room some weeks before. Norris was just a year younger than Michael, slim, rather delicate and not especially good-looking but with a vulnerable quality to which Michael was drawn. Indianapolis-born, he had become stage-struck at Princeton before his early professional experience, primarily as a designer, at Falmouth in Massachusetts with the University Players, a stock company run on co-operative lines which had also given early breaks to such young talent as Henry Fonda, Margaret

Sullavan and Joshua Logan. Norris had written two books, the more recent an account of his time spent in Moscow observing Russian theatre, *Moscow Rehearsals*. He was a passionate advocate of non-profit and regional theatre, and of theatres as essential parts of the community, all of which struck chords with Michael too. When they met, Norris had just arrived in England, working at the American embassy for the US Naval Reserve. The immediate passion between them, now interrupted by Norris's temporary return to Washington, together with the strain of the ceaseless work on *Uncle Harry*, had built up in Michael on tour in Edinburgh: 'Willie lunches with me but I feel so rotten I go up and lie down. R. comes in and sits on bed and I cannot go on without telling her about N. After a time and after she has been pretty wonderful and I have cried, into a deep sleep. Woke feeling differently. R. says, "It's silly but I feel quite happy about it." '

The tour involved a good deal of extra-curricular activity too, with both Michael and Bea often booked to speak at local Equity meetings and in Glasgow Michael had several meetings with Michael Powell, who was still keen to find a project for them both. He was also drinking too much: 'Should by rights be alarmed at the amount of whisky I manage to put away in an evening. . . . At Aberdeen, the manager gave me a bottle and on the first night I gave twice as good a performance, with the lamentable result that I feel I need it for the last act.'

By the time the tour was coming to an end, Norris was back in London and Michael was impatient to see him:

> I can't really subscribe to the theory that men attract towards themselves the events they deserve, attractive though it be. But I have no doubt that if you go on wanting a thing enough, the force with which you want it helps you to take hold of it when it comes your way. And, war or no war, and even in the face of the Atlantic Ocean, I mean to wear you, Norris, in my heart's core.

In the week in London prior to *Uncle Harry*'s opening at the Garrick, Michael noted that he was in the White Room 'every night this week', usually with Norris. He was also seeing Norris at his service flat in Sussex Square where they would listen to music often (Haydn at this time) or they would walk through London together:

> We walk in park and sit for some time. He becomes sad and says the beauty of the day makes him so. I remember that yesterday I thought of Blake's line about catching joy as it flies. Then to the Meurice where I book a room and arrange we stay there. . . . I talk about Charlotte Wolff. He about the psychiatrist who says there was no reason why he should not overcome his fear of women.

Michael returned home a few nights later – a period of suddenly intensified bombing had begun – and to an understanding Rachel after Norris's departure on another Washington trip: 'R. tells me of strange dream she had of Norris and she and I all living together "as if I had two husbands".'

Willie and Michael were still making final adjustments to *Uncle Harry* right up to dress rehearsals in those days without previews, Michael making a last-minute change of incidental music to use William Walton's 'Duets for Children', a clever choice, just right for a play whose central trio remain locked in the stifling embrace of their childhood. He felt, worryingly, 'flat, with that deadly calm' – the mood of inertia rather than adrenalin, a feeling dreaded by actors – before the first night, but an actress in a small role having a temperament about her curtain call position fired him up so that he forgot to be nervous and gave, unusually for him once he had become successful, a performance on the first night better than any previously on tour.

He was amazed – as were his guests – to see among his dressing-room visitors after the enthusiastic reception the weighty figure of James Agate who extravagantly presented '*mes hommages*', adding, 'Now you can stop being an intellectual and be a real actor,' a phrase he repeated in his *Sunday Times* notice.

Without exception, *Uncle Harry* received *hommages* across the board, unqualified praise going to Michael for a chilling transformation into the flaccid murderer, holding hysteria in reserve just simmering beneath a pliable exterior until, with an impact those who saw it never forgot, it erupted into the most hideous violence. Willie cried with joy at one of his biggest successes – protesting, as usual, that the tears were only because of his snuff – later writing to Michael: 'It's one of the most delightful experiences I've ever had in my perplexing life in the theatre. I've never "directed" anyone more helpful and sympathetic and easy. If I go on like this, I'll cry again and that is bad for my chest.'

Both Bea Lehmann and Ena Burrill had been stimulated by Michael's refusal to stop work on the play until it was right, and by his unusual experiments and exercises to keep it fresh, as Bea expressed: 'How satisfactory and delightful working with you has been. For the first time I have felt we were cutting a patch through all the dreadful tangle of bad old habits and attitudes of mind.'

During the play's run Michael was always determined to keep the quality of the production and of his own performance up to scratch. He would, for instance, decide to focus for a few performances on a different object-ive, such as Harry's vanity ('I'll prove I'm cleverer than you are') to avoid staleness. After a few weeks of the run, when Willie and he both sensed a slight routine quality creeping in, he called a long, challenging rehearsal to outline the problem and then to spend time with each character improvising: 'This I find illuminating and each person to me reflected in their improvisation no basic difficulty with the part. The performance gives me more delight than for a long while. It sounds fresh again.' This kind of post-opening work was highly unusual then, and while a few diehards muttered resentfully, Michael was grateful to Bea, Ena and Rachel for taking part so committedly in the work. Even something unexpected, like seeing the huge but fastidious Sydney Greenstreet's performance in *The Mask of Demetrios* at the cinema, gave him ideas for maintaining his own spontaneity: 'Makes me play Harry in the evening a shade more *delicately*, which is not without effect. I am so averse to the idea of deliberation in acting. I do not like anything to be precisely the same – the information I like most is the one which surprises me.'

How he found the energy for this application to the play seems surprising, set against the life he was leading for the early part of the run. Rachel then was seeing Charlotte Wolff regularly, reporting to Michael that now she was enjoying days on end without what she called her 'Zero hour' low point. Michael saw Charlotte less regularly: 'She says, principally, to trust it will be all right. R's longing for certain ties is a natural result of her fear ... my conflict is independent of R. (although directed at her) as hers of me (tho' directed at me).'

Something of the nervous edge of Harry seemed to possess Michael after the play had opened. He was rarely at home, staying often at the Cavendish or the Meurice even when Norris was away from London, was usually in the White Room after the show and was beginning a frantic period of, in Oscar Wilde's phrase, 'feasting with panthers'. One diary entry, reintroducing Tony Hyndman, is typical: 'The day ends with a visit to W.R. with Tommy. We eat sandwiches. With him, Pat, Bill and others to Music Box!! And there to flat in Chelsea and really this is going too far and yet it seemed a necessary degradation at the time.' Sometimes he would take hair-raising risks, one night slipping a Gordon Highlander he had met at the White Room into his hotel after a performance of *Uncle Harry*, this not long after Max's sentence and at a time when Ivor Novello had been jailed for a relatively minor petrol-rationing offence: 'E. has to be at Marylebone at 9. He dresses and looks as dashing as a really Michelangelo figure in a kilt can look. At theatre, fireman whispered to me "Did you sleep well last night?" I think all will be well, but after Ivor's publicity this sort of thing is scary.'

Many entries record similar reckless escapades dicing with danger in mindless promiscuity. He finally took a room at the Savoy, often insomniac, his mind restless, sometimes walking in the small hours solitarily across Waterloo Bridge in the moonlight, when no amount of blackout could totally mask the Thames, like a silver ribbon linked bank to bank by the bridges which provided such a target for the Luftwaffe. He knew, in his rational mind, that Charlotte Wolff was right, as he had written after one gaudy night back at the Savoy: 'Woke full of self-recrimination. Never seen more clearly truth of Charlotte's statement about danger of divorcing sex from love' – and yet, the same night as that entry he was back in the White Room and on most nights on to the Music Box, the Gargoyle, the Blue Lagoon or wherever, spending far too much, drinking far too much, as if to blot out his other, 'real', life. His work did not seem to suffer; *Uncle Harry* continued to play to capacity and he was working on a new project with Diana Gould, back in London after the tour of *The Merry Widow* and a broken love affair.

Diana had been writing to him, approaching him, only half-jokingly, as a remote figure – 'a baroque Castle set on a craggy height with a drawbridge' – who could vanish behind a portcullis, emerging occasionally for what she described as 'a few enchanting meetings'. He let down his drawbridge enough to ask her to work with him on an adaptation of *Amoureuse* by Porto-Riche – Diana spoke perfect French – which he was contemplating directing. Work began happily enough, although she found his reserve a barrier, shrewdly noting that it resulted from a combination of nerves, self-consciousness and fear. When he arrived for a third session, seeming withdrawn, she tackled him, reminding him she'd had a theatrical kiss on the first session and a handshake on the second, adding: ' "If the next time you're going to address me through your lawyers, just let me know in time to shut the door in your face." He swept me up in a bear-hug, roaring with laughter, and from then on we shared the fondest of *amitiés amoureuses*.'

Michael was enchanted by Diana's beauty, vivacity and candour. At one point during their collaboration he wrote: 'I think she would like to have an affair, but this would be a great mistake and would end in our not speaking. ... She is very attractive, but ... but ...' Whether or not Diana ever had set her cap at Michael – she was certainly never a woman to be content with an average man – it was at this time, when they both attended a lunch party of her mother's, that Diana met Yehudi Menuhin who, after a courtship complicated by the geography of his concert bookings, married her a year later, with both Menuhins becoming lifelong friends of Michael and Rachel.

There were other new friends at this time, too, including the French star Françoise Rosay, a favourite of Michael's from *Un Carnet de Bal*, who had fled France just before the Nazi occupation. She thought Michael the best contemporary British actor, especially strong on film: 'She says I act

with inner emotion which expresses itself through my face.' Rosay joined
Michael and Vivian Cox for lunch on occasion at Prunier's in St James's
where, most unexpectedly with wartime restrictions, they were able to
enjoy massive aperitifs of Dubonnet, with Michael marvelling how even
the resourceful Madame Prunier had procured it. Rosay, who had begun
her career as a lion tamer and cared little for other impressive French-
women, retorted: 'Madame Prunier is so fucking peess-*elegante*, she probably pees Dubonnet.'

There was also a reunion with Michel Saint-Denis, now with Suria
Magito, briefly in London from Paris where, as Jacques Duchesne on Free
French Radio, 'His popularity is such that he could ask a million francs
tomorrow: "for anything – and *get* eet! Eet's terrifying".' Michael confided
in them his dream of a company to play in repertoire after the war, hoping
that both would be somehow involved. Binkie continued inscrutably
uncommitted, although at a recent lunch he had made a point of stressing
to Michael how expensive to run the John Gielgud season at the Haymarket that year was proving. He also was cool about Michael's Pinero
suggestions of *The Second Mrs Tanqueray* (for Peggy) and *Trelawny of the
'Wells'*, which had the plus of a supporting role, an old-fashioned melodrama actress, for Daisy who was always calmer when working. Michael
had reason to worry that Binkie might not come through for him.

He had other reasons to be worried. He was the victim of a serious
blackmail threat, something which he had always dreaded. It came, too,
against the background of the horrible news from Ceylon that Dick
Green had been sentenced to two years' military detention for 'conduct
unbecoming' when caught in flagrante with a Sinhalese rickshaw driver
(Vivian Cox, then based with his ship in Colombo, did his best at the trial
as Dick's 'Prisoner's Friend'). A note arrived at the Garrick stage door,
threatening that unless Michael paid up, Rachel and the Savoy (where
Michael had been as careless as Wilde) would be told of his private
activities. The following day Rachel received a note from the same man
telling her to meet him that night in Trafalgar Square. Michael pacified
her and took action; after the show he went immediately to Nelson's
Column to meet 'G' (as he is referred to simply), made the man realise
that Rachel was fully aware of his nature and read a note Michael had
written on the consequences of blackmail and sign it, admitting what he
had done. On another occasion during the run of *Uncle Harry*, Michael
asked Vivian Cox to follow him at a distance from the Garrick Theatre
after the show, again to Trafalgar Square, while he dealt with another
blackmail attempt, this time by a guardsman who had also stolen Michael's
wristwatch (which he recovered).

When the offer came for Michael to appear in a new film, then called

Rendezvous, about early Battle of Britain pilots and their American back-up, to be directed by Anthony Asquith and scripted by Terence Rattigan, he was very keen to accept, even though his character was killed halfway through. He admired the script and also was deep in trouble financially – owing over £2000 in back tax and with an overdraft nudging £1000 at the bank. Edith Hargreaves, who as 'secretary' guarded Michael like Cerberus, never liked to bother him with mundane matters like tax, often shoving the brown envelopes into drawers. Rachel was none too keen on Edith as an organiser and she was a bone of contention with Daisy who resented her manner of granting access to Michael. Michael rented what became known somewhat euphemistically as 'the office', a room in Goodwin's Court, then a rather raffish alley off St Martin's Lane, which Edith could use during the day and which Michael could have as a *chambre d'assignation* by night.

Binkie was happy at a time when air raids were affecting West End business to take *Uncle Harry* back on the road for a few weeks, put it on ice while Michael did his location scenes and then bring it back to London. Michael and Rachel had time for a brief Bromyard visit ('Don't know what we should have done without these two women,' he wrote of Cousin Lucy and Nanny Randall), where they found Vanessa and Corin closely bonded with their private codes and games (one, invented when they sim-ultaneously had measles, had them both with imaginary fathers – the boxers Joe Louis and Bruce Woodcock) while Lynn, unsurprisingly, was very shy. They had a family picnic with everyone together on Corin's birthday before the opening of *Uncle Harry* in Liverpool, where a nasty shock was waiting, a letter from the bank refusing to cash further cheques until Michael's overdraft was 'significantly reduced'. They still had time to celebrate their ninth wedding anniversary, in the city where they had met, with an Adelphi supper ('Afterwards, we get very hot but happy').

When the tour moved on to Hull, Norris joined them for a few days, he and Michael having one morning in Beverley to themselves (where they talked of 'the holiday we would one day like to take together'). Michael wrote in Hull, 'Dick, Rachel and Norris seem to me the 3 great people of my life. With each of them I have been ecstatically happy, creatively happy.'

Michael joined the location shoot for the film (Dunfee had negotiated a £7000 fee, the first instalment of which soothed the bank manager) at a disused RAF station at Catterick, the background for the airfield in *The Way to the Stars* as it was now titled. Michael knew 'Puffin' Asquith – he had been among the guests at Mrs Gould's lunch for Yehudi Menuhin – but had never worked with him and was at once impressed by his evident careful preparation and by the relaxed but concentrated on-set atmosphere, reminiscent of Carol Reed. Gentle and quietly spoken, usually dressed in frayed blue overalls (Ingrid Bergman initially mistook him for a studio technician), he was the son of Herbert Asquith, Liberal Prime Minister 1908–16, and the formidable Margot, besotted by films since his Winchester schooldays although politically of the left (and proud of his long service as president of the film technicians' union ACCT). He had directed Rattigan on stage and was ideal for the dramatist's oblique handling of emotion and his spare, understated style.

Michael had been sorry to leave Rachel at Bromyard from where she wrote regularly, making him jealous about breakfasts of porridge and cream and fresh farm eggs, and vividly describing the plays written and presented by Vanessa, Corin and their friend Stephen Croft, with proper rehearsals, tickets for admission and electric light bulbs for footlights (shades of Roy and his sister Lena). But *The Way to the Stars* was a delight to make, the location atmosphere taking on the elated wartime camaraderie of the picture; Michael, John Mills and Basil Radford, his old colleague from *The Lady Vanishes* and *Climbing High*, all had a good time on and off the set. The film captured something, too, of that hectic good-fellowship mixed with danger and sentiment between airmen during the Battle of Britain. Rather as *The Way Ahead* had treated the Army, *The Way to the Stars* combined an involving story with a semi-documentary treatment in a film of two halves. The first part of the picture is the story of the flight-lieutenant played by Michael who is killed not long after his marriage and the birth of his child, the second part the story of an American pilot (Douglass Montgomery) who falls for the widow. The pilots never meet in the film but the two stories intermesh cunningly in Rattigan's screenplay, although the film does perceptibly dim in its later stages with Montgomery's rather bland performance unequally matched with Michael's.

At one point Asquith, Rattigan and producer Anatole de Grunwald were so impressed by Michael's work that they had the idea of him doubling with the American pilot whose scenes were scheduled for later, and had got as far as make-up and tests before dropping the notion. Only subsequently did Michael discover that it was largely because both Van Heflin and Burgess Meredith had turned down the part and they were panicking that they might not be able to cast an American actor.

Emotional restraint is the essence of Rattigan's best work and that quality infuses all the scenes between Michael and Rosamund John as his hotel manageress wife, scenes which both actors play with extraordinarily affecting finesse, charging everyday, intimate exchanges with a depth of feeling and of fear (although neither voices the thought of imminent death). One of the most moving moments in the film is Michael's quiet, restrained delivery of the epitaph which his character, a would-be poet, has written for himself, borrowed from a John Pudney poem but seemingly here to belong by right to every flyer –

> Do not despair
> For Johnny Head-in-air
> He sleeps as sound
> As Johnny underground
>
> . . .
>
> Better by far
> For Johnny-the-Bright-Star
> To keep your head
> And see his children fed

– a poem which, with what Michael saw as its 'strong socialist undercurrent', remained a lifelong favourite.

Michael left location hoping that he might work with Asquith again. During the shooting, the music-mad Puffin had lent him Donald Tovey's book on the concerto, in which Michael was struck by a sentence which might have served as a kind of credo for both Asquith and himself: 'One of the first essentials of creative art is the habit of imagining the most familiar things as vividly as the most surprising.'

Returning to London to prepare to relaunch *Uncle Harry*, Michael was reunited with Norris, although there was a brief *froideur* when Norris went off for a Devon weekend, Michael having planned to join him, telling Michael at the last minute that he was 'expecting a friend there'. Michael was honest enough to write that it was his vanity that had been hurt as much as anything (he had already packed a suitcase), but it seemed to mark a stage in the relationship. Yet the next day he wrote: 'Seeing US Navy uniforms in street reminds me constantly of him.'

With the frets of a fairly new relationship it must have been odd for him to be reminded of a past one as he and Edith Evans rehearsed for a BBC radio broadcast of *As You Like It*: 'Some of the magic of 1936 comes back at the sound of those lines.' Edith had insisted on Michael for Orlando, saying that she would simply not be able to re-create her Rosalind without him.

Norris and Michael were together again briefly and as intensely as previously before Norris was sent by the Naval Reserve to Paris while *Uncle Harry* resumed its run, its box office only slightly affected by the threat of buzz-bombs. Michael and Rachel were also thinking of moving again with Rivermead Court not quite big enough, although Michael was not entirely convinced by John Fowler's argument that now they needed 'a background house' ('I'm all for background if there are some staff to be had in the foreground'). There had been some talk of Michael taking over Chapel Street from Andy, but although it was usefully central, he was reluctant. Relations between Daisy and Michael had been strained for much of the year, with her old bilious spite about his career and about Rachel often on display, sometimes making meetings impossible: 'I realise my greatest fault is timidity, much of which is derived from being "protected" by her.' Very few people – Diana Gould was one, Bea Lehmann and John Fowler others – saw behind the façade to Michael's insecurities. Once, on the *Uncle Harry* tour, Ena Burrill had been taken aback when, twitting Michael about his manner with headwaiters (a vague look with his mouth slightly open), he had replied honestly: 'The reason is I am afraid of such people.'

John Fowler had come up with some likely houses, Michael taking particularly to one in Thurloe Square (£1250 and £110 per annum rates) but nobody else was keen. In late November a house came up for sale on the river at Chiswick. Michael bicycled from Putney to look at it: "Wander all over it, talking to myself – "My God", "But this is incredible" – for it has everything. And so it should for £12,000.' Next day Michael, Rachel, John Fowler and Diana Gould visited it and despite dry rot in the basement, all were enthusiastic. John Fowler immediately got on to his solicitor saying, 'You *must* get it for them!' and by doing so Fay Blackett-Gill became the Redgraves' solicitor too. A dynamic, chic woman, she had set up her own firm in Staple Inn after qualifying at twenty-eight, at a time when women were hardly taken seriously in the legal profession, building up a clientele predominantly from the theatrical and fashion worlds. She was able to arrange a building society mortgage – just over £600 a year for twenty years – which was not tiny then, but easily possible on Michael's likely future income. The house needed a good deal of exterior work, the garden total reclaiming, but both Michael and Rachel instinctively felt positive about the move.

Bedford House was the Redgrave home for the next eleven years. It was one of the large, dark-brick houses of a beautiful Queen Anne terrace in Chiswick Mall, on the river just up from Thames Eyot, with a bakery at one end and a brewery, scenting the air with hops, at the other. The Dove pub was just up the road on the river, close to the house where William Morris had lived and from where he would take the whole family by river to Kelmscott. The area was then a mixture of working families from the nearby brewery and the Cherry Blossom shoe-polish factory, and upper-middle-class neighbours including A. P. Herbert and his wife Gwen, their stage-designer daughter Jocelyn, then married to the solicitor and painter Anthony Lousada, George and Sophie Devine, Julian

Trevelyan and, next door, Tom and Mary Nelson, both doctors, with Alec and Merula Guinness nearby in St Peter's Square. The friendship interrupted by the war was important to both Alec and Michael, both inhibited men but who could relax feeling at ease in each other's company. Michael would often 'drop in' on Alec and Corin, who played with Matthew at St. Peter's Square, later speculated that 'they probably confided in each other quite a lot. My father always carried quite a burden of guilt vis-à-vis my mother and us children.' The diaries which Alec kept throughout most of his adult life touch on the kind of confessional aspect to their discussions (one is described as a 'fascinating heart to heart and hair down talk') but beyond the mention of their exchanging notes 'on our drunken mums' he did not note specific details.

The garden was a jungle, completely taken over by couch grass, and the house had lost a few windows, but with considerable help from Mr Owers the gardener and from John Fowler, a genius at using inexpensive materials (book-binding canvas as curtains), the house and garden began to take on new life. Rachel, too, always had a special gift for making homes, while in the garden she and Michael (a more occasional gardener) planted old roses and hundreds of bulbs, reclaiming a pergola near the drawing-room french windows as a summer patio, the rest of the garden sloping down to the river where tugboats still travelled with their cargo and on which swans glided at high tide. Their first social event was a children's party before Christmas, with a huge tree and other children – young Matthew Guinness, the Lousada children – joining the family. Rachel was heartened to hear Michael tell her that he loved Bedford House – and nearby Chiswick Park with its Inigo Jones gateway, where he walked the dog and learnt lines, communing with the shades of Pope and Hogarth – and that he 'should want to stay at home more'.

And yet his diary continues to record the ceaseless battle between that instinct and his other desires. Alternating with entries such as: 'Home and talk about new house. R. says last days have been so happy. Tonight certainly was,' regularly he records another feast with his panthers: 'To W. R. Mean to ring R. up and don't. Meet T., had only vague idea of appointment. V. satisfactory and so home, where I can't apologise to R. ... At breakfast R. justifiably very angry. ... Promise to try to do better.'

Uncle Harry was becoming more of a strain; sex, Benzedrine and drink were all necessary to fuel the demanding nervous intensity of the part. He was often ill – respiratory trouble, involving nasal douches – resorting to colonic irrigation to clear his system of ailments real and imaginary. Also, he took to arriving as late as possible at the theatre – most uncharacteristically – as if dreading each curtain rise and taking his performance closer to the edge of danger. He was even starting to drink before curtain-up: 'To W. R. and drink quite a few too many whiskies. By the end of the play my speech is definitely slowed down. Why do I do it?'

In the end, after nearly a year with the play ('a year of hurly-burly') he was close to a breakdown and the play closed. Binkie, to Michael's dismay, seemed from his silence displeased at closing a play still making money, although in fact Michael had originally contracted to play Harry for three months only.

Work was piling up for the future, with planned films including an Ealing anthology film, *Dead of Night*, and an adaptation of Graham Greene's *The Man Within*. Michael still had tax debts to clear and to meet expenses on Bedford House, but he also decided to fit in another play, again with a part for Rachel, which he would co-present, direct and in which he would also star.

Jacobowsky and the Colonel – its self-deprecating American adaptor, S. N. Behrman, loved the cartoon of two bearded East Side New York Jews looking at the theatre marquee, one asking the other, 'Jacobowsky and the *what*?' – had come to him from a new producer, Peter Daubeny, an ex-actor who had lost an arm at Salerno. The play had been a Broadway hit directed by Elia Kazan; set against the fall of France, it seemed to find its moment in America just as *Thunder Rock* had in London. A humorous parable dramatising the ego of an aristocratic Polish colonel contrasted with the shrewd survival instinct of the resourceful Jewish and also Polish Jacobowsky, its background was based on the experiences of the original author, Franz Werfel, who had been trapped in France while escaping Hitler's Germany making for America with his wife, the scalphuntress Alma Mahler. It had a cast of over twenty and several sets as it moved from Paris to the Atlantic coast against the events of 1940 and needed top-flight casting.

In New York the best part, the wily Jacobowsky, had been played by the great Viennese actor Oscar Karlweiss (a legendary Orlovsky in *Die Fledermaus*), the sole actor Behrman ever felt was equipped to play his hero, Montaigne. For London, it was played by Karel Stepanek, husband of *Winged Victory*'s Wanda Rotha, a fine actor but lacking the ability effortlessly to beguile an audience, vital for the part. Michael's role, the egocentric, quixotically feudal Colonel Stjerbinsky ('You have one of the finest minds of the fifteenth century. Unfortunately we live in the twentieth,' Jacobowsky tells him), initially outraged at having to travel with a Jew, and who believes that modern civilisation lacks heroism and poetry, is a magnificent dinosaur, but it is a one-note part and it was not one of his best performances. A character of such blissful self-assurance he found difficult and although he looked convincingly dashing, the performance was over-stiff and subject to a law of diminishing comedic returns. Rachel, too, was basically miscast as Marianne, emblematic of indomitable France. Diana Gould doubled as a cast-off girlfriend of the Colonel's and a tango-dancer in tight satin in a waterfront café, and Frith Banbury, in one of his last performances before his producer-director career, was very effective as an *'Allo, 'Allo*-style lisping Gestapo man.

In London, the play came over rather as the Broadway mogul Lee Shubert had described it: 'Potash and Perlmutter with class!' (a London wag subtitled it *Veni, Vidi, Vichy*) and while Kazan's kinetically charged Broadway staging of the play as a kind of ballet of ideas had papered over its repetitiveness, Michael's production never fused its comedic style with its tragic theme. The reviews, apart from a rave from an emotional Ivor Novello as Guest Critic for the *Sunday Chronicle*, were tepid. Agate was unusually savage, using his piece as yet another chance to insist that Michael should never play comedy and shooting Rachel down for having 'drenched the south-west corner of France with the authentic perfume of Wimbledon'. Running costs were too high to nurse the play when receipts dipped after a strong start and it ran only a couple of months.

For the rest of the year Michael was hardly out of the film studios, moving from one set to another, creating some friction with Jack Dunfee with whom he had never had the same easy relationship as he had with Bill Linnit. During rehearsals for *Jacobowsky*, VE-Day had been celebrated – Michael and the cast moved into the packed streets, a crazy mixture of celebration and catharsis – and all the opportunities seemed now ready for a post-war British film renaissance, with Michael hoping for more scripts of the quality of *The Way to the Stars*, which had been a big critical and public success.

He was excited about the idea of the first of his scheduled pictures. *The Captive Heart* was one of the first British films to deal with the subject of prisoners of war, an Ealing film which had been suggested by Aileen Balcon (wife of Ealing's chief Michael Balcon), who had been with the Red Cross during the war. Michael was not necessarily expecting an English *La Grande Illusion* but the script was a disappointment (he was even more disappointed with the publicity, which advertised it as 'The Strangest Love Story Ever Told'). Angus MacPhail and Guy Morgan (an ex-POW) began their treatment with an almost documentary approach, with several sequences, superbly shot by Basil Dearden, of the hapless marching of wounded soldiers captured at Dunkirk beneath lowering grey cloudscapes. They then moved into the camp (shot on location at Marlag only six weeks after the Nazis abandoned it), gradually establishing the relationships and tensions between a disparate group of men (including Basil Radford in one of his best performances as a colonel trying to preserve morale). Then another narrative begins to dominate, tracing the story of Hasek, a Czech soldier escaped from a concentration camp who has taken the clothes and identity of a dead British officer, a stratagem which compels him to continue correspondence with the dead man's waiting wife (Rachel), falling in love with her photograph and finally reaching England, presumably to marry her.

Michael's performance is extremely subtle, dangerously but absorbingly low-key to start with as Hasek tries to efface himself in the camp, with just an occasional facial muscle or an unusual inflection betraying his inner tension. C. A. Lejeune, who, like most critics, felt the unforced truth of the early scenes was somewhat compromised by the romantic element, still rated Michael's performance highly, recognising the difficulty of playing a character forced to mask most emotion: 'Time and again, his skilful way with a line gives it a kind of isolated warmth and beauty.'

Like so many screenwriters for British films then, the team for *The Captive Heart* wrote poorly for women. The leading role in *The Years Between* is a woman (Valerie Hobson), created by a woman (Daphne du Maurier adapting her own successful play), but although the film raises a potentially rich subject – a prisoner of war's return to an altered post-war world – the writing is stamped with all the vices of cliché, class-bound convention and sexlessness of so much British cinema of the period. Its story of a woman who, believing her husband killed, falls in love with another man and then sees her husband return need not necessarily have developed into such a novelettish affair, full of the uncritical feudalism of gnomic postmen and comic-relief parlourmaids in ATS uniform automatically saluting the gentry, and wasting Flora Robson as a loyal old retainer. The film was from the same team (producer Sydney Box, director Compton Bennett) responsible for the enormously popular *The Seventh Veil* and yet again all the really interesting issues raised, including a husband having to adjust to a world in which his wife has taken over his parliamentary seat, are dissipated in the stress on the romantic triangle. Michael enters the film late – he does not appear until just before halfway – as it crawls along while Valerie Hobson treats the House of Commons like the filling in a sandwich between Harrods and the hair salon, and for a while he manages to give it some interest, significantly finding his best opportunity in a scene without dialogue. This is a long sequence, virtually silent, in which he moves through his beautiful country house with an odd air of wary contentment shot through with a suggestion of unease, on his return from a POW camp and finding the fabric of his life altered. Sex, of course, goes unmentioned, but in one short scene, when Michael suddenly pulls Valerie Hobson into his arms in a burst of physical desire, the moment seems peculiarly, shockingly human amid the *Mrs Miniver* corn.

A film which did take sex on board, as it were, although in a somewhat unexpected way, was the lumpy colour version of Graham Greene's first published novel, *The Man Within*. Very different from the later novels of Greeneland, in 1929 this had sold remarkably well for a first effort, although Greene tended to dismiss it. It was mostly seen as a spirited canter over the country of one of Michael's favourite writers of his adolescence, Stanley Weyman. A tale of Regency smuggling in Sussex, this cast Michael as Carlyon, commander of the smugglers' ship, opposite a young Richard Attenborough (with an alarming Nature-Boy hairdo) as the craven young smuggler Francis, orphan son of Carlyon's closest friend who tips off the Excisemen. On the run, pursued by Carlyon, he becomes involved with two women, an innocent farm girl (an unlikely Joan Greenwood, essaying her RADA wench dialect) and a sensual older woman played, with a good deal of ringlet-tossing, by Jean Kent ('she puts the sex into Sussex' as one review, somewhat overstating the case, put it).

The title is taken from Sir Thomas Browne: 'There is another man within me and he is angry with me.' Greene's original story of cowardice becoming courage laid more stress on the spiritual and sexual conflicts within Francis than on the suspense between smugglers and Excisemen. In the book the sexual pull between the respective purity and carnality of the two women is the fulcrum of Francis's craving for the physical, but the screenplay (Muriel and Sydney Box) and the direction (Bernard Knowles) lay a more surprising stress on the bond between Carlyon and Francis, lending the film a homoerotic subtext surprisingly strong for the time. There is a heavy emphasis on punishment, the film opening with a torture scene before flashbacking to the main story with Carlyon promising to 'take care' of the lad on leaving school, insisting he move into his cabin on board and reading poetry together. Francis comes to see Carlyon as a replacement for his hated father, the epitome of everything he admires. But Carlyon's sadistic side emerges when envious shipmates plant money from stolen brandy on Francis, for which he is stripped, tied to the mast and flogged by Carlyon himself (cut to screaming seagulls).

On board, Michael's Carlyon is often moodily bare-chested, with lots of lowering, enigmatic looks between him and Francis, and when Carlyon is pursuing the boy over the moors, the camera frequently silhouettes him in his cape and tricorn hat against swirling mists. In the final reel, with Francis confronted by a captured, stripped and whipped Carlyon, whom he finally decides not to betray again, Carlyon chooses death so that Francis can go free, their last goodbye whispered, like lovers, through prison bars. By then, we are in an exceedingly rum film indeed, an exotic hybrid of Georgette Heyer and Jean Genet, although in a post-war climate which saw cinema attendances boom, it did good business. It rather depressed Michael that queues could form for it while the public stayed away from a film he had passionately wanted to do, *Fame is the Spur*.

Reuniting him with the Boulting brothers, this was an ambitious and, for the time, big-budget (£350,000) film, based on the 1940 best-seller by Howard Spring. One theory for its disappointing takings was that by presenting a character based on Ramsay MacDonald and implicitly criticising the 1945 Attlee Labour government, the film's coincidence with a mood of post-war disillusion made it off-putting to the public, although as film historians have said, the screenplay by novelist Nigel Balchin had been finished only a year after Labour's election victory when strikes and disastrous internal divisions had not yet scarred it. The Boultings insisted – and Michael agreed – that to attack the Labour government was not the film's aim, pointing out that, in Spring's novel as well as in the script, the story of party compromises carried lessons for the future.

Like *The Stars Look Down*, the film had to slim down a three-part multi-narrative novel. The spine is the story of Hamer Radshaw, born illegitimate in Manchester's Ancoats district, paralleling his personal story with the fate of the book's central symbol, the sabre rescued from the Peterloo Massacre by Hamer's activist grandfather. In the novel, Hamer's son throws the sword into the sea before his death in the Spanish Civil War; Balchin retained it right until the closing scene when the old and now isolated Hamer cannot reach it on the wall. Whole sequences, sadly including a meeting between Hamer and Friedrich Engels in a Manchester bookshop, are cut, while Balchin's script reinforces the contrast between Hamer, prepared to compromise for the greater good, and his lifelong friend Ryerson who maintains all his early ideals, appalled when Hamer evasively does not publicly support the 1929 hunger strike marchers. Against the canvas of New Labour, some of Hamer's arguments, as when he refutes Ryerson's charge of selling out with a ruthlessly pragmatic counter-attack, saying, 'The Party indulges in too much sentimental talk about "the old days"! We're no longer a little bunch of enthusiasts at street corners,' seem remarkably familiar.

Michael brought great skill and sympathy to a very difficult part, which took him through many years. The problem is that, more in screenplay than in Spring's novel, Hamer is a one-note character, even if not the Ramsay MacDonald clone some critics alleged. The book's Hamer is more complex and essentially, truthfully anti-heroic, whereas the film, which repeatedly reinforces his abandonment of principle for expediency, increases the difficulty of responding to him sympathetically. But in some scenes Michael's eyes, always an index to his involvement with a character, dull and cloud over with shame most movingly as he accepts an accusation of compromise, while they blaze in the early scenes when conviction and dreams still burn. All through he keeps the character and the film alive and engaged. The *Daily Worker*, perhaps inevitably, gave it its best review, urging that 'All Labour leaders should see the film twice', but even in the unlikely event that they did, attendance figures remained low.

Of all the films he made in that crowded 1945–46, he was always most proud of his contribution to the Ealing compendium film *Dead of Night*. His agents were none too keen – a short episode, *The Ventriloquist's Dummy*, in a five-story film seemed infra dig – but Michael was completely enthralled by the script and charmed by the unassuming, Brazilian-born director Alberto de Cavalcanti ('Cav') who had made only a few films, including the splendid *Went the Day Well?*, based on a Graham Greene story about a British village infiltrated by Nazis.

Ventriloquists always intrigued Michael – he often hired one for children's parties – and he had much admired the haunting performance by Erich von Stroheim in *The Great Gabbo*, an early talkie of 1929 which had von Stroheim as a pitiful, obsessed ventriloquist attacking his dummy Otto and using him as an outlet for feelings he cannot express. Since then the screen had ignored a profitable subject, except for guest appearances by professional ventriloquists such as the American Edgar Bergen with his dummy Charlie MacCarthy. *The Ventriloquist's Dummy* was written by John V. Baines and is a perfect screenplay-in-miniature, easily the strongest section of the film's stories of phantoms, possession and premonition, linked by the character (Mervyn Johns) who meets the people in his recurring dreams. The combination of the taut lean story, Cavalcanti's subtle direction and an hypnotic piece of screen acting from Michael lift it clear from any suggestion of being just a horror story to the level of art.

The subject surely taps into something primal, the dread of the disembodied voice which must go back to the Oracles of Greece or the dybbuks of ancient civilisations of Israel. The fear is compounded by the fact that for most people there is something menacing and curiously unsettling about a ventriloquist's dummy, the assemblage of papier mâché, rolling but vacant glass eyes and little-man miniature body suggesting that the dummy may be inhabited by some familiar that could at any time take on a life and personality of its own. The sinister hint of violence and dismemberment seems fundamental to the very concept of the disembodied voice, something that Baines' script cleverly exploits, as Gerald Kersh had also done in the scary title-story of his 1944 collection, *The Extraordinarily Horrible Dummy*; in no more than four terse pages it casts a similarly sweaty spell in the tale of Ecco, a sad, haunted ventriloquist whose ghoulish dummy is possessed by a human spirit. Film – after all a ventriloquial medium – can exploit these terrors uniquely and no other film on the subject (certainly not Richard Attenborough's pale Xerox, *Magic*) can come close to *The Ventriloquist's Dummy*'s authentic horror.

Michael plays Maxwell Frere, a successful ventriloquist who, at the start of the film performing in Elisabeth Welch's nightclub, is clearly already disturbed as his dummy, Hugo, escalates the process of taking him over. Drink does nothing to calm his nerves and Frere also becomes convinced that a rival ventriloquist, Sylvester (Hartley Power), is out to steal Hugo. A tale of possession and dual personality mounts in tension until Frere is driven mad, locked in an asylum's padded cell before the film springs its most chilling twist. After Frere has violently destroyed Hugo, stamping him brutally to bits, a genuinely concerned Sylvester visits him. As Frere's eyes swivel to his 'rival' his mouth lolls open but what emerges is not recognisable speech but a nightmarish '*Exorcist*'-like cacophony of chokes and gaggings like a record or tape on fast-forward before finally, when speech comes, it is Hugo's voice emerging from Frere's mouth with 'Why, hello, Sylvester, I've been expecting you'. Michael's eyes in Cavalcanti's final shots match anything from Anthony Perkins and Hitchcock at the end of *Psycho*.

For a short episode, it is an extraordinarily dense film, not only tapping into basic fears and superstitions but capable of different interpretations. More recently it has been seen as the story of a repressed homosexual – Frere's gay sensibility evident from details such as Hugo's photograph on his dressing table, his jealousy if another person touches Hugo, with the 'rival' Sylvester viewed as a threat to Frere and Hugo, while Hugo 'flirts' with Sylvester ('We two could make beautiful music together'). That Cavalcanti was homosexual is occasionally added as supporting evidence of the film's 'subtext'. It is unlikely that that is what Baines, Cavalcanti and Michael consciously intended, but it is also an earnest of the film's unsettling density that, when viewed again, it can take on totally new colours in the light of such readings.

Michael refused to use wires or tricks for the Frere–Hugo sequences, working hard with Diana Graves, his friend from Old Vic days, helping him plan Hugo's voice and the intricate timing involved. He also worked with the ventriloquist Peter Brough of radio's *Educating Archie* to advise on the kind of cheeky-chappie, irrepressible persona he wanted for Hugo. His performance was praised but the film itself was treated as little more than at best superior Grand Guignol (Agate dismissed it as 'a mess'). Only the writer Lesley Blanch, discussing it in *The Leader*, saw the film's real originality, comparing Cavalcanti's and Michael's work with the kind of film which emerged from the Ufa studios, directed by Lang, Murnau or Robert Weine, and starring Conrad Veidt or Werner Krauss, when magic was an accepted force in German cinema.

Moving from the neurosis of Harry Quincey to the macabre, patho-
logical mind of Maxwell Frere had been a strain on Michael's nerves. He
was having more nightmares, one inspired by Elizabeth Bowen's story
'The Inherited Clock' when he woke up screaming for Rachel and
knowing the real meaning of the phrase about the tongue cleaving to the
roof of the mouth. Bedford House, which, like his children, he saw little
of during a long period of continuous filming – undoubtedly making for
subsequent awkward shyness between him and Lynn in particular – could
soothe some of the stress, and he and Rachel worked on in the garden,
planting more old and climbing roses alongside almond and japonica
trees.

The Chiswick social life was often lively, although it tended to be
informal. Michael and Rachel hosted their first real dinner party in March
when their guests included Guinnesses, Lousadas, Topolskis and Nelsons
along with the novelist William Gerhardi. Michael was somewhat surprised when Gerhardi asked him to be a subject for the 'Character' series
of profiles, based on the subject's answers to some set questions, in the
News Chronicle, which continued to be Michael's newspaper and for which
Gerhardi occasionally wrote. Titled 'Michael Redgrave: The Summing-
Up', it refuted C. P. Snow's dotty remark that actors' temperament is akin
to that of footballers, claiming that Michael was 'the actor poet': ·

> How honest, how self-searching, are your answers – they reflect the poet's
> thought, the scholar's scruple that make you the most exquisite of our
> actors. . . . A practical idealist, you have in spite of all remained starry-eyed.
> On the negative side, there is a good deal of undigested hero-worship –
> due, perhaps, to some unacknowledged reverence for a parent.

Gerhardi, who then did not know Michael well, indeed touched on some
key areas of his personality. The series ended before the *News Chronicle*
printed it but Michael always kept the typescript Gerhardi gave him.
He also, in a rare assertion of parental authority (other than constantly
chivvying his children about their posture – 'Sit up! Sit up!'), took the
News Chronicle regularly to the children, suggesting it might be an idea to
read another paper besides Nanny Randall's *Daily Mail* or *Empire News*.
He had been somewhat alarmed on location to hear from Rachel during
the coal crisis of that freezing winter and the Labour government's State
of Emergency: 'Corin and Vanessa, always conservative, now rail against
Attlee and Shinwell, come out with streams of statistics and generally
seem to know almost more than any of us.'

Although his immediate future was filled with work, longer-term plans
were still nebulous. Alexander Korda, even harder to pin down than most
film tycoons, had offered Michael a four-year contract for six pictures

with six months off to do stage work after every second film, at a fee of a then remarkable £20,000 a film. This had been negotiated by Michael's new agent, Cecil Tennant, to whom he had gone after *Uncle Harry* closed, no longer happy with Jack Dunfee. Tennant – 'Uncle Cecil' to Olivier and Vivien Leigh, two of his clients – was the sort of man of whom Michael was always somewhat in awe. Tall – taller even than Michael – he was impeccably groomed, self-confident (Eton and the Guards background), decisive, with a perfect 'trophy' wife, the ex-ballerina Irina Baronova. An extremely smooth business operator, in partnership with the American Myron Selznick in the English branch of MCA (Music Corporation of America), he represented only stars and major earners, working hard for his clients (although there were those who said he really worked hard for MCA's percentage) and was on familiar terms with all the theatre and film power brokers. Rachel was always somewhat cool about him, feeling he rather regarded her as not truly 'A list'. However, at that time, even Tennant could not track down Korda, supposedly in America, finally to sign Michael's contract (he never did).

Nor had Binkie committed to the scheme of Michael's West End company. He had even gone to talk to representatives from J. Arthur Rank and some interest had been expressed in Rank funding the company in return for Michael's commitment to Rank pictures. With Michael worried about the quality of Rank scripts – and Cecil worried about what Rank could pay – he had no confidence that route would be happy.

In more private areas, Norris (who returned to America before the end of the war) and Michael wrote often to each other (according to Michael's diary) although the cooling of their affair had not been helped by their separation. More or less simultaneously, it would seem, each had decided that the other was not the great love of his life. Great fondness remained, however, and they still hoped to work together. Norris now was involved, with several partners, in a new non-profit organisation in New York, Theater Incorporated, which had recently produced a successful revival of *Pygmalion* with Gertrude Lawrence (whose husband, Richard Aldrich, was a Theater Inc. partner). Norris had suggested de Flores in *The Change-ling* as a possible part for Michael to play for the company before long.

Michael was keen to work in America, especially in his adored New York to which he had not returned since 1941, and frustratingly he had recently had to turn down a reprise of *The Beggar's Opera* for Broadway, tantalisingly with a Duke Ellington score; the dates could not synchronise with his film schedule. In addition, the world of British films, his sole province for over a year, often depressed him with its lack of vision and readiness to settle for the average, the work of a few directors excepted.

One high spot among all the activity of 1946 had been Dick Green's return to England 'from his long ordeal' in military prison: 'And, thank God and D's sense of philosophy, more or less unscathed – in fact, fortified, I think.' Michael immediately offered Dick the use of a small studio he had bought near Bedford House where Dick could readjust and pick up the reins of his writing before deciding his future. Rachel, who had always liked Dick, was also glad to see him seemingly undamaged. Before he moved in, Michael accompanied him to his parents' Buxton home, spending the time walking the moors with him: 'with chat about all the more sordid and comic aspects of our lives during the past six years.' On returning to Bedford House, the new family labrador, Rudi, 'was so pleased to see me he peed down the front of my coat' and he also found waiting for him a new offer via Cecil for him to ponder.

Hollywood had made overtures to Michael previously – the producer Sam Howard once offering him a fortune for a picture he was not available to do in any event – but now Cecil had an offer for two consecutive Hollywood films. Both sounded tempting. The first would be directed by his revered Fritz Lang who had been in Hollywood since before the war, a *film noir* called *Secret Beyond the Door*, followed by a film version of Eugene O'Neill's mighty *Mourning Becomes Electra*, scripted and directed by Dudley Nichols, with Michael again as an Orestes-figure, Orin Mannon, in O'Neill's reworking of Aeschylus. Cecil had also negotiated excellent money – $47,000 for the Lang film – and although Michael knew it would mean a long absence from home, his instinct, fully backed by Rachel (it was decided that she should come over for part of the time), was to accept.

Booked to sail in early January 1947, having two films – *The Man Within* and *Fame is the Spur* – awaiting release in England while he was away, his spirits were high over that Christmas at Bedford House with the now ritual family present opening on the parental bed. And just before the year's end he lunched with Binkie when it was agreed that provided Tennent's could arrange some funding from CEMA (the forerunner of the Arts Council) he would present *Macbeth* with Michael in the West End, after a provincial tour, on his return from Hollywood. Michael had always dreamt of being more the master of his own career after the war and it must have seemed then as if this coming year of Hollywood films and classic work in London was the perfect combination with which to launch that ideal.

Twelve
HOLLYWOOD DREAMS

From an arctic London where the stores had run out of candles and oil lamps with the threat of a total electricity breakdown, Rachel replied to Michael's early letters from Hollywood: 'Everything sounds wonderful and the whole life like a sort of fairy tale.' Michael could only agree. He had sailed in luxury on the *America* and in New York at the Sherry-Netherland Hotel was taken shopping for new suits and shirts at Saks (all on Universal Studio expenses). He had time for a brief reunion at the Stork Club with Norris before travelling on the Twentieth Century to Chicago (lunch en route with Gertrude Lawrence); he changed there to the Super Chief for Pasadena where the press gathered to photograph him being met by Fritz Lang, in vicuña coat and with his trademark monocle in place, before he was whisked off to a suite in the Bel Air Hotel.

As he was required initially at the studio only for costume and make-up tests, his life at first was indeed 'a sort of fairy tale'. There were lunches with the Hollywood Raj – David Niven, Gladys Cooper, Ivor Novello and the vanishing lady, Dame May Whitty – drinks with Lang and his beautiful forthcoming co-star Joan Bennett, and a prized Sunday lunch invitation from the aristocrat of Hollywood's social scene, director George Cukor, to whom he had been introduced by Novello, and at whose table he joined Katharine Hepburn, Fanny Brice, Beatrice Lillie and Greta Garbo. Michael was so tongue-tied by sharing a car home with Garbo that when she eagerly enquired about the extent of British Buddhism he could only stammer that there wasn't a lot of it about, which ended that – and indeed all – conversation. He was literally dumbstruck by her beauty, writing to Rachel of her 'eyelids quivering like butterflies' wings when the insect is resting on a flower.'

He was occasionally taken to informal gatherings at the Santa Monica home of Berthold Viertel (Bea Lehmann's ex-lover) and his wife Salka, a close friend of Garbo's and a legendary hostess, known as 'The Mother of us All', a warm, flame-haired woman to whom most of the émigrés who had left Europe for Hollywood in the 1930s gravitated. There Michael met for the first time Franz Werfel, author of the original *Jacobowsky and the Colonel* as well as Thomas and Heinrich Mann, Arnold Schoenberg and Bertolt Brecht. He also heard a good deal of fascinating gossip about Fritz Lang, an occasional but not very popular visitor to the Viertels' – did he really murder his first wife? Was he really asked by Goebbels to head the German film industry? – and began to comprehend something of the myths around his director.

At the Bel Air he could bask in or beside the huge pool, walk in the hills behind the hotel and sometimes take to its squash club, only slightly fazed by a stark-naked Mickey Rooney offering him his cologne in the showers. There were further Cukor starry lunches – other guests including Ethel Barrymore, Moss Hart, Olivia De Havilland and, disconcertingly, a sweaty and tetchy Evelyn Waugh, who was there on *Brideshead Revisited* business – before filming began on *Secret Beyond the Door*.

The experience of the film came like an icy shower after his balmy introduction to Hollywood. Michael had not seen a completed script until shortly before going in front of the cameras (he never found out that James Mason had already turned down the part) and only then did he begin to get some idea of the hornet's nest he had entered. The script was by Sylvia Richards, one of Lang's girlfriends – she introduced this most Teutonic of directors to square-dancing – who worked in the offices of his production company. It had been based on a *Redbook* pulp-fiction serial (source of many a *film noir*) but most of the plot had been changed, with extensive tinkering by Lang. The director had also had an affair with Joan Bennett who had starred in four of his American films, most recently in *Scarlet Street* as a floozie known as 'Lazy Legs'. The film was being made as a venture of Diana Productions, a company formed by Lang and Joan Bennett's producer husband Walter Wanger – they and Bennett were the principal stockholders – under a deal with Universal.

The set-up did not give Lang quite the power he had been used to at the Ufa Studios in the 1920s, but he still behaved like a parody of the despotic Teutonic director on set, with tantrums and tirades against cast and crew, and screaming rows with the cinematographer Stanley Cortez (who had photographed Orson Welles' *The Magnificent Ambersons*). Lang wanted Cortez fired (although his contribution is one of the few virtues of the movie) but Joan Bennett was fully aware of how well Cortez photographed women, and he remained on the film. Wanger, perhaps wisely, mostly avoided the set throughout.

Even with all the background tensions and internecine squabbles, a decent film might have emerged. But *Secret Beyond the Door* was hamstrung from the start by its screenplay, so *noir* as to be often impenetrable, a mish-mash of a 'woman's picture', the Bluebeard legend and all the recently fashionable oneiric and Freudian trappings used by Hitchcock in *Spellbound* – Daliesque dream sequences, turgid analysis of repressed-memory syndrome and a moody, fragmented score (Lang even used the same composer as *Spellbound* – Miklos Rosza). Lang added to an already over-burdened script all his favourite leitmotifs and trademark elements of water (a wishing-well sequence) and fire, with a near immolation at the end, reminiscent of *Rebecca* and complete with a Mrs Danvers figure.

The film opens wonderfully, with a Mexican sequence full of shadows and virtuoso tracking shots, all handled with authoritative flair, but once into the story the script shoots the picture in the foot. Although Lang was often fascinated by the dualism of his male 'heroes' (in *Scarlet Street* he is even named Chris Cross), Michael's publisher Mark Lamphere – rather like Gregory Peck in *Spellbound*, alternately outgoing and withdrawn – his demons based on a guilt complex rooted in a childhood trauma, is a mass of contradictions rather than conflicts, and he is saddled with some ludicrous dialogue, not least in a bizarre trial sequence when he has to both prosecute and defend himself.

Michael grew very fond of Joan Bennett – she and her sister Constance, daughters of the stage star Richard Bennett, knew all the Hollywood ropes – and their shared humour helped get them through a film both knew early on was never going to have a chance, as Michael reflected: 'Am frankly bored with the film. Fritz's passion for detail seems silly and maddening.'

The disillusion with Lang and disappointment over what he had hoped would be a new departure in film, away from the parochial world of the British studios, were alleviated by his continuing glamorous social life. Gene Kelly and his wife Betsey often had him over for brunch or volleyball, other guests including Judy Garland, her then husband Vincente Minnelli and Phil Silvers. He was now also a regular at Cukor's elegant Sunday lunches at his exquisite Italianate house, full of Renoirs and the Sargent drawings of his adored Ethel Barrymore, on Cordell Drive on a spreading hillside estate behind high walls with a large pool in the cypress-planted garden.

It was round the pool that Cukor's rather different Sunday late-afternoon parties were held, rivalling those hosted by Cole Porter – all-male affairs for the more discreet gay Hollywood or visiting society along with a weekly selection of handsome young men, some of them hustlers. And it was after Michael had stayed on for such an occasion that his diary has the first mention of a new name: 'Bob Michell drives me home. $\frac{1}{4}$ Indian.' The following day's entry is simply: 'To pool for breakfast. Studio p.m. Home and met by Bob.' And the next: 'Drinks with Lang. To see some rushes. Home and out with Bob. He stays night.'

Bob Michell, Michael's new lover, was to become an integral part of his life for the next decade. Ten years younger than Michael – he was twenty-nine when they met – he was born Leroy John Meyers (his child-hood nickname was 'Bud') in Ohio, son of a convicted conman, Charles Meyers, who had worked as a policeman in Los Angeles briefly before serving time in San Quentin for bilking old ladies of money. He was married at least four times. Bob's mother Hazel was also from Ohio; after Meyers deserted her she lived for a while with Jack Michell, who made her young son sell newspapers on street corners to help support the household. When he was just over fourteen Hazel pulled the boy out of school and, falsifying his age, sent him to work in the Californian CCC (Roosevelt's Civil Conservation Corps), which provided work for men of eighteen or older. He repaired roads throughout the state – a tough life for which he never forgave his mother, especially after the trauma of being gang-raped one night by workmates. This drove Bob to go AWOL from the CCC and into the Western Union Telegraph Company, initially as a bike messenger. During the war he had served in the US Army's Combined Services for four years, working in communications for Marine landings in the Pacific, returning to LA after the war.

He was back at Western Union, in the Hollywood office, when Michael met him. Bob, at six foot three inches, was as tall as Michael and was extremely attractive, with dark hair, remarkably smooth skin, deep-set eyes (he claimed to have Iroquois blood) and a brilliant, captivating smile. Of all Michael's principal lovers Bob, something of a gentle giant, was the one everybody seemed to like most, perhaps because he did not seem to want anything professionally from Michael. He was bisexual – there was a girlfriend, Nelya, in the background then – although at that time he was a fairly regular face around the Cukor pool on Sundays.

Michael's diary records spending at least part of every day with Bob for the next few weeks, usually at the Bel Air, more rarely at Bob's modest rented home in the valley. When Rachel arrived in mid-March, Bob returned there while Michael met her at Pasadena in a chauffeured studio car: 'V. moved in car and nearly cry. How can one love two people so much?' adding the next day: 'This is the first day in 4 weeks I have not even phoned Bob.' Following the pattern of the Norris affair, the next day he writes: 'After lunch I burst to tell R. about B. and do so and she takes it generously.'

A few days later, on his birthday, Michael gave a party at the Bel Air, before which Rachel and Bob met for the first time (he remained always her favourite of Michael's male lovers). He invited also Fritz Lang, Katina Paxinou (the Greek actress soon to play his mother in *Mourning Becomes Electra*) and her husband Alex Minotis as well as Leo Genn (the British actor cast as Adam Brandt in the film) and his casting-director wife Margaret.

For a while, the air was not without its tensions, Michael once more clearly feeling his old guilt and fear of the future as well as bursts of euphoria. He was shocked, too, by belated news from England of Andy's death. Andy had been in poor health for some time and had been virtually blind in his final few years, but Michael's adult opinion of Andy (he never forgot his mother's parenthetic 'good man' mention of their Café Royal date) as 'a remarkable character' had only increased with the years. He also heard with some alarm that Daisy had booked to come to Hollywood.

Nothing seemed finally resolved, as Michael said after dining out one night with Rachel, 'When we get back we talk and weep much till 2.30.'

Rachel and her friend Jenny Nicholson, daughter of the poet Robert Graves, left for a brief trip to San Francisco, leaving Bob and Michael to spend most of the time together. On Rachel's return, slowly the situation clarified: 'R. and I dine and discuss Leo and she says I am right to do what I want to do.' What Michael wanted to do, having fallen deeply in love with Bob, was to go on with the affair; even then he was contemplating asking Bob to return with him to England at the end of filming. As well as the physical intoxication with Bob, Michael also responded to something damaged and vulnerable in Bob's personality. In turn, Bob was used to the attentions of successful older men in the Cukor world but from the start he simply adored and idolised Michael. On Rachel's part, she had over her time in Hollywood grown ever closer to Leo Genn.

Both Redgraves had known Genn slightly in England. Tall, polite and beautifully spoken – Hollywood's ideal of an English gentleman – he had read Law at Cambridge and practised as a barrister before going on the stage. After a time at the Old Vic, West End and Broadway work had led him to Hollywood. Her sessions with Charlotte Wolff had led Rachel to realise that while she, like Michael, wanted their marriage to continue, other relationships on her side need not be out of the question. She and Genn began an affair – Margaret, otherwise involved elsewhere herself, had no objection – which Rachel told Michael about (he liked Genn but found him a remarkably dull actor). It all seemed very civilised, at least on the surface. But there were undercurrents, with Bob beseeching Michael, 'Don't show me the presents you buy Rachel,' and Michael often stabbed by uncertainty (a first tiff with Bob and he begins to doubt the wisdom of future plans together) and guilt whenever Rachel seemed tense.

Shortly before Daisy's arrival, dreaded by Michael and Rachel alike, they moved into a rented house on Angelo Drive, where the early days of the *ménage à trois* were sometimes tricky: 'Bob stays night. Wake about 5 and go to see him. R. rather upset in the morning. We have it out, or part of it.'

Daisy managed to time her arrival to coincide with Michael's first day on *Mourning Becomes Electra* and even on her first evening Michael noted, 'Mother fairly tight by bedtime.' A few days later things were worse: 'Mother seems resentful and wants to return home. Demands "stiff drink".' She had quite a few old friends and colleagues in the English community in Hollywood but even with May Whitty she seemed tetchy and ready to pick quarrels; her bad moods were always worse when other people were working.

Michael certainly had to work extremely hard on *Mourning Becomes Electra*, which turned out another crushing disappointment. He had seen O'Neill's trilogy in 1937 in London – with Bea Lehmann giving a performance touching hands with greatness as Lavinia, the Electra figure – and was well aware that it was going to be a difficult piece to transfer to the screen. O'Neill had consistently refused permission for a film but finally consented when RKO agreed that Dudley Nichols, a screenwriter friend of the playwright, would direct as well as adapt the massive work for the screen, cutting it to two and a half hours (it still feels like ten).

Nichols' dogged fidelity is the key problem with a film that needed radical rethinking ever to work in screen terms, but apart from a few scenes – General Ezra Mannon's return from the war, brother and sister Orin and Lavinia witnessing their mother Christine with her lover Adam Brandt on his ship – the film stays rigidly faithful to the original's mansion setting and for the most part, using stagy groupings broken up with close-ups, it seems simply a ploddingly photographed play. The most imaginative touches are in the music – repeated variations of 'Shenandoah'.

The Babel of accents further undermines O'Neill's brooding power. Katina Paxinou – cast presumably because of her Oscar for *A Farewell to Arms*, rather a different challenge – is hopelessly at sea with the demands of O'Neill's language and rhythms (her best scene is wordless – an awful, animal moan and collapse when she hears of her lover s death), Leo Genn seems to be in White's Club, chiming very oddly with Raymond Massey's Canadian Ezra, while Rosalind Russell, hilariously miscast as Lavinia and in her black crinoline looking like an inverted umbrella, sounds like a brisk Saks salegirl. Michael's accent is more than creditable and in other circumstances his Orin might have been a major performance. Certainly, of all the haunted New England Mannons in that Civil War version of the House of Atreus, he is the only one remotely convincing, with a frightening immediacy suggesting the segments of Orin's disturbed mind, communicating all the love for his mother which slowly turns to an unbalanced hate. He alone seems to comprehend that in this play O'Neill's characters wear masks as if to hide their secrets and Orin's tension in trying to maintain his mask is palpable, most tellingly in the extraordinary scene in one of the Mannon mansion's pillared rooms, hung with gilt-framed ancestors, in which he muses over the body of his dead father, whereas with all the other performances it is hard to forget Shaw's description of the play as 'banshee Shakespeare'.

Michael was staggered when his Orin subsequently won him an Oscar 'best actor' nomination. It emptied cinemas across America and was not released in the UK until seven years later when, despite some unexpectedly good reviews, it did equally poor business. Hollywood was just beginning to change, during Michael's time there, away from the all-powerful studio system and nobody seemed to have any idea of how to present him to the American public. 'He's tall! He's rangy!' had been Universal's notion, while RKO tried to create a bookish, intellectual image for what they saw as a 'literary' film. Nothing, however, helped at the box office.

Apart from Bob, one other good thing had come out of his Hollywood experience. The house on Angelo Drive was rented from the screenwriter John Balderston who had co-adapted the play *Berkeley Square* from Henry James's story *The Sense of the Past*, and its library had an extensive James collection. During one weekend Michael reread James's *The Aspern Papers*, his story of late nineteenth-century Venice, and began to think that the tale, with three leading characters caught in a cat-and-mouse game and that fine Jamesian sense of suspense, might make a play. During the rest of his stay he made notes, roughed out a scene division and even mapped out an opening scene of *Juliana* (the name of the aged recluse at the centre of the story) as he then titled it. It would be over a decade and after much reshaping before it saw the stage, but the germ of its success lay in that shaded library in Hollywood, first imagined in that period of complex – even Jamesian – doubts and scruples in Michael's mind.

Rachel had tested for and won a good part in *A Woman's Vengeance* with Charles Boyer and so stayed on in Hollywood – Leo Genn was to return there soon – while Michael and Bob (who took leave from Western Union) travelled to New York for a hectic social round with a Sardi's lunch with Gielgud and John Mills, catching *Oklahoma!* and *Brigadoon*, nightclubbing at the Copacabana or the Stork Club and meeting up with Norris. It had been agreed that Norris would co-direct *Macbeth* in London with Michael, although only Norris would be billed as director. This was not such an unusual set-up then; with Donald Wolfit, in some of his fellow actors' eyes, somewhat degrading the term 'actor-manager' in staging his productions as showcases for his ego with supporting actors kept well in their place, actor-directors such as Gielgud had used director-dons (including Dadie Rylands or Nevill Coghill for his 1944 Haymarket season) as 'cover' directors while they effectively steered rehearsals.

Binkie may have raised his eyebrows – many did – at the idea of a major West End classical production being even nominally directed by an American with virtually no professional directorial experience, but Binkie's perennial philosophy was to keep his stars happy and, in any event, he had confidence in Michael as actor-director. Dates were fixed provisionally for October rehearsals.

After a whistle-stop Canadian publicity tour at J. Arthur Rank's request, Michael sailed with Bob, seen off by Norris. They arrived in style at Southampton, met by a Rolls-Royce (1936 vintage) and a chauffeur, Ken Parker, both new to the Redgrave household (Bedford House had acquired also a cook and a full-time gardener in Mr Owers).

Bob was given the tourist's guide – St Paul's, Buckingham Palace, Green Park and Michael's favourite Waterloo Bridge – before they were driven to Bexhill to join the children and Nanny Randall on holiday. With the Rolls and the presents – Hershey Bars and records of *Annie Get Your Gun* – it was another visiting potentate's arrival. From the start, all the children took to Bob – he loved children and had a happy knack of being able to entertain them without obvious effort. It was only a short break for them – Rachel, back from her film (another poor screenplay), was able to join them all for a few days before Michael and Bob returned to London to prepare for *Macbeth*. In an interview just before the production went into rehearsal, Michael had said, 'It is extremely nice to have success, but it is important to have failure as well.'

Few great actors have had much luck with *Macbeth* – Gielgud, Olivier in his first effort, Guinness and Paul Scofield could not count it a triumph, while for Richardson (directed by Gielgud) it was a famous disaster, if not quite on the Peter O'Toole scale later. Michael's Macbeth was a success, but a distinctly qualified one. The pity about the whole enterprise was that Michael should have mixed private affection with professional commitment, and Norris was grievously over-parted. It made the situation awkward for both. Although most people liked Norris, he was seen, inevitably, as a weak and indecisive director; should an actor query a point in rehearsal, Norris's usual reply was that he would 'think about it', which most of the company assumed meant that he would discuss it with Michael later. This, also inevitably, made the company's attitude to Michael ambivalent too; aware of this, always hypersensitive to atmospheres, he would often retreat inside an aloof mask, behind which, of course, his anxieties on Norris's behalf only increased.

Macbeth lived up to its reputation as Shakespeare's ill-starred play. The initial auguries were good – Michael had made a clear early decision, typically unorthodox, to have no truck with any conventional conception of Macbeth as a noble but flawed man driven to evil by an ambitious wife. This Macbeth was to be played as a towering figure in a savage tribal society with murder already lurking in his mind and needing only a spousal nudge to send him on his course to a fate for which he was destined. He wanted an actress with a strong sexual presence as Lady Macbeth and Ena Burrill was cast.

Norris, who agreed with Michael that the supernatural element must be very strong, had come up with a novel idea to add to the three witches another trio ('The Three' as they were billed), monolithic warlock shapes who dominated the witches. But this idea, together with a risible notion of dispensing with Banquo's ghost in the Banquet Scene, suggesting his presence by a special-effects empty chair with a movable arm operated by remote control (it never worked and had to be cut), seemed an imposed visual conceit, not organic to a design (by Paul Sherriff, designer of Olivier's *Henry V* film) strong on cloudy, livid backcloths but weak in practical terms (the banquet scene was a particular mess, with most of the guests – and their crucial reactions – invisible to the audience).

The production started badly. Norris – used to New York's tougher ways – had suggested that only after a scheduled first week of readings would the minor roles be definitely assigned, eager actors sometimes reading different parts on different days. With a huge pool of younger actors returned from the war to draw on, competition was fierce and of course, after a tense week, some hopes were dashed and feelings hurt. It may have been done with good intentions but it was badly handled and, as Richard Bebb – making his first London appearance in a small part – said, 'a recipe for disaster', creating a resentful and divisive atmosphere at an early stage.

The tour opened in Liverpool – its only competition was *Naughty Girls of 1947* (at the Shakespeare Theatre) – to capacity business and strong reviews, which continued throughout the pre-London tour, apart from a freezing week in a Glasgow shrouded in sooty fog where business was only average. The *Macbeth* company were glad to mix with the actors headed by Micheál MacLiammóir and Hilton Edwards from Dublin's Gate Theatre, playing the Citizens', who introduced them to a Gorbals Italian deli with a snug café serving minestrone for 6d.

Michael had high hopes of success in London and was optimistic after the Aldwych opening – 'Quite the best performance we have given. Breathless, coughless house. Binkie over the moon' – but the *Macbeth* notices were completely divided. Several critics remarked that this Macbeth grew in power as the evening progressed and that in the second half Michael inhabited a large and awesome picture of a man not dead to fear or remorse being torn apart on the rack of conscience. The final violent duel with Macduff – fisticuffs, swords and daggers – and some inventive touches (Macbeth just a second late in drawing his sword to

salute Malcolm as Prince of Cumberland) were all praised but the production overall was judged patchy, while the main criticism of Michael's
performance (not wholly to his surprise) was that it lacked 'poetry'. He
had consciously roughened his voice as part of his concept of Macbeth as
a violent man in a barbaric society. One critic, in a long and careful piece
in the *New Statesman*, admired both the production and the ideals behind
it: 'It is an attempt to give a considered and rounded version of The
Play instead of a series of virtuoso performances. They play as a group,
subordinated to the over-riding presence of an idea. A bit Moscow Arts?
Certainly and what a welcome infusion.' His performance had passionate
admirers – Binkie wrote, 'I shall never forget and always be more than
grateful,' while Puffin Asquith said, 'I haven't been so excited for a long
time' – and the box office, even over a freezing New Year period, was
strong (this *Macbeth* actually made a profit in London).

Some bitter aftertastes remained, including the end of Michael's friendship with Ena Burrill who did not hide what she thought of Norris's
inadequacies and who was hurt to be told that for the planned Broadway
production the producers were insisting on a star to replace her. That was
true, but Michael had never been happy with Ena's performance which
he found unsubtle (she, of course, could counter that she had had no real
help). And although Michael's friendship with Norris survived unimpaired
there had been problems, with Norris being forced to ask Michael to
'defer' to him more to give him some authority. The whole situation,
however, had been Michael's own fault and the backstage atmosphere
undeniably made his own performances erratic. Richard Bebb said, 'I have
never worked with any actor whose performances varied so much,' adding
that at least as far as his Macbeth was concerned: 'You can't discuss a
Redgrave performance with someone unless you were both there on the
same night.'

Michael's anxiousness on Norris's behalf compromised the production
and the company atmosphere, not helped by an unusual retreat behind
his portcullis on this production with his Rolls-Royce lifestyle and lofty
habit during the run of giving notes on performances by sending them on
personalised stationery ('A note from Michael Redgrave') which, not
surprisingly, tended to be greeted irreverently backstage.

Domestically, although Rachel was temporarily parted from Leo Genn,
still in Hollywood, life at Bedford House seemed more settled: 'Rachel
and I have happy day. It is nowadays as if I had shed all pretence.'

Bob Michell had returned before Christmas to America and his job –
Michael once noting the fear that he might marry Nelya – but it had been
agreed that he and Michael would meet up when *Macbeth* crossed the
Atlantic. Michael's old nagging frets never left him entirely, however; at

the end of his 1947 diary there is a jotting about his 'forever-forthcoming' autobiography, musing on a chapter on 'Why I am so unpopular' with two sub-headings of 'Why I deserve to be' and 'Why I don't think I ought to be'. One cause he suggests is his desire to court popularity with one hand while hitting it over the head with the other, and he then goes on to describe another, 'historical', cause:

> I share with some of my generation the desire for some kind of suicide. So far as we are concerned Spengler was right. A slow social suicide seems to be my ticket. What a pity! But is it entirely? I do not like being called decadent but that is what I am. And the fact that I know it and say so before anyone else says so in my hearing is typical of my case. My unpopularity, my decadence, is my tubercule.

Flora Robson replaced Ena for Broadway as Lady Macbeth (she had played it to Charles Laughton's poorly received Old Vic Macbeth and was keen to have another chance and to act with Michael). The production was revised somewhat for Broadway – the banquet scene redesigned – and Michael felt that despite her warm voice Flora was a splendidly incisive Lady. He redefined a good deal of his own performance too and with a predominantly new company ('a stronger cast than London,' he noted), the production opened in Montreal, playing to capacity and excellent notices.

Michael knew that in New York memories were still vivid of a successful *Macbeth* with Maurice Evans and Judith Anderson (very much along the conventional lines of weak man and fiendish woman) only six years before and, indeed, that was held up as an exemplar in several reviews. The critical reaction was even more divided than in London, with the *New York Times* hailing the whole evening and Michael in particular ('No one else in the contemporary theatre has drawn so much horror and ferocity out of it') and while the relative lack of 'poetry' mattered less in New York, the production still came in for a good deal of criticism.

The recasting included some clever talent spotting, young beginners including Julie Harris as a witch (the sole actress from the Aldwych on Broadway, Gillian Webb – another witch – remembered how she was determined to make the witches' movement different from London) and Martin Balsam as one of 'The Three', and it was altogether a much happier company than London. And Michael made a lifelong friend in Lehman Engel (who had worked with Orson Welles in the stirring days of the Federal Theater Project), who conducted Alan Bush's shrieking score. But with the heavy running costs for a large cast and orchestra, and with only the cheaper seats for a younger audience selling strongly, the business was not enough to sustain *Macbeth* beyond half of its scheduled season.

Bob had been found a $50 per week dresser's job on the production, and he and Michael shared an East 64th Street apartment, enjoying the usual social life even with eight performances a week – a weekend with Ruth Gordon and husband Garson Kanin in Connecticut, visits to the Penthouse or the Blue Angel to catch favourite jazz singers Maxine Sullivan or Nan Wynn, and a farewell brunch party hosted by Richard Aldrich of Theater Inc. with Coward, Bea Lillie, Gertrude Lawrence and *le tout* British New York. After a few NBC Radio broadcasts and catching Marlon Brando and Jessica Tandy in *A Streetcar Named Desire* ('a really thrilling evening'), Michael treated Bob to a week in Bermuda, swimming nude in the caves of the bay near their rented cottage and discussing a possible future in England for Bob, who had given up his Western Union job but was still undecided about leaving America.

Laden with presents for Rachel and Schwartz's gifts for the children, back in England he was elated to find Lynn now less shy with him. Rachel was working in the West End in *The Paragon*, but his first diary entry after his return reads, 'It is good to be home. R. and I share my room just as when I left.' She was glad to have his support then; Eric, her father, who had had a heart attack, died two weeks after Michael's return, a devastating loss for Rachel who had remained so close always to Eric whose fundamental socialist principles, mostly drawn from his hero Robert Owen, underpinned her own views. Michael made sure he was with her as much as possible; at home, he was also learning to work with a new secretary, Joan Sparks, ostensibly to 'help' Edith Hargreaves although she was no longer working full-time for Michael. Mrs Sparks, a widow with a young son, carried on working for Noël Coward as well. She remained with the Redgraves for some thirty years. Michael took the children off Rachel's hands when he could – taking them all to see *The Red Shoes* film – and also went with them down to Bexhill where Dick Green joined them in their rented house. It was a lazily relaxed hot summer, mostly spent on the beach with Michael constructing baroque-statued sandcastles and with evenings of gin rummy or darts at the local Bell pub. Rachel joined them at weekends: 'R. arrives and I am v. excited and happy at thought of meeting her. Think I am happier than I have been for years.'

Yet the old compulsive pattern soon reasserted itself once he was back in London. His diary records many September meetings with 'F', usually at 'the office' in Goodwin's Court and frequently with champagne: 'In the middle of night wake v. depressed and feel I have let B. down by renewing this matter.' 'F' was Frederick F. LeGrand (known as 'Foff'), one of the three strikingly handsome and musical sons of a Swedish colonel, all educated at Cranleigh, although Foff had left before Michael's arrival. Blond and often melancholy, a talented painter as well as pianist, Foff was also a one-time boyfriend of the Viennese-born actor Anton Walbrook. Michael saw him regularly for most of the rest of that year, apart from a break from London when he took Rachel on their first post-war holiday abroad, going for the first time to Venice, immediately a favourite city for both, about which Michael could wax extra lyrical, writing of it as viewed from the air: 'Suspended, one might have thought, between sea and sky, like a slightly rusty but glittering scimitar on a silver plate ... in the nacreous, fostering and protective womb of the sea.'

Michael described it as 'that week of pure gold', staying at the Danieli, visiting the Arsenale with its strange sculpted guardian beasts, learning the difference between a campo and a piazza, eating ices at Florian's and sometimes breakfasting on the Riva degli Schiavoni during a mild October. The visit was memorably enlivened by meeting the startlingly peroxided and white-suited aesthete Stephen Tennant, once Siegfried Sassoon's lover (when asked, along with his more conventional siblings when young, by his ultra-conventional father, what he wanted to be, Stephen's reply was 'A great beauty, sir'). He was in Venice with his friend Edith Lewis, who had been companion to the American writer Willa Cather, and the foursome took gondola trips together and dined at La Luna after Stephen had demonstrated what he thought of currency restrictions by entering the Redgraves' bedroom to throw 1000-lire notes all over the room. They also took a trip to Milan where Massenet's *Werther*, even in a poor La Scala production, delighted them. Rachel remained enchanted by Stephen, later occasionally visiting him in his Wiltshire rococo bower at Wilsford; having heard about Stephen's epic verse dramas – one, 'an experiment in blank verse', was called *Wake, Wild Visionary!* – Michael remained rather more circumspect.

Daisy created problems as soon as they returned. Since Andy's death she was drinking more and this new bout was serious enough to warrant another drying-out 'cure' in Brighton, Coral Browne offering to accompany her. Perhaps because of his anxieties, Michael was seeing 'F' again and, more dangerously, was often 'cruising' at Victoria or Hyde Park, typical diary entries being, 'Go down to Victoria. Something says I am making a fool of myself,' or, 'To Hyde Park Corner – back to office with J. Home by hired car.' This on-the-edge behaviour was perhaps also part of the need to charge himself for one of his most challenging parts, demanding reservoirs of nervous energy – the Captain in Strindberg's *The Father*, which he had agreed to play at the Embassy in Swiss Cottage. This was an adventurous off-West End theatre – it seated about 500 – run by the actor Anthony Hawtrey (the illegitimate son of actor-manager Charles Hawtrey by his mistress – Garrick Club rumour, which he did nothing to discourage, had it that he had been conceived in a telephone box), an irrepressible Casanova, debonair and always immaculately tailored. Michael liked him and the easy atmosphere of the Embassy, as did most actors.

The Father was directed by Dennis Arundell – he and Michael had not worked together since Cambridge – with an undervalued actress, Freda Jackson, extremely powerful as Laura, the Captain's wife who helps harry him into madness so that he can be forcibly restrained from altering her plans for their daughter. Strindberg – *Miss Julie* aside – was hardly known in England; *The Father* had not been seen in London for over twenty-five years when Michael's old hero Robert Loraine played the Captain who is not master of his fate.

The portrayal of a mind already unbalanced slowly disintegrating became in Michael's performance almost unbearably frightening and ultimately moving to watch (the final scene when he was coaxed, like a baby, into a straitjacket by Lilly Kann as the old nurse held audiences breathless). All the facets of a notoriously complex role – childlike help-lessness, yearning dependence, the desire to be comforted and the final retreat into the Captain's apparent madness – were all superbly charted and balanced.

Quite a few notices compared his Captain with Robert Loraine's per-formance, remembered for its 'nobility' in particular. Although his per-sonal reviews were extremely favourable, Michael once more – irked by critics' laziness and ignorance of an accessible text – fired off a broadside, this time in *World Review*, arguing eloquently that Strindberg never intended the Captain to be a 'noble' character and that he is no con-ventional tragic hero: 'I have been criticised for making it appear that the Captain seeks refuge in madness. This is precisely what I intended and what I believe Strindberg intended. It is, of course, less "noble".' Rightly he pointed out that Loraine often went against the text and stage directions, aiming a climactic pistol into his own mouth rather than, as specified, at his daughter's head. He also reported that Loraine's widow when she saw the new Embassy production told him that Loraine 'cut all the crossgrain', every reference which might make the Captain seem weak, no doubt giving a 'noble' performance but traducing the play.

He was delighted by so much enthusiastic fan mail in reaction to *The Father*, especially by a letter from Charlotte Wolff. She had seen the play twenty years previously with the great German star Paul Wegener, an extremely macho actor who had a big success as the Captain: 'But it is now clear to me that Strindberg's Father can only be played as you do – the hypersensitive man with a "feminine" ambivalence in himself and, of course, towards the woman.'

Somewhat to Michael's surprise, the Embassy run was so successful that a transfer was arranged for early 1949. The break gave him the chance of a rare work-free Christmas and he was able to meet Bob, who had after all decided to come to England to be with Michael. After Dick Green had left the Bedford House studio in Thames Street it had for a while been occupied by Vivian Cox, now working in film production, who vacated it for Bob. Rachel sorted out studio furniture and details such as a ration book for Bob. Christmas morning was the ritual of the three children and their parents opening their family presents on the marital four-poster, Bob joining the family later. Michael seemed still to spend most nights with Rachel – a recurrent phase in his diary then was '*le lit arrange tout*' – and the *ménage à trois* had established itself without too much drama, one reason undoubtedly being Rachel's fondness for Bob.

There was some talk of Bob trying an acting career and he did play tiny parts in an Embassy revival of Kaufman and Hart's *You Can't Take It with You* and in the Peter Brook-directed *Dark of the Moon* at the Lyric, Hammersmith, but the combination of his diffidence and the difficulty of obtaining a work permit for him led to Bob's own suggestion that he should work for Michael as typist or driver when needed and help generally at Bedford House.

Michael turned down lucrative offers – including a musical of *Quality Street* which would have paid £300 per week – to transfer with *The Father* to the Duchess where it continued to play to strong business for the strictly limited run to which he had agreed. He continued in lower-paid work to direct and act in *Amoureuse* which was finally titled *A Woman in Love*, returning him to the Embassy. He and Diana Gould (now married to Yehudi Menuhin) had done an excellent job in their version of George de Porto Riche's 1891 comedy, honouring its acerbic tone for what was its first English production. Rather like *Parisienne*, it looked at love, sex and marriage with sceptical, adult French eyes, somewhat to the disquiet of audiences and critics during a try-out week in Brighton. The *Sussex Daily News* described the heroine, Germaine, a Maupassant-like character, as 'a woman of the most staggeringly amorous disposition' which, even for Brighton, was something of an overreaction to a woman with one husband and one lover.

Michael played Etienne, the husband who both resents and is enchanted by Germaine's ardour but who becomes so jealous of Pascal, her artist lover, that he takes her back, with the curtain falling on a happy *ménage à trois*. Some metropolitan critics also displayed a curious *pudeur* in their reactions, as if they had stumbled into the wrong bedroom in a honeymoon hotel. The air of Constant's *Adolphe* which pervades the play makes English audiences uneasy; its unblinking view of marriage as an institution in which each partner may want something different is alien to Anglo-Saxon conventions of sex and marriage. Elegantly suited and sharply bearded, stomping around the drawing room in alternate fits of rapture and raging jealousy, Michael was extremely funny in a high-comedy part, as was a bone-dry Michael Hordern as Pascal. Margaret Rawlings (Michael had wanted Coral Browne, but she was ill) was deemed generally somewhat charmless as Germaine, but the main problem was the English response to a play which, as the great French critic, Sarcey, said is unusual in that 'its charm is at once bizarre and attractive, bewitching and disquieting'.

The real-life *ménage à trois* had its upheavals occasionally also, Michael ruefully noting after a tiff with Bob: 'To see B. and my nerves coil back on me. R, seeing my eyes swollen as I get into bed says "poor M, you get it from *both* sides".'

Since Hollywood Michael had not earned serious money and finances loomed large at this time, especially as he had (against Cecil Tennant's advice) committed to a season at the Old Vic from the autumn. Binkie had, as he had always feared, not come through for his West End company ambitions. They had had a major row when Michael once again broke the H. M. Tennent 'rules' by rebuking an unruly matinée schools audience during *Macbeth*, although the real reason was undoubtedly, for the profit-conscious Binkie, the risk of high running-costs repertoire in the commercial sector. And so, when the new Old Vic director, Hugh Hunt, was able to offer Michael Hamlet (which clinched the deal for him, whatever the financial loss involved) as well as Berowne in *Love's Labour's Lost*, another chance to explore Rakitin (to be directed by Michel Saint-Denis) and young Marlow in *She Stoops to Conquer*, his acceptance was immediate.

He had, in the interim, to earn some significant money and so, somewhat against his own judgement, agreed to co-star with Celia Johnson (wife) and Margaret Leighton (mistress) as Faber, the torn psychiatrist whose guilt pushes him to suicide in the film of one of Coward's short plays from the 1936 *Tonight at 8.30* sequence, *The Astonished Heart*. The producers doubtless banked on it repeating the success of another film based on a play from the sequence, *Brief Encounter*, but they overlooked the fact that while *Still Life*, the *Brief Encounter* original, is a touching miniature, *The Astonished Heart* is Coward at his worst, a misguided attempt at earnest psychodrama (the title comes from Deuteronomy's admonition to those flouting the commandments: 'The Lord shall smite thee with madness, and blindness and astonishment of the heart'). As the best of Coward's critics, John Lahr, has rightly observed, 'Only at his most frivolous is Coward in any sense profound,' and the play – and screenplay – is a trivial anecdote with risibly elevated dialogue, everyone suffering nobly in clenched Anglo-Saxon style. Michael thought the script poor but kept his views to himself and got down to it, loving working with both leading ladies and during on-set waits thinking up rhymes for *Oklahoma!* with the word-game-addicted Celia Johnson. He was rather disconcerted, then, when not long into filming Coward, back unexpectedly early from a Jamaican holiday, swept with his entourage into Pinewood Studios to see the rushes and declared himself unhappy. After a good deal of fuss, Michael offered to withdraw, for Coward to say he would take over on condition Michael received his fee in full. What Michael did not know was that Coward had originally cast himself in the picture but pulled out in pique when Celia Johnson turned it down, reacting with even more pique when, after Michael's casting, she changed her mind (after the switch of leading man she called Michael to say she had only accepted for the chance to act with him). As it turned out, Michael was well rid of the film in which Coward's performance of ravaged heterosexual ardour is riotous; it was panned by the press and lost a great deal of money.

With a summer unexpectedly vacant – and paid for – there was time for some fun, including the now annual Boat Race party at Bedford House, guests including Guinnesses, Oliviers, Millses, Menuhins, Goughs, Diana Wynyard and Binkie, all marvelling at Michael's lung power cheering for Cambridge. He also went back – inevitably with Dick – to Mortehoe in July for a relaxed holiday of bathing, reading Balzac and *Hamlet*, with the bonus of John and Mary Mills staying near by, although there were some worrying times caused by Dick's ever increasing drink problem.

From Mortehoe it was back to the family favourite of Bexhill and the charms of Monopoly with the family, Bob and Nanny Randall, the cinema or shove-ha'penny and darts in the pubs. Also, as usual at Bexhill and rather relishing the contrast between its world of whitewash and hydrangeas and the decaying palazzos of Venice, Michael worked quietly on *Juliana*.

It had not been an unproductive time – *The Father* a particular high spot since his return from Broadway – but that determination to be more the helmsman of his own career had not quite brought the results of which he had dreamt. Financially Cecil Tennant, he knew, had a point but for Michael there was no question but that he had to go to the Old Vic ('You make your own luck'), especially with the chance – at last – to take on *Hamlet*.

Thirteen
'THE READINESS IS ALL'

Climbing the staircase to the top-floor rehearsal rooms at the Old Vic again brought many memories for Michael. The company would rehearse there but play at the New Theatre until the Vic auditorium was finally refurbished after its bomb damage.

His keyed-up excitement seemed to infect the building. The Vic had suffered from post-war infighting and the boardroom squabbles still rumbled – Olivier and Richardson had departed while Michel Saint-Denis, George Devine and Glen Byam Shaw at the Old Vic School, now in Dulwich, felt increasingly threatened. The Vic's new director, Hugh Hunt, had a lot riding on his first season. Intelligent and experienced – he had been artistic director of the Abbey in Dublin – Hunt was perhaps not the most visionary of directors, but he was a shrewd choice to steer the Vic into safer waters. His own productions tended to be bland and at times pedantic – his published pre-rehearsal talks, *Old Vic Prefaces*, confirm that reputation – but with the opening *Love's Labour's Lost*, perhaps catching fire from Michael's enthusiasm, he came up with a fleet and poised production, helped by a crack team of clever comedic actors – a sort of Old Vic Crazy Gang – as the often dreary Worthies.

Hunt and Michael agreed in seeing Berowne, the most articulate of the four young men in the King of Navarre's court who forswear love for Academe only to recant when the Princess of France and her ladies arrive, as Shakespeare's reflection of himself as a young realist, with a zest for life and laughter. They both also felt that inside the masque-like prettiness and verbal fireworks of an often undervalued comedy, there is a play with its own passion, and Hunt elegiacally phrased the growing darker side to the fun, suddenly clouding on Mercade's entrance with intimations of mortality. Michael was in ebullient mood throughout, heartened by Bob's and Rachel's reactions after a dress rehearsal when the company felt slightly swamped by wigs and costumes ('Rachel says I look twenty-two!') The comedians – especially Miles Malleson, codfish jowls quivering as a bemused Sir Nathaniel – were widely praised, but it was Michael's Berowne who dominated the evening and the reviews. A performance of quicksilver wit, most eloquent in Berowne's rejection of austerity and great hymn to love, he had a mental alertness and rueful gaiety throughout that helped charge Hunt's production with a spring-heeled buoyancy. With what was often a difficult play to sell, the box office was busy as soon as the reviews appeared.

Love's Labour's had rehearsed simultaneously with Goldsmith's *She Stoops to Conquer*, which opened shortly afterwards, directed by Michael Benthall, a dapper old Etonian whose partner was the actor-dancer Robert Helpmann, who choreographed the dances. Benthall had a tendency towards fussiness and Michael had to bite his lip in rehearsal: 'Michael B. overlays the play with business and before we have had any chance to play it for its own values.' It was designed like a Rowlandson cartoon, although some performances tended more towards Gilray – in a play pivoting on social distinctions it seemed perverse to have Mrs Hardcastle (Michael's old Clifton role), the lady of the house, as vulgar as a caricature charwoman – and there was a good deal of 'comedy-servant' acting with running exits and grotesque make-up.

Michael quietly got on amid the strenuous frolics with creating a real original out of Marlow. He seized on Goldsmith's hint of a speech impediment ('This stammer in my address') affecting him whenever he speaks to a woman of his own class, although with Kate Hardcastle as 'barmaid' he is free and easy, to develop a character who could move without contradiction from bashful courtship to reckless wooing. He found a fundamental shyness in the man as the bedrock of the character. It developed into an unexpectedly hilarious performance, best of all in his scenes of social panic with the 'lady' Kate, his body like a wilting stalk, gentle stammer – his lips locking mutinously on every word beginning with 'M' – fading away into strangled falsetto, and it drew some of the best notices of his career, even from those who found the production coarse. Michael had said that he could never have taken on Marlow if Agate had still been writing – the critic had once said, continuing to dismiss Michael's comedic gift, that Michael tackling Marlow would be like Bob Hope taking on King Lear – so when he was unable to resist looking at the press after the opening and read *The Times* description of his 'triumphant' high-comedy performance he was ecstatic: 'Burst into tears on bed and wake R. Overjoyed. Have seldom been happier.'

His euphoria at the Vic and the continuing rapture of his relationship with Bob cushioned ever present money worries. The brief flirtation with the high life of chauffeured Rolls-Royces was over; the car was sold (£600) and, providentially, chauffeur Ken Parker married Birdie, the cook at Bedford House, leaving to set up his own business. But Michael was behind with surtax payments and also overdrawn again on his personal account. Edith Hargreaves had to be told – a tricky situation, dealing with someone also a family friend and Lynn's godmother – that she would have to take second secretarial place to Joan Sparks, much more financially efficient. Michael's ideas of economising were hardly draconian – he would stomp about the house switching off the lights – although for a time during his demanding schedule in the early days of his Vic season he was cutting back on the social life, a good many diary entries then ending with 'To bed with Ovaltine'.

The reunion with Michel Saint-Denis on *A Month in the Country* had been so anticipated by both that Michael dreaded an anticlimax but he felt 'much stimulated' once again during the early rehearsals although it took time to adjust to a new translation (Constance Garnett) and a very different production from the St James's version. If Emlyn Williams's had been somewhat superficial, Michel's was an in-depth exploration of a society and a little colony of people in a specific era. Michael still found Michel – whose English seemed to have got no better – the most inspiring director, even if his candour was at times unsettling: 'Michel says I am "too discreet". Not "positive" enough. Am put out, but know he is right.'

Now well into the rhythm of the season, and at a time of high professional excitement, Michael began to slip off the rails at night: 'Home via Victoria and Knightsbridge. To office. Very foolish and great regret and disgust after.' Post-performance adrenalin, that 'high' familiar to most performers, was another factor leading him to crave these anonymous encounters, fleeting sex, usually with guardsmen or soldiers making – as Tony Hyndman had done – a bit extra on top of Army pay. What was new and disturbing – and what surely explains the mentions of shame and self-recrimination – was the element of increasingly seeking some form of expiation as well as solace or escape in those brief encounters, often with 'rough trade'. He must have known what dangerous territory he had entered and tried hard to resist, often vowing, 'Home late after what I *swear* shall be the last mistake of this kind,' but usually it was not long before another 'office' incident and more shame, more remorse.

Also at this time he often could not control his drinking; it never affected performances noticeably, but after a first night of Rachel's – Christopher Fry's *Venus Observed* – at a party given by the Oliviers Michael got extremely drunk, even insulting Cecil Tennant ('Why, *why* did I do it?'). He was also deeply troubled by the progress on *A Month in the Country* which, after his disappointment with the St James's version, he desperately wanted to succeed. In rehearsal, however, it had become clear that Angela Baddeley – offbeat casting for Natalya in the first place – was not going to deliver the goods. Michael and Michel did all they could to help her but she was fundamentally adrift and Natalya's volatility, the swiftness of her mood changes, continued to elude her.

Michel's production looked ravishing in Tanya Moiseiwitsch's sets, especially the garden scene, warm and summery, with receding lines of raspberry canes, although it was generally accused of being too slow. Michael's second Rakitin was judged by those who had seen the 1943 production to be even better ('more subtle,' said Philip Hope-Wallace who – exceptionally – thought the whole evening the best production of a Russian play in London since Michel's *Three Sisters*). About some aspects of this perfect Platonist Michael himself was more happy this time, feeling that he had better judged the distance from himself at which Rakitin stands – that which the ironist normally maintains, provided he is untouched – although he still felt that he had unfinished business with a play that continued to fascinate him.

After three personal successes Michael might well have been worried that his luck would run out on *Hamlet*. His diary is a blank for the rehearsal period but on dress rehearsal day he was recording that feeling common to many actors at that stage – 'Wearing anxiety alternating with complete apathy: Is it all worth it?' – and, after a second dress rehearsal, the afternoon of the opening: 'I feel nowhere inspired and do not feel I am much good.' Yet he had sounded more positive in a rehearsal interview for *Theatre World*: 'I refuse to look upon my forthcoming appearance as Hamlet as an ordeal. I have the consolation of knowing that no actor has ever completely failed as Hamlet just as none has completely succeeded as Macbeth.'

In the event, the ovation and ten curtain calls (Olivier raced by cab with Rachel from *Venus Observed* to catch the end while Vanessa went with Daisy) were not just welcoming the company back to its newly decorated red-and-grey Waterloo Road home; the Old Vic core audience's cheers were acknowledgement of both a great performance and Michael's loyalty to the company.

Michael guessed that his would be compared with Gielgud's Hamlet, which he himself considered the finest of his time; he saw Gielgud's first Old Vic Hamlet, avoiding his subsequent three ('I did not want to be unduly influenced by him when my own turn came'). The notices took him genuinely by surprise. He had expected very mixed reactions whereas, a coolish *Times* excepted (and even that acknowledged 'only minor faults'), that first Hamlet was recognised as of the very top rank, several using the word 'great'. In the event, comparisons with Gielgud, the verse-speaker of his era, seemed to be to Michael's advantage; there was a general sense that the poetic pre-war sensitive son had matured away from little-boy-lost self-pity. Even his handling of the verse, the soliloquies in particular, was singled out for praise. T. C. Worsley spoke for many in highlighting Michael's absolute mastery of the vocal line 'without tricks, without

mannerisms or affectation, but immensely various, always absolutely true
... the sense, we feel, has been mastered as a whole'.

Michael shared with Gielgud a great gift in playing Shakespeare – the
ability to mint each thought on the moment without sacrificing the overall
structure of the verse, and always moving thought with a forward impetus.
He may have chosen to play all the soliloquies downstage and very still
(his last scene in *The White Guard* had taught him how potent stillness
could be) but they were far from inert dramatically, full of self-questioning
and constantly active. That quality was always part of his special talent for
inhabiting the solitary confinement of the soul.

The Old Vic School students were given tickets for *Hamlet*, told by
Michel to take special note of Michael's handling of the soliloquies. A
young Joan Plowright, then at the school, wrote a letter home praising
Michael's performance above that in the film version from Olivier:

> He took the famous 'To be or not to be' well down near the front of the
> stage, and so quietly and simply ... he had his hands behind him and just
> brought his right hand forward at the end to make one significant gesture
> which was the more beautiful for being the only one.

All his Hamlets were rooted in a paralysing grief for his dead father;
Michael was pleased that an Old Vic regular, Wilfred Walter, was cast as
the Ghost – a human figure rather than the lurid fluorescent spook so
often seen. His Vic performance charted superbly the gradual emergence
from a state of frozen numbness, clearly coming through the terrible
events of the central sections of the play (and, crucially, the absence
when sent to England) towards a spiritual reawakening and growth, at its
supreme best when, finally calm – serene, even, in 'the readiness is all'
with Horatio, a scene which touched the heart – he died on the throne-
dais, clutching the crown usurped by Claudius.

The production itself was not much more than efficient – the designs,
by Irving's grandson, Laurence Irving, sometimes open to reveal stormy
seascapes, then narrowing to contain more private scenes, did not please
everybody – and blighted by too many of the mid-century Shakespearean
production clichés (the ambassadors played with the conventional bleating
voices of castrated clergymen). Michael imported a few effective pieces of
business, such as William Poel's touch in *Fratricide Punished* which he had
seen in Daisy's Fellowship of Players' version, of having Gertrude's wig
on a block in the Closet scene, revealing her white hair, and throughout
his performance was informed with new stresses and meanings.

It became a sold-out success at once. Visitors crowded his dressing
room after every *Hamlet* evening – Anthony Blunt, John Lehmann, a
moist-eyed Willie Armstrong, the Menuhins, David Loveday and, alone

at a matinée, Edith, who wrote of her admiration: 'you made it entirely your own and it seemed so fresh and holding. It was lovely.' And he was touched by a letter from Thornton Wilder, who saw it twice, remarking on the intellectual strength combined with the unremitting mental anguish of the performance, praising its 'unbroken line of inner life'.

The intense emotion of the play spilt over into life. On the same day as Bob gave him 'an anniversary present' celebrating three years since meeting, Rachel told him she was pregnant again: 'I am so happy that she is so happy.' Two days later they met up after their respective shows for supper: 'and so home, and we are truly happier in every way than for a long time.' And then, nearly a month later: 'R. in bed as she fears losing baby.' After four days the only entry is a bleak two sentences: 'Dot Hyson [Anthony Quayle's wife] has baby. At about same time R. loses hers.' Although Rachel was in no danger she was briefly admitted to the Chelsea Hospital for Women and Michael visited every day. His diary is then blank for several weeks. Both would have liked another child, although this one was not conceived to patch up a marriage – Michael in particular had been keen on the idea of another boy – and while both knew how lucky they were compared with couples who could not have children, the miscarriage remained a sadness for some time.

Rachel luckily was back home before Michael had to fly to Copenhagen one April weekend to read two Hans Christian Andersen stories as part of a broadcast to celebrate Andersen's birthday. It was broadcast from Andersen's childhood home, a small whitewashed house in Odense, with Michael sitting in the author's chair surrounded by his hats, umbrellas and the portmanteau with which he had travelled to England to meet Dickens. It was a highly successful visit, laying down much goodwill for the Old Vic's summer European tour; the Danes always appreciated Michael's understanding of Andersen as much more than just a writer of tales for children.

With all four of his plays successes at the Vic, Michael could be jus-tifiably pleased that his decision to accept Hugh Hunt's offer had worked out so well. Cecil Tennant's percentage of Michael's £50 per week would not buy many Scott's or Chez Victor lunches, however, and he was insistent that Michael must do at least one film. Hunt was wooing Michael for the following season and also trying to persuade Peggy Ashcroft; Michael was prepared to play Orsino in *Twelfth Night* to her Viola, the other suggested play for them being *Antony and Cleopatra*. He took Peggy to lunch to discuss it, but her attitude to Cleopatra ('Well ... it would be a *challenge*') and her lack of enthusiasm for Hunt as her director did not seem quite enough for Michael.

An old friend from the great days of Gielgud's 1930s companies,

Anthony Quayle, had taken over as director at Stratford-upon-Avon and Michael was more drawn to the suggestion of leading the Festival of Britain company there, especially when Quayle told him of his exciting plan to present a History Cycle – *Richard II*, both parts of *Henry IV* and *Henry V* – in repertoire, opening consecutively. As it happened, the Stratford governors insisted on a 'safe' play too – *The Tempest* – which foiled Quayle's dream (a *Wars of the Roses*-style project ahead of its time). But, remarkably swiftly – one phone call, one meeting – Michael agreed to play Richard II, Hotspur in *Henry IV, Part 1*, to direct *Henry IV, Part 2*, and play Prospero and Chorus in *Henry V* the following year.

Presented with this plan as a fait accompli – Stratford paid £10 per week more than the Vic – Cecil insisted even more forcefully that Michael must get before the camera as soon as possible. Then, by one of the few major strokes of luck in his film career, Eric Portman's unavailability to re-create his stage role in the film of Terence Rattigan's *The Browning Version*, to be directed by Puffin Asquith, floated the film in Michael's direction. He had been surprised when Rattigan first mentioned it to him at a Sibyl Colefax party, but now – although no contract had been agreed – it was looking likely.

The Old Vic season ended in late April – Bob, Michael, Rachel and Leo Genn, back from Hollywood, all dined at Besitto's after the protracted curtain calls – and then the company took off on a short UK tour, including Liverpool, where Michael felt the usual 'sort of nostalgic poetry' and where he received the screenplay of *The Browning Version* ('I long to do it'). But still with no final contract, Cecil put him into *Dangerous Meeting* in which he would co-star with Anouk Aimée, filming in France, although Michael thought the script incoherent.

First he led the Old Vic company on a European tour which began in Zurich before travelling to Denmark where *Hamlet* would be the first British company to play at Elsinore since before the war. Michael loved Elsinore at first sight – a seaside shipyard town reached by a lovely coastal road from Copenhagen, with over 3000 people at each performance crowded into the flagstoned courtyard of Kronborg Castle ('Hamlet's Castle' to Danes). The castle was open to tourists by day and so only two late-night rehearsals were possible while Hugh Hunt adapted the production to a very different space. The company had a lot to live up to – memories of Gielgud and Olivier – and were also expected to efface memories of the previous year's American company in an updated version set in the Wild West using rifles instead of rapiers ('Hamlet Get Your Gun' it was dubbed).

It was a daunting start – trumpets and cannonades heralding Hamlet stepping out on to the haunted platform where his destiny had been worked out centuries ago – in the presence of Danish royalty, Eleanor Roosevelt and the British ambassador, but an overwhelming success. It was especially sweet for Michael that *The Times* sent its critic to reassess his Hamlet and that, among the ecstatic Danish reviews, the paper's verdict was that Elsinore's third English Hamlet had been the best and that his performance had been electric, reaching real greatness.

But for Michael the high spot of his Danish visit came two days later when he was invited to lunch, with Daisy (who – with a minder – had come to Elsinore) and his Ophelia, Yvonne Mitchell, by Baroness Blixen, Karen Blixen, alias Isak Dinesen, author of the *Seven Gothic Tales* (for Michael an authentic masterpiece) as well as *Out of Africa*. It was a glorious summer's day when they were driven to her house at Rungsted near the harbour, a low whitewashed building amid pasture land, full of light from the sea and the walls covered with lion skins and Masai swords. He was impressed beyond words by this impossibly frail woman, limbs like twigs but with the most alive, glittering eyes. Michael and she talked of Shakespeare, Henry James and of the America she wanted to visit once more; for him it was an unforgettable meeting.

She Stoops joined *Hamlet* in The Hague for the company's last touring date for the Holland Festival, where Michael also, with Dick Keigwin accompanying him, delighted Amsterdam audiences with more of Dick's versions of Andersen stories. Together they realised now from reactions so far that his Andersen readings could have a future at home and in Europe.

There was time for a brief holiday with Bob in France before *Dangerous Meeting* began location filming, and while they were in Juan Les Pins they often met up with Anouk Aimée and her entourage. As it happened she was the only one to come out of the film with anything to show for it (two couture dresses) – it became obvious early in shooting that the film company had run out of money and the picture ended in messy collapse. Shrugging it off as one of those disasters not uncommon in the movie world, Michael travelled on to Paris where Rachel joined him while Bob returned to London. It turned out a happy holiday although funds were low; they dined most nights at the cheap but congenial Le Coucou in rue Casanova, visited most of the art galleries and spent hours exploring the Marais district, which neither had known before.

The good news coinciding with the day of their return was that his contract for *The Browning Version* had come through, the start date giving him enough time to take Rachel and the children to Wollacombe Bay. It was a lazy family holiday of beach games, the new craze of Canasta, and for Michael long walks along the beach letting *The Browning Version* and the History Cycle plays begin to 'lie fallow' in his mind.

The early stages of the film were extremely tricky. Professionally he had the problem of shooting out of continuity, especially difficult on a script so specific in its short time-frame and with such a concentrated emotional arc for its leading actor. Climactic scenes had to be shot first, which on this occasion Michael found unsettling. Privately there were now deeply upsetting incidents with Daisy, out of work and drinking heavily. After only a few days' filming Michael was called by Daisy's neighbour to warn him she had 'started a bout'; at once he went to her flat and stayed all evening with her. A week later he had to ask Puffin to be released before the end of his call, 'When I hear that the Club is talking of calling the police for Mother. Spend frightful time with her.' These were agonising scenes for Michael, with Daisy alternately incoherent and spitting jealous tirades, or turning up at the Garrick Club demanding to see him. It was horrible for him to watch, helpless, as she turned into a vengeful Fury. Having to cloak his private distress helped him play the emotionally repressed Andrew Crocker-Harris, the public-school Classics master dubbed by his pupils 'The Himmler of the Lower Fifth', so masterfully. It ranks with *Dead of Night* as one of his greatest pieces of screen acting.

Michael took infinite pains to transform himself into this prematurely aged failure in whom it is just possible still to discern (as one pupil does) the idealist he had been before disappointment and an unhappy, incompatible marriage to a woman whose sexual needs he cannot satisfy (Rattigan's perennial theme – 'two kinds of love') led him to develop the dry, pedantic shell mocked by the boys. He dyed his hair so that on film (black and white) it would look lifeless (he also shaved a briefly glimpsed bald spot) and experimented with spectacles until he found the right rimless pair which would not mask his eyes (vital in a film of repression of gesture) and, bodily, developed a scholar's stoop which makes him seem much less than his usual commanding height. He also insisted on voice tests before filming; he wanted to pitch his voice to a 'head' voice, slightly higher than his own, with a humourless, silky rasp for the precise, parenthetical Crocker-Harris tones.

Corin Redgrave, who played Crocker-Harris on stage half a century later, rightly has pointed out that for the first few frames the nasal, dry voice seems fleetingly too much: 'Don't! You can't possibly sustain it' is the fellow actor's response. But, extraordinarily, he does; it is a performance on the edge, a high-wire piece of acting ('And it has no safety-net,' adds Corin). It gradually suggests that the real 'Crock' has become petrified behind his mask of ironic pedantry (one reason, perhaps, why some Rattigan apologists read many of his plays as paradigms of his buttoned-up homosexuality) until it has stuck.

The most astonishing scene in the film, much helped by Asquith's unerring touch and by the truth of Brian Smith as the boy, Taplow, occurs when Taplow gives 'the Crock' a leaving present, a copy of Browning's translation of Aeschylus' *Agamemnon*, which produces the most devastating reaction. Crocker-Harris, only just holding on to his emotions, sends Taplow to fetch some medicine and, alone, in a catharsis of emotion – grief, gratitude, shame – against which, for once, he has no defences, the mask peels off in scaldingly helpless, hopeless tears. It is one of those moments at which Michael excelled, when the audience (in cinema or theatre) suddenly becomes so directly privy to a character's soul that it feels like an intrusion.

It seems a pity that Rattigan felt he had to 'open out' the play so much, especially with an unnecessary underlining of the worm turning at the close. And it is even more of a shame that Margaret Lockwood (Michael's suggestion) turned down Millie Crocker-Harris; Jean Kent's stagy exhibition, full of busy eyebrow work, is a waste of a good part. But Michael's performance, so delicately tracing each flicker of the seemingly dead eyes, each barely perceptible tic of a facial muscle, seems still unforced, true and profoundly touching. Puffin wrote to him after he had just seen a 'demi-semi-final cut' to say:

> You deliberately from the start – and our schedule was no help! – chose a very apparently small range of colour – say pale to dark grey. But within those self-imposed limits what a fantastic gradation of tones, half-tones, quarter-tones, etc! Yours is an iceberg performance. We may not see much above the surface but we know how huge a mass lies *beneath* the water.

As a bonus the film did excellent business at the box office and won him a first Best Actor Award for a British actor at the Cannes Film Festival. It was an enormous hit in France particularly, as *L'Ombre d'un Homme*. Only in America, where Rattigan never had much luck, did it fail to draw a public.

Michael had planned a break before starting what he knew would be an exhausting Stratford season, but he and Dick Keigwin flew to Amsterdam to perform some different Andersen tales for the impresario Jan de Blieck. And as a favour to Dennis Arundell he agreed to narrate the rarity of Debussy's *Le Martyre de Saint Sébastien* at the Royal Albert Hall. Arundell had translated Gabriele d'Annunzio's libretto, a modern attempt at a mystery play, an oddity of florid, perfumed mythology crossed with nature worship, originally staged with Ida Rubinstein at Covent Garden in 1911. The concert version was an ambitious undertaking involving a huge choir and orchestra, with little rehearsal time. The uncontrapuntal choral writing is by far the most rewarding part of a demanding evening, but

Michael thoroughly relished the experience of working with such enormous musical resources.

Early in the new year Bob drove Michael and Rachel to Stratford to meet the genial general manager, George Hume, to see possible apartments for the season – they ended up with a large flat in Avoncliffe, on the edge of the town, its garden running down to the Avon – and for Michael to have meetings with Quayle and Tanya Moiseiwitsch, the designer of the History Cycle.

Anthony Quayle remains one of the unsung great figures of the post-war British stage. A burly, vigorous personality, after a distinguished naval wartime career he had been offered a Hollywood contract by MGM which, at thirty-five, he turned down in order to accept Stratford, a choice born out of his strong moral sense: 'It would be an artistic achievement and a political one – it could help bond the nations together.' Some friends warned him that the job could be a poisoned chalice; the outgoing director, Sir Barry Jackson, certainly did not make the changeover easy for Quayle and financially the theatre was in frighteningly poor shape. But there was an element of Guthrie's field marshal instinct in Quayle too and he turned Stratford round remarkably quickly, wooing friends such as Gielgud, Peggy Ashcroft and Paul Scofield to the Avon. He had a touch of the devious businessman in him as well; it was a clever ploy to bring Binkie, a useful earpiece to the stars, on to the Board of Governors.

For the 1951 season he had planned to rehearse the four History plays simultaneously and open them on consecutive nights, terrifying a notoriously conservative Board, worried enough already by the scheme devised by Quayle and Michael to have a permanent set for the cycle. As well as having to accept *The Tempest*, Quayle had to agree to open the plays at monthly intervals, compromising his vision of a national epic tracing Shakespeare's concept of kingship and leading to precisely what he and Michael had hoped to avoid, critical expectation of the plays as separate 'star vehicles'.

Quayle and Michael still kept to the intention to present Richard as the last of the medieval absolute monarchs inculcated in the Divine Right of Kingship, Henry IV as the inheritor of his curse, haunted as any Orestes, and Henry V as a pragmatic modern monarch of inner doubts and scruples. Although influenced by E. M. W. Tillyard's writing, it was not an academic concept and should have been recognised as both revelatory and revolutionary. As it was, traditionalist critics moaned that Richard was not 'sympathetic', Falstaff not 'merry' enough and Henry V not 'patriotic' enough; had they seen all the plays together as planned, possibly they might have asked themselves if this might not have been deliberate. The same diehards also felt short-changed by seeing the same set on four separate Stratford visits. Moiseiwitsch, who had worked extensively for Guthrie, came up with a mould-breaking and influential design. Her permanent set recalled the Elizabethan stage – a central gallery with steps at either side and vast double doors below, fluid and versatile for court and Eastcheap scenes alike, and bringing the action closer (she covered the pit – the musicians were in the wings – and used no curtain), just as Quayle was trying to make the tricky Memorial Theatre interior and auditorium more audience-friendly. Detractors said the simple wooden structure was dull, and yet, although miles away from the Stratford pictorial tradition, her design could still provide breathtaking visual coups like the season's opening when to a great blast of trumpets, the massive doors opened as Richard's pages, in tabards bearing his emblem of the white hart, made way for the entrance of Michael's golden King.

Everything about him in the early scenes seemed gilded, like a watery sun – hair, a delicate beard just tracing the jawline, crown and jewels, toying with a flower while capriciously playing power games with his court. The first night was a trial for Michael who was in great pain from a chipped bone in his foot (a dress rehearsal accident) and thrown by a late start while the audience took in the refurbished auditorium. Olivier (who, with Vivien Leigh, was in the first-night house, further disconcerting Michael) said later how much he admired Michael's 'courage' in playing Richard as 'an out-and-out pussy queen'. That exaggerated, but it was a bold, calculatedly homosexual interpretation, a sometimes feline, wilful and indulged monarch who fully believed himself to be God's deputy on earth, humbled and made human in the recognition of his own pride. The cornerstone of Michael's performance was in the return from Ireland when Richard has to hear of Bolingbroke's successes, where he found the bridge between the self-conscious autocrat and the later contemplative man. Once again the keynote was shame, the self-abasement of a once arrogant man forced to admit to his few remaining followers that he is, after all, as human as they, his voice unforgettably cracking after a daringly long pause between the confession 'I live with bread like you, feel want, taste grief' and the half-statement, half-plea of 'need friends'. He filled the pause with a world of emotion – hurt, bewilderment and shame – in another of those startlingly piercing moments of self-recognition that marked some of his greatest performances.

Michael had private reservations about some of Quayle's production – he strongly disagreed with the Guthrie-ish mischief of turning York (Michael Gwynn) into a craven compromiser with no textual evidence – but their working relationship was one of the happiest of his career.

They went at once into *Henry IV, Part 1* rehearsals, Michael set again to defy convention as a Hotspur without a stammer, instead using a distinctive Northumbrian accent. He had worked hard on the accent during the pre-rehearsal weeks, even going up to Alnwick to stay with the Duke and Duchess of Northumberland in his visit to Percy country. He studied the accent with the castle piper, Jack Armstrong, recording local voices (Barbara Jefford – Lady Percy – recalled 'a tape recorder almost as big as himself').

Hotspur emerged as one of his most free and relaxed performances, vivid and fiery, a man so impetuous that his words tumbled over themselves in guttural impatience to articulate his speeding thoughts. Even in moments of repose he seemed perpetually balanced on the balls of his feet, as if ready to spring at any opponent. Michael admired Barbara Jefford – he had auditioned her for *Amoureuse* – and their scenes together had an unusually strong sexual charge ('He just *threw* himself into Hotspur and he was wonderful in it,' she said). With Harry Andrews a broodingly awesome Henry IV, Richard Burton emerging into potential greatness as Hal and with such strong support as Alan Badel's impudent Poins (he doubled with a Shallow of delirious dotage), this was a powerful cast and evening.

'The next 4½ weeks are going to be purgatory,' Michael wrote in his diary as he began rehearsals as director of *Henry IV, Part 2* while playing eight shows a week. The second part is usually thought of as the weaker play, some skimpy historical scenes linking the Falstaff story, but when played in sequence this never seems the case. Michael had done his homework and had the plus of a company who now knew how to work together. He was never a brilliant improvisatory director ('a bit of a schoolmaster,' remembered Barbara Jefford) but he certainly coaxed a much less obvious Falstaff from Quayle (helped by a simplified make-up – he seemed to disappear behind beard and wig in Part 1) and staged bustling street and Boar's Head scenes, with a stunning moment, strongly focused, of Hal's rejection of Falstaff on 'I know thee not, old man'. He fused the buoyancy of Eastcheap with the more elegiac country scenes quite beautifully.

With Part 2 launched at last he had the occasional night off. Rachel had come up sometimes – she had acted as his dresser when his was ill – and now came back with all the children, watching their father on stage together (Lynn in tears at *Richard II* – 'It's so *sad*'). He was able to enjoy some punting with them on the Avon and bike trips into the Warwickshire countryside, remarkably lush that summer. But he also had to buckle down to Prospero, which he had hardly had time to glance at since Mortehoe: 'Walking with *Tempest* for lines. Man on bike with girl on pillion shouts – "Poetry, poetry – that's the life!"'

With that workload he could have done without Dick Green's arrival during *Tempest* rehearsals, especially when, after arranging with some difficulty a ticket for Dick to see *Henry IV, Part 1*, he reached his dressing room after Hotspur's first scene to find a sozzled Dick asleep in his chair. The following night he was even more drunk and made an embarrassing scene at the stage door from where he was sent home in deep disgrace. There was no real rupture in their friendship – which continued to puzzle many of Michael's friends – but he did read the riot act to Dick about his drinking.

Those who had felt starved of the pictorial in the Histories were amply rewarded by *The Tempest* as directed by Michael Benthall and designed by a young Australian, Loudon Sainthill. Even the rococo imagination of Stephen Tennant, who adored marine design, would have been sated by the amount of nacreous shell motifs on display. There was in addition a curtain, a grey-green front gauze evocative of a Jules Verne fathoms-deep world, backlit at the opening with the hissing of waves rising to fury to reveal the ocean as the undulating arms of sea nymphs before the ship and Michael's Blake-like Prospero, with a huge, blasted branch as his magic staff, were revealed. On the masque Sainthill really went to town, with goblins and sea monsters out of Bosch and Brueghel and an epithalmic spectacle of descending, garlanded goddesses.

So busy was Benthall with this 'Captain Nemo Night at the Atlantis Copacabana' side of the production that Michael more or less had to fend for himself. Luckily, he had a very clear idea of Prospero. For him it was, indeed, 'rough magic' that this non-professional magician practised. With enormous skill he was able to band-aid over the pontificating aspects of a character who can often be a bore, to leaven his rage with humanity, creating an empirical magician whose every spell is practised with effort, his hands trembling with doubt of his own powers. For once, the exhaustion of Prospero, his longing for secluded peace, at the end of the play seemed justified. He had to compete with a finale staging – anticipating *The Phantom of the Opera* with candelabra all over the floor, slowly fading into a growing dawn – of some busyness, but at the close of this *Tempest* it seemed as if a human beneficence had triumphed in a malignant world.

Michael especially enjoyed his scenes with Alan Badel as a near naked Ariel, no Peter Pan androgyne but a fiercely spirited boy, torn between a love for his enslaver and the instinct to be free. But every aspect of his performance was praised in an almost unanimous set of notices, the Sunday ones of which he was able to enjoy with Rachel when they stayed (as they did several times that summer) at Notley Abbey, the Oliviers' stately weekend Buckinghamshire home. Other guests on that occasion included Danny Kaye, Ralph Richardson and Orson Welles, the latter massively crouched over a tiny portable typewriter in the garden bashing out a novel, *Mr Arkadin*. Also, there was the Australian-born actor Peter Finch, who had begun an affair with Vivien Leigh; she had used Rachel as her main confidante about this since the beginning and they continued close as her marriage to Olivier frayed.

Olivier and Michael had not met since a review for Michael's Richard II had appeared, with a bold headline: 'LOOK OUT LARRY, THERE'S A REDGRAVE ON YOUR TAIL!', whipping up a 'rivalry' between them by suggesting Michael might usurp Olivier's place at the top of the classical acting tree. Michael, well aware of Olivier's famous touchiness and ambition, had been rather trepidatious about the weekend, much of which they spent together dead-heading roses in the garden. Olivier never mentioned it, although Michael also noticed that neither did he mention that day's *Tempest* notices.

With the Stratford season doing record business, Michael was besieged by requests for tickets from friends – Robert Ardrey, Bea and Rosamond Lehmann (Bea could be a caustic critic and Michael was thrilled by how much she had admired what he had achieved in *Richard II* particularly), Dennis Robertson and Dadie Rylands from Cambridge, Benn Levy and Constance Cummings, and Charles Laughton, who wept at the close of *The Tempest*. But Michael still had Chorus in *Henry V* to rehearse, not the most taxing of his season's roles but one he enjoyed playing – and he genuinely admired the watchful, guarded Henry from Richard Burton. With Quayle celebrating in Festival of Britain year what he saw as Shakespeare the embodiment of Englishness, Michael as Chorus was the spirit of the 'epic of England' concept, voice blazing and confiding alternately as he set the scene for the events in Moiseiwitsch's approximation of the wooden 'O'.

The final night was an emotional occasion. Even if not presented according to his original dream, Quayle had taken both cycle and season home to remain as one of the great Stratford post-war peaks. He and Michael loved the *Variety* headline: 'STRATFORD BARD BOFF BIZ', trumpeting the season's phenomenal success. For the final curtain call, Michael, Harry Andrews and Burton all took their bows in the costume of their respective king to one of the most heartfelt ovations ever heard in the building. Afterwards Quayle, Michael and their wives had a quiet, reflective supper. It had been an exhausting time but for both men deeply fulfilling. Michael pledged that – Cecil willing – he would try to come back as soon as possible.

One old friendship was revived during the final week when Max Adrian returned to England after some time in America. He and Michael had a joyous reunion, at once reviving their old Bigolo–Frattocini rivalry fantasia, with Michael, the showbiz bible's Stratford headline still in his mind, inventing a story of the ageing tenor Frattocini about to marry the widow of a Wisconsin wheat baron – 'WOP WEDS WHEAT WID WED'. Michael had suggested his old friend as possible casting for the butler, Lane, to Puffin Asquith for the movie version of Oscar Wilde's *The Importance of Being Earnest*, which was soon to start filming, but Max's dates did not fit. Michael had agreed to play Jack Worthing with some qualms; not only would he be following John Gielgud's stage success but he would be replacing him opposite Edith Evans' now legendary gorgon of Lady Bracknell. He was also – not the only one – somewhat dubious about such a perfect artificial comedy working on screen at all, but Cecil was nagging and he felt, too, that if any director could find the right style it would be Asquith.

There was time for only a brief Bexhill holiday that year, the favourite familiar routine of sandcastles and improvised meals, with Michael again travelling in his mind to Venice as he continued work on *The Aspern Papers*. Rachel wrote to him after he left to begin filming following one of their most idyllic Bexhill weeks: 'Beloved Mikie-Baba, Oh I was so happy with you and I still have in my limbs the reminder of our early morning's loving.'

Not since his first day in Gielgud's company had Michael been so nervous as he was at Pinewood at the start of *The Importance*, not least because it would be the first time he had worked with Edith (broadcasts excepted) since *As You Like It*. The butterflies vanished quickly; he found that acting with her, even in a very different medium (and she did not make her first film until she was sixty), was still like swimming through silk. The magnificent battleship – in full sail with every gun blazing – that she had made of Lady Bracknell did not greatly change for the screen, largely because of Asquith's decision to turn the apparent drawback of the play's heartless artificiality into an advantage by making a film which threw the principles of filmcraft aside to emphasise the piece's staginess. He stressed it right from the credits – presented as a theatre programme – with a couple settling into a box to see the curtain rise, and bringing the curtain down on a final stage tableau at the close.

For some the approach meant a denial of all that cinema should be, while the film's champions insisted that Asquith's way was the only one possible (it certainly worked considerably better than Oliver Parker's 2001 version). Puffin insisted on a Rolls-Royce production, with Carmen Dillon's art direction providing *le dernier cri* bamboo in Worthing's Albany set and a Paxton-style conservatory, and 'Bumble' Dawson's costumes giving Edith bird-bedecked hats which were a tribute to the taxidermist's art and putting Michael in a white flannel suit trimmed with braiding for the country, reminding him of Andy's outfits when visiting Stratford in the summer of 1921.

Puffin's passion was music, and it shows in his scoring of the play's intricate verbal rhythms, confident enough – as Billy Wilder was with his comedies – to know when to leave pauses for laughs and when subtly to crank up the pace. He had a flair for casting too; experienced bliss from Margaret Rutherford and Miles Malleson as Prism and Chasuble, like two wobbling jellies, but also the newcomer of a young Dorothy Tutin (Michael's suggestion) as Cecily, a rose only just in bud but already with a few sharp thorns. Michael is a beefier Jack than usual – but then George Alexander and the males of St James's original company were tweedy Victorian squires rather than sylphs – and he has an airy surface blandness only just cloaking the secret Bunburying life (a queasy panic is visible behind the façade when Algy rumbles his hidden life). He also shapes and phrases Jack's complex, articulately fashioned sentences with superbly inflectioned breath control.

Michael felt disappointed, finding the film slightly slow on viewing a rough cut, liked it more when seeing it with an audience, and it finally became one of his favourite films. Agate's ex-assistant Alan Dent had expressed his scepticism of the film's success, telling Michael that it would have to combine the airiness of Rossini and the best rococo architecture with the style of René Clair's work, but after seeing it he agreed that it had succeeded.

The making of an Asquith film coincided again (Puffin was most understanding) with a fully fledged Daisy crisis; during the shooting she finally had to be taken into a clinic in Ticehurst where, this time, she had to stay for a period of months (with the alcoholic's cunning she still managed to sneak gin inside somehow).

Michael was beset by anxieties after finishing *The Importance*. Financially, tax and overdrafts had caught up with him again (he owed the Inland Revenue £16,000). Although Cecil had fixed him up with a top accountant (Walter Smee) to supervise his accounts on a monthly audit basis and to persuade the Revenue to accept weekly payments of back tax rather than a lump sum, there were warnings that there could still be trouble ahead. Visiting Daisy, which he did dutifully, was often harrowing, while Bob was away on his annual American trip.

Michael and Bob had seen comparatively less of each other during the Stratford season, when Rachel was more frequently at Avoncliffe. Their relationship was still extremely close; Bob knew of Michael's occasional London nocturnal wanderings, but he knew too that they were essentially apart from and no real threat to their particular bond. But that year Michael's diary occasionally worried about Bob's low spirits, while Corin had noticed that although Bob's eyes still smiled, the rest of his face sometimes looked sad. Bob loved Michael's family almost as much as he loved Michael; he gladly acted *in loco parentis* when Michael and Rachel were away, taking Vanessa and Lynn to school at Queen's Gate (Corin, removed from a school in Malvern which he had hated, was shortly to go to Westminster) and driving them to Stratford. But it was perhaps around this time, as he saw the children growing up, that Bob's desire for a family of his own began to grow more strong.

Also, as always fretting about the critical perception of him as an artist, Michael had a new bogey to replace Agate. Michael had been – without arrogance – proud of the Old Vic and Stratford work he had done, genuinely feeling that his performances there had been, as he described, more 'free'. As ever hypersensitive, he was both puzzled and hurt by the attitude to his work of the wunderkind Kenneth Tynan as he made his meteor-like impact on English dramatic criticism.

Michael had been intrigued by what he read about Tynan's under-graduate production at Oxford of the Quarto-text *Hamlet* for the OUDS and made a point of seeing it when it briefly visited London at the Rudolf Steiner Hall, finding it 'a fascinating if rather wrong-headed approach, stimulating and alive'. Like many of his generation – surely influenced by Gielgud's example – he was always encouraging to the gifted young and after seeing the OUDS *Hamlet* he wrote to Tynan offering what help he could if he was contemplating a career in the theatre. Tynan's reply was speedy – he had at that time ambitions as a director – and at Michael's invitation Tynan came to talk to him at length. Soon afterwards Michael reviewed Tynan's precocious first book, *He that Plays the King*, in encour-aging terms although subsequently he used to say, only half-jokingly in the light of a sustained critical battering: 'I have often thought what a mistake I made in getting in touch with him.'

Tynan's perspective from the outset – and it very rarely varied – followed the familiar Agatean line that Michael was an 'intellectual' actor, prone to internalise rather than communicate. Most of his *obiter dicta* on Michael – that his eyes transmitted little beyond effort, that he was an actor of mind rather than heart – were not only irritating in their magisterial assumptions but, crucially, based on false criteria. Even before his Brechtian conversion later in the 1950s Tynan had several agendas – besides making a con-troversial name for himself in a hurry – and, breathtaking stylist that he was, his arguments could be extremely persuasive. Principally they involved creating a continuing (and highly exaggerated) antithesis between Olivier and Gielgud in order to elevate what Tynan regarded in Edmund Burke's terms as Olivier's awesome Sublime over Gielgud's harmonious but less challenging Beautiful. It was clear even at the start of Tynan's career that he wished to exalt Olivier over all his contemporaries. Recently, in a new biography of Tynan, his first wife, Elaine Dundy, asserted that from the outset of his life as a critic his unconditional adoration (it was nothing less) of Olivier was part of a canny long-term stratagem eventually to work for and with his idol, ideally at a National Theatre, the drive towards which was a regular Tynan campaign platform.

Whatever the truth of that, and allowing that a critic's job is not necessarily to be right but primarily to convey an opinion as well as possible (Tynan certainly would usually pass that test), what has to be borne in mind is that, partly coloured by his main agenda, Tynan's judgements on acting were often wide of the mark. Most strikingly he refused to grant Gielgud any talent for comedy (*Forty Years On? Brideshead Revisited?*) or in modern work (an Indian summer in Pinter, Edward Bond and David Storey?), while he also relentlessly dismissed any suggestion that Vivien Leigh, in his view no equal talent as consort for his hero, might have any gift apart from her beauty. He also turned savagely on Donald Wolfit, whose Lear he had admired as a would-be critic, alarmed by a suggestion at one time in the *Daily Telegraph* that Wolfit might be a likely leader of a National Theatre. These verdicts could be almost gleefully cruel.

In an early column for the *Evening Standard* Tynan wrote a piece on Michael with special stress on his 'intellectual' approach, what Tynan termed his 'self-deception' as an actor, the distinct implication being that Michael was a rung or three down the Great Acting Ladder from Olivier. Then, with his curious habit of wishing to ingratiate himself with his victims, he wrote to Michael saying that he hoped that Michael could 'learn to forgive' him. In a drafted reply – never posted – Michael, touchingly self-revelatory, mildly acknowledged that the cerebral label was hardly novel, but added that he wanted Tynan to understand that it perhaps had its origins not in any feeling of intellectual superiority but on the contrary in 'a feeling of insecurity and a lack of belief in my own powers', conceding that this lack of security he at times compensated with 'a slightly pompous manner'. Michael also took issue, although still in mild terms, with Tynan over the accusation of internalisation, quoting Edith's description (she compared the process to the peeling of an onion layer by layer) of learning over the years how to act without self-consciousness, and adding: 'Something of the same process is happening with me. . . . I was always happier playing definite character parts or when able to hide behind a pair of spectacles or a strange moustache. But the basic fear is something that partly consciously but partly by the process of living, I have been trying to overcome in life and in acting.'

Michael knew very well when he wrote in reply to Tynan that his next stage excursion would be a demanding test of that effort; perhaps he finally decided to let that performance speak for him rather than take up the cudgels with a critic (which most actors are usually reluctant to do). Out of many offers to choose from – Binkie was pressing hard for him to sign for a new Terence Rattigan play in particular – he had accepted an unusually demanding part in a new American play for the West End and on Boxing Day he had his first meeting with the American Sam Wanamaker who had left an America increasingly allowing Senator McCarthy power and who was to co-produce, co-star and direct: 'Sam Wanamaker over. Alarms me at first, but leaves me more excited about the part than even before.' The part was that of Frank Elgin, a once great and now near forgotten alcoholic actor attempting a Broadway comeback under a tough young director (to be played by Wanamaker). The play, by Clifford Odets, was called *Winter Journey*.

Fourteen
ANNUS MIRABILIS

Somewhat to the surprise of the family, Michael decided on a real winter journey as a break before the Odets play began rehearsals. With Bob, a much more experienced skier, he went to Montana in the Swiss Alps where they stayed at the Hotel Savoy in a tiny individual chalet called 'Paradis'. It became less paradisial for Michael after some early days on the nursery slopes when he fell – walking, not skiing – wrenching his ankle. Bob had to ski alone for their last days while Michael sat writing letters and studying *Winter Journey*.

As planned, they moved on to Paris, where it was Bob's turn to be introduced to meals at Le Coucou and onion soup at Le Pied de Cochon during a highly social trip; there were suppers with Erik Chasell (composer of *White Horse Inn*,) dinner at Maxim's with *Winter Journey*'s bon viveur co-producer Henry Sherek and the great French star Edwige Feuillère, and the high spot of the visit for Michael, a reunion with Louis le Breton.

Michael had not seen Louis since before the war. Now working in the Louvre, still preoccupied with his own painting and his gardening, Louis was also still the gentle personality, prone to melancholy, who had been so close to him at Cambridge. He had a meeting alone with Louis over drinks at the Ritz, while the family – including Louis's brother Pierre and his elegant mother Hélène – gave a small party for Michael and Bob, a happy evening including 'talk of Beaucé all those years ago'.

Only on the Channel crossing was the elated mood clouded; opening a packet of forwarded mail, Michael found a letter from Daisy in her clinic imploring him to take her away. She was in a bad way at this time and continued to harry him and his half-sister Peg, who sometimes had Daisy to stay, during the early rehearsals for *Winter Journey*.

Originally titled *The Country Girl*, Odets's play had had a Broadway success two years before, notable for an electrifying performance by Uta Hagen as Georgie, Frank Elgin's long-suffering wife (Googie Withers in London). The general consensus was that in New York Paul Kelly as Frank had never quite convinced as an actor with a great past career. The other main role in an essentially triangular drama is that of the feisty young director Bernie, who takes a chance on Frank, remembering his prime, as the lead in a Broadway-bound play, a journey troubled by Frank's struggle to stay on the wagon and by Bernie's growing attraction to Georgie. After a long absence in Hollywood, Odets's comeback play charted familiar ground; the text acknowledges the inspiration of Laurette Taylor, a luminous star whose drinking ruined her career before a legendary return in Tennessee Williams' *The Glass Menagerie*, while both Emlyn Williams in *The Light of Heart* and Ivor Novello in *Downhill* had written English comeback trail backstage dramas. What was more novel for English audiences in *Winter Journey* was the jagged authenticity of its theatre world and a terrific early scene in which Frank comes to towering life when encouraged by Bernie to improvise, the voltage of such episodes helping to cloak some queasier passages in later scenes.

Almost from the start the production was bedevilled by difficulties and clashes of personality. Sam Wanamaker was only thirty-two and although his work had included an appearance with Ingrid Bergman in *Joan of Lorraine* on Broadway and a couple of low-budget British films, he was unknown on the London stage where he was now aiming for a triple-whammy as co-star, director and co-producer. No two producers could have been more different. Henry Sherek, son of a variety booker, raised in a Bloomsbury house amid personalities such as Caruso and Melba besides acrobats and performing seals, was an ebullient personality who produced T. S. Eliot alongside the lightest of boulevard frivols. Wan-amaker was ambitious, pugnacious and combative – all qualities which helped get his Globe Theatre project on London's South Bank finally built, but which made an incendiary mix in the West End of 1952.

Devoted then to the teaching of Stanislavsky (although later, in a Brechtian conversion, he underwent a dramatic de-Stanislavskification), Wanamaker encouraged improvisation and in-depth character analysis in rehearsal, all very innovatory in an insular, hierarchical West End where actors wore suits and ties and hats and gloves to rehearsal. In his T-shirt and bomber jacket, often unshaven, Wanamaker was like a gale-force wind of change in this atmosphere.

Everything seemed set fair at the start. Michael's only comment on the first rehearsal day was: 'Read play. Sounds even better as it reads. Googie v. good. Afternoon, S. talks, perhaps a little too much.' The warning signs were in that caveat. Michael had agreed enthusiastically to such novelties (for the period) as making the first-act improvisation scene genuinely so, different at every performance, instead of repeating the slickly written apparently improvisatory scene scripted by Odets. This was a surprise to the company; Patricia Marmont, beginning her West End career understudying Georgie prior to her later career as an agent, remembered, 'Improvisation was not at all common at that time. It was part of a whole new post-war experience.' And of course improvisation exposes stars, refusing to take on board their specialness, although that bothered Michael not at all. But as Patricia Marmont noticed early in proceedings, 'Sam was not very good at handling stars.'

Early in rehearsals Wanamaker asked Michael and Googie each to write out a background, a biography of their characters; he was especially insistent that they focus on the accident which killed the Elgins' only child, which he considered a vital element in their relationship. Neither Michael nor Googie necessarily would have disagreed with that, but they both felt extremely strongly that it was too early in the rehearsal process for them to make such decisions about characters they had only just begun to explore together. From that point on, despite the usual publicity photographs of the central trio 'sharing a joke', the experience began to sour. Wanamaker was a touchy personality. To him, of course, the West End of the early 1950s probably seemed a clannishly tight little enclave, snobbishly resistant to change, but he also insisted that the British theatre was rotten with anti-Semitism ('You don't acknowledge Jewish actors,' he told Patricia Marmont who thought, like many others, that 'Sam's Achilles heel was anti-Semitism'). He had besides felt his authority undermined by his stars' reluctance to create their backgrounds when asked; at the end of the first rehearsal week he called on Googie at home, complaining that she was resisting his direction, finally challenging her:

'You don't like me, do you?'
'Not very much, no.'
'You don't like me because I'm a Jew and a Red.'
'No, it's because I don't like you.'

She never changed her opinion of Wanamaker ('A dreadful man. A monster'), although she thought he directed the play well. Michael tried to maintain some equilibrium, although he knew too that the tensions would not necessarily harm a play with so many adversarial scenes, and indeed sometimes wondered if some of the hostility stirred up by Wanamaker might be deliberate.

He was thrown in turn by Wanamaker's changed attitude to him. Feeling that Michael was on Googie's side, Wanamaker ('relentlessly macho' according to Patricia Marmont) had not known before rehearsals about either Michael's bisexuality or his drinking. Not famed for fidelity himself, he distrusted drinkers and homosexuals ('Sam had an impatience with self-destruction,' said Patricia Marmont).

Still Michael stayed loyal to the production, feeling that Wanamaker was infusing it with an edgy, tensile adrenalin new to the English stage, and in rehearsal he felt that familiar surge of expectation when the character began to fit him like another layer of skin. He dropped early ideas for a complex make-up, using only a base and one 'special effect', a pair of prosthetic half-circles under his eyes for post-drinking scenes, giving his face a puffy, pouched look.

Michael had insisted on a pre-London tour – he dreaded the Old Vic and Stratford systems of opening 'cold' with a single preview or public dress rehearsal – and all the family came to King's Cross to see him off to Edinburgh ('You'd have thought he was going to the North Pole,' marvelled Googie). Despite a gruelling dress rehearsal (the play has three sets), the opening in Edinburgh had the audience enthralled and Sherek was extremely happy. In Manchester, hearing of a young company called Theatre Workshop (the MP Tom Driberg, a champion of their work, had tipped off Michael to look out for them), Michael took Sam Wanamaker with him one morning to their damp and chilly church hall rehearsal room to watch, fascinated, their improvisatory but highly disciplined rehearsal methods. Meeting the director, Joan Littlewood, and the actors after the rehearsal, Michael – backed by Wanamaker – said he thought the company's work should be more widely seen and promised to do what he could to spread the word about them.

Other weeks were less cordial. There was a distinct *froideur* in Bournemouth where Daisy, on a few days' trial leave from her clinic, joined Michael; while she was lunching with him and Googie one day, Michael abstractedly disappearing behind a mask of unconcern as Daisy downed the drink, Wanamaker came up to the table in high good humour to announce that they now definitely had a West End theatre booked – 'And boy, have we got a theatre! The St James's.' Michael was about to reply – it was a favourite theatre of his – when Daisy, well gone on the gin, spoke up: 'The St James's,' she boomed, 'is a very *common* theatre.' Michael's mask descended once more as Wanamaker vanished.

And the rest of the tour established a pattern; the more the play looked like a success, the more the backstage tension mounted. Perhaps sensing from the audience reactions that Michael was now taking Frank Elgin into unexpected areas of great acting ('You absolutely totally believed he had been this great star,' said Patricia Marmont), Wanamaker increasingly tried to compete, although with no other eyes to monitor him his performance began to lose its edge. He quarrelled furiously with Sherek who, because of shingles, had not seen the play since Edinburgh until Bournemouth when he felt as co-producer he must tell Wanamaker that his now over-gesturing performance reminded him of a Habimah Players actor. Tactless perhaps, but Wanamaker's reaction was to order Sherek, accusing him of anti-Semitism, out of his room and he hardly spoke to him again for the rest of the run.

The same overreaction lay in wait for Michael just after the play had opened in London. On the first Saturday, Michael was called at home after the two performances by an irate Wanamaker: '$1\frac{1}{2}$ hours of furious quarrelling. Am called anti-semitic and I know not what.' That night in the first-act scene of Frank's initially stumbling attempt to improvise, which grows into a revelation of the awesome emotional power of which he is capable, Frank/Michael had called Bernie/Sam 'a tyke'. As Michael allowed, a Yorkshire epithet was perhaps not very appropriate in the context of a New York audition, but in the heat of the moment he had used it. Wanamaker, though, kept insisting that he had been called 'a kike', so much so that relations between the two became impossible and backstage at the St James's even more of a war zone, Wanamaker now communicating with his co-stars by written notes only.

Michael loathed and was bemused by the state of affairs. Wanamaker – in all three of his capacities – had come out very well from the production. Even when the 'feud' had got to a ludicrous stage, with Wanamaker threatening to report Michael to Equity for altering moves and lines (all in a scene which it had been mutually agreed should be left improvisatory), Michael stressed to Henry Sherek: 'I have always maintained that Sam Wanamaker has done a good production. I have also repeated that in spite of criticism of his performance it has been of more help to the play than a more considerate or circumspect performance would have been.' Several of those associated with the production felt a main problem was that in the acting stakes Wanamaker's Bernie, good as it was, simply was not in the same league as Michael's Frank Elgin, as was reflected in the reviews. Even Tynan had no reservations about this searing display of great acting on the St James's stage. Everything Odets suggested about this has-been with a flickering spark of genius still in him, forever battling with himself, alternating a pathetic jauntiness with sudden bursts of almost uncontrollable power, was in absolute focus. It was a brilliant depiction of a lush, which Michael certainly knew how to play – the slightly shaky hands, the half-hysterical leaps from despair to euphoria, the eyes trying not to reveal where his dressing-room booze is hidden – and of a man still cocooned in a desire to be protected and mothered. For all the play's occasional manipulative glibness and shameless last-act sentimentality, Michael injected it with a sense of the primal, most forcefully in that crucial early improvisation scene which demands an extraordinary gear change from the actor as Elgin's buried genius begins to surface. One of the best chroniclers of mid-twentieth-century acting (an ex-actor himself), Laurence Kitchin, ranked the scene with Michael's execution scene in *The*

White Guard as a summit of his career: 'I don't know how far that improvisation varied from performance to performance, but the night I was
there it left the audience alone with Redgrave and a current of shocks not
to be had before or since in the London theatre.'

The 'House Full' boards were up outside the St James's nearly every
night, with London audiences fascinated by what seemed then an unusual
confrontation of acting styles, Michael's supposed classicism against a
rawer American realism. Except that the 'classical' actor proved able to
yoke that background (so potent in suggesting the character's past career)
to anything that the looser, supposedly more emotionally free actor could
throw at him. Later Michael said that one of the reasons he took the part,
opting to pass on the virtually certain hit of Rattigan's *The Deep Blue Sea*
as Peggy Ashcroft's husband for Binkie, was that Frank's background was
the very opposite of that of a Stanislavsky-trained actor.

The atmosphere backstage – even if it might have helped the play – was
enough for him not to extend his six-month contract and Sherek allowed
Googie to leave then, too, replacing them with Alexander Knox and
Constance Cummings, Wanamaker and the rest of the cast staying on. But
business collapsed as soon as the new cast went in and Sherek had to close
Winter Journey quickly. He always felt miserable about the whole experience; in his subsequent autobiography he mused on what might have
happened if, as once was mooted, Alec Guinness had played Frank: 'As I
know him, he would have just walked out without a word, certain that I
would not sue him for breach of contract. He would have been right.'

From early on, knowing that *Winter Journey* would run at least six
months, Michael was in a mood to think of escaping from the commercial
theatre jungle for a return to the company ethos of the Old Vic or
Stratford. Michael Benthall, now leading the Vic, had suggested a second
Macbeth and possibly Benedick, but Michael was more drawn to the Avon
where the Coronation year company was to be divided between Stratford
under Glen Byam Shaw and an Australian tour under Tony Quayle,
especially when *King Lear* was offered and then Antony, finally, opposite
Peggy's Cleopatra (she felt confident with Glen Byam Shaw directing it).
So delighted was Michael that he impulsively agreed, to help Stratford's
budget, to start earlier than originally suggested and play Shylock too.
This meant there would be no decent amount of time to fit in a lucrative
film between *Winter Journey*'s closure and Stratford rehearsals early in
1953 and Cecil, once more, was not best pleased. Writing from the
hothouse atmosphere of the St James's to Glen in the ensemble world of
Stratford, Michael enthused: 'I am having a hard struggle to prevent
myself going over the moon at the whole thing, simply because it seems
such a dreadful long time to have to wait! But oh, I am so happy!'

Despite all the problems with Wanamaker, Michael had gone ahead with his attempts to help Theatre Workshop. He persuaded the Embassy to house the company for a short season in May, the billing reading 'Michael Redgrave Presents' (he put up some of the capitalisation, too), in Ewan MacColl's anti-nuclear play *Uranium 235*. It was an unusually contrasted first night, with the play using every agit-prop and Living Newspaper device, and the audience full of glamorous celebrities, from George Cukor to Laurence Olivier and Vivien Leigh. This kind of theatre was not on the critical beaten path in the early 1950s (although Theatre Workshop had toured and played the Edinburgh Festival, their work was unsubsidised and little known) and the metropolitan critics were left slightly flummoxed ('But it is openly political!' the *Daily Mirror* complained). Joan Littlewood's inventive production and the multi-role acting (Theatre Workshop then included Harry H. Corbett and George A. Cooper) were widely praised, but its mixture of polemic and political satire meant that the company would be more honoured abroad than at home for some years yet. Littlewood wrote to Michael to thank him for his help and a generous programme note: 'I was deeply touched by your tribute to our work. We have often felt isolated by our curious way of life.' In turn, Michael never lost his admiration for Littlewood and Theatre Workshop, and was delighted when, the following year, they based themselves at the old Theatre Royal in Stratford E15, visiting many productions and sending the children there to see an alternative approach to classical acting and new plays alike.

To the press, sniffing out a story from backstage rumours at the St James's, Michael had said that he was 'exhausted' by the part, which was true enough. A holiday was not possible; some time before he had accepted an invitation to deliver four Rockefeller Foundation lectures at Bristol University, in the pioneering Department of Drama, the first one to be public, the other three to university students. A condition of the lectureship was that the talks should be published, which imposed a particular discipline on Michael as well as broadening his audience; he found a congenial publisher in Edward Thompson of Heinemann Educational Books, a gentleman publisher of the old school, impeccably courteous with a troubled private life, who became a good friend of both Michael (in whom he often confided) and Rachel.

Michael began to map out his lectures during the latter part of the *Winter Journey* run, continuing to work on them during a Scandinavian trip in October. He had thought very carefully about *The Merchant of Venice*. The most impressive Shylock for Michael remained one he had seen as an adolescent when the Dutch actor, Louis Bouwmeester, played in London. A large man with a huge voice, Bouwmeester had a kind of superhuman fury, famous for a terrifying throat sound of anger. Michael had asked his friend, the Dutch impresario Jan de Blieck, to help him with his research and de Blieck put him on to Johan de Meester, a leading director, coincidentally rehearsing *The Merchant of Venice* for Amsterdam's Stadschouwburg, who told him of Bouwmeester: 'He was as beautiful and impossible to control as a fighting tiger; there was not much of the sadness of the Jews in him, but there was all the fury and the power-to-hate of hundreds of generations of tortured ghetto-Jews from all over Europe.'

Michael had no intention of replicating Bouwmeester's performance (which he could remember only in broad outline in any case) but he did not want to make his Shylock a German, Italian or Spanish Jew and he finally decided to play him as originally from the Amsterdam ghetto. He could only see Shylock as a tragic hero whose 'fatal flaw' is that he tries to turn the law, from which he and his race have suffered so much, into an instrument of revenge. The sound of the part absorbed him – less a question of accent (he had made an early decision to avoid a strong foreign or East End Yiddish accent) more one of voice – especially since he wanted to make as strong a contrast as possible to all the vocal colours he would use as Lear.

With de Blieck's help, he arranged a trip to Amsterdam, seeing the opening of de Meester's powerful production of *The Merchant*, talking with Paul Saalborn who had played Shylock and with other Dutch actors. He also visited Amsterdam synagogues and Jewish shops, in one of which he bought a silver bracelet and buckle to use as part of his costume. Additionally, he fitted in a hop over to Sweden, where Dick Keigwin waited for him in Stockholm, to give a Hans Christian Andersen performance in the delightfully preserved eighteenth-century little theatre at Drottningholm.

On his return he had less than a month in which to finalise his four lectures. The first of these would be to an audience of well over 1000 and he was distinctly nervous. In it he was nailing his colours to the mast in the words of Harley Granville-Barker to Jacques Copeau: 'The art of the theatre is the art of acting, first, last, and all the time,' and he was fearful that a lay audience might find it recondite or over-reverent. He need not have fretted; artfully weaving a handful of good anecdotes into his text, he could quote from sources as varied as Longinus, Aristotle, Quintilian, Diderot, Stanislavsky, Shaw and Edward Gordon Craig without falling into the trap of pedantry. A few listeners may have guessed, from mentions of Dennis Robertson and 'Goldie' Lowes Dickinson, that Michael had been to Cambridge and had had Bloomsbury links, but there was little that was abstruse in his opening discursive review of the actor's art. The three following were more informal, ranging widely over the actor's challenges and problems, including a sparkling survey of Stanislavsky's theories, rightly claiming that a more accurate title of *An Actor Prepares* would be *An Actor's Work on Himself*; Michael's fundamental attitude to Stanislavsky's work was always that it should be seen as a practical aid to an ideal, especially as a help to the actor, servant of the play, to find the correct creative mood.

Edward Thompson was delighted with the lectures, which needed little alteration for publication. Still in print after half a century (the enterprising Nick Hern Books reissued it, with an Introduction by Vanessa, in 1995), the book of *The Actor's Ways and Means* remains fresh and challenging. From the outset Michael stressed that he would raise many questions without providing necessarily definite answers; he saw the lectures as a chance to air mid-twentieth-century actors' concerns, throughout implying that the constant stimulus to and feeding of the imagination is a cornerstone of the art of acting. He was addressing mainly drama students, and the extraordinary thing is that all these decades on, despite a transformed theatre in which the repertory system in which Michael and his contemporaries cut their teeth has all but vanished and despite today's voracious consumption of young talent by agents and television, his book remains an inspiration to young actors. Michael is not so unworldly as to forget that rent and mortgages have to be paid but he returns often to stress the value of building a worthwhile career; if it emphasises – although he does not quote – Yeats's 'fascination of what's difficult', it is only as part of the attempt to upgrade the standing of the actor's work.

The published version was well received. Michael was touched by the generosity of old friends such as Arthur Marshall, reviewing it enthusiastically in the *New Statesman*, but even more impressed by Harold Clurman (whose own book on the Group Theater, *The Fervent Years*, was one of his favourites) who wrote on it for *The Nation* in glowing terms, especially impressed by the 'dignity' of Michael's attitude to acting and by his remark: 'We as actors can never rest on our laurels, for if we do we are likely to be smothered by them.' Charlotte Wolff, to whom he sent a copy, wrote of how fascinating she found it: 'I love the all-round awareness of the many sides of each question, the awareness of our natural ambivalence.' The only sour note was in a radio programme produced by John Davenport in which Tyrone Guthrie, who distrusted everything about Stanislavsky, came up with the old reproach to Michael of being 'too serious', simultaneously betraying an oddly spinsterish reaction to the whole subject: 'The topic is, in my opinion, too subjective, too intimate. ... The work of artistic creation is analogous to the work of physical procreation.'

Towards the end of the year Michael finally got away – to New York – although he had to combine this trip with work, too, doing publicity for the film of *The Importance of Being Earnest*, just opening in America, as well as several broadcasts and two TV appearances. Bob had sailed in advance and had booked them into the unfashionable but comfortable Park Chambers Hotel, very central on West 58th Street, and Michael set his usual hectic New York pace. In their three weeks in his magic city they saw virtually every show on Broadway in a vintage season which included *Pal Joey*, *The Crucible*, Eartha Kitt in *New Faces* and the new musical, *Wish You Were Here*, notable for its on-stage swimming pool and for its unusually large quota, even for a Joshua Logan show, of male beefcake. He and Bob also renewed their friendship with Bette Davis – they had visited her Laguna house several times during Michael's 1947 Hollywood time – backstage after seeing her revue *Two's Company*.

There were parties thrown for them by Lehman Engel and by Manhattan's powerful showbusiness couple, attorney Arnold Weissberger and agent Milton Goldman, and they dined quietly with Norris Houghton, then setting up the non-profit Phoenix Theatre venture. Among all the social rounds he had to fit in personal appearances to promote *The Importance* (well received in America), three radio plays and a TV production of Chekhov's *The Bear* opposite June Havoc, as well as the anarchic fun of an appearance on the top TV comedy show *Your Show of Shows* in a sketch opposite Sid Caesar, which Michael loved doing, rating Caesar a nimble-witted genius.

Hardly surprisingly, by the end of the trip he had a bad cold and a boil, although even those could not cloud the sheer delight of *Guys and Dolls*, which was to remain his lifelong favourite Broadway musical. He identified especially with Sky Masterson's song of nocturnal city wandering in 'My Time of Day':

> My time of day is the dark time,
> A couple of deals before dawn.

Sky Masterson left New York for Havana, while Michael decided to visit Jamaica for the first time since his brief wartime idyll of a stopover. He had a standing invitation from Noël Coward to visit his Blue Harbour home, but although Michael was glad to be met by Coward and Cole Lesley, now a permanent fixture among his entourage, he and Bob stayed at the Castle Gordon Hotel, visiting Blue Harbour to swim and for drinks. Michael worked on his Shylock lines during the day, although nights were busy, including a grand party at King's House for the visiting Winston Churchill, to whom Michael spent some time talking, writing to Daisy: 'I am *not* a Conservative, but I have always thought him a truly great man, even though, like the truly great, he can be occasionally much less than great. He seemed awfully tired, but his complexion is amazing – like a baby's bottom.'

Coward also took them along for dinner with Ian Fleming and his wife Ann, one of London's leading hostesses, at their house, Goldeneye, an evening which threatened to become sticky when Coward, as could happen when he took a drop too much, was at his most philistine. Ann Fleming reported back to Cecil Beaton:

> We had an epic evening with Noël, Cole, Michael Redgrave and Bob Michell; Noël insisted that Clemence Dane would have more posterity fame than Cyril Connolly and said Cyril's only claim to fame was the good fortune he had had in being sent to Eton. It is difficult to protect Cyril but that was going too far. Seconds later, he laid down that Shakespeare, thank God, was no intellectual. I managed to kick Redgrave into the argument and was amazed how intelligently and tactfully he routed Noël without giving offence.

They sailed home, arriving at Southampton with only a weekend at Bedford House before Stratford rehearsals. Michael had time to see Daisy ('in a bad way but not abusive') in her clinic and to spend an evening playing and singing *Guys and Dolls* songs with Vanessa and Bob before Bob drove him up in deep snow to Stratford to join Rachel. She was in the company too – Octavia in *Antony and Cleopatra* and Regan in *King Lear* among her roles – and had gone up in advance to arrange their flat (Peggy had Avoncliffe that season). Bob left them together – they had not seen each other for two months – to drive back to London.

Michael's diary sadly is blank for most of 1953, which for him was a genuine *annus mirabilis*. He arrived in a snowy Stratford bronzed and fit after Jamaica, and seemed unusually energised that season, walking or cycling to rehearsals each day. He and Peggy were leading a strong company – Harry Andrews, Marius Goring, Rachel, Yvonne Mitchell, Tony Britton and newcomers including Donald Pleasence and Robert Shaw – and although Glen Byam Shaw had been anxious beforehand (Rachel had found him, the night before rehearsals commenced, in his room at the theatre with Percy Harris, cleaning countless pairs of shoes from Wardrobe to calm his nerves), the atmosphere in the 'Jam Factory', as the squat brick building was familiarly known, was buoyant as spring started to thaw the snow.

Michael began and continued in confident mood as Shylock. The slight Dutch accent he had refined, sibilant and throaty, helped fuse the performance with the full-blooded gusto and power for which he was aiming. There was a hint of Fagin and of Beerbohm Tree's Svengali about his Shylock, with black mittens on his hands, ready-reckoner round his waist and the badge of the Star of David worn proudly on his shoulder. And although there was a shattering force, something sublime, in his passion for revenge, it was also only too clear that this was something which must be checked. The great scene of denunciation to Tubal was an astonishing feat, one of those key moments in his best performances when the vividly present-tense immediacy of his emotion – here scalding and corrosive – was almost scarily intimate to watch. He wrote to Daisy during late rehearsals:

> It is a joy to be back here. What I enjoy most is playing Shylock. But I must confess that rehearsing the Tubal scene and the trial makes me quite ill and I'm glad I'm not playing him for a run. To be mad with blind revenge and hatred is something which doesn't come easily to me. For years – in fact all one's life – one rejects thoughts of hatred and revenge, but when one lets those thoughts go and gives them their head they develop frightening power. I think the glimpse I had, last summer at the St James's, of what a feeling of persecution can do to a person was a great help for me as poor old Shylock.

Unfortunately this was another instance of a great performance in an indifferent production. *The Merchant* was directed by Denis Carey, who had won golden opinions at the Bristol Old Vic but here, not helped by an insipid set of gilded arcades which did little to distinguish Venice from Belmont, his work was fussy and uncertain in tone, with some dismal comedy scenes and, surprisingly, an off-form and pallid Portia from Peggy.

Critically Michael came out of it extremely well, and he must have been happy on the following Sunday to read Harold Hobson (Agate's *Sunday Times* successor) who wrote a somewhat teasing notice, beginning by referring to the old 'intellectual' tag round Michael's neck, although gradually it becomes apparent that he is not using the word as a term of reproach, going on to compare Michael with Macready ('who had as much emotional explosiveness as could be mustered by half the contemporary stage together, as well as a brain as active as Mr Redgrave's'). For Hobson, Michael's brooding Shylock, erupting into obsession close to madness, was no abstract conception but a characterisation fully inhabited and 'presented with overwhelming theatrical bravura'.

To turn to Kenneth Tynan would have robbed him of the pleasure of reading Hobson. Tynan's piece, less a review than an essay illustrating his questionable theory that Shylock can be properly acted only by a Continental actor able to switch moods with lightning speed, extended his exaltation of Olivier in a discussion of great acting. To Tynan, the gulf between good and great acting is one which Olivier, animal-like, leaps over like a pole-vaulter, and which Gielgud crosses by tightrope using a parasol as balance, while only Redgrave has to battle it out with the current, the hardest way. Diametrically opposed to Hobson, while granting the intelligence of Michael's conception of Shylock he refuses to allow its execution a theatrical validity. But then – not for the first time – Tynan was using a performance to illustrate a theory, and his notion that English actors are incapable of the rapid gear changes required for Shylock has been disproved by more than a few Anglo-Saxon actors besides Michael, who had in *Winter Journey* the previous year amply demonstrated a rare ability to accelerate from a standing start, which Tynan seemed somehow to forget.

Michael had never especially craved a chance to play Antony. He was well aware that no actor in recent memory had made a significant success in the part (Godfrey Tearle opposite Edith and Olivier with Vivien Leigh had failed to pull it off) and he could see all the dangers: 'There is no plain sailing in Antony, no point of rest where the words will carry you along, no safe haven until Antony's death. It is a part that calls on all the strength one possesses and tests out every weakness.' It is a curious leading role if only because the character has all the appearances of nobility and strength whereas Antony in fact is often a weak man; Enobarbus touches on some heroism, but he is never seen as doing anything especially noble. The actor has somehow convincingly to create the image of a man who held part of the world in thrall. Possibly, he felt, because both Tearle and Olivier had insisted what a tough part it was to learn, for the first time ever Michael had trouble learning his lines, having to ask Glen or Rachel to hear him at night well after the stage when he would normally have even a big role under his belt. For a while, the 'Actor's Nightmare', his hideous dream of his dissolving made-up face, recurred and the dress rehearsal of *Antony and Cleopatra* became an horrific ordeal (also given fictional form in *The Mountebank's Tale* subsequently) of fluffs and dries, alarming the whole company as well as Michael. Peggy, nervous herself, knew something of what he was going through (but had seen thrilling glimpses of greatness in rehearsal) and reassured him in a scribbled first-night note: 'Egypt has no gifts for Antony, but so *much* love and deepest, heartfelt wishes. You not only look like him – you *are* him.'

On the first night, Michael – taking Peggy with him – soared into the stratosphere. Their first entrance had been his own suggestion to Glen – Cleopatra running on leading Antony ensnared in a rope of waterlilies, both clearly not long out of bed and keen to be back there. The whole production had a hurtling, restless force from that unforgettable image onwards, helped by Glen and Percy Harris deciding to have a simple set, a permanent stepped structure against a vast cyclorama which could switch instantly from Egypt's baking heat to the cooler world of Rome. There were a few emblematic flown pieces – a metal campaign map, the Roman Eagle – and they used the elaborate Stratford stage machinery only for the closing Monument scenes. Throughout, the stress was on speed, with no cumbersome scene changes or heavy furniture, with everything geared to keep the pace of the play cumulatively fleet.

Peggy, in her red ponytail wig and with a pale make-up, was an unconventional-looking Cleopatra, but the mistress of English cool surprised and entranced nearly everyone with the sexual power and range of a performance which moved from a tigress's rages to flooding sensuality and finally into incandescent ecstasy as she prepared for death, recalling her Antony:

> I dreamt there was an Emperor Antony.
> O, such another sleep, that I might see
> But such another man.
> ...
> His face was as the heav'ns and therein stuck
> A sun and moon, which kept their course and lighted
> The little O, th'earth.

Even allowing for Cleopatra's hyperbole, any Antony must suggest something of this demigod. Michael's looks helped him here; with his height and physique, breastplate open to reveal a broad, bronzed chest, tousled auburn-gold hair and beard, he looked like something out of a Veronese allegorical painting, but there was nothing allegorical or abstract about his performance. As Richard Findlater wrote, he simply *looked* so right: 'With a careless, laughing and abandoned magnificence ... when he speaks, one sees his past spread around him like a scarlet cloak.'

The performance took on all the aspects of a multifaceted role, from the careless relapses into a heedless sensuality, the near psychotic rages (the whipping of Cleopatra's messenger, appalling to watch), the marvellous defiance as he calls his 'sad captains' to him for one more gaudy night 'to mock the midnight bell', the instinctive courage to the petty weaknesses. Most impressive was the way he manoeuvred into the very heart of Antony in the most difficult scenes of the play as he approaches his end. In speeches fraught with pitfalls – often they seem self-pitying and peevish – once again Michael found the key in a character's sense of shame. Because his Antony, although greedy and weak, had been unmistakably great, his fall was all the greater and in his closing scenes, beautifully staged by Byam Shaw, isolating Antony in increasing shadows, his vocal power amazed as he traced – like a surfer – the long, soaring and cresting cadenzas of grief and loss, reaching that sense of a man's deep sense of shame, with lines such as 'I have lost command' and 'I have offended reputation'

becoming freighted with self-laceration, holding the house utterly rapt as
he finally turned to Eros for: 'Unarm, Eros: the long day's task is done,
and we must sleep.'

This time Tynan reserved his lash for Peggy. Headlining his notice
'CLEOPATRA FROM SLOANE SQUARE' he mocked her 'Kensingtonian'
vowels and, switching sexes from *The Merchant*, now insisted that Cleopatra is a part only within the range of Continental actresses able to switch
gears quickly (so much for Judi Dench, Maggie Smith, Helen Mirren *et
al.*). Michael thought this was nonsense; for him Peggy's acting tran-
scended vowel sounds, and he had the same feelings of security and
freedom on stage with her as he had had with Edith. The production,
greeted everywhere else with acclaim, became Stratford's hottest ever
ticket and Michael had a packed dressing room after every performance.
He had scores of letters about it, including one from J. B. Priestley, who
described his Antony as 'easily the best I have ever seen – and I may add
that this is my favourite play of Shakespeare'. And he had a letter from an
American director now living in England, Joseph Losey, whom he had
met in the French Club. Losey marvelled at what he described as the
'hugeness of spirit' of this Antony: 'The destruction and ruin of a man,
the inevitability of his passion and its nobility. How seldom it happens in
the theatre that one must cheer!'

With two down and the big one still to come, Michael had a few days
of idyllic Stratford sunshine when the children and Nanny Randall came
up from London and there was time for punting on the Avon (just as he
had done with Daisy over thirty years before), tennis and picnics before
he had to go into rehearsal under George Devine for *King Lear*. He also
entered the public arena – extremely forcefully – taking a passionate line
in the *New Statesman* against the Labour MP George Strauss's suggestions
that the Old Vic should be the home of a National Theatre, that the
government funds (then a paltry £1 million) allocated to a new building
should be shared out by all the country's repertory theatres and that the
South Bank site should be scrapped. In a trenchant, angry letter Michael
described a 'wicked nonsense' Strauss's notion that another South Bank
theatre would mean the end of the Vic. He was to return to this subject
often over the next few years, always vigilant for any lapse in what he saw
as the government's duty to have a National Theatre built.

On *Lear*, although as a classical director Devine tended to be methodical
rather than inspired, Michael and he had a happy partnership, united in
their view of it as an essentially pagan play into which Christian values of
forgiveness and repentance gradually enter. Michael's only real quibble
was over the design. Devine had wanted Henry Moore for the production
(there was a short-lived vogue then for using artists and sculptors in the

theatre – Barbara Hepworth designed an Old Vic *Electra* two years before) and when Moore proved unavailable Devine bravely asked the wayward Scottish artist Robert Colquhoun, then living, tempestuously as always, with his equally anarchic artist partner Robert MacBryde. When designs were slow in arriving, a young Frank Dunlop, an ex-Old Vic School student not yet embarked on his directorial career, was packed off to an isolated cottage at the end of a muddy track in Essex to chivvy Colquhoun along. That was easier said than done, Dunlop finding the pair engaged nightly in enthusiastic bouts of S & M activities (MacBryde descending for breakfast each morning with a fresh set of bruises). Also staying was Elizabeth Smart, the writer of *By Grand Central Station, I Sat Down and Wept*, with her children by the poet George Barker. Colquhoun, MacBryde and Smart, all epic drinkers, spent most of the time in the local pub and finally it was Dunlop who more or less interpreted Colquhoun's drawings and made the set model. It was along vaguely Blakean lines with, in prominent centre-stage position, a monolithic Stonehenge-ish structure variously compared to a bunch of Stone Age bananas and a Cubist sliced pomegranate.

Many Lears – Irving and Gielgud included – have disappointed on their first nights, but on this occasion, completing an astonishing hat-trick season, Michael rose to the heights, even surprising many of his fellow actors. He did not forget everything of his Cranleigh *Lear*; here too this was a signally old Lear, agonised by failing powers, a sometimes near clinical study of senility in the workings of his lower jaw or the way in which his body, straining to draw his broadsword, failed to match the force of his fury when Lear turns on Kent. Unconventionally, the early scenes presented no peevish old dotard tyrant but a king who was by then on the way to bring a 'fond and foolish' old man, absurd in his parade of power. In the taxing central Heath scenes he played a man already shattered, whose throwing himself on the mercy of Goneril and Regan became a version of self-immolation, a kind of death wish. The later scenes took off, as they must, into the empyrean of real tragedy. In the Dover scene and the scene with the flowers he was heartbreaking – a man seeking in madness a haven from a reality too intolerable to be borne – and he invested the reconciliation scene with a Lazarus quality, using a wisp of his own hair as the feather to test Cordelia's breath, holding the audience coughless, almost breathless.

Of all the superb notices for *Lear* (even Tynan, if somewhat grudgingly, had to admit its power) he was most pleased by that of Robert Speaight, actor as well as leading Shakespeare scholar: 'Critics have a habit of qualifying Mr Redgrave as a "character actor" as though there were something limited in this. This Lear is indeed characterised, but it touches the universal for all that; time and again we are caught up by the sweep and the surprise of great acting.'

The production had some lapses – Marius Goring's prancing ninny of the Fool included – although Rachel's Regan, a chill-voiced domestic tyrant who finds she likes sadism, was widely praised. Her work that season took wing, undoubtedly partly because she had just begun a love affair. She and Glen Byam Shaw had known each other since Old Vic days in the 1930s and there had been incidents – dancing together during Rachel's first pregnancy, a Buckingham Palace Garden Party when Glen, as he told her years later, had been transfixed by Rachel's beauty in a white dress – when there had been tremors in the air. That summer they began an affair which was the most important relationship with another man besides Michael in Rachel's life, much deeper than that with Leo Genn.

Glen had something of Michael's combination of handsome strength and sensitive vulnerability. Son of the artist Byam Shaw, as a beautiful young man he had been the lover of Siegfried Sassoon (both had been bruised emotionally previously by Ivor Novello) who became almost obsessed with him before Glen, always a gentle man, eventually had to extricate himself from what was an unequal relationship. He later married the actress Angela Baddeley and they had two children. Michael and Angela both understood the situation (Angela, said Rachel, 'loved Glen so much that she would put up with anything he did, as I had with Michael') and the parallel situation continued for most of the rest of Glen's life. In the early stages of the affair John Fowler would lend them his Hampshire country house where they often met. Michael was happy for Rachel and he was devoted to Glen. All Rachel said of this aspect of the quadrilateral relationship in her memoirs was that 'Michael, being tolerant in these matters, was understanding and in a sense relieved'. But there were times for both Rachel and Glen, the understanding being that they would not leave their marriages, when the realisation of that fact could be suddenly painful, although those feelings ebbed with time.

The scale of *Antony and Cleopatra*'s success led to a transfer to London, where for a six-week season it filled every seat in the vast Prince's (now Shaftesbury) Theatre. It had been an astounding year for Michael and he had a European tour of *Antony* under Jan de Blieck's auspices early in the new year to crown the production's triumph. But the end of 1953 brought him a most unwelcome early Christmas present. On 19 December he received a letter at Bedford House from the Solicitor's Office of the Inland Revenue threatening that unless he paid at once £6122 in outstanding surtax, a bankruptcy notice would be issued against him. This panicked him into inertia; somehow he carried on, apparently unconcerned, during a regular Chiswick Christmas of tree, carols and presents, before taking off for The Hague on the first leg of the tour of *Antony and Cleopatra*, a sold-out success everywhere, although on its last date, playing Paris's huge Théâtre des Nations, critics more used to the declamatory notes of Marie Bell's Cleopatra in Gide's version for the Comédie Française were disturbed by the earthy sexuality of Peggy's scenes with Michael.

Early in the new year when Michael had gone on the *Antony* tour the Solicitor's Office called at Chiswick, threatening to come again shortly with a bankruptcy notice. Joan Sparks went into action, contacting Walter Smee's office, and Smee, with Cecil's connivance, eventually pacified the Inland Revenue with an offer to pay £10,000 of a forthcoming fee (£12,500) for a Michael Powell movie, settling his surtax debt and first tax instalment for the new tax year. But now Cecil was merciless with Michael; after the *Antony* tour there could be no question of any stage appearances until Michael had worked himself into the black in the film studios.

Along with all this, Michael was going through another drama of his own. During the Stratford season he had been approached by the film producer Filippo del Giudice ('Del') who had produced Olivier's films of *Henry V* and *Hamlet*, to film *Antony and Cleopatra* in Italy with Michael to star, write the screenplay and direct. Olivier, he was assured by Del, had said when first approached that after his stage Antony he had no desire to film it. Michael, although at first trepidatious, began to relish the challenge; he felt that the play was by far Shakespeare's most cinematic and was soon bursting with ideas both visual and textual. Peggy had no enthusiasm for films but Margaret Leighton was thrilled at the idea of Cleopatra (which she played memorably later on stage) and Michael also came up with a bonus of Orson Welles as Enobarbus. Welles had just coincidentally offered Michael a part in a film in Spain based on his novel, *Mr Arkadin*, which he had been writing when they last met at Notley, and in return for Michael's acceptance offered reciprocally to appear in Michael's film (whether he would have honoured a verbal promise had the movie finally gone ahead is, of course, another matter).

Del was a capricious character, wily and often secretive in money matters, although he had pioneered what he boasted as 'my Method' of deferred payments and profit participation. He had a habit, when pressed on financial details, of delaying tactics, often claiming food poisoning, when his English would become as fractured as that of Michel Saint-Denis' ('I have been intoxicated by the fishes').

The film's announcement was widely covered in the press and while Del explored fund-raising possibilities in Milan, Michael worked extremely hard on his screenplay. Reading the yellowing pages today it is easy to understand why the venture remained one of the few really hurtful disappointments of Michael's career. The script – inevitably having to cut a long play but managing to leave both main story and essential themes intact – is genuinely imaginative, totally thought through in screen terms. Key images of water, sun, desert and sky predominate – as in the play – and his solution throughout in rethinking the play for film is to avoid the kind of gaudy realism of the later Elizabeth Taylor version.

As an instance, when working on Enobarbus's great description of Cleopatra to Caesar's lieutenants ('I will tell you …'), he knew that no visuals could match Shakespeare's words and that an impressionist approach would work best. He wrote it so that the camera would cut out Agrippa and Maecenas, moving in on Enobarbus closing his eyes as if to key up his powers of recollection, the camera then circling round him, pulling back so that we are no longer in Caesar's house where the scene takes place:

> We see a broad expanse of water, with the sound of flutes. On 'The barge she sat in …' we pan forward and see *not* the barge itself but the *reflection* of a great golden barge and the purple sails in the ripples made by the oars. Then back to a shot of Enob. looking younger as he was at the time of Antony's meeting Cleopatra, as if on the rails of an adjacent ship, surrounded by officers of Antony's retinue. Then slowly fade sounds and images and camera pans back to behind Enob. And then to his face as the speech ends.

The script is packed with similarly striking marriages of sound and image, and Del, Margaret Leighton and Loudon Sainthill, who was to design both a Tiepolo-inspired Rome and an exotic Egypt, were all enthused by the work Michael had done and the clarity of his vision of the film. Del seemed confident that the bulk of the financing was virtually in place and began to issue contracts.

A bombshell hit Michael on his return with the Stratford company from Paris when he discovered that a disturbing rumour of a planned rival film of *Antony and Cleopatra* was true; it would star Olivier and Vivien Leigh, with Olivier directing his own screenplay, to be produced by Alexander Korda and filmed at Rome's Cinecittà. With extraordinary generosity Michael wired Del: 'Had supper with Larry. Tells me of A & C for Korda. Told him "May Best Man Win". But if it would help you to do it with Larry and Viv I would be content to wait for Tempest next year.'

He was in more combative mood a few days later, however, after hearing from Leighton's agent, the respected Vere Barker, 'that he regarded the whole Alex–Larry–Viv project as pure *sabotage*' (Leighton was devastated by the behaviour of Korda, whose protégée on film she had been). Michael also heard from Michael Benthall and Robert Helpmann, close friends of Vivien Leigh (and prize gossips), 'who told me a number of things concerning "jealousy" and ambition which I would not have thought possible'.

Michael was becoming increasingly mistrustful of Cecil's role in what was beginning to seem a suspiciously murky affair; not only was Cecil Olivier's agent, he was also a director, as was Korda, of LOP Ltd (Olivier's production company). He telephoned Olivier, telling him that he and Leighton would stick to Del and that he would be seeing Cecil, adding – deliberately casually – 'I hope not for the last time'. Pricking up his ears, as Michael intended, Olivier asked, 'Oh, what *do* you mean, old boy?' Michael understandably enough replied that he could not employ an agent who was also Olivier's when such clashes arose. He then postponed seeing Cecil while, as he rightly guessed, Olivier and Cecil conferred.

Olivier's casuistry could be breathtaking as he kept wriggling on the moral hook to Michael, insisting that there was no master plan, that he was only, as a jobbing actor, accepting 'an offer' from Korda, that Korda kept telling him that Del would not raise the funding for Michael's film and so on. Michael wrote back to Olivier unusually bluntly: 'What I think is wrong, completely and utterly wrong, is that Alex should proceed on the assumption that Del will fail to secure the money. That is not for even a financial wizard like Alex to know, and as for Cinecittà's project, how many plans has Alex not from time to time abandoned?' The short-term outcome was that the Olivier project shelved a public announcement for the time being, but the rumour mill had already done its damage, with potential investors now unsure about putting up money for Del with a rival and potentially starrier version hovering. Olivier wrote a blustering letter in reply to Michael, *faux-naif* in accusing him of sounding 'bitter and disappointed, old boy', to which Michael responded, saying that that was not how he felt (he pointed out, with some silkiness, that he had been surprised that Olivier had never even acknowledged that he had offered to retire in Olivier's favour to help Del), continuing: 'I felt it necessary to write to you because I did not think it was quite fair to let you assume I was putting most of the blame on Alex, and I still think that there might be a chance that Alex and Cinecittà could prevent Del from getting full backing.' Which was exactly what happened. In increasingly poor health, Del battled on over four more years trying to complete his funding – in Canada, Ireland and the UK – before the project petered out in 1958. The Korda–Olivier version also, of course, never went ahead, sceptics even at the time saying that there was no intention of ever making the film, only of stopping Michael's from being made. Olivier's last word to Michael on the subject was an acknowledgement of Michael's letter, in a tangle of mixed metaphors describing himself as 'not being able to see the wood for the trees when any knotty problems blankets itself around me (the difference, I suppose, between a BIG man and not a big one)'.

The 'jealousy' which Michael had been told so much about undoubtedly came into play in Olivier's behaviour over *Antony and Cleopatra*. At the centre of the whole business surely lay the niggling memory in Olivier's mind that in the same week as Michael had opened so spectacularly as Antony in London, he had opened, much less spectacularly, in Rattigan's 'occasional comedy' *The Sleeping Prince* with Vivien Leigh, and as Michael wrote to Del: 'Olivier has been heavily criticised for doing a charming but lightweight Rattigan play and wants to restore his position as the leading English classical actor *and also* make a lot of money. I don't blame him for that. I do blame him for kicking his friends aside in order to do it.' Furthermore, Olivier to date had been the only English actor to script, direct and star in Shakespeare on screen. It is hard, given the evidence, to see another motive for the sudden and short-lived rival *Antony* film than the desire to prevent Michael – increasingly presented in the press as not only a rival but also a surpasser of Olivier ('an ageing matinée idol' had been a recent description of Olivier) – from scoring a possible similar film success, particularly in a role in which he had triumphed on stage while it had been for Olivier a rare classical disappointment.

Corin remembered his father at that time:

Michael was wrapped in thought in the window of the drawing room at Bedford House looking out towards the river. I asked him if anything was wrong and he said, with a very sad smile: 'There are times when you find out who are your friends and who are not.' I think it hurt him more that Olivier, whom he thought the world of and valued as a friend, should have acted against him without his knowledge than he minded about losing the chance to act in and direct A & C.

With 'the realisation of our glorious project', as Michael described *Antony* to Del, looking increasingly unlikely, he had to buckle down to the films lined up for him by Cecil, including three days' work in Madrid for Welles on *Confidential Report* (as *Mr Arkadin* had been retitled). Michael once described Welles during this period of self-imposed European exile from America as 'a wandering star of spasmodic incandescence. You never know what he will be doing next.'

The movie likewise is of distinctly 'spasmodic incandescence'. Some Wellesians make high claims for it as a companion piece to *Citizen Kane*, both featuring Welles as a megalomaniac millionaire, both featuring bravura camera work, broken or overlapping music and dialogue, and both centred round a quest – a search for identity in *Kane*, for a past in *Confidential Report*. But while *Kane* had Herman Mankiewicz's vital input on the script Welles's screenplay for *Confidential Report* is, like the novel *Mr Arkadin*, a lazy affair. Its narrative, set against a neo-Jamesian corrupt

heroics and, crucially, allowing time to develop the characters, although Michael's performance has such absorbing mental energy that the later bombing-raid sequences involving Richard Todd, when Wallis takes second place to action, seem oddly less involving. Michael's quiet, dogged patience, even in scenes in which Whitehall mandarins treat him like a quack pedlar, the just perceptible shiver as Wallis waits in the ops room, cocoa untasted, for the results of his experiment, and a beautifully played scene when the inventor of destruction feels he must ask two pilots eating prior to taking off on a raid if his joining them at their table disturbs them, all underpin a performance on a level with his Crocker-Harris for the craft of screen acting. With its kind of inspired and unsentimental humility, it is a deeply human piece of work.

The treadmill of film appearances seemed to involve him in back-to-back pictures. He worked once more for Michael Anderson, but neither was happy with a low-budget version of *1984*, which traduced Orwell's satire with an altered ending to have Winston die a hero's death. Intriguingly, many reviews said that the film would have benefited had Michael played the tortured victim instead of the bland American Edmond O'Brien. As it was, the scenes between Winston and interrogator (name changed unaccountably to O'Connor in the film) lost that sickly-sweet intimacy which can grow between victim and torturer – Orwell understood this as much as Patrick Hamilton – although Michael, vocally hypnotic, managed to suggest some of the civilised irony that is so urbanely chilling in Orwell's character.

The film of this time to which Michael had most looked forward turned out a really crushing disappointment. Although the wartime *49th Parallel* had not worked out, Michael Powell had kept trying to find a film on which they might work together and when the offer came for Michael to star in the third of a series of films by the Archers (Powell, Emeric Pressburger and their creative team – a kind of movie co-operative) he was thrilled, having admired the Archers' films for their risks, particularly their use of colour and sound in a manner unusually bold in a convention-bound British cinema. After *The Red Shoes* (ballet) and *The Tales of Hoffmann* (opera, collaborating with Sir Thomas Beecham), the Archers' final movie in a planned artistic triptych was to be their adaptation of Richard Strauss's operetta, *Die Fledermaus*. Powell, knowing that Michael had been offered simultaneously the film of Rattigan's *The Deep Blue Sea* with Vivien Leigh and having failed to cast original choices such as Maurice Chevalier, pursued him with shameless flattery to play Eisenstein in *Oh, Rosalinda!!* (beware films with two exclamation marks) as it was now called: 'You must play this mad, innocent blue-eyed French husband. Nobody else can. *And* you must sing him too.'

By far his happiest time on the film was the period in Vienna at the end of 1954 recording his own songs – with the Vienna Symphony Orchestra, no less – as did Annelise Rothenberger (Adèle) and Tony Quayle (Orlofsky), Rosalinda – Eisenstein's wife – was dubbed by the operetta star Sari Barrabas ('a plump partridge with amusing "shrieks"', Michael described her) and was played by a Powell favourite, the ballerina Ludmila Tcherina ('rather too like Bobby Helpmann's imitation to be comfortable'). The new lyrics were by Dennis Arundell who was in Vienna for the recording, tempting Michael from the plush comforts of the Hotel Sacher to explore some more louche Viennese nightlife, a bonus one evening being a surprise encounter with Cavalcanti, peripatetic as always and still hoping to work with Michael again.

The film itself was purgatory to make. The script reset the story in a post-war Vienna of the Four Powers with Anton Walbrook as Dr Falke ('The Bat') hotting things up for a Frenchman (Michael), a Russian (Quayle), an Englishman (Dennis Price) and an American (Mel Ferrer, cast only because the Archers wanted Mrs Ferrer – Audrey Hepburn – to film Giraudoux's *Ondine*, and charmless). There was an idea there, but the laboured Iron Curtain jokes and the overstuffed, nudging style were fatally at war with Strauss's music. Perversely, Tcherina – certainly no comedienne – dances not at all and although Walbrook has a casual aplomb, nowhere does the film come near the *La Ronde* style of sophisticated wit to which it aspires. Extraordinarily for an Archers film, it is vulgar; even the designs, the work of an authentic genius, Hein Heckroth, veteran of the Viennese operatic stage and of *The Red Shoes*, are garish and coarse-grained, like a shoddy touring version of *White Horse Inn* in the hotel exterior set.

Michael's diary – resumed briefly then – records his misery: 'Think I am going to hate the next 7 weeks.' The Elstree set was oppressively hot and the atmosphere often tense. Anton Walbrook, who had left Germany in the early 1930s, would not speak to either Rothenberger (extremely temperamental) or Oskar Sima (playing Frosch, in the film a signally unfunny interpreter), both of whom he claimed had been Nazis, while Powell was at his most snappily autocratic. He was uncomfortable about homosexuality; Walbrook was gay and he and Michael had 'Foff' LeGrand in common (a serious relationship for Walbrook, a fling for Michael). Powell became, curiously and erroneously, convinced that 'Anton and Mike were in love with each other'. One of those who believe that homosexuality is an evasion of adult responsibilities, a refusal fully to grow up, Powell wrote of Michael after showing *Oh, Rosalinda!!* years later to his disciple Martin Scorsese in New York: 'I saw now what I had never seen before, either in rehearsal or in performance. Michael Redgrave was a child. He had the open heart of a child, the innocence and cunning of a child.'

The friendship with Walbrook, a civilised, ironic and melancholy man, was the only good thing for Michael to come out of the film. He is far from at his best in it; he looks overweight, his scenes with Tcherina seem endless and only in snatches, mostly in his few scenes with Walbrook, does he find the nonchalant insouciance the film so often fails to capture.

He was consoled amid the laboured frou-frou of *Oh, Rosalinda!!* by the anticipation of a return to the stage. During what was for him a long absence – nearly two years – he had had to turn down a good deal of theatre work including Binkie's offerings of Christopher Fry's *The Dark is Light Enough* opposite Edith and a surefire comedy, *Simon and Laura*, with Coral Browne, as well as Benthall's suggestions of Falstaff and *Timon of Athens* for the Old Vic (neither of which he ever played). But this time, whatever Cecil might think, he was not going to pass on the chance to play, finally, Hector in Giraudoux's *La Guerre de Troie n'aura pas Lieu*, now freshly and incisively translated by Christopher Fry, with the bonus of a production by his revered Harold Clurman, who had also always hungered to do the play. He turned down many other offers to take on Hector, including Higgins in *My Fair Lady*. The producer Herman Levin had pursued him for some time, calling him early in 1955 from New York to try to clinch the deal ('He suggests I could get out of Clurman and Giraudoux commitment'); although dates were adjusted, the offer was withdrawn when Michael refused to sign for more than a year, allowing Rex Harrison the chance of his career.

His diary entries for this period quite often note 'Rachel with G'. Glen and Rachel had now settled into a pattern of meeting whenever they could, usually at John Fowler's. Michael and Bob were much more together at this period, Bob often joining him at Elstree, going together to the cinema or out to friends (Bob was a special favourite of Vivien Leigh's) or working together laying paths in the Bedford House garden. Michael was also thrilled that Vanessa, who had accepted that she would be too tall for her first love of the ballet, had taken so happily to her early drama school training ('Oh, Daddy, it was sheer bliss,' he reported her reaction to the first day at Central School). Corin and Vanessa still had that unusually strong bond from their closely shared childhood while Lynn, originally the odd child out, shy with most adults (although she adored Bob instantly) and often sickly when young, had bloomed with her teenage passion for riding (her godmother, Edith Hargreaves, gave her a pony, christened – even after the reviews of the film – Rosalinda). Michael, although tired, was in good humour when filming for Powell finished as preparations for the Giraudoux play were under way: 'A wonderful feeling of being free, brought to state of elation by being called to St James's to see auditions: "This is the life," I think, as I swing my umbrella down St James's St.'

Fifteen
AMERICAN STAGES

Even the prospect of imminent rehearsals could not make Michael do without the ritual annual Bedford House weekend Boat Race party with the guests that year including Guinnesses, Menuhins, Millses, Edith Evans, Diana Wynyard and the producers of the Giraudoux play who became alarmed for their star's voice as he bawled support for Cambridge (they won).

He had wanted as strong a company as possible for *Tiger at the Gates* as the play, at Michael's suggestion, was now to be called, the producers vetoing a literal translation of the title as uncommercial. He had written to the co-producers, Scottish-born Stephen Mitchell and the American Robert Joseph: 'Above all, it is a team play, surely.'

With twenty-seven actors – a big commercial venture even in the palmier days of 1950s Shaftesbury Avenue – it was cast to the hilt and Michael had suggested some strong actors including Barbara Jefford who had the right warmth and sensuality for Hector's wife Andromache, Catherine Lacey (from *The Family Reunion*) as Hecuba and, in the late-appearing but crucial role of Ulysses, who has a taxing near climactic scene with Hector, the formidable Walter Fitzgerald. Newer talent included the stunning young Diane Cilento as a Helen of Troy far removed from Marlowe's 'face that launched a thousand ships', more of a pragmatic minx (Michael agreed with Clurman that the casting would be controversial in London but trusted to his judgement that New York audiences would understand this Helen at once), Robert Shaw and Leo Ciceri as a sun-bronzed Paris.

Michael and Clurman had corresponded regularly in the months prior to rehearsals. After the failure to include the play in the pre-war Phoenix season, Michael had tried to interest T. S. Eliot in working on an English version, but Eliot had demurred and it had been Clurman's bright suggestion to approach the benignly urbane Fry, ideal for Giraudoux's comedy with a grave theme, often mordant in tone. Fry was not the fastest of workers and Michael received his script only in tantalising instalments but, like Clurman, he was delighted with the precision and wit of Fry's version, which also kept the underlying gravitas of the more rhetorical passages in focus. Clurman, in the midst of directing William Inge's *Bus Stop* on Broadway, wrote to Michael: 'No project that I have engaged in for the past ten years or more has so endeared itself to my imagination.'

Excited and anticipatory as the atmosphere was when rehearsals began in late March, all concerned were aware that the play was a risk in a West End increasingly given over to middlebrow escapism, and Giraudoux had had more previous luck in New York (the Lunts had dazzled in *Amphitryon 38*) than in London. A career diplomat at the Quai d'Orsay for much of his life, Giraudoux in his plays, detachedly ironic and exquisitely poised, often adapted or subverted fairy tales (*Ondine*), or myths, as in *Siegfried*, a caustic tale of identity with a French soldier transformed into a German during 1914–18. He had been a great admirer of Jacques Copeau's work – they had a similarly sophisticated intelligence – and of Louis Jouvet who created Hector in the play's première. In translation his style, artificial and rhetorical but in the right hands capable of sardonic, richly textured drama, can be hard to capture with its unusual equipoise between the mythologist and the Parisian boulevardier, but Fry, who would go on to work similar magic on Jean Anouilh, had succeeded beyond Michael's expectations.

Clurman was only seven years Michael's senior but his background as critic, producer and director – work for New York's Theater Guild as well as co-founding the Group Theater, his experience with Copeau in New York and Stanislavsky in Russia – inevitably made him for Michael one of those figures to be hero-worshipped. Not all actors agreed with his veneration of Clurman; Diana Wynyard, who accepted a few years later an offer to appear in a Broadway *Heartbreak House* to be directed by him at Michael's urging, was severely disillusioned, telling Michael that while she would concede that Clurman had a fine mind she thought him basically lazy and hopeless at staging a play. But Michael would later tell Clurman that his time on the play was 'one of the greatest experiences of my life'.

Rehearsals went well, although according to Barbara Jefford, Clurman and Michael were 'not always on the same lines' and there were occasional clashes – discussions rather than temperamental rows – probably inevitable with a piece of such elusive style. At one rehearsal, aiming for a drier tone from Michael, Clurman asked him to go back over a key late speech of Hector's, the great Oration to the Dead, and to play it as he imagined Louis Jouvet might have done. The company held its collective breath – it was unheard of then for an English star actor to be given such direction – but after an infinitesimal pause, Michael obeyed, remarking to Bob Joseph later: 'Imagine such a direction! But I *was* better when I tried to comply with it.' For his part Clurman was mightily impressed by the homework Michael had done: 'I was astonished at the first company reading to see that he had got everything right, anticipated my every desire.' Fascinated by Michael's complex personality, he added: 'He is so intelligent he destroys all by himself the silly notion that actors are or ought to be stupid. That actors are often childlike is certainly fine, but that is not to be counted against them. The child in all of us is to be cherished.'

It was the usual short West End rehearsal period, held in the empty St James's Theatre. With Clurman's permission Vanessa and Corin, now alike drawn towards the theatre, sat in on rehearsals at the back; Bob Joseph recalled Vanessa 'devouring it like a dedicated mouse'. Michael had to take a few days off in the middle to honour a long-standing commitment in Denmark. He was, much to his delight, invested with the prestigious Order of the Danneborg by the Danish ambassador at the embassy in London ('a very handsome affair') before flying with Dick Keigwin to Copenhagen for a Hans Christian Andersen birthday celebration, an enormous function with TV cameras, full evening dress 'and decorations' (Michael proudly sporting the showy new Order which rather overshadowed his more modest CBE, awarded three years previously) and the Danish royal family arriving for his Andersen readings, followed by a formal banquet and speeches the next day at the Hotel Angleterre.

So it was a slightly breathless Manchester opening for *Tiger at the Gates* after a tiring and epic dress rehearsal, with the company's first exposure to Loudon Sainthill's set – a seductive background of Aegean-blue sea and a positive death trap of multilevel and steeply raked platforms ('The set is *purgatory* to play on,' moaned Michael). Perhaps because of the tension, poor local notices and long rehearsals each day, Michael slipped back into some of his old ways after the show at night, hooking up with Eric Portman's friend Maurice Mendleson: 'He undertakes to show me the Manchester I don't know, and indeed I don't.' It became a week of after-hours bars, clubs and parties as well as work, contrasting sharply with the next two more sober weeks in Scotland, marred only by the perennial complaint of the touring actor about noisy hotels (with his insomnia, Michael was convinced that every early-morning bus outside or Hoover in the corridor was a personal affront). In Edinburgh he had a joyous reunion with Max Adrian, playing at the Empire, reviving over a long supper their fantasy fading soprano, Bigolo (Michael assured Max that he had found her a job playing the Eunuch, Mardian, in his *Antony*). He also continued his Edinburgh habit of lunching with Professor John Dover Wilson, one of the Shakespeare scholars he most admired who had helped him so much with his preparations for Shylock.

In Glasgow Rachel joined him for the week and suddenly everything was very different. They stayed outside the city in a small hotel at Drymen

and with Clurman absent that week and no daytime rehearsals it was an
idyllic time: 'We are like honeymooners as we drive up the east side of
Loch Lomond. Long walk up foothills, moss violets and bluebells coming.
Sit on R's coat and lie in the sun, kissing. Very, very happy.' They walked
several times in the hills after driving up to Tarbert and although even the
supposedly tranquil countryside conspired against him ('bloody tractors
and farm noises outside window') he was sad when Rachel had to leave on
the Saturday. *Tiger* was in good shape, although privately Michael agreed
over dinner in Glasgow with the Broadway dramatist George S. Kaufman
(whose then wife, Leueen MacGrath, played Cassandra), famous for his
lean style and method of cutting to the bone with his collaborators on the
road, that Clurman had cut so much that some of the essential Giraudoux
tone had been lost. A number of key passages were subsequently restored.

The final touring week, in Michael's least favourite theatre, the Oxford
New, in his least favourite touring date, became extremely tense and his
jitters began to surface. Clurman came back from a brief Paris visit, gave
copious notes after seeing an Oxford midweek performance, only to vanish
during the next day's matinée. When an irate Michael called him on a
cross company's behalf, Clurman said he was unable to rehearse the
following day because he had to meet his wife, the strong-willed and
extremely voluble actress Stella Adler (Robert Lewis, a Group Theater
member, once said that Clurman's autobiography, *pace* Stanislavsky, should
be called *My Wife in Art*). But when he heard Michael on the line –
'Never mind your wife! You've got a show to get on!' – he came back to
Oxford.

Tiger at the Gates opened in London at the Apollo – its auditorium the
ideal size for the play's style although the stage dimensions meant a tight
squeeze for Sainthill's obstacle course set, on which Michael tripped on
his first entrance – and while Michael had one of the best critical receptions
of his career (he always claimed that his initial stumble completely calmed
his nerves), the play came in for oddly mixed reactions with most of the
popular press taking, with curious logic, the line that the anti-war theme
was no longer relevant. The suggestion that a play written in 1935 when
Giraudoux feared that civilisation was in peril from the barbarian horde
was somehow no longer admonitory because most of the world was now
at peace was roundly trounced by both Hobson and Tynan (the latter now
on the *Observer*) in the Sunday notices, emphasising that the play would
remain burningly relevant while any threat of any war existed.

When Michael had first read it he had wondered if Hector was perhaps,
in Edith's phrase, a 'white role', meaning one with little or no development.
But as he worked with Clurman he began to see much more of a subtle
shape to the role, one of his most challenging to date. Hector's warm, still

youthful idealism he was at home with, but the part's demands include charting a series of long speeches, climaxing in a searing, discriminatory oration to the war dead and a tense, closely argued final clash with Ulysses. His musical sense helped him here; he was able to find a different colour and dramatic value in each speech, infusing all of them with intelligence and fire. It was, too, a very human performance, markedly in the clear expression of his love for the pregnant Andromache. Barbara Jefford remembered that they aimed for 'the sense of sexuality between Hector and Andromache, as opposed to marble statues. He had such tremendous energy, virility and total commitment to the part.'

As anticipated, Diane Cilento's flattish voice, at times betraying her Australian origins, came in for criticism, but she and Michael worked hard during the run and he was delighted with her progress. Clurman left Michael and Fry jointly in charge of his production while he returned to the States. Fry was dutiful about monitoring the run, reporting to Clurman at one stage on the performance of Wyndham Goldie, a much-loved but somewhat indulgent actor, describing his pauses as now no longer pregnant but in labour.

With so many strong actors playing comparatively minor roles, hardly surprisingly some of them tried, consciously or not, to build up or embellish their performances; Robert Shaw constantly had to be pulled back, as the Topman, from playing his scene too libidinously, as Clurman had cautioned him, while the crafty Scottish actor John Laurie as the poet Demekos began, according to Michael, 'to imagine that he is Danny Kaye' and had to be slapped down. Michael – always clearing his notes with Clurman in advance – held several company sessions to keep the production on its toes, his principal note for a rhetorical play being an urgent reminder to the cast to recall the difference between 'active' and 'passive' listening on stage, vital to avoid staleness. But the Apollo run was a happy time, although he found Hector a taxing and tiring part to play.

Shortly after the West End opening two New York critics – Brooks Atkinson of the *Times* and Richard Watts of the *Post* – filed rave notices from London and plans were at once put in motion to take the production to Broadway, with as many of the original cast as possible, to open in late September. Michael had not agreed to Broadway in advance and with the Inland Revenue making familiar growling noises and more lucrative offers from both London and New York (including a proposed musical with Lena Horne), it was only his commitment to the play and the cast as well as Clurman which made him sign. Once he had, he was maddened by Bob Joseph ('the most fantastic wishful-thinker that I have ever come across'), who was offering ridiculously low salaries. The respected stage manager Diana Bodington, who both Michael and Clurman had insisted must come to New York, had to turn down Joseph's offer, which would have left her out of pocket; Clurman and Michael had to kick up an almighty fuss until he saw sense. It made Michael worry what New York might hold.

That summer in London, Rachel was often away working, including playing Mrs Elvsted in *Hedda Gabler* with Peggy Ashcroft, a production taken over by Glen. She and Michael remained in constant touch; she wrote to him after one weekend of the happy time they had shared: 'I think perhaps the only positive happiness one can have is in love that is not physical or let us say in love that survives the "splendours and miseries" of physical love. I think my idea is not original, I think Micheál Mac-Liammóir said it too. But I begin to recognize that fact. Anyway, my darling, whatever way it is, I love *you* very truly.'

She knew how much he worried about Daisy, who continued to be unpredictable. At times she was ensconced, like a character in Rattigan's *Separate Tables*, in a room at the Tudor Court Hotel ($8\frac{1}{2}$ guineas a week, which included three meals a day) in the Cromwell Road, which she described as full of 'gargoyles', although her old friend Dorothy Green lived near by and was a loyal visitor. At other times, when she hit the bottle and became impossible – sometimes turning up at Bedford House at all hours or writing Michael long screeds accusing him of ingratitude – she had to be taken into a clinic, usually a newer and stricter establishment in King's Langley. Michael's distress when confronted by Daisy during one of her 'dos' was upsetting for those close to him; sometimes after a visit to his mother or when she came to see him in one of her black moods, he would just sit silently for hours. The children saw little of him even though he was working in London; he slept until late and the atmosphere in the house (as every actor's child knows) was always more sombre when he was appearing in a serious play such as *Tiger*. Although he was physically present, it was often as if only his essence – an aura combining the scents of his Dunhill 'My Mixture' pipe tobacco and Knize, his favourite cologne – was there.

Michael tried hard to get Bob attached to the New York production on the stage management side to give him something definite to do and to provide him with some extra cash. Bob had never been able to obtain a work permit in England and could in effect only be employed as Michael's personal assistant; Bob Joseph and Arnold Weissberger had said they would try to help but Michael had to sail before anything had been fixed definitely.

It was nearly a decade since *Macbeth* and Michael, now well known from British movies in America, was interviewed in countless magazines and newspapers, most of them taking the hoary old 'Egghead Actor' line (one piece called him 'a professor with stardust in his eyes'), which he swiped at to one reporter who seemed to think acting easy: 'That's absolute rubbish and based on a romantic notion of acting that has one rising from bed one fine day able to perform *Oedipus* perfectly. I'm as instinctive as anyone else, but that doesn't mean I didn't have to learn technique and method.'

When they opened at the Fulton Theater, the Broadway notices were virtually all superlatives, with few of the London cavils about the play, while Clurman's prediction of New York's reception of the sexpot Helen of Diane Cilento was accurate enough ('AVA GARDNER, LOOK OUT!' headlined one notice). Michael's performance had altered, inevitably, since the Apollo, growing perceptibly more awesomely powerful near the close when Hector becomes as possessed with violence as the warmongers, drawing his sword on Ajax with an animal roar in his throat as frightening as anything Bouwmeester could ever have produced. All the reviews praised the heroic dimensions and the warm, simple humanity of the performance ('one of the most memorable characterisations of the modern theatre'), and the production, Michael's biggest success in New York, was a solid hit, breaking the house record in its eighth week, in a season stiff with competition including *The Lark*, *Inherit the Wind* and *The Diary of Anne Frank*.

As he settled into his apartment on East 52nd Street for what the box office signalled was to be a good run, few other aspects of his life were so certain. The worst financial crisis of his professional career began to loom when Peter Wenham of Walter Smee's office contacted him with the grim statistics that he owed £10,000 tax, with outstanding UK bills totalling £2000. With his anticipated gross earnings at the end of the tax year closing in March 1957 (estimated at around £30,000) he would be liable to both further tax and surtax. The chill advice was to sell Bedford House, for which £18,000 had been offered, and to aim for another £4000 for the studio (mortgages on both totalled £7500). High drama raged, with Rachel and Joan Hirst (as Joan Sparks had become when she recently remarried) cautioning him not to rush into accepting the Bedford House offer, desperately hoping that a painting of Michael's (reputedly a Constable) might be sold to save the day.

Glen's brother, Jim Byam Shaw, an art dealer and sympathetic to their cause, took the picture to various experts but the consensus was clearly that it was not a Constable and so, by the end of the year, with the utmost reluctance Rachel – listening also to their lawyer neighbour Anthony Lousada's advice – agreed that she would look for an alternative house or flat. Everything seemed to be altering on Chiswick Mall. Two other houses had recently changed owners and now the Nelsons next door had decided to move to Haslemere, Mary Nelson writing to Michael in New York: 'It will not be easy to leave Chiswick Mall, there is something about these old houses and the ever-changing scene on the river.'

With the success of *Tiger at the Gates*, offers had flooded in for Michael in America, although agreeing to direct *A Month in the Country* for the Phoenix Theater Company, which was run by Norris Houghton and T. Edward Hambleton (total fee $500), was hardly going to make Cecil or Walter Smee happy. But with extremely heavy persuasion from Binkie and Cecil, together with a great deal of flattery from Terence Rattigan, Michael agreed to return to New York later in the year under Gilbert Miller's management to direct and co-star with Barbara Bel Geddes (then having a big success in Tennessee Williams's *Cat on a Hot Tin Roof*) in Rattigan's *The Sleeping Prince*. MCA's New York office drove a hard bargain, obtaining a deal which would pay Michael $3500 as a fee plus expenses and a weekly 2 per cent of the gross as director to add to his 10 per cent of the gross against a weekly $1500 as actor; if the production was a hit, it could make him a tidy sum. For both these contracts Michael requested an extra clause, that his 'Assistant Director' should be Fred Sadoff. This was a new love in Michael's life – the last of his three major American male love affairs – who would be close to him privately and professionally for over a decade. They met during the run of *Tiger at the Gates* after an Actors' Studio session which Michael had attended, although Michael had in fact seen him once before – on stage as one of the chorus in *Wish You Were Here* which he had seen with Bob in 1953.

Fred's personality polarised people; he had some loyal lifelong friends but others, especially an older generation in England, found him self-serving, pushy and undoubtedly out for what he could get. But Michael was again besotted; Fred, eighteen years younger, slim, with intense dark eyes (photographs, emphasising his swarthiness, rarely did Fred justice), vital, street-smart and funny, an early member of the Actors' Studio, seemed part of a vibrant, fresh American scene. He was from a Russian-immigrant background ('gypsies' Fred liked to claim), born and raised in California – he hinted always that his family was uncommunicative emotionally – and came to New York as a stage-obsessed teenager, working in the chorus of *South Pacific* and *Wish You Were Here* while attending Studio classes under Lee Strasberg, although he venerated even more the work of another teacher, the ex-Group Theater actor Sanford Meisner. As he was devoted to the earnestness of the Studio and the extrovert brassiness of big Broadway musicals alike, his infectious energy and opti-mism quite captivated Michael, who was equally impressed by Fred's ambitions to direct and write as well as act. Of all Michael's love affairs, that with Fred had the strongest overtones of the Pygmalion myth. Fred hitherto had been bisexual; his sex life, about which he could be disconcertingly candid, had been enthusiastically busy and he seemed remarkably free from any guilt or remorse in his sexual attitudes. He liked, in a then hip phrase, to 'cover the waterfront'.

This new passion brought Michael's relationship with Bob to a stage that had been approaching the inevitable even before Fred turned up in Michael's life. In England Bob had realised more and more that much as he loved Michael and the family, his life essentially was being lived through others. He missed America and he also had decided that he could possibly have a marriage and the children of his own for whom he now genuinely longed. If he left it much longer he might never leave. Saying goodbye to the family he found heartbreaking. Corin, then aged sixteen, recalled Bob – although his face seemed to be smiling – crying silently for days prior to his departure. The day before he left he took Corin's face in his hands and said, 'I will never forget you children,' and it is abundantly clear that he never did forget his years with the family from the letters he subsequently wrote to Michael: 'Besides the wonderful years of my life that you have made possible, you also gave me a background of life and home that is a continual blessing.'

Michael paid Bob's passage back to America and they had an emotional meeting in New York, where Bob had been further upset by news of the death of one of his oldest friends, Carol Bowen, in Ohio. Through Arnold Weissberger Michael arranged for $500 to go to Bob in Ohio to help him while he took care of Carol's funeral, and he also had Weissberger arrange for $75 a week to go to Bob out of his *Sleeping Prince* salary later in the year until he had found his feet.

Before going into the blessed security of rehearsals for a favourite play, *A Month in the Country*, Michael had once more to put on his mental mortarboard for another academic engagement. He had accepted a flattering invitation from Harvard's Professor of English, Harry Levin, to deliver the Theodore Spencer Memorial Lecture, following T. S. Eliot, Elia Kazan and Arthur Miller to the podium. He gave his lecture the title 'Mask or Face' (subtitled 'Reflections in an Actor's Mirror') and it provided the basis of the book of the same title published by Edward Thompson. Surprisingly, it is less formally academic in some respects than *The Actor's Ways and Means*, not least in a long virtuoso opening section, a dressing-table mirror's view of different actors in dressing rooms across the globe getting ready for a show – West End, Broadway, off-Broadway, Paris left-bank cellar theatre, Berlin, Kabuki theatre in Tokyo – a deftly evocative series of pen pictures and one of the best things Michael ever wrote. More contentious, at least in America, was his section on 'The Method', respectful to the likes of Kazan, Marlon Brando or Julie Harris but pulling few punches when he turns to Lee Strasberg, pointing out a crucial dichotomy. For Michael, it is crystal clear that while Stanislavsky meant that his stress on 'the actor's work on himself' must include work on the role and on the play, 'too many of Mr Strasberg's pupils seem to believe that the actor's work begins and ends in himself'.

His second book was also well received, a strikingly understanding review being John Barton's in the *Spectator*, admiring Michael's presentation of how the Stanislavsky method, designed to help refresh actors, had been often traduced by being elevated to the level of a code, almost a religion. Michael was touched by the reaction from Diana Menuhin, to whom he had sent a copy. Perennially on the move with Yehudi, she typically headed her letter 'The Desert, California', in it congratulating him for avoiding what she calls 'the inevitable salesmanship which is the sin of our times'. Diana understood Michael better than most of his friends even if geography those days kept them often apart: 'I genuinely find myself always wanting to know, to argue with you, to exchange, to bandy even to fight, and above all to pierce that thicket which you do not erect around you so much as weave, right on top of your undershirt and which is so well worth getting through, even with one's hair full of splinters.'

Uta Hagen, who played Natalya in *A Month in the Country*, a dedicated teacher as well as a Broadway star, would have agreed with much of Michael's Harvard lecture (the title of her own later book, *Respect for Acting*, is one which Michael could have used). Michael had never seen her previously on stage, trusting colleagues' opinions of her, and he found her a delight to work with, telling Binkie that she was 'the most wonderful *worker* – co-operative to the extent of losing nearly a stone in weight and really looks gorgeous – she strongly reminds me of Edwige Feuillère'.

With a low budget at the non-profit Phoenix, based at the old Yiddish Art Theater on Second Avenue, Michael – with Norris designing – insisted on non-naturalistic sets, using just a few well-chosen items of essential furniture for each scene on a revolve without heavy changes or waits and spending more on Alvin Colt's costumes so that the play could move with fluid grace. *A Month in the Country* was little known in New York, last seen in 1930 with Nazimova oddly cast and playing Natalya like a cobra woman, and Michael was careful in publicity to stress that the play, set in the 1840s, should not be compared too much with Chekhov despite their similar silken subtlety, pointing out that Turgenev was more influenced by French than Russian theatre, taking the main situation from Balzac's play of the late 1840s, *La Marâtre*.

His production captivated critics and audiences with Uta Hagen, best known for heavyweight roles such as Blanche in *A Streetcar Named Desire* or Georgie in *Winter Journey*, a revelation with a performance of quicksilver volatility, deeply touching and truthful with a most delicate comedy touch too. She was especially notable in the scene with Vera, Natalya's ward, in love with the handsome tutor to Natalya's young son (as is Natalya), a scene brilliantly staged and played, with Natalya circling the girl, advancing on her and backing away almost simultaneously, so contradictory are her emotions. Throughout Michael kept the action light and swift while also subtly charting the tornado-strength disturbances beneath Turgenev's limpid surface, with just the right amount of broader comedy from the supporting performers. They included Luther Adler, Stella Adler's brother, both children of the great Yiddish theatre star Jacob Adler. As he made his debut aged five in 1908 and later worked for ten years with the Group Theater, there was very little that Luther Adler did not know of stagecraft and Michael worked delightedly with him in making the venal doctor, Shpichelsky, a wonderfully rich and rounded character, one that was acclaimed as showing Adler's best work for years. The Phoenix, which had had see-saw fortunes in the past, had a solid hit with *A Month in the Country*, which played to capacity throughout its season.

Michael had initially dreaded coming home after *Tiger at the Gates* closed to say farewell to Bedford House. He sailed on the *Queen Elizabeth* with Fred, who had been helped by the New York producer Roger Stevens to direct a production of the recent Broadway play *The Young and the Beautiful* at the Arts Theatre club in London. In the event, the return to Chiswick, knowing the house was sold, 'was not so bad. And we imme-diately found a large, hideous but convenient flat behind Harrods.' This was no. 3 Hans Crescent, a sprawling apartment of four bedrooms (plus separate quarters for Nanny Randall), a large, panelled reception room, a dining room, study and two bathrooms. With Rachel about to join a new company at the Royal Court – the English Stage Company – under George Devine, it would be more convenient than Chiswick for her, for Vanessa at Central, Corin at Westminster and Lynn still at Queen's Gate. It was dark compared with Bedford House with its rooms flooded by Thames-reflected light, but it remained the Redgrave London base for fifteen years. In the meantime they spent their last weeks in Bedford House with Fred in the studio ('it ached with the absence of Bob,' noted Michael). With his charm and aura of New York cool, and his easy talk of the Actors' Studio, the children all took greatly to Fred, although Rachel initially found him less immediately simpatico than Bob, whom she had both loved and admired.

There was, providentially, some cushioning of the blow of leaving Chiswick, with John Fowler once again acting as the Redgraves' benevo-lent godfather. He had bought a small but uniquely charming hunting lodge, set amid the woods near Odiham in Hampshire, accessible by both car and train from London. Local legend had it that once wild boar had been hunted in the woods and that the lodge had been used by Henry VIII. In the grounds was a dilapidated cottage which Fowler had not wanted to sell while its tenant of sixty years, old Granny Porter, was alive, but with her recent death he suggested that Rachel buy it. It needed a great deal of work to be made properly habitable; the cottage had several bricked-in windows, from the days of the window tax, and it desperately needed a damp course installed, while the gardens had degenerated into a wild-wood wilderness and the stream running along the property was choked almost as much as a boggy area, once the old 'stews' (breeding ground for fish for the local manor) which were silted up.

Equally providentially, Cousin Lucy Kempson, still vital at eighty-two despite cataract problems with her eyes, generously had offered to lend Rachel some money (£2000), which she would be left in Lucy's will in any event, to buy a small property to compensate for the loss of Bedford House, which Lucy too had loved whenever she visited. Walter Smee, who had a soft spot for Rachel, arranged that she should have £500 from the Bedford House sale to put in proper drainage and a septic tank in Hampshire. When the sale went through, Rachel and John Fowler had marathon sessions with secateurs and sickles; together with a local gardener they fought back the worst of the overgrowth in the garden while work went ahead on the cottage – Wilks Water as it was known – eventually perhaps the happiest Redgrave house. It never was a grand country pile like Notley Abbey; even when the house was enlarged with a modest lake with a tiny island made out of the old 'stews' turning it into a haunt of coots and moorhens, and with the glorious garden and orchard created by Rachel (a proper 'gloves-off' gardener by now), it never lost its unpretentious quality, at its best perhaps in summer when the sun warmed the rose-pink bricks.

But it was not entirely unexpected that the move in London, the work at Wilks Water and the Royal Court venture should lead to further health problems for Rachel, diagnosed eventually as a troublesome ulcer. She was also having to deal with her ailing mother, with whom her relationship had never been totally comfortable, writing to Michael of her own illness: 'I can't but believe that a lot of it is inherited from my ma, and that upsets me still more.' Rachel spent some time recuperating in the peace of Bromyard, from where Lucy had written to Michael: 'The nuns of her youth seem to have convinced Rachel that indigestion was a necessary concomitant of piety.' Vanessa, whose political commitment was dawning with her reaction to the Russian invasion of Hungary, had also been at Bromyard. Lucy wrote to Michael thoroughly approving of her zeal: 'But when, after a long course of Hungary, she ended up with "Cousin Lucy, what is inflation?" I gave up. You can do that one.'

Cecil had fixed a quick cameo appearance in a film directed by Gene Kelly – who specifically asked for Michael – filming in Paris, which Michael combined with a brief holiday with Fred. For Fred, just plucked out of the chorus line, as it were, it must have been like a dream – on a first evening's stopover in Paris he found himself having drinks with Noël Coward and Marlene Dietrich before dinner at, of course, Le Coucou and onion soup at Le Pied de Cochon. Michael also introduced him to Louis and his mother, and Louis and Michael had a long walk together – each had no secrets from the other – through the Tuileries Gardens. Then they drove – Fred at the wheel – through Avignon and Les Baux, and on to Cassis where they wrote poems to each other before returning to Paris, to be lodged in luxury at the Trianon Palace courtesy of the film company.

Kelly's film, *This Way to Paris*, was a somewhat cutesy trifle of two winsome moppets running off to Paris to rejoin their respective single parents (Kelly and Barbara Looge). By far the best sequences involve some Jacques Tati-style slapstick, the high spot being an episode in which the children stray into a massive NATO operation. Michael's role, which he had a happy few days working on under Kelly's relaxed but disciplined direction, was that of a pipe-smoking British general with a bristling Auchinleck moustache who barges into elephantine action ('Operation Meatloaf'), vowing to 'catch the little nippers', brass-brained and barking into four telephones simultaneously in a splendid spoof of modern military manoeuvres. Kelly wrote of his delight at Michael's performance after seeing a rough-cut and when the movie was released, retitled *The Happy Road*, Michael's contribution stole all the notices.

Harder work waited for him back home when the hope of working with Joseph Losey – they had met on a few occasions to discuss possible projects – finally materialised. One of several bright directors – Edward Dmytryk and Jules Dassin were others – to have crossed the Atlantic as the Senator McCarthy investigations expanded, Losey had not yet made a film in England under his own name (because of the blacklist). However, Michael had seen and admired *The Sleeping Tiger* of 1954 with Dirk Bogarde who had taken a gamble on Losey, and he had also seen his striking American political allegory, *The Boy with Green Hair*. Losey, who had worked extensively in radical New York theatre as well as with Brecht in Los Angeles, fascinated Michael. His passion and energy, combined with a kind of American puritan austerity, made him a complex mixture, and when the script of *Time Without Pity* arrived (based on an indifferent Emlyn Williams play, *Someone Waiting*), although it was not strikingly original, Michael was intrigued enough to take a risk like Bogarde.

It turned out an invigorating experience. In the hands of Losey and his then regular script collaborator, Ben Barzman, Williams' play was turned inside out, jettisoning the whodunnit element to reveal the killer in a baroque pre-credit sequence, and a workaday low budget black-and-white British filler becomes a minor work of art. This owes something to Losey's gift of looking at situations – here an alcoholic father trying to save his estranged son from going to the gallows for a murder he swears he did not commit and the father's pursuit of clues to find the murderer – through a lens which invests them with an edgy network of fear, revenge, guilt and moral tension, as well as to extraordinarily imaginative and ingenious art direction, in this instance often using paintings or props to reflect the tone of interior scenes. A routine enough episode in the script, of Michael questioning a slightly tipsy old woman (Renée Houston) who might have valuable information, gains a riveting atmospheric touch by filling her overstuffed little room with alarm clocks, their unsettling ticking and unexpected ringing underpinning a story driven partly by the sense of a race against time. And a sequence set backstage at a Windmill-style theatre where Michael's David Graham tries to talk to the dead girl's sister (Joan Plowright, suggested to Losey for her first film by Michael who had seen her Royal Court work), is played against the crowded activity in the wings during a scene change. For Joan Plowright as a saucer-eyed chorine it was a first experience of working with Michael and he rather surprised her by not wanting to rehearse their scene too much: 'He wanted from his point of view to be spontaneous on film – it was my first lesson in screen acting. I grew more confident in working Michael's way – it made me convincingly taken by surprise by his questions. I didn't feel at all straitjacketed.'

Michael's performance as the troubled alcoholic, tempted progressively to fall off the wagon as his fight to clear his son's name runs out of time, gives the picture a strong core, and all his scenes with Leo McKern, the bull-like tycoon and real killer – scenes often filmed from unexpected angles, full of shadows and reflections – are extraordinary in their full-blooded commitment, quite unlike the prevailing costive restraint of most 1950s British films, more like a Warner Brothers melodrama of the 1930s and all the more startling accordingly. Michael finished the film admiring Losey's ability to bring it in on budget within a tight schedule, and also convinced that this was a film maker with whom he definitely would want to work again. Losey later admitted that he had somewhat dreaded the experience – when calling from London to discuss the film with Michael in New York he had formed the distinct impression of possible alcohol problems – but on set there was nothing but discipline and concentration. Losey began immediately to think of possible future collaborations.

Just before Michael and Fred sailed back to New York for *The Sleeping Prince* rehearsals, Fred's Arts Theatre production of Sally Benson's wispy adaptation of a group of F. Scott Fitzgerald stories of 1915 Chicago opened. *The Young and the Beautiful* had been only a moderate success in New York the previous year and it seemed a strange choice for London, where its slender plot of flirty adolescent girl avid for experience emerged as flat as well as small beer. The reviews were poor, Fred's production being generally criticised as heavy-handed, while even Lois Smith reprising her Broadway role as the coquette Josephine failed to find favour.

If Fred's venture appeared out of place in London, Rattigan's fairy tale Ruritanian comedy, *The Sleeping Prince*, seemed to breathe the wrong air on Broadway. It was written as an 'occasional' play for the 1953 Coronation and set during George V's coronation of 1911 in the Carpathian Legation with the rigidly protocol-ruled Prince Regent falling for a beguiling American showgirl, and the Oliviers' star power had given the play a West End success. But with the 'occasion' of the Coronation well past, together with a patronising attitude to Americans and, by 1956, some sticky references to Hungary and British imperialism (Suez still was in the news), which Rattigan misguidedly refused to alter or cut, this feather-light comedy was a dubious proposition for Broadway.

Michael felt something of this, at one stage even trying to extricate himself from the project during the summer without effect. He found in the pre-rehearsal period a dismaying lack of organisation from the management. Gilbert Miller seemed permanently away on his social rounds and Michael became caught in the middle of some embarrassing situations. Cathleen Nesbitt had been offered the part of the Grand Duchess and had accepted, handing in her notice to *My Fair Lady* in which she had created Mrs Higgins, when (without first consulting Michael) the Miller office became excited at the possibility of casting the Broadway star Ina Claire. In the event Claire's prevarications and demands – costumes by Balmain, star dressing room – ruled her out but Michael had been placed in a most awkward situation with an understandably upset Cathleen Nesbitt. Miller, who liked to see himself as the Binkie of Broadway (although he lacked Binkie's serpentine guile and shrewdness), specialising in costume plays and classy West End imports, continued to plague Michael with his extraordinary meanness over costumes (designer Alvin Colt was being offered minimum fees) and refusals to pay for the live music which the script demanded.

Rehearsals were pleasant enough (again Fred was billed as 'Assistant' to Michael) and Michael liked his cast, including Barbara Bel Geddes who looked enchanting in her 'simple white dress' (a Mainbocher couture number) in a set of rose-pink and green, lit seductively by candlelight, designed by Norris. The out-of-town try-out dates were extremely successful, although Miller – Michael called him 'the hippopotamus' to Binkie – totally ignored Michael throughout the tour and, worried about the comedy quotient (just like the Broadway producers who tried to persuade Alan Ayckbourn to reverse the order of the last two scenes of *Absurd Person Singular* because the penultimate one got more laughs), tried unsuccessfully to bring in an embarrassed Cyril Ritchard, a comedy specialist and a friend of Michael's, to 'beef up the laughs'. By the time it opened, Michael felt that the management's mistrust had affected the cast and his confidence flagged. His dressing room on the opening night was a bower of flowers and cards. Coward sent a slyly affectionate message to his 'Dearest China' with 'A great big kiss, but of *course* in the strictly continental sense. Perhaps I don't quite mean that.'

But it was a sticky opening, with a typically overdressed Park Avenue Miller first-night crowd and Michael simply 'froze' – one of his worst ever first nights (they rarely saw him at his best) when he got through the evening on technique alone – and without the underlying touching vulnerability of the character it seemed a gelid and tight performance. The notices were actually much better than he anticipated but the play's thinness was widely criticised; advance bookings for theatre parties were strong enough to keep it going for three months, but for Michael it had been a miserable experience.

Much as he loved New York and being in the city with Fred, to be back home working in a company was what Michael really wanted. He knew that the Rattigan play was not top-flight material and was cross with himself for allowing himself to be sweet-talked into doing it. It belonged to a past theatre and Michael's own instincts had nearly always been to respond to the new. The high spot of his theatregoing during the summer in London had been at the Royal Court where he and Rachel had gone to the first night of John Osborne's *Look Back in Anger*, which both had found thrilling, Michael immediately writing to Norris to tell him to snap up the play for the Phoenix (he was outbid). But yet again, with his financial problems forcing him to take Cecil's advice and film work, he seemed to have lost hold of the reins of his career after such a glorious run of work.

While in New York he and Glen had been in touch, and Glen had offered Michael the Stratford 1958 season, suggesting Benedick in *Much Ado About Nothing*, possibly *Pericles* and a second Hamlet. Michael initially worried about his age – he would be fifty in 1958 and perhaps the days when actors could go on in leading classic roles at fifty were past in a new era of youth culture just under way – but Glen, who had never directed *Hamlet* and had considered Michael's Old Vic performance touched greatness, insisted there was no problem, assuring 'darling Mikey': 'This theatre needs you desperately. There is no-one who can make the Trumpets sound like you.' Michael gave Glen a verbal commitment to 1958 but in the meantime, with the Rattigan running only half of its anticipated six months, money was yet again a problem, solved in the short term by two American offers.

After surprising New York audiences, unaware of his musical ability, with his Macheath in a concert version of *The Beggar's Opera*, organised and conducted by Lehman Engel in Carnegie Hall, he was offered the title role in a live colour TV Special of Henry Leon Wilson's novel of 1913 rural America, *Ruggles of Red Gap*. No sooner had he accepted than Audrey Wood of MCA's New York office told him that he had also been offered the part of Fowler, the disenchanted English foreign correspondent in 1952 Saigon, in Joseph L. Mankiewicz's film of Graham Greene's novel *The Quiet American* to be filmed on location in Saigon and at Cinecittà in Rome. Although no contract for *Ruggles* had been signed, he definitely had a moral commitment, but he had wanted to work for Mankiewicz for some time – he was unavailable when he had been offered Brutus in Mankiewicz's film of *Julius Caesar* with Brando and Gielgud – he had read and admired Greene's novel, and MCA were urging him to drop the television job, reminding him that they had negotiated a $45,000 fee plus a profit participation for the movie. An almighty fuss erupted and Michael had to hire an expensive lawyer to untangle '*L'Affaire Americain Tranquil*' as he described it to Rachel, finally pacifying the Swift Meat Packaging Co. (sponsors of *Ruggles*) when the film rescheduled to allow him a later start in Saigon so that he could do both jobs.

Ruggles was a cut-price adaptation, reducing Michael's gentleman's gentleman, won in a poker game by Americans on the Grand Tour and transported to Red Gap, to a caricature in order to make room for some hoedown choreography and sub-standard Jule Styne songs, mainly for the saccharine Jane Powell. The emotional impact of one sequence which remained intact – Michael's recitation of the Declaration of Independence – was a high spot which took viewers by surprise, although having survived (just) the ordeal of a major live TV musical, Michael was in no great hurry to repeat the experience.

At his suggestion Fred had been cast in *The Quiet American* as Dominguez, Fowler's sidekick, and had flown out earlier, meeting Nicholas, Rachel's brother, in Hong Kong en route. Fred wrote often to Michael as he toiled through *Ruggles*, his first letter written on his Pan-Am stratocruiser: 'I've already started counting the days till your arrival.' And from Saigon, using Michael's old childhood diminutive petname: 'My Mikey doodlums – you'll be here shortly, I'm so excited. I'll say a silent prayer tonight so that the next week will pass quickly. Oh, Mikey ...'

After a circuitous and seemingly endless journey, Michael arrived in Saigon to be met by a mahogany-tanned Fred and the news that Audie

Murphy, cast in the title role, had been laid low with appendicitis and so scenes had had to be rescheduled once again. This gave Michael some time to explore Saigon, which he found a beguiling city. As he knew it, Saigon was still 'the Paris of the Orient', with wide streets and boulevards, a handsome Presidential Palace, once the home of Indo-China's puppet emperor, gracious villas and fashionable shops and cafés all along the central streets, lined by tamarind and rubber trees, although the traffic ('rather like the dodgems,' he said to Rachel) made him glad that he did not drive.

He and Fred were together in an enormous suite, cooled by ceiling fans, in the Hotel Majestic, and the Saigon filming once fully under way was painless apart from the problems of acting with Audie Murphy and with Georgia Moll, a German actress, as Phuong, Fowler's girl friend (Mankiewicz unaccountably claimed that he could find no suitable Asian actress, although the talented France Nuyen had been available). Murphy was the most decorated US war hero but, with his disconcertingly unvarying preppy smile and unblinking eyes, he was a problem to act opposite. As Michael observed to Mankiewicz, it is easier to direct an amateur actor than to act with one, and Moll was similarly wooden.

The part of Fowler absorbed Michael, however, and he and Mankiewicz, both fascinated by other cultures and by words (Mankiewicz nicknamed Michael 'the semantic philosopher'), had a great deal in common, spending many evenings together after filming. At that time Mankiewicz was under stress, with his marriage falling apart under the strain of his wife's nervous troubles, and his own company, Figaro Productions, had a major stake in what was an expensive film. The script came up for discussion often between them, with Michael still disappointed – as he had been on a first reading – by the radically changed ending which whitewashed the American, Pyle (Greene just smiled whenever asked if he had deliberately chosen the name to imply 'a pain in the ass'), who is unnamed in the film, but Mankiewicz insisted that quite simply the film would never have been made with an ending 'condoning' complicity in murder and 'anti-American' to boot.

From Saigon the unit moved to the Cinecittà Studios in Rome, where Michael and Fred had an apartment with a huge roof terrace, with views all over the city, in the Corso Umberto. Mail began to catch up with him, including letters from Rachel filling him in on Wilks Water's progress. Writing looking out on drifts of aconites and narcissi, she described the planting of old and climbing roses around the new porch and against a favourite Oeil de Boeuf wall, while on the interior John Fowler again had helped, providing inexpensive plain linens and Rachel's simple floral chintzes for sofas, cushions and curtains. The whole family were coming out to Rome before shooting ended; although at that time none of his children knew of the real nature of his relationships with Bob or Fred, Rachel had by this stage wholly accepted Fred too: 'I am glad all goes well with you, Darling Mike. Do you know, I envy you being able always to be with the one you love with *no* restrictions or difficulties of any sort. I don't envy you in a horrid way but I hope you feel pleased in the wonderfulness of that. It must give you calm and strength.'

Rachel, as reflected in that letter, had seen comparatively little of Glen, with her Royal Court work and his commitments at Stratford where he was now sole director making meetings difficult. But it was Rachel to whom Glen turned to act as go-between when a major crisis blew up around him, jeopardising all his carefully planned future programme. Cecil, who could be devious in business, had insisted to Glen that Michael was not formally contracted to Stratford for the 1958 season and was threatening now that for financial reasons he was unlikely to be able to come (he had not mentioned this to Michael). Cecil would have argued that he was simply protecting his client's interests, not allowing him to commit himself so far ahead in case of better offers (to Cecil that meant more rewarding movie work). Glen, a quiet man who could on occasion be extremely emotional, was so shocked that he refused to speak to Cecil. After he had told Rachel, she sent a passionate letter – the longest she ever wrote – to Michael in Rome, outlining her version of what, with some understatement, she described as 'un joli kettle de poisson'.

On her own initiative Rachel had called Walter Smee who, while owning that Stratford's money was atrocious (actors in effect subsidised the Memorial Theatre), felt that moral commitments should be honoured. Rachel was clever here; she knew that Smee and Cecil tended to disagree, and she was also able to spike Cecil's guns by shooting down his argument to Michael that he could delay Stratford until 1959. Because of her closeness to Vivien Leigh, she already knew that Olivier (a Cecil client) was booked to lead the company for that season. Furthermore, it was clear that Cecil was panicking Michael by exaggerating his likely tax debt by July 1958, with Smee giving a significantly lower figure: 'Cecil quite simply says he sees no reason for you to go there. Well, I'm sorry, I completely disagree under the circumstances and you can imagine how Glen feels about it. Cecil will argue black is white for ever.' Glen, who hated flying, even went out to Rome to talk over the problem (Michael declined Cecil's offer in a letter to fly out too, to 'protect' him) during the time Rachel and the children were there. There was actually little discussion, with Michael saying that he would of course honour his promise to play Benedick and Hamlet, although he was glad when Glen released him from *Pericles* to which he had never been much attracted. On his return, Glen wrote to Michael of a time when both Rachel and Michael each had their respective lover in Rome: 'I shall remember you always, striding ahead with supreme enthusiasm to show us the marvels of Rome and your delightful little jokes that expelled any possible feelings of torture or embarrassment. I know what that decision has meant to you. It is what dear Percy always says – the great people in life always have real generosity of spirit.'

During the last weeks on *The Quiet American* Michael had been putting into motion the formation of a company for Fred (FES Plays) which could present productions in partnership with Michael's own company. Joan Hirst also had arranged with Anthony Lousada the lease of a tiny studio flat in Egerton Garden Mews, off the Brompton Road and near Hans Crescent, as Fred's personal and business address.

Fred returned to London to settle into the studio at the end of his filming, while Rachel joined Michael in Italy for another visit to their beloved Venice and then on to Ischia for the first time. Uncomfortable in the overdecorated grandeur of the Regina Isabella, they moved to a smaller hotel and had a gloriously happy time, much of it in the exuberant company of Iris Tree, one of Beerbohm Tree's legitimate daughters. She had been part of Reinhardt's epic of *The Miracle* with her great friend Lady Diana Cooper and was still stage-struck; with her unvarying page-boy hairstyle, vast eyes and colourful, eccentric clothes, Iris was a true original. When Fred returned, they all visited Pompeii with her and late one moonlit night Michael recited Prospero in the deserted stone theatre, while they also sat talking and drinking, often until dawn, in a bar run by a usually plastered ex-actor, Phillipo, who might recount stories of his many theatrical disasters. She wrote to Rachel after the Redgraves reluctantly left for home: 'I miss Michael painfully all over. As for ambivalence, there's more to it than we touched on. It's a deeper cleavage – it's to be or not to be, it's to not believe the things one bets on. It's to marry the hunter and weep with the deer.'

In London, word started to filter back from America of *The Quiet American*; Mankiewicz's partner in Figaro, Robert Lantz, cabled Michael after the Washington première that it was a smash hit, that the notices were great and that Michael had scored a big personal success. Only the latter was strictly accurate. After Michael first saw the (heavily cut) film at a private Wardour Street screening with the family, he wrote at once to Lantz, 'I was, frankly, very disappointed at the general diminution of character all round. What could have been a great picture has missed its mark by a mile.' He assured Lantz that of course he would say nothing in public against the film but he wrote to Dick Green: '*The Quiet American* was one of the biggest disappointments of my life. By hoping to present it as an action picture they cut almost all that was not action or plot, and what should have been the stripping, by painful skin after skin, of a man's character, became – well, nothing very much.'

The problems with the film really lay deeper, beginning with Mankiewicz's distortion of Greene's novel. The world-weary reporter Fowler in the book not only escapes punishment for any implication in the American's murder but keeps the girl, Phuong, while in the film a manipulative Hollywood ending sees Fowler, isolated amid a Saigon crowd, sentenced to a lifetime of guilt-haunted solitude. Mankiewicz, in a cheating trick which must have made Greene even angrier than he admitted in public, also cut the crucial first half of the book's final sentence in Michael's closing voice-over, robbing it of both its irony and sadness.

Mankiewicz built up the part of Vigot, the French police chief (well played by Claude Dauphin), writing a lengthy late duologue between him and Fowler which never reaches the Dostoevskyan level to which it aspires, revealing Fowler as a dupe of the Communists, another betrayal of Greene's intentions. The novel's layers of coruscating irony are further traduced by his reduction of Pyle to the vacant grin of Audie Murphy, a dangerous innocent abroad in Greene whose good intentions cause the deaths and mutilation of innocent people in a Saigon explosion, but whose involvement in plastics in the film is reduced to the making of toys, not bombs. Had Montgomery Clift, as originally intended, played Pyle perhaps even Mankiewicz's sanitised version might have retained some of the character's disquieting ambivalence, but Murphy's blandness leaves Michael little to play off. The wonder is that against all the odds – a complex story reduced to a conventional love triangle ('Three Caught in the Shadow-World of the Seething Orient' ran the publicity) – his performance remains so absorbing.

Fowler, of course, is not allowed to be seen smoking opium on screen, as he does in the novel, but Michael still conveys the character's mixture of escapism into pipe dreams and his corrosive sense of *accidie*. The whiplash, mordant wit cuts like a knife (asking Murphy for a cigarette and being offered a whole packet, he snaps, 'I asked for a cigarette, not economic aid') and gradually he shapes an in-depth portrait of a man reduced to a hollow shell, his self-betrayal by his servile values and terror of loneliness worse than anything he does to Pyle.

When it was re-released and re-reviewed in 2002 for a season at the National Film Theatre in London, press and public responded with astonishment to this Fowler. Even up against a near simultaneous remake with a script faithful to Greene, Brendan Fraser's excellent Pyle and Michael Caine as Fowler, the aching spiritual void at the heart of Michael's Fowler remained way ahead of anything in Philip Noyce's movie.

It was while finishing *The Quiet American* that Michael had heard from Hélène le Breton the shockingly unexpected news of Louis's death. At the family's country home to which he had come from Paris for the weekend he had been working in his cherished gardens when he had a heart attack. Unable to get to the funeral, Michael had written to a completely grief-stricken Hélène who later replied: 'Dear Michael, you were Louis' dear friend, but also mine – don't forget it.'

News from Bob, who wrote only rarely at first after returning to America, was sketchy. He had been ill after relocating to Los Angeles, and Michael had sent him some money; Bob probably did not want to reveal too much about some hard times when he had driven a cab and worked on commission selling china. Finally he wrote that he had been taken on again at Western Union from which point his letters were more frequent. Even with his affair with Fred still at its most initially intense, Michael would not forget Bob easily – a *Guys and Dolls* song on the radio or old friends asking after him could be potent reminders – after their years together.

The business of getting Fred a work permit to be employed as an actor in England proved endlessly frustrating despite the efforts of everyone Michael called into play – George Devine, Anthony Lousada, Cecil and Glen and George Hume from Stratford, where Glen had agreed to have Fred as assistant director in 1958. There are only a handful of scattered diary entries for the later 1950s, but they mostly agonise about 'Fred, poor lamb' or 'poor dear Fred' who at one point threatened to return to the States although Michael persuaded him to be patient (which Fred rarely found easy), reassuring him that at least once FES (Plays) was up and running he would be able to produce and direct. Everyone tended to be calmer at Wilks Water, where Michael now had a separate annexe across the stream from the main house where Rachel and John Fowler had done miracles in a short time. The contrast with Notley – 'much developed and overcrowded since I last saw it' – struck Michael when he and Rachel spent the weekend there in November. Olivier was then appearing in Osborne's *The Entertainer*, allying himself with the new wave of English dramatists (and falling in love with Joan Plowright as his marriage to Vivien Leigh fell apart). Michael was not jealous – one reason why he never accepted any of his various offers to play Othello – but he could not help reflecting that Osborne's play was more exciting than the new one he had recently accepted from Binkie.

Originally called *Rich Man, Poor Man*, it was by Binkie's dream play-wright N. C. Hunter who had a golden streak in the 1950s with his reassuringly middlebrow dramas, always studded with well-crafted roles for Binkie's preferred glossy star casts, the biggest success of which had been *Waters of the Moon* with Edith and Sybil Thorndike, directed by Frith Banbury who was slated to direct this latest piece. Often misleadingly and to his own embarrassment labelled 'the English Chekhov', Hunter in his new play, an examination of the corrupting effects of exposure to wealth on a English schoolteacher's family, seemed to have attempted an Ibsenite play, but for Michael it was too schematic and he had turned it down. The wily Binkie then told Hunter all of Michael's criticisms, with the result that the dramatist sat down and rewrote the play in light of them, retitling it *A Touch of the Sun*. Michael responded much more positively to the new version, especially when, after auditioning her, Banbury and Binkie cast Vanessa as his daughter in the play. Not long out of drama school and after a summer season of weekly rep in Frinton, Vanessa now made her West End debut. Michael was even happier when Diana Wynyard, with whom he had always hoped to work again, was signed to play his wife, joining one of his favourite character actors, Ronald Squire, as his father.

He had an unexpected preview of Vanessa as his daughter when she was also cast in a film with him shortly before *A Touch of the Sun* was due to rehearse. *Behind the Mask*, based on John Rowan Wilson's novel *The Pack*, was a medical drama set in a large hospital in which the progressives and the dodos (led by Michael as an eminent surgeon, Sir Arthur Benson) become locked in opposition during an inquiry into a patient's death. Unfortunately, a potentially involving ethical drama becomes smothered by a Mills and Boon hospital romance involving an idealistic surgeon (Tony Britton) who marries Sir Arthur's daughter and then jeopardises his career. Vanessa was given the full 1950s British starlet make-over – tight perm, cakes of make-up and tailored costumes – although critics greeted her as a fresh talent (she was widely compared with Diana Wynyard), while Michael's subtlety in suggesting a deep parental warmth under Sir Arthur's suave pomposity also helped a stodgy film. It was directed by Brian Desmond Hurst ('Desdemona' to his chums), a famously lazy director who got by for years by employing brilliant technicians. He was a gregarious, outrageously roguish old reprobate; Michael knew him through Vivian Cox, who for a time was a lodger in the somewhat alarmingly bijou Knightsbridge mews house owned by Hurst, who had private means and a swanky open-top Rolls. He threw occasional parties à la Cukor, albeit with no pool, frequented by handsome young guests, several of which Michael attended. He liked Hurst, who was full of good stories, mostly about his early years after leaving Ireland for Hollywood where he had been John Ford's assistant on several films, but Michael privately felt that *Behind the Mask* was no more than routine.

But when he had seen the first rushes of Vanessa in the film he had 'wept with joy', recognising the real thing, even under her layers of pancake. At the same time Corin thrilled him by winning a scholarship to Cambridge (noted in big, bold letters as a single entry in his diary), while he, Rachel, Nanny Randall and Edith Hargreaves all attended Lynn's confirmation at Holy Trinity, Brompton, that same day. The following week he and Vanessa took the Tube together to the first rehearsal of *A Touch of the Sun*, with Michael quaking more internally than Vanessa, far more nervous for her than on his own behalf.

Sixteen
ROLLER-COASTER RIDE

Occasionally a production has a glow of success about it from the outset and *A Touch of the Sun* was an immediate hit on tour and in London, filling the barn of the Saville Theatre – usually considered an unlucky London house, at the quieter end of Shaftesbury Avenue – for as long as Michael could stay with it.

The only shadows across the project were in his own mind during rehearsals. Much concerned about 'piteous darling Fred' and his permit problems, Michael began to worry that he was not on top of the script, after nearly three weeks noting: 'Rehearsals. Begin to feel concerned about words. Still nowhere near putting book down.' The next day he wrote: 'Late to rise after night tortured with angst about F. Have not so far "done my homework" on this play.' Because of Fred's problems and the rewrites – virtually a completely new text – which Hunter had done on the piece, Michael had not had the time to allow the play to soak, sponge-like, into his mind: 'I prefer to allow a part to drop into my head a long time in advance, while my mind is lying fallow. Things pop in – they can surface or not much later.'

Michael thought that Frith Banbury handled the play and his cast – established stars and newcomers alike – extremely well. Banbury remained always guarded in his response to Michael, admiring his talent but feeling that while the character of the idealistic schoolmaster he played in *A Touch of the Sun* could finally face up to his problems and flaws, Michael could or would not. Although Banbury understood the awful difficulties with Daisy, with whom he had once acted – he recalled one occasion of working with Michael at Hans Crescent prior to rehearsals when Daisy, already well fuelled on gin, arrived before lunch to demand more drink and to bully Michael in front of Banbury, berating his talent and his handling of his career – nevertheless he made it abundantly plain in Charles Duff's book *The Last Summer* that to his mind Michael's 'self-indulgence' was the source of all his problems. The happily adjusted, always in control homosexual Banbury was perplexed by Michael's compulsion to dice with danger and by the covert strain in his nature, that urge to secrecy which led him, for instance, to omit even any mention of Fred from his autobiography. On this first collaboration, however, the two men worked well together, and Banbury had respect and admiration for Michael's performance, although he was aware of Michael's lingering reservations about the play.

The dress rehearsal in Liverpool found him 'depressed about the play', although he also noted how good he thought Vanessa was. Then, after an afternoon opening-day rehearsal made inaudible by gale-force winds: '1st perf. goes wonderfully, astonishingly well. Play last act as good as I've yet done it. Vanessa a distinct hit with audience (and Binkie).'

Apart from having to say goodbye to Fred, who was returning to New York to deal with his apartment, the next few weeks were rosy, with a happy company enjoying full houses and breaking Brighton's house records. Michael made a new and enduring friend on the production, Anthony Oliver, who played his brother. Oliver was gay, living with his partner Peter Sutton who worked for the BBC (they also had an antiques business together) in Pimlico, and their flat became, during rehearsals and for many years afterwards, one of Michael's regular late-night stops, where he could be sure always of a drink, cards or just a sympathetic ear and a completely understanding ambience.

A Touch of the Sun needed little rewriting on the road. It was superbly cast, Frith Banbury was the master of this kind of naturalistic, middlebrow play, and Binkie made sure that the production values were top-drawer Tennentry, with an applause-grabbing Reece Pemberton setting for the second-act Riviera villa terrace and Balmain outfits for Louise Allbritton as a rich American. Still Michael characteristically fretted over details other actors might have ignored, particularly his final exit very near the end of the play after a touching scene in which Philip Lester, an idealistic schoolmaster in danger of souring and losing his hope, finally can admit his failings and envy to his wife. On tour, he was getting an exit round as he left the stage at every performance, something many actors would be thrilled by; Michael felt that it made the real ending, a brief but heartfelt speech by Diana Wynyard to Ronald Squire, anticlimactic and he rehearsed with them for nearly two hours in Blackpool to find a way of killing his applause. Michael saw a solution – if he underplayed his last few lines and then exited, without closing the door behind him, more unobtrusively. That night he left the stage in pindrop silence, which gave Diana Wynyard exactly the right springboard for her final lines, the curtain falling to more even than the usual applause.

A young ASM on the production, also understudying Vanessa – they became close lifelong friends – was Thelma Holt, an actress before her producing career. She noticed one night in Brighton that in a scene involving Michael and Anthony Oliver playing chess, the board accidentally was knocked over and that Michael put the pieces back mal-adroitly. With the courage born of a company drink in the long-vanished 'Single Gulp' backstage bar at the Theatre Royal, she told Michael that she had noticed it was evident that he did not really play chess and offered to mark places for him on the board so that he could make the right moves. Michael told her that he would rather she taught him something about chess and she was able to give him a crash course in the basics. Thelma Holt said of Michael: 'My lessons from him were lessons of how to behave in this profession.'

Vanessa had to go her separate ways on tour; while Michael and Diana Wynyard were in the best hotels, she, Thelma Holt and Dinsdale Landen (playing Michael's son) all had to find their own digs. There were no special favours – although occasionally the girls were allowed to use his hotel bathrooms to wash their hair – because she was the star's daughter. She was much in demand for publicity, nonetheless, described as 'a Big Bonny Girl' with photographs captioned 'the Sweet Smile of Success' in Liverpool.

The play opened in London the day following Vanessa's twenty-first birthday, her party having to wait until the weekend. The glow around it continued, Diana Wynyard saying: 'There was a sort of glitter on the first night of *A Touch of the Sun*.' In a play not in the same league as *Tiger at the Gates* or even *Winter Journey* Michael still managed to create an original and compelling character in Philip Lester. Teaching at what his cynical, ex-bankrupt father describes as a 'Dothebrats Hall for mentally defective cubs', a Surrey school for backward boys, he and his family find themselves amid Riviera privilege and wealth visiting Philip's brother and his rich American wife. Both his children seem to him to be glamourised by their surroundings, and he guesses his wife Mary's attraction to a suave playboy (who murmurs seductively in her ear, 'I know a little beach near Théoule'), and Philip retreats, in what he sees as humiliation, into a shell of righteous resentment. Back in Surrey, when he comprehends that Mary has after all chosen to stay with him and realises how close he has come to a kind of death of the heart, he can admit that he was envious of the freedom money can buy but is convinced by her of the continuing worth of his work. His horn-rimmed spectacles, rather floppy hair and the very slightest suggestion of a stammer just touched in something boyish still inside the man, a kernel of gallantry and idealism at the centre of someone not quite worn down into priggishness by the academic grindstone. He often managed to find or suggest a depth of subtext to Hunter's dialogue, most beautifully in a second-act scene on the moonlit terrace with Vanessa as his daughter, flushed with wine for the first time and exuding a kind of radiant benevolence to which her impassive, silent father cannot respond.

The problem with the play was that having set up a potentially rich clash of worlds, Hunter had very little original to say about it and the last act, back in Surrey's Subtopia, is full of dangerously stiff, clenched dialogue that often teeters on the verge of bathos. Audiences loved it, however, and the notices, even when coolish towards the play, were unreservedly excellent for the cast; with Michael Gwynn replacing Michael, the production was still strong enough at the box office to move to the Prince's to continue its run. Michael won the *Evening Standard* Best Actor Award for Philip, and was much touched by a letter from the disarmingly modest Hunter after Michael had left for Stratford (performances there did not qualify for the *Standard* Awards): 'This is, as so often in life, probably the right award for the wrong reason – I'm told by those who saw it that your Hamlet *was* Hamlet.' Glen wrote to him after the opening: 'It was beautiful to see all your family together on the first night and all looking so happy and so enchanting. You never *asked* for our sympathy. There was no self-pity, only a deep conviction of being in the right. And that is what made it so tremendously moving and real.' For Michael perhaps the happiest aspect of a happy venture was Vanessa's success; Binkie said to him after the Saville first night, reminding him of Olivier's words at the Old Vic the night of her birth: 'Tonight a great actress has been born.'

Fred returned to London at the end of Michael's run at the Saville, and with only a short time before *Hamlet* rehearsals, they took off for the Capri villa owned by Cavalcanti and Graham Greene. The somewhat vague Cav had claimed he had told the 'Guardian' supposedly looking after the house of their arrival, but nothing seemed to have been organised and it turned into rather a bleak holiday. It rained continuously for eight of the ten days they were on the island, most of their time spent huddled over a weakly smoking fire 'in a very damp casa', hardly the sunny, calm time Michael had wanted before a Stratford season. Yet in a photograph of him, presumably taken by Fred, en route to Tiberius' villa on Capri, he looks at his most happily relaxed. It was a copy of that photograph which he sent to Dick Green, asking for one of Dick in return, moved to do so perhaps by an emotional meeting in Paris when he was returning to England with Hélène le Breton, who never really recovered from Louis's death (she died three years later); she had given Michael a photograph of Louis amid the profusion of his garden in the country. Michael was only just past fifty, but Louis's death seemed to act as a nudge to keep those friendships most dear to him in good repair.

Dick had at last settled down, having even given up drink for some years ('nothing stronger than tea') and he had formed an enduring partnership with the cheerful, strong Roy King, a Dorset farmer's son. With some money from a family trust Dick had bought a seventeenth-century house with extensive grounds, including a walled rose garden, somewhat neglected, in the idyllic village of Batcombe, a few miles south of Frome on the Somerset–Wiltshire border. He, Roy and Roy's parents had settled there after Dick and Roy had done a great deal of work restoring the house's many rooms, while Gervase Smith, living near by in a folly (known as the Convent) in the gardens of Stourhead, had begun work on the gardens. Rockwells House, as it was known, became for Michael what Mortehoe and Bromyard had offered: a haven of relaxation among people with whom he could be totally at ease. Dick wanted to lure Michael to their valley – 'Avalon, no less' – promising: 'I think you will like the local girls and boys – especially one who I can only think is the origin of all desire under the elms.' Dick and Michael could often josh each other in this way, yet in the letter accompanying the Capri photograph, which talked of his happiness with Fred, he asked Dick to make sure he did not 'leave it lying around'. The old habits of secrecy died hard.

Michael must have been aware of the raised eyebrows at Stratford in the summer. Rachel was again also in the company – playing Lady Capulet in *Romeo and Juliet* and Margaret in *Much Ado* – and she joined him at Avoncliffe, much spruced up since they had last occupied it in 1951, with Fred there too, in the downstairs room. Glen somewhat startled the company on the first day of *Hamlet* rehearsals, introducing Fred as more or less his equal, implying a status as virtually co-director, causing a certain amount of speculation and sniggering behind hands, although Fred's eternal optimism and good spirits won a lot of people round, especially the younger company members, fascinated by the breath of air from an apparently more dynamic American theatre.

Michael had reconsidered his Hamlet with great care, which was just as well because Glen's production was sadly routine, surprisingly poorly designed by Percy Harris. The costumes, mostly High Renaissance with crimson and gold predominating and Fortinbras's troops all in white, were fine, but the stage was often reduced to an enormous bare space. That had worked well for most of *Antony and Cleopatra* but in *Hamlet* it left vital scenes such as Hamlet's closet scene with Gertrude looking forlornly stranded with the eavesdropping Polonius a ridiculously long distance away. There was little sense of a world within Elsinore, with static group-ings like an old-fashioned opera production. It often happens in the theatre that a director wants to tackle a play for so long that when it finally comes along the original impulse has lost its spark. Also, Glen had been under enormous pressure at Stratford – he was much more of a worrier than Tony Quayle – and he was not working at his best during the 1958 season.

Michael's reading was infinitely more subtle and rich than his Old Vic performance, and much more, too, a riposte to Olivier's theory, voiced in his film version, that *Hamlet* is the story of 'a man who cannot make up his mind'. He retained that sense of a near paralysing grief at the loss of an obviously adored father in the early scenes, but now it was noticeably yoked to a more active, participatory perspective on events in Elsinore. At the Old Vic in the first court scene he had been isolated downstage, removed spatially and emotionally from the court, while at Stratford he was still downstage, this time with his back (unusual in those days) to the audience, but very much watching and noting everything around him. The essentially sceptical side of Hamlet's intellect was also considerably more in focus; this was perceptibly the quickest brain in Elsinore, becoming caught in the trap of events so that on this occasion Hamlet's tragedy resulted less from a weakness of will or inability to take action than from being faced with situations so complex and subtle that they cannot be easily simplified.

Although this was still a son shocked by the suddenness of death and by his mother's remarriage, there were also some completely fresh appraisals of key scenes, including taking the risk of playing the whole of 'Now might I do it pat' as Hamlet encounters Claudius at prayer in a whisper (audible to the back row) and an electrifying approach to the scene with Ophelia (Dorothy Tutin). The knowledge that she is being used as a dupe by Claudius and Polonius invested Hamlet here with the contradictory emotions of a fierce but unhysterical rage and affection, frightening both Ophelia and himself. Tutin found acting with Michael on stage exhilarating, with something fresh to play off at every performance. She echoed Michael's description of acting with Edith when talking of acting with him: 'It was impossible to get stale with Michael. It wasn't frightening when things were different – the groundwork of the scene had been well laid so that you still feel absolutely safe, no matter what changed. He always acted *with* you, it was always *mutual*.'

The theatre historian Muriel St Clare Byrne, whose Hamlets went back to Forbes Robertson, was thrilled by what she saw as a fusion of the classical and the modern in Michael's Hamlet, describing his 'How all occasions do inform against me' soliloquy, outlined against the cyclorama sky, as looking 'breathtakingly like the Lawrence portrait of Kemble as Hamlet and just as majestic', while elsewhere the urgency and tenderness of his playing belonged to an entirely assimilated psychological portrait, most powerful in the serenity of the closing sections. At Michael's request Glen had not made the customary cuts in Act V Scene 2 in which Hamlet describes his foiling of Claudius's plot, which helped him enormously to push Hamlet's thoughts and actions back into gear. This is Hamlet describing his deeds not, as in his soliloquies, his thoughts, and it gave him the taking-off point into the altered man of the last scenes, ready for whatever providence or destiny might have in store. Vocally he was in superb condition, able to shift from a whisper to the astonishing haunted cry of 'My fate cries out' after meeting the spectre of his father, a spine-tingling leap right off the starting block into top gear, literally delivered 'at the top of his voice' and charging the house with a palpably electric tension.

After the opening few performances Michael flew to Paris for a weekend to visit Corin who was living near Versailles before Cambridge. They read Tynan's *Observer* notice together. According to Corin, they were able to laugh resignedly at it and go off for a walk in the Père Lachaise Cemetery before going on to Chantilly for lunch with Duff and Diana Cooper, although Michael must have been stung by its tone. It was Tynan at his most bitchy, dishing out lethal back-handed compliments, as he had done to Gielgud in describing him as 'the finest actor, from the neck up, in the world today'. Reviewing *Hamlet*, Tynan cited his idol, quoting Olivier as saying he would rather, as an actor, lose his hands than his eyes, claiming that Michael, who 'persistently suggests the Cyclops', lacked the basic ability to connect with other actors, for all his unrivalled intellectual grasp of a classical text. But virtually all the actors who played opposite Michael – Tutin (her Ophelia dismissed by Tynan but cheered by every other critic), Edith, Olivier himself when they played together in *Uncle Vanya*, Joan Plowright, Peggy Ashcroft heading the list – stressed his 'giving' qualities as an actor, and Michael always considered the eyes as the visa on an actor's passport. Of all Tynan's lofty judgements on Michael's work, that particular one is the widest of the mark and, for posterity, the most damning and damaging.

There were long queues round the Memorial Theatre for every *Hamlet*, Michael's performance seeming to reach and touch audiences even more than in 1950. The children all came up to see it – Corin then nursing a hopeless adolescent crush on Dorothy Tutin – as did Dick with Roy King, Norris Houghton revisiting England, David Loveday who had left Cranleigh to return to the Church and now was Bishop of Dorchester, Dadie Rylands and Dennis Robertson, and an unexpected visit from Glen's old lover Siegfried Sassoon, who wrote to Michael: 'Thank you for a lovely Hamlet, magnificently sustained and real and true in feeling. I shall always remember your "Alas, poor Yorick" passage for its perfect naturalness and tenderness.' Iris Tree also visited Stratford to catch the performance, afterwards driving back with Michael and Rachel for a Wilks Water Sunday, a rare sunny interlude in a rain-sodden summer. The lake was now finished, the unblocked stream edged with marsh marigolds and the new roses – Albertines and the foamy white Madame Alfred

Carrière – all in bloom as they had a strawberry picnic on the lawn. Increasingly, they found it hard to leave Wilks Water when it was at the height of its tranquil beauty.

When *Much Ado* went into rehearsal Michael and Rachel (playing Margaret) often walked to the theatre; everyone needed to be fit for an athletic production with several dances. The critics were generally somewhat sniffy about this production by Douglas Seale, who had mounted a rare staging of the trilogy of *Henry VI* at Birmingham Rep, but it was a genuine crowd pleaser, rather anticipating Franco Zeffirelli's Neopolitan ice cream of a production for the early days of the National Theatre. In a beautiful design by Tanya Moiseiwitsch, Seale set the play in 1850s Italy, with the men clearly returning from one of Garibaldi's campaigns, the women in crinolines, Don Pedro like a young Prince Albert and Richard Johnson as Don John resembling a Delacroix. Throughout, the emphasis was on sunlight and brightness – the threatened punishments for Don John were cut – except for the chiaroscuro of a candlelit church scene when Michael and Googie Withers (Beatrice) hushed the auditorium with 'Kill Claudio'.

Michael made an elegant, dandyish Benedick, whether in military uniform, white linen suit and panama hat or topper and tails for the wedding scene and he and Googie had a delightfully sophisticated raillery in their scenes together (a recurrent critical comparison was with Alfred Lunt and Lynn Fontanne), while Michael found a valuable vein of rueful comedy in his portrait of a man surprised by late-flowering love. Although it was enjoyable to play to capacity houses, he rather agreed with the critic who said that the production should follow *My Fair Lady* into Drury Lane. It was somewhat too like a musical, relentlessly busy with such endless invention – Hero being laced into stays for her marriage, much business with dance cards during a lengthy ball scene with complex waltzes – that often the basic narrative was swamped. A production which might have suggested Stendhal set to music by Verdi ended up more a marriage of Ouida and Rossini.

Michael's old friendly rival for school drama laurels, John Garrett, who had left Whitgift and was now head of Bristol Grammar School, was in charge of the series of talks and lectures each season at Stratford. Michael had given talks during his previous summers there and protested this time that he really had nothing new to say on acting, but the persistent Garrett wooed him into a talk, given the advance, usefully all-purpose title 'Character and Characters', to be delivered as the closing lecture of the 1958 season. On the day the Conference Hall at Stratford (now the Swan Theatre) was packed and Michael surprised his audience after opening a fat spring-back file when he announced that he would not be giving a lecture but telling a story, the first version of what became his only published work of fiction, *The Mountebank's Tale*. He gave it then the Pirandellian subtitle of 'Right You Are if You Think You Are'. For over an hour he kept his audience enthralled by his tale of mixed identity, the story of a great actor, Josef Charles, and the slightly younger doppelgänger who takes his place. In this first version Michael had a journalist as the narrator and the narrative was a simpler affair than it was to become. He had described it self-deprecatingly as 'a Harlequinade to Mr John Garrett's season', but the buzzing reaction convinced him that he had the germ of a strong story which needed revision. He was right. Far from having nothing left to say on acting, *The Mountebank's Tale* in its final form would emerge as the most revelatory of all his writing on the subject.

He would have settled down in Avoncliffe to revise the story now both his plays were in repertoire, but he became sidetracked by his involvement once more in the protracted saga of the National Theatre building. At a lunch to welcome the Comédie Française to London, Michael was pugnacious about the need for endless agitation against the English enemy of indifference in order to match the House of Molière, with the planned National Theatre building as yet with only a mouldering foundation stone to show for it: 'Like an out-of-work actor, it is "resting".' Then Harold Hobson in the *Sunday Times* wrote a calculatedly provocative and characteristically whimsical piece, describing the establishment of a National Theatre as a cultural disaster, rejoicing in the foundation stone's decay, insisting a National Theatre building was unnecessary with both Stratford and the Old Vic, which should simply add new plays to their repertoires. Michael, backing a reply from Lord Esher, a National Theatre trustee, wrote a splendid riposte, cleverly hitting back at Hobson, the self-appointed champion of the French stage (Edwige Feuillère was his special goddess), by attacking such 'cultural philistinism' using a French comparison. He described how on a recent trip to Paris he mused on the paradox that France, the Western country with the most heavily subsidised theatre, should have so many leading actors (Marie Bell, Jean-Louis Barrault, Gérard Philippe) who regularly return to Molière and Racine while simultaneously there seemed to be no shortage of new French plays. His blood still warmed quickly at any threat to the ideal of a National Theatre.

At this stage of his career Michael was pouring as much energy into off-stage theatrical activities as he had once done into political life. He had no trace of the slightly embarrassed condescension of many actors towards amateur theatre; in 1958 he agreed to be president of the Questors' Theatre in Ealing, impressed by its work and by the passionate, persuasive enthusiasm of its leading light, Alfred Emmett. Even with a busy Stratford schedule he made several trips to Ealing that summer – to welcome actors from Moscow, to open a new rehearsal room (appositely named after Stanislavsky) and helping to launch the fund-raising drive towards a new theatre to replace the old tin-roofed Mattocks Lane building. His commitment to the Questors' was solid for twenty years, while he continued, too, as a vice-president of the Actors' Orphanage and a trustee of the emergent British Theatre Museum.

Shortly before the end of the Stratford season Daisy's health deteriorated badly. Michael was able to visit her at the Stanmore nursing home where she continued to weaken. When the home called him at Stratford one morning to tell him that Daisy's death was imminent he was driven at once to Stanmore and he held her hand while she was still semi-conscious before he had to leave for a matinée. He was driven back between performances but she had died during the afternoon. Michael kept no diary of this time but her death while he was at Stratford must have had certain resonances for him. His happiest memories of his early years included the never forgotten 1921 summer when his mother had acted at the old theatre. And among the ugly, drunken scenes of more recent years there had been one tranquil interlude in 1951 when Daisy, for a while on the wagon, came to Stratford for a week, seeing the History Cycle while preparing to rehearse a new play in London. Michael would hear her lines and she would reminisce, often with astonishing recall, about the Stratford of thirty years before, sharing many memories.

Daisy's funeral was a quiet affair, with family and a few close friends including Dorothy Green. The later memorial service was at St Paul's, Covent Garden, the 'Actors' Church', with an orotund and mostly incomprehensible lesson by the sonorous-voiced Robert Atkins. Corin recalled that the night before the service, Michael went to the piano and played E. J. H. Moeran's setting of a Walter de la Mare poem, continuing to play while tears streamed down his face. The contrast between Daisy when she was poor and struggling and when, moving to Chapel Street with Andy, she became affluent and moderately successful, was so sharp that for Michael it must have been like dealing with two different women. Some of his friends believed that Daisy was the source of Michael's confusions and his demons, heaping guilt on him with her jealousy of his success, her accusations of ingratitude and the blame she burdened him with for the life to which she had committed herself to give him, Peg and herself security. She might well have coped better with the frustrations of her life had he been only averagely successful. As it is, as Corin put it: 'In fact, all his life seems to me a baffled unsuccessful attempt to earn her gratitude and praise.'

In a letter to Bob – like all Michael's letters to him, it has not survived –

Michael must have revealed some of his distress; Bob, who had consoled Michael through many aftermaths of Daisy's behaviour, was infinitely understanding in reply, reminding Michael that in every way, including financially (Andy left Daisy comfortably off but she had gone through it all before her final years), he had done all he could to help his unhappy mother. Bob's own news that year – which delighted both Michael and Rachel – was of his marriage. In New York he had met Betty, a pretty, dark-eyed Catholic girl from La Rochelle, and after she had visited him in California they had been married back in New York. Bob also had just been promoted within Western Union, and he and Betty seemed happily settled in Los Angeles.

Another tense situation erupted in Stratford before the end of the season. The company had been invited through the British Council by the Soviet Ministry of Culture to make its first visit to Russia with *Twelfth Night* in Peter Hall's production and Glen's productions of *Romeo and Juliet* and *Hamlet*, a huge undertaking involving over seventy actors, musicians and technicians, hundreds of costumes and tons of scenery. It had taken endless planning but late in the day Cecil – perhaps still smarting from having lost the previous year's tussle with Glen – again rocked the boat by telling Glen that Michael (who, like the rest of the company, had not known of the tour when he signed for the Stratford season) would not be able to join them if a film contract should clash with the Russian dates. He pointed out that others had been replaced – Googie Withers had to return to Australia and was to be replaced as Gertrude by Coral Browne. On this occasion Michael overrode Cecil at once. He was well aware of the importance of the trip at a sensitive time of a thaw in the Cold War and he had also always wanted to visit Russia.

With the women swathed in still acceptable leopard skin and mink, and Michael sporting a black chapka, the company arrived in a Moscow so cold (–17 degrees) that Zoe Caldwell's nose bled, and they were not much warmer on the train whisking them to Leningrad. Most of them stayed up drinking hot lemon tea and vodka, arriving as sunrise was hitting the roof of the Hermitage in a Leningrad where the Neva was iced over and the wide streets packed with frozen snow. Michael was glad that *Romeo* would be opening the tour, the first visit to Leningrad of a British company since the Revolution, sparing him the endless wait for the first performance to begin while speeches were made and a forty-piece military band played assorted anthems. He also had some time to get used to the uniquely hideous theatre housing them in the Palace of Co-operative Workers, a cavernous brown auditorium seating nearly 3000, designed to resemble a municipal swimming pool. The reception for all the plays from packed houses who loved Shakespeare enough to save for 50-rouble tickets (double Bolshoi prices) was unprecedented for the company; flowers, notes, even watches showered the stage during the countless curtain calls Michael had to take after his first *Hamlet*, a performance which he (and Glen) considered by far the finest he had ever given.

In Moscow Michael was proud to be playing the Moscow Art Theatre, haunted by history for him and much more intimate than their Leningrad space. Audiences were if anything even more demonstrative. Russian actors wanted to meet them; Andrei Popov held a big party for the company in the Actors' Club on Gorky Street with Bolshoi musicians and an octet from the Red Army Choir (they included 'Tipperary' in their selection) and an enormous Russian-style buffet. They celebrated Christmas with carols in their hotel; Zoe Caldwell had bought little wooden candleholders and candles which the company lit, Michael sitting on the floor holding his to lead the singing of 'Away in a Manger'.

It was after a Moscow *Hamlet* performance that Michael had his memorable reunion with Guy Burgess, living in Moscow since his defection and flight with Donald Maclean, when he came round very tipsy and accompanied by the young boyfriend helpfully provided by the State to congratulate his old Cambridge friend, although only after being sick, with obviously well-practised aim, into Michael's washbasin. Michael had a surreally melancholy lunch with Burgess at his Moscow flat, with only pâté de foie gras to eat, the planned hare having been ruined by being cooked with its gall bladder still inside, having to listen to a progressively drunken litany of complaints about Russian life. Coral Browne, elegantly couture clad and with the vocabulary of a Sydney stevedore, had been much intrigued by Burgess – Michael introduced them in his dressing room – and it was her subsequent lunch with him which Alan Bennett later dramatised in his TV and stage play, *An Englishman Abroad*.

Michael crammed as much theatregoing as possible into his evenings off, although most of what he saw depressed him, showing all the institutional-theatre blights of tired productions, actors clinging on to roles they were too old for and shabby scenery. But there were surprises and delights too; he was fascinated by another Bulgakov play, *Escape*, at the Pushkin Theatre with the great Cherkassov as a tragic White general during the Revolution, he loved Popov at the Moscow Circus and, most of all, reminding him of childhood afternoons at the illusionists Maskelyne and Devant's in Langham Place, he became a child again at a Hansel and Gretel-style story at Leningrad's Children's Theatre: 'I wonder whether it was also the child who is so much the father to every actor, which made the performance the most exciting theatrical event I saw in Russia?'

He had to take off on his travels again almost as soon as the Stratford company returned to London, visiting Vienna – ensconced once more at the Sacher – to deliver two lectures for the British Council, one on modern English theatre, the other a repeat of his Stratford story. He had revised *The Mountebank's Tale* slightly since then but in the city where so much of the story is set and after an absorbing tour of the Old Burgtheater he began to think of further changes to what had clearly seized the imagination of the Vienna listeners as much as it had engrossed at Stratford.

He had many offers on the table for future plays on his return. Clurman wanted him for O'Neill's rarely staged *A Touch of the Poet* and for *Heartbreak House* on Broadway, and for London Peter Daubeny was wooing him for Archibald MacLeish's Biblical play *J. B.*, but he passed on all of them, determined to buckle down to make something of his novella and also, finally, to finish his version of *The Aspern Papers*.

In early February 1959 he immured himself at Batcombe, where Dick's and Roy's house enchanted him, as did Roy's mother, Mrs King, who looked like a benevolent Carabosse and spent most of her time in the kitchen creating delicious meals. Also a permanent resident of Rockwells was a lodger, 'The Commander', a rotund Billy Bunterish and perennially cheerful old soak who joined in games of Canasta, taken ferociously seriously, at which Michael, with his ability to keep his face an impenetrable mask, was a master of double bluff. Dick and Michael occasionally went for long walks or to Frome to potter around antique shops, but for the most part Michael worked hard on reshaping *The Mountebank's Tale*.

While he was with Dick, a script of a play by Robert Bolt arrived from Frith Banbury and Michael reacted positively to it on a first reading. It had its origins in a 1955 television play, *Last of the Wine*, in which a London family face nuclear disaster. Bolt had reworked it to centre it around an Oxbridge academic family but the central concern about the nuclear threat was still at the core of the play. It was now called *The Tiger and the Horse*, from Blake's 'The Tygers of Wrath are Wiser than the Horses of Instruction' ('Proverbs from Hell'). The horse was Michael's role, Jack Dean, a detached ex-astronomer academic up for election as Master of his college who refuses to sign a CND petition organised by his daughter's don boyfriend in case it should harm his election chances. The tiger in the play is Gwen, his wife, who since her husband's sexual estrangement from her has devoted herself to her garden; concerned about deformities in babies caused by nuclear tests, slowly driven to breakdown during the play, Gwen destroys a priceless Holbein belonging to the College, which restoration has revealed to include a hunchback child, pinning the petition with her signature to the picture, an act which finally brings Dean out of his shell of detached non-commitment.

Reduced to bare plot it sounds like a C. P. Snow novel or a thesis play but it is more than polemic. The CND theme was something about which Michael felt strongly – he sang that year in a Festival Hall CND concert organised by Peggy Ashcroft (and talking to Bolt of the CND issues effectively began Vanessa's involvement in radical politics) – but he was also drawn to the characters in the play. Right from the outset, however, he felt keenly that Bolt had not totally realised Dean and that for too many stretches of the play he seemed obtuse rather than uncommitted. He expressed his enthusiasm – and his doubts – to Banbury, but agreeing with the bait of the suggestion that Vanessa might again play his daughter, a passionately committed, ardent woman in this play: 'She has the vulnerability and also the emotional youthfulness. Also she has, like her mother, a conscience the size of Grand Central Station.' Bolt at that time lived in Somerset, not far from Batcombe, although soon afterwards he moved to affluent Richmond splendour, and Michael visited him and his first wife Jo. A big, burly and affably demonstrative man, Bolt took to Michael at once and they had long discussions about the play, Bolt writing delightedly to Michael later: 'I don't know where else we should have found anyone to embody the difficult combination of the potent scholar and red-blooded man consumed by elegance of mind.'

Binkie and Banbury joined forces with silent partnership from FES (Plays) to present the play, but with Michael's 1959 film plans already set and since Peter Daubeny had agreed to produce *The Aspern Papers* (Michael dropped *Juliana* as a title when several people asked why he had written a play about the Queen of the Netherlands), it could not be until well into 1960 before *The Tiger and the Horse* could be put into production ('God in heaven, what a rat race it all is,' as Bolt said to Banbury about the mills of the commercial theatre). Michael had hoped that Peggy Ashcroft would play Gwen, but she turned it down, feeling that the Gwen–Dean relationship was not worked enough in the text. He stressed the coincidence of her reaction with his feelings to Binkie and Bolt did some revisions to their scenes; Banbury always felt that had she seen the rewritten script, Peggy might have changed her mind (Catherine Lacey was cast). But Michael continued to worry away, still not entirely happy with the part although he was committed totally to the play.

Bolt in fact saw his next play – *A Man for All Seasons* – produced by Binkie in the West End before *The Tiger and the Horse* opened. Impatient though he was and disappointed that the plays could not be seen in their order of writing, he had agreed with Banbury that they should wait for Michael: 'How extraordinary to find a man who can both act and think.' They kept in touch, and when Bolt moved to Richmond he occasionally came to drinks or parties at Hans Crescent: 'I went to Redgrave's last Sunday and was puzzled by the plushy atmosphere which successful people of the theatre seem to drift into. I had the impression that Redgrave was puzzled by it too, as though he had woken up one morning to find it all grown up around him . . .'

Before rehearsals of *The Aspern Papers* began Michael had a good deal of revision to do on the script, and once again he took himself off to Batcombe where he could work without distractions at Dick's. Fred had been worrying him: 'much troubled by Fred, who is a bit hysterical about P. Daubeny and share in *Aspern*'. In the train to Batcombe he thought more about the problems: 'Write long letter to Fred, about why he must not think everyone is trying to do him down.' Faced with the silky-smooth operators of the West End the inexperienced Fred, whose main problems always were impatience and the conviction that he could do it all, often felt patronised and could lash out accordingly. Michael still had a con-suming love for Fred but he knew also that their future as co-producers might be rocky if Fred resorted to scenes and sulks. At Michael's sug-gestion, FES would start off with an uncomplicated production, a one-set, small-cast thriller, *The Sound of Murder*, which would hopefully give Fred a grounding in the basics of commercial management.

In Rockwells' Chekhovian atmosphere Michael worked long hours on what he called 'the carpentry' of *The Aspern Papers*, reducing to 'a jigsaw' James's subtle and complex skein of motive and ploy before reassembling it, and he finished a new draft in good time. Fred came down to collect the manuscript and have it typed in London. Dick, although always perfectly polite and saying nothing to Michael, never cared for Fred, perhaps to some extent because he had liked Bob so much; Dick was always of the camp who believed that there was something manipulative in Fred's character and that he was out for what he could get.

From Dick's seclusion, Michael had to return immediately to the film studios, as Cecil had been urging for some time. His latest film had just been released, a little-known but happy comedy, *Law and Disorder* (all concerned were relieved when the title was changed from the original *The Windy Side*). Interviewed on location, he was made in some press pieces to sound less than a barrel of laughs ('He does not have the capacity of being at ease with people, perhaps because he is not at ease with himself.') But then Michael was never much good at the instant assumed bonhomie of movie publicity. In fact, he had been completely at ease filming what was not an Ealing comedy as such but which was out of the Ealing stable with a script by T. E. B. ('Tibby') Clarke; not perhaps quite in the same league as his *Lavender Hill Mob* or *The Titfield Thunderbolt* but fresh and funny, and with an Ealing director, Charles Crichton. Michael had great fun playing a genial conman trying to keep his prison record secret from his son, now a judge's marshal. The plot involved smuggling jewels inside a shark, car chases and his multiple disguises – a bishop, a missionary, a Customs official included – and Michael, like the film, has a larky zest throughout, an outstanding sequence being a very funny scene in the back of a Black Maria between Michael and Robert Morley at his most splenetically magisterial as the judge.

For Michael Anderson, and for the chance to appear in a film with James Cagney, an actor he revered, Michael agreed to play the small but key part of an IRA chief, 'The General', in *Shake Hands with the Devil*, shot at Ardmore Studios in Ireland. Even for this three-day job Michael took his customary care, consulting photographs of Michael Collins, the prototype for 'The General' (noting he wore soft collars with civilian clothes), and finding through Brian Desmond Hurst a teacher from Cork to coach him in the accent. He was, he told Anderson, 'very, very, proud to think I will be in a film with James Cagney' and he admired Cagney's intense, low-key performance in a piece of unexpected casting (Cagney was proud of his Irish roots and wanted to film there) as an eminent Dublin surgeon with a covert life as a fanatical revolutionary. Again, the movie is little known but despite some lurches into melodrama it is often a gripping film and Michael's scene with Cagney, intimately tense and shot mostly in close-up, is played with masterly economy by both actors.

For different reasons – the Jamesian in him could not resist – he also accepted a small part at the opening of Jack Clayton's film *The Innocents*, based on Henry James's story *The Turn of the Screw*. With his own experience of adapting James, Michael had great respect for the script, based on William Archibald's stage version with work by Truman Capote and John Mortimer. The film goes along with Edmund Wilson's theory that it is not Miles and Flora, the children, who are possessed, but Miss Giddens (Deborah Kerr), their new governess at Bly House, whose repressed sexual longings have been buried in what James called 'her small smothered life'. As the children's guardian in the preliminary London interview with the governess, Michael has exactly the right kind of charm, both innate and calculated, of a rich and cosmopolitan man used to getting what he wants. Helped greatly by the photography of Freddie Francis, giving the entire film a misty, dreamy edge like the photographs of Julia Margaret Cameron, Clayton is able to hint – even although the scene has only one tactile moment, a handshake – at a sublimated attraction to the guardian on the part of the governess, a parson's daughter, which triggers her descent into hell. Although his own contribution was small, Michael thought highly of Clayton's work on a difficult film.

It was while rehearsing his last job before *The Aspern Papers* – a television version of *A Touch of the Sun* alongside Rachel (replacing an ill Diana Wynyard) and old friends Constance Cummings and Roger Livesey – that

Michael went back to his diary to note: 'I suppose I will remember this as one of the most happy of all my days. Happy as much as anything because of Rachel's happiness at the news.' He was being offered a knighthood, to join Richardson, Olivier and Gielgud (the latter being, surprisingly, the last of that trio to be honoured). For Michael it justified all those early years and the decision to make the stage the focus of his career despite the siren lure of films. Very early he had decided the kind of actor he wanted to be and he had always kept the bargain he had made with himself ('He never renegotiated the contract,' remarked Corin). Surely, too, he wished Daisy could have known. When the press announcement came he was genuinely moved by the mountain of letters and telegrams which arrived, and was unable to resist dropping in to lunch at the Garrick ('Everyone most kind') and at the weekend at Wilks Water: 'R. and I go into Odiham, partly on my part to be congratulated.' The newspapers carried prominent photographs of Michael – on the set of Michael Anderson's film of Hammond Innes's *The Wreck of the Mary Deare*, in which he had a dull role – being congratulated by co-stars Gary Cooper and Charlton Heston. The congratulatory letters included one from Bob, who also gave Michael the news of the birth of a first child, a girl to be called Leigh, for Betty and him.

The Aspern Papers rehearsed at the end of June. It had been cast extraordinarily painlessly, with Beatrix Lehmann (herself an occasional novelist and a Jamesian) accepting Juliana at once, although she saw clearly, as she said to Michael, 'You have written yourself a hard part, through loyalty to Henry James.' Flora Robson – who had played the governess in *The Innocents* on stage in London – similarly responded immediately to the role of Miss Bordereau's niece (Michael gave her the more euphonious stage name of Miss Tina rather than Tita) and because of her casting Peter Daubeny had suggested Basil Dean to direct. Dean had been a dominant West End figure between the wars although his star had dimmed since, largely because of his notoriously acerbic personality. But he and Robson had worked together at the start of her career and often thereafter; Daubney thought that Dean would be able to curb Flora Robson's well-known tendency to play for sympathy. She was what was known as a *jolie laide* – she had once been engaged to Tyrone Guthrie in the 1930s but he asked to be released from his promise and she had never married – and she seemed to need to be loved by audiences, leaving directors and fellow actors often tearing their hair while with her lambent voice and wounded eyes she manipulated a script to distortion in performance. Michael had not wanted to direct a play which he had also adapted and was appearing in, and so readily accepted Daubeny's suggestion.

It made for a disastrous start. Michael White, then Daubeny's assistant before launching his own distinguished managerial career, remembered Dean as 'a very grumpy old man. Like a great sportsman who has gone off the boil.' By the second day Michael was noting: 'Basil's method of giving inflections is very hard for me to take, but I swallow it to support him.' Two weeks into rehearsal and he was in despair. Dean had reverted to type, endlessly correcting Flora Robson with sarcastic criticism (typically for a bully, he did not go for Beatrix Lehmann who would have made mincemeat of him). Michael hated such atmospheres: 'By the end of the day's rehearsal am all churned up inside by Basil's finicking. Speak of this and he sulks. Later it happens that Bea rings up and says "You've got to make up your mind, you know".' He did and Daubeny told Dean to leave the production (Michael, mindful of his help on the text and of his pride, insisted that he should retain his directorial credit and have half his agreed royalty). With Michael taking over, he described the next two weeks as 'rather a nightmare, but less so than the previous two', although he knew that he was neglecting his own part to get the play ready to open. And he had a hectic time prior to leaving to open in Newcastle: his investiture, a lightning trip to Stratford to catch Vanessa's Helena in *A Midsummer Night's Dream* while Rachel was coaching Lynn in drama school audition speeches, she too having decided to act (she followed Vanessa to Central). Michael was moved in Stratford to hear Vanessa say, apropos their family relationships: 'Ours is a family that rejoices in each other.'

During the pre-London tour there was time to keep fine-tuning *The Aspern Papers*, Michael's only worry being a muted Flora Robson: 'Flora a little subdued and I feel she thinks (from a remark she made) that Bea "steals the play".'

It had taken over a decade for the play to reach the stage from that first impulse in Hollywood but in that time, over many restructurings and rewrites, Michael had finally produced the most successful of all the many stage adaptations from Henry James, the kind of success that poor James had so craved for himself in the theatre. Unnecessary elements had been stripped away; originally his version opened in the Venice hotel room of Mrs Prest, the American friend of the story's narrator (called H. J. in the play) and included extra characters, but over the years Michael refined it to just one setting, the dilapidated old *sala* in the palazzo of Miss Bordereau, the ancient lady believed to have been the lover of the great early American poet-in-exile Jeffrey Aspern and to have letters and papers of his in her possession, and her shy, unworldly niece. Mrs Prest remained, and Michael cleverly touched in two servants' roles, but – as in James – it is an essentially triangular drama.

Completely loyal to James in spirit and tone, some changes were still necessary for the stage. It was impossible to dramatise literally the story's ending with the narrator hastily leaving the palazzo and going into Venice, so Michael created a new ending, a climax to top the *coup de théâtre* of the penultimate scene when the macabre spectre figure of the old lady finds H. J. about to examine her papers before her fatal heart attack. The play's ending, in a nod towards *Hedda Gabler* which Michael hoped the Ibsenite in James would have smiled upon, has the rejected Miss Tina light the stove and begin to burn the papers.

In the original 1947 notes he made for himself Michael wrote: 'Broadly speaking, the writing needs to be in a higher dramatic key than the original. James's special quality of creating situation and atmosphere by implication cannot be transferred to the stage (hence his personal failure as a dramatist).' Michael accordingly crucially heightens the stakes, giving Aspern's life a deeper and more romantic colour, making him a Byronic figure but also a voice from America's youth; his letters would unlock the mystery surrounding much of his European life and give any scholar involved great *réclame*. And he slightly heightened the cat-and-mouse game of James, the old lady almost a mummy but with the fiery particles of her brain still alight, 'on' to H. J. from the start. Similarly, he tightened the tension in the great scene following Juliana's death when Miss Tina obliquely offers herself to H. J. in exchange for the papers, a scene which had the most profound impact on stage with its layers of emotion – Flora Robson's almost abject hints, Michael's stammered 'Ah, Miss Tina, it wouldn't do – it wouldn't do' and her burning embarrassment, eyes lowered, at his rejection. Miraculously, James's opaline quality, so haunting in the story, was not coarsened in the adaptation process. Michael intuitively understood that the key element in the original was suspense – sometimes invisible but always there, 'like the high-wire above our heads at the circus' as he put it.

It was cheered to the echo at the Queen's Theatre opening, the audience responding to an evening of high quality in all departments. And it was wondrously acted. Beatrix Lehmann, wheelchair-bound and with her eyes shaded as specified in James for most of the evening, was denied the use of so much of the actor's equipment, but the sheer force of will and cunning which transmitted itself from her shrunken frame was formidable. Her last scene, catching H. J. about to rob her as she thinks, when she cried 'You publishing scoundrel!' like the last sound of a dying animal, was spellbinding. As Miss Tina, another in her long line of thwarted spinsters, Flora Robson had all the ingenuous directness, the naïveté of a nun who realises that she is near to disloyalty to her religion (her aunt), of James's great creation. And, for the early performances at least, she emerged in the last act as a genuinely tragic figure.

As Beatrix Lehmann had spotted, Michael had written for himself the most thankless role of the triangle. He played H. J. as a Europeanised American – there was a residual New England accent – and as a man of personable, plausible charm. But – his main achievement – always present too was the obsessed scholar who has admitted to Mrs Prest that to use 'hypocrisy and duplicity' is his only chance to insinuate himself into the Bordereaus' lives. His scenes with Juliana became accordingly a tensely involving struggle between the elderly seclusion of a survivor of a bygone era and a more rapacious age of enlightenment.

Of all the praise for the play Michael was most heartened by a letter from Leon Edel, the outstanding James scholar and biographer, who congratulated him in appropriately Jamesian style:

> I was aware every moment of the difficulties you were surmounting, not least the brilliant way in which you keep 'H. J.' from being the cad he would seem if he were shorn of the easy innocence of his own obsession. You and your actors have caught the fine nuances and the beautiful fetters of the thing.

The business at the Queen's was soon a sell-out, good news for Michael – on percentages as adaptor (he insisted James's name be billed first), star and part-director as well as being part of the management set-up – although the run was not easy. Before very long, Flora Robson had started to sentimentalise Miss Tina and she reacted very badly to Michael's attempts to get her back on track. The production manager would often watch the show, since Michael could not monitor it from the front, and reported several times that a key line of Miss Tina's was inaudible. When Michael passed this on to Flora she lost her temper, shouting that no director had ever criticised her diction before and then, literally, she showed him her dressing-room door. She had at the beginning of the run played with such unerring truth that their disagreements saddened and upset Michael. They were different kinds of actor, of course. For Flora the audience mattered most and she wanted to please them and win their sympathy. For Michael the text was – always – paramount.

The difference in acting approaches was also at the centre of *The Mountebank's Tale* as finally published shortly after *The Aspern Papers* had opened; Edward Thompson enjoyed taking Michael off from the launch party in Albany down Piccadilly to Hatchard's bookshop, which had an entire window stacked with copies. It had altered considerably since its first Stratford outing, with a more sophisticated tale-within-a-tale struc-ture and with an actor rather than a journalist as narrator of the outer tale, while the backstage episodes in Vienna had gained in texture from his British Council visit. In a letter to an American friend, Arnold Marlé,

Michael admitted that he had based a good deal of his central figure, the great actor Josef Charles, on the Viennese star Josef Kainz who is mentioned en passant in the revised text ('But that,' Michael added teasingly, 'could be just to deceive the knowing reader'). Anton Walbrook had once given Michael a present of a book of photographs of Kainz, the ideal of the dedicated great actor, and certainly the portrait of Josef Charles is much denser in texture in the post-Vienna version.

The core of his story remained unaltered, with the actor-narrator in his opening section trying to solve the mystery of Josef Charles's disappearance, leaving his own double, a younger Englishman, to take his place. The crux of Charles's self-effacement lies in a realisation when he exchanges roles with his double in a two-hander play to act the subordinate role and the *jeu d'esprit* goes awry as Charles has to watch his protégé entrance the audience with showy tricks and flourishes, so disillusioning Charles that he, for the first time in his career, 'dries' – forgets his lines. The suggestion is that this was the key moment when Charles, as it were, 'saw through' the theatre and which triggered his vanishing act. However, his double, it seems, can see beyond it; and it is on the quality of experience shared with his beautiful and loving daughter Perdita, who is herself now studying singing and acting in turn, that the main story ends, redolent with echoes and resonances of Shakespeare's late romances of reconciliation and reunion, *The Magic Flute* and *Der Rosenkavalier*.

At its first Stratford reading Michael had added a coda of a reading of Shakespeare's Sonnet XXIX ('When in disgrace with fortune and men's eyes') with the poet expressing his habit of 'desiring this man's art and that man's scope'. And therein lay a clue to the allegory at the heart of the story. Michael's friend Doris Langley Moore, costume expert and Byron scholar, wrote to him congratulating him on his scrutiny of the shadowy gulf between a performance of genius and a performance of high talent, perceptively adding, 'My theory is that the actor and his double are one and the same person.' She was right. At the centre of *The Mountebank's Tale* is the dissonance in Michael as an actor himself, with Joseph Charles the *acteur*, the artist, while his doppelgänger, his physical image but antithesis in temperament, is the *comédien*, the showman with a gift for the crowd-pleasing flourish, that he could not be. The double sums it up with the mountebank's glibness: 'Josef Charles had every quality of greatness except that one. That he could not ever learn because he did not wish to learn it. I did not have to learn it. It was part of my nature. I was a born Mountebank.' In the same way as Josef Charles, Michael lacked, as he knew – he once or twice touches on it in his diaries – the mountebank's instinct for showmanship, that ability to paper over a crack in a play or performance with a bravura flourish, the knack that was second nature to an actor like Roy, his father or, in his own theatre, Olivier.

The book sold well, having been favourably reviewed, compared in turn with James (the James of *The Tragic Muse*) – although Michael's friend the novelist and dramatist Enid Bagnold was reminded of M. R. James – E. F. Benson, Somerset Maugham, Hans Christian Andersen (Dick Keigwin recalled 'The Shadow') and David Garnett. His real exemplar, as he admitted to Dick Green, was Baroness Blixen when he described his first outline of the story, then called *The Lonesome Eucalyptus*, as 'a long short story in the Dinesen manner (I wish I could say her style but that is, I think you'd agree, inimitable)'. She had written her early stories to be read aloud on her African farm to the Africans she thought by far the best audiences for her tales and she had told Michael at Rungsted that stories should always be written as if they would be read out loud. From her, too, he borrowed devices such as giving a landscape an unexpected twist (an apparently Cotswolds house with a eucalyptus in the garden – in California, it transpires – in Michael's story) and her way of using a narrator figure to frame the tale. Michael, craftily, makes his narrator, whom he introduces in a London club clearly based on the Garrick, a leading actor rather like himself; it acts as a clever deflection, the reader overlooking that in fact it is Josef Charles who is really himself. Even Corin admits that it was only on a later reading that he spotted the legerdemain, adding of Michael: 'He was both actor and double artist and showman, mask and face, and as often as not these two contradictory sides of his talent were at war.'

There was a certain amount of war – within Michael and on the production – when *The Tiger and the Horse* finally went into rehearsal, Bolt having writhed for well over a year in the Kafka-esque toils of Shaftesbury Avenue. Michael was never very happy in the play, as he wrote to Googie Withers later: 'I must confess I didn't enjoy it much except for Vanessa's tremendous personal success. Frith did a terrible production, beastly sets and bad bits of casting.' Any production, especially a troubled one, becomes after the event like the Japanese story *Rashomon*, each participant having a different version of events. For Banbury, as he made clear in a television documentary for Corin and even clearer in Charles Duff's book, *The Lost Summer*, covering the West End's post-war heyday, Michael's drinking and what Banbury considered the desire of a recently knighted and now grand actor to play Jack Dean for sympathy ruined the play. His perspective was simple: 'Michael Redgrave fucked it up.'

According to Banbury, Bolt agreed with him and could not bear to go to the Queen's Theatre after the opening because of Michael's distortion of his character. Trying to untangle the truth is far from easy. It is undeniable that Michael drank more than usual during this time; he was anxious about Fred and deeply worried about the play and about Banbury's production. Bolt, too, although fond of and grateful to Banbury who had given him his first West End success with *Flowering Cherry*, was unhappy with aspects of *Tiger*. Banbury was unrivalled as a director of plays of atmospheric naturalism but increasingly Bolt was unhappy with the restrictions of the naturalistic proscenium stage. *Flowering Cherry* had hinted at another dimension with its closing image of the hero's dream orchard, and in *A Man for All Seasons* he moved, under Brecht's influence, altogether away from naturalism. As a halfway house *The Tiger and the Horse* is often uneasy, with some heightened passages – Dean's speeches on astronomy in the second act most strikingly – which are awkwardly pitched within the bounds of the realistic play. Bolt could not always clearly articulate his intentions; on tour prior to London he suddenly decided that the play's opening should be 'symbolic' and insisted that it be tried with Vanessa as Dean's daughter Stella discovered as the curtain rose posed as Rodin's *Thinker* instead of wrapping a parcel as in the script (it went in for one performance only).

Banbury was clearly given a hard time by a volatile and anxious Bolt, but some of the problems on *The Tiger and the Horse* lay on his own shoulders. Bolt had asked that an art master friend from his schoolteaching days, Sam Lock, design the sets although he had never designed a professional play previously, giving strict instructions to Lock to avoid anything too naturalistic. The play has three settings and all of them in Lock's designs were hideous – neither stylised nor realistic – and crudely executed with badly painted flats in the interiors and ridiculous plywood cut-out trees for the garden scene. The mystery is why Banbury (a co-producer as well as the play's director) and, even more surprisingly, Binkie, who took pride in Tennent's classy production values, should have allowed such work ever to see the stage. After two commercial successes, Bolt was certainly in a strong position, but for the management to let such botched amateur work go ahead was a cardinal error and an admission of weakness. Many of the reviews commented on the damaging ugliness of the designs, particularly of the exterior; Elisabeth Bergner, in a letter to Michael, said that they came close to scuppering the play.

Although the script had been partially revised, Bolt's rewrites never entirely solved the schematic nature of the play or (Michael's continuing main reservation) the background of the Deans' marriage, despite Bolt's attempt to strengthen Gwen's feelings of unworthiness because such a great man as her husband has ceased to love her. There were certainly problems in rehearsal, with Michael uncharacteristically extremely slow to learn his lines – at one point late in rehearsal Banbury felt he had to warn Binkie that the production might not be ready to open its pre-West End tour in Brighton as scheduled, although in the event it just got by – and on tour when Michael's drinking and insecurities (on the lines and with his performance) dragged out the play's running time. Banbury blamed an actor refusing to face the unsympathetic side of his character (perhaps because aspects of Dean were too close to home for comfort) while Michael knew he was still struggling to make sense of one of the most awkward roles (in terms of motive) which he had ever taken on. It was precisely in such a situation that he could have done with even a small amount of the bravura showmanship of Josef Charles's doppelgänger mountebank, but at the very inner core of Michael's being as an actor was the inability to resort to such a compromise. And the more fretful he became, frustrated by his own contribution and worried by Banbury's inability to help him in rehearsal or in notes sessions to 'unlock' Dean, the more he drank; he had noticeably cut down on the alcohol towards the end of the tour when his performance began to come together more persuasively, but he was never entirely satisfied with his work in *The Tiger and the Horse*.

Duff's book *The Lost Summer* asserts that despite all the problems, the play received in London 'ecstatic reviews from every paper except *The Times*', but the evidence of the notices does not at all support that claim. Bernard Levin, at the beginning of his fulsome public worship of Vanessa (who received unanimous bravos), was indeed 'ecstatic' and another influential critic of the period, Robert Muller, ranked Bolt almost with Ibsen, but elsewhere there was considerably less rapture, with many criticisms of the play's air of the textbook (Bolt candidly once described it as 'a large play but cramped in places' – an accurate assessment) while Banbury's production was in fact very poorly received, described variously as 'muffed' and 'lacking both verve and dramatic rhythm'. A long, considered review by Richard Findlater argued that Bolt had not fully realised his main character ('The Master is unfinished as a role and as a man'), going on to analyse the main problem of Bolt's attempt to break free from the constraints of the fourth-wall convention and the realistic 'well-made' play. He suggested that Bolt's efforts had been in effect straitjacketed by Banbury and that the play needed another director, 'not a remorselessly realistic perfectionist like Frith Banbury, who time and again cramps an out-of-the-rut play into a naturalistic mould which is neat, tidy, but dangerously wrong'.

The Tiger and the Horse did not see Michael at his best; another factor in his unease as the detached Dean may well have been the reminder of his own apparent withdrawal from commitment after the affair of the People's Convention but at base the problems with both play and production inhibited the growth of this performance into something on the very highest level. His director always claimed that Michael on this occasion was marked by the star actor's Achilles heel of wanting the audience's sympathy (not a characteristic of his usually, it must be said) but, *contra* Banbury, he was widely praised for the chilly, aloof grandeur with which he invested Dean's detachment. He did more than perhaps any other actor could have done to fill the vacuum inside Bolt's character who is, like T. S. Eliot's Elder Statesman, a hollow man. The play and Michael reached real heights in the second act in a variation of the central father–daughter relationship of *A Touch of the Sun*, a scene with Vanessa as Stella who has been looking through the telescope Dean used before abandoning astronomy, during which she tells him she is pregnant by her lover, the CND-campaigning don. Even in Lock's unlovely set, the scene in the sunset of the autumn garden touched the heart – Stella trying to get through to her austerely remote parent through his old love of the stars and planets, new life within her, while he who once had the universe for his compass retreats into a wintry, uninvolved isolation. Vanessa's glowing combination of tender yearning and self-reliance, Michael's backing away into his protective shell of detachment ('I am not involved'), the whole scene eddying with half-voiced emotional surges, saw superlative acting by both.

Bolt reacted to the performance somewhat differently from Banbury's recollections. He wrote to Michael after the Queen's Theatre London opening: 'I experienced an accelerating lightness of the heart as I observed the sharp, clear and athletic attack you made upon the trunk and roots of the play. Inevitably the rest of the cast took their tone from you. Our considerable amount of success stems from your performance and from that.' And Bolt certainly visited the Queen's subsequently, writing to Michael again after three months of the run to say how much he had liked new touches in Michael's development of the character.

As on many productions, probably faults were on various sides. But Thelma Holt shrewdly later assessed the main issue on *The Tiger and the Horse*, noting how Michael worked – 'He would *hone* his way into a role – he never took easy short cuts. He skied off the piste – always exciting to watch' – a way of working on a difficult new role that may have disconcerted Banbury. He and Michael had collaborated happily on *A Touch of the Sun*, but somehow Banbury seemed unable to be of much help to Michael with Jack Dean. According to Thelma Holt: 'Frith was a man of his time and a director of his time. Michael was not a man of his time, but a man of the future, as an actor and as a man of the theatre.'

Other people's achievements often seemed to give Michael more pleasure than his own. Just as he was delighted with Vanessa's continuing advance, so he was thrilled that Fred had had a success with *The Sound of Murder*, his first independent venture into management, which went into modest profit over a healthy run. Shortly afterwards Fred and Michael jointly presented Coward's new play of old actresses in a retirement home, *Waiting in the Wings*. Michael, with memories of Daisy, Dorothy Green and their chums, and the play's director Margaret Webster, daughter of actors Ben Webster and *The Lady Vanishes'* Dame May Whitty, were understandably attracted to the world of the play, although – like most of Coward's post-war work – it is overwritten and diffuse. The usual producer of Coward's work was Binkie but he had passed (with some duplicity) on this new piece and Coward was displeased with what he saw as sloppy management scheduling compared with the smooth running of the Tennent production line. After a string of critical post-war flops (several of which had also failed at the box office) Coward was distinctly nervy during the run-up to *Waiting in the Wings*; he had a hectoring streak and there was a good deal of shouting and banging of tables by the tetchy playwright. Coward had tried hard in the 1950s to promote his protégé–lover Graham Payn as a star in London and New York with no success (Payn had only a supporting role in *Waiting in the Wings*), while now here was Michael in turn giving his new flame a boost in the professional arena, another factor underlying the tensions between Coward and his management on the production. However, the friction seemed to have abated by the time of the play's London opening, coinciding with the Redgraves' Silver Wedding anniversary; at a crowded Hans Crescent party which Coward attended his gift was in a prominent place – a silver-framed photograph of him in profile, gazing at a bust of himself and signed (in case of any confusion) 'Noël Coward'.

Fred was effectively in charge of the pre-London try-out while Michael continued in *The Tiger and the Horse* (Coward's play opened in Dublin, which Michael had to miss) and despite Coward's initial reservations he was popular with the large cast, mostly of veteran actresses, and became adept at smoothing over the not infrequent backstage rivalries. The critics panned *Waiting in the Wings* but, with a strong cast headed by Sybil Thorndike and Marie Lohr, it managed to run for over six months and just made it into the black. Together with stakes in *The Aspern Papers* and *The Tiger and the Horse* it had been by no means a discreditable start for Fred and the company. Although he had no acting work permit Fred could still direct as well as produce but FES had less success with his work on *My Friend Judas*, a shrewd adaptation by Andrew Sinclair of his much-praised novel of Cambridge life during May Week. Sinclair had given Fred considerable help in absorbing the background to the play (and was persuaded to invest in it) but he and a strong cast led by Dinsdale Landen as the rebel undergraduate Ben Birt were left stranded by Fred's direction, generally criticised as messy, with no sense of a Cambridge atmosphere. Its Arts Theatre run lost a considerable sum. And the company's ill-considered involvement with a New York friend of Fred's, Robert Lavin, on a shambolically produced musical, *The Dancing Heiress*, developed into a tangle of feuds and threatened litigation. Its foreshortened Lyric, Hammersmith run involved Michael having to dip into his own pocket to settle the bills. It seemed worryingly clear that Fred's impetuousness could still run away with him.

The team did well with *The Importance of Being Oscar*, Micheál Mac-Liammóir's solo Oscar Wilde evening, directed by Hilton Edwards, his partner in life and at Dublin's Gate Theatre (Dublin knew them, with immense affection, as 'The Boys' or 'Sodom and Begorrah'). This one was Michael's idea; after reading a *Times* review of the show's Dublin opening, he at once flew with Fred to catch it for London. He had always been fascinated by MacLiammóir since their 1947 Glasgow meeting (and Rachel had loved working with him on *Hedda Gabler*). A genuine spell-binder, MacLiammóir – originally Alfred Wilmore from Kensal Rise – had arrived in Ireland at twenty-eight when he fell in love with Edwards and all the seductiveness of the Celtic Twilight, staying on to reinvent himself and to reject England. With his Black Velvet voice and outsize personality – until old age he wore a jet-black toupée and full theatrical make-up all day – he delighted Michael with his stories of Orson Welles (another self-mythist, who had a volatile relationship with MacLiammóir) and with his conversation, even when he moaned about his audiences on Broadway when Michael and Fred co-presented *Oscar*, swearing that when he languorously recited Wilde's hymns to youths called Jonquil, Hyacinth or Narcissus they thought he was going through the Woolworth's spring-bulb catalogue.

After *The Tiger and the Horse* Michael's own plans took him back to Broadway. He aimed for third time lucky with Graham Greene, this time playing Victor Rhodes, the cuckolded suburban dentist created by Ralph Richardson in London in Greene's *The Complaisant Lover*, an acidulous comedy with a central episode of adultery surprised in an Amsterdam hotel out of Feydeau. Michael was unsure of the play's Broadway chances but he was under pressure from Glen (directing) and Cecil as well as from its producer, the daunting Irene Mayer Selznick.

She was the daughter of one Hollywood mogul and ex-wife of another, and her post-divorce Broadway life had produced hits including *A Streetcar Named Desire* and *The Chalk Garden* (on which she sacked George Cukor as director and even intimidated the usually imperious Enid Bagnold). A classic control freak, she noticed out of town that Michael had become friendly with Anne Kaufman Schneider, the daughter of George S. Kaufman and wife of Selznick's patient production manager Irving Schneider. Anne was bright, funny and well read, and Michael enjoyed morning walks on Boston Common talking with her, but she was ordered back to New York by Selznick, who did not want her star 'distracted'.

It was not an easy time. Fred accompanied Michael; billed again as 'Assistant', his main job was to make sure Michael stayed off the drink after rehearsals and learnt his lines ('He did not,' remembered Googie Withers who played the adulterous wife, 'notably succeed'). Richard Johnson as the lover was sacked and then reinstated, while Googie Withers became Selznick's whipping girl when, with that uncanny ability of some producers to focus on the wrong problem, she decided that Googie's figure was all wrong and made her for a time wear a rubber bodysuit. After that it was her make-up that was wrong. She was more wary of Michael; after two weeks of rehearsal, as she sat glowering and chain-smoking, terrifying an already nervous Glen into near panic, Michael advanced one day – 'to a silent cheer from the company' according to Googie – to say: 'Mrs Selznick, will you please leave this rehearsal and at once. I cannot and will not have you sitting there blowing smoke at us. You are a distraction. And a bad one.'

They opened extremely shakily in New Haven with Michael all over the place on his lines, but by Boston he had pulled himself together. The senior Boston critic Eliot Norton reviewed it lukewarmly on the opening but, most unusually, returned before the end of the run there and completely revised his opinion, based on the galvanic change in Michael's performance, which he noted had now grown so that all of Victor's embarrassing practical jokes with whoopee cushions and trick glasses at north London dinner parties at the start and the farce of the second act led to a deeply affecting end – 'he had achieved a small masterpiece,' wrote Norton.

The play had only a moderate run at the Ethel Barrymore Theater in New York. Michael's talk about it in pre-opening interviews had raised some eyebrows, as he stressed that he saw it as a play about love rather than adultery: 'But adultery is irrelevant in love. If people would realise that marriage isn't always perfect sexually after a while, we wouldn't all be such hypocrites. We all have some private suffering torturing us.' Most of the notices, however, concentrated on the high-jinks in the second act, with an hilarious early performance from Gene Wilder – just out of the Actors' Studio – as a bemused but ineffably polite hotel valet. Michael was very different from Ralph Richardson, with a more melancholy edge, but he managed to make Victor, the British Babbitt, clumsily endearing and was superb in another of his piercing moments of self-discovery when

Victor finally comprehends his cuckolding ('His face looks as deserted as a broken window' was one critic's description). Googie Withers thought that as he had a sort of deep genuine shyness in life 'that came out in a real, embarrassed way', so on stage 'He was wonderful at moments of real, desperate unhappiness. Right through his career there were always moments in a play, often of embarrassment or self-reproach, when you saw something so moving.'

Broadway in the early 1960s was also less than the ideal climate for *The Aspern Papers*, which went through convoluted management and casting muddles before it crossed the Atlantic. It had been successful throughout Europe, with the Rome production memorable for the Juliana of the great Emma Grammatica, well into her eighties, who had acted with Duse. Michael managed to see the Paris production – at one point, tantalisingly, Pierre Fresnay seemed likely for H. J. – directed by Raymond Rouleau (who played H. J., finally), described by Michael as 'one of those rare, unforgettable theatrical experiences'. The mouldering palazzo setting for Paris, designed by the reclusive genius Lila de Nobili, he thought one of the best he had ever seen and he tried, vainly, to persuade the Broadway producers to use it. The New York production, directed by Margaret Webster with Michael, still playing Victor, helping when he could, never gelled. Michael's old wartime friend, Françoise Rosay, was unable to disguise her natural forcefulness, while the H. J. of Maurice Evans was a strangely neuter, over-elocuted performance with nothing to suggest that Miss Tina (Wendy Hiller, truthfully touching) could be attracted to him. In a British-dominated Broadway season *The Aspern Papers* had a struggle to survive and it too managed only a disappointing run.

Michael had not had the happiest experience on Broadway that time, although nothing could ever make him tire of New York. But he could not disguise to his American friends his joy to be returning to the kind of theatre he understood best. While playing in *The Complaisant Lover*, he received a telegram from Olivier, asking him to consider joining the company for the first season of the Chichester Festival Theatre under his direction to play Uncle Vanya with Olivier as Astrov, Joan Plowright (now Olivier's wife) as Sonya and Sybil Thorndike as the Nurse. Michael did not need to consider; he called Cecil at once telling him to accept, not even asking about money (he assumed – rightly – it would be minimal) or billing. Olivier cabled back: 'Dear Mike. Overjoyed hear lovely news from Cecil. Looking forward to it madly and so dearly grateful for your thrilling co-operation. Love Larry.' Rachel was less bowled over. She never totally trusted Olivier (who had given her an icy reception when, well-meaning if ill-advisedly, she had at Vivien Leigh's request tried to mediate between her friend and Olivier as their marriage fell apart) but for Michael the omens – the combination of the new theatre and his old, often thwarted ambition to play Vanya, a part he had virtually re-signed himself to forgetting – seemed among the most auspicious of his entire career.

Seventeen
SHOCKS OF THE NEW

His absences in New York and on movie locations left Michael feeling somewhat isolated from the family. Rachel and he wrote often. Her letters, now that the children all were busy, were always crammed with news updating him on all their activities. He was desperately sorry to miss Vanessa's historic Rosalind at Stratford – 'her romantic springtime' Rachel called it – which catapulted her into the top flight of younger English actresses. Her increasing political involvement continued; she was now on the Committee of 100, and was arrested for disturbing the peace at a demonstration and had been imprisoned overnight (Tony Oliver, always a loyal friend, waited with a car to collect her on her release in the morning). It was not so much the political confrontations that concerned Michael as the effects on her voice of such regular speeches at meetings and rallies. Rachel was usually able to soothe his anxieties, despite her own complaints that Hans Crescent had 'become a sort of Committee headquarters', writing after a much publicised Trafalgar Square CND meeting, 'You would have been very proud of our lovely Vanessa. Her voice rang out as she read the speech from Sir Herbert Read.'

All during his absences she had kept him informed as much as she could about Corin's final Cambridge terms. Corin had been something of a shooting star even in a glorious era of undergraduate theatre – Ian McKellen, Clive Swift, Derek Jacobi were contemporaries – with Dadie Rylands still monitoring young talent. Busy as he had been as student actor and director while at King's, he still achieved a remarkable First and was now working as an assistant at the Royal Court where Tony Richardson, George Devine's associate at the English Stage Company, had cast him as Lysander in *A Midsummer Night's Dream* to launch his professional acting career.

Richardson had also offered Lynn the chance of Helena although she would have to leave the Central School early to accept. She called Michael on the muffled transatlantic line available then to find him not wholly in favour, feeling she should complete her training (possibly his opinion was coloured by his less than committed enthusiasm for Richardson as a stage director), but she went ahead and took the part. Michael's relationship with Lynn had never been as easy as those with Vanessa and Corin. Undoubtedly stemming from his absences in Hollywood and on British locations in her early years, her shyness with her father – and his with her – had continued into teenage years. Corin, intriguingly, once speculated: 'My father, who never liked to enter a race unless he had decided to win it, seemed to give up the challenge of winning her affection.' More recently Michael, deservedly, had been in deep domestic disgrace. When he attended Lynn's school play in 1959 she was playing Theseus in *A Midsummer Night's Dream* and was of course most anxious to impress Michael but she saw on looking through a hole in the curtain that after her first scene he had left. Michael probably argued that Theseus does not appear again until close to the end of the play and may have thought he had seen all he needed, but it was extremely ill-judged behaviour and he really could offer little protest against the near Coventry to which he was consigned for a period. Yet he never reproached Lynn for ignoring his advice, taking comfort from Rachel's opinion, based on watching Lynn at Central: 'I think we have got another tip-top actress in her.'

Rachel had her own worries at the time. Apart from having eight performances a week in a dull part in a poor play about St Teresa of Avila with Sybil Thorndike, her mother – a woman who at times derived happiness by draining it from others – was ill and demanding, while she also had great anxiety over Glen. She had learnt – Angela Baddeley telephoned her – that Glen had had a heart attack ('You will guess my unhappiness – it strikes at my heart, Mikey darling') but she had to respect Angela's insistence on no visits or letters until he had recovered. He was slow to improve, but by the time Michael was about to return to England in the spring of 1962 he had been able to spend some time at Wilks Water with Rachel. They and John Fowler had enjoyed walking in the woods or sipping hot rum beside bonfires next to the lake and they could also spend time with George Devine, now living with Jocelyn Herbert at a cottage ('Andrews') near by.

Some of their friends – aware of the quadrilateral arrangement and with the children all now on their way – wondered why Michael and Rachel stayed married. That was to overlook their interdependence; each was the fixed point, the lodestar, in the other's life and despite the fading of the sexual bond the stronger tie of love remained. Rachel touched on this in her first letter after Michael had left for America: 'I was truly dreadfully sad at parting and I felt as if it was the end of something so magic, and as if you and I reached a new unspoken peace and understanding. The lover relationship is always difficult, God knows.'

Rachel was as happy as Michael that *Uncle Vanya* would be his first stage appearance on his return; she had feared he might feel he had to accept the far better financial West End offer from Binkie of N. C. Hunter's new play *The Tulip Tree* opposite Celia Johnson (in which Lynn made her West End debut). Like Michael, she was convinced that the new venture of Chichester was more exciting, despite her wariness of Olivier.

With Chichester salaries so low, Michael had to take on a busy workload before rehearsals for *Vanya*. He also knew – although he had to keep it secret from all but Rachel in the meantime – that he would before too long have another low-income period. He had been approached by Alderman A. W. Graham Brown, chairman of the Guildford Theatre Trust, to be director of a festival to inaugurate a new Guildford theatre, planned to open in 1964, and he had accepted. As well as his own past Guildford ties from Cranleigh days, there was another connection: Rachel's brother Nicholas, now retired from the Navy and living near Guildford, was the theatre's appeals organiser. New theatres were close to Michael's heart and the prospect of being involved with two potentially exciting ventures was irresistible.

In the meantime he landed a much needed lucrative job when he joined the cast of a television version of *Hedda Gabler* with Ingrid Bergman, somewhat unlikely casting but a major star still, Ralph Richardson as Judge Brack, Trevor Howard as Lovborg and Michael as Tesman, Hedda's husband. The cash was from America through David Susskind's company, with CBS backing and the BBC providing production facilities. Rehearsing in the unglamorous surroundings of the Drill Hall in the Brompton Road, it was not the most searching production; Ingrid Bergman, still ravishing, was serenely tender throughout, a heroine on the rack, not entirely what Ibsen had in mind, and utterly without Hedda's gallows humour. Michael, like everyone else on the production, was captivated by her, although he was aware that she was miscast. The original aspect of the venture was the casting of Richardson, for once asked to be incisive and rapier-sharp, and of Michael playing the fussy, pedantic bumbler, whereas a less imaginative casting director might simply have cast it to type, the other way round.

Although it was a low-budget film, Michael accepted the chance to be in the film of Alan Sillitoe's *The Loneliness of the Long-Distance Runner* at once. He was a Sillitoe fan, first alerted to his work by Dick Green, of whom in turn Sillitoe was an admirer (he wrote a sympathetic introduction to Dick's reissued novel, *Land Without Heroes*). The director was Tony Richardson, who impressed Michael when they met to discuss the film, stressing that he did not want Michael's Borstal Governor played as a Blimp and that there would be no dilution of the book's chilly rage. Michael, moreover, sensed a new mood in British cinema and indeed, with *This Sporting Life*, *A Kind of Loving*, *A Taste of Honey*, *Saturday Night and Sunday Morning* and *The Loneliness of the Long-Distance Runner*, a brief New Cinema golden age was under way.

Some of Richardson's film has dated – the larky *nouvelle-vague*-ish speeded-up sequences and an ending which alters Sillitoe (in which Colin Smith is anti-authority throughout), to make Colin opt for his calculated defiance at the last minute with his climactic running showily and modishly intercut with flashbacks. But Walter Lassally's grainy black-and-white photography remains superb and it is one of the best-acted British films of its era, down to the tiniest role (including James Fox's movie debut as a well-intentioned public schoolboy). Michael was most impressed by Tom Courtenay's fiercely unsentimental Colin, his hard, watchful eyes and flat voice giving no quarter. He played Colin from the character's point of view, which was also Michael's approach to the Governor. He put on a little weight for the part – catching the heaviness of a man in a sedentary job, a ruthless haircut allowing an incipient roll of fat above the back of his collar to be glimpsed. But while the obvious route would have been to play for easy laughs as a cliché authority figure, Michael and Richardson respected the character enough to create a genuinely well-intentioned man, progressive according to his lights, only slightly absurd – there is a lovely shot of the Governor looking at the runners prior to the final race through binoculars as if inspecting bloodstock at a horse race – and baffled by the decision of the young anarch who will not play by the rules.

There was little time to enjoy Wilks Water in its summer bloom. Michael had to spend time in London planning a new West End play, *Out of Bounds*, for his old friend Henry Sherek who would produce it after *Vanya* in partnership with Fred and Michael. Fred's lease on his studio had expired and he now moved to a flat in Rutland Street (Michael nicknamed it 'Rutstrasse'), although he spent a good deal of each day and evening at Hans Crescent. Nanny Randall had finally retired; Rachel had taken considerable trouble in helping her to find a cottage (she named it Hans Cottage) in the small town of Dereham in Norfolk, with Michael paying for the installation of a new bathroom. Nanny Randall had never particularly cared for Fred, much preferring Bob, from whom Michael had recently had the news of a second child, a boy to be called Michael: 'Were you pleased I named my son after you? I had to have a M. around to always remind me of you.'

Before Chichester, Michael suddenly found himself busier on television than he had ever been in his entire career, with a newspaper headline claiming that over a brief period in one week he had 'pulled in' 80 million viewers. These appearances included a turn as Mystery Guest on *What's My Line?* on which he bamboozled the panel by singing all his answers, and he also became a quasi-regular on the most original programme of early 1960s television, *That Was the Week that Was*. Most memorable of his contributions to *TW3* was perhaps Caryl Brahms's wry and touching elegy on the melting down of Madame Tussaud's figures, celebrities such as Marilyn Monroe making way for more sensational Chamber of Horrors exhibits like James Hanratty.

He was able to stay in London for the early *Uncle Vanya* rehearsals, which began encouragingly, despite the pressure on the production, the last of the opening season's three. The Chichester experiment had begun disappointingly. The theatre itself, a hexagonal building of glass, concrete and steel partly cantilevered over the foyer area ('The Mushroom' detractors called it), had been the brainchild of a local solicitor, Leslie Evershed-Martin, inspired by the example of Stratford, Ontario under Guthrie, and it had also been his idea to invite Olivier to be its first director. The building, sited splendidly in oak-studded parkland, had been widely welcomed, but Olivier's first two productions, John Fletcher's forgotten Jacobean comedy *The Chances* and John Ford's *The Broken Heart*, had been poorly received, with Tynan implying that the hexagon might be hexed.

In an unprecedented public scolding just before *Vanya* opened, reviewing Chichester to date in the form of an Open Letter to Olivier in his *Observer* column, Tynan took his idol to task not only for a poor performance in *The Broken Heart* but also for two below-par productions. He added a strong urging that Olivier should take on co-directors or advisers. More than a few saw this as Tynan's public application for a job under Olivier at a National Theatre, now rumoured behind the scenes to be soon in the offing with Olivier as the first director. If so, his strategy worked; in part because of Joan Plowright's advocacy of Tynan as a potentially non-Establishment participant in the institution of a National Theatre, his appointment as the National's literary manager (he wanted the title of dramaturg) was announced soon after Olivier's appointment was made public later that year. Tynan's *Observer* piece inevitably heightened the pressure on *Uncle Vanya*; the box office may have sold out in advance of the opening but should the third production of the season fail critically, the whole Chichester enterprise could be threatened.

Uncle Vanya was cast in depth; neither of Olivier's top choices for Yelena – Margaret Leighton and Claire Bloom – had worked out and he settled for Joan Greenwood ('Well, well, we'll just have to pray, that's all,' he wrote to Michael), but with even minor parts such as Maman, the Nurse and Waffles taken by Fay Compton, Sybil Thorndike and Lewis Casson, Olivier had confidence that he was off to a good start. He anticipated quibbles about the design; given the English love of Chekhov as ersatz country-house drama, Sean Kenny's spartan set of stripped wood and basic furniture without a silver birch in sight would inevitably upset traditionalists.

Olivier in rehearsal gave little sign of the stress he was under. He had prepared impeccably; his working script is a mass of planned stage patterns and moves, alert to the open stage's demands, orchestrating complex key scenes such as Vanya's attempted shooting of the professor with military precision. Michael felt relaxed and free, with no qualms about the open stage, so clearly was Olivier taking its requirements into consideration in his staging. He had decided to avoid wiggery and false hair; he grew his own beard and simply let his hair become longer than usual (he also washed it before each performance to give it the floppy look he wanted). Olivier fully supported him: 'The least wigging and make-up the better I think for this theatre – the furthest seat is only about a cricket-pitch away.' In rehearsal Michael's only slight worry was Joan Greenwood's performance – her mannered drawl made her delivery rather slow – which seemed to him out of kilter with the rest of the performances, especially Joan Plowright's Sonya, button-eyed, doggedly loyal and loving and utterly truthful, for which he had boundless admiration.

Moving down to Sussex as the mid-July opening approached, Michael rented a house in South Pallant close by. Named Cawley Priory, it sounded grand but in fact it was on what Michael described as the 'twee' side, always referring to it by Dick Green's nickname of 'Teapot Towers'. Final stage rehearsals confirmed his hopes for the production, and he was only slightly put out after a late rehearsal by Olivier's somewhat bitchy and inaccurate note of 'Loud echoes of Sir John' in his performance. The dress rehearsal developed into a mixture of farce and disaster, with sound effects going so haywire that Waffles's strumming on his guitar emerged from the speakers as barking dogs, but, for once, Michael seemed remarkably unconcerned amid everyone else's anxieties. This was a part he knew he had – in Edith's old phrase – 'in his soulcase'.

The myth has grown up that *Uncle Vanya*, unquestionably one of the finest achievements of post-war British theatre, was an immediately unqualified triumph. At the box office it certainly was, but although most critics had little but praise for the acting (Joan Greenwood, as Michael feared, had poor notices, however) many of them voiced their dislike of seeing it on the open stage in rooms without walls, saying it would have worked better behind the proscenium arch ('My idea of heaven is Bayreuth – total darkness, picture glowing' – Philip Hope-Wallace's reactionary view was by no means a lone voice). In fact, the open stage and the democracy of Chichester's auditorium – still relative novelties in the 1960s – gave the production there a palpable emotional groundswell which was never quite recaptured at the same level when it subsequently moved to a proscenium stage. The effect almost of a cinematic close-up possible at Chichester when Vanya, in the wrong place and, characteristically, at the wrong time, brings his flowers for Yelena to find her in Astrov's embrace, Michael's eyes filling with bewildered embarrassment, or the desolation of Sonya's aching attempt to console her uncle at the close – those moments and others at Chichester had a heart-stopping immediacy never quite recaptured.

Although Michael used little make-up and no wig, this was another of his transforming performances; with a kind of unquantifiable alchemy he seemed to make his own body podgy, slightly gone to flab (he used no padding, but reminded costume designer 'Bumble' Dawson of Michel Saint-Denis's old trick of clothes just a fraction too tight), his arms often loose and helplessly dangling as if not quite in phase with the rest of his limbs. In repose he could look comparatively dandyish, but under pressure both voice and body seemed to lose control and an hysterical childishness possessed him. Almost out of left field, when Vanya realises the implications of the Professor's plan to sell the estate – robbing Vanya of any dream of making a new start in life – his voice took off into a strangled falsetto, building to the rush for his revolver and – superbly staged by Olivier – the tragi-comic attempt to shoot the Professor. It was heart-breakingly moving but also often side-splittingly funny. Michael loved the knife-edge danger of this fusion and wrote to reassure those patrons who commiserated with him that there had been so much laughter:

> The pathos and humour and fun of *life* are closely intertwined. Less than a minute after Vanya has been laughing with the doctor he is in tears because Sonya looks at him 'So like your dear mother'. And, as Astrov says of him, he is something of a buffoon. Every single one of them has an element of absurdity in him or her. There is nothing solemn about Chekhov – to act in it has been the greatest joy of my professional life.

How anyone could ever say that this was an actor of head rather than heart is beyond comprehension. Joan Plowright said that everyone involved thought of the production as 'something special', all of them loving the play and also aware that *Vanya* was 'the crunch' after the failure of the opening plays. She had not acted on stage with Michael before; having been struck by his force of concentration on set for Losey, she found in the theatre: 'He had an emotional energy in rehearsal – he never wasted a minute. And in performance – when you're with this man, who is absolutely quivering with emotion, you don't really have to act, you react. He was a giver. He did give so much. His anguish as Vanya was palpable.'

Halfway through that first season Olivier asked Michael to come back for another *Vanya* run the following year and Michael, enjoying one of his happiest summers, accepted at once. He was also genuinely delighted on

Olivier's behalf when Olivier in secrecy told him that the next Chichester season and company would form the nucleus of the National Theatre under Olivier to be based at the Old Vic until the South Bank site was ready. Michael had never ceased campaigning on behalf of a National Theatre. Only recently, replying to Gerald Croasdell, Equity's secretary, who had asked Michael for his opinion of an Equity memorandum to the Arts Council, he had been vociferous in supporting Equity's objection to a characteristically wimpish Arts Council suggestion of starting a National Theatre Company and only then, depending on its effectiveness, to prepare a home for it: 'What it boils down to is that Granville-Barker was right. I think that those of us who have for so long cried out for a National Theatre have become touched with fear similar to that of political prisoners waiting from month to month for news of a possible release.' He was adamantly opposed to the compromise of settling for anything rather than nothing and so the news that the South Bank plans would proceed and the suggestion of his being part of the very first National Theatre Company elated him immeasurably.

To follow the sublime of Vanya with a character called Lancelot Dodd (BA, Cantab.), headmaster of a minor English public school in a West End comedy, was, for some critics, a descent to the ridiculous. *Out of Bounds* was by Arthur Watkyn, forgotten now but in his day an able confectioner of the kind of amusing trifle that had no other aim but to divert a pre-dinner audience, the sort of play at one time described as 'ideal for the tired businessman'. The plot was a sheer frivol; up for a Test match at Lord's with his mackintosh and neatly packed sandwiches, Dodd instead finds himself at MI5 Headquarters. The doppelgänger of a master criminal and spy, he is coaxed into impersonating the enemy in an entrapment scheme in a London hotel where he finds, under the influence of a little alcohol and an attractive Whitehall secretary, an unexpected relish in saving the nation's secrets.

With his owlish spectacles, unruly forelock, concertina'd socks and nervous giggle, like a cross between Will Hay and an elongated Billy Bunter, Michael deftly spun the play into a de luxe comedy zone, genuinely endearing in the way Dodd, suddenly removed from the familiar rituals of dormitory duty, begins to inhabit a different world and persona. Henry Sherek and Michael made sure it was a Rolls-Royce cast; he was reunited with Pauline Jameson (Mrs Prest in *The Aspern Papers*) as the secretary and the hilarious Charles Heslop, still larcenously appropriating scenes in his eighties, was like some spluttering, rampant walrus as a bibulously confused solicitor. Most of the reviews – as Michael anticipated – took him to task for appearing in such froth, but he made no apologies ('Every actor is entitled to an occasional *capriccioso*'), adding that this kind of farcical light comedy – seemingly effortless – was far from easy to play: 'On the contrary it is like playing ping-pong for two hours – standing way back from the table.'

Tom Stoppard, then writing for *Scene* magazine, reviewed *Out of Bounds*, taking his aunt with him to see what the fuss ('as if Richard Dimbleby had turned up on *Juke Box Jury*') was about. He too regretted the lack of good parts in contemporary plays for great actors – although Pinter, Bond, Bennett, Storey and Stoppard himself in *Jumpers* would rectify that before long – but added, keeping it in perspective, how genuinely watchable and 'uplifting' Michael's performance was, a welcome chance to see a new facet of a distinguished actor. He predicted, rightly, a long run ('It is doubtless already heavily booked ahead with other people's aunts'). *Out of Bounds* made for a happy time; Michael was mostly relaxed amongst a strong company and now was also chivvied by a remarkable new dresser. Christopher Downes, half-Irish, burly, cheerful and funny came to him after a varied previous career which had included stints as a bookshop manager for the then-fledgling tycoon Robert Maxwell, as a gents' out-fitter and, not entirely gloriously, briefly as a jazz singer in a Swedish nightclub. The ideal mixture of organised nanny and simpatico sounding-board for Michael's occasional Macreadyish frets and fusses, Downes had also a passion for Milton's verse, a useful bonus at a time when Michael was contemplating a revival of *Samson Agonistes* for his Guildford project; the atmosphere at Wyndham's Theatre during the run of Watkyn's trifle was contrastedly enlivened by the backstage booming of chunks of *Paradise* both *Lost* and *Regained* by Michael and Downes in Miltonic harmony. Sherek tried hard to persuade Michael to stay in a money-making hit instead of returning to Chichester to repeat a performance. Michael promised his old friend 'to do everything in his power, short of committing bankruptcy, to keep us all happy' and did stay with it for longer than his contracted stint, but he told Sherek,

> I know it is quixotic of me to have made this promise to Larry, but every now and then comes along THE PART for This or That Actor. I am sure too that you will understand there is the sheer joy – the all too seldom sheer joy – of doing something that you think you can do, shall we say, better than anybody. That is rare you know. And I am not being conceited. I know exactly what I mean.

Michael never really believed that a performance could be 'definitive' but his Vanya has remained, for many who saw it, unmatched. There have been several splendid subsequent Vanyas – Nicol Williamson and Simon Russell Beale included – who have come close to Michael's achievement, without ever quite surpassing it.

But before leaving *Out of Bounds* to return to Chichester, letting 'Teapot Towers' once again, Michael had to hold Fred's hand while he launched a new London venture. Collaborating again with American friends, Fred had put together an evening of short Eugene O'Neill plays using a linking commentary by Ted Allan Lewis, with Nan Martin as the solo performer in *Before Breakfast* and Burgess Meredith in *Hughie*. It was a laudable undertaking although more suited perhaps to a Fringe theatre than the Shaftesbury Avenue spotlight and it predictably flopped at the Duchess. It was not an easy production, with Burgess Meredith drinking and Fred again not entirely in control, leading to an atmosphere troubled enough for Ted Allan Lewis to voice his concerns about Fred to Michael:

> Allowing his greed to think for him, Fred is thinking in terms of the West End so that success will bring him to Broadway. He should be thinking in terms of the Arts or Royal Court so that success will bring him recognition in his new country. This is *not* basically a West End property. My real problem with Fred is his lack of conviction in his own opinions and his own taste. . . . One longs for greater strength.

Peter Eyre, then just beginning his acting career, who had met Lewis in Paris, had the unenviable job of trying to keep a hard-drinking Burgess Meredith to the task of learning his lines for *Hughie*, and he came to know Fred well in the 1960s. Like many others he responded to Fred's 'zippy American energy' but he also came to notice 'a slightly sinister trait' in him. Fred liked to manipulate people, arranging and 'fixing', doing deals both professional and private, including nudging Eyre closer to Lynn; they went out together for nearly two years and during that time Eyre increasingly realised Fred's interest in power.

Michael's life had become progressively compartmentalised, with his Rockwells existence (of which Rachel never and Fred only rarely was a part) and the established metropolitan network of a few trusted gay friends or couples such as Tony Oliver and Peter Sutton, Max and Laurier Lister and the writer Paul Dehn and his partner, the composer James Bernard co-existing with the conventional Knightsbridge and country-retreat worlds of a knighted actor. Peter Eyre could at times be 'confused, even embarrassed' by the contrasts; with Fred in Rutland Street the atmosphere was confidential, gossipy, mischievous while when at Hans Crescent or at Wilks Water his persona was altogether more discreetly deferential. There the outward appearances were correct, so much so that it was some time before the children came to comprehend the real nature of Michael's friendship and partnership with Fred. Corin has said that he intuited his father's bisexuality as a teenager, while Vanessa was over twenty before she too came to understand it; there was a good deal of knowing whispering behind fans in the gossipy world of the 1960 West End when Vanessa appeared in a play (*Look on Tempests*) as a young wife unaware of her husband's clandestine homosexual life, still then herself unaware of Michael's secret. Eyre saw also that Lynn did not know; it was only after she had left home and married that she fully grasped the extent of Fred's role in Michael's life. Peter Eyre was fascinated by the family: 'One thing about the Redgraves – there's a sort of purity about the way they see the world. It's like a true aristocracy.' To a degree the household's mixture of innocence and worldliness stemmed from the way the children had been brought up to have an intellectual as well as artistic view of the theatre, in addition to the secrecy of some subjects.

In all of this, Fred was much exercised by the opinions of others; he was always asking Eyre what the children thought about him ('it was a way of getting a hold over the family'). The whole complex set-up seemed at times very unusual in atmosphere to Peter Eyre: 'I remember thinking that if I was a fiction-writer I could write something extraordinary, some-thing almost out of Henry James – I knew all these things about these people that not all of them knew themselves.'

There were a few cast changes for the 1963 *Uncle Vanya* revival, with Olivier using some talent later to be part of the National Theatre Company. Rosemary Harris replaced Joan Greenwood and, to Michael's great pleasure, Max Adrian was cast as the old Professor. Derek Jacobi played smallish roles that season and understudied Michael as Vanya; Olivier was insistent that understudies, who were rehearsed regularly, repeat the principals' performances to the letter, and naturally a keen Jacobi also watched the performance often, noticing that although super-ficially Michael's performances varied little in the essentials from night to night, 'He made it look totally of the moment. I thought it would be easy to reproduce but it wasn't at all, it looked so utterly spontaneous. A great lesson for me to learn.'

The revival of *Vanya* had sold out in advance and was even better with its cast changes. Michael's performance, reacting to the quality of Rosemary Harris to some extent, slightly heightened the element of the arrested adolescent – it informed the turn from innate gentleness to sexual frustration and envy with more edge – the desperate laughter which overcame him at times (laughter on stage is normally never easy to sustain) seeming even more natural and unforced. Harold Hobson paid the company the ultimate compliment of comparing the ensemble work with that of Edwige Feuillère, Jean-Louis Barrault, Pierre Brasseur and Jean Desailly in Claudel's *Partage du Midi*, for him the yardstick of great acting. Michael was never quite sure who was meant to compare with whom.

The audience reaction to *Vanya* nightly seemed to reflect Edward

Thompson's feelings as expressed to Michael: 'God, how everyone adores a great play, played greatly!' If possible, the acting was praised even more in that second season, with some splendid descriptions of individual performances. *The Times* was especially vivid on Michael's Vanya:

> ... a tousle-haired delayed adolescent who has awoken in middle age to the fact that life has passed him by, undergoing the most spectacular development. It is a portrait of a gentle nature devoured with spleen and sexual frustration, and the collision between violence and tenderness is both pitiful and explosively funny. His body is at odds with itself; menacing speeches and threatening advances being suddenly cancelled out in aimlessly flapping hand gestures and swoopingly deflated vocal inflections.

Michael was most pleased, however, by Bernard Levin, who wrote: 'Sir Michael dominates the evening without – it is his greatest achievement – ever unbalancing it'.

Friends unable to find tickets the previous year descended on Chichester in hordes; even Dick Green who loved the theatre but hated audiences ('I am a positive Ludwig') came with Roy King, in his new toy of a vintage Jaguar with red leather upholstery ('it's the wonder of East Somerset') to see the play as well as Michael. Enid Bagnold, with whom Michael occasionally stayed at Rottingdean at weekends, Iris Tree and Diana Cooper, Wynyard Browne, David Loveday and Dennis Robertson all visited, as did the Menuhins for whom Michael had performed at their Bath Festival with his Andersen readings. There were cheers all round when it was announced that this already historic *Vanya*, along with that season's *Saint Joan* with Joan Plowright, would form part of the opening season of the National at the old Vic. For many, the end of that second Chichester season, the *Vanya* curtain-call with Michael and Olivier together, clasping each other's hand and beaming at the centre of an astonishing line-up through a prolonged ovation, was never to be forgotten. It seemed to be a promise of further individual and company triumphs to come at the Waterloo Road.

In typical British fashion, having been delayed by endless setbacks and Whitehall bureaucracy for decades, suddenly everything to do with the National Theatre had to happen in a rush when it was decided that the Old Vic company would finish at the theatre, vacating it for the new National company, in the autumn of 1963. The hectic pace was both exhilarating and daunting. Working out of old Portakabins in nearby Aquinas Street in Waterloo with rats scurrying under the floorboards, Olivier and his team had to put plans into motion quickly, working against the clock to have the major adjustments to stage and auditorium finished in time. Olivier chose to open predictably with *Hamlet* (the Eternity version) and although he had trumpeted the intended ensemble ethic of the company, he cast Peter O'Toole, then at the height of his film fame, to play Hamlet only, leaving the company after a relatively brief period in the repertoire.

That surprised Michael too. He had been so overjoyed at the thought of being part of a venture for which he had campaigned so long that he had agreed, unwisely in light of events and ignoring Rachel's qualms that he was overburdened, to play 'as cast'. Cecil would never have advised that (Michael's workload during that season effectively prohibited outside work and Old Vic salaries were not lavish) but Cecil had recently ceased to be Michael's agent. Caught up in the American anti-trust laws, MCA had to drop its agency activities in order to continue as a production company, and in England Cecil had helped open a new agency, London Artists, taking many of his old clients with him. Michael used the opportunity to leave Cecil, which he had never quite plucked up the courage to do previously; Cecil's commanding, assured personality was one of which Michael stood always in some awe.

He chose to join the long-established Christopher Mann firm – other clients included his friends Carol Reed, Sybil Thorndike and Anton Walbrook – where his affairs were looked after by Aubrey Blackburn. Another 'gentleman-agent' and a shrewd ex-casting director in films, Blackburn was neat, impeccably groomed with slicked-back hair and Savile Row's most discreet tailoring to mask a tendency to portliness, with considerable and lethal charm (he was one of the very few agents to battle Binkie and sometimes win). Michael, however, had committed himself to Claudius in *Hamlet*, Vanya, Henry Horatio Hobson in *Hobson's Choice* and Solness in Ibsen's *The Master Builder* in Emlyn Williams' new version. When asked why he had taken on Claudius and Hobson he would reply that in a company – just as at Liverpool under Willie Armstrong – occasionally an actor had to take on parts for which there might be no better-suited actor available. In the case of Hobson, distinctly unexpected casting, it was Olivier who had answered Michael's own questioning of his casting with the argument that he was the company's best character actor, also reminding him of his success with a north country accent in *Uncle Harry*.

Stories by the dozen have accreted round the first National Theatre season, which in the event was far from the happy time of which Michael had dreamt. Many of them focus on Olivier's fear of his star being dimmed by competition – they point out that he never cast himself in parts like Hobson and that he never appeared with Gielgud, Richardson, Guinness or Scofield on the National stage (and only in *Vanya* with Michael) – and they also stress his jealousy of other actors, even suggesting that he deliberately miscast Michael.

Of Olivier's level of jealousy there is ample evidence – more than Michael noted the edgy glint in Olivier's eye when, after Michael and Joan Plowright had won *Evening Standard* Awards for *Vanya*, he insisted on their presentations being backstage rather than at the formal Awards lunch, saying apparently jokingly, 'I don't really approve of these Awards. Unless I'm getting one' – and alongside a capacity for kindness, there are also many recorded instances of his less than gracious reaction to individual acclaimed performances by others at the National, although the charge of a Machiavellian plot to damage Michael's career is hard to believe. But by the end of the season, baffled and annoyed by Michael's unhappiness (which not only Olivier ascribed partly to alcohol), he was certainly capable of behaving with extraordinary lack of grace. Yet the notion of Michael's entire season at the National (*Vanya* excepted) being disastrous does not hold water either.

Hamlet was certainly a major disappointment as an opening production. Having opted for the play, Olivier seemed without any ideas to bring to it, although a woolly programme note touched on Angry Young Men as well as his old Oedipus complex notions from 1937. O'Toole resembled a clone of Olivier from the film version – winsomely blond with Little Lord Fauntleroy collar – but he was out of condition vocally, with no resources left by the end of each soliloquy. Nobody was helped by the set, one of the rare poor designs from Sean Kenny: a monolith of thrusting stone curving up to a sharp vertical rock tower which could serve as throne or bedhead depending on the sloping ramp's position on a revolve. It was a nightmare to rehearse on, not aided by the rubble in the auditorium and wind howling through holes in the stage wall during refurbishments (Max Adrian, playing Polonius, picking his way through the chaos, snarled at his fellow Irishman Kenny, 'I suppose this is your revenge on the English'). The set's weight caused it to jam regularly (the cast christened the revolve 'The Revolt'), a standby procedure being devised for an emergency with supporting players pushing it into place. Derek Jacobi had to appear with Michael on top of the ramp as it swung round at one point; early in the run, it stuck and all the court lords and ladies got off to push it round, which they had not quite succeeded in doing before the music covering the change ran out. At which point the voice of an enterprising Court Lady, keenly ad libbing to cover, was heard clearly to say, 'I thought Hamlet looked a bit down at the wedding,' causing even more wobbling on the ramp from a giggling Michael, Jacobi and assorted court.

Michael violently detested the set. His first entrance with Diana Wyn-yard's Gertrude asked them to descend the steep ramp, come through an arch and then move to their thrones. Kenny had designed an arch only six feet high and Michael, saddled with a large crown as part of the first of several elaborate costumes, was easily several inches taller, making him have to duck through, hardly a commanding start, by which time all attack had deserted him. He and Diana had looked forward greatly to the venture – they had written to each other and met to talk about the play and Granville-Barker's ideas of Claudius and Gertrude (they wanted to stress the sexual charge between them) – but Olivier, with constant demands on his attention and having to spend more time on O'Toole than he perhaps had bargained for, gave them very little guidance.

After a glamorous first night with celebrities from Princess Margaret to Shirley Bassey out front, the notices were at best polite, with Michael's performance, in a production without much of a Prince, dominating in the acting stakes, many appreciating an unusual Claudius, no villainous voluptuary but a beefily ruddy, genially shallow opportunist, oozing surface charm and sex appeal but revealing towards the close both a conscience and unexpected bravery. The grab-all politician in Claudius, affable enough to cover his tracks, was only too recognisable and the performance had much illuminating detail: 'His elegant naturalism (he has a splendid frivolous giggle after dismissing the Fortinbras problem – 'So much for him!') is skintight to character.'

It had been a disappointing start for the Company and Michael had been surprised by the lack of imagination in *Hamlet*; he had also been rather hurt by Olivier's note to him in front of the company after a dress rehearsal: 'When you came on as Macbeth it was if you said "Fuck you, I am Macbeth!". When you come on as Claudius you are dim!' Nevertheless he had been impressed by the strength and enthusiasm of a company which had taken on younger talent such as Jacobi, Robert Stephens, Frank Finlay and John Stride, the walk-ons initially including Lynn (who had a difficult first season watching her father's increasing unease) and Michael Gambon. But he never felt entirely at home in this Elsinore, always worried by the set and occasionally, surprisingly to everyone including himself, fluffing his lines, as Jacobi noticed: 'There were several occasions when the lines went but he would carry on, making up – quite brilliantly – blank verse until back on course.'

The return of *Uncle Vanya* as part of the National's repertoire, playing to standing room only at every performance, helped him recover some of his equilibrium and he began *Hobson's Choice* rehearsals under John Dexter with Joan Plowright as Maggie Hobson and Frank Finlay as the turning worm Willy Mossop in good form. He was not natural casting for Harold Brighouse's tinpot domestic tyrant, but a good deal of the character was within his range. Joan Plowright thought he was very good in rehearsal ('He had his own quirky way of doing it') but gradually his confidence drained away. He had never had problems with accent before, but the 'bite', the harder grain of Salford, was tricky for the timbre of his voice and this became a major worry (although often an actor's worry about an accent or vocal problem is indicative of an underlying acting problem). Again he found lines difficult to retain – during a late run-through the waspish Dexter was heard to sigh, 'Only another 364 dries to curtain-down' – most probably because the part asked from him one quality not in his armoury, coarseness. In the great second-act scene when Hobson condescends to visit the newly-wed Maggie and Willy, moving from tipsy confusion to cursing rage like a Northern Lear, he was magnificent ('He knew what he was about in that scene,' Joan Plowright observed) while some of the more routine comedy of the first act, on paper much easier, eluded him.

Despite his private fears he 'got away with' his Salford Bacchus, looking oddly like a bibulous W. G. Grace with his spade beard, with only a few notices even remarking on the inconsistency of his accent. There were continuing troubling signs, however. When the repertoire included *Hamlet* and *Vanya* while he was also rehearsing *Hobson's Choice*, during one matinée of *Vanya* he entered to shoot the Professor and then stopped, looking as Joan Plowright said: 'a bit distraught. He pointed the gun eventually but couldn't say the lines. We all started to ad lib, Max shrieking and so on and we got through. We took it as a blip, due to tiredness.' Michael was used to tough schedules – filming by day, playing in the theatre at night – although it was a long time since he had played in such demanding repertoire. He remembered 'only a great feeling of tiredness' from this period, often catching himself fixedly staring at some object, beginning to wonder if he was ill. Then, on *The Master Builder*, the final production of the opening National season, everything gradually seemed to pile on top of him: 'Once again, the lines would not stick. I had the feeling that the rest of the company were whispering about me. More and more I retreated into myself. I found myself at odds with everything.' Yet he had looked forward to playing the brooding Solness, guilt-haunted by the past with a dread of the future, almost as much as he had anticipated *Vanya*. The director Peter Wood he knew from Batcombe – Wood had recently bought a barn to convert, close to Rockwells – Diana Wynyard was playing his wife, with Max Adrian also in the cast and, playing Hilde Wangel, the voice of the younger generation knocking on Solness's door, was Maggie Smith, an actress he greatly admired.

Wood's production was more ground-breaking than was acknowledged at the time, set in soaring Rudolf Heinrich designs (a huge diagonal shelf bisecting the architect's office, the second-act interior using an enormous bookcase and skewered window) and taking a defiantly non-naturalistic approach to a dramatist usually cocooned in Anglo-Saxon realism. Against this, the obsessive Nordic Prometheus struggling in the coils of private guilt for having sacrificed his wife's happiness to his ambition should have been an ideal part and Wood's approach its ideal frame for Michael.

In rehearsal he could be impressive, especially in the Wagnerian defiance of the great final scene, although some wondered if Maggie Smith's Hilde, Ibsen's younger and conscienceless version of Rebecca West, might not be perhaps too contemporary, too much of the King's Road, opposite Michael. She, like the rest of the cast, was sympathetic to his problems, especially when halfway through the rehearsal period came the dreadful shock of Diana Wynyard's death. In those heady 1960s days all sorts of pills were popped and passed around backstage – 'uppers', 'downers' and appetite suppressants – and Diana, always obsessive about her figure and impressed by Lynn's weight loss, went to the same Harley Street doctor for 'slimming' injections with a strict diet, hardly helpful to someone with an existing kidney condition. She had been in poor health for some time and in fact was suffering from cancer. Her death affected Michael deeply; he looked terrible, gaunt and shaky, at her funeral. Not many grasped the closeness of the long friendship between Michael and Diana; he often spent hours with her at her jewel box of a house near Regent's Park, hung with exquisite pictures, including a Boudin, and each, with a complex private life, had never had many secrets from the other. Michael was grief-stricken: 'I loved her for her beauty, her gaiety and the sense of lightheartedness she un-leashed in me.' Celia Johnson more than capably took over Mrs Solness but the production seemed somehow jinxed from that point, and Michael was struggling to keep a grip on his lines. He was, however, unexpectedly 'per-fectly fluent on the text,' Peter Wood stressed, at a run-through towards the end of the rehearsal-period attended by Olivier who afterwards dis-concerted everyone – not least Michael – by making no comment on pro-duction or performances, remarking only, with some evident surprise, of Solness: 'God, it's a wonderful part!' He had witnessed a display of heroic acting which revealed the richness of a role both challenging and then unfamiliar (*The Master Builder* had had few major London revivals). In this performance and production, actor and director honed in on the play's Wag-nerian dimensions ('He did see himself as Siegfried' Wood said of Michael) and very likely some memories of the spellbinding silver images of Fritz Lang's *Die Nibelungen* with Paul Richter's Siegfried in Heidelberg informed the subterranean 'soulcase' of this Solness. The first of only two previews was a nervy, sticky occasion with recalcitrant sets and Michael in uncon-vincing shape (Olivier had said, tactlessly, following a dress rehearsal with Michael shaky again on his lines that it was too late for him to take over the role) although the second, according to Peter Wood, was 'very good' and moods mostly lifted. Michael remained deeply anxious however, as did

Lynn who had to watch her father throughout a good section of the last act as the maid of the Solness household. He kept going over his lines with a concerned and understanding Christopher Downes (Michael insisted on his employment at the National), still fearful that they would not stick.

The first night, last opening of a rocky season, was an extremely tense evening. Michael never had to take an audible prompt but for the first act in particular was markedly nervous (those in the front rows could see how heavily he was sweating); Maggie Smith helped him out whenever possible, on more than one occasion altering her staging to move downstage of him to feed him a line. Wood, as was his directorial custom, was sitting alone at the end of a row close to the Pass Door on to the stage, watching his production just about get by, with Michael finally showing some of his slow-release power in the final act. The curtain fell to a strong enough reception. Suddenly Wood felt a hand grasp his and he was yanked to his feet from his aisle seat, through the Pass Door and backstage before he had fully registered that it was Olivier, who had watched from the back of the stalls, pulling him in a vice-like grip, dragging him upstage and round the corridor at the back of the Old Vic stage to the star dressing rooms. The actors were still coming off stage, then Michael came past them and into his tiny dressing room, the door held open by Olivier who asked 'with silky politeness' if he and Wood could come in.

Three men were now squeezed into the small space, Olivier never letting go his grip on Wood's hand. Michael, at his dressing-table mirror, finally broke an obviously awkward silence by asking, 'Well, how do you think it went?' Even after forty years the scene remained etched in Wood's memory, as did every syllable of Olivier's reply which began, 'Well, you must know how it went. You certainly don't need to ask us.' In Wood's view 'the masochistic side of Michael was ready to be made mincemeat of'. And Olivier, whom Derek Jacobi is by no means alone in describing as possessing 'a great capacity for cruelty', (to Wood he could 'drill like a dentist' into people's vulnerable spots) held a dangerous pause, Michael just staring at him in his mirror, before he continued, as Wood remembered:

> 'You must know that this evening you made a fool of yourself. You have made a fool of the other actors. You have made a fool of Peter here, and you have made a fool of the young National Theatre. And you have made a fool of me. Next season we will commence the season with this production. I will play Solness. Maggie and Joan will alternate Hilde. I cordially invite you to the first performance.'

Wood, shell-shocked by the evening and the dressing-room scene, had no chance to speak before he was pulled out of the room. He was never able to decide whether or not Olivier had prepared his devastating speech: 'It was *so* Mafioso, a demonstration of the most appalling anger. Under Olivier's lash Michael's genius was rebuked as Antony's was by Caesar.'

Olivier, of course, like others, assumed that Michael's troubles were self-inflicted, that he laid this *via dolorosa* for himself, all because of alcohol, although ironically Michael had cut down during *The Master Builder*. It had been a frustrating and problem-ridden season for Olivier and he possibly felt that Michael would be best served by such shaming, but for one actor to treat another in such a manner, especially at such a vulnerable time, is beyond excuse. The irony too is that, as promised, Olivier did take over Solness during the next season and it was on that production that his 'terrors' began, his own terrible period of stage fright. The supreme technician in Olivier never quite understood – perhaps was envious of – Michael's particular genius and the special prismatics of his work. Great acting makes its own rules – it can be wayward, awkward, at times even ugly. Michael on his best nights could take an audience to those areas, as Wood felt he often did in the great choric sections of *The Master Builder*'s final act, 'where even life itself has never provided for you those levels of emotion'.

Critical reaction to *The Master Builder* was extraordinarily polarised, to a degree reflecting divided Anglo-Saxon attitudes to and wariness of Ibsen's later plays. For Bernard Levin the whole production was 'a catastrophe' and he was one of those hardest on Maggie Smith whose Hilde – a boldly unconventional performance which, at least on the first night, sacrificed something of its impact to help Michael – was rather unfairly taken to task. Most agreed with Laurence Kitchin who found her disconcertingly contemporary; he also felt that her style was uneasily matched with this Solness ('Sir Michael's fireworks will have to wait until there are people on the stage with him to generate the necessary "friction" '). J. C. Trewin, not subject to overnight deadlines and aware that first nights seldom saw Michael at his best, reviewed the second performance, declaring:

> *The Master Builder* is Michael Redgrave's play. He can persuade us at once of the man's towering domination, mental and physical. When he, who had once been triumphant youth, confesses 'Youth to me is change, new banners, retribution', the words are driven from him. We can credit the haunted, ruthless, ambitious (and often curiously winning) man, the builder of whom Ibsen – establishing his play against a strange personal background – said once 'Solness is a man somewhat related to me'. Redgrave is the actor for Ibsen.

But the most absorbing view of *The Master Builder* appeared when Olivier replaced Michael in November. Ronald Bryden, then theatre critic for the *New Statesman*, wrote a fascinating, long and considered piece, scrupulously avoiding odious comparisons in acknowledging that each actor had mined his different set of values from the play and that 'both readings fit'. It reflected Peter Wood's feeling when left 'punch-drunk' following what he described as the 'gladiatorial' dressing-room scene after Michael's opening night that indeed 'There were two Solnesses in this juxtaposition of mighty talents' ('There really were giants in those days', he reflected). Bryden's description of Michael captured the scale of the performance, describing it as:

> a Wagner hero wrestling amid green and cloudy glooms with the primal guilt on his soul. His Solness was a giant neurotic, obsessed like Brand with his offence against God and a sleepwalking wife whose happiness he had sacrificed to his ambitions. Redgrave paced like a captive wolf in the cage of advancing years and his wife's contempt.

Bryden felt that this self-willed tyrant – one who rarely raised his voice, even to his underlings, until the final scene when his voice began to ring out like a trumpet – was a performance on a slow-burning fuse while the very different actor's instincts of Olivier dictated an utterly opposite route into the role. Reminding Bryden of his portrayal of another small-town petty dictator in the Hollywood version of Theodore Dreiser's *Sister Carrie*, Olivier's performance brimmed with the most brilliantly-observed naturalistic detail, often sharply comic in the earlier scenes and definitely more credibly balanced with the scale of both Maggie Smith and Joan Plowright. Bryden wrote of Olivier as Solness:

> He must toil to amass a characterisation which Redgrave, almost too perfectly cast, could exude in romantic acting ... He is no Nietzschean hero, as Redgrave was. Olivier's builder exists socially in a social play.

With Olivier at its centre, the physical production and particularly Heinrich's neo-operatic sets seemed out of kilter with the altered amperage of the acting. Michael's performance was geared to Wood's view of the play as symbolic autobiography, while all the naturalistic detail and social realism informing Olivier's reading (he cleverly suggested a parvenu in Solness) raised throughout the first two acts the question whether he had laid the foundations for the rise to the demands of the last act's awesome defiance of God. Bryden wrote:

> It is a smaller nobility than Redgrave's ... Olivier's *Master Builder* is early Ibsen, thick with reality. Redgrave's last act, all abstract fire and horn-music, came nearer to the summit of that late, mountainous poetry.

Olivier's Solness was undoubtedly more accessible to Anglo-Saxon sensibilities, while Michael's – and on his best nights it was like watching lava gradually build in heat and pressure before a terrible, molten eruption – was keyed to an approach acknowledging Ibsen's avowed intention in writing for a modern European theatre: 'to torpedo the Ark'.

However, even his better notices, those which grasped something of the production's attempt to blow off Ibsenite cobwebs, could not settle Michael's dreads and Olivier's behaviour was a lasting (if cloaked) hurt. He saw out its scheduled number of performances until the end of that first National season, although he came literally to dread every *Master Builder* evening; he would begin to sweat and shake as his car crossed Waterloo Bridge and although he sent a telegram to Olivier on his first night in the production the following season (quoting Solness's line 'It will be wonderful, wonderful') he never could bring himself to see it. There was some polite talk of Michael returning to the Waterloo Road, and the businessman in Olivier did not want to lose the hot ticket of *Uncle Vanya*, but Michael – who had the Guildford project looming – equally politely declined. Subsequently when Olivier was trying to put together an American tour for the National a few years later and with the American organisers desperate to have that legendary *Vanya*, Michael was wooed again by Olivier. But no other part was on offer and he chose not to repeat one former glory.

That he was deeply worried about the National experience – his memory lapses, the overwhelming tiredness – is evident in a letter from Rachel who had asked a local doctor friend to find help for Michael:

> Dr Macley thinks he had found exactly the right doctor for your problem. He says he is in fact a Psychiatrist, but in your case he would not give you psychiatric treatment but would go into your problems and endeavour to give you the confidence to know all is really well. Dr Macley said he thinks you'd 'hit it off' with him and that he would be for you a sort of father figure. This is interesting as I had not mentioned that word but Macley feels that is part of what you need.

Michael did seek medical advice – physical and psychological – with several exhaustive check-ups, all of which were concluded with prescriptions for tranquillisers (the last thing he needed as it turned out) or vague reassurances of minor blood pressure problems plus instructions to cut back on the drink (which he obeyed).

Nothing much seemed to go right for him at this time. In the summer of 1964 Fred, with misplaced confidence but infinite optimism and Michael's backing, decided to present, appear in and direct a double bill, *Games*, which he had also written, at the Arts Theatre. Disarmingly, whenever taxed about the wisdom of writing, producing, acting and directing at one time, his reply was 'Noël Coward does it' (in fact, Coward did not produce

much of his own work). In no department, however, was *Games* up to the
level of even minor Coward. Trevor Bentham, then resident stage manager
at the Arts, had a difficult time during rehearsals on days when things
simply ground to a halt, an excellent cast including the stylish Faith Brook
'all quite bewildered' and more or less having to resort to directing
themselves. Bentham, who ended up working twice as hard as usual to
help get the production ready, reflected many people's opinion of Fred: 'I
didn't dislike him – he just didn't have the talent.' The physical production
turned out to be something of a poorly organised shambles. The design,
on a shoestring, supposedly representing two Manhattan locations, was a
problem, the dress rehearsal revealing a hessian backdrop creased and
badly painted when hung. Bentham recalled: 'Suddenly an army of Redgraves appeared. Corin jumped into a taxi to fetch curtains from Hans
Crescent to disguise the worst folds. Vanessa, Lynn and Rachel all got
paintbrushes and touched up the worst parts of the set while Michael
consoled Fred.'

Faith Brook suffered *in extremis* under Fred, a weak director and, she
thought, no great shakes as an actor, at least in his own plays. She also
found 'something of the Mafia' in him: 'Watchful, sharp, always on the
make for attention, anything that would further his career.' *Games*, as even
the ever optimistic Fred must have appreciated from the awful reviews,
rightly describing his pieces as little more than Edward Albee *réchauffé*,
was not going to further his career in any department. 'I preferred him
arrogant,' said Faith Brook when he was so pathetically cast down after
his drubbing in the press and with very small houses during the brief Arts
run.

After the searing experience of the National Michael spent some time
at the haven of Wilks Water, often with a now slightly expanded family.
Vanessa had married Tony Richardson, then at the height of his 1960s
success (Rachel privately to Michael gave the marriage 'around five years'
and she was right) and Corin had also married, his bride an attractive
1960s extrovert, Deirdre Hamilton-Hill (Fred acted as his best man). The
children's careers were about to take off – Vanessa in movies after *Blow-
Up* for Antonioni, Corin in Wesker at the Royal Court and on Broadway,
Lynn following with a delightful performance in *The Girl with Green Eyes* –
and with 'The Redgraves' phenomenon burgeoning it was another reason
for Michael to take some time out. He often also retreated to Batcombe
where the cottage attached to Rockwells – Vine Cottage – had been leased
by Vivian Cox, yet another old and trusted friend, now regularly at a
favourite bolt-hole.

He was very far from idle. Guildford, scheduled definitely to open in
1965, occupied him a great deal and he also spent long days in the

recording studios completing his work on the ambitious and revelatory twenty-six-part BBC series *The Great War*, for which he provided the understated but compelling narration, as well as happily returning often to *TW3* for Ned Sherrin.

He had time, before Guildford claimed him exclusively, to play on film one of his favourite poets, W. B. Yeats (his 'Prayer for My Daughter' was a poetry-reading standby of Michael's), in *Young Cassidy*. Another venture which went sadly awry, this was based on Sean O'Casey's autobiographies, although John Whiting's script, with the US distributors in mind, air-brushed out a good deal of the soul-destroying dirt-poor O'Casey background (the urchins playing by the Liffey all look remarkably clean and healthy), not to mention the playwright's Communism and virulent anti-Catholicism. The story was further compromised by casting as the stick-thin, myopically malnourished young O'Casey (rechristened, for no good reason, Cassidy) the powerfully built and exuberantly healthy Australian, Rod Taylor. Michael had been tempted by the news that John Ford, the great Hollywood veteran, would direct but even before his scenes were scheduled Ford, who had arrived in Dublin drunk and stayed drunk for most of the brief time he worked on the picture, had been sent back home and replaced by Jack Cardiff.

Michael's first day on the film reunited him with Edith, playing O'Casey's substitute mother figure of Lady Gregory. Entering a waiting room set aside for the principals, Michael found her sitting with Rod Taylor. She rose with a surprised cry and swooped on him in a delighted embrace. Taylor muttered mock-hurt that he had not been accorded such treatment, to which Edith, still with that unmistakable 'dive' in her voice, laughed – 'Ah, but you see, Michael and I are *old* lovers!' *Young Cassidy* is no great film, despite some lovely work from Maggie Smith as Taylor's girlfriend, but Michael has two good scenes as Yeats, especially his magnificent (if not entirely historically accurate) rebuke to the unruly audience at the Abbey Theatre première of *The Plough and the Stars*.

After the Dublin filming he felt distinctly rejuvenated and with the National experience behind him, was ready once again for the theatre, looking ahead now to most of the next year occupied with the new venture at Guildford.

Eighteen
FRESH WOODS

The Guildford theatre project – the building was named the Yvonne Arnaud Theatre after the popular Parisienne former child pianist who became a musical and comedy West End star, living with her husband on a farm near Guildford for thirty years – had appealed to Michael for many reasons, not the least of which were the site and design of the new building. The redevelopment of the riverside along the River Wey included a new department store and just down the river, on a small isthmus of land next to the original mill-race and Mill House (leased as a scenery store), surrounded by a necklace of water and trees with views to the hills beyond, was the theatre site.

Like the Chichester venture, the Yvonne Arnaud used a mixture of glass, steel and concrete – in the absence of a foundation stone, Vanessa's footprint was immortalised in cement – creating a horseshoe-curved two-level auditorium not dissimilar to the new Nottingham Playhouse. Usefully, the contractors were those who had already had experience of a riverside site in creating Bernard Miles' Mermaid Theatre on the Thames at Puddle Dock out of a derelict blitzed warehouse. Austere at an initial viewing, the theatre's lines were softened by the comfort of the auditorium, the sweeping, generous bar and foyer space, and touches such as the portrait of a welcoming, beaming Yvonne Arnaud and a bust of Michael by a local sculptor, Lorne McKean, 'the only artist who has succeeded in making me look like something other than a startled fish'.

Michael and Rachel, genuinely enthused by both building and the level of local support, threw themselves into the pre-opening activities and fund-raising, attending countless balls, garden fêtes and concerts. Michael persuaded Yehudi Menuhin to give a solo Bach sonata concert as a fund-raiser and in 1964, on Shakespeare's birthday, Vivien Leigh and Diana Wynyard had joined him on a platform cantilevered over the river for a recital. Six swans paused in their regal progress upstream while Michael performed the Chorus speech from *Henry V* – 'O, for a muse of fire!'

Planning the 1965 opening festival season gave him several headaches. He had from the start of the project indicated that he would appear in two out of three productions, but since then the effects on his confidence of the National experience had gone deeper than anybody, even Rachel, realised. Now Michael had a real fear, even terror, of forgetting his lines and the exposure would be all the greater on the wide Guildford stage, which would make any prompting glaringly obvious. After a great deal of thought his selection resulted in playing safe with *A Month in the Country*, which he knew inside-out and would once more direct (also playing Rakitin again) – he could argue that Michel Saint-Denis's Old Vic production of 1951 had played only fifteen performances – and *Samson Agonistes* in another familiar role in a play which he had always felt drawn to try again with the full resources of a modern theatre. The final choice was the rarity of Isaac Bickerstaff's ballad opera *Lionel and Clarissa* with music mostly by Charles Dibdin, a mid-eighteenth-century success comparable to that of *The Beggar's Opera*. Michael had enjoyed the 1920s Lyric, Hammersmith production; it would also show off the theatre's orchestra pit and provide good contrasting roles for many of the season's hand-picked company.

Despite the low salaries (Michael's fee for the season, which also covered the unpaid years of pre-opening planning, was £3500) an extremely strong company was formed. Some old friends included Max Adrian, Fay Compton, Patricia Jessel and Faith Brook, younger talent numbering Daniel Massey and Jennifer Hilary, with Rachel loyally agreeing to join the Chorus of *Samson* as well as appear in *Lionel and Clarissa*, the latter directed by Laurier Lister, still living with Max and joining Guildford's operation after two Chichester seasons as Olivier's associate director. For much of this period Michael was without Fred, who had gone to South Africa with a production of *Who's Afraid of Virginia Woolf?* in which, away from the pressures of London, he gave – according to a fellow cast member Jerome Kilty – a fine performance.

Press and box office interest went through the roof at Guildford when Michael announced that Natalya in *A Month in the Country* would be played by Ingrid Bergman. They had enjoyed each other's company on *Hedda Gabler* and she responded with interest at once to Michael's personal approach, her only worry being that the Guildford period would prevent her annual holiday on a Swedish island with her various children and husband Lars Schmidt. Michael pitched heavy woo, however, offering her Dirk Bogarde's suggestion (he was a godson of Yvonne Arnaud's) of the guest suite in his Surrey house near Hascombe. Shrugging off the belated qualm that Natalya is meant to be twenty-nine (Bergman was fifty) she wrote to Michael that she would sacrifice the vacation.

Michael chose his season's designers well. Initially he had approached Cecil Beaton to design *A Month in the Country* – it turned out to be one of Beaton's favourite plays too – but his Metropolitan Opera work on

Turandot finally prevented that and Michael turned to Alix Stone who was known to him from her Stratford work with Tanya Moiseiwitsch. She produced a seductive world of summery pastels and muslins, moving to the darker shades of the play's later scenes, her garden setting – like Moiseiwitsch's for Saint-Denis – being especially beguiling, with soft-focus trees and romantic leafy arbours. It was a breathless rehearsal period – just four weeks for a complex play and with a leading lady working in a language not her own – which made Bergman more than slightly hesitant. She was most conscientious and had studied her lines thoroughly in advance, but she was not able genuinely to inhabit the role fully by the opening. She found Michael's habit of rarely giving praise as a director – inherited from Saint-Denis possibly, and by no means uncommon – initially somewhat daunting and, as Faith Brook (who had generously agreed to understudy Natalya as well as play Dalila in *Samson*) remembered, there were a couple of occasions when Michael – off on a bender in London the night before – failed to appear for morning rehearsals, which did not endear him to his star: 'We thought we might do line-rehearsals, but no. She would sit waiting, flicking through *Vogue* and other magazines. She was not going to rehearse without her director.'

There were over 5000 applications for first-night seats (theatre founders were balloted) and the opening-night audience, spilling out on to the terraces during the interval, included the American and French ambassadors, Olivier and Joan Plowright, Sybil Thorndike and Lewis Casson and Dirk Bogarde, who read a specially written prologue by Christopher Fry. It was an evening slow to catch fire, with an understandably tense Bergman in the early scenes and Michael, too, feeling his way gradually into Rakitin, and at Guildford the production never quite achieved Turgenev's delicate balance, the texture which Stanislavsky called 'the lace-work' of the piece, although Max was at his finest as Shpichelsky, the scheming doctor who proposes marriage as if detailing a prescription.

Everyone agreed on Bergman's radiant stage presence, even if as yet her performance did not go much beyond the picturesque. Harold Hobson, doing comparative obeisance yet again at the shrine of Edwige Feuillère, for him perhaps the only actress capable of fusing the tremulous poetry of Natalya with her troubling desires, was representative of the polite but reserved critical reaction to her performance.

Bergman's presence of course had ensured the sell-out success of the entire festival, but those able to obtain tickets only for *Samson Agonistes* may have felt short-changed; as Michael owned, they came, but visibly 'bracing themselves for the ordeal'. He still felt, as at Cranleigh, that Milton's 'Dramatick Poem' was viable as a theatrical experience, although he was aware that the rare previous professional attempts had proved unsuccessful – Max Beerbohm had found William Poel's St Martin-in-the-Fields version 'very dull indeed' (Michael had been much intrigued, however, by what he had heard of Kenneth Tynan's showy undergraduate staging at Oxford).

Milton's location is given as 'outside the prison in Gaza' but Michael, working closely with designer Michael Annals, came up with 'a desert place near Samson's prison', mainly to show fully the width of the stage and its cyclorama, lit with sweeping skyscapes to match the mighty harmonies of the verse. He nagged Annals hard on the costumes, finding some much too grand, not barbaric as he wanted, particularly the Chorus of Danite women – 'who must look poor, primitive and defeated' – when he wanted to heighten the subliminal notion that Milton intended the Danites as Puritans and the Philistines as Royalists. One costume he emphatically did want to be opulent was Faith Brook's as Dalila: 'Make her *rich* as hell, but be careful not to suggest for a second the Place Pigalle.'

At one stage Michael had planned a short Afterpiece to *Samson*, asking as varied a cross-section of writers as T. S. Eliot, Peter Shaffer, Harold Pinter and the American John Cheever, whose story 'Montraldo' (it had one of Michael's all time favourite opening lines – 'The first time I robbed Tiffany's, it was raining.') he thought might adapt well. Finally he opted for Milton unadorned, adding only his old prologue from the Book of Judges as used at Cranleigh, well aware that the evening would be caviare to the general, although in fact it had some passionate defenders. Michael looked and sounded impressively large-scale – chained, blinded and ragged, it was a bravely unglamorous portrayal and vocally awesome, finding an extraordinary build to the crescendo of defiance in the scene with the Philistine champion. Where the production needed to throw off its Cranleigh fetters was in the treatment of the Chorus, which Michael unwisely did not fundamentally re-examine. The music by his friend James Bernard, like Bowyer's at Cranleigh, was heavily percussive, using oboe and tambourine imaginatively under Dalila's entrance, but it was mostly safe stuff, as was Pauline Grant's choreography, very Anglo-Saxon with its inescapable suggestions of a Women's Institute class in Eurhythmics. The notices, like the audiences, were respectful, mostly along the lines of Penelope Gilliatt's judgement that although the evening, like Michael, had an 'extraordinary, intractable splendour', it was 'impressive, but not captivating, like Roman architecture, or haggis'.

There were few complaints about *Lionel and Clarissa*, a soufflé-light and tuneful confection of two pairs of Sheridanesque lovers temporarily thwarted, against glowing Henry Bardon sets with romantic David Walker costumes, showing off the theatre's revolving stage. It was performed at just the right pitch of satire, with a wonderfully ripe Max as a furiously gouty, lecherous aged parent and Rachel happily given a rare comedic chance as a fluttering Lady Mary Oldboy, constantly collapsing into fits of the vapours.

Lionel and Clarissa also played to full houses and Michael by the season's close could feel confident that he had achieved what he had been hired to do, with Guildford now launched successfully as part of the 1960s burgeoning regional theatre scene; Laurier Lister was appointed the Arnaud's director and he steered it successfully for the next decade. The size of the opening company and the seemingly inevitable loss by any new theatrical organisation on catering meant that the first festival led to a deficit, but that was recouped (and more) by the theatre's share in the subsequent West End transfer of *A Month in the Country*.

It had played fewer than twenty Guildford performances in repertoire, with a thriving black market in tickets; clearly it had a future in London and there was no shortage of panting producers anticipating a killing with Ingrid Bergman's name up in lights. In the event – to the deep displeasure of Binkie (who had tried in vain before to lure Bergman to London) and others – Michael and Fred (whose company was involved in the transfer) opted to partner Emile Littler, a West End veteran known mainly for musicals but with the crucial advantage of controlling the Cambridge Theatre. Because of its wide stage and depth, Alix Stone's sets could move without the adaptation which more favoured Shaftesbury Avenue houses would have involved.

Some recasting was necessary, with Jeremy Brett and Joanna Dunham replacing Daniel Massey and Jennifer Hilary, and the transfer also involved a blip in Michael's long friendship with Max. In the gap between Guildford and the West End, Max had not been well; he also seemed to become distinctly grand during negotiations, he or his agent demanding – according to Littler's records – an unusually high salary and billing with Bergman and Michael above the title and in newspaper advertising. All contracts and negotiations were handled solely by the Littler office but when Max's terms were refused (Emlyn Williams replaced him) he wrote tearfully to Michael, putting the blame on him and threatening legal action (which came to nothing). Michael was distressed; managerially he had to agree with Littler's decision that Max's demands were unacceptable, but he did not want to lose a cherished friend (he did offer Max a loan should he genuinely suffer a bad patch of unemployment and Max finally simmered down). Ingrid Bergman was characteristically pragmatic about the change, writing to Michael that she had cried when she read in a letter from him that Max was out, but that when she read on to find that Emlyn Williams would take over she quickly dried her tears.

This latest – and last – scrutiny of a favourite play, although much improved from Guildford, still was not quite the version of Michael's dreams. Ingrid Bergman was a much more varied Natalya; she admitted to the press that she had not been ready at Guildford ('I knew my lines but I probably didn't know them profoundly') but at the Cambridge in key scenes such as her jealous cross-examination of Vera she no longer had trouble with the character's swift, volatile caprices and changes of mood. She just could not quite pull off the sudden stabs of malice in a love-transformed Natalya; her radiant good nature, the quality for which audiences adored her, always shone through. Emlyn Williams in place of Max's crafty comedy offered a more evidently signalled opportunist but Jeremy Brett and Joanna Dunham, both with the gaucherie of youth and unforced charm, communicated subtly that sense of becoming aware of sexuality for the first time. Brett found himself fascinated by the seemingly effortless craft of Michael's performance with its now perfectly pitched balance of exterior elegant dandyism and inner tensions. One moment in particular he would watch nightly from the wings attempting to gauge how Michael did it; when Natalya first confesses to Rakitin her love for the handsome young tutor, Michael's rapid, involuntary swallow and almost imperceptible return to unruffled composure was a tiny detail but so cleanly projected – without 'pulling focus' – that it had the effect of suggesting an internal emotional cauldron, another of his stage 'close-ups' when the audience could read in a detail a seismic but suppressed sea change in a character.

Originally announced for an eight-week season, the run was twice extended – it became as hot a ticket as Olivier's *Othello* – and although the weekly running costs were high, the production went tidily into profit over an enjoyable run. Ingrid Bergman wrote to Michael shortly after the close: 'Oh, what a happy time it was!! I wish I could give you a little pat or a slight hug or a flighty kiss like I could do before our first garden scene.'

Michael did not appear on stage again for six years. He turned down interesting and sometimes lucrative work and continued to do so – Anthony Shaffer's *Sleuth*, his old friend Wynyard Browne's play of 1880s revolutionary Russia, *A Choice of Heroes*, for Binkie, David Lean's film of *Dr Zhivago* and several tempting Broadway offers, often involving Harold Clurman. But for whatever reason or combination of reasons – fear, fatigue, the desire to allow the family increasingly to take the spotlight, his worry over Fred's career – he was often content to take a few days' well-paid film commentary work rather than a movie on location or (one sadly aborted project aside) a play.

One new departure, which gave him some of his most rewarding directorial times – although hardly financially, with a fee of £1000 covering preparation and rehearsals – was his work in opera at Glyndebourne. Now run by George Christie, the founder's son, the opera house had approached Michael on several previous occasions but always he had been unavailable or unable to commit to the long-distance planning of the opera world. When he was asked to direct a favourite piece, however, Jules Massenet's *Werther* (last seen with Rachel and Stephen Tennant in Milan), *A Month in the Country* was set for a long West End run and although Tony Richardson was pressing him to be in his new film, *The Charge of the Light Brigade*, Michael gave a commitment to Glyndebourne.

A bonus of the engagement was the reunion with his *Beggar's Opera* coach Jani Strasser, still at Glyndebourne as head of music staff, who had often urged him to work in the entrancing surroundings of an opera house set in the middle of some of Sussex's most beautiful countryside, and they worked harmoniously together, Strasser being of great help to Michael in preparing his score. Moran Caplat, Glyndebourne's general manager, had rightly pointed out that *Werther*, an unusual departure for the house into the French repertoire, needed a particular touch for which he thought Michael ideal: 'It needs exactly that delicate approach which is needed for Chekhov.'

Michael worked hard on *Werther* during his run at the Cambridge, using the piano score and LPs to familiarise himself with a little-known opera, and he and Rachel took the chance of a brief Christmas break to visit Vienna for some research. Based on Goethe's 'Sturm und Drang' novel, *The Sorrows of Young Werther*, drawing on his own Wetzlar meeting with Charlotte Buff, its story of Werther's romantic agony and suicide for the love of Charlotte, betrothed and then married to another, is set against the background of German provincial life. It was enormously popular in its day (first produced in 1892) at a time when Massenet's lyric work, a halfway house between music drama and *opéra comique*, chimed perfectly with the tastes of a sedately bourgeois public. Michael's immediate feeling was that the tone of the opera would be served best by a romantic, painterly design; sadly, his dream of working with Lila de Nobili, the great romantic *verismo* designer of her era, was frustrated by her unavailability and he turned to the Guildford team of Henry Bardon and David Walker who did him and the piece proud with four beautifully realised sets moving from the evergreens and flowered gazebo of a sun-washed first act, through a ravishingly handled moonlit orchestral interlude with night closing in and the sounds of the little town fading underneath the entry of the cellos as Charlotte and Werther return from the ball, to the deep-toned domestic interiors of the later scenes.

Part of a mould-breaking Glyndebourne season, with four out of five productions premières (including Janet Baker in Purcell's *Dido and Aeneas*),

Michael's operatic debut successfully reclaimed an opera thought by many to be too saccharine for modern tastes. His sense of detail and character helped find the glowing, tender sensibility of the piece, scaling it beautifully to the size of the house. His three principals were all making Glyndebourne debuts and although he had to work hard to prevent Jean Brazzi as Werther from semaphoring, his dark good looks ('like a Corsican Elvis Presley,' said one critic) worked well opposite Hélia T'Hezan as Charlotte.

The Glyndebourne team – like an extended family and meticulously organised (the only aspect of which Michael had any criticism was the dreadful food in the staff canteen) – all enjoyed working on *Werther* with Michael; it was earmarked for future revival and he accepted also an invitation to direct the very first Glyndebourne production of *La Bohème* the following year. His only stipulations were that he would like singers 'as young and *lean* as possible' and that although he did not want simply 'to do another *Werther*' he would want the same design team.

The experience of Glyndebourne, although happy, did not seem greatly to reactivate him. For the only period during the 1960s he resumed occasional diary entries for 1967 (between January and April). Both the front page and the space following the final entry carry the same carefully transcribed quotation: 'Time cannot be remedied – we cannot alter the past.' And yet he seemed to continue apathetic towards theatre work. Offered the title role in Brecht's *Galileo* at New York's Lincoln Center, he instructed Aubrey Blackburn 'No' at once. Many entries record his routine on Sundays (*The Critics* on radio, walk, rest), his late-night stops on his nocturnal wanderings at Fred's or Tony Oliver's flat ('an armchair and a nightcap any time you're passing, you know that,' Tony always offered), visits to Rockwells at Batcombe in January and February, the house snug and welcoming with fires in all the rooms (even bedrooms) but with Michael doing little but reading or playing endless games of Canasta. At times he simply records worries about what he calls his 'closed-circuit life':

> Exhausted and dripping with sweat. Why?
> I can remember nothing – not even a 5-min telephone call – unless I take notes.
> I feel I'm getting lazier every day.

On one occasion he went with Rachel to see Alexei Arbuzov's *The Promise* with Judi Dench and Ian McKellen but he collapsed in the interval as he went for some air: 'I am all right in a few minutes of fresh air – but it is alarming and a bit shaming.'

Apart from a few planning meetings for *La Bohème*, he worked very little at this period. He was roused briefly when Federico Fellini came to talk to him about a film in which Michael would play a dead cellist ('who doesn't know he's dead. Very exciting'), but nothing came of this at the time (it later was the basis of *The Orchestra*). But he seemed happy to potter, reviewing Malcolm Lowry's Letters for the *Sunday Times* (he had been touched that Lowry had remembered him, sending a pre-publication copy of *Under the Volcano*), taking part in a recital for the Italian Arts Rescue Fund at the Haymarket, considerably enlivened at rehearsal by Ralph Richardson's refusal to sit on stage while 'a German' (Dietrich Fischer-Dieskau) sang, or doing the occasional lucrative broadcast or commentary (*The Lost Peace* followed *The Great War*).

Only one possible English theatre project interested him enough to take further. The eupeptic American-born producer, Toby Rowland, who had once worked for Binkie, planned to present Edward Albee's *A Delicate Balance* in London with Michael to co-star for the first time with Vivien Leigh, directed by John Dexter, but it had to be postponed when Vivien Leigh's old enemy of TB flared up once more. Michael often walked from Hans Crescent to her impeccably decorated Eaton Square apartment where he would go through the lines of their scenes together in her flower-filled bedroom while she, defying all her doctors, smoked away. Both felt genuinely challenged by a play they found one of the most intriguing to have come along for some time.

No production date could be fixed until Leigh's doctors agreed, and Michael had also been pursued by New York's Theater Guild to star in a new musical based on Arnold Bennett's novel *Buried Alive*, then called *The Great Adventure*, with lyrics by E. Y. ('Yip') Harburg and score by Jule Styne. His moderate interest in this project increased when he realised that he could time a visit to discuss the show with the Guild to coincide with a trip with Rachel for Lynn's New York wedding in early April to a British-born ex-actor, John Clark. The news had come rather unexpectedly – Lynn was enjoying a Broadway success in Peter Shaffer's *Black Comedy* – but both parents were thrilled.

It was a lightning trip. They stayed at the Algonquin – Michael always liked the slightly faded atmosphere and literary associations of its wood-panelled lobby bar – before meeting Lynn and, for the first time, her husband-to-be ('at first seems brash and unattractive to me,' noted Michael). Sidney Lumet and his wife Gail had helped to plan the wedding, very secretly to elude the press, holding it at their downtown Lexington Avenue apartment, decorated with ivy and white gardenias. The ceremony was performed by a Minister from the non-denominational Ethical Church, with Michael 'leading Lynn in', before a wedding supper at Luchow's Restaurant, Michael beaming throughout with the pride of a paterfamilias, enjoying – as he always did – the cornerstone ceremonies of weddings or christenings: 'Lynn looks gorgeous. Rachel looks divine all day. We have been so happy. Later we walk down 5th Avenue together.'

The meetings for *The Great Adventure* were amicable and Michael certainly thought Styne's score superior to *Ruggles of Red Gap*, also meeting the promising young Stephen Vinaver who was to direct. He was careful not to commit himself, however, and his enthusiasm for the idea of a Broadway musical appearance was tempered slightly by seeing Angela Lansbury after *Mame* at a matinée ('sounds like a circus audience,' he thought): 'Cannot help thinking – "*This*, *twice* on matinée days!!" She says in dressing room: "It's sleep, eat and the theatre."'

With Glyndebourne in mind he took Rachel to *La Bohème* at the Metropolitan ('Bad production – Musetta looked like Betty Grable in a 1940s film').

Rachel flew to California with Lynn (just closing in *Black Comedy*) and John Clark where they could join Vanessa, filming *Camelot* (and just embarking on her love affair with co-star Franco Nero) in Hollywood. There was an enormous amount of press interest with the Oscars imminent and both Redgrave sisters nominated (Vanessa for *Morgan*, Lynn for *Georgy Girl* – Elizabeth Taylor won). Column after column hinted at rivalry between the sisters and within the family; Michael chose to ignore all the flimflam and get back to London, passing on the chance to revisit Los Angeles and Hollywood, for which he never much cared.

He found Fred in low spirits. Fred was not at all keen on the idea of Michael going to Broadway for a musical which would offer him no opportunity. After a stint working in television for Rediffusion he was trying to revive stage production plans and was doing his best to persuade Michael to drop out of a still unscheduled *A Delicate Balance* and to appear instead with Vivien Leigh in Fred's production of Patrick Hamilton's old warhorse *Gaslight* or even in a whole season of melodrama under Fred. With Michael in his current undecided frame of mind and with Fred out of his professional Glyndebourne future (the opera house had its own assistant directors) their relationship could be at times tense, Michael on his nocturnal wanderings for a while ending up more often at Tony Oliver's in Pimlico than at Fred's in Rutland Street.

It was shortly after returning from New York that Michael for the only time 'outed' himself to one of his children when he spoke to Corin one evening late after arriving back at Hans Crescent from a return visit to *The Promise*, this time with Fred and Lehman Engel, visiting from New York. Corin was staying the night at Hans Crescent; Deirdre had just given birth in hospital to Luke, their second child (a fourth grandchild for Rachel and Michael following Vanessa's daughters Natasha and Joely

by Tony Richardson and Corin and Deirdre's daughter Jemma, who was
with Deirdre's parents). Once Lehman Engel and Fred had left after a
nightcap, Corin and Michael sat talking about Engel and his emotional
problems (his love life tended to be unhappy), with Michael adding to
Corin, 'Lehman, as you've probably guessed, is homosexual,' which Corin
indeed understood. After 'an interminably long pause', Michael – without
any preamble – spoke again to utter with markedly laboured breathing an
oddly qualified sentence which, with more long pauses between its careful
punctuation, seemed to take an eternity for him to articulate: 'I think I
ought to tell you that I am, to say the least of it, bisexual.' He stared at
Corin almost accusingly, as if he had been forced to speak and then, in
Corin's description, came three huge, heaving sobs, 'Aaagh … aaagh …
aaagh.' Then the dam burst and his grief and rage came out in a terrible,
heaving cascade. Michael cried readily – at weddings, funerals, the
theatre – but this, inevitably recalling the cracking of Crocker-Harris's
carapace in *The Browning Version*, was completely new, 'a grief so awful
that it seemed to undo him'. Corin crossed to Michael, sitting on the arm
of his chair to comfort him, embracing him and saying 'I know' while
Michael gradually composed himself. After another long pause he resumed
the conversation as if the subject had never been raised. But for Michael,
perhaps at least some quietus was made in that tortured, protracted confession of the most secret part of his psyche. The subject was never
referred to again, however, and Michael never spoke of his bisexuality to
either of his daughters.

Before rehearsals at Glyndebourne he stayed once again with Enid
Bagnold at Rottingdean; he liked her tough, acerbic conversation with its
baroque flourishes, and her slightly shabby-grand house where pictures
were liable to drop off the walls in the night. *La Bohème* was part of an
Italian-biased season, including Cavalli's *L'Ormindo* and Donizetti's *L'Elisir
d'amore* as Glyndebourne continued to extend its repertoire. Once again
he had considered the visual side of the work with great care. He had
travelled with an ancient Baedeker for one research weekend in Paris,
trying to pinpoint the Café Momus, normally designed as a noisy Left
Bank restaurant but visualised by Michael and Henry Bardon as more of
a fashionable central meeting place for various classes, not unlike a *fin de
siècle* French Café Royal, accommodating Musetta with Alcindoro and
Bohemians alike, a clever solution to the libretto's problem of a freezing
Act I attic and then a curious alfresco Christmas Eve meal. Michael wanted
to create a sense of exterior cold throughout until the final ray of wintry
sunshine falls on the face of the dead Mimi, and Bardon concentrated
accordingly on creating his sets with a colour palette restricted to greys
and blacks, with a frosted effect like an old lithograph, while David

Walker's costumes were also predominantly monochromatic, with touches of pale blue and mauve echoing the lilac tone of the lamplight in the streets. The effect was stunning, like a series of Gavarni engravings, the whole production evocative of Henri Murger's realism in *La Vie de Bohème*, and a grave, stimulating reappraisal of an old favourite.

The shame was that on this occasion Glyndebourne's casting let the production down; the principals, mostly making their British debuts, were young as Michael had requested, and Anna Novelli gave a touchingly detailed performance as Mimi (purists tutted at her death scene – in a chair rather than the chaise of convention) but Ottavio Garaventa's Rodolfo was a coarse, unsubtle effort, hard as Michael tried to wean him away from his stock gestures and out-front acting. 'The Glyndebourne cast has been unable to realise Redgrave's intentions' was typical of the music press's reactions.

This most popular of operas drew many friends to Sussex for a summer treat and interval picnic, although Enid Bagnold, never the most quiescent of authors in the theatre, was puzzled by the different working methods of the opera world: 'How *extraordinary* about not being needed – or *desired* – at musical rehearsals. Just like all directors' attitude to me!'

The Glyndebourne management knew that they had found a director popular with singers who could also bring a fresh perspective to romantic works, and they were anxious to hold on to him. Both Berlioz's *Beatrice and Benedick* and one of his favourites – Tchaikovsky's *Eugene Onegin* – were suggested for the 1968 season. The latter, with Elisabeth Söderström as Tatyana, might well have come to pass had Michael been able to realise his dream of working with Lila de Nobili but she was already engaged to design it for Peter Hall at Covent Garden. Also the Glyndebourne commitment, including preparation and rehearsals totalling a considerable period for such basic fees, meant that, as at Stratford and the Old Vic, Michael was in effect subsidising his own work. Once again tax troubles were threatening and reluctantly he had to pass on *Onegin*, although he was able to return to Glyndebourne one more time, in 1969 when he revived *Werther*. The production came up glowing afresh, much enhanced by a magnificently sung and most touchingly acted Charlotte by Josephine Veasey, which made it possible to understand why the role had appealed so much to Lotte Lehmann.

With few interesting parts on offer from the film studios Michael began to think again of writing his own script and turned to his version of *The Aspern Papers* to rethink it in cinematic terms. For long periods he was happily ensconced at Rockwells (where Fred rarely came), the evenings spent playing Canasta or 'The Game', a keenly disputed precursor to the TV programme *Call My Bluff*, at which Michael, with his mask of deadpan inscrutability, was usually the winner. Vivian Cox in the cottage often had mutual friends to stay, including the director-choreographer Wendy Toye, and Rockwells in the 1960s became even more of a congenial second home for him. His work on *The Aspern Papers* went encouragingly; as with *Antony and Cleopatra*, it was a complete rescrutiny of the piece in visual terms and has some brilliantly imaginative touches, including a pre-credit sequence with the ancient Miss Bordereau's hand sorting through her trunk of Aspern's relics and papers as the screen slowly bleeds into colour from sepia, and a gripping new treatment of the final confrontation between Miss Tina and H. J., using a photograph of Aspern as the camera's point of view at crucial points.

Coincidentally Michael discovered that the Czech director Jiri Weiss was planning to film the story, although after reading Michael's version he decided that it caught the Jamesian spirit so well that it would provide the basis of his film. Over the next few years Michael – with a great deal of work from Aubrey Blackburn also – tried hard to interest film makers in *The Aspern Papers*. Initial reactions were always the same – professed admiration for a superb script but reservations about the chances of a 'literary' film in the contemporary youth-dominated market. Then Michael tried adding actors to the package; he had a rapid response from Bette Davis – 'what a really fine, good film this would be to make' – but even with Weiss, Davis and Edith Evans (as Juliana) producers and directors remained wary, some using the excuse that the story had been previously filmed (*The Lost Moment*), albeit in a much looser version. Bryan Forbes, then running Associated British Productions at Elstree, Anatole de Grunwald, Carlo Ponti, Sidney Lumet, Karel Reisz – all were admirers of the script but it was always 'too special' for general audiences. Michael's disappointment over the failure of *The Aspern Papers* to reach the screen was never so deep as his regret over *Antony*, but it remained a sadness, especially as he was only too aware that his recent film work had been comparatively humdrum.

There had been a few movies with leading directors. For Sidney Lumet he had a good part in *The Hill*, a powerful all-male story of a Middle-East detention camp during the war in which a weak CO allows a martinet sergeant-major's regime to slip into sadism. It was strongly cast, with Sean Connery, Michael's old Stratford colleague Harry Andrews, and Michael as a shifty, weak-willed medical officer, but it made only a modest impression at the box office.

Michael also worked for Hollywood's Anthony Mann (*El Cid*, *Winchester '73*) in an action picture, *The Heroes of Telemark*, much of which was taken up by Kirk Douglas and Richard Harris (both unlikely Norwegians) trying to outstare each other. The script was written by Iris Tree's son Ivan

Moffat and Losey's old colleague Ben Barzman, based on a true episode of the Norwegian Resistance preventing the Nazis from obtaining heavy water for atomic research, but did little more than string various action set pieces together. Michael as 'Uncle', a senior Resistance figure, had little to do but offer sage advice while puffing on his pipe and die an heroic death. The part was typical of offers now coming in, unremarkable but extremely well paid (£15,000 for a brief period on the Norwegian location and three Pinewood days) supporting roles to add a touch of class to routine product.

Television offered even more such opportunities and throughout the 1960s Michael took part in rather too many big-budget TV Specials, usually internationally funded. There was a dismal version of Wilde's *The Canterville Ghost*, dismembered by Burt Shevelove, and he appeared as a gruffly bearded grandfather in a lavish adaptation of Johanna Spiri's *Heidi* with Jean Simmons and Maxmilian Schell, directed by Delbert Mann and filmed in Munich. Mann also directed a most peculiar version of Dickens' own 'favourite child', *David Copperfield*. This structured the story as a series of flashbacks when David returns from Switzerland to Yarmouth and, while staring endlessly at the sea, tries to reconstruct his fragmented life. Some of the book's most absorbing characters – Rosa Dartle, Mrs Gummidge – simply disappear in this reworking of the novel as the casebook of a contemporary man with writer's block and an identity crisis. The producers, as if realising the script's weaknesses, showered the project with luxury casting – Ralph Richardson as Micawber (heavily cut), Edith as Betsey Trotwood, Cyril Cusack as Barkis, a ripe double act from Olivier and Richard Attenborough as Creakle and Tungay, and Corin as the faithless Steerforth. Most of the scenes involving Michael as Peggotty were filmed on location at Southwold with 'Peggotty's Hut', based on Phiz's illustrations, made out of old ships' timbers on the beach, although the scenes were ruthlessly trimmed. Michael's performance, featuring an oddly uncertain accent and possibly the most extravagantly whiskery of all his false-hair jobs, was not exactly subtle, although that was hardly what the film was aiming for. One review said that it proved Michael 'can ham as well as Lionel Barrymore' (in George Cukor's MGM film), which is not necessarily a complement.

The most prodigally lavish of all these assignments was Peter Wood's production of *Hamlet*, one of the Hallmark series, with Richard Chamberlain, still a major star from *Dr Kildare* on television, having what can be best described as 'a brave stab' at the title role, a highly romantic, dreamy-eyed and gentle Prince of Denmark. Wood surrounded Chamberlain with a sumptuous cast for the filming at Raby Castle in Northumberland, including Gielgud as the Ghost, Margaret Leighton a tippling

Gertrude and Alan Bennett a memorably camp Osric, and he gave the play the glossiest of production values, including a full heavenly choir to sing Hamlet to his rest. Cut – by John Barton – to two hours, it could never be much more than a *Reader's Digest* version, although Michael's Polonius was relatively unaffected by the surgery. It was a very unexpected and effective reading; with his stock, stick and cane (Wood used a Regency setting), he suggested a courtier out of Dickens (there was more than a touch of Micawber in his advice to Laertes) with a crumbling dignity, hinting at a past of real strength and power now on the wane. It was an aptly fine and fresh performance to mark his final appearance in the play, and it dominated all the coverage, especially in the USA.

The television projects Michael responded to with most enthusiasm tended to be rather more unusual ventures. He was one of the first of what ended up as a remarkable cast to commit to the TV film of Lewis Carroll's *Alice in Wonderland*, to be directed by Jonathan Miller. The fuss kicked up by this in 1966 was extraordinary. Miller, not a little influenced by Michael's old friend William Empson and his suggestions of Freudian layers in the dreamscape world of *Alice* in *Some Versions of Pastoral*, stripped away the familiar Tenniel trappings to reveal the adult figures beneath in what developed fascinatingly into a fantasy of repression and identity, featuring superbly inventive designs by Julia Trevelyan Oman, evoking all Carroll's overstuffed Victoriana within Miller's focus on *Alice* as having the context of a dream, an askew oneiric world with characters only a footstep away from lunacy in some cases, and a grave, inquisitive and sometimes distinctly tetchy Alice, mercifully free from the hair-banded pert child of convention.

One of the most imaginative films to come out of television, it was widely accused at the time of perverting a classic and, extraordinarily, was described by the BBC as 'unsuitable' for children under twelve. This ceaselessly searching treatment of Carroll's classic as a Victorian fantasy of growing up had a glittering cast, including a lovely pairing of Gielgud and Malcolm Muggeridge as the Mock Turtle and the Gryphon, Peter Cook as the Mad Hatter, a sublimely somnolent Wilfred Lawson as the Dormouse and Peter Sellers as the King of Hearts. Michael was a magnificently bemused Caterpillar, filmed in the Sir John Soane Museum (just one of Oman's inspired choices of location) in an odd, eerie sequence in which his near senile, hookah-smoking figure cast an elegiac but slightly sinister spell.

Michael also took on – simply because he liked the project and those involved – a version for television of the institution of the J. B. Morton 'Beachcomber' column from the *Daily Telegraph* with Spike Milligan. There were definite Carrollian echoes in pieces such as the 'Trial of Red-

Bearded Dwarves' and also in Michael's main contributions, a weekly extract from Beachcomber's 'Anthology of Huntingdonshire Cabmen', to which he brought an inspiredly solemn dottiness. The highlight was the lethal send-up of poetry reading, not excluding his own.

Still the theatre, for which offers continued to crowd in on Aubrey Blackburn, seemed to have lost its lure. A Broadway musical had always been an ambition, but Michael finally turned down the vanishing artist-hero Priam Farll in the Theater Guild's Arnold Bennett musical and, just as with *My Fair Lady*, he had no regrets. As it resulted, he was well out of *Darling of the Day*, as the show was finally titled; it turned into a classic case of a Broadway musical 'in trouble on the road', with changes of cast, director and songs as well as title, and even though Patricia Routledge had a personal success opposite a miscast Vincent Price, it managed only a month's run, losing a fortune.

A Delicate Balance ended in misery with Vivien Leigh's sudden death in 1967, a shock compounded by Cecil Tennant's death in a car crash following her funeral. Harold Clurman tried hard to revive Michael's interest in the play the following year, suggesting Celia Johnson and Irene Worth as possible co-stars, but again Michael politely passed. He and Rachel – she, as a loving, staunch friend more intimately – had been close to Vivien Leigh in her later years after the collapse of her marriage to Olivier, and he had worked so closely with her on the script that the thought of the play without her could not rouse him, for all Clurman's attempts to persuade him. As shocked as anyone at the news of Vivien Leigh's death had been Bob, to whom she had always been a loyal friend, meeting up with him whenever she was in Los Angeles. Bob wrote to Michael of his sadness at the news, but also marvelling at the children's success, especially Lynn's: 'As you said, remember that gawky little girl! Now she can be up for the Oscars!' Bob and Betty were planning to move to Seattle where Bob had been offered a better Western Union job. He added to Michael that he would like to see him: 'Somehow it must be arranged, for in our lifetime and after all that we have meant to each other, not to meet again would be very sad.'

Instead of the theatre, Michael spent his time increasingly on location or in the studios, usually as Establishment figures in mostly indifferent pictures – a spy chief in *Assignment K* and a blank of a part as an air vice-marshal subordinate to Olivier's Lord Dowding in *The Battle of Britain*. He partnered Olivier again in Richard Attenborough's film version of the Joan Littlewood and Theatre Workshop production of *Oh! What a Lovely War*, cleverly underplaying against Olivier's harrumphing blimpishness. This was another cast of all the talents – Olivier, Richardson, Gielgud, Dirk Bogarde, Vanessa (as Mrs Pankhurst), Maggie Smith and Corin as

'Brother Bertie'. Michael played Sir Henry Wilson, Deputy Chief of Staff (his bicycle trips round France impressed his superiors somewhat more than any record against the Germans), and he and Olivier as Sir John French shared two slyly funny scenes, displaying hilariously envious snobbery at the sight of Haig (John Mills) – clearly risen from 'trade' – and blinkered jingoism ('We're not under any obligation to the French – we have our own war to fight'). Attenborough's film, underpinned by Len Deighton's notion of substituting Brighton Pier for the original's pierrot show, in full colour and glittering with guest stars, inevitably lacked the visceral punch of Theatre Workshop's production but it seemed a gem in the desert of mediocrity of so much British cinema at the time.

Sadly more representative of the level of material coming Michael's way was *Goodbye Gemini*, a film of surprising meretriciousness which turned an accomplished novel, *Ask Agamemnon* by Jenni Hall, into an ogling trip round 'swinging London'. Michael was cast as an MP well known as a champion of alienated youth who becomes dangerously involved with twins (Martin Potter and the all-purpose 1960s nymphet Judy Geeson), who come from a broken world of their own (the Agamemnon of the book is their teddy bear). Blackmail, murder, hints of incest and sexual shenanigans (Michael inevitably ends up in bed with Judy Geeson) are all thrown into a voyeuristic and tawdry film, a sad spectacle in which Michael seems more ill at ease than in any other movie.

He had higher hopes – dashed at the box office – for his only film with Bette Davis, *Connecting Rooms*. Davis was unusually cast as Wanda, a cellist from the vanished elegance of the Café de Paris reduced to busking for cinema queues and exploited by a charmingly amoral conman. To her Bayswater boarding house comes Michael as Wallraven, sacked from a public schoolmaster's post for his involvement (innocent) in a scandal and now working as a janitor in an art school. A study of character, ruthless youth against middle-aged compassion, it is a low-key and sometimes sentimental film but it is truthfully and affectingly acted, especially by Kay Walsh as a prying landlady and by Michael and Bette Davis as they trace the unlikely, quiet friendship which develops between Wanda and Wallraven.

Michael knew that *Connecting Rooms* had few of the obvious ingredients for major commercial success but he was keen to work with Davis and stressed in interviews how much he had enjoyed acting with her and how her approach matched his: 'We don't talk too much about it. We just get up and give it a go.' She could seem a sad figure, however; Gabrielle Drake, making her first film, remembered her as lonely on the set, while Michael and Rachel had a sticky evening when they took her to dinner at the Garrick. She did not want either Vanessa or Lynn present – younger women were not welcome – and seemed still bitter at the inevitable passing of her glory days of studio stardom, with little to say in praise of any contemporary cinema.

Connecting Rooms was poles apart from the big-budget and extremely ill-advised remake of *Goodbye, Mr Chips* in a musical version with Peter O'Toole as the eponymous schoolmaster and Petula Clark his unlikely musical-star wife, with Michael as the headmaster. Herbert Ross, directing his first film, chose to have the songs – lacklustre, even by Leslie Bricusse's standards – warbled off screen while the principals pranced around to the soundtrack. He did little to enliven a sluggish script by Terence Rattigan (Michael's last association with the dramatist) and the picture seems to sprawl very slowly for hours. Michael, bumbling and thickening perceptibly over the years covered in the film, and an outrageous Siân Phillips as a Tallulah Bankhead figure of a visiting theatrical, emerged relatively unscathed but he must have been despairing of ever receiving a good part in a first-rate script again.

He had been working on another script of his own, intended as a film for television to be produced by Fred, who had now switched his ambitions from the theatre. Michael once again turned to Henry James, adapting his novel *Washington Square*, although the timing was poor; film and television producers then seemed little interested in 'literary' period projects and Fred, who moved between London and Hollywood trying to drum up interest, was becoming very discouraged indeed. On his own initiative Fred had also developed a screenplay of Edward Caddick's novel *Paddy on Sundays*, but that too proved frustratingly difficult to sell and eventually Fred lost his rights in the property. On *Washington Square* as a last gambit he tried at various points using the family connection to include Vanessa or Lynn as the jilted heiress Catherine Sloper opposite Michael's planned Sloper *père* as part of the package, not a notion to fill Michael with delight (he always dismissed out of hand any of the many 1960s offers for American TV specials to feature some or all of 'The Redgraves').

In the event, the argument from putative producers that there already existed a perfectly sound version of James's story as *The Heiress* was enough to squash Fred's hopes of seeing the project come to fruition. It was a difficult time in Fred's relationship with Michael and Fred was uncharacteristically gloomy for long periods, writing to Michael from Hollywood: 'It is agonising to wake up to another day of nothingness – the frustration of having worked with so little result makes it a bit difficult for me at the moment.' A bout of hepatitis could hardly help his depression and he had also to realise that he had little chance of reactivating his career as a director in England and that Michael's continuing absence from the stage (in addition to a big drop in his earnings) offered him few chances as a producer either.

Shortly before going off to Madrid for yet another dull supporting part, as a tsarist general this time, in a lavish all-star-cast film (*Nicholas and Alexandra*, for which producer Sam Spiegel went on a buying spree through British theatre), Michael took some time off to revisit Liverpool. He had never lost contact with the Playhouse, visiting with Rachel in 1968 to open a new Circle Bar called the 'Redgrave Room'. That same year saw him also realise a secret dream – one of his few remaining ambitions – to follow his mother (and Rachel and Vanessa for that matter) by including a pantomime among his stage credits. For the OUDS at the Oxford Playhouse he appeared in *Cinderella* as recast by Gyles Brandreth from H. J. Byron's 1860s original – the student cast featured a future MI5 chief in Eliza Manningham-Buller as the Fairy Queen and the choreography was the work of a later drama critic, Michael Coveney – to recite a specially written rhyming couplet prologue by Nevill Coghill:

> I don't know what to say about Dandini -
> I think I ought to warn you, he's a meanie!

He returned to Liverpool in 1971 to attend what he found a surprisingly moving occasion – recalling 'the most exciting Whitsun of my life' when he first visited the city to meet Willie Armstrong in 1934 – the theatre's Diamond Jubilee, a gala affair with a magnificent civic banquet and many reunions.

This renewed involvement with the theatre, whether at Liverpool, or at Farnham, not far from Wilks Water, where he had been asked to lend his name to a new theatre, or in Ealing where he continued to visit the Questors' Theatre regularly to open each new stage of its redevelopment, appeared to be the catalyst of his decision to return to the stage. His feelings of continual lethargy seemed to be abating, especially after long breaks among the tranquil peace of Wilks Water or at Rockwells, and when he read the script of William Trevor's play *The Old Boys*, adapted from his Hawthornden prizewinning novel, he was immediately intrigued. It was to be produced at the riverside Mermaid Theatre, run by his old friend Bernard Miles, and although inevitably there were some butterflies of nerves at the prospect of returning to the theatre in a demanding new part after an absence of six years (his longest ever), all his inclinations were that he should end a self-imposed exile.

Nineteen
THE WALL OF FEAR

When Michael's appearance in *The Old Boys* was announced at a Mermaid press conference in June 1971 shortly before rehearsals began, he was clearly both surprised and gratified by the amount of interest; the reception was packed and for once he seemed to be able to relax and even enjoy the event, talking enthusiastically about the Mermaid, his previous associations with Bernard Miles and describing William Trevor's play, to which he had been attracted at once, as 'funny and rather touching'. He offered no special reason to explain such a long absence, only that after the tiring period of Chichester, the opening of the National and the Guildford project in succession, a planned sabbatical period simply extended into a longer break. He genuinely felt that his fears and phobias were behind him, the only sign of possible anxiety being his request for six weeks' rehearsal rather than the Mermaid's customary four; with the box office already healthy, Miles thought that he could easily afford the extra amount of rehearsal salary (even with a fifteen-strong cast) on the budget.

William Trevor was then a new name in British fiction but *The Old Boys*, a mordantly funny but compassionate study of old age centred round the rivalry of two ex-public schoolboys for the presidency of the Old Boy Association, had been greeted as the work of an unusual talent. With much of the novel conducted in dialogue – precise, formal, literate – there were inevitable comparisons with Ivy Compton-Burnett but Trevor's tone from the start of his career was very much his own. Like most of his earlier fiction its story inhabits a slightly run-down suburban London – SW19 here, in Crimea Road, aptly named arena for a plot of domestic and institutional warfare. Mr and Mrs Jaraby battle over his beloved ageing cat Monmouth and her worshipped but to him disgraced son Basil, while Jaraby, considered the obvious candidate as the new OB Association president, unexpectedly finds himself opposed by Nox, an old enemy who goes to the lengths of hiring a seedy private eye, Mr Swingler, to ferret out any useful exploitable secrets in the Jaraby household. The action moves between Crimea Road and the ante-chamber to death that is the Rimini Hotel, an establishment populated by Old Boys of the school and run by the Venus flytrap of Miss Burdock whose matronly exterior masks a dragon of exploitative control. She, like Swingler, sees the elderly as victims.

After a first adaptation for television (which hardly included Swingler), still the novelist's hand showed at times in the writing but the play provided rewarding acting opportunities and was cast quickly and extremely strongly. Michael had a few old colleagues in the company – Peter Copley (his Old Vic Laertes in 1950) as Nox and, as the meek, bird-loving widower Mr Turtle, John Kidd from the 1951 Stratford company. With Sylvia Coleridge as Mrs Jaraby, the redoubtable Margaret Courtenay as Miss Burdock, Bernard Hepton making Swingler a memorable latter-day Jacobean villain prowling south-west London, and many distinguished senior actors as the denizens of the Rimini Hotel, it was a first-rate cast.

All involved were exhilarated by the early rehearsals in the Chelsea rehearsal room, when Michael seemed in magnificent form, investing Jaraby with a touching, snuffly dignity even in his obsessive preoccupation with the past, and building in power to an astonishing crescendo when, now a widower with his cat Monmouth dead, he arrives at the Rimini for a memorable confrontation with Miss Burdock, leading to glory in a defiant rebellion of the residents against her restrictive regime. Sylvia Coleridge, who had often acted with Michael on radio, was convinced it was shaping to be one of his finest performances.

Then, almost imperceptibly at first, in the final stages of rehearsals – during which photographers and interviewers seemed constantly around, inevitably reminding him of the looming opening – all his confidence began to ebb. Lines which had been ringing with assurance now were stumbled for or escaped him completely, and even with Sylvia Coleridge and Peter Copley helping him go through his part in the evening at Hans Crescent, his insecurities increased. Touchingly, there were no reproaches from his fellow actors, all of whom understood that this *crise de nerfs* was due not to drink or laziness but to something much deeper (and, like most older actors there was, too, that sense of 'There but for the grace of ...').

When the production moved on to the Mermaid stage it was clear during the dress rehearsals that there was a major problem with Michael's memory. At this point the biographer has to enter the narrative. I was directing *The Old Boys*; as associate director of the Mermaid then, I had recently had a success with a revival of Shaw's *John Bull's Other Island* and when Trevor's agent sent his play to the theatre it was offered to me to direct. Michael was my choice of casting; I had seen many of his performances and – not alone of my generation – had been influenced towards a theatre career by *Uncle Vanya* in particular. Like the author and cast, I was often moved and impressed beyond expectations by his emotional wattage in earlier rehearsals. Star actors often can drain energy from the rest of a cast in rehearsal. It can be a deliberate ploy, to bag the lion's share of rehearsal-time, but more often it is unconscious, the result of a kind of *droit de seigneur* power built into their theatrical DNA. This – in my experience at least – was never the case with Michael, who throughout the rehearsal period of *The Old Boys* was always open to suggestion, willing to experiment and, vitally, fully alert to anything new coming to him from the other actors.

When 'the wall of fear', as Michael later called it, descended I talked to Bernard Miles who, to his eternal credit, never even voiced the possibility of replacing Michael. But after the first of only two previews, which developed into a nightmare duet between Michael and the prompting stage manager, drastic action had to be taken. It was Miles who came up with the solution; he had heard of a walkie-talkie prompting system whereby the actor wore a hearing aid (providentially completely in character for Mr Jaraby) and when necessary was prompted (inaudibly to the audience) through the earpiece from a microphone set up off stage. The old Mermaid prior to its redevelopment had an unbroken continuity of auditorium and stage walls with no wing space or conventional proscenium house prompt corner. There were two narrow cubbyholes, no more than slits, in the brick of the right-hand auditorium wall close to the stage, accessible by ladders (once inside, one was there until the interval or after the play), both with complete stage views, in one of which the stage manager had a place while the other usually held lighting or sound equipment.

In *The Old Boys* the stage manager had a busy time – dressing-room calls, stage staff alerts, lighting and sound cues – and for her to keep her attention on Michael too and also to prompt was asking the impossible. I had the advantage that over the later rehearsal period I had developed the ability to anticipate when Michael was about to dry and so at rehearsal the next afternoon, Michael was fitted up with his hearing aid while I climbed up the ladder into the concealed spare space in the wall to crouch over the miniature microphone.

Something of a black farce ensued. In his anxiety Michael had twiddled the hearing aid's volume control in his breast pocket and so quiet prompts emerged in a crackling fusillade from the earpiece, completely incomprehensible to him. Sylvia Coleridge gamely tried to help him out as he struggled with the controls, in the course of which the hearing aid came to pieces in their hands and fell in fragments to the floor (Michael, never one to lose the chance of a self-deprecating story, in his autobiography has the accident happening on the opening night). Things slowly ground to a halt and then, for the only time in my experience, Michael wept in despair, slumped in Jaraby's chair and sobbing that he was letting everyone down, that he should never have attempted to work on stage again.

Before I could get down from my eyrie Peter Copley, who had been waiting off stage to enter, swiftly came on, crossed to Michael to sit beside him, his arm round his shoulder, and reassured him gently that everybody in the cast could appreciate what he was going through. Then we persuaded him to have another attempt using the stand-by earpiece. For the rest of that run-through he was beginning to be able to use the system with more confidence and at the second preview, although his performance was still somewhat tentative and slowed down by occasional pauses for prompts, the audience could not tell that there was a major problem.

The first night must to him have reared like a Beecher's Brook. When I went to his dressing room to see him before climbing up my ladder to the prompt spot, I was inevitably reminded of *The Mountebank's Tale* – his hands were ice-cold, the coldest I have ever held, and his eyes were filled with apprehension. He had no friendly support out front; Rachel was filming, Fred in California and the children were all busy too. The loneliness of which so many actors speak on opening nights for him was multiplied *in extremis*.

He began tentatively but Sylvia Coleridge cleverly avoided one disaster area when he jumped several pages by improvising a few lines as a link before getting him back to where he should have been and he took the half-dozen or so prompts required with no obvious waits. When I saw him in the interval – not my custom – I was heartened to find him quite angry with himself, the iciness gone and the eyes alive. Despite a bad fluff early in the second half and a few prompts, the latter stages were like watching a racehorse revive after a flagging start, and by the time he arrived at the Rimini Hotel to face Miss Burdock, startling her and marshalling the residents to his side with a long (unprompted) Yeatsian speech of rebellion asserting the rights of the elderly to anarchic joy in defiance of the approach of death, the performance was soaring.

A handful of notices mentioned his occasional hesitancy on the lines, but extraordinarily from so close to complete disaster he had pulled off, if not a triumph, at least a definite success ('HEAD BOY REDGRAVE GIVES A LESSON IN ACTING' headlined one review). Michael Billington's *Guardian* notice rightly spotted that the performance was not quite there yet but found many 'moments of greatness' and described Michael as still possessing all his uncanny ability to evoke a feeling of bottled hysteria. The critic-dramatist Frank Marcus thought Michael very nearly at his supreme best, especially in the final scene: 'He shuffles into the Committee meeting in a crumpled raincoat and shows us why he is regarded as one of our great actors. He is always at his best when called upon to undermine the effect of his tall, handsome presence with suggestions of nervous tensions amounting to terror.'

During the Mermaid run, as his performance continued to expand once his wall of fear had lifted (although psychologically he clung on to his prompt system – I spent much of a clammy summer in that Black Hole in the Mermaid wall – he needed it less and less), Michael talked frankly in an interview about that frightening opening period, berating himself as a 'duffer' and stressing that panic had overwhelmed him rather than a failing memory: 'Acting to an audience whose expectations are high is a little like bull-fighting. A slip – and the crowd as well as the bull can turn into your enemy. And once you have felt yourself slipping into that abyss, it is hard to re-master your nerve.' He admitted the 'terrors' of the National experience for the first time publicly, but added that he thought the intervening years had cured him of 'that absolute horror' of having to face an audience feeling insecure. The interviewer, Peter Lewis, was not the first to notice the disjunction between Michael's urbane, collected appearance and tone, and his vocabulary of 'dread', 'fear' and 'horror'. Lewis had been back to see Michael's Jaraby a second time, describing it as a performance now as rich and deep as any of his past successes, a judgement reinforced during the run by American critics in their summer London surveys (the *New York Times* hailed it as 'a great performance') and by the notices on the long regional tour (without hearing-aid) which followed the London run. It finished in Oxford, about which Michael revised his opinion during a week of sold-out houses and coughless audiences; after the final performance there was a 'lock-in' in the pub behind the New Theatre while the whole cast, many of whom must have guessed that *The Old Boys* might be their last stage appearance, drank and sang the songs of their youth until dawn in a touching echo of the play's last scene.

As if in confirmation of his seemingly restored theatrical power, at last a film opened of which Michael could be genuinely proud. It may seem a high claim that one of his smallest film roles should also be one of his greatest, but in *The Go-Between*, even with only a handful of lines and a total of just a few minutes' screen time, he gives a demonstration of screen acting as fine as anything in *The Browning Version* or *The Stars Look Down*. It reunited him with Joseph Losey after a frustrating period earlier in the 1960s when Losey had planned a film of Roy Fuller's novel *Carnal Island*, the story of a distinguished man of letters visited by a younger publisher, planned for Michael and Alan Bates but for which finance was always collapsing. More recently Losey's involvement with what Dirk Bogarde deplored as 'the lolly and the lushness' of his infatuation with mega-budgets and the Elizabeth Taylor–Richard Burton hoopla of overblown films like *Boom!* or *Secret Ceremony* had to some signalled the atrophy of a major talent, but by returning to his most sympathetic collaborator, Harold Pinter, on *The Go-Between* he directed his finest film. Despite the outward period trappings, the film is just as rooted in the closed world and coded undercurrents of Anglo-Saxon class and manners, both sexual and social, which underpin their previous collaborations on *The Servant* and *Accident*, although neither film is as daring as *The Go-Between* in its handling of time.

L. P. Hartley's 1953 novel, based on experiences of his own boyhood, is a haunting story of lost innocence, repression and betrayal. A young fatherless boy, Leo, from a relatively poor background, finds himself when invited by a school friend in a seductive Eden, a leisured country house world during a last, long Victorian summer. Used by Marian, the beautiful daughter of the family, to carry assignation notes between her and her farmer lover (although her ambitious mother has matched her to a viscount), Leo sees his holiday end in tragedy, affecting him well into his later years ('You flew too near the sun and you were scorched').

Other film makers had tried to bring the book to the screen before, including Puffin Asquith and Korda, who planned it as a vehicle for Margaret Leighton as Marian (she is superb as her watchful mother for Losey) with a script by Nancy Mitford, but the rights – as Losey and producer John Heyman found too – were problematic. When they were secured, Pinter at first turned down the project, thinking the book almost too perfect to film, but his eventual script, catching all the nuances of the novel and crucially understanding that *The Go-Between* is Hartley's search for lost time, makes it all the sadder that he and Losey were never able to film Proust together.

The most ingenious stroke is Pinter's solution to the contrast between and confluence of tenses in the novel. Whereas the body of the story is one extended flashback book-ended by a prologue and an epilogue which would have been extremely clunky as a film device, Pinter had the idea of 'flash-forwards', initially short enough to miss if one blinks and then progressively longer until the final scene, also in the present, between the older Leo and Marian in old age (Julie Christie in a not entirely successful latex mask). Pinter's solution, which became the making of the film, was fiercely opposed by virtually everyone (Heyman included) in the production and distributing departments, and yet on screen it is impossible to imagine the alternation between present and past handled any other way. Losey's treatment of the 'flash-forwards' is masterly, giving a crucial slight dislocation between sound and image to the earlier ones and also using for all of them a completely different lighting, bleached and chill in contrast to the warm, heat-hazed Renoir glow of the 1900 scenes.

Michael loved Hartley's novel – 'that wondrous book' he called it to

Edward Thompson – and it is hard to think of another actor who could have inhabited the haunted older Leo so completely. In the gleaming black beetle of the chauffeured Daimler in which he revisits the Norfolk lost paradise of his boyhood trauma, he seems to be inside a second carapace in his buttoned-up raincoat, with his tightly furled brolly and bowler hat. From his opening voice-over of Hartley's first sentence – 'The past is a foreign country. They do things differently there' – through each glimpse of him during the film until the interview with Marian, he suggests with the most remarkable finesse the tension between the bright and hopeful boy of young Leo and the tight-lipped, repressed old man, flinching as if struck at the accuracy of Marian's description of him as 'dried up'. The unforgettable final image of the film, of the elder Leo being driven away, the house of the past (looking now lifeless in contrast to the bustle of its 1900 heyday) still seen through the Daimler's rain-spattered rear window, has Michael's face close in on itself in wintry isolation, the eyes deadening, mouth tightening, as Leo sinks back into his armour of repressed, fearful denial of feeling. No other actor could have conveyed so much with such economy.

With his scenes separate from the main story, Michael had disappointingly little contact with a happy unit, with Alan Bates, Julie Christie, Edward Fox and Dominic Guard (young Leo) enjoying long summer days and cricket matches between shots on location in Norfolk. But he loved working again with Losey and wired his congratulations when *The Go-Between* won the Palme d'Or at Cannes, beating a more fancied film from another Marxist romantic, Visconti's *Death in Venice*. And he in turn was proud to receive a letter from Pinter after the film was finished: 'Your performance in *The Go-Between* is quite superb and of enormous importance to the film. Because of your remarkable delicacy and subtlety the film is now essentially about Leo and the pain of time. That was our intention. Now it has been achieved.'

While on tour with *The Old Boys* Michael had been asked by Michael Codron, who had succeeded Binkie as the West End's most prestigious producer, to replace Alec Guinness in John Mortimer's success, *Voyage Round My Father*, at the Haymarket. Michael had no qualms about taking over from another actor; he admired Alec's performance but he also realised that it was a part which could be played in a very different way. Mortimer's play was an undisguised family memoir about his relationship over thirty years with his barrister father who goes blind in mid-life but continues with both his life and practice as though nothing had happened, carrying on his nocturnal battles with earwigs in his garden, a crafty, occasionally malicious but not unsympathetic character. Guinness's performance, technically impeccable and fastidiously funny as the Father flicks off his aphorisms ('Nothing narrows the mind as much as foreign travel'), nevertheless for some was rather clinical and somewhat bland overall. 'I'm always angry when I'm dying,' the character rages at one stage, but Guinness's anger was very low-key (sent by his director to coax more fire out of the star, Mortimer was countered rather huffily by Guinness: 'I tap my boiled egg in the breakfast scene quite crossly').

Michael latched on to the Father's rage at once: 'I think I'm rather like the character in the play, although I'm not a bully. But I can ignore things I don't want to see. What really fascinates me is the son's introduction to the audience in the first act. He says: "He had a great capacity for rage but never against the universe." This, to me, makes sense.' The detail of the blindness absorbed him even before rehearsals. At Cambridge he had had a friend, Elisabeth Wiskemann, an able modern historian who was going blind slowly, and he remembered details of her behaviour, especially the delicate motion of her hands feeling for surfaces and objects.

Once again he had gone into rehearsals optimistic, convinced after he had proved during *The Old Boys* run that he could finally remember a new role that all would be well. And once again what seemed to him 'the wall of fear' descended and, late in rehearsals, the hearing aid was sent for (again the device was in character). The West End gossip mill soon spread all sorts of stories about Michael and his device on *Voyage*, including the incident of a radio taxi company cutting into the system's frequency so that Michael turned to the startled actress playing his wife to tell her, 'I am to proceed immediately to Flask Walk, Hampstead' (sadly apocryphal, like most of the other tales). With the pressure of opening behind him he was able to settle into his favourite West End theatre, happy in a company which included his old Liverpool colleague Jane Baxter as his wife and Amanda Murray, playing his daughter-in-law, who became a good friend. His richly textured and detailed portrayal of this Edwardian original was covered by few major critics, although many of those who caught it thought his performance richer than Guinness's with its curious nimbus of sanctity. Michael found a completely new subtext to the character; in his hands this was a man clearly staving off disguised terror and the spectre of death. The *Observer* described it as 'one of the most quietly astonishing performances in London' and Michael, on 10 per cent of the box office, which continued strongly after his takeover, was once more earning significant money, much needed at that time.

With the children all now dispersed, Hans Crescent was too large and too expensive to run, and in 1972 it was sold while Michael and Rachel moved to a charming, eccentrically laid-out leasehold house in Lower Belgrave Street, with Fay Blackett Gill organising a bank loan to fund the extra £15,000 needed (the surrender of the Hans Crescent lease raised only £6000) using Wilks Water as security. A three-storey house with a striking canary-yellow front door, tucked between a florist's and an off-licence, it had a long, narrow corridor on the ground floor with just one room, an office, off it and then a light, attractive sitting room–dining room and kitchen on the first floor with a small roof garden (Rachel was thumbing through the rose catalogues even before they moved in) with bedrooms on the third floor. John Fowler once again helped Rachel decorate, using as much as possible from Hans Crescent. With Fred now so often absent in California Michael had surrendered the lease on Rutland Street, but he also took over the tenancy of a tiny one-up, one-down studio flat in the neighbouring Ebury Mews.

No sooner had that been arranged than he had to fly to Canada for a few weeks of *Voyage Round My Father* where the play had a chilly reception, before moving on for a season in Australia. Michael had dithered about accepting, only partly joking in explanation: 'I've not taken the chances offered before because of this uncomfortable feeling that my mother was so unhappy there. Australia was almost my cradle and I've always felt it might be my grave.' But in one of the advance interviews to the Australian press to publicise the tour, he took a different line: 'One of the things I would rather like to do is visit my father's grave. I suppose it would make me a sort of Australian. I don't know exactly where the grave is.' This last claim is odd. Among the boxes of papers and letters which came to Michael after Daisy's death and which he had gone through carefully – at one stage in 1963, as he told Caryl Brahms and Ned Sherrin among others, he was considering writing a book on the story of Roy and Daisy – was Sister Cyril's letter with the details of Roy's death, his burial and the mention of the South Head Cemetery grave. Either Michael had forgotten, which seems unlikely, or some atavistic superstition or dread made him reluctant to visit the grave of the father he had never known.

The season opened in Melbourne with an Australian supporting cast directed by Euan Smith, who had previously assisted *Voyage's* London director Ronald Eyre and with whom Michael enjoyed working. At the Comedy Theatre he wrote to Rachel after a dress rehearsal that he thought they had a flop – 'a big fat flop' – on their hands, but the reviews were some of the best he had ever had, noting his performance's canny rejection of easy sentiment and its underlying wonder at the mystery of familial relationships, and he came to remember his Melbourne time with affection. Although officially autumn, it was still warm and in the middle of a city which surprised him by its leafy beauty he found a favourite park where he sat to write home: 'I still visit my lovely adjacent park each day and am writing this in the late afternoon sunshine by a secluded lily pond.' Often, as he admitted, he was 'very homesick', especially as Rachel's letters, at a time at home of the miners' strike and Edward Heath's three-day week, were often worrying with upsetting news of problems in Corin's marriage (he and Deirdre parted in 1974), her anxiety about his and Vanessa's increasing dedication to the Workers' Revolutionary Party and her concerns for the grandchildren. Also in Melbourne he had the shock of hearing of the closely consecutive deaths of Binkie Beaumont and Noël Coward, two men so important in his own life who both, despite occasional differences, had always remained close friends.

There was some consolation from other old friends when he was able to enjoy a few days with Yehudi and Diana ('so loving and warm') while the Menuhins were in Melbourne, and in hearing that for his next engagement, an American tour later in the year of the RSC's anthology *The Hollow Crown*, Peggy Ashcroft would be joining him. Also, Googie Withers was ceaselessly hospitable and altogether he was sad to leave for Sydney and the grim John Clancy Auditorium ('Crematorium' he dubbed it), writing to Amanda Murray and Rachel of its echoing acoustics and narrow stage, on which the company had to do some rapid restaging. Tony Guthrie when directing *Oedipus* there had described the antiseptic, cavernous auditorium as a pyramid for a dwarf pharaoh. But by sheer force of concentration and projection Michael seemed to tame the space, leading a critic who had vowed previously never again to see a play there to describe the evening as 'Sir Michael's Miracle': 'It is monumental in the sum of its minutiae, pieced together with compassion and dimension . . . there is a capacity for acting above and beyond the lines, of a way of giving a lifetime of experience to a playwright which simply does not exist in this country. The word to describe this performance is wisdom.' In Sydney he never visited South Head Cemetery to look for Roy's grave. He was now keen to be home, writing to Rachel: 'Oh, I can't tell you how I long to get home! To hear all your news, to hold you in my arms and I do long to hug and kiss you.'

There was time for most of July at Wilks Water together, the garden at its finest that year, and they often saw John Fowler and Jocelyn Herbert, who spent most of each summer in the country following George Devine's death. Rachel still saw a good deal of Glen Byam Shaw, who visited Wilks Water often during Michael's absences; fully back to health, he was usually extremely busy with Sadler's Wells Opera of which he was now director. But at the end of July 1973 Michael had to pack again and with Peggy, Roy Dotrice and Brewster Mason fly to Denver where *The Hollow Crown*, with so little rehearsal it was only just pulled together in time, opened at the Central City Opera House.

John Barton's compilation, by and about the kings and queens of England, was an audience-pleasing entertainment of readings mixing poetry, letters, chronicles, Jane Austen's *History* and royal writings with music concerning or by them. The setting – five stately chairs and a lectern – was simple enough for lengthy touring; the men wore casual dress while Peggy was more resplendent in a red kaftan. By far Michael's best opportunities were James I's splenetic 'Counterblast to Tobacco', a delightful piece from the ambassador to the Neapolitan court answering questions from Henry VII about the possibility of the Queen of Naples as a prospective bride while delicately deflecting such problems as her perceptible moustache, and a moving valedictory piece from Malory's *Morte d'Arthur*. The altitude in Central City gave him problems; he found he could do little during the day and he felt worryingly tired often. But he was happy in the production, telling Rachel: 'Peg is *twin towers* of strength and I hope and trust she feels *something* of that in me.'

There was one visit which, however tired, Michael was determined to make during his only brief break during this American trip. Earlier in the year Rachel had heard from Betty Michell that Bob was dying. He had been diagnosed as suffering from terminal cancer, which had begun in his throat, and by the time Michael was able to visit the Michells in Nevada had undergone a laryngectomy, removing his voice box, at a Reno hospital. It must have been a moving final meeting – Michael seemed much frailer after nearly twenty years while Bob, usually weighing around 200 pounds, had shrunk dramatically to less than half that. Whether Betty had any idea of the reality of her husband's previous life with Michael is uncertain; Bob always wrote to Michael when Betty was at Mass or out, and Michael's letters to Bob, none of which has survived, were probably among the possessions which Bob stored in a brown suitcase, always kept locked (only after his death did Betty notice that it had disappeared, Bob presumably having destroyed it at some stage when he knew he was dying).

Michael had only a couple of days before leaving to rejoin *The Hollow Crown*, but the family tactfully left them together as much as possible, Bob occasionally scribbling on the notebook he used to communicate with visitors, Michael giving him updates of all the children's activities and surely also telling him of Fred's decision to remain in California. Most people at home felt that Fred had exploited Michael and had simply decided to stay in America when Michael could not be of much use to him any more. Michael did not take that view; he was grateful for the good times he had had with Fred and realised that Fred, no longer young, would have as difficult a time rebuilding an American career as he would have had constantly trying to find a real niche in London. Bob and Michael must have touched on past times, too, and all that they had shared; of all Michael's male lovers, it would seem that Bob always had the most secure place in his heart. Betty drove Michael to Reno airport with Bob; as Michael finally had to make for the departure lounge Bob quickly scribbled a note for him: 'I won't stay to wave you off. I know I should start crying.'

The Hollow Crown and another RSC compilation of readings, Terry Hands' *Pleasure and Repentance*, a scrutiny of love in prose and verse, profitably employed Michael and various different casts sporadically over the next few years. Early 1974 involved a strenuous twelve-city US tour, giving him a final New York appearance at the Brooklyn Academy of Music while Lynn was having a Broadway hit in *My Fat Friend* and they saw a good deal of each other, their relationship now freer from the constraints of the past. New York had not seen *Pleasure and Repentance* previously and it went down well, Michael scoring heavily with Charles Lamb's ironic 'Complaint about Married People', his quietly devastating delivery of that chilling tale of a suburban Othello, W. H. Auden's poem 'Victor' and, most enjoyably for him, the chance to let his hair down as narrator of a piece of classic Mickey Spillane pulp fiction with the gangster's moll played by a favourite younger actress of his, Sara Kestelman of the husky voice, to whom he wrote:

> O Sara, great Sara,
> O how do you do it?
> Making grown men shed tears
> When you say 'Pass the cruet'.

It was his last batch of New York notices – he and Rachel later turned down all the efforts of producer Herman Shumlin to co-star them on Broadway in William Douglas-Home's *Lloyd George Knew My Father* – and all were glowing for him. The *New York Times* praised 'the touching beauty' of his voice and his ability to handle verse so that the technique of the poem evaporates into air, leaving behind only the essence of the piece.

That tour ended with the company's return at a fund-raiser for the Redgrave Theatre, Farnham, which had opened in May while Michael was touring America; Rachel and Peggy deputised for him at the opening. It had been just before the final American dates that Michael had news of Bob Michell's death. Rachel heard in a telephone call that Michael was upset by 'a friend's' death and intuited at once that this must mean Bob, writing to Michael immediately: 'Oh dear! Oh dear! What can one say? He, the bravest and the best, it's unbelievably cruel. I know how terribly upset you will be, and so was and so *am* I.'

Rachel was then having to cope also with letting Wilks Water for a time – through Peggy Ashcroft it was let to Harold Pinter, who wrote *No Man's Land* there – because of their financial situation. Although Michael could still command handsome touring salaries, there were now increasingly long gaps between engagements with no money coming in.

At sixty-six and after two years of extensive touring, Michael was not unduly worried that he once again felt continually exhausted, and it was Rachel who badgered him into seeing a doctor and then a specialist. At the National Hospital for Nervous Diseases finally – explaining all the terrors, the feelings of persecution at the National, the increasing involuntary 'mask' of facial immobility of over a decade – Michael was diagnosed as suffering from Parkinson's disease. The diagnosis of PD came at a depressing time – continuing money problems, no work on Michael's horizon until another *Hollow Crown* tour early in 1975 and the death of a favourite family dog, Barney (named for Barnes Wallis and, for Rachel, 'ever faithful, ever true') – but Michael was remarkably resilient. Surely, despite the prognosis (there is still no cure for Parkinson's disease) he was glad to have an explanation of what had been wrong with him and to disprove the theories of others that his self-indulgence or weakness might be to blame for his memory problems and physical deterioration. Some friends were puzzled that he was not angry at such a belated diagnosis but the techniques now common to examine the brain were then not widely available and Michael refused to waste time on useless recriminations.

He understood the implications for his career. The illness works on the central nervous system and as brain cells producing dopamine (the chemical which acts as a messenger to the brain) reduce, the normal systems of communication to the brain begin to break down. Usually those neurons which control motor function begin to show signs of damage first, as another actor sufferer, Michael J. Fox, has explained: 'Like a car without motor oil, a brain without dopamine is going to slowly but inevitably break down.'

Michael's handwriting, discernibly shakier in letters from Australia in 1973, had got worse and now his speech often could sound slurred, although there were as yet only occasional signs of the tremor of Parkinson's ('the shaking palsy' was its old name). Fox, diagnosed remarkably young (Young Onset Parkinson's is much rarer), was initially tempted – like many stricken – to see the disease as 'payback', a metaphor (in Susan Sontag's sense in *Illness as Metaphor*), the bill finally presented for a banquet underappreciated, but Michael did not react in that way even initially. Prescribed the drug L-Dopa (Levodopa), he immediately found it of great benefit, but by the beginning of 1975 he was often tired again, and frequently sleepy and nauseous, part of L-Dopa's side effects. Rachel saw him off at Heathrow on a freezing early January morning to begin another *Hollow Crown* and *Pleasure and Repentance* tour, this time to America and Australia, writing in her first letter:

Oh my darling,

It has seemed the most painfully sad day. Your braveness in going off this morning when you were feeling obviously so low and exhausted tore my poor heart which has ached *literally* all the day.

But once he had had time to acclimatise, Michael was sounding astonishingly revived in Palm Beach ('even more Babylonian than Fort Lauderdale') and happy in a company including Brenda Bruce, Paul Hardwick and Derek Jacobi. Like the rest, Jacobi took care to include Michael as much as possible in off-stage activities, although they all had to accept that there were times, often triggered by memory lapses about his medication, when 'his illness could make him very selfish and sometimes cantankerous'. Meals could be particularly tricky with Michael liable sometimes to fall asleep in mid-course, but Jacobi more often remembered very happy times. At Fort Lauderdale the company all went to the famous gay bar, the Marlin Beach, where Michael was enthralled by the exotic clientele at the *thés dansants* and by the stories of the owner, an ex-actor called Jim Eilers who had outrageous anecdotes of his times working with Diana Dors when she was still Diana Fluck of Swindon. Another high spot was Honolulu where Terence Knapp, who had been in the National Theatre's first company, now professor of drama at Honolulu University, took them all to a riotous bar: 'Michael dropped 20 years – afterwards we all walked back to our hotel over Waikiki Beach singing, with Michael suddenly younger and happy and in his element.'

The Australian segment of the tour was extremely social, with many Sydney functions and junketings with the cast from the RSC's touring *Hedda Gabler* headed by a rather dour Glenda Jackson but also including Peter Eyre and Timothy West. On this second Sydney stay, again it would seem that he did not track down South Head Cemetery to look for his father's grave. Michael was homesick by now, as he wrote to Rachel, also touching on his current reading, Nigel Nicolson's *Portrait of a Marriage*, covering the relationship of his parents Harold Nicolson and Vita Sackville-West, involving bisexuality on both sides in a marriage even more unorthodox than that of Michael and Rachel: 'I find it a very irritating book. No marriage could survive such a lot of verbiage. The world *love*, *love, love* loses its value when it sprawls over so many pages.'

On his return he was able to join Rachel back at Wilks Water where Pinter had left a script of *No Man's Land*, which Michael could only read wistfully. Gielgud and Richardson co-starred in it subsequently; Michael in his prime could have played either leading role, but the chances of his ever being able to create a demanding new part were slim while the disease insidiously destroyed his short-term memory, its most cruel manifestation for an actor.

Rachel, too, was at a low ebb, her confidence badly shaken by con-secutive unhappy experiences in the theatre, recently in a miserable time at the National with a new Peter Nichols play *The Freeway*, something of a catastrophe which nearly drove her to a breakdown and which she left early. Their finances, as always, seemed in disarray; running both Wilks Water and Lower Belgrave Street seemed to eat up the solid sums Michael could bank from his tours. But *The Hollow Crown* and *Pleasure and Repent-ance* were beginning to run out of touring dates while filming was impos-sible because of his memory and the increasing unpredictability of his movement. Aubrey Blackburn's heart trouble had now forced him to stand down from the agency business although Michael was happy (and Rachel joined him) to be represented by Ann Hutton, an extremely capable and trusted agent who had worked with Blackburn and who built up an enviable client list.

Even though he never entirely lost his Micawberish streak, with so many options closed to him he must have had occasional anxieties about an uncertain future. Shortly after returning from Australia, with no work in sight, he took part in a Stratford fund-raising gala which covered the generations back to his own golden days with Tony Quayle as Falstaff, Peggy as Queen Margaret, Judi Dench as Fanny Kemble and Alan Howard as Oberon, while Michael played Lear's awakening which Peter Hall, one of four Stratford directors on stage at the end – Quayle, Glen and Trevor Nunn joined him – found both 'an amazing trip down memory lane' and deeply affecting: 'Michael Redgrave, weak with Parkinson's disease, performed Lear ... Redgrave has always been a favourite of mine. Tonight he was simple, direct and very moving. I cried.'

Twenty
CLOSE OF PLAY

At that point in 1975 I joined another project involving Michael, which arose out of a production including Rachel. That year I was to direct Julian Mitchell's distillation of Ivy Compton-Burnett's basilisk scrutiny of Edwardian landed family life, *A Family and a Fortune*, produced by Michael Codron in the West End, and Rachel had been offered a part which ended with her character's moving deathbed scene at the close of the first half. She turned it down, something of a blow as she was ideal for the role of Blanche Gaveston, a seemingly scatterbrained wife with a detached husband and unloving children, who emerges as perhaps the wisest character in the play. All of us involved in the production assumed that Rachel had considered the part too small. Coincidentally, I had been invited for a Wilks Water weekend at that time and of course mentioned our collective disappointment; it emerged that in fact she had really liked both play and part but she was insecure after what she called 'the haunt' of her recent theatre experiences, genuinely feeling that her nerve had gone and that she should concentrate on television in future. I could reassure her that *A Family and a Fortune* would reunite her with old friends – Alec Guinness and Margaret Leighton included – and that Percy Harris, one of the Motley trio and a friend for forty years, would be designing. Finally she reconsidered and she was outstanding in the part.

But it was clear at Wilks Water that although Michael truly was delighted by the offers coming in for Rachel, he was despondent about his own career. He talked frankly about his illness, now completely aware of and mostly resigned to the reality that he was unlikely ever again to be able to take on a major new role, even if his memory for parts he had played in the past, particularly his great classical roles, was unimpaired. Although physically at times distinctly diminished, he seemed when his medication was working properly almost as commanding a presence as ever; his features would lose their mask-like rigidity, and with his hair still thick, he looked when in top form less than his sixty-seven years. I promised him that I would try to come up with some ideas for the theatre that we might consider involving him.

Considerably activated by Joan Hirst and Ann Hutton, a kind of 'Save

Michael' campaign was already in operation to explore the possibilities still open to him. Paul Elliott, an engagingly affable West End producer and the impresario Michael trusted and liked by far the most of those who had managed the tours of *The Old Boys* and *The Hollow Crown*, had recently gone solo and under his management it was agreed that I should devise and direct a programme for Michael which would use a small supporting company, shaping the evening round major extracts from his Shakespearean repertoire. It was not as ideal as a new play but hopefully it could keep him working and earning for several years to come.

Shakespeare's People, as the evening was called, was structured in four seasonal sections, moving from the springtime of the early comedies through the histories and tragedies to the winter of *King Lear* and the late romances of reconciliation and forgiveness, designed to give Michael a relatively gentle start and to provide crucial rests for him throughout the evening; it also used sonnets, songs and related lighter pieces such as a wonderfully indignant outburst on the insensitivity of audiences to his *Macbeth* from Macready's *Journals*. Three actors – David Dodimead (an ex-Old Vic and Stratford regular), Philip Bowen and Elizabeth Counsell, with a brilliant guitarist, lute player and singer, Rod Wilmott – supported Michael, playing against a large Elizabethan tapestry, variously lit, with the company on stage throughout, the men in black trousers and loose white shirts, the solo woman in a trouser suit for the androgyny of Rosalind and Viola, then a long silk gown for later scenes.

For Michael the major responsibilities included the long bravura scene of Richard II's return from Ireland, the scenes with Lady Macbeth prior to and following the murder of Duncan, Prospero's renunciation of his magic and, nearly always the most memorable, King Lear's emergence from his 'great rage' to be reunited with Cordelia. He was in good physical shape during the summer rehearsals in Chelsea, at times astonishing the company with his power – his voice seemed to have recovered much of its delicacy of shading – and he was obviously elated to be working at full throttle again rather than having to resort to readings such as *The Hollow Crown*; although the staging of *Shakespeare's People* was uncluttered and necessarily simple, it gave him the freedom to use his body and gestures – magnificent invocations with his arms and hands during Prospero's 'Ye elves of hills' speech – as well as his still matchless voice.

Paul Elliott did things in style. The flight to Johannesburg on the first tour of *Shakespeare's People* to South Africa involved an eight-hour Paris stopover which the company dreaded. They were met by a smart people carrier and mysteriously driven from Charles de Gaulle Airport around the perimeter of Paris to arrive at a beautiful, moated and mellow-stoned chateau for an epic lunch worthy of several Michelin stars. But it was still a gruelling flight and the South African management, low-profile to say the least, was not in Elliott's league; a badly jet-lagged Michael (the time differences confused him also when it came to his medication) had to stay in Johannesburg for press interviews while the others flew on to the first date in a gale-lashed East London and by the time he joined he was completely exhausted. The first performance was for a local charity – Books for African Schoolchildren – in a bleak, cheerless hall rather than a theatre (the stage management had to spend a day covering its large windows with blackout material) and was a predictable disaster, with Michael so adrift he was never quite sure what piece was next and only just getting through the evening because of the ever supportive quick thinking of his fellow actors.

At the next date, Port Elizabeth, where their competition was another British import, Barbara Windsor in *Barbara Carries On* (which was rather more popular), the company feared the worst; arriving on their first day for a poolside lunch, Michael 'looked about 110 and dropped most of his lunch on the floor' as David Dodimead noted in one of the audiotapes he made on *Shakespeare's People*. Dodimead anticipated another evening of artfully sotto-voce prompts, 'but, suddenly – Bingo! – he's all right again and gives a wonderful performance'.

Moving on to their main date in Johannesburg, the production opened to excellent reviews but poor business – 'Johannesburg and Shakespeare are not exactly lovers' was Dodimead's verdict – although now that he was acclimatised, and nannied by the discreetly tactful company manager employed by Elliott, a quietly droll, quizzical reformed alcoholic, Grimmond Henderson, who monitored his medication, Michael's demeanour on stage had something of the majesty of his glory days. The social life in Johannesburg was lively and there were guided tours of unexpected pleasures such as the city's art gallery with its great El Greco of the Apostle Thomas and some major Impressionists, but Michael never felt happy there ('I did not much enjoy that town,' he told Rachel, writing to her of the shock of seeing 'Whites Only' signs on taxis and the bizarre anomaly of a Supremes concert which turned out to be for an exclusively white audience). Michael was in markedly reflective mood in Johannesburg; often I joined him for a nightcap in his depressingly gloomy hotel suite, and as he talked of books, of past performances and of aspects of his life I sometimes wondered if he was musing aloud with his autobiography in mind. I noted in a journal at that time: 'What a chasm of confusions – confusion rather than guilt. He appears always to be attempting to puzzle out what has happened to him, but still looking at himself from a certain distance.'

Everything changed in Cape Town where they all relaxed, playing to large and wildly responsive houses in the Nico Milan Theatre, a well-designed modern auditorium with outstanding acoustics. Michael wrote to Rachel, 'There is none of the Blacks and Whites oppressiveness here – or I have as yet seen none – and we play entirely to multi-racial audiences.' He was ensconced in the opulently rose-pink Edwardian Mount Nelson Hotel with its spectacular views of Table Mountain, although he always felt uncomfortable when staying apart from the company. There was a large pool in the hotel grounds – one of Michael's foibles was his love of swimming in the rain and he considerably diverted hotel guests by padding out in his baggy trunks to swim whenever there was a shower – and he gave several lunch parties round the pool so that the company could swim, at one memorable occasion (on their day off) providing copious champagne and performing his repertoire (extensive) of Noël Coward songs.

Mail took for ever to arrive from home; Lynn's letters from America (where she and John Clark were now permanently based with their three children) reached him more quickly than those from London ('I absolutely worship her,' he told Dodimead after receiving one of her letters) but despite occasional homesickness, for most of the time in South Africa his spirits seemed high. His supporting company all came to love him, the unpredictabilities notwithstanding. Dodimead noted in many of his tapes performances when 'the old magic' was as potent as ever, powerful enough for audiences to forget the slightly palsied hand. But there were other nights when Dodimead, Bowen and Elizabeth Counsell all had to be extra vigilant when Michael's stage brain was underpowered, and Dodimead in a final South African tape guessed that below the surface of the bonhomie, Michael often was 'a really worried man' when he contemplated his disease and its implications for his long-term future.

Back in London, Michael seemed outwardly confident enough. He felt that provided his schedules allowed him time to adjust to each new venue after travelling, *Shakespeare's People* could be a lifeline for him in the immediate future and Paul Elliott, with his new business associate Bernard Jay, soon put together a tour for the autumn of 1976. Michael and all the members of the original company found it irresistible on reading an itinerary that began with rehearsals above a London pub in Drury Lane, opened in Buenos Aires followed by a string of South American dates and then to Canada before a luxury return on board the *QE2* during which they would present one informal performance without scenery.

The only apparent lowering of his rejuvenated spirits while at home was when the news came of Edith Evans' death. Michael and Rachel – both with many memories – attended the memorial celebration of her life held in a jam-packed St Paul's, Covent Garden, with Michael delivering one of her favourite poems, Wordsworth's 'Westminster Bridge'. He was, as most press reports remarked, slightly stooped that day, but he read the poem beautifully, simply and without a tremor in his voice.

Before re-rehearsals for *Shakespeare's People*, still clinging on to a shred of hope that at least some remission of his PD might be possible, Michael flew to America to consult Dr Irving Cooper, a leading specialist in the condition, at St Barnabas Hospital in New York's Bronx. Largely at the urging of several Americans, including an old friend, Dr Nicky Ruzzo, who were not entirely convinced by Michael's treatment at home and also encouraged by Lynn who had met Cooper's medical associate, Dr. Joe Walz, he was now determined to explore the possibilities of a pioneering operation which might alleviate the worst PD symptoms. This operation required the utmost precision in boring a hole in the skull to target a nucleus of cells (the VIM nucleus) in the thalamus of the brain which controls movement, the object being then to disable those cells which affect the trademark PD 'tremor'. Today, with advances in surgery and computer screen back-up (Michael J. Fox successfully underwent a thalamotomy in 1998) the operation is less rare; in 1976 there was a strong risk of bleeding in the brain and, of course, even if the operation helped reduce the tremor it could not – still cannot – totally arrest the stealthy progress of the disease itself.

Michael certainly would have risked the operation had it been considered advisable but Dr Cooper, after extensive tests, counselled against it. Still, as Michael wrote gratefully to the Actors' Fund of America which (approached by Lynn) had contributed to his expenses: 'I feel immensely fortified.' While he was in St Barnabas Vanessa and Lynn, both then in New York, often visited and they were occasionally allowed to take him out to picnic in a nearby park for the afternoon, Vanessa sometimes bringing Michael's new grandson, Carlo, her child by her *Camelot* co-star Franco Nero.

In St Barnabas Michael was put on a new drug, Sinemet, a combination of Levodopa and Carbidopa, the latter designed to prevent the former from being metabolised in the body's organs, allowing more of it to reach the brain. It definitely reduced Michael's tremor initially and he found the new drug's side effects considerably less worrying than the nausea and frequent vomiting of L-Dopa. He sounded remarkably sanguine in his letters to Rachel, usually written in St Barnabas's azalea-packed gardens (although his handwriting is often discernibly shakier), cheered greatly by the news that his Sinemet dosage, originally prescribed for eight times a day, had been reduced to only three times.

Paul Elliott, always sensitive to Michael's problems, provided more back-up for him on the South American and Canadian tour, and Ron Lucas, a cheerful and exuberant character in contrast to Grimmond Henderson's laconic personality, became his personal dresser, both of them having the knack of organising and unobtrusively assisting Michael without fuss. The whole company noticed the difference which Sinemet seemed to have made and the 1976 journeys made up one of his happiest ever tours; the audiotapes which David Dodimead continued to make reflect the whole company's enjoyment. They were at first startled and then delighted by the unexpectedly demonstrative receptions in South America with cheering audiences showing their love of Shakespeare and gratitude for the performances with flowers which rained down from the tiered boxes in some beautifully maintained *fin de siècle* theatres. Reactions in Canada were similar, with Michael's cherished *Variety* reporting the Ottawa performance as receiving 'a well-deserved vertical ovation'.

In Toronto he was especially pleased by one notice, which spotted in his performance a detail of which he was secretly rather proud. At the end of the first half of *Shakespeare's People* he came forward downstage as the lighting changed to deliver Jacques' 'Seven Ages of Man' from *As You Like It* and, towards the end of the speech, he elaborated in performance a piece of 'business' which had happened involuntarily because of his PD tremor in the rehearsal room and which everyone present insisted he should reproduce and incorporate in performance. It happened just after Jacques has reached the final age of 'second childhood and mere oblivion', and as the Toronto critic noticed:

> He has a slightly palsied shake in his left hand which he controlled perfectly all evening – except here. Suddenly he seemed not to be able to stop it. And then when he had everyone on the edge of the seat, he blurted out the famous last line: 'Sans teeth, sans eyes, sans taste, sans everything'. What a ruse! And how brilliantly he did it! Mocking infirmity is just one facet of Sir Michael's new profile. The performance he gave last night was the essence of memorability. To have seen him do Jacques was to have seen something grand and splendid; a gesture in the face of all the littleness that lurks around us.

There were further successful Canadian dates in early 1977 – again with the same loyal company – which included Vancouver. And it was in that gleaming modern city, in an encounter born out of secretive and complex Edwardian-era love affairs thousands of miles away and which must to him have carried around it something of the aura of a Shakespearean late romance, where Michael met for the first and only time his half-brother Victor. This was Victor Parrett, Roy's son by the actress Ettie Carlisle who had been with Roy in South Africa and Australia, although Victor had thought for all his early life that his father was the actor Henry Parrett, to whom Ettie was married in South Africa on the rebound from Roy, only for Roy to pursue her. She had abandoned Henry Parrett, unable to resist Roy's charms, returning to England with Roy from Australia when pregnant to give birth to Victor ('the boy' of Roy's letters to Daisy), only to be abandoned in turn by Roy after Daisy's bombshell of her pregnancy. So, like Michael, Victor never knew his father. He only discovered his true paternity at twenty-one (his mother Ettie had died five years before) when he required his birth certificate which, obtained from Somerset House, revealed to his surprise that his father was George Ellsworthy (Roy) Redgrave. Victor had closely followed Michael's career once he realised the link between them and in 1977 in Vancouver, where he and his wife were living, he finally contacted him. They talked for a time one winter afternoon, with Michael at his most shy, in a conversation animated mostly by Victor, who was left not much wiser about their father's extraordinary character, his subterfuges and his secrets.

But in turn Michael kept secret his Vancouver encounter; although he and others of the family had met the son (another Roy) of Robin Redgrave, first child of the marriage between Roy and Judith Kyrle, he never told his family of the meeting with Victor, not even when subsequently working closely with Corin on his autobiography. That had other secrets and omissions, of course; there was no mention, for instance, of his relationship with Tony Hyndman or anything of the long involvement with Fred, although the astute reader would be able to gather how crucial a part Bob had played in his life. The secrecy about Victor seems somehow characteristic; perhaps he simply forgot to tell the family or, more likely, it amused him to save up yet another of Roy's surprising secrets to be revealed, or not, at a later stage. It was not in fact until 1994 when Lynn was in Vancouver and was contacted by Victor that anyone of Michael's family had any inkling that he had met Roy's 'boy', his near contemporary half-brother.

There was another long gap before the next, and most exhausting, tour of *Shakespeare's People* was scheduled to begin in San Francisco. Most of the summer was spent at Wilks Water; Lower Belgrave Street, with its steep awkward stairs and expensive to maintain, had been sold, so now only the tiny cottage of Ebury Mews remained as a London base. But Michael was content enough among the wildlife and the gardens in Hampshire, watching the moorhens on the water, still reading widely and increasingly just resting while Rachel's career seemed properly at last to have come into its own; she was in considerable demand for prestige television work and now was preparing for the theatre again with Alan Bennett's *The Old Country* opposite Alec Guinness, in which she gave one of her finest, subtlest performances as the disillusioned wife of an exiled traitor living out a sad life in a Russian dacha.

For Equity reasons only David Dodimead (who had a Green Card) was able to accompany Michael on this next long tour, covering most of the American states. Using American actors in the other roles, this version of *Shakespeare's People* was mounted jointly with the American Conservatory Theater of San Francisco and was directed by the ACT's Ed Hastings.

Dodimead called it 'this mad tour' and indeed the itinerary – rehearsals in San Francisco before opening at the other end of the USA in New Jersey, then slowly and often circuitously moving south and finally back across to California – involved some epic journeys (one day in October the company went through five states in a single twelve-hour journey) and was often exhausting. Yet Dodimead also described it as 'wonderful, wonderful, wonderful'. He and Michael were both Americanophiles but knew little of the landscape outside New York and California, while this tour took them, often speechless with wonder, from the ravishing autumnal woods of New England to the astounding beauty of the Blue Ridge Mountains of West Virginia and through the snows of Kentucky at 3000 feet above sea level before returning to their last sun-bleached dates in California.

Michael missed his other supporting actors who, after the various tours of *Shakespeare's People*, had blended into an unusually strong ensemble, familiar with his difficulties, but with Grimmond Henderson and Ron Lucas besides Dodimead he had enough friends to cushion the rigours of such a demanding tour. The dates were mostly one-night stands, with occasional rest days, touring in a bus with overnight stops usually at the staple Howard Johnsons (Michael found their uniformity oddly reassuring) or Quality Inns. Sometimes they played handsome, intimate old theatres, at others characterless modern university halls or improbably vast venues such as in Boston where they played (and filled) the 2600-seat Symphony Hall; in such huge houses, much to their distaste, the actors would have to be miked (with footlight microphones – 'like little river rats on the floor in front of us,' said Dodimead).

Only rarely was there any opportunity for enjoying hospitality – normally it was a case of changing after a show and back to the hotel or into the bus to drive some of the distance towards the next date – although in Virginia an old friend of Michael's from his Navy wartime days there, Anne Cone, with whom he had always kept in touch, threw a lavish party with lashings of vintage Dom Perignon for a delighted company. Initially, with a tiring schedule and while adjusting to new actors, Michael's performances were often erratic; in the early stages of this tour Dodimead's skill as a subtle prompter was often required, but after the first busy period in New England and Virginia his old form returned.

He was blissfully happy. Michael genuinely loved touring – he was certainly Roy Redgrave's son in that regard – and he relished playing towns whose evocative names he knew only from American novels (he was reading William Faulkner and F. Scott Fitzgerald on this tour), films or popular songs, places like Chattanooga, St Louis, Kalamazoo, Terre Haute and Des Moines. It was a gruelling schedule, even for a young and fit actor; there was something heroic about Michael, a PD sufferer approaching seventy, still responding to the nightly challenges of a new town, an unfamiliar auditorium, a different audience.

He was glad of his sympathetic companions when, late in the tour, he heard the devastating news of Dick Green's death. Only Rachel, perhaps, could fully comprehend the depth of his feelings for Dick; many of his friends could never quite appreciate Michael's loyalty over forty years, but despite his earlier 'crazing' and the drinking problems, Dick remained for Michael always the truest of his friends, the one to whom he could reveal himself most fully. Michael accepted his friends flaws and all, and his admiration for Dick's unusual character – a complex, witty but fundamentally melancholy man whose convinced Stoicism helped him cope with an often troubled life – did not diminish with the knowledge that Dick, Senecan to the last, had killed himself knowing that he was hopelessly riddled with lung cancer.

Soon after he had heard the news, he was visited by Vanessa and her partner at that time, Timothy Dalton, who caught him in *Shakespeare's People* in magical form in San Francisco. Even the brief time with them cheered him somewhat but Dick's loss still weighed heavily, as he wrote to Rachel ('I am thinking of Dick a good deal of the time and I am apt to get morbid'). And yet, as he said in a notably unsentimental interview shortly afterwards for his seventieth birthday, referring to himself as 'not a very nostalgic man' and only briefly mentioning the death of 'a great Cambridge friend': 'The great thing is not to dwell on it but to go on.'

Rachel, who had always been fond of Dick, although she was never part of life at Rockwells, was saddened too but she had reasons of her own for unhappiness then also. For a quarter of a century she and Glen had continued their close relationship, never entirely easy for either of them but in the good times a solace and a deep bond for both. But Glen's wife, Angela Baddeley, who had enjoyed late-life television stardom as the truculent Mrs Bridges, the cook in *Upstairs, Downstairs*, had recently died, since when – seemingly out of some profound, belated sense of paralysing guilt – Glen had ceased all contact with Rachel, her letters and calls going unreturned. She was inwardly devastated and with Michael and her daughters in America, Corin mostly in Yorkshire and now also without the familiar counsel and unfailing support of John Fowler (he too died in

1977), Rachel then was at her absolute loneliest; her sense of isolation must have been exacerbated for a time by the shock of Michael's belated revelation of his affair with Edith Evans all those years ago. For some while afterwards she was prone to some very black spells of deep, despairing unhappiness.

It was also becoming increasingly clear, once Michael had been back home for a while, that his working life was drawing to a close. Paul Elliott still had future bookings for *Shakespeare's People*, including a successful UK regional tour, joined by a new member of the company, Rosalind Shanks (Michael felt as comfortable with her as he had with Elizabeth Counsell and she was similarly helpful with reminders to him of his 'dolly-mixtures', as he called the Sinemet tablets), and a Scandinavian visit which included his last performance in Copenhagen.

Most successful of all was an enchanted fortnight at the Bermuda Festival, which involved endless jaunts and hospitality, including a bibulous late-night party at the Police Headquarters Club, and much publicity, which became equally riotous on the occasion when Dodimead, quizzed on television as to the nature of *Shakespeare's People*, described it as 'loosely hung about Sir Michael's great parts'. Elliott joined the company in Bermuda; he, like them, felt that the festival performances saw Michael at his very best, voice and physical presence almost undimmed. He needed no prompting and the notices unquestionably were among the best he had ever received. Philip Bowen, always intrigued by the mix of humility and self-consciousness, even vanity, in Michael's personality, was with him when he read the glowing praise: 'His eyes were streaming with tears. These sort of notices still mean so much to him. It's sad in a way because he's been through so much fame in his time.'

Sinemet had been of great initial benefit, but after the latest rounds of *Shakespeare's People* the tremor began to return more frequently and, most desolatingly for him, his voice was losing its elasticity and distinctive timbre. Professionally, a void lay ahead; he had to tell Ann Hutton and Elliott that no more tours were possible and even radio and recording work was becoming difficult. Michael had made countless recordings throughout his career – including many Hans Christian Andersen stories, always using Dick Keigwin's translations and artfully highlighting the element of the surreal in a favourite teller of tales. He had also worked often for Dadie Rylands (appearing many times for Apollo Society poetry readings), who was still remarkably active and occasionally tempting Michael into the studios; of all his work for Dadie, Michael was most pleased with his recordings of Gerald Manley Hopkins' verse (often partnered by Barbara Jefford) and the epic undertaking of *Paradise Lost*, in which his Satan conveyed a compelling malignity, freighted too with that sense of the fathomless sorrow of those his favourite Faulkner called 'the unhomed angels'.

On radio he had managed to play several key roles which he never had the chance to tackle in the theatre – the arch dreamer Peer Gynt was the most special for him – and more Chekhov, Trigorin in *The Seagull* (with Guinness as Konstantin) early in his career, and a later *Ivanov* included. Over the years he had worked with most of a Golden Age of radio producers – R. D. ('Reggie') Smith, for whom he starred in the journalist James Cameron's Prix Italia-winning play structured round a heart operation, *The Pump*, Val Gielgud, Donald MacWhinnie, Douglas Cleverdon, Rayner Heppenstall and John Tydeman among them.

In 1976 the producer John Theocharis had approached Michael, somewhat tentatively, hoping that he might consider a small but key role in Euripides' *The Sons of Oedipus* (the title David Thompson's new version gave *The Phoenician Women*), the last of his plays dealing with the age-old theme of power lust through the Theban legend. The masterpiece of Euripides' later years, the play ends with Oedipus in obdurate old age, blind and bitter, still refusing to come to terms with his downfall. Theocharis knew that the late appearance of Oedipus was central to any successful version of the play: 'I needed a great actor who was somehow not now at his very greatest – his whole presence as Oedipus has to suggest *past* glories.' Ann Hutton had warned Michael that the actual size of the role was small but when Theocharis telephoned him, reinforcing his feeling that 'every line the character has is a giant' and illustrating his point with Oedipus' line of greeting to Jocasta ('My wife, my mother'), he accepted the part immediately.

In its depth of tragic feeling it remains a towering performance; Michael was especially pleased that it had been noticed by one of a new generation of critics, Nicholas de Jongh in the *Guardian*, who described this now rare instance of a Michael performance in the UK as 'a remarkable one ... his emergence into the terrible light of day at the play's close is chillingly memorable'. So successful was this venture that BBC Radio, for Michael's seventieth birthday in 1978, set up a major new production of Sophocles' *Oedipus*, in Edward Fitzgerald's version, directed by Theocharis. Two years since their last collaboration saw Michael considerably diminished and the project began disastrously one morning with Michael, clearly ailing and vocally distressingly frail, pleading quietly in the studio, 'Can I go home now, please?' Talking to Rachel, Theocharis discovered that Michael's medication meant that usually he was stronger in the afternoons. He made the next call a post-lunch session; Michael on arrival flung open the studio door, calling 'How's this?' in his most resonant voice and ready to work all afternoon. His voice had unquestionably lost something of its resilience but the broadcast was still an astonishing demonstration of vocal skill and sensitivity to a text without ever allowing the technique underpinning that art to show, most marked in the sense of awe communicated as Oedipus realises the sacredness of Colonnus and the final submission to his destiny.

For Theocharis Michael ranked – with Gielgud, Peggy Ashcroft, Judi Dench and Leo McKern (Olivier was never happy with only the microphone) – among the great radio actors. All shared the rare gift of 'being able to generate energy on air' and although all had very individual vocal qualities, they could mint thought with a mysterious, almost electric transmission: 'You can hear it through the voice. If they *think* right, the vocal quality becomes right.' Theocharis's words on radio acting could almost be those of Michel Saint-Denis talking of the stage.

Publicly Michael seemed cheerful enough and indeed, for someone so hypochondriacal in earlier life that a cough instantly became consumption, it was extraordinary how uncomplainingly he reacted to such a debilitating illness. There were only a few times when privately he sank into silent brooding, never jealous of others of his generation still active and employed but inevitably saddened by his enforced inactivity.

Socially he was of necessity much less active and if he and Rachel were both in London, the doll's house of Ebury Mews could become claustrophobic. Michael might take himself off on one of his mysterious nocturnal jaunts or take up invitations from newer friends such as the composer Lionel Bart or a personable and gregarious young actor-photographer, Alan Warren; at both their flats there would be a floating population of visiting American showbusiness personalities and young gay men in relaxed, congenial atmospheres in which he would be perfectly happy just sitting with a drink. Wilks Water was quieter, especially after John Fowler's death. However, his hunting lodge was eventually tenanted by the writer and interior designer Nicholas Haslam who had known Fowler well and who was always kind to Michael when Rachel was away on location, often inviting him over for drinks or supper.

The actress Patricia Hodge and her husband Peter Owen were Haslam's guests one weekend when Michael joined them belatedly for dinner. She was surprised by his initial appearance – dishevelled, shaky, clumsy with his food – and then by the transformation once, evidently, his medication had taken full effect. He seemed another man, joining her and fellow guests around the piano, exuberantly singing Gilbert and Sullivan and, memorably, his party piece of 'My Time of Day' from *Guys and Dolls*. Patricia Hodge remembered the evening for that and even more for the 'charismatic effect', despite his illness, of what she called 'his devastating charm'.

Just when it looked seriously as if Michael would never work again, late in 1978 Harold Pinter called Rachel to ask her if she thought he might consider taking on a vital but – apart from one line near the end – virtually silent role in Simon Gray's new *Close of Play*, which Pinter was to direct at the National Theatre the following year. There was no special pleading in the argument that the role of Jasper needed a special actor. The play, one of Gray's best, was a jet-black comedy, often also achingly moving, of a dysfunctional middle-class family, the paterfamilias of which sits silent in the sitting room throughout, immobilised by a stroke, while his two sons and their wives use him as a surrogate confessor, spilling out all sorts of secrets and guilts to this impassive patriarch. Only at the close, when the play moves away from naturalism into an eerie, choric sequence, does Jasper speak ('The door is open') after he has struggled to rise from his chair, 'his eyes fixed in wonder'.

Already cast in this unsettling family reunion were Michael Gambon as the shambling doctor son, John Standing as the other, a hopelessly alcoholic BBC producer, and Anna Massey. A bonus for Michael was that Peggy Ashcroft was to play the leading role of – of all names – Daisy, nicknamed 'Nanty', a cousin of Jasper's late wife, bustling around constantly, chattering non-stop, worrying about off-stage grandchildren using a soup tureen as a potty and seemingly oblivious to the collapsing lives and marriages round her. It was a wonderful part and Michael at once saw how Peggy could pierce to the truth of the character without making her irritating to the audience.

When he was first told of the offer, Michael cried with joy. The idea of playing on the National Theatre stage on the South Bank, the site of which he had helped battle for, in a new play directed by Pinter was to him a godsend beyond anything he could have imagined. It mattered not a jot to him that he had only that single line; he knew from the script that all of Jasper's reactions, his every expression, would be vital to the other actors and to the play.

The cast certainly found that so. John Standing as the drunk Benedict understood keenly how much Michael helped him – 'in the hands of a lesser actor it would have been very difficult' – especially in a crucial lengthy confessional speech with only Michael's eyes and slight movements for reactions: 'He was so helpful, so immensely generous. He would always feed you. ... For me, what was especially wonderful was that when I had a pathetic, drunk breakdown scene, this self-destructive son breaking apart, Michael's look of disgust was so right to act off.' *Close of Play* went into rehearsal in February 1979 against a background of industrial action on the South Bank. Peter Hall attended the first reading as the National Theatre's director:

I was moved to see Michael Redgrave there, Crocker-Harris to the life, sitting listening attentively to the other actors and gazing quizzically over his half glasses. This was one of my favourite actors in his prime. Now he is slow and gentle, and ravaged by Parkinson's disease. It's a miracle this part exists to get him back onto the stage – a part with no words, but the face having to convey infinite feeling.

Michael, nearly always first to arrive at each day's rehearsal, was impressed by Pinter's quiet authority and also felt that Peggy was well on the way, even in the early stages, to creating one of her most memorable performances as Daisy. And then, in a grim replay of the 1943 *A Month in the Country*, an injury – this time to her knee, which she had damaged before rehearsals – forced her, to her distress and Michael's desolation, to withdraw. Under the circumstances her replacement, Anne Leon, gave an excellent performance, but something had gone out of the heart of the play. Rehearsals were then further disjointed by picketing as the industrial unrest turned bitter; Michael's taxi was stopped as he arrived to rehearse and despite his illness and mobility problems he had to hobble the length of the building to reach the stage door. The first night was twice postponed, Gray's play finally opening almost two months later than scheduled.

The first image – and the last – of *Close of Play* was Michael's spotlit face, a majestically impassive ruin of a demigod, rigid in his chair against a void of inky darkness (more than one critic saw the play as Jasper's dream of imminent death). A few notices remarked on the mesmerising subtlety of Michael's contribution to the evening, but it was surprising how many echoed Frith Banbury's verdict that his appearance in a one-line part was sad (one even insisted that the casting was 'exploitative'). They were wrong. Michael was an actor; an actor acts.

Close of Play played in repertoire and on performance days Michael was always perceptibly much brighter, anticipating the evening. Towards the end of the National run there was a crisis when a planned week in Dublin as part of the Theatre Festival was threatened by worries for the company's security in Ireland in the aftermath of Lord Mountbatten's assassination. At a company meeting called at the National, among those present was the Dublin Festival's young director, Michael Colgan, who, facing the loss of the prize of his first programme, had flown over to attend. Sitting anxiously next to Michael, just before a show-of-hands vote on whether or not to go ahead, Colgan felt Michael's hand shakily reach for his to pat it reassuringly before quickly putting it up to be the first to vote to ignore the IRA by playing in Dublin.

Although saddened by Peggy's withdrawal, Michael was happy through-out the run of the play. On the last night at the National Peter Hall dropped in to say his goodbyes: 'Michael Redgrave in tears. I think he feels that this was his last time on the stage. He said to me, "Do remember I can learn more than four words." His illness has resulted in such a loss to us all.'

Money remained a constant problem; the top salary at the National was £150 per week and there was no prospect of future work, with only Rachel's earnings to keep them going. Before long Michael also had to have a full-time carer; in another odd twist, this turned out to be Stephen Croft, the Westminster schoolboy who had been so close to Corin and Vanessa at Bromyard during the war.

Good-humoured and tirelessly patient, Stephen 'lived in' at Wilks Water when caring for Michael. He knew the area well, having acted as caretaker for a time for the National Trust which had been left the freehold of John Fowler's hunting lodge. Stephen was theatre and film literate, and he also understood Michael's moods well, always remembering the essential need for gentleness in the physical handling of PD sufferers; he also quickly learnt that should Michael on occasion over-indulge in alcohol, it was wiser to make no comment (his usual riposte if challenged was to pour an even more massive vodka).

To act as Michael's chauffeur was also part of Stephen's job and it was because of driving him at times to London that he became aware that Michael, despite his frailty, had a lover whom he would occasionally visit there. This, Michael's 'Last Attachment', was Alan – Michael never told anyone his surname – of whom tantalisingly little is known except that he was around fifty, married, and lived in north London. Stephen's description of Alan was 'rough trade' and he formed the impression that he was either a cab driver or a lorry driver, but when visiting him Michael always asked to be dropped some distance away and so Stephen never knew Alan's exact address. Rachel had met Alan once or twice, but only fleetingly, and Michael also told Corin of his existence. But he remained a shadowy figure; Michael's sense of secrecy never entirely left him.

The label of 'rough trade' is misleading, however; even if intended only as a physical description of Alan it suggests the casual anonymity of the one-night stand, whereas although Michael never talked of Alan at any length, much more was involved. From the little that he did say – and from the length of the association over his final years – it is clear that there was an emotional as well as a sexual bond, certainly for Michael and probably for both men. Corin remembered one time in 1982 when his father mentioned that after spending the night together in Ebury Mews, he and Alan had kissed goodbye on the doorstep in the morning before realising that they had been witnessed by the wealthy dowager who lived opposite. Corin tried to reassure his father, telling him that the woman was probably liberal-minded, but Michael remained unconvinced: ' "Oh, you don't know," said my father, and shuddered as if pinched by a cold draught.'

Some of that reticence, to a large extent born surely out of the prejudice – and the law – which marked most of his lifetime, informed the autobiography on which Corin and Michael were working during that hot summer, Corin coaxing patiently as much material as he could when Michael's energy was low. At that time Corin had abandoned his theatrical career, devoting his time to the Workers' Revolutionary Party, but he travelled regularly from the Party's Yorkshire base to help on a project vital to Michael's immediate financial future; the book had attracted a handsome advance and there were promising prospects of serialisation rights.

They worked in the Wilks Water studio, although Michael no longer slept there. A year before in the winter, when the stream between studio and main house was in full spate, late at night he had stumbled and fallen off on his way across the little bridge, landing heavily face down in the icy water. Stephen Croft was not at Wilks Water that night, but eventually somehow Rachel heard Michael's faint cries and with almost superhuman strength – Michael even in old age was never a lightweight – she managed to lift him and drag him back into the house. Afterwards, he was more frequently sleepy and often dizzy, but through the hot days of the following summer Corin, with infinite patience, finally had the manuscript of Michael's autobiography in shape, with the book ending (almost as strongly as the first two chapters, written so many years before) on an oddly affecting dreamlike note in a coda which Michael dictated in one sitting without a single correction.

During the writing of *In My Mind's Eye* he once said to Corin: 'I don't feel old. I just feel slow.' The prospect of activity always seemed to revive him, however; he was stimulated by all the business of proof-reading and pre-publication publicity, and delighted by his selection for a Foyle's Literary Luncheon. The book had been respectfully reviewed and Michael was touched by so many letters of praise from old friends going back as far as Clifton days. The bookshop's event was a crowded occasion with many of those old friends and colleagues present – Peggy Ashcroft, John Clements (who had always been kind to Daisy), Alec Guinness and John Mills among them. Although under no obligation to speak – certainly in light of his illness – Michael had planned to amuse the guests afterwards by ending the speeches with a playful old party piece which he normally had no trouble remembering, a jaunty cockney monologue that had been in the repertoire of Little Tich (Michael may have first heard it seventy years before with Uncle Willie in the gods of the music hall at Portsmouth), but when he rose before the microphone he completely 'dried' and not a word emerged as he stood opening and closing his mouth like a goldfish, blinking at the audience, until after an epic pause he smiled gently and finally said, 'I think I'd better sit down, don't you?' Many guests, including the notoriously unsentimental Clements, were in tears and, the main business completed, the room began to empty, but curiously it was not a depressing spectacle, as Peggy Ashcroft reassured him: 'How can I put into words all – or anything! – of what I felt and still feel about Wednesday's lunch? I shall always remember it. Like they say drowning is – so much of the past swims up into one's mind. Shared pasts. I felt proud to be sitting next to you. So wonderful to see Rachel in all her beauty. In fact everything had a glow to it, radiating from you.'

In My Mind's Eye sold solidly in the UK, although many of his friends wished that he had written more of it before his illness was so advanced. It used an unusually informal cover photograph of a pensive Michael taken by Franco Nero, catching him in a non-professional unguarded pose reflecting Googie Withers' description of his eyes: 'I have a picture of Michael always in my mind – of eyes that are slightly sad. He looks as if he's just been hurt. That's Michael to me. I always had that feeling – which Rachel had too, I suppose – for a child that isn't quite the same as the others. You always love that child more.'

There was one last junket to his adored New York for the book's American publication when, once again, the prospect of activity buoyed him up. During this brief visit his old friends Milton Goldman and Arnold Weissberger, always splendid hosts, threw a lavish party for him at a mid-town restaurant glittering with famous names – Anthony Hopkins, Sam Spiegel, Carol Channing, Hermione Gingold, Douglas Fairbanks Jr – but also there, at Michael's request, were less high-profile but valued American friends including Anne Cone, Norris Houghton (it was their last meeting) and Lehman Engel.

On his return, as all those close to him noticed, he seemed to go downhill rapidly. He had managed, with extraordinary will-power, to perform the Lear–Cordelia reconciliation scene from *King Lear* twice for benefit performances in aid of the Young Socialists' Training Centres with Vanessa, once making his very last appearance on his first professional stage at the Liverpool Playhouse (going through his lines with Stephen Croft at the Adelphi beforehand, he tartly told Stephen that his Cordelia needed work, reminding Croft later of the scene involving *Lear* between the King and his doctor in Alan Bennett's *The Madness of George III*). The second *Lear* extract – his valedictory performance – was at London's Round House, a less happy occasion with Michael clearly ailing, almost too moving and painful to watch (Thelma Holt, rarely lachrymose, found herself awash with tears).

Yet he had one final flourish in him, again responding to the prospect of activity even if he could no longer appear. Although he was not much directly involved with the 1984 revival of *The Aspern Papers* he followed its progress keenly, attending some rehearsals and, nostalgically for him, the try-out at the Yvonne Arnaud, Guildford. It was a fine production, impeccably staged by Frith Banbury and magically lit by Joe Davis (one of his final jobs) to suggest the shimmering reflected light from the canal outside the Bordereau palazzo. Vanessa was at her best as Miss Tina, a hibernating creature blinking into the light, opposite Wendy Hiller graduating into an eerily macabre Miss Bordereau, with – to massive publicity – Christopher Reeve as H. J., giving a stylish performance, much admired by Michael, which silenced those who had sneered in advance at 'Superman casting'.

Michael, who in those days could look distinctly unkempt at home, in old clothes with his now permanent beard full of crumbs, spruced up markedly for all his attendances at *The Aspern Papers*, beaming his approval from a box at the London opening, his last visit to his favourite Haymarket.

The royalties during a sold-out limited season were welcome, but both money worries and Michael's condition – by now he was often in a wheelchair, awkward at Wilks Water – dictated the dreadful wrench of selling the Hampshire house. It was worst for Rachel, who had poured such work and love into Wilks Water, but all the family were sad, even the grandchildren, the younger ones perhaps not yet appreciating the place of the house in their parents' and grandparents' lives but still loving its atmosphere and the adventure playground of its surrounding woodland.

The grandchildren – there were now ten altogether – could tire him quickly, but he always welcomed them and on form could entrance them with his stories and fantasias. In the Wilks Water days he invented for them a firm of solicitors, close cousins of *Private Eye*'s Sue, Grabbit and Runne, called Scratchem, Grabbit and Nabbem, based in 'Antshire', as whose bigwig Nathaniel Nabbem he wrote mock-threatening letters on behalf of the Wilks Water family dogs to the hedgerow mice warning them, in an anthropomorphic version of Robert Ardrey's *Territorial Imperative*, that a certain Mr Art Dodger (Michael's cat Dodge, named after the Artful Dodger) might be called upon 'to make sure all mice kept a respectful distance'.

After the melancholy business of disposing of both Wilks Water and Ebury Mews, Michael and Rachel moved into a Chelsea flat in Rossetti Mansions, but soon he was showing increasing signs of frailty and was admitted to the London Hospital in Whitechapel. His neurologist, Professor Watkins, who was familiar with his case, wanted Michael to remain for a time while his levels of medication were checked. Dosages of Sinemet require the most precise measurement and regular monitoring; an insufficient amount increases tremor and concomitant depression, while too much often causes hallucinations (which was beginning to happen in Michael's case, making him imagine accusing, gibing voices at times). But as soon as his dosage was adjusted he discharged himself from Whitechapel and, in one last defiantly anarchic replay of his past wanderings, he had not returned home to Chelsea but had hailed a cab and disappeared. Corin imagined that he had gone to find Alan, adding, 'It was comforting to suppose him still independent and on the loose.' He was back at Rossetti Mansions before long but very soon required a nurse by day and another at night. A few weeks later when Corin telephoned from Yorkshire to check on Michael's progress, the nurse said she thought that perhaps Corin should come to London (Rachel and Vanessa were both working, and Lynn was in America). Corin arrived to find his father that night in bed, Dodge the cat asleep on his unusually distended stomach; his eyes were half-open and he looked dreadfully ill. Glimpsing Corin in the doorway, he opened his eyes fully and whispered to his son the remarkable phrase, 'You put the wind in my sails.'

According to the doctor waiting for Corin in the kitchen, Michael was extremely ill. With his voluntary muscles beginning to fail, urine retention was slowly poisoning his system and he required immediate hospitalisation to save his life. Although, the doctor added more slowly, Corin might just perhaps think it better, with Michael's disease so far advanced, to 'allow it to run its course'. In effect, Corin was being given life or death choice over his father: 'Michael must have known that this was happening, with his hyper-acute hearing and extra sensitivity. Was that why he had greeted me tonight as if I were his rescuer?'

Corin insisted on Michael's hospitalisation and that night he was admitted to St Bartholomew's in the City of London, recovering surprisingly quickly after treatment. The family visited often and Lynn flew from America to see him. In her solo play, *Shakespeare for My Father*, later Lynn described the dark comedy of one visit when she and Vanessa were together by his bedside. The curtains round his bed were drawn and Michael, again hallucinating before his Sinemet was finally adjusted, was imagining that the curtains were the house tabs of a theatre and the murmur of voices from other patients and their visitors the buzz of an anticipatory audience. At one point when Lynn peeped through a gap in the curtains he was aghast, scolding her, 'Don't be so unprofessional! Never look through the curtain when the audience is in front!' Vanessa corrected Michael – 'my sister, the Marxist realist!' said Lynn wryly – telling him that he was not actually in a theatre but in a hospital and that the noise was from all the other patients. She then left to make a phone call. Michael, in his mind, remained happily inside a theatre and Lynn ('no realist, me') helped keep him there, reassuring him when he asked her, 'By the way, how's the house?' that he had a capacity audience and that on all the posters his billing, of course, was above the title.

Michael spent just over a month in Bart's, the consultant specialist then explaining to the family that the hospital had done all that could be done for him in his current condition. Rossetti Mansions was not equipped to cope with the round-the-clock care he now required and so in January 1985 he was admitted to a nursing home close to the film studios in Denham, Buckinghamshire, where he had often worked. With astonishing adaptability and good humour he rather took to life in this establishment, run by the Licensed Victuallers Association (some of his older cronies saw a pleasing aptness in that) principally for the benefit of retired publicans. He had a bed in a small room with only three others, one occupied by Duncan, a cheerfully chain-smoking patient (suffering from emphysema) who had once run a Shaftesbury Avenue pub frequented by actors. A passionate movie buff, he had seen virtually every film Michael had made and, in what sounds like a comic variation on the black finale of Evelyn Waugh's *A Handful of Dust*, Michael was regularly regaled by word-perfect re-enactments, punctuated by hacking bursts of coughing, of scenes from Duncan's special favourite, *The Way to the Stars*.

Rachel and Vanessa visited whenever her work allowed, as did Joan Hirst and Corin with his second wife Kika Markham, daughter of Michael's old colleague from *The Stars Look Down*, David Markham (his wife Olive had knitted the shawl for the infant Corin). They would push him in his wheelchair in the grounds on morning visits, learning early on to move sharpish when the bell signalled pre-prandial opening time to beat the stampede of retired publicans to the smoke-filled bar.

A few long-standing friends also made the trip to Denham, including Peggy Ashcroft and John and Mary Mills who lived near by. Yehudi and Diana Menuhin, despite their still hectic international schedule, drove down to spend some hours with him early in 1985 and, like others, wondered at how accepting, even happy, he seemed. And it was true that there was never any Job-like repining at the confines of his now restricted life. He had never been one for major regrets; as far as the theatre was concerned he might have enjoyed another chance to play Lear or to tackle Timon of Athens but it never bothered him that he, alone of the great quartet of his generation, had never played Othello ('I don't understand the jealousy,' he told Stephen Croft once). In the cinema there was only one major sadness – the lost *Antony and Cleopatra* opportunity – and a wistful 'if only' in the shape of *The Leopard*, di Lampedusa's great novel of revolutionary nineteenth-century Sicily, one of his very favourite books

(Burt Lancaster was cast as Prince Salina, a role in which Michael would have excelled, in Visconti's film which he thought a masterpiece).

Diana Menuhin spoke some years later of her visit to Denham with Yehudi, who admired Michael above all contemporary actors and who understood the deep attachment which bound Diana and Michael. Although she saw him only occasionally in later years, the closeness between them since the 1940s never slackened and she, more than most of his friends, understood his emotional defensiveness and secret dreads, instantly intuiting, for instance, the extent to which Michael wrote himself, in a manner almost coded, into *The Mountebank's Tale*. Looking as chic in old age as when Michael met her in her stylishly impecunious youth, she spoke of him in a 1996 television programme directed by Roger Michell (another old Cliftonian) to coincide with the publication of Corin's *Michael Redgrave, My Father*, remarking how struck she had been by Michael's gentleness and graceful resignation at Denham: 'He seemed very beautiful, very relaxed, very sweet – there was no need to battle, no need to fight – he always seemed to need to fight. He didn't have to be frightened any more.'

By then speech was often difficult for him and his silences could be epic, but he was happy enough to sit and listen to others. Although he tired easily he was anxious to take up the suggestion of a now rare theatre visit to see his eldest grandchild, Natasha Richardson, play Ophelia in a Young Vic *Hamlet*. It was a matinée, crowded with an initially restless, whispering schools audience, which was finally organised for him. He sat – in the wheelchair which by now he needed constantly – quietly apart at the back to watch the play unfold he knew better than any other and hearing the young audience soon grow hushed and absorbed in David Thacker's fast and uncluttered production with Natasha a stronger than usual Ophelia whose collapse into fragmented madness was beautifully charted opposite a vigorous Hamlet from Matthew Marsh. On the drive back to Denham with Vanessa at the wheel Michael was very quiet; the family were used to his silences, usually signifying deep thought. It was quite close to Denham before he spoke, clearly having gone through the performance – in his mind's eye – to give his verdict: 'She is a true actress.'

On 20 March 1985 Michael was seventy-seven and Corin visited Denham that day – Rachel was filming and both Vanessa and Lynn were in America – but during the afternoon Michael developed a temperature which continued to rise; even a change of bedding and a cooling fan seemed to give him little relief. Corin returned the next morning, realising as soon as he entered the room that his father was close to death. He sat down beside Michael, talking to him without properly knowing if he could hear the comfort of his voice. Michael's breaths gradually grew deeper and more rasping. While sitting, Corin began to leaf through the new softback edition of *In My Mind's Eye*, the book falling open at the passage from Michael's 1940 diary in which he talked of Roy's decline and death to Rachel, trying to describe his own sense of troubled resemblance to the haunted hero of *The Family Reunion* as 'the consciousness' of his family, 'its bird sent flying through the purgatorial flame'. Looking up to check on his father, Corin suddenly had the thought that perhaps he should somehow have attempted to trace Alan in case Michael had wanted to see him: 'It was too late. He took a deep breath, then paused, as it seemed for a long time, took one more deep breath and a sigh, and then no more.'

That evening from the stage of the National Theatre at the end of a performance – apt coincidence of author – of Chekhov's *Platonov* in Michael Frayn's version as *Wild Honey*, Ian McKellen at the curtain call asked the audience to rise for a minute's silence 'in memory of a great actor'. Later that night, while Vanessa and Lynn were flying home, Rachel, Corin, Kika and Rachel's brother Nicholas all walked together in the cold over Michael's favourite Waterloo Bridge. They noticed that the National Theatre's brightly flashing illuminated electronic signboard in place of the usual box office information had put up the announcement:

MICHAEL REDGRAVE: ACTOR 1908–1985

Whoever was responsible for the National's tribute could not possibly have been aware that its wording so closely echoed that of another quietus which Michael had previously made. After a *Close of Play* performance which Lynn had attended, she suggested that she take Michael for a post-show supper at the Savoy Grill where he had so often dined during the war years and later. He was delighted at the idea and thrilled to be recognised by the maître d' and other diners. Lynn and he had champagne as she filled in her father with all her news, in particular of a recent visit to Australia.

After some sleuthing in Sydney she finally had gone to South Head Cemetery, high up on a hill just outside the city near the open sea with two white lighthouses prominent on the cliffs. Through the gravekeeper's office she was able to find, next to a grassy pathway, the grave she was searching for. Roy Redgrave's last resting place, the records showed, had been paid for (15 shillings) by Minnie, Roy's last 'wife', but – with Roy leaving only debts, Minnie presumably had no extra money – there was no headstone. Now it would be possible, Lynn felt, to erect a stone and mark Roy's grave. Eagerly she asked Michael what he would like carved on the stone as his father's epitaph. Some lines of poetry? A quotation from Shakespeare? Was there anything he would like? Michael did not immediately reply; as so often before, Lynn found it difficult to read his thoughts.

Then Lynn noticed that her father's hand had begun to tremble, whether from emotion or Parkinson's she could not tell. Perhaps he felt sad – even ashamed – that he had not been the one to find South Head and Roy's unmarked grave beside the sea. At all events the pause continued for a long time before finally, quietly, Michael spoke: 'Just put "Actor" ', he said.

In Australia some years later Lynn returned to South Head where to mark Roy's grave now stood a modest red-brown headstone. Along with the dates of his birth and death the inscription read:

ROY REDGRAVE
ACTOR
MARKED BY HIS SON MICHAEL

EPILOGUE

Michael's funeral took place on a blustery late March day at Mortlake Crematorium, across Chiswick Bridge not far from his favourite London home of Bedford House. Rachel, in a cream-coloured coat with a bright silk scarf at her throat, was at her most beautiful, supported by all the family and the inner circle of the Redgraves' closest friends.

It was a simple ceremony with just a few readings; Peggy Ashcroft, plagued by injury and illness in her later years, was unable to attend and Dorothy Tutin read a Shakespeare sonnet in her place. Natasha Richardson, voice uncannily reminiscent of her mother's, evoked youthful new life, even in a ceremony structured round a death, as she read a speech of Perdita's from *The Winter's Tale*, reminding those present who had read *The Mountebank's Tale* – which also features a character named Perdita – of the closing sections of resolution and harmony in Michael's story. Both Corin and Ian McKellen spoke eloquently of Michael's uncompromising commitment to a life in the theatre; neither quoted Daisy's exact words but implicitly both reinforced the truth of what she had said to Michael when it became clear during his Cranleigh years that the theatre after all was to be his destiny: 'Most people go into the theatre for what they can get out of it. Not enough think about what they can put into it.'

Something of a blackish farce of misunderstandings ensued subsequently over the final resting place of Michael's ashes. Following an oddly prurient item some time later in the 'Londoner's Diary' of the London *Evening Standard* 'exposing' the fact that Michael's ashes remained at Mortlake, Corin retrieved them from the crematorium. They then spent a time in the boot of his car while the family pondered the various possibilities. At one stage, having bought a modest plot in Highgate Cemetery (Karl Marx is possibly its most celebrated resident), Corin hoped that his father's ashes might rest there but finally, mainly because of Rachel's wishes, they were buried in the earth of the churchyard of St Paul's, Covent Garden. Lynn and Vanessa together planted a rose on the spot in Michael's memory.

The saga of his ashes would have hugely diverted him, although with his uncompromisingly materialist belief that each of us has only one life, and with a good deal of the philosophy which he had absorbed from Dick Green, it is unlikely that he would have had passionate feelings on the subject of his remains' final resting place.

The informality and accidents of his funeral – Lynn's flowers mistakenly were left outside with the other 'floral tributes' – and of the episode of his ashes were worlds away from the sober ritual of the more conventionally formal Thanksgiving Service held at the Actors' Church in Covent Garden at the height of a blazing summer.

Michael would have been gratified by the capacity house of St Paul's, packed even upstairs next to the organ with fellow actors and the public alongside the great and the good. All the stepping stones of his career – Clifton, Magdalene, Cranleigh, Liverpool Playhouse, the National Theatre, the Royal Shakespeare Company, Equity, the Questors' Theatre, the Theatre Museum, the Garrick Club, the Redgrave Theatre, the Yvonne Arnaud Theatre, for most of which institutions he had done no small service – were represented, along with colleagues going back to Jane Baxter from Liverpool (she read from *A Hundred Years Old*, in which she had appeared with Michael half a century before) through Gielgud, Guinness and Peggy from the 1930s heady days when he was making a first mark in London, to those with whom he had travelled the world on his later tours.

Yehudi Menuhin played Bach's Partita in E Minor, Peggy read from Eliot's *Four Quartets* and Nicholas Kempson, now living in Cranleigh, touchingly read Joyce Grenfell's poem on death. Gielgud's still spell-binding voice – that day like the silver trumpet muffled in silk of Alec Guinness's simile – filled St Paul's with Shakespeare's Sonnet XXX and, in a different key, Googie Withers delighted the congregation with Roy's 'Little X', the poem for an actor's son which had marked Michael's first stage appearance in Melbourne in 1910 and which only the family had heard before.

Most affecting of all, totally hushing the church, was John Mills's simple, direct reading of John Pudney's 'For Johnny' from *The Way to the Stars*. It always ranked high among Michael's favourite poems; although brief, the emotional impact of its stress on a basic humanity – to a degree the poem is a gloss on Oliver Baldwin's reminders to the impressionable adolescent Michael that each human being has responsibilities to others – was for him as potent as anything in his pantheon of Yeats, Keats, Hardy or Hopkins.

And yet, of all the occasions and commemorations in the aftermath of his death, Michael probably would have been best pleased and moved by the most informally secular, a Tribute Evening on 1 September, organised principally by Thelma Holt and Corin. It was held, appropriately, at the Old Vic, home of his breakthrough London appearances, his first professional Hamlet and of one of the greatest performances of its era, his Uncle Vanya. The evening gave an extraordinarily vivid picture of the forces which helped shape Michael and of his special place among the stage greats of his time.

As he had always ruefully predicted, his obituaries – for the most part carelessly written and betraying their cuttings library origins – recycled the shopworn 'intellectual actor' label inherited from Agate and Tynan. With the exceptions of *The Times* and the *Guardian*, there were no attempts at even a cursory scrutiny of those special influences which made Michael an actor not easily classifiable within the English mainstream tradition but no less great because of that. Only in the American and European papers was he written of without qualification as unquestionably a great actor; all the main American obituaries ranked him with Gielgud, Olivier and Richardson (the *New York Post* rated him the subtlest of that group). For the British press his career had simply ended in 1972 when his Parkinson's disease was diagnosed; of course, between 1973 and 1978 he toured all over the globe and, as Corin pointed out at Michael's funeral, in that time he played in more theatres and halls than he had appeared in during the whole of his previous career.

It is too simple, however, to blame Michael's decline and the fall of his reputation among twentieth-century actors on his illness alone. There was, along with all his other tensions and schisms, another crucial duality in Michael which surfaced in middle-age, a tug-of-war between the strength of his ambition to build and then maintain his career as an *acteur* – as far as possible, given the financial, domestic and market-place constraints of most actors' lives, to be at the helm of his own life in the theatre – and a certain passivity, a weakness in his nature. It was Jung who stressed that artists often must pay dearly for the 'divine gift' (a phrase Michael once used for the young Vanessa's quality) of creative fire; each human being, Jung claimed, is born with a limited store of energy, and in the artist creativeness usually absorbs that energy, the price paid being often some sort of 'deficit' in life's other areas. And almost every major artist at a certain age loses – or, at best, has a struggle to preserve – the vital capacity for self-renewal and development. John Gielgud, for instance, suffered a serious decline in vigour in his fifties when he seemed cut off from an English stage which once he had ruled before a later-career remarkable renaissance, and Michael too seemed to lose his way in the 1950s for a period. It was a time coinciding both with his knighthood, which for a while undeniably did lead to his divorce from the sheer blood-and-sand realities of the theatre and to a certain remoteness, and with his love-affair with Fred Sadoff. For an artist, such as Michael had chosen to be, these both could be considered misfortunes.

Amongst his contemporaries Michael was especially distinguished by his discrimination, his taste (that essentially was what critics were talking about when they used the pejorative 'intellectual' label) and by an unusually wholehearted commitment to the art of acting. He was a true exemplar of the dictum of Stanislavsky's which he often quoted to his children – 'You must love the art in yourself and not yourself in art' – and for most of his career he had a unique balance between confidence in his own judgement and genuine modesty. But for a time that equipoise was shakily insecure, evidenced during *The Tiger and the Horse* and – even more seriously for an actor whose instincts had usually been to ally himself with the innovatory – by such second-rate choices as *The Sleeping Prince* or *The Complaisant Lover*, when too often he merely acquiesced with the plans or advice of others such as Binkie, Cecil Tennant or Fred, who was always keen to be allied with Michael in New York where there were fewer accusations of his holding on to Michael's coat-tails to find success. At times Michael seemed dimly aware of such weakness; he did at one stage attempt to extricate himself from *The Sleeping Prince* but he did not fight his own corner with much conviction, quickly climbing down when faced with Binkie, Cecil and Rattigan in a united front and with the pleas of Fred, anxious to be back in Manhattan.

There was, too, the mostly unadventurous and often troubled managerial record with Fred and FES (Plays); besotted and blinded by love in their early days together, Michael continued to find it difficult to refuse Fred (at times their relationship illustrated a recurrent theme in Terence Rattigan's plays – how the seemingly weaker partner in a relationship can often exert a terrible, clinging strength), although he too came to realise that not only did Fred have at best merely a slender talent but also, and more damagingly, he had no taste at all. Then, appallingly, just when it seemed as if he had woken up from this period of self-induced torpor and that his own instincts and sense of timing ('You make your own luck') had resurfaced to take him to the glory of *Uncle Vanya* and the promise of a whole new era back in the kind of ensemble theatre of his initial dreams and of his early career, the seeds of his disease were beginning their insidious growth.

Richard Findlater, always a critic unusually perceptive about Michael's particular qualities – he understood too that first nights rarely saw him at his best (although as Michael ruefully accepted: 'The history of the theatre is the history of first nights') and would often catch subsequent performances – seemed to sense something of the imbalance within Michael at that vital mid-career stage when writing of the dilemmas of the mid-twentieth-century actor in his 1956 book *Michael Redgrave, Actor*:

His career reflects the problems of actors of his generation tugged between behaviourism and theatricalism, psychology and tradition, cinema and stage, the long run and the classic repertoire. They have to work against the paralysing effect of English middle-class emotional etiquette with its exaltation of understatement; against the persistent anti-theatrical strand in intellectual life; against the deflationary pressures of post-Freudian, post-Marxist conditioning; against the general sterility of acting values in new drama.

Few of the obituaries of Michael reflected even partially Findlater's perspective. Moreover, what so many missed was a point crucial to any understanding of Michael as an actor, that the crucibles in which his work was fashioned – his adolescent times in Heidelberg and France, exposing him to a German cinematic revolution and to Louis Jouvet, the seminal influence of Michel Saint-Denis (through whom Stanislavsky was refracted and refined) and his early response to an American dynamic with the Group Theater ideal – were all essentially outside the Anglo-Saxon theatrical tradition.

Michael was not at all a typically English actor; more than anything else, that lies behind the more wary or purblind critical perception of his work. His Group Theater hero Harold Clurman, inevitably one of his 'father figures', in his book *Lies Like Truth* made the unpalatable but accurate assertion that despite the brilliant technical sheen of its acting the British theatre of the mid-twentieth century was fashioned mostly from theatre itself rather than from reality. In effect, at that time life was used rather than created in the acting on British stages and screens.

However, at the very core of Michael's being as an actor, confirmed by everything that he had absorbed from Saint-Denis (and as *The Mountebank's Tale* transmuted into metaphor), was the impulse to start from the living natural processes of which the actor must be conscious. This almost sacerdotal belief, which led showmen such as Guthrie or actors schooled and happy in the easy West End world's attitude of 'Just say the lines and don't bump into the furniture' to describe Michael as at times 'difficult' or over-serious, was grounded in what he took from Stanislavsky and Saint-Denis, based always on the latter's insistence that in all acting the key question should always be 'Why?' rather than 'How?'. The base conviction was that the starting point and development of any part in any play was never the individual role in isolation but the unfolding of a whole course of events and the evolving relationship of each role to the others within the course of the actions in the play, taking place at a specific time and under particular conditions. It was something of this burning-glass lucidity of focus on the role within its wider context which so impressed

Michael's old Cambridge friend Wynyard Browne when he wrote to him after seeing his first Rakitin with his attempt to analyse Michael's ability to act in three dimensions simultaneously. That too was behind Thornton Wilder's reaction to Michael's first *Hamlet*, marked above all by its transmission, often electric, of 'an unbroken line of inner life', as Wilder put it.

Today, Michael's approach to acting would be regarded as less than revolutionary but in the theatre of his formative years and beyond he was, if not unique, certainly most unusual. As Vanessa wrote in *News Line* soon after Michael's death, 'It was very demanding working with my father – he would not allow me or anyone else to slip back into mechanical repetition of what we had achieved previously, however skilful.' Vanessa went on to stress how much her father absorbed from Saint-Denis of Stanislavsky's essential principles:

> At each and every moment he would be listening to and looking at the other actors on the stage, as if for the first time, and allow the events, what they did and said, to activate his actions, thoughts and words.

His allegiance to such disciplines in his work was inevitably another factor in the 'intellectual' labelling, which he countered unusually combatively in a lucid Preface contributed to a biography of Louis Jouvet by Bettina Knapp published in America in 1957. Michael had, of course, tackled roles previously associated with Jouvet – Hector in *Tiger at the Gates* most notably – but also everything that he had heard from Michel Saint-Denis, alongside whose uncle, Jacques Copeau, Jouvet had worked in a rich post-1918 era at the Vieux Colombier (the Parisian theatre in the Left Bank street where reputedly Racine and Molière would visit Boileau), confirmed his adolescent impression of the actor on seeing him on stage in Touraine as 'the true artist':

> Jouvet has been criticised as an elocutionist, a pedant and a schoolteacher. The first epithet needs little defence: better an excess of clarity than confusion. Pedant and schoolteacher are the common terms of contempt used by the lazy or the dull, with whom Jouvet, who was a reformer as well as an artist, had little patience. These epithets lose their sting when applied to a true actor and *homme du théâtre*, and in these days when the eccentric, subjective, the wild and – in a word – selfish performance often wins very high acclaim, it is a good thing to remember that here was an actor and a mentor who believed that the playwright's word was the playwright's bond and the actor's brief.

Michael wrote his piece on Jouvet in America at a time when, however intrigued and impressed by the work of such figures as Elia Kazan, Marlon Brando or Julie Harris, he was more sceptical of some of the less disciplined but often indulged work from some of Lee Strasberg's disciples. But his robust defence of Jouvet undoubtedly also reflects something of his reaction to some of the criticism received at home by his own work.

Something of that approach to the actor's art and an impression of those varied forces which shaped Michael's talent shone through the Old Vic Tribute Evening in 1985. Kika Markham read from Daisy's account of her runaway teenage pantomime audition while Corin incarnated his grandfather in some of Roy's bravura letters from Australia. Peggy Ashcroft appeared as a pugnacious Lilian Baylis, Rachel read a favourite Hardy poem 'The Ruin'd Maid', Gielgud performed Prospero's valediction to his magic and Ian Charleson, not long before his death, sang Michael's favourite, Sky Masterson's valentine to nocturnal Manhattan, 'My Time of Day' from *Guys and Dolls*, in the National Theatre production of which he had appeared.

Reflecting the wide and international range of Michael's influences, the evening also included an appearance by Popov (so admired at the Moscow Circus by Michael), New York's Acting Company led by Orson Welles' old colleague from the Federal Theater Project and Mercury Theater, John Houseman (another old Cliftonian), in an extract from Marc Blitzstein's *The Cradle Will Rock*, and a scene from *Richard III* performed by the visiting actors who had so impressed London, the Rustaveli Company from Georgia.

From Roy and Daisy the Redgrave line that night travelled down the generations. Lynn was working in America but Vanessa reprised her tremulous Miss Tina with Wendy Hiller in an extract from *The Aspern Papers*, while the grandchildren were represented by Jemma Redgrave's Katharina from *The Taming of the Shrew* and Natasha Richardson as Nina in a scene from *The Seagull*. That same year in the West End Natasha appeared as the aspirant actress Nina to her mother's Arkadina; previously, of course, Vanessa had inhabited Nina for Tony Richardson on stage and for Sidney Lumet on film.

It becomes difficult to avoid mention of gene pools when reaching the more recent Redgraves. Latest credits include a short film directed by Luke Redgrave (*Strangers*, with a duality one might describe as archetypally Redgrave in the tension between its central character's outward Anglo-Saxon politesse and his internal violent rage – against his wife's sexual betrayal) and a screen project of Wallace Shawn's play *The Fever* directed by Carlo Nero and starring his mother, Vanessa. Michael had ambivalent feelings about the whole phenomenon of 'The Redgraves' and of descriptions of him as the founder of a 'dynasty'. As he pointed out – although he conceded that it made less colourful copy – the theatrical strain in the Redgraves genes went back further than him, further even than Roy, back to Cornelius in his Drury Lane shop or to the Zoe Ellsworthy who acted opposite the great Fechter at the Lyceum. He would often stress, too, that the tribes of Redgraves, Scudamores, Ellsworthys, Kempsons, Markhams and Clarks included, equally vitally, sailors, boat-builders, clergymen and farmers.

Nevertheless he was quietly, fiercely proud of the careers of all his children, seeing many of his daughters' films and West End or Broadway successes. He did not live to witness Corin's remarkable theatrical rebirth when he returned to the profession, including a young Vic *Coriolanus* (1989) with Rachel in blazing form as an indomitable Volumnia (once Michael had had adolescent dreams of playing Coriolanus to Daisy's Volumnia). Intriguingly, Corin also took on several parts previously inhabited by his father, including Frank Elgin in *Winter Journey* (with Kika Markham as Georgie) and, especially memorable for its portrait of emotional repression breaking down under pressure, Crocker-Harris in *The Browning Version*. He also seemed to share Michael's special talent for playing riven characters, in performances as real-life men with double lives including Wilde, Roger Casement and, in 2002 in his own play at Chichester, Anthony Blunt in *Blunt Speaking*, basing his play around the exposure of his father's old Cambridge colleague on *The Venture* as a traitor.

Michael would have taken pride too in some 'family' productions, including a *Three Sisters* with Vanessa, Lynn and Jemma Redgrave in 1991 at the Queen's Theatre (home of his 1937 Tusenbach) produced by Thelma Holt and directed by the Georgian Robert Sturua, a scrutiny of Chekhov as mould-breaking as that of Michel Saint-Denis had been in its day. Corin, Vanessa and Kika Markham appeared together (as writer, ex-mistress and wife) in a West End revival of Noël Coward's *A Song at Twilight* in which they fused the study of a famous, closeted author forced to keep secret an entire area of his sexual life with compelling subterranean currents. And later Corin and Vanessa played brother and sister in *The Cherry Orchard* at the National Theatre as part of the 2000 Ensemble under Trevor Nunn.

If there is a common thread linking the acting generations of the Redgraves it has to do not only with an ability to inhabit the covert and the duplicitous (in an absorbing piece coinciding with the British Theatre Museum's Redgrave Exhibition in 2003 the critic Michael Billington echoed Wynyard Browne when he described this duality as the ability to live in different dimensions simultaneously on stage) but also, even more remarkably perhaps, with a special transparency in their acting, an emotional candour – even nakedness – which can jolt and startle an audience in theatre and cinema alike.

One of Michael's greatest gifts – unrivalled among his generation – was his present-tense immediacy of thought and communication of emotion. This could be almost literally mesmerising, unforgettable in such trans-fixing episodes as Vanya's bleak comprehension of his barren future, Rakitin's conflicting feelings towards Natalya's infatuation, Frank Elgin's awesome exhumation of dormant genius, Crocker-Harris's reaction to Taplow's farewell gift in *The Browning Version* or in the life projected in *Dead of Night* in which the dummy Hugo's voice becomes hideously more real than that of its creator, Maxwell Frere. Even within the discipline of the iambic line this ability was a constant. Shaw may never have been his favourite dramatist (he always claimed that his plays left nothing for the actor to contribute) but he was more valued as a critic and Michael agreed with Shaw on acting Shakespeare: 'Shakespeare should be played on the line and to the line with the utterance and acting simultaneous, insep-arable, and in fact identical'. Time and again, yoked to his mastery of the vocal line and his inner truth, this immediacy informed his greatest clas-sical performances also, piercing to the realisation of 'the thing itself' in *King Lear*, launching Hamlet's rite of passage ('My fate cries out') and travelling to the growth of his accommodation to the idea of death ('The readiness is all') and, supremely, unerringly tracing the emotional arc from self-abasement and corrosive shame to the nobility of the high Roman fashion through Antony's perilous later scenes in *Antony and Cleopatra*. In all of these – and many more instances – he had the capacity which might be described as the square root of the equation of great acting, the ability to make it seem as if his characters were coining their emotions and thoughts on the instant, for the very first and only time, even after months of performances or multiple takes, as if those thoughts, those words were those of his characters, not of their dramatists or screenwriters.

Something of this on-the-moment immediacy of thought on stage was evident when coincidentally both Vanessa and Lynn were working in New York in 2003. Lynn seemingly effortlessly sailed over the hurdles of the solo play in Alan Bennett's *Talking Heads*, most impressively in *Miss Fozzard Finds her Feet* as the apparently repressed spinster who ends as the dom-inatrix of a shoe-fetishist chiropodist, both wildly funny and heart-breakingly touching. Vanessa was one of the few Redgraves never to have visited Elsinore, but as more than one critic remarked, her portrayal of the morphine-addicted Mary, mother of the haunted Tyrones in Eugene O'Neill's *Long Day's Journey into Night*, had overtones of Ophelia, most of all in the climactic scene when Mary, lost in a drugged fog of memory, comes down from the attic holding her old wedding dress ('The mad scene. Enter Ophelia.' says her elder son), a scene which capped a searing performance. A recurrent point in the reviews was the sisters' gift for the total inhabiting of thought on stage. Their faces – like Michael's so often – could become almost translucent, revealing and communicating the most fleeting subterranean thought and feeling. Both performances convinced audiences, in the words of one critic, that they were 'living every moment in the play for the first and only time'.

In the same period Natasha Richardson returned to act in London for the first time since moving to America nearly a decade before. There she had often successfully taken on American parts, including the title role of O'Neill's *Anna Christie* (the primal emotional demands of O'Neill seem to suit the Redgraves) on stage and Patty Hearst on screen, but her London return was, challengingly, once again in another role previously inhabited magnetically by her mother, Ellida in Ibsen's *The Lady from the Sea*. London critics, like their brethren in New York analysing Vanessa and Lynn, tried to anatomise Natasha's gift for inhabiting totally the skin of another character. She seems to use the research into her characters – shades of Michael visiting the Amsterdam ghettoes prior to his Stratford Shylock, for instance – as a kind of stepping stone to complete emotional identification. At one stage she may have tried to throw off the family 'baggage', as she referred to it, by moving to the USA but as the critic Peter Conrad noted in an astute profile of Natasha, she – like Hamlet with his father's spectre – cannot evade 'the dictation of her past'. In a sense, when after making his final theatre visit to see *Hamlet* Michael finally pronounced – to her mother – that Natasha was 'a true actress', he was announcing, and legitimising, close to his own death, a matter of succession.

Rachel's genes too – her committed allegiance to family, her passionate loyalties – took root in the succeeding generations. After Michael's death her career continued to flourish, with distinguished work on stage (especially striking in a West End revival of T. S. Eliot's *The Cocktail Party*) and late-flowering film and television roles, nowhere stronger than as the redoubtable Lady Manners, ignoring the prejudices of an old-guard Indian Raj, in *The Jewel in the Crown* television series, the last of the many productions on which she worked with Peggy Ashcroft. She took enormous pride in heading the family's representation at a major film event in Paris in 2000 when, as part of the 'Typiquement British' Festival at the Pompidou Centre, a special 'Redgrave Season' was included. It opened with Michael and Rachel together in *The Captive Heart* and then covered an astonishing range from the 1930s British Hitchcock of *The Lady Vanishes* through the 'Swinging London' world of the 1960s with Vanessa in *Blow Up* and Lynn in *Smashing Time* to early film appearances by Natasha and Joely Richardson in films by directors such as Paul Schrader and Peter Greenaway.

At ninety Rachel was still in remarkable form. She had outlived most of her close contemporaries; Glen Byam Shaw had died in 1986 without ever resuming contact with her after Angela Baddeley's death. Of Michael's loves, Tony Hyndman died back in his native Wales in 1982 and Norris Houghton in 2001. Fred Sadoff had initially found it hard to pick up the threads of an American career but gradually acting work began to come his way; he eventually established a solid if unspectacular career on US television, appearing in many episodes of series such as *The Streets of San Francisco* or *Barney Miller*, often cast as doctors or psychiatrists. Financially, Fred had no worries latterly; he played the stock market with profitable shrewdness and had apartments in New York and Los Angeles, occasionally teaching acting in both cities. He gave up the Manhattan base in the late 1980s when he was diagnosed as HIV-positive; Fred died of AIDS in Los Angeles in 1994, leaving the bulk of a considerable estate to AIDS charities. Memorial services were held at the Actors' Studio's New York and Los Angeles branches; on both occasions affectionate messages sent by Corin and Vanessa were read out on behalf of the Redgrave family.

Slowly but perceptibly after the Pompidou Centre Festival Rachel's health began to decline; she suffered a series of relatively minor but cumulatively debilitating strokes and her memory, too, began to fail. She still looked beautiful – that remarkable, chiselled bone structure remained until her extreme old age – particularly on one of her last outings to the theatre, smiling happily in a Haymarket box (from which she had also watched Lynn in *Shakespeare for My Father*) at the opening of a revival of Wilde's *Lady Windermere's Fan* with Vanessa and Joely Richardson playing mother and (secret) daughter.

Rachel stayed on in Chelsea – always a favourite London area – after Michael's death, active in local affairs until she finally moved into Vanessa's apartment where she could be better cared for. Among those possessions which she took with her one was particularly prized – the Anthony Devas wartime portrait of her, commissioned by Michael, which catches her at the peak of her beauty – to grace the walls of her final London home.

When Vanessa went to New York early in 2003 to rehearse for the Broadway production of *Long Day's Journey into Night* Rachel travelled with her and when Natasha Richardson crossed to London for *Lady from the Sea* Vanessa and Rachel stayed in the house belonging to Natasha and her husband Liam Neeson in New York State. Rachel died there peacefully in May 2003. By then Lynn was also working in New York while Corin, who had just finished a run at the National Theatre, had flown to America to visit his mother and to see his sisters' plays. So Rachel died with all three of her children close.

In a book of her own – she called it *A Family and Its Fortunes*, a nod to Ivy Compton-Burnett, with whose novels of Edwardian family secrets and schisms her own story had some aspects in common – Rachel wrote artlessly but most touchingly and revealingly of Michael and of their marriage. Had he lived just a few more months they would have celebrated their Golden Wedding anniversary. Some people could never comprehend the ties between them. Margaret Leighton, a compassionate woman, was nevertheless one of those hard on Michael; she saw his serial infidelities and what she regarded as his 'weakness' as selfishly cruel to Rachel.

Yet for all its sometime tempests and despite endless gossip both fascinated and malicious, the marriage between Michael and Rachel was one of the most profound mutual love and cemented loyalties. Rachel never pretended that the dissonance at the centre of Michael's personality did not on occasion cause her acute unhappiness and suffering. Corin has talked of how he could be so affected as a young man by seeing Rachel's transparent distress at times that he would implore her to leave Michael, believing that she surely must be happier apart from him. Lynn, too, on occasion in her younger years suggested to Rachel that she should leave Michael ('He could be pretty bad to her') although she came to realise how strongly rooted was Rachel's sense of duty and commitment in her upbringing ('In another era their marriage would probably not have lasted') and to understand her conviction that love was more important than sexual fidelity ('Good girl! With all the difficulties you've stuck it out,' Edith Evans, also a woman with another generation's sense of duty, once said to Rachel). But of course Rachel knew too – had known since they first met in Liverpool in 1935 – the guilty unhappiness and suffering that the bifurcation of his sexual nature could cause Michael. And, as her children all in their maturity came to comprehend, she had no inclination to complain.

Rachel's book carried an incidental reminder of what for her became a maxim for living, taken from a favourite Shakespearean quotation. It was first absorbed in 1933 as a Stratford walk-on in *Richard II* and confirmed in 1951, again in Stratford, when Michael gave what in Rachel's view was one of his greatest performances as that gilded and finally humbled, humanised monarch. The words, which for Michael and Rachel alike carried echoes of Dick Green's stalwarts of Zeno and Seneca, come from Richard's rebuke to Thomas Mowbray:

> It boots thee not to be compassionate;
> After our sentence, 'plaining comes too late.

ACKNOWLEDGEMENTS

The bulk of this book's source-material, most of it being published for the first time, comes from the Michael Redgrave Archive in the Theatre Museum. The material could have been sold overseas for a sum greatly in excess of that which the scandalously underfunded Theatre Museum (even with the assistance of a Heritage Lottery grant) could possibly afford; the Theatre Museum was a cause very important to Michael – he was one of its first trustees – and it is pleasingly appropriate that his papers should remain in the UK and be housed there.

It is a rich and varied Archive; it contains a great deal of photographic material, both professional and private, the surviving letters between Michael's parents, unpublished family recollections, the diaries which Michael kept sporadically and in varying detail throughout his life, many family letters, correspondence from colleagues and friends, scripts, recordings, press-cuttings and scrapbooks. Acquired by the Theatre Museum in 2001, the Archive was catalogued speedily and efficiently by Alexia Byrne whose work greatly facilitated my research. I am indebted to the Theatre Museum's Archivist, Guy Baxter, and to all the unfailingly helpful staff at the Blythe Road, Olympia premises (which seemed virtually my home for over a year) where the Archive is housed, and also at Covent Garden.

I must especially thank Corin Redgrave; no less professionally busy than his sisters, he was usually geographically closer to hand and he answered my many questions with enviable patience. Any factual errors undoubtedly remain mine.

Other organisations and institutions to which I gratefully acknowledge thanks for assistance and research facilities include:

The Australian Film Corporation
The British Film Institute
The British Library (and Kathryn Johnson, the Olivier Archive)
The Clifton College Society (and T. C. W. Gover and Margaret Kelly)
Cranleigh School
The Garrick Club (and Enid Foster, Librarian)
Glyndebourne Opera
The Illustrated London News Group

The Isle of Wight County Record Office
The London Library
Magdalene College, Cambridge (and Dr. R. Hyam, Litt. D., College Archivist,
    and Mrs. Aude Fitzsimons, Asst. Librarian)
The Mander and Mitchenson Theatre Collection
The Parkinson's Disease Society
Portsmouth City Reference Library
Princeton University Library, Princeton, New Jersey
The Registrar General's Office, Sydney
The Shakespeare Birthplace Trust, Stratford-upon-Avon
The Theater Collection, Lincoln Center, New York
The Victoria and Albert Museum

As a first-time biographer, I have been touched by the generosity of more experienced practitioners. I particularly thank Jonathan Croall who lent me notes made
when researching his biography of Sir John Gielgud, John Coldstream (Dirk
Bogarde's biographer) for information on Joseph Losey, Bryan Forbes, biographer
of Edith Evans, Selina Hastings whose biography of Rosamond Lehmann pointed
me in the direction of Michael's letters to John Lehmann, and Professor John
Sutherland who kindly permitted me to read the manuscript of his unpublished
biography of Stephen Spender.

Michael Michell provided information about the early life of his father Robert
(Bob) Michell which would have been difficult to find elsewhere. I am also grateful
to Philip Bowen who lent me the audio-tapes made by the late David Dodimead
in his possession.

The following individuals, the majority in personal interviews, provided valued
guidance and information:

John Ainsworth, Frith Banbury, Peter Bartrum, the late Sir Alan Bates, Jennifer
Beattie, Richard Bebb, Trevor Bentham, Philip Bowen, Faith Brook, Michael
Codron, John Coldstream, Michael Colgan, Elizabeth Counsell, Michael
Coveney, Vivian Cox, Jonathan Croall, Stephen Croft, Gabrielle Drake, Frank
Dunlop, Peter Eyre, Bryan Forbes, Mrs. Jane Garrett, Christopher Godwin,
Nickolas Grace, Jacki Harding, the late Margaret (Percy) Harris, Selina Hastings,
the late Joan Hirst, Patricia Hodge, Sir Derek Jacobi, Barbara Jefford, Jerome
Kilty, the late Dinsdale Landen, the late Donald Lindsay, Patricia Macnaughton,
Iain Mackintosh, Richard Mangan, Patricia Marmont, Michael Michell, Amanda
Murray, Kathleen Nolan, Gaydon Phillips, Dame Joan Plowright (Lady Olivier),
Corin Redgrave, Lynn Redgrave, Vanessa Redgrave, Anne Kaufman Schneider,
Rosalind Shanks, Katie Simpson, Andrew Sinclair, Sir Donald Sinden, John
Standing, Professor John Sutherland, John Theocharis, the late Dame Dorothy
Tutin, John Tydeman, Gillian Webb, Michael White, Nigel Williams, Googie
Withers, Peter Wood.

The germ of this book lay in a suggestion by Sue Rolfe, the Press Officer for the Theatre Museum, that I might like to see the Archive; then uncatalogued, it was a huge pile of bursting boxes and files, but even a glimpse was enough to indicate that it contained priceless original material for a biography. I should also like to thank Annabel Freyberg, then the outstanding Arts Editor of the London *Evening Standard*, who commissioned an article on the Archive, leading to the commissioning of this book by Ion Trewin; most encouragingly considerate of editors and publishers, he made even what became a tricky process of finalising the book a pleasure. I am also grateful to his Assistant at Weidenfeld & Nicolson, Victoria Webb, and to Ilsa Yardley for her eagle-eyed copy-editing. I was lucky enough to have as my Literary Agent the remarkable Giles Gordon, whose untimely death came just as this book was going to press. It was especially reassuring to me that he had read and approved of the book when it was in manuscript and I shall always remember his enthusiasm and help. Thanks are also due to Jacki Harding for tolerant assistance to an E-Mail virgin and to Toni Smith and, especially, Liz Lomas for their skill with my original manuscript.

After the long research period, mostly in noisy cities, I eventually wrote this book in an isolated house on a mountain in remote rural Majorca, not perhaps the most practical location – especially over an unusually wet winter – for a non-driver. I owe a great deal to supportive friends on the island (particularly Iris Read of Read's Hotel) without whom this book would have taken much longer to complete.

The author and publishers gratefully acknowledge permission to quote from the following copyright material:

Max Adrian correspondence: The Mander and Mitchenson Theatre Collection
Anthony Asquith letter: The Estate of Anthony Asquith
W. H. Auden ('Look, Stranger'): Faber & Faber Ltd.
J. M. Barrie letter: by permission of Samuel French Ltd. on behalf of the Estate of J. M. Barrie
Kitty Black (*Upper Circle*): Kitty Black and Methuen Ltd.
Robert Bolt letters: Sarah Miles, by kind permission
Noël Coward letter: by kind permission of the Noël Coward Estate
T. S. Eliot (*The Family Reunion*): Faber & Faber Ltd.
Edith Evans letters: by kind permission of Bryan Forbes and the Estate of Dame Edith Evans
Ann Fleming letter: courtesy of Mark Amory
John Gielgud letter: Ian Bradshaw and the Estate of Sir John Gielgud
Dick Green letters: Vivian Cox (Literary Executor) for the Estate of the late Richard Green
Peter Hall (*Diaries*): Sir Peter Hall and Hamish Hamilton Ltd.
Christopher Isherwood (*Christopher and his Kind*): Random House Publishing
Frank Loesser ('My Time of Day' from *Guys and Dolls*)
Bob Michell letters: Michael Michell

Laurence Olivier correspondence: by kind permission of Lady Olivier on behalf of the Estate of Lord Olivier

Harold Pinter letter: by kind permission of Harold Pinter

Joan Plowright (*And That's Not All*): Joan Plowright and Weidenfeld & Nicolson Ltd.

J. B. Priestley (*Cornelius*): Reproduced from the play by J. B. Priestley (Copyright Estate of J. B. Priestley, 1935) by permission of PFD on behalf of the Estate of J. B. Priestley.

John Pudney ('For Johnny'): the Estate of John Pudney and David Higham Associates

Corin Redgrave (*Michael Redgrave, my Father*): Corin Redgrave and Richard Cohen Brooks

Michael Redgrave (*In my Mind's Eye*): the Estate of Sir Michael Redgrave and Weidenfeld & Nicolson Ltd.

George Rylands correspondence: Unpublished writings of G. H. W. Rylands, copyright The Provost and Scholars of King's College, Cambridge, 2004

Siegfried Sassoon letter: by permission of George Sassoon

Every effort has been made to contact copyright-holders; omissions or errors will be corrected in future printings.

BIBLIOGRAPHY

Of the books consulted during research, the following were particularly useful:

AGATE James, *The Contemporary Theatre* (Harrap, 1946)

ALDGATE Antony & RICHARDS Jeffrey, *Best of British: Cinema and Society from 1930* (I. B. Tauris, 2001)

ANGELIDES Steven, *A History of Bisexuality* (University of Chicago, 2001)

ANNAN Noël, *The Dons* (Harper Collins, 1999)

BARR Charles, *English Hitchcock* (Cameron & Hollis, 1994)

BEAUMAN Sally, *The Royal Shakespeare Company* (OUP, 1982)

BILLINGTON Michael, *Peggy Ashcroft* (Mandarin, 1991)

BLACK Kitty, *Upper Circle* (Methuen, 1984)

BOURNE Stephen, *Brief Encounters* (Cassell, 1996)

BURTON Hal (ed.), *Great Acting* (BBC, 1964)

CALDWELL Zoe, *I Will Be Cleopatra* (W. W. Norton & Co., 2001)

CARTER Miranda, *Anthony Blunt, his Lives* (Macmillan, 2001)

CAUTE David, *Joseph Losey: A Revenge on Life* (Faber & Faber, 1994)

CHAMBERS Colin, *Peggy: The Life of Margaret Ramsay* (Nick Hern Books, 1987)

CLURMAN Harold, *All People Are Famous* (Harcourt, Brace, Jovanovich, NY, 1984)

CONNOR Steven, *Dumbstruck* (OUP, 2000)

COVENEY Michael, *Maggie Smith* (Gollancz, 1992)

CROALL Jonathan, *John Gielgud* (Methuen, 2000)

DUFF Charles, *The Lost Summer* (Nick Hern Books, 1995)

FINDLATER Richard, *Michael Redgrave, Actor* (Heinemann, 1956)
          The Player Kings (Weidenfeld & Nicolson, 1971)

FORBES Bryan, *Ned's Girl* (Elm Tree Books, 1977)

FORSYTH James, *Tyrone Guthrie* (Hamish Hamilton, 1976)

FOX Michael J., *Lucky Man* (Ebury Press, 2002)

GARBER Marjorie, *Vice-Versa – Bisexuality and the Eroticism of Everyday Life* (Simon & Schuster, NY, 1995)

GREEN Chloe and MACLEAN A. D. (eds.) *A Skilled Hand: a Collection of Stories and Writings by Dick Green* (Macmillan, 1980)

GUNNING, Tom, *The Films of Fritz Lang* (BFI, 2000)

HALL Peter, (ed. John Goodwin), *Diaries* (Hamish Hamilton, 1983)

HARPER Sue, *Picturing the Past* (BFI, 1994)

HASTINGS Selina, *Rosamond Lehmann* (Chatto & Windus, 2002)

HOARE Philip, *Noël Coward* (Sinclair Stevenson, 1995)

JONES Nigel, *Through a Glass Darkly – the Life of Patrick Hamilton* (Scribner's, 1991)

KEMPSON Rachel, *A Family and its Fortunes* (Duckworth, 1984)

KNAPP Bettina (Introduction by Michael Redgrave), *Louis Jouvet, Man of the Theatre* (Columbia University Press, NY, 1957)

LEEMING David, *Stephen Spender, a Life in Modernism* (Duckworth, 1999)

LEHMANN John, *In the Purely Pagan Sense* (Blond & Briggs, 1976)

LEWIS Roger, *Laurence Olivier* (Century, 1996)

LITTLEWOOD Joan, *Joan's Book* (Methuen, 1994)

MACDONALD Kevin, *Emeric Pressburger* (Faber & Faber, 1994)

McGILLIGAN Patrick, *George Cukor* (St. Martin's Press, NY, 1991)

MATTHEWS Jessie, *Over My Shoulder* (W. H. Allen, 1974)

MEGAHEY A. J., *A History of Cranleigh School* (Collins, 1983)

MENUHIN Diana, *A Glimpse of Olympus* (Methuen, 1996)

MULLIN Michael, *Design by Motley* (Delaware, 1996)

O'CONNOR Garry, *Alec Guinness* (Hodder & Stoughton, 1994)

OLIVIER Laurence, *Confessions of an Actor* (Weidenfeld & Nicolson, 1982)

PERRY George, *Forever Ealing* (Pavilion, 1981)

PLOWRIGHT Joan, *And That's Not All* (Weidenfeld & Nicolson, 2001)

POWELL Dilys (ed. George Perry), *The Golden Screen* (Pavilion, 1989)

POWELL Michael, *Million-Dollar Movie* (Heinemann, 1993)

QUAYLE Anthony, *A Time to Speak* (Barrie & Jenkins, 1990)

READ, Piers Paul, *Alec Guinness* (Simon and Schuster, 2003)

REDGRAVE Corin, *Michael Redgrave, my Father* (Richard Cohen Books, 1995)

REDGRAVE Deirdre & BROOK Danaë, *To Be a Redgrave* (Robson Books, 1983)

REDGRAVE Lynn, *Shakespeare for my Father* (Samuel French, NY, 2001)

REDGRAVE Michael, *In My Mind's Eye* (Weidenfeld & Nicolson, 1983)

REDGRAVE Vanessa, *Autobiography* (Hutchinson, 1991)

ROWELL George, *The Old Vic Theatre* (CUP, 1993)

SEYMOUR-JONES Carole, *Painted Shadow: The Life of Vivienne Eliot* (Constable, 2001)

SHELLARD Dominic, *Kenneth Tynan* (Yale University Press, 2003)

SHEREK Henry, *Not in Front of the Children* (Heinemann, 1959)

SMELIANSKY Anatoly, *Is Comrade Bulgakov Dead?* (Methuen, 1993)

STEPHENS Robert with COVENEY Michael, *Knight Errant: Memoirs of a Vagabond Actor* (Hodder & Stoughton, 1996)

THOMSON David, *Rosebud: The Story of Orson Welles* (Little, Brown, 1996)

TREVELYAN Julian, *Indigo Days* (MacGibbon & Kee, 1957)

TREWIN J. C., *A Play Tonight* (Elek, 1952)

TURNER Adrian, *Robert Bolt* (Hutchinson, 1998)

TYNAN Kenneth, *Curtains* (Longmans, Green, 1961)

     Tynan Right and Left (Longmans, Green, 1967)

VICKERS Hugo, *Vivien Leigh* (Hamish Hamilton, 1988)

WAPSHOTT Nicholas, *The Man Between: The Life of Carol Reed* (Chatto & Windus, 1990)

WARDLE Irving, *The Theatres of George Devine* (Jonathan Cape, 1978)

WILLIAMSON Audrey, *Old Vic Drama* (Rockliff, 1951)

WORSLEY T. C., *The Fugitive Art* (John Lehmann, 1952)

WRIGHT Adrian, *John Lehmann: A Pagan Life* (Duckworth, 1998)

NOTES ON SOURCES

PROLOGUE: The letter quoted (p. 2) is from Michael's Cranleigh colleague Maurice Allen (18/3/68).

Although this is, as stated, the first full biography of Michael Redgrave to be published, it should be mentioned that a previous book was written. This was begun in the late 1970s by the Redgraves' friend Yvonne Mitchell, who had written successful novels and plays in addition to her acting career (she was Michael's 1950 Ophelia and Cordelia to his 1953 Stratford King Lear). She died before completing the book, which was subsequently finished by her daughter Cordelia Monsey, but there were disagreements over it and the book was not published. I have not read the M.S. or any copy.

ONE: ANCESTRAL VOICES: Most of the material in this chapter is from unpublished sources – Michael's Garrick Club Dinner speech of 1960, notes on Redgrave family history by his aunt Lena Doughty and his great-uncle Hyma Henry Redgrave, and Daisy Scudamore's notes on her early career. All of this material is in the Michael Redgrave Archive.

TWO: FAMILY SECRETS: The surviving correspondence between Michael's parents, and his mother's later reminiscences – all also in the Archive – provide the main sources for this period.

THREE: BRISTOL-FASHIONED: Michael's earliest diary (covering 1925–26) and that briefly covering part of his time in Heidelberg have been drawn on. The information on Roy's death comes mainly from Daisy's papers in the Archive. Oliver Baldwin's autobiography, *The Questing Beast*, was also a helpful source, as were letters from David Loveday, personal recollections from Michael's Clifton schoolfriend Peter Bartrum, and material published in the school magazine, *The Cliftonian*.

FOUR: TREADING THE WIND: The bulk of the material on Michael's undergraduate years is in his letters and in letters from his contemporaries at Cambridge including Louis le Breton, Anthony Blunt, Mary Coss, Michael Garrett and Geoffrey Hayward, together with correspondence from David Loveday and Dadie Rylands. The letters from Rylands to John Lehmann are in the Lehmann Collection at Princeton University Library, as are Michael's letters to Lehmann; Rylands's letters to Michael are in the Archive. Other sources include issues of *Granta*, *The Venture* and the *Cambridge Review*. Archive material at Magdalene College was also consulted.

FIVE: EARLY STAGES: Vivian Cox's personal recollections were especially useful in illuminating Michael's Cranleigh period. The prompt-scripts of most of his Cranleigh productions are in the Archive, along with some incomplete scrapbooks and albums of his time at Liverpool Playhouse. Basil Dean's auto-biography, *Seven Ages*, provided information on the Playhouse's early years. Michael's occasional brief entries in a 1935 diary and the unpublished memoirs of Eric Kempson also provided material on the Liverpool period. The late Paul Eddington provided delightful reminiscences of Willie Armstrong.

SIX: TAKING THE TOWN: Much of the background to the 1936–37 Old Vic season is vividly conveyed in James Forsyth's *Tyrone Guthrie* (the source of the Ernest Milton anecdote on p. 119). The material covering the relationship between Michael and Edith Evans is mainly from their correspondence, much of it previously unpublished, and from Bryan Forbes's biography *Ned's Girl*. Edith Evans's description of rehearsing Rosalind (p. 123) appeared in *The Birmingham Post* (17/4/64), Diana Graves's recollections of *As You Like It* (p. 125) in an article in *Woman's Weekly* (10/6/57), and Michael's description of acting with Edith (p. 125) in *The New Yorker* (1961) in 'The Player' by Lilian Ross. Michael's verdict on Olivier's Hamlet (p. 128) was quoted in *Olivier* (ed. Logan Gourlay, p. 68). The letter from Rachel quoted (p. 139) was written to Bryan Forbes (September, 1977).

SEVEN: COMING OF AGE: Michael's correspondence and the few entries in his diary in 1939 provide material for this period. Irving Wardle's *The Theatres of George Devine* was extremely useful on the work of Michel Saint-Denis, as were Carole Seymour-Jones's biography of Vivienne Haigh-Wood, *Painted Shadow*, and Peter Ackroyd's *T. S. Eliot* on the background of *The Family Reunion*. Michael's letter to Max Adrian (p. 156) is from the collection of his letters to Max Adrian in the Mander and Mitchenson Theatre Collection, as are the other quoted letters to Max.

EIGHT: SOUND STAGES: Michael wrote on the cinema in *In My Mind's Eye* and in a lecture ('I Am Not a Camera') for the British Film Institute at the Edinburgh Festival. Pauline Kael wrote on Elisabeth Bergner (p. 164) and on *The Stars Look Down* (p. 168) in *Kiss, Kiss, Bang-Bang* (1970, p. 260 and pp. 349–351).

NINE: LOVE AND WAR: Unpublished letters and Michael's sporadically-kept diaries cover much of the early wartime period. For material on Tony Hyndman I have gratefully drawn on John Sutherland's biography of Stephen Spender. Virginia Woolf's remarks (p. 177) appear in a letter to Quentin Bell in *The Letters of Virginia Woolf*, Vol. V (ed. Nigel Nicolson, 1971, p. 275). Christopher Isherwood's description (p. 177) of Tony as Jimmy Younger appears in *Christopher and his Kind* (2001, p. 220) and Barbara Skelton's description of Spender (p. 178) in *Tears Before Bedtime* (1987, p. 48). The description of *Thunder Rock* during the Blitz (p. 184) is from Kitty Black's *Upper Circle* (1984, p. 50).

TEN: POLITICS AND WAR: Michael's letters and diaries – the latter often fairly detailed (especially for his first visit to New York in 1941) – provide the main sources for this period. Information on Michael's relationship with Noël Coward is in Philip Hoare's biography *Noël Coward*, while Diana Menuhin wrote of her friendship with Michael in her first volume of autobiography, *A Glimpse of Olympus*.

ELEVEN: HURLY-BURLY: Michael's relationship with Norris Houghton is partially detailed in his 1944 diary, as is the latter part of the *Uncle Harry* tour and some of its London run. Frith Banbury provided information on The White Room. *Alec Guinness* by Piers Paul Read (p. 246) had useful material on Michael's friendship with Guinness (p. 230) and on its mentions in Guinness's diaries. Steven Connor's fascinating study of ventriloquism, *Dumbstruck*, was enlightening on aspects of *Dead of Night*, as was Stephen Bourne's *Brief Encounters*.

TWELVE: HOLLYWOOD DREAMS: Michael's Hollywood period is covered fairly comprehensively in his 1947 diary. Both Richard Bebb and Gillian Webb had vivid memories of the 1947 London *Macbeth* and Gillian Webb also recalled the Broadway production. The Redgraves' meeting with Stephen Tennant in Venice is also documented in Philip Hoare's *Serious Pleasures*. Vivian Cox provided information on F. F. ('Foff') LeGrand, and on the film of *The Astonished Heart*.

THIRTEEN: THE READINESS IS ALL: Comparatively regular diary entries for 1949–50 fill in much of the background of Michael's Old Vic season. Joan Plowright's description of his Hamlet (p. 262) is taken from her autobiography, *And That's Not All* (2001, p. 22). Anthony Asquith's comments on *The Browning Version* (p. 267) are contained in a letter to Michael (27/11/50); Anthony Quayle on his aims for Stratford (p. 268) is in *A Time to Speak* (1990, p. 85), while Barbara Jefford had extremely fresh recollections of the 1951 Stratford season. Michael's unposted letter to Kenneth Tynan is in his Archive, and the opinions of Elaine Dundy (p. 276) appear in Dominic Shellard's *Kenneth Tynan, a Life* (2003, p. 49).

FOURTEEN: ANNUS MIRABILIS: The progress of *Winter Journey* was described in the personal recollections of Patricia Marmont and Googie Withers, and also in Henry Sherek's autobiography *Not in Front of the Children*. Laurence Kitchin's description of Michael's Frank Elgin (p. 283) appeared in *Plays and Players* (February, 1964). Ann Fleming's account of dinner at Goldeneye (p. 288) is from *The Letters of Ann Fleming* (ed. Mark Amory, 1985, p. 122). Richard Findlater's description of Michael as Antony (p. 291) appeared in *Tribune* (20/11/53) and Robert Speaight reviewed *King Lear* (p. 293) in *The Tablet* (22/8/53). The filmscript of the projected *Antony and Cleopatra* film is in the

Archive. Michael Powell's autobiography *Million-Dollar Movie* (1992, p. 278 & p. 280) refers to Michael's appearance in *Oh, Rosalinda!!* (p. 302 & p. 303).

FIFTEEN: AMERICAN STAGES: Barbara Jefford had useful memories of the production of *Tiger at the Gates*. Harold Clurman's comments on Michael (p. 307) appeared in his book *All People Are Famous* (1974, p. 120). Michael's diary is fairly detailed for this period also. Joan Plowright recalled the filming of *Time Without Pity*. Some of Fred Sadoff's surviving American friends, particularly Kathleen Nolan, provided valuable information about his earlier life. Kenneth L. Geist's *Pictures Will Talk*, his biography of Joseph L. Mankiewicz, and Michael Shelden's *Life of Graham Greene* covered aspects of the 1957 film of *The Quiet American*.

SIXTEEN: ROLLER-COASTER RIDE: *A Touch of the Sun* is covered in some detail in Michael's 1957 diary, the last to contain significant consecutive entries, and Thelma Holt's memories of the production were also most helpful. The 1958 Stratford season was recalled by Dame Dorothy Tutin not long before her death. Michael White's recollections contributed to the section on *The Aspern Papers*, the many draft versions of which are in the Redgrave Archive. Leon Edel's comments on the production (p. 348) are in a letter to Michael (1/9/59).

The production of *The Tiger and the Horse* is covered from different perspectives in the biographies of Robert Bolt (by Adrian Turner) and his agent Margaret Ramsay (*Peggy, the Life of Margaret Ramsay*, by Colin Chambers), in Charles Duff's survey of the post-war West End and the career of Frith Banbury in *The Lost Summer* as well as in the recollections of Frith Banbury and Thelma Holt and partially in Michael's diary. Andrew Sinclair recalled the tribulations of his play *My Friend Judas*. The background to *The Complaisant Lover* on Broadway, discussed in Irene Mayer Selznick's autobiography, *A Private View*, was reinforced by the recollections of Anne Kaufman Schneider and Googie Withers. Laurence Olivier's reaction to Michael's acceptance of *Uncle Vanya* at Chichester (p. 357) was in a cable to Michael in New York (14/12/1962).

SEVENTEEN: SHOCKS OF THE NEW: Letters between Michael and Rachel cover some of this time. Corin Redgrave's remarks (p. 360) on the relationship between his father and his sister Lynn appear in his book *Michael Redgrave, my Father* (1995, p. 88) – as do other quotations. Joan Plowright contributed her recollections of the Chichester *Uncle Vanya* and of *Hobson's Choice* for the National Theatre at the Old Vic. Tom Stoppard's notice of *Out of Bounds* (p. 367) appeared in *Scene* magazine (2/11/63). The remarks on Fred Sadoff (p. 368) by Ted Allen Lewis were in a letter by Lewis to Michael (9/10/63). Detailed valuable recollections of the first National Theatre season included material from Sir Derek Jacobi and Peter Wood. The notices of *The Master Builder* are by Laurence Kitchin (on radio's 'The Critics', printed in *The Listener* 25/6/64), J. C. Trewin (*Birmingham Post* 10/6/64) and Ronald Bryden (*New Statesman* 27/11/64). On Fred Sadoff and his productions recollections from Faith Brook, Trevor Bentham and Peter Eyre were especially illuminating. The troubled early shooting of *Young Cassidy* is covered in *Print the Legend*, Scott Eyman's biography of John Ford.

EIGHTEEN: FRESH WOODS: The Redgrave Archive includes an extensive amount of material covering the planning and opening of the Yvonne Arnaud Theatre. Penelope Gilliatt's review of *Samson Agonistes* (p. 385) appeared in *The Observer* (20/6/65). The Glyndebourne Archives have material on the background to Michael's opera productions. The screenplay for *The Aspern Papers* is in the Archive.

NINETEEN: THE WALL OF FEAR: The notices of *The Old Boys* referred to (pp. 404–5) are from Michael Billington in *The Guardian* (30/7/71), Frank Marcus in *The Sunday Telegraph* (2/8/71) and Clive Barnes in the *New York Times* (27/8/71). The interview with Peter Lewis appeared in *The Daily Mail* (10/8/71). Michael's comments on *Voyage Round my Father* (p. 409) appeared in *The Australian Women's Weekly* (28/2/72) and *The Age* (17/2/72). The review in *The Observer* of *Voyage Round my Father* appeared on 10/9/72 while the notice of the Australian production in Sydney (p. 410) was in *The Australian* (20/5/72). Sir Derek Jacobi contributed recollections of touring with *The Hollow Crown*. Michael J. Fox's *Lucky Man* (2002, p. 145) provided information on Parkinson's Disease. Peter Hall's description of the Stratford Gala in 1975 (p. 415) appears in his *Diaries* (ed. John Goodwin, 1983, p. 173).

TWENTY: CLOSE OF PLAY: David Dodimead's audio-tapes provide much of the background to the tours of *Shakespeare's People*. The Toronto review by John Fraser (p. 421) appeared in *The Toronto Globe and Mail* (29/10/76). The interview for Michael's seventieth birthday referred to (p. 424) was with Sheridan Morley in *The Times* (20/3/78). John Theocharis recalled Michael's later radio work; the review quoted (p. 426) of *The Sons of Oedipus* was by Nicholas de Jongh in *The Guardian* (28/2/76). John Standing contributed sharp memories of the production of *Close of Play* and Peter Hall's descriptions (p. 429) of Michael at the National Theatre on the South Bank are in his *Diaries* (p. 416 and p. 469). Stephen Croft had many memories of his time as Michael's carer. Peggy Ashcroft's description of Michael's Foyle's Literary Luncheon (p. 431) comes from a letter to Michael (September, 1983) and Googie Withers's description of Michael (p. 432) is from her recollections. Both Corin Redgrave in his memoir and Lynn Redgrave in *Shakespeare for my Father* wrote movingly of their father's later years.

EPILOGUE: Richard Findlater's view of Michael's career (p. 443) appeared in *Michael Redgrave, Actor* (1956, p. 228). Michael's writing on Louis Jouvet (p. 444) is from his Preface to Bettina Knapp's *Louis Jouvet* (1957, pp. viii–ix). The review of *Long Day's Journey into Night* (p. 447) referred to, by Benedict Nightingale, appeared in *The Times* (7/5/2003). Peter Conrad's Profile of Natasha Richardson – 'The Redgraves, the Richardsons and Rebirth' – appears in his collection, *Feasting with Panthers, or, The Importance of Being Famous*. Michael Billington's article – 'The Secrets of their Success' – appeared in *The Guardian* (9/7/2003).

INDEX

Performances and works by Michael Redgrave are given under his name in alphabetical order. Theatres are in London unless otherwise indicated.
Abbreviations are used as follows:
F. A. = Fortunatus Augustus Scudamore
RK = Rachel Kempson
MR = Michael Redgrave
RR = Roy Redgrave
DS = Daisy Scudamore